VAN BUR
DECATU   W9-BUS-793

Dogs
ALL-IN-ONE

FOR

DUMMIES®

DISCARDED

Dogs
ALL-IN-ONE
FOR
DUMMIES®

by Eve Adamson, Richard G. Beauchamp,
Margaret H. Bonham, Stanley Coren,
Miriam Fields-Babineau, Sarah Hodgson,
Connie Isbell, Susan McCullough,
Gina Spadafori, Jack and Wendy Volhard,
Chris Walkowicz, M. Christine Zink, DVM, PhD

WILEY

Wiley Publishing, Inc.

636.7088
Dog

Dogs All-in-One For Dummies®

Published by
Wiley Publishing, Inc.
111 River St.
Hoboken, NJ 07030-5774
www.wiley.com

Copyright © 2010 by Wiley Publishing, Inc., Indianapolis, Indiana

Published by Wiley Publishing, Inc., Indianapolis, Indiana

Published simultaneously in Canada

No part of this publication may be reproduced, stored in a retrieval system, or transmitted in any form
or by any means, electronic, mechanical, photocopying, recording, scanning or otherwise, except as
permitted under Sections 107 or 108 of the 1976 United States Copyright Act, without either the prior
written permission of the Publisher, or authorization through payment of the appropriate per-copy fee to
the Copyright Clearance Center, 222 Rosewood Drive, Danvers, MA 01923, 978-750-8400, fax 978-646-8600.
Requests to the Publisher for permission should be addressed to the Permissions Department, John Wiley
& Sons, Inc., 111 River Street, Hoboken, NJ 07030, 201-748-6011, fax 201-748-6008, or online at http://
www.wiley.com/go/permissions.

Trademarks: Wiley, the Wiley Publishing logo, For Dummies, the Dummies Man logo, A Reference for the
Rest of Us!, The Dummies Way, Dummies Daily, The Fun and Easy Way, Dummies.com, Making Everything
Easier, and related trade dress are trademarks or registered trademarks of John Wiley & Sons, Inc., and/
or its affiliates in the United States and other countries, and may not be used without written permission.
All other trademarks are the property of their respective owners. Wiley Publishing, Inc., is not associated
with any product or vendor mentioned in this book.

LIMIT OF LIABILITY/DISCLAIMER OF WARRANTY: THE PUBLISHER AND THE AUTHOR MAKE NO
REPRESENTATIONS OR WARRANTIES WITH RESPECT TO THE ACCURACY OR COMPLETENESS OF
THE CONTENTS OF THIS WORK AND SPECIFICALLY DISCLAIM ALL WARRANTIES, INCLUDING WITH-
OUT LIMITATION WARRANTIES OF FITNESS FOR A PARTICULAR PURPOSE. NO WARRANTY MAY BE
CREATED OR EXTENDED BY SALES OR PROMOTIONAL MATERIALS. THE ADVICE AND STRATEGIES
CONTAINED HEREIN MAY NOT BE SUITABLE FOR EVERY SITUATION. THIS WORK IS SOLD WITH THE
UNDERSTANDING THAT THE PUBLISHER IS NOT ENGAGED IN RENDERING LEGAL, ACCOUNTING, OR
OTHER PROFESSIONAL SERVICES. IF PROFESSIONAL ASSISTANCE IS REQUIRED, THE SERVICES OF
A COMPETENT PROFESSIONAL PERSON SHOULD BE SOUGHT. NEITHER THE PUBLISHER NOR THE
AUTHOR SHALL BE LIABLE FOR DAMAGES ARISING HEREFROM. THE FACT THAT AN ORGANIZA-
TION OR WEBSITE IS REFERRED TO IN THIS WORK AS A CITATION AND/OR A POTENTIAL SOURCE
OF FURTHER INFORMATION DOES NOT MEAN THAT THE AUTHOR OR THE PUBLISHER ENDORSES
THE INFORMATION THE ORGANIZATION OR WEBSITE MAY PROVIDE OR RECOMMENDATIONS IT
MAY MAKE. FURTHER, READERS SHOULD BE AWARE THAT INTERNET WEBSITES LISTED IN THIS
WORK MAY HAVE CHANGED OR DISAPPEARED BETWEEN WHEN THIS WORK WAS WRITTEN AND
WHEN IT IS READ.

For general information on our other products and services, please contact our Customer Care
Department within the U.S. at 1-877-762-2974, outside the U.S. at 317-572-3993, or fax 317-572-4002.

For technical support, please visit www.wiley.com/techsupport.

Wiley also publishes its books in a variety of electronic formats. Some content that appears in print may
not be available in electronic books.

Library of Congress Control Number: 2010922045

ISBN: 978-0-470-52978-2

Manufactured in the United States of America. This book is printed on recycled paper.

10 9 8 7 6 5 4 3 2 1

WILEY

†/11
3↵

About the Authors

Eve Adamson is an award-winning pet writer and the author or coauthor of more than 30 books, including *Labrador Retrievers For Dummies* and *Dachshunds For Dummies.* She is a contributing editor for *Dog Fancy* magazine and writes frequently for many pet publications; among them are *Your Dog, Dogs USA, Puppies USA, Cat Fancy, Cats USA, Kittens USA, Veterinary Practice News,* and *Popular Pets,* including the issues on *Guinea Pigs, Rats,* and many issues on dog training and behavior. She writes the "Good Grooming" column for *AKC Family Dog* magazine and a breed profile column and a natural dog care column for *Pet Product News,* and she is a member of the Dog Writers Association of America and the Cat Writers Association of America.

Eve is an active supporter of the Iowa City/Coralville Animal Adoption Center, where she adopted her terrier, Sally, in 1999. She lives with her family in Iowa City, which includes partner Ben Minkler, sons Angus and Emmett, terriers Sally and Jack, a parakeet named Snugglebunny, a dwarf hamster named Mr. Hampy, and three little fish ceremoniously dubbed Little Fishies 1, 2, and 3. You can find out more about Eve and her most recent publications at her Web site, www.eveadamson.com.

Richard G. ("Rick") Beauchamp has been successfully involved in practically every facet of purebred dogs. He has bred them as well as trained and handled them professionally in the show ring. For many years, he owned and managed a publishing house devoted almost entirely to books and periodicals about purebred dogs. He is a published author of numerous breed and all-breed dog books and has lectured extensively on purebred dogs throughout the world.

As a breeder-exhibitor, he has been actively involved in breeds of nearly all the variety Groups, including top-quality Chow Chows, Dachshunds, Salukis, and Irish Setters. His Beau Monde Kennel has produced champion Boxers, American Cocker Spaniels, Poodles, Wire Fox Terriers, Bull Terriers, Pembroke Welsh Corgis, Cavalier King Charles Spaniels, and Chinese Shar-Pei. Rick is particularly associated with the Bichon Frise, a breed he has specialized in since its earliest days in America.

As a judge of all breeds with the Federacion Cynologique Internationale, Rick has had the distinct pleasure of judging championship events in Mexico and throughout the United Kingdom, Scandinavia, Europe, Australia, New Zealand, South Africa, the Orient, Central America, and South America. Rick now judges throughout North America for the American Kennel Club, the Canadian Kennel Club, and the United Kennel Club.

In his other life, Rick has had a lifelong interest in film and theater and spent several years as a copy editor and reporter for the television and film industry bible, *Daily Variety.* He lives in Cambria, California, a coastal village situated midway between Los Angeles and San Francisco.

Margaret H. "Maggie" Bonham is a four-time award-winning professional dog, cat, and science fiction and fantasy author who lives in Colorado. She has worked as a vet tech, grooming dogs for clients. She also has groomed various dogs as pets and for show. She has trained more than 50 dogs in sledding, agility, packing, obedience, weight pulling, and conformation, earning multiple titles on several of her own dogs. She has written educational coursework (dog agility and activities) for dog trainers with Thomson Education Direct. She also is a professional member of Association of Pet Dog Trainers (APDT).

Maggie has been a professional writer since 1995, writing novels, nonfiction books, short stories, courses, educational materials, and articles. Her books include *Having Fun with Agility; A Dog's Wisdom: A Heartwarming View of Life; The Complete Guide to Mutts: Selection, Care and Celebration from Puppyhood to Senior; Bring Me Home: Dogs Make Great Pets; Bring Me Home: Cats Make Great Pets; The Complete Idiot's Guide to Labrador Retrievers; The Complete Idiot's Guide to Dog Health and Nutrition; The Complete Idiot's Guide to Designer Dogs; The Complete Idiot's Guide to Golden Retrievers; Soft Coated Wheaten Terriers; An Introduction to Dog Agility; Northern Breeds: The Simple Guide to Getting Active with Your Dog; Cancer and Your Pet: The Complete Guide to the Latest Research, Treatments, and Options; Your Siberian Husky's Life: Your Complete Guide to Raising Your Pet from Puppy to Companion;* and *Prophecy of Swords.* Her work has appeared in various national publications, including *Dog Fancy, Dog World, Dog and Kennel, Pet Life, Pet View, The Dog Daily, The Daily Cat, Catnip, Natural Pet, Contract Professional,* and *Mushing* magazine. She has been a columnist and contributing editor for *Dog and Kennel* and *PetView* magazines, and she was a frequent contributor to Pets.com and Vetmedcenter.com Internet sites. She is the editor of *Merial PawPrints,* a newsletter that covers topics about dogs and cats and is distributed to veterinarians for their clients.

Maggie currently trains various breeds for agility, sled-dog racing, obedience, and conformation. She lives with many purebred and mixed breed dogs, and one cat.

Stanley Coren is best known to the public for his popular books on dogs and on general psychological issues. However, within the scientific world, he's also a highly respected scientist, a Professor of Psychology at the University of British Columbia, and a Fellow of the Royal Society of Canada.

His engaging writing style and his broad knowledge about the behavior of dogs and people have made his books *The Intelligence of Dogs, Why We Love the Dogs We Do, What Do Dogs Know? How to Speak Dog, The Pawprints of History, How Dogs Think, Why Do Dogs Have Wet Noses?,* and *Why Does My Dog Do That?* all bestsellers. Roger Caras, President of the ASPCA, and himself a best-selling author of dog books, noted, "Stanley Coren has an incredible gift — the ability to take the most complex matters and make it all seem so simple and clear." Perhaps this is why Coren was named Writer of the Year by the International Positive Dog Training Association and is a sought-after contributor to a number of national dog and pet magazines, including *Pets Magazine, Modern Dog, AnimalSense, Dog and Puppy Basics,* and *AKC Gazette.*

Many professional associations have recognized Coren's work with service dogs, and he has received awards from several major police dog organizations, including the California Canine Narcotic Dog Association and the British Columbia Police Canine Association. His work with and knowledge of dogs has often caught the attention of the media, and he has been the subject of feature articles in *People Magazine, USA Today, Time Magazine, Maclean's, US News & World Report, New York Times, Los Angeles Times, San Francisco Chronicle, Washington Post,* and others. His affable manner has also made him a popular guest with the broadcast media, and he has been featured on numerous television programs, including *Oprah, Larry King Live, Dateline, 20/20, Maurie Povich, Good Morning America, Charlie Rose,* and the *Today Show.* He currently hosts the national TV series *Good Dog!* in Canada.

Miriam Fields-Babineau has been a professional animal trainer since 1978 and has enjoyed exhibiting horses and dogs since childhood. She holds degrees in psychology and zoology from the University of Maryland. She is a member of the Dog Writers Association and the Cat Writers Association and is listed in numerous editions of *Who's Who in America.*

Fields-Babineau has been writing professionally since her first article was published in *Canine Chronicle* in 1986. She is the author of 35 books, including *Click & Easy: Clicker Training for Dogs; Cat Training in 10 Minutes; Labradoodle: Comprehensive Owner's Guide; The ABCs of Positive Training; Training Your Mixed Breed; Training Your Puppy in 5 Minutes; Raising Dogs the Natural Way; The Perfect Retriever;* and *Multiple Dog Households.* She has also published three short stories (one of which appeared in *Christmas Cats: A Literary Anthology,* for Penguin, USA) and two novels: *The Tocharian,* a romantic fantasy-adventure, and *Evil,* a thriller.

She has provided animal actors for media productions since 1983, participating in the filming of commercials, advertisements, TV programs, videos, and feature films.

Fields-Babineau also designed the Comfort Trainer head halter for dogs, the All-in-One Leash, and the Clicker Spoon training tool for cats. Fields-Babineau currently resides in beautiful Amherst, Virginia, with her husband, Mike; son, Brendon Kyle; four dogs; four cats; and two horses.

Sarah Hodgson, president of Simply Sarah Incorporated, has been a trainer of dogs and their people in Westchester, New York, and southern Connecticut for more than 20 years. She's the author of eight dog-training books, including *Puppies For Dummies, Dog Tricks For Dummies, Puppy Raising & Training Diary For Dummies, Teach Yourself Visually Dog Training, You and Your Puppy* (coauthored with James DeBitetto), *DogPerfect, 2nd Edition, PuppyPerfect,* and *Miss Sarah's Guide to Etiquette for Dogs & Their People.* In addition, Sarah has produced two videos, patented a dog training leash (the Teaching Lead), and invented many other products to simplify the shared lives of dogs and people.

Sarah is frequently featured as a dog training specialist on network television, on radio, and in print media, including *The New York Times,* NBC, CBS, Animal Planet (Disney syndicate), FOX, CNN, WOR, Hollywood Pets, *Parenthood* magazine, and others. She has worked with many famous persons' dogs, including TV personality Katie Couric, actors Richard Gere, Glenn Close, Chazz Palminteri, Chevy Chase, and Lucie Arnaz; business moguls George Soros, Tommy Hilfiger, Tommy Mottola, and Michael Fuchs; and sports greats Bobby Valentine and Alan Houston.

In addition, Sarah is a behavior consultant and education facilitator at the Adopt-A-Dog shelter in Armonk, New York, where she holds training and socialization programs, conditioning each of the dogs within a fully decorated home environment before their formal adoption. For more information on everything Sarah, visit her Web site at www.dogperfect.com.

Sarah also writes a weekly column and balances all with her top priorities: her family and pets.

Connie Isbell, the author of *Rabbits For Dummies* and *Rabbit Adoption For Dummies,* grew up in rural New York State where she spent time with creatures of all kinds — companion, farm, and wild alike. Connie carried this interest in animals and nature into her work as an editor and writer for *Audubon* magazine. She has also edited countless pet books, on everything from adopting an ex-racing greyhound to training parrots and dogs. Connie now works from her home on the coast of New Jersey, where she lives with her husband, two daughters, and an assortment of pets.

Susan McCullough writes about all things dog for print and online outlets across the United States. She is a contributing editor to *Dog Fancy,* and her work has also appeared in the *AKC Gazette, AKC Family Dog, Your Dog,* the *Popular Dogs* magazine series, *Studio One Networks, The Washington Post,* and *Family Circle.* Her dog care books include *Senior Dogs For Dummies* and *Beagles For Dummies* (Wiley).

Susan is vice president of the Dog Writers Association of America (DWAA) and belongs to the Association of Pet Dog Trainers (APDT). She is a five-time winner of the DWAA's Maxwell Award for excellence in writing about dogs, and she also won the 2001 Eukanuba Canine Health Award for outstanding writing about canine health.

When she's not writing or hanging out with friends and family (both two-legged and four-legged), Susan counsels puzzled people on how to deal with canine potty problems and other dog-related quandaries. She lives in Vienna, Virginia, with her husband, Stan Chappell; their daughter, Julie Chappell (when Julie's on break from college); and the family's Golden Retriever, Allie.

Visit Susan's Web site at www.susanmc.com and read her blog, *The Allie Chronicles,* at thealliechronicles.blogspot.com.

Gina Spadafori writes an award-winning column on pets and their care, which appears in newspapers across the country through the Universal Press Syndicate. Her writing also appears frequently on Pets.com, where she is the special correspondent and essayist, and on the Veterinary Information Network's Pet Care Forum Web site.

Gina has served on the boards of directors of both the Cat Writers Association and the Dog Writers Association of America. She is a three-time recipient of the DWAA's Maxwell Medallion for the best newspaper column, and her column has also been honored with a certificate of excellence by the CWA.

The first edition of her *Dogs For Dummies* was given the President's Award for the best writing on dogs, and the Maxwell Medallion for the best general reference work, both by the Dog Writers Association of America.

Along with coauthor Dr. Paul D. Pion, she was given the CWA's awards for the best work on feline nutrition, best work on feline behavior, and best work on responsible cat care for *Cats For Dummies.* With top avian specialist Dr. Brian L. Speer, she has also written *Birds For Dummies.*

Gina is affiliated with the Veterinary Information Network, Inc., of Davis, California, the world's largest online service for veterinary professionals. She and her pets divide their time between Northern California and south Georgia/north Florida.

Jack and Wendy Volhard share their home with two Labrador Retrievers, a Landseer Newfoundland, three Standard Wirehaired Dachshunds, and one cat. The dogs are more or less well trained, depending on whom you ask, and the cat does his own thing. All are allowed on the furniture but do get off when told. The Volhards are true practitioners — they have obtained more than 50 conformation and performance titles with their dogs.

Through their classes, lectures, seminars, and training camps in the United States, Canada, and England, the Volhards have taught countless owners how to communicate more effectively with their pets. Individuals from almost every state and 15 countries have attended their training camps. Veterinarians, breeders, trainers, and dog owners like you regularly consult them on questions about behavior, heath, nutrition, and training. Internationally recognized as "trainers of trainers," they're also award-winning authors, and their books have been translated into three languages.

In addition to their work together, both Jack and Wendy are well recognized in the training community for their individual accomplishments.

Jack is the recipient of five awards from the Dog Writers Association of America (DWAA) and has been an American Kennel Club obedience judge for 30 years. He's the author of more than 100 articles for various dog publications and the senior author of *Teaching Dog Obedience Classes: The Manual for Instructors,* known as "the bible" for trainers, and *Training Your Dog: The Step-by-Step Manual,* named Best Care and Training Book for 1983 by the DWAA.

Wendy is the recipient of four awards from the DWAA. She's the author of numerous articles, a regular columnist for the *American Kennel Gazette,* and the coauthor of five books, including the *Canine Good Citizen: Every Dog Can be One,* named Best Care and Training Book for 1995 by the DWAA, and *The Holistic Guide for a Healthy Dog,* now in its second edition.

Wendy, whose expertise extends to helping owners gain a better understanding of why their pets do what they do, developed the *Canine Personality Profile,* and her two-part series, "Drives — A New Look at an Old Concept," was named Best Article for 1991 in a Specialty Magazine by the DWAA. She also developed the most widely used system for evaluating and selecting puppies, and her film, *Puppy Aptitude Testing,* was named Best Film on Dogs for 1980 by the DWAA. Wendy specializes in behavior, nutrition, and alternative sources of health care for dogs, such as acupuncture and homeopathy, and has formulated a balanced homemade diet for dogs.

Chris Walkowicz has been deeply involved with the dog world since 1965. She and her husband, Ed, have raised and shown German Shepherds and Bearded Collies under the Walkoway banner (along with three sons and a daughter, under the Walkowicz banner).

Chris is an AKC dog show judge, as well as an award-winning author of dog books, columns, and articles. She is active in rescue, and her goal is to put all rescue groups out of business — by helping all dogs to find loving homes. The best way to accomplish this is through advising prospective buyers how, why, when, and where to find the perfect dog. Her book *Choosing a Dog For Dummies* does this, in addition to helping people determine who should — or shouldn't — own a dog. And for those who are ready for the adventure, this book can help you determine which breed to choose.

Chris is the president of the Dog Writers Association of America. Among her accomplishments are DWAA Best Book, the DWAA Communicators Award, and the title of FIDO Woman of the Year. But more important, she says, is her philosophy: "If I can save just one dog's life, my work will be worthwhile."

M. Christine Zink, DVM, PhD got her first dog, an Irish Wolfhound, the day she graduated from Ontario Veterinary College with her DVM. From an initial interest in obedience, mainly as a survival tactic, she gradually became fascinated with all aspects of canine performance. While competing in performance events throughout Canada and the United States, Chris recognized a significant information gap. Owners and trainers wanted to know more about how canine structure and medical or physical conditions affect their dogs' performance, and how to keep their canine teammates healthy and injury-free. Yet little information was available. She therefore wrote the award-winning *Peak Performance: Coaching the Canine Athlete,* a comprehensive guide to the dog as an athlete. Her second book, *Jumping from A to Z: Teach Your Dog to Soar*, coauthored with Julie Daniels, has become the gold standard for jump training.

Chris presents Coaching the Canine Athlete seminars worldwide to rave reviews and regularly writes for dog magazines. She is also a consultant on canine sports medicine, evaluating canine structure and locomotion and designing individualized conditioning programs for active dogs. Chris has put out more than 50 titles in agility, obedience, hunting, tracking, and conformation on dogs of several different breeds from the Sporting, Working, and Hound groups.

In her other life, Chris is a professor at Johns Hopkins University School of Medicine and is credited with more than 100 scientific publications. There she teaches medical and veterinary students and does AIDS research.

Publisher's Acknowledgments

We're proud of this book; please send us your comments at http://dummies.custhelp.com. For other comments, please contact our Customer Care Department within the U.S. at 1-877-762-2974, outside the U.S. at 317-572-3993, or fax 317-572-4002.

Some of the people who helped bring this book to market include the following:

Acquisitions, Editorial, and Media Development

Editor: Corbin Collins

Copy Editor: Krista Hansing

Acquisitions Editor: Tracy Boggier

Assistant Editor: Erin Calligan Mooney

Editorial Program Coordinator: Joe Niesen

Technical Editor: Patty Kovach

Senior Editorial Manager: Jennifer Ehrlich

Editorial Supervisor and Reprint Editor: Carmen Krikorian

Editorial Assistant: Jennette ElNaggar

Cover Photos: © Don Mason

Cartoons: Rich Tennant (www.the5thwave.com)

Composition Services

Project Coordinator: Sheree Montgomery

Layout and Graphics: Yovonne Grego, Joyce Haughey, Christin Swinford

Special Art: Kathryn Born

Proofreaders: Lauren Mandelbaum, Bonnie Mikkelson

Indexer: Glassman Indexing Services

Special Help: Alicia South

Publishing and Editorial for Consumer Dummies

Diane Graves Steele, Vice President and Publisher, Consumer Dummies

Kristin Ferguson-Wagstaffe, Product Development Director, Consumer Dummies

Ensley Eikenburg, Associate Publisher, Travel

Kelly Regan, Editorial Director, Travel

Publishing for Technology Dummies

Andy Cummings, Vice President and Publisher, Dummies Technology/General User

Composition Services

Debbie Stailey, Director of Composition Services

Contents at a Glance

Table of Contents

Introduction

● ●

*W*elcome to *Dogs All-in-One For Dummies!* This book is just what the title implies: a soup-to-nuts reference on all things dog. Dog health, dog training — not to mention dog gear, dog grooming, dog breeds and breeding, even dog sports. Whether you're looking to adopt a dog, trying to improve your relationship with one you have, or trying to come up with fun things to do with your furry pal, this book contains something for you.

No other animal has had such a long and close relationship with humans. Wolves started becoming domesticated some 15,000 years ago, by some estimates, and spread all over the world. They helped protect early human settlements, they were with the ancient Romans and Greeks and Egyptians in their glory days, and they may have even accompanied the first migration from Siberia across the Bering Strait into North America.

Dogs have always had jobs to do. Whether it was herding other animals, helping hunters and fishermen earn their living, going to war, protecting royalty, keeping communities rodent free, or pulling sleds, dogs have earned their place in history and in the hearts of animal lovers everywhere. Thousands of years of breeding to do those different kinds of work have shaped the sometimes wildly different bodies and personalities of hundreds of breeds. They've come a long way from their gray wolf ancestors, who were attracted to campfires and hoping for a handout.

Nowadays dogs are mainly companions. It's this slight discrepancy between what dogs *think* we still want them to do — what we bred them to do for so long — and what we *actually* want them to do now that is the source of much misunderstanding between the canine and human worlds. This book aims to correct some of that by helping you see things from the dog's point of view.

About This Book

First, here's what this book is not: It's not a textbook, nor a long-winded history, nor a rote learning tool. Lots of those kinds of books are on the market, if that's what you're looking for. No, *Dogs All-in-One For Dummies* is a generous conglomeration of practical material from several *For Dummies* dog books. It aims to cover the gamut, from what those funny "thumbs" are called (dewclaws), to picking out a crate, to the fine art of getting around dog-hostile rules and regulations.

Most of the material within these pages is relevant to any breed and any age of dog, though there are special sections for puppies, and the chapters in Book V cover each breed recognized by the American Kennel Club, one at a time.

Conventions Used in This Book

Important words are defined in *italic*. Key words in lists that bring important ideas to your attention are in **bold.** And all Web addresses are in `monofont` to set them apart.

Most of the time, the word *dog* is used to refer to any individual of the species *Canis lupus familiaris*. However, among the more exclusive world of dog breeding and showing, a *dog* means the male form, and the female, to the delight of Bart Simpson, is called a *bitch*.

The names of proper, recognized breeds are capitalized.

What You're Not to Read

There are many sidebars (in shaded gray boxes) in this book that you don't really need to read to follow the chapter text. They contain extra information or background stories and history that you may be interested in, or not. Feel free to skip anything marked with the Technical Stuff icon, too.

Foolish Assumptions

Dogs All-in-One For Dummies doesn't assume that you know anything about dogs to begin with. It starts from zero and builds from the ground up — and then keeps going and going. It contains straightforward, informal explanations of processes such as choosing to adopt a dog, grooming, going to the vet, exercising and training, and so forth.

This book is designed for just about anyone who loves dogs or wants to know more about them. It is as useful for people who have never had a dog in their lives as it is for those who have always had dogs. Even advanced dog lovers or even devotees of specific breeds will find plenty of valuable information in these pages, including teaching tricks, performing first aid, competing in a dog show, and even the magical art of breeding itself.

Regardless of your situation, experience, or motives, this book's goal is to give you enough information so that, ultimately, you can enjoy and find out more about dogs on your own.

How This Book Is Organized

Dogs All-in-One For Dummies is sorted into six "books," organized around general areas of interest, so you can drill down and find what you need to know quickly.

Book 1: Choosing and Bringing Home a Dog

This is probably the most important step in dog ownership, yet it's one most people don't spend nearly enough time on. The wrong choice here can and does haunt frustrated folks for years. Chapters 1 through 4 are devoted to different aspects of what to consider when picking out your new companion. Chapter 5 looks at the delicate process of bringing your adopted dog into your home. Chapter 6 helps you accessorize, discussing all that great stuff you see in pet stores and describing what you definitely need — and what you may just want to get because it's fun. Chapter 7 gets a bit into dog psychology and tries to help you understand the world from your canine roommate's point of view. And Chapter 8 looks at the various laws and regulations society places on our four-legged friends.

Book 11: Dog Nutrition and Health

The chapters in this book focus on various aspects of keeping your dog bright-eyed and bushy-tailed. Chapter 1 gives you the scoop on dog food, including what kind to buy, what to avoid, and how much to feed. Chapters 2 through 4 look at vaccinations and health issues, canine first aid, and visits to the veterinarian. Chapter 5 is all about one of the most important things you can do to make your dog's life full and wonderful: exercise, and plenty of it. Chapter 6 considers special issues in caring for an aging dog. Sooner or later, all dogs head into their twilight years, which brings up painful decisions. Chapter 7 is for readers who are crazy enough about their breed — or just crazy enough, period — to attempt their own breeding program.

Book III: Cleanliness Is Next to Dogliness: Grooming

Your dog may be your best friend, but at the end of the day, she's still a hairy animal, and something has to be done about that to maintain a certain reasonable level of hygiene and, shall we say, acceptable odor and appearance. Chapter 1 delivers the basic of dog grooming, including the tools you need to get and how to use them. Chapter 2 delves into the fine art of brushing and bathing your furry pal. In Chapter 3, you discover how to take care of your dog's eyes, nose, teeth, ears, and a place or two you might be surprised, if not alarmed, to find needs your attention. In the last chapter of this book, Chapter 4, you get to play barber.

Book IV: Training, Agility, and Shows

You *can* teach an old dog new tricks, it turns out. And you can train almost any dog to do a lot more than you thought, probably. First things first, though: housetraining in Chapter 1. Chapters 2 and 3 cover teaching your dog manners and basic commands, respectively. In Chapter 4, you start to get into fun and fancy tricks, and Chapter 5 might be the most fun of all. If you haven't seen dogs run an obstacle course, you're really missing out. Finally, in Chapter 6, you step into the klieg lights and get a taste of what it takes to become one of those people running around a ring with a dog.

Book V: Meet the Breeds

The sheer variety of dogs in the world is truly amazing. The American Kennel club recognizes 192 breeds, and each of them is profiled here in these chapters. Dog breeds are organized into "groups," and the chapters follow that organization. Hence, you find chapters on the Toy, Working, Herding, Hunting, Terrier, Sporting, and Non-Sporting breeds. And last but not least, you find a chapter on those lovable mutts, the mixed breeds, and discover that some mixed breeds are becoming nearly as popular as standard breeds.

Book VI: Resources

Finally, after you've come so far in your dog study, you may want to go even farther. A world of dog information of every conceivable kind is out there just waiting for you to explore. This book offers two chapters. One is a glossary of terms to help you interpret some of the things your vet or true dog-fanatic friends might say. The other is a treasure trove of dog resources to feed your fascination even more.

Icons Used in This Book

You'll see five icons scattered around the margins of the text. Each icon points out a certain type of information about the world of dogs. They go as follows:

This icon notes something you should keep in mind. It may refer to something covered earlier in the book, or it may highlight something you ought to remember in the future.

This icon flags the boring (but sometimes helpful) stuff. Feel free to skip text with this icon. On the other hand, you may be interested to know extra details or little-known trivia about the topic at hand — in that case, by all means, read away.

Information marked with this icon usually tells you something that can come in really handy, saving you time, money, or heartache. Sometimes it refers to especially helpful ideas and advice that can enrich your canine experience.

This icon points out stuff you should avoid or things that may be dangerous to you or your dog.

This one flags information that's especially for dogs under a year old.

Where to Go from Here

If you're a true dog neophyte, you may as well start with Chapter 1 and follow along from there. If you don't have a dog yet, head straight to Chapters 2 through 5 in Book I. If you just adopted a dog and are wondering what you do now, head to Chapters 5 through 8 in Book I.

Otherwise, use the index and table of contents to zoom in on whatever your particular area of interest may be. Feel free to skip around and explore!

Book I
Choosing and Bringing Home a Dog

In this book . . .

Picking out the right dog for your temperament and lifestyle may be the most important dog-related thing you ever do. The first few chapters here cover the history of dogs and the universe of things to consider when choosing your new pal. The rest of the chapters help you bring your adopted dog into your life, decide what your dog needs in terms of accessories, comprehend your dog's point of view, and understand the laws that govern dogs in society.

Chapter 1

What Are Dogs and Why Do They Behave That Way?

In This Chapter

▶ Going back in time to see how dogs became dogs

▶ Seeing how evolution affects your relationship with your pooch

▶ Helping your dog successfully learn

▶ Finding out why dogs behave the way they do

You can offer your dog no greater gift than to understand her and her whole being. In other words, you need to walk a mile in her paws. Even though money can buy a lot of dog biscuits and squeaky toys — and those pricey obedience classes can encourage greater responsiveness to you — a lot more is going on behind the scenes than the simple recognition of the "Sit" command. This chapter begins your journey of discovering the mystery that is your dog. You discover the evolution of your dog and how it affects your relationship.

The History Behind the Beast: How Dogs Came to Be Dogs

The goal of this book is to help you understand your dog from her vantage point. It helps you to discover what it must feel like to be a dog and to understand your role and capacity to shape your dog's behavior after you've developed empathy for her experience.

Remember that your dog isn't merely a four-footed person in a fur coat. Your dog isn't a wolf in disguise either. Though some proponents of dog psychology emphasize the common ancestry between dog and wolf, your dog is more than a tamed version of any of its wild descendants, be it wolf, jackal, fox, coyote, or dingo. Your dog and these other canine species do share a lot of characteristics, both in physical makeup and behavior, but humans share a lot of physical and behavioral characteristics with apes. Does that mean we're just like other apes? Not exactly.

Wolves and dogs are part of the larger order *Carnivora* (animals that are meat eaters and mostly live by hunting). Even though each dog has a secondary classification specifying its distinctions, all are categorized by biologists as *canines* and members of the same biological family, *Canidae* — as are wolves, foxes, jackals, and coyotes.

If you were to line up all modern domesticated animals in the order in which they were domesticated, you would see that dogs lead the pack. In fact, dogs were brought into the human circle well before humans even knew how to grow their own food.

Recent evidence based on the fossil record suggests that dogs were domesticated between 17,000 and 14,000 years ago, which is much earlier than sheep (11,000 years ago) or cats (7,000 years ago). Domestication seems to have occurred at different times in different places, with dogs first domesticated in Asia and Russia, and then separately in the Middle East, Europe, and North America.

In this section, we explore a little canine history.

In the beginning

From the beginning, dogs and humans naturally formed an everlasting relationship. Both species were hunters that lived and survived through a dependency on a close-knit hierarchical group. The main advantage humans had over canines was the ability to learn and reason. However, in comparison to others in the animal kingdom, canines also were (and still are) intellectually advanced.

Even though the wild ancestors of dogs were efficient and daring pack hunters, they also scavenged when the opportunity arose. Scavenging around human campfires proved fruitful and was certainly less dangerous than hunting some of the larger hoofed animals that could kick and gore. When they were regularly presented with free meals, wolf packs weren't above taking advantage of leftovers. Such leftovers were often dumped just outside the camp or village in heaps that archeologists call *middens.* For the wolves, middens were a veritable buffet of free food that was being continually renewed.

What sensible wolf would rather hunt when such easy pickings were available? And perfectly happy to oblige, the humans appreciated the value of having another species about that would make use of their waste while simultaneously keeping their camp varmint and odor free.

Now perhaps if the relationship had just stopped there, no further domestication would have occurred. However, humans and canines share another important similarity — namely, both are territorial. Wild canines came to view the area around the camp as their territory. As a result, when a threatening wild animal or a marauding band of strangers came close to the encampment, the canines created a commotion. The noise gave enough warning for the inhabitants of the camp to rally some form of defense, which was especially useful at night. As a result of the vigilance of these canines, the lives of the nearby humans became much safer.

Wolves initiate domestication

The domestication of dogs wasn't simply a matter of some Stone Age man finding a wolf pup and bringing it home where it would be fed, sheltered, and treated like a dog. It may sound surprising, but the first stages of domestication were probably initiated by the wolves themselves.

The only wolves that could benefit from discarded food were those that could comfortably coexist with humans. If a particular wolf was aggressive or threatening, he was simply killed by the human residents as a matter of safety. This process began a kind of human-enforced natural selection — the genetic elimination of the most destructive individuals. Animals that were friendlier and less fearful could stay closer to the settlement. In addition to the free meals, the close proximity to humans provided them protection from predators that preferred to avoid human contact. When these friendlier canines began to interbreed, they ultimately generated a race of animals that were much more doglike. In these new animals, the genes for tameness were predominant.

Domestication takes more than simply taming a wild animal. A *tame* animal allows a human to care for it and accepts human presence and control to some degree. A *domesticated* animal, however, is actually genetically modified. Humans exert control over its breeding patterns, which leads to an animal that's drastically different in both physical appearance and behavior than its wild ancestors. Certainly no one would ever mistake a Pekingese or a bulldog for a gray wolf based on what they look like and how they act.

Book I

Choosing and Bringing Home a Dog

Don't try to tame a wolf

Research shows that instantaneous domestication just isn't possible. Researchers have often tried hand-feeding wolf puppies from birth and rearing them with a human family. The results have been far from satisfactory. In virtually all the scientific studies, as the wolf cubs matured, they became more wolflike in their behavior. The previously "tame" cubs, for instance, began to stalk and hunt farm animals, other house pets, and even children, growing ever more socially dominant and challenging their people for control. Even though tame wolf puppies can learn basic obedience commands, they stop responding to them when they're adults and begin challenging the authority and status of humans. Many reports tell of supposedly domesticated wolves attacking and biting their handlers.

Consider some research done by the Russian geneticist Dmitry K. Belyaev, who was trying to re-create the domestication of dogs. He decided not to use wolves because, in many areas, evidence suggests that domestic dogs have interbred with wolves and any dog genes would contaminate the data. Instead, he used another canine species: the silver fox. Also, because silver fox fur is prized for making expensive garments, he saw the potential for some economic benefits if he could domesticate these foxes and make them easier to raise on a farm.

The form of genetic manipulation that Belyaev used was similar to what occurred naturally around prehistoric villages with wild canines. He looked for the animals who were the tamest — the least fearful and least aggressive. The tamest and friendliest animals were bred with other tame and friendly animals, and after only six generations, noticeable differences existed between the tame and wild foxes. After 35 generations, this research created animals who looked and acted so much like dogs that they could be sold as pets and live in a human family. If you saw one of them walking down a street, you'd most likely believe that you were looking at some exotic breed of domestic dog.

What really happened to change a fox into a dog? Genetic changes aren't governed by a simple process. Because of the ways that our chromosomes are constructed, it turns out that if you want to change one specific feature genetically, you often end up changing other characteristics as well. That's exactly what happened when researchers began to breed foxes in a way that encouraged the genes associated with friendliness and tameness. It happens that these traits are linked to other genes so that selective breeding for tameness actually changed Belyaev's foxes physically and behaviorally. The resulting genetic mix actually changed the timing and rate of physical and psychological development in these new "dogs" so that they physically appear more doglike as well.

Humans make the second move

Because the wild canines hanging around the prehistoric camps were more docile and friendly, some clever Stone Age person realized that if the canines would protect whole camps, why couldn't one protect an individual hut? Protection at a personal level. Hmmm. . . . This development turned out to be a fortunate choice because, in the end, dogs would demonstrate other behaviors that would help keep early man (and his successors) alive by doing the following:

- ✔ Acting as a warrior or comrade in arms
- ✔ Assisting in herding flocks of animals
- ✔ Finding items by scent, including food, lost people, and property
- ✔ Participating in military actions or acting as a guard against attack
- ✔ Serving as a hunting partner to flush, run down, and capture game

The end result: Perpetual puppies

In truth, what the domestication process accomplished was to arrest dog development in a very puppylike state. In essence, domestic dogs are the Peter Pans of the canine world.

Neoteny refers to certain features normally found only in infants and young juveniles but which in certain animals persist into adulthood. In Figure 1-1, you can see that many physical features of an adult domestic dog resemble those of a wolf puppy more than those of an adult wolf. Common physical differences between wolves and dogs come about because of neoteny. As you move down the arrow, you move farther away from adult characteristics and toward more puppylike features.

In terms of human relationships with dogs, the behavioral aspects of neoteny are most important. Dogs keep a number of puppylike behaviors that wolves lose as they mature. These puppy behaviors are what make dogs fine companions (versus the adult canine behavior that makes wolves so difficult to tame). Table 1-1 offers an interesting look at what the adult wolf behavioral characteristics are like compared to the wolf-puppy characteristics that you see in dogs.

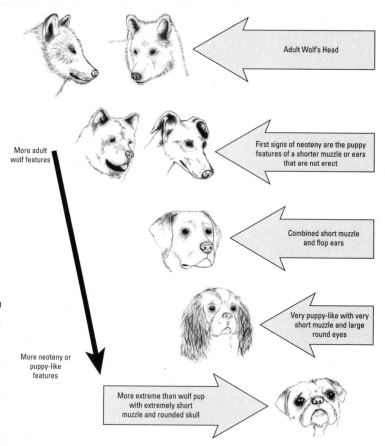

Adult Wolf's Head

More adult wolf features

First signs of neoteny are the puppy features of a shorter muzzle or ears that are not erect

Combined short muzzle and flop ears

Very puppy-like with very short muzzle and large round eyes

More neoteny or puppy-like features

More extreme than wolf pup with extremely short muzzle and rounded skull

Figure 1-1:
The ranging charac-teristics between adult wolves and perpet-ual puppies.

Table 1-1   Dogs Act More Like Wolf Puppies Than Wolf Adults

Behavioral Trait or Characteristic	Adult Version Seen in Wolves	Puppylike Version Seen in Dogs
Fear of strangers (xenophobia)	Common and not easily changed	Usually friendly and approach strangers if brought up with ade-quate human contact
Acceptance of leadership	Often challenges for leadership and dominance	Usually accept humans as leaders and challenges are rare
Dependence	Independent	Tend to look to humans or other dogs for guidance

Behavioral Trait or Characteristic	Adult Version Seen in Wolves	Puppylike Version Seen in Dogs
Play behaviors	Very rare in adults and then only shown around puppies	Urge to play continues throughout life
Trainability	Minimal; obedience commands learned when young often aren't responded to when adult	Much more trainable than wolves; furthermore, obedience training can occur throughout life, and trainability is retained through adulthood
Barking	Rare and brief — only in warning or surprise	Common in many settings, with variations serving as communication
Yelping	Absent except in pups	Common in many settings
Group howling	Common social activity	Less common in dogs; much like pups, when it does occur, it includes barks and yelps
Muzzle biting and pinning canines to the ground	Common as part of the ritual display of dominance	Rare except in the most wolflike breeds (such as Malamutes)
Licking as a greeting	Occurs only occasionally and for short duration	Quite frequent, especially in the most puppylike breeds

Understanding the Evolution of the Dog and Human Relationship

Is your dog a wolf in sheep's clothing? Well, yes and no. Suffice it to say that dogs approached domestication at their own speed. There was no cosmic moment when some brave young child, holding a wolf pup, approached his father and said, "Please, Dad, can we keep it?" Instead, domestication was a slow evolutionary process involving a gradual progression that began with curious wolves who drew closer and closer to our ancestors' campfires. Domestication shows the marked physical changes that characterize the dogs we know today. This section gives you a brief history of the evolution.

Which wild canines became dogs?

More than 30 different species of wild canines are candidates for the first animal that humans domesticated into a dog, but which species did humans actually take into their homes and make their closest animal companion?

DNA evidence suggests that the first wild canine that was domesticated was the gray wolf. However, other types of wolves and also jackals, coyotes, wild dogs, dingoes, and even some varieties of fox got into the mix as well. As a result, any one dog may have a combination of genes from all these various members of the canine family. Researchers know this fact because domestic dogs can interbreed with any of these species (the exception being some of the common fox species, such as the red fox, which have the wrong number of chromosomes). The offspring from such matings are live, healthy, and fertile, which is usually taken as evidence that they're all the same species or, according to evolutionary theory, at least have a relatively recent common ancestor.

This research suggests that the dog at your side may be some random mix of genes, descended from perhaps 40 percent wolf, 30 percent jackal, and 30 percent coyote, while another breed may be 60 percent wolf, 10 percent jackal, 15 percent arctic fox, and 15 percent dingo. No wonder so many different breeds have so many different physical appearances, behavioral styles, and personalities.

People and dogs: A parallel evolution

Our relationship with dogs began during a time when survival was our only focus. During this time, dogs provided personal protection and hunting assistance.

For eons, dogs and humans evolved in parallel. During the agricultural era, for example, we modified our selection process to produce dogs who would cull the varmint population and others who would herd livestock. As kingdoms grew, massive dog breeds were shaped by a process of manual selection to guard castles and aid wars. The selection process has continued throughout time, and today more than 400 different dog breeds — all developed for particular tasks — populate our globe.

Except for in a few instances, most dogs' special talents are rarely needed. But don't tell your dog that; it would be too depressing for him, because he thinks his abilities are still in high demand.

Seeing how domestication shaped dogs' personalities

Dogs' devotion to people was hard wired upon domestication. The canine species is the only species that will look to and take direction from another species (humans) as if it were their own.

In Chapter 3 in Book I, you discover how to identify your dog's temperament and how it shapes her understanding of the world you share. For example, a dominant dog assesses everyone who enters, whereas a timid dog hides under the table when the doorbell rings. Embracing your dog's personality helps you orchestrate a training program to normalize your life together.

Unlike humans, who learn by listening, your dog is much more attuned to nonverbal communication — from how you hold your body (especially in moments of tension or stress) to where you focus your eyes. Understanding your dog's concept of language can help you understand her behavior and be understood in kind.

If you consistently look at your dog, she may interpret your interest as a need for leadership. So remember this little jingle: The more you look *at* your dog, the less she'll look *to* you.

A dog's senses never change: Dealing with sensory overload

To really consider life from your dog's perspective, you need a new nose. Dogs rely most heavily on their sense of smell to interpret even the most minor aspects of their surroundings, such as when another animal may have passed through or even the stress hormone of a visitor in your home.

In your dog, the sense of sight (a human's strongest sense) is blurred and limited. Your dog only can recognize a limited range of colors and is more attuned to the motion of an object than its particulars. Dogs don't rely on the recognition of fine details of objects. Rather they were born to be hunters with the motto, "If it moves it might be food, and I'll chase and catch it!"

Your dog's hearing abilities are much different than your own, and this difference can be traced to the evolution of our separate species. Humans are more sharply attuned to the sound of other human voices, whereas dogs are capable of hearing higher frequencies and fainter sounds. Because dogs evolved from hunters, their hearing is more attuned to the sounds that their potential prey might make.

Unfortunately, dogs' sensory strengths are rarely appreciated today. An apartment dog is admonished each time he alerts to the sound of a footstep; hounds are scolded for getting into the trash; and all breeds are reprimanded for chasing the family cat. In our world, dogs are on sensory overload and yet they're expected to ignore everything.

Influencing Your Dog's Learning

Dogs love to learn and feel connected to group activities. So how you develop as a teacher and translator directly affects their enthusiasm for learning and, in turn, for life. Think of each lesson and highlighted word as though you were teaching a foreigner your language. Lift "Sit," "Wait," "Down," and "Good" beyond mere command status; instead, make them verbal directions that show your dog how to act in everyday situations.

Book IV lays out all the tricks of the trade, exploring learning influences and emotional responses. In addition, the chapters in that part help you make sense of the different schools and methods of training your dog.

Keeping age in mind

Whether you have a puppy or an older dog, you can appreciate that time and experience will make a difference in your dog's behavior. A young puppy, who's often interpreting many of life's nuances for the first time, watches your actions carefully and is influenced by how you behave. An older dog, however, who may have studied many human responses, may be less influenced by your activities — unless, of course, they're unusual or unexpected.

Chapter 5 in Book I highlights how to best acclimate your puppy and lists the ideal lessons to introduce at different stages. It also stresses the critical importance of early socialization and how encounters with various people and places can change your dog's life forever.

Dogs age quickly. Even though many of their life processes mirror ours, their timeline accelerates at ten times our rate. By age 3, your dog is a mature adult, by 7 most have reached middle age, and by 10, many are heading into their twilight years. It's a reality that can't be ignored or avoided. Chapter 6 in Book II is devoted to the care of an aging dog.

Putting commands to work

Book I

Choosing and Bringing Home a Dog

There's no one approach to encouraging good behavior. Each dog is unique and may respond better to one technique than another. A clearly orchestrated attempt to educate yourself and understand the different methods available will keep your training effort fresh and alive.

Even though a dog can recognize up to 165 different *commands,* or word cues, your goals need not be so lofty. Table 1-2 lists six example commands that are most useful for navigating your life together. After you have these directions firmly planted in your dog's memory bank, they form the foundation for controlling your dog's behavior. Their use reassures your dog of her place in your family and her vital inclusion in your world.

Table 1-2	Six Commands That Make a Difference
Command	*Daily Uses*
Follow/heel	When walking about town or off your property, or to encourage attention in your home
Wait — okay	To get your dog to stop and check in before entering or exiting your home or new buildings as well as when you cross the street and approach stairs
No (and other derivations, such as Not now, Leave it, Don't think about it)	To alert your dog that a given impulse is not in her best interest (for example, stealing food, chasing an object or animal, and so on)
Stay	Enforces impulse to control; ideally used when you need your dog to be still or to relax
Down (and Settle down)	Directs your dog into a submissive, relaxed pose or to her bed
Come	Directs your dog to stop whatever he's doing and go to you

Ain't Misbehavin': Examining Dog Behaviors and Human Responses

No matter how livid you feel when your dog disobeys you or damages prized possessions, you won't influence his routines until you sit down and listen to his side of the story. Sure, your half-eaten pair of shoes cost $95, but to your dog, its enticing aroma (a perfume called "You") was impossible to pass by. This section leads you through the most common frustrations, from house-training to anxiety-driven behavior and on to aggression, in an effort to shape your ability to respond in a manner that your dog understands.

Why dogs act out

Just as people do, many dogs act out when they feel misunderstood, restless, or needy. If you walk around claiming that your dog is reacting out of spite, then in your mind, her every reaction will be tainted by that view — even though "spite" is not an emotion that dogs have. If you keep shouting "Bad dog!" every time your dog makes a wrong move, what option does she have?

Dogs, like children, are motivated by what gets attention. However, it often appears that dogs can't differentiate positive attention from negative. So if an action gets a reaction — any reaction — it will get repeated.

Furthermore, negative attention can be misperceived as being rough play or confrontation. Thus, a dog who steals from the counter may feel *prize envy* when her people react uproariously. A smart dog will simply wait until people have left the room and then (minus competition) carry the prize off to a more secluded space. Chapter 2 in Book IV examines what can be done to address misbehavior.

Dissecting daily frustrations

You may have a real issue with some of your dog's behaviors, but it's unlikely that he's even aware of the issues. Even though a pee-stained carpet can raise your blood pressure, from his point of view the carpet is just as absorbent as the grass, and whether his accident was motivated by need or distraction, he did what came naturally.

Now, don't get stressed. You don't have to live with a dog who urinates on the carpet, jumps on company, or chews your slippers. However, recognizing that your dog's behavior isn't motivated by spite, vengeance, or guilt can ease your frustration.

Common complaints that dog owners have about living with their dog include barking, chewing, jumping, and house soiling. Each behavior, though disruptive and aggravating, may be a perfectly normal sign of a dog who has bonded well and is trying to get along within the family unit. Reorganizing his outlook may require some effort and intervention, but the process usually takes less time and is less stressful than coping with the current frustrations that have become status quo.

Reality bites: Inside canine aggression

Aggression is the one behavior that warrants a red flag on any playing field. Though biting is sometimes perfectly understandable, dogs simply aren't allowed to bite human beings (or other animals) — unless, of course, they've been trained to such ends or are legitimately defending their territory.

Dogs who bite are excluded from activities, relinquished to shelters, or euthanized. So before your dog shows any signs of aggression, it's wise to understand what motivates her and do what you can to prevent it. The chapters in Book IV cover many aspects of training.

No book for home use can address the needs of a dog who's exhibiting a full-blown aggressive response and threatening the safety of family members, neighbors, or other animals. Even though this book gives you the means to recognize the nature of your dog's behavior and some ways to deal with it, if your dog has seriously bitten someone, or is really scaring you because she's threatening to bite, you must seek professional advice.

Chapter 2

Ready, Set, Stop: What You Need to Know Before You Choose a Dog

You're on the mark. You're set. You're ready to run . . . straight to the nearest pair of wistful puppy eyes. Whoa, there! Ever hear about those times when people could kick themselves? Mm-hmm. This is one of them.

If you buy a shirt that doesn't fit, it's no big deal. You simply return it or give it away. Poor magazine choices can be recycled or canceled. When you cave in to puppy love, though, it's a dog of a different color. The time for making decisions about whether to buy — as well as how, when, and where to do it — is *before* you look into those big brown eyes. Putting a cute pup down and walking away is downright impossible, especially after she snuggles close to you and licks the tip of your nose.

The wide and wonderful world of dogs boasts more than 400 breeds of canines. Finding a puppy seems like a simple task, but it can be overwhelming when it comes to finding just the right dog — the perfect dog — for you. This chapter helps you sort through the whens, wheres, and hows of finding a dog.

If everyone buying or breeding dogs were to strive to become responsible pet owners, then the people who are involved with rescues and shelters could turn their energies toward raising funds for veterinary research, conducting education seminars, or simply having more time with their own dogs.

After getting them home, dogs must have physical care to thrive. The necessities of life include shelter, coat care, fresh water, good-quality food, prevention of illness, companionship, and medical treatment when needed. Over the centuries, human society has changed wild, self-sufficient canines into domesticated pets who can't provide for themselves. True, as long as the large, white porcelain water bowl in the bathroom is kept flushed, all but the smallest dogs can find water. Oh, and yeah, occasionally a bread crust is nibbled beneath the baby's chair or a steak is snarfed from the countertop. But other than those accidental waterings and feedings, dogs are pretty much dependent upon us.

Returning a pup after human and canine hearts become connected is painful for all involved. Similarly, disposing of a dog because you've satisfied a temporary whim is unfair. And, last but not least, impulse decisions can lead to a lifetime of regret. So right now — before you buy — is the time to examine your lifestyle, facilities, and pocketbook. Forethought eliminates later pain for dogs and people. This chapter can help you decide whether you're ready for the commitment. After your self-examination, you may find that a dog isn't a good choice for you at all. You may find that you'd be better off with a cat, a fish, or a pet rock.

Considering Your Lifestyle

Before your heart is set on a new dog, you need to ask yourself the following questions:

- ✔ Is this the right time for adding a dog to my life?
- ✔ Am I emotionally capable of devoting a lot of time and energy to taking care of a living creature's every need, from now to perhaps a dozen or more years down the road?
- ✔ Does my work schedule allow for time to take care of a dog?
- ✔ Is my household/neighborhood a good place for a dog to live?
- ✔ Who's going to watch the pup when I go away?

Contemplate all aspects of your life, present and future. Even though you may not currently have small children, consider the possibility of becoming a parent. Also think about visitors, neighbors, or grandchildren. Everything involves some risk. Children can love dogs too much by hugging them too tightly, and they can also fall on them, pick them up in the wrong way, or even drop and seriously injure them, especially Toy breeds or puppies.

However, it isn't always the dog who's injured. Rowdy canine play can result in a child being knocked over or scratched. Small or timid dogs can snap if cornered. Herding dogs sometimes instinctively round up their charges by nipping at heels or behinds. Guardian breeds may take their jobs too seriously, especially when "intruders," such as visiting children, engage in rough, noisy play. You still can choose your ideal dog even though you have children, but you may want to wait until they're a few years older.

Scheduling a family meeting and obtaining the approval of everyone who'll share the household with the pet is a good idea, even if you'll be the main caretaker. The dad who grudgingly buys Junior a dog hoping to teach the lad responsibility will be up to his neck in doggie doo within a week. When a sullen teenager promises he'll take care of the pup, you need to get real.

Some people who have grown up with pets know that a dog is a treasured friend. For some, it doesn't make any difference how busy they are; they simply wouldn't think of being without a dog — no matter what the obligations — any more than they would decide to isolate themselves from human family or friends. But even lifelong dog lovers need to realize that circumstances may change regarding finances, living quarters, or leisure time. Perhaps having a dog still is possible, but you must choose wisely. You pay the price, and the dog suffers the consequences when you make the wrong decision.

Don't *ever* buy a dog as a surprise gift for someone. Buying a pet for an unsuspecting friend or relative is one of the worst ideas you can ever have — dumber even than getting matching his-and-hers socket wrench kits for your anniversary.

The Money Angle: Keeping Canine Expenses in Mind

Dogs truly are love that money *can* buy. But the expense surely doesn't end with the purchase. Even a dog given to you by a puppy-burdened co-worker doesn't come without expensive needs. Sure, the love and affection are free, but unfortunately, other life necessities are not. Even free dogs cost money.

A medium-sized dog can easily eat, chew, and barf his way through more than $900 a year. No skimping on generic dog food for this prince of a pup, so figure $300 for quality food. Dog tags average anywhere from $10 to $50. Even if your dog is healthy all year, his veterinarian bill can still runs $200 or more for exams, vaccinations, flea control, and heartworm prevention. For a dog who needs professional grooming, tack on at least another $150 per year. Oh, and do you like to go on vacation? If you don't take the dog with you every time, you may have to pay someone to dogsit. If you add in the occasional dog walker, you can tack on another $100 a year. You like to buy fancy treats, right — and Frisbees, tennis balls, real bones, and elaborate dog toys and accessories? Add another $100. That's *without* replacing the chewed baseboards, couch cushions, and shoes. Not to mention all those training classes you'll want to try.

Large-sized dogs, such as Labs, Great Danes, and Mastiffs, have bigger tummies to fill and more square inches to groom. They also need larger doses of medications and preventives as well as bigger and more expensive collars and housing.

The first year of dog ownership is often the costliest. Puppies need lots of supplies and preventive care to start a good life. Bowls, housing, blankets, brushes and combs, nail clippers, collars, and leashes all need to be on your list of supplies to buy. Other smart investments include training classes and fencing for either your yard or an exercise area.

If you're interested in a purebred pup, also keep in mind that prices can be quite hefty depending on the breed and the breeder's reputation. Dogs with impressive pedigrees and real show prospects are almost always more expensive.

Last but not least, what about you? What shape are your finances in? Are you starting a new business or saving for a new home? If so, you may want to wait a bit of time to get a pet. After all, if unexpected and unplanned expenses occur lifewise or dogwise, will that extra mouth to feed still be considered a valuable part of the family — or another albatross around your neck? Writing out the check to the dog breeder won't be the last time your pup cracks open your checkbook or picks your pocket (sometimes literally).

Recognizing Your Responsibilities

Responsibility. You know how much you hated that word when your folks first lectured you about it? Well, it follows you the rest of your life. When you adopt a four-legged dependent and take this hairy creature into your home, you're as responsible for him as much as if you'd brought him into the world. He deserves to be fed, housed, and given vet care for the rest of his life. A pup needs boundaries set for behavior, and these boundaries must be taught to him in a fair, humane manner — otherwise he'll go as far out of bounds as any normal human teenager. The difference is that most human kids don't bite when they're out of control.

Dogs need exercise and mental stimulation to be mentally and physically healthy. They can't do this by themselves, however. Even with a huge, safely fenced area, they won't constantly run around and play unless someone can join their pack and share in the fun. They also may pick inappropriate ways to entertain themselves when left to their own devices — chewing the siding off the house, digging in the prize petunia patch, or barking at imaginary friends.

Some dog owners view the responsibilities of ownership as a pleasure. When you compare caring for a dog with some other responsibilities, such as teaching a teen to drive (and actually handing over the keys), paying bills, and covering college tuition, your dog's needs are relatively simple:

- ✔ Exercise
- ✔ Food and water
- ✔ Safety
- ✔ Shelter
- ✔ Training
- ✔ Vet care

Even though they're simple, the items in the preceding list are essential. Provide these things, and you ensure that you have an appreciative, loving buddy for a long time to come.

Without these essentials, however, you not only compromise your dog's health, but you also risk turning him into a creature with less than desirable habits, including

- ✔ Barking all night
- ✔ Biting
- ✔ Making the Persian rug the puppy potty
- ✔ Stealing food
- ✔ Turning the antique credenza into toothpicks

Before you buy a dog, be sure that you're ready to accept the responsibilities of ownership — all of them. When you're truly ready to be a dog owner, the rewards are many.

Besides nurturing your exciting new relationship with your new best friend, you're also responsible for developing at least one more with your veterinarian. Good vets (and there should be no other kind) recommend everything you need to do to ensure the health of your dog for many years. You can find more on vets in Chapter 4 in Book II. You may also have a new bond with a breeder. A responsible — there's that word again — breeder always answers your questions, cheers you on, and shares your sorrow a dozen years down the road. See Chapters 3 and 4 in Book I for more information on breeders.

Choose vet relationships wisely. During conversations with the doctor and his staff, you'll have good or bad vibes. Pay attention to them. Someone may have referred you to this person, but you're the one who has to deal with him in person or on the phone. Follow your gut feeling; if it doesn't feel right, walk away.

Keeping your dog safe

Being a good puppy or dog parent means making certain that your four-legged friend is safe at all times. Unlike the old days when someone almost always was at home, many demands are placed on the time of today's family, whose members are often away from the home front. Puppies are much like human toddlers. They're curious, and when left to their own devices they will eventually provide entertainment (and danger) for themselves. This can mean chewing on electrical cords, visiting the kids across the highway, or swallowing the pork chop bones left in the trash. So it's important to puppy-proof your home when you're away. See Chapter 5 in Book I for more on how to do this.

Exercising your pooch

No dog park? No yard? You still can give your dog exercise without jeopardizing her safety — but exercise she must! Jog with her. Enroll in agility classes. Get a *retractable leash.* These leashes extend the dog's roaming freedom from 16 feet to a whopping 32 feet. However, be sure that you're adept at using one and that plenty of space is open so the dog doesn't wind the leash around trees or legs (painful rope burns!), or, worse, dart in front of a car. See Chapter 6 in Book I for more on leashes.

Providing adequate shelter

If you leave your dog outdoors for any length of time, he needs suitable shelter from the sun, rain, snow, and extreme temperatures as well as a respite from the public eye. Every dog wants to be alone now and then. He seeks a protected place for a nap, for example. And of course fresh water must be available at all times, indoors and out.

Here are a few good shelter options that can keep your dog from running loose and possibly causing injury to himself or others:

- ✔ A kennel run (at least 3 x 10 feet, or larger for a big dog) with a house
- ✔ A crate under a deck or overhang
- ✔ A doggy door into a garage pen, basement, or house

Whatever you do, don't *ever* chain a dog and leave him. A chain makes a dog feel vulnerable and that he must defend himself. And never use a trolley with a sliding attachment; these devices incite dogs to run back and forth. In fact, dogs can hang themselves on these contraptions (and have done so) when unsupervised. Neighbors are likely to take a dim view of both techniques as well, and then you could get an embarrassing visit from an animal protection agency.

When you can't be around to supervise your pet, provide a safe house or room. The best place — especially for puppies — is a dog kennel. You can use either a crate indoors or a secure fenced area outdoors. Some owners prefer putting a pup in a kitchen, bathroom, or laundry room while they're gone. Usually these areas can be shut off with a door or baby gate, have little to damage, and are easily cleaned when messes occur. If accessible to little paws or needle-sharp teeth, items still may be damaged, but at least his life won't be endangered. Try putting a favorite toy — one that's given to him only when he's confined — in the area and move other items out of reach.

Taking part in training

Training classes make your dog a treasured family member and good citizen. In fact, the AKC has a test for all dogs — registered, purebred, or mixed — called the Canine Good Citizen (CGC) test. A basic training class teaches your dog to become a CGC. Large metropolitan areas offer many choices for owners who want to train their dogs. But even out in the boonies, you usually can find a club or private trainer within a half-hour's drive. Whether you introduce your pooch to training classes or not, be sure to check out Book IV, which provides a lot of information on training your dog.

Classes are great, not only for the camaraderie but also for the socialization of the dog with others of all sizes and breeds. However, the private trainer offers a couple pluses, too. You can arrange training according to your schedule, and the trainer's attention isn't divided among a dozen students, enabling the trainer to focus on your needs and your dog's quirks.

Puppy kindergarten offers the basics in good house manners. You usually are recommended to begin these classes as soon as the pup has been inoculated. Formal obedience training can begin any time after the dog reaches 4 months of age. These classes aren't just for competition or for good citizenship. They can save your dog's life. One of the more important lessons is the *recall*, in which your pup learns to come when you call her. Imagine if your dog escapes and runs toward a busy street — you can yell, "DOWN!" or "COME!" and she'll do it!

You may have such a good time with the basics that you consider handling or agility classes. Usually only those people who intend to show in the breed ring attend handling classes. But agility training is for anyone and everyone — all sizes and breeds. Agility gives your dog good exercise as you race together through an obstacle course. Sometimes it's difficult to tell who's having a better time — the owner or the dog. Even though speed is necessary for top prizes, many disabled, elderly, or just plain clumsy people compete for the fun of it.

Not all training clubs or private trainers are listed in the phone book. Call your vet or the Better Business Bureau for a referral. Talk to other owners who've been pleased with their training experiences as well.

Remembering essential vet care

A pup needs inoculations to protect against various canine diseases, including rabies, distemper, and parvovirus. Each year a dog needs a physical exam, any necessary boosters, and heartworm tests. A preventive for this dangerous parasite is advised in most areas as well. You also may want to consider flea and tick prevention. Regular vet checks help to establish a patient-doctor relationship that's beneficial if an illness or injury occurs.

Routine intestinal parasite screenings (fecal exams) are also a good idea, particularly for pups, because they often carry parasites that are contagious to humans.

Testing Your Readiness: Rent-a-Dog

So you've just about decided to take the leap and bring a dog into your world. A life is involved here, though, so you want to make sure that this is the right decision for you. What can you do to make sure that you're not making a mistake? Many people do a little dogsitting sometime before making the plunge into pet parenthood. Then they're aware of some of the agonies of guardianship (albeit temporary) as well as the many ecstasies. Thus, the answer to your question is: Borrow a dog.

Offer to help a neighbor who has a new puppy and can't make it home during the lunch hour. You'll be introduced to overturned water bowls and housetraining accidents. And you'll swear that the shark from *Jaws,* rather than a 10-pound pup, has you by the ankle. Pray that it's winter so you'll at least be wearing long pants as a protection against those nails when the little darling claws its way up your legs to lick you from ear to ear. An earsplitting yodel greets you as you arrive, and another mourns your departure.

Thinking about a giant breed? The puppies are so cute and cuddly! But babies do have a way of growing up — and fast. Dogsit a Great Pyrenees for the week someone's on vacation. Mop up great goobers. Clean up elephantine droppings from the yard. If you're really brave, let the beast romp in a mud puddle and follow it up with a brushing and a bath. Prepare yourself for walks by lifting weights. Long white hair will decorate your wool suit, clog your drains, and keep the dog in your memory long after he has returned home.

Volunteer to provide foster care for a dog when the Humane Society is full. If you're considering a particular breed, contact the rescue organization for the breed's local or national clubs. Just like traumatized children, abandoned or abused dogs have nightmares and tortures in their pasts. And like children, they need love and attention now. A rescued dog will thank you with a tail wag and a lick, and by laying his head upon your knee.

After a dog enters your home, she may never leave. Even if she physically leaves, she takes a little piece of your heart. Corny? Maybe. Also true.

If you've finally decided that you want to take the plunge and introduce a dog into your life — perhaps one of the biggest decisions you'll ever make — congratulations! Now you face numerous other choices as you work your way toward dog ownership. You need to think about whether you want an adult dog or a puppy — both have their advantages. Male or female? Pure breed or mixed breed? Great dogs can be found in plenty of places — through reputable breeders, humane societies, and breed rescue organizations, to name a few. But when you get to the place where you'll choose a dog, you still need to know what you're looking for in an individual dog. Chapters 3 and 4 in Book I help you make these decisions (and many more) in narrowing down the choices and making sure that you get the right dog for you. And of course, all the chapters in Book V introduce you to the unique characteristics of the various breeds.

Chapter 3

Considering All the Options

· ·

In This Chapter

▶ Thinking about your new dog's age

▶ Determining the importance of gender and size

▶ Factoring in energy and temperament

▶ Identifying signs of a healthy dog

▶ Picking the perfect puppy

· ·

So many adorable dogs are out there, barking and wiggling to get your attention. If only you could take them all home! Of course, you can't. But you can pick the right dog for you by focusing on exactly what you want and need in a dog, and determining what kind of dog works best in your home and with your lifestyle. The fact that animal shelters are full of dogs is proof that too many people buy dogs who aren't right for them. This chapter helps you make smart decisions about the issues involved in selecting a dog so that when you do choose yours, you'll know you've considered all the factors.

Sure, you can listen to your heart, but let your brain have the final say.

Puppies Are Precious, but . . .

Just look at that fluffy ball of fuzz, those big innocent eyes, that madly wagging tail! Many people who want to adopt a dog are hoping to adopt a puppy, and that's no surprise. Puppies can be practically irresistible. Shelters have a much easier time placing puppies than they do older dogs. The downside, however, is that many of these puppies wind up back at the shelter as soon as they hit that difficult adolescent period — when they're big, rambunctious, and particularly challenging.

Before you insist on a puppy, take a good look at your options. Sometimes breed, size, or temperament is more important than a dog's age. A chubby, round, yellow Labrador Retriever puppy may be the cutest thing you've ever seen, but how will you feel when he grows to 75 pounds of explosive energy and knocks favorite knickknacks off your coffee table with his big tail? Adopting a puppy and adopting an adult dog have distinct advantages and disadvantages, so consider the pros and cons of each before making a decision.

Pros and cons of adopting a puppy

They're tiny, they're cute, and they pull at your heartstrings with that ferocious little tug-of-war puppy growl. But do you really want to adopt a puppy?

The *pros* of puppy adoption include the following:

- Control over exactly when and how well the puppy is socialized and trained, so your puppy learns good behavior early

- An opportunity for you and your puppy to bond right from the beginning

- A fun, playful, adorable companion

- Short-lived high energy that often (but not always) mellows into mature adolescence in one to two years

- A longer amount of time together than if you adopt an older dog

The *cons* of puppy adoption can saddle you with this stuff:

- A pet with behaviors you don't like, if you fail to control exactly how well the puppy is socialized and trained.

- The chore of housetraining your puppy, a time-consuming and sometimes frustrating task. If you aren't consistent with your training, you'll have puppy puddles and piles to clean up for what seems like forever.

- Chewed up, well, everything. Puppies need to chew . . . a lot. You must provide them with appropriate items to chew and keep things they are *not* allowed to chew out of reach. If you tend to leave your expensive shoes on your bedroom floor, a puppy may not be right for you.

- A seemingly inexhaustible need for more exercise and stimulation than most adult dogs. Puppies, by nature, are energetic.

- Ill-mannered behaviors. Granted, *manners* are all human, and puppy behaviors are entirely natural. Even so, in our human world, puppies have no manners whatsoever. They may nip fingers, jump on people, bark at everything, pull on the leash, pick on other pets, dig holes in your yard, try to escape the fence to play with the neighbors, and keep you up at night because they still want to play. You have to teach them *everything.*

✔ **An uncertain adult appearance.** If you adopt your puppy through a shelter or you choose a mixed breed, you can't be sure of your puppy's parents and you won't know what the puppy will look like when it grows up. Many shelter puppies who look like purebreds grow up to look much different as adults.

If you have your heart set on a puppy, check out the tips for picking the perfect one later in this chapter.

Pros and cons of adopting an adult dog

Adult dogs can make absolutely wonderful adopted pets. After adopting a puppy, many people decide never to do *that* again and vow to adopt only adult dogs in the future.

Many adult dogs in shelters are well-behaved family pets who lost their homes through no fault of their own. Some dogs are there because their owners didn't know how to manage perfectly natural dog behavior. Others are there because their owners got divorced, moved, or died. Others are there because they're no longer the cute puppies to which their owners first were attracted. The most common age for dogs to be surrendered to shelters is in the difficult adolescent phase and early adulthood, usually between about 9 months and 2 years, when dogs typically develop some challenging behaviors backed up by a full-grown size. Instead of working on these issues with training and socialization, pet owners often just give up.

Before you decide that you want an adult dog, consider the advantages and disadvantages within the context of your lifestyle. An adult dog may be the perfect fit for you because it may already be

✔ **Housetrained:** Many dogs housetrain young and never forget.

✔ **Finished teething:** Adult dogs typically don't chew and nip the way puppies do, although exceptions do exist.

✔ **Well versed in basic training:** They know how to walk on a leash, obey basic cues like "Sit" and "Come," and generally behave appropriately in the house.

✔ **Well socialized:** Many adult dogs are friendly and accustomed to different kinds of people and situations.

✔ **More laid back:** Adult dogs aren't quite as wild and energetic as puppies.

Dogging it indoors or out

Before you choose a dog, think about where you're planning to keep him. Certain breeds must live indoors because they suffer in extreme temperatures. Others adapt to virtually any weather, as long as they have adequate shelter.

But all dogs do better living inside with the family at least part of every day. Bonding is even easier when your pet is your shadow by day and your foot warmer at night.

✔ **Almost finished with adolescence:** Although adolescent dogs initially may have high energy, they often (but not always) mellow out, especially if you provide plenty of outlets for that energy.

✔ **More adaptable:** Adult dogs are usually willing to bond closely with anyone who takes them in, feeds them, and gives them a home and some attention.

Many people claim that adult dogs they adopted from shelters and rescue groups seem to know that they've been given a second chance. These pet owners say they get a strong sense of gratitude from their dogs.

✔ **A quick study:** Adult dogs typically learn quickly and enjoy training sessions as a fun way to spend time with you. You *can* teach old dogs new tricks.

✔ **More readily available:** Shelters have a harder time placing adult dogs. Adopting one saves an animal who may otherwise never find a home.

Despite all the wonderful aspects of adult dogs, they may present their own challenges. Be aware of these considerations before you decide to adopt one:

✔ **Behavioral problems:** Resource guarding — snapping when you try to take away food or treats — is a common problem. Others can include dislike of children or displays of aggression or self-mutilation in response to anxiety.

✔ **Bad habits that take extra training to undo:** Examples include excessive barking, digging in the yard, and chewing on shoes.

✔ **A lengthy adjustment period because the dog was in another home for so long:** Dogs may mourn lost loved ones or seem depressed.

✔ **Difficulty bonding:** Some dogs need to be taught to trust humans again.

✔ **Too short a time in your life:** You may have only a few more years with an adult dog. Larger breeds, especially, have life spans of only six to eight years. If your adopted Great Dane is already 4 years old, well, you do the math.

Book I

Choosing
and
Bringing
Home a
Dog

Considering Sex and Size

Just as some shelters have a harder time finding homes for adult dogs than they do for puppies, many have a more difficult time finding homes for male dogs than they do for female dogs. Potential pet owners often say they want a female, a factor that sometimes is even more important to them than breed.

Yet males and females exhibit virtually no consistent difference in behavior. In some breeds, males actually make more affectionate pets, and females are more independent and exhibit a higher drive to work. In other breeds, males tend to be more aggressive and females are more laid back. But even these generalizations have many exceptions. And when pets are spayed or neutered, these differences become even less significant.

Trying to predict a dog's personality based on gender is impossible. Instead of merely choosing male or female, look at breed, age, grooming needs, and temperament. You may find that your canine soul mate is the opposite sex you thought you wanted.

Likewise, size isn't always an obvious advantage or disadvantage. A lethargic giant may take up less space than a tiny dynamo dashing from sofa to windowsill to front door and back to sofa. Given proper exercise, even bigger breeds can do just as well in the city as in the country.

Similarly, tiny breeds aren't necessarily the ideal choice for a family with small tots. In fact, many big dogs have a reputation for being easygoing and patient with children. Large breeds also aren't as likely to be injured by a slamming door or a toddler teething on an ear. To protect herself, a big dog can simply get up and move; she doesn't need to retaliate with teeth to protect herself.

Keep in mind, of course, that a larger breed can be more difficult to manage simply because of mass weight. Nudging a Komondor over a car seat is a little harder than shoving even the most defiant toy breed.

Choosing a Pooch to Match Your Pep

As you're thinking about what kind of dog you want, consider your own level of activity: Are you more like a marathon runner or a couch potato? Choose a dog with an energy level similar to your own so you can enjoy activities together.

Beware of dog

Statistics show that people, homes, and businesses with doggie doorbells are less frequently victims of break-ins and attacks. Think about whether you want a dog who will simply announce visitors or one who will protect your home. And remember, if you're looking for protection, your choice isn't limited to large breeds. Dwarf or giant, dogs make a lot of noise — yaps, growls, and booming barks serve as canine alarm systems. For would-be burglars, shunning the dog and moving on to the next place is simpler than wading into an unknown situation. After all, little teeth can hurt as much as big ones.

The amount of activity a dog requires depends not on his size, but on his attitude. Some of the giant breeds, for instance, are happiest when snoozing in the sun, whereas high-energy breeds demand vigorous daily exercise. Frisky dogs are more in tune with hikers than 80-year-old quilting devotees.

Whatever your hobby may be, you can find a breed of dog eager to join the fun. Some dogs are content to lie on the sofa; others require regular, exhaustive exercise. (Also see Book V for descriptions of specific breeds' needs.)

Factoring In Temperament

Many shelters do temperament testing on the animals they hope to offer for adoption. Testing gives them a clear idea of the kind of home that best suits the pet and enables them to separate dogs who won't be able to thrive in a home because of bad temperament. Temperament testing can be as simple as checking a dog's behavior with other dogs and people, giving her basic commands to see whether she has had previous training, and testing her with cats and children.

Some shelters do more intensive temperament testing that follows specific methods recommended by certain trainers. Ask your shelter what type of temperament testing it has done and whether you can read the test results.

Be wary of a shelter that refuses to let you read the results, because it may be trying to hide the fact that it doesn't do any temperament testing. The dog may be perfectly adoptable, but you want to know as much as possible about the animal you plan to adopt.

Evaluating a dog's temperament is extremely important. It can spell the difference between a loving relationship with a trustworthy, trainable family pet and disaster in the form of injured people, angry neighbors, lawsuits, eviction, and a death sentence for the dog. A pet dog with a bad temperament is a serious liability. Bad temperament isn't the same as behaviors you don't like, such as failing in housetraining or barking too much. Dogs with bad temperaments cannot be trusted around humans or other pets because they are either aggressive or so painfully shy or unsocialized that their quality of life suffers and they can't form healthy relationships with people. Remember, shy dogs often bite out of fear.

Beyond bad temperaments are variable temperaments. Some dogs are outgoing; some are reserved. Some are vocal, pushy, and assertive; some are shy, retiring, and quiet. Temperament is akin to personality and comes in many different guises. Understanding a potential pet's temperament — and your own — helps you choose a dog you can live with.

Not everyone agrees that accurately analyzing the canine temperament is even possible in just a few minutes or after just a few meetings. Determining a dog's temperament is never quick and easy. It involves a careful process of observing and interacting with the animal. Some signs of bad temperament are obvious — growling, snarling, constantly quaking with fear — but many signs are not. Other aspects of temperament unfold slowly as the dog becomes more comfortable in your presence. Before you adopt a dog, arrange several extended visits. The more comfortable the dog is around you, the more her real temperament will come out.

Exploring breed temperament

Assessing the temperament of any given dog is tricky, at best. Complicating matters are temperaments that once were accepted as part of a dog's breed but now are no longer suitable for pets. For example, working sled dogs, hound dogs, guardian dogs, and herding dogs needed extremely high levels of energy and endurance, an instinct to run long distances to track down game, strong territorial instincts, or instincts for nipping at heels to keep livestock in one place. If you're adopting one of these dogs, you need to know about these breed traits.

The breed or mix of breeds in a dog has a big impact on that dog's temperament and physical traits, such as his coat and size. Mixed breeds that have some sporting dog in them (like Labrador Retrievers, Golden Retrievers, and German Shorthaired Pointers) are relatively large and have high energy. Labrador Retriever mixes (see Figure 3-1) are among the most common dogs in animal shelters, often because people expect a placid temperament but are overwhelmed with the activity needs of a younger Lab or Lab mix.

Figure 3-1:
Lab mixes make devoted, intelligent, trainable companions as long as you give them a lot of exercise.

Knowing a dog's natural tendencies is an important key to matching it with an individual or family. You can't expect a Border Collie to act like a couch potato or a Jack Russell Terrier not to bark; it simply isn't in their nature. If you do, you're just setting yourself up for failure and your dog up for disappointment.

Ask the shelter or rescue group for help in determining the breed or mix of the animal you're thinking about adopting. Most shelters and rescue groups label dogs as a breed or breed mix to give you an idea of what you can expect. Consider this information as a guideline for helping you choose a dog, but remember that no test can predict or guarantee exact behavior a few months down the road. Some general trends in breed temperament include the following, but remember that many exceptions exist for every rule:

- **Sporting breeds:** Retrievers, Pointers, and Spaniels are high energy and need plenty of activity, but they're generally easier than many other breeds to train.

- **Large working breeds:** Rottweilers, Doberman Pinschers, Great Danes, and Boxers tend to be territorial and protective. They need to be thoroughly socialized to keep them from becoming aggressive.

- **Terriers:** Jack Russell Terriers, Fox Terriers, Westies, and Schnauzers are high energy and bark a lot. They like to dig and jump, and can rarely be deterred from chasing small furry animals.

- **Hounds:** Beagles, Dachshunds, and Greyhounds follow scents or moving targets without regard to you, traffic, or anything else. They are independent and can be difficult to train.

Book I

Choosing
and
Bringing
Home a
Dog

✔ **Northern breeds**: Siberian Huskies and Malamutes are extremely high energy, independent, and notoriously difficult to train. They are great at sports like sled pulling but can become destructive without enough mental and physical challenge.

✔ **Toy breeds:** Chihuahuas, Shih Tzu, and Maltese tend to bark a lot and can be prone to shyness (as a protective mechanism caused by their diminutive size) or aggression when they're unsocialized or overly protected. See Figure 3-2 for an example of a toy breed mix.

✔ **Herding breeds:** Border Collies, Shelties, and Australian Shepherds are highly intelligent and trainable. They need a challenging job and plenty of exercise, or they can become destructive. Some herding breeds tend to nip at heels to keep children, other pets, or anyone else in the herd.

Figure 3-2: Small mixed breeds like this Miniature Pinscher/ Pug cross probably have toy breed and/ or terrier in their genetic mix.

For more information about breed characteristics, check out Book V.

Understanding the basics of temperament

So how do you know what's good or bad about a dog's temperament?

First, observe how the dog acts in the shelter or foster home. Is she active or laid back? Does she seem nervous or calm? Does she follow people or stay closely focused on them? Or is she more concerned with doing her own thing, exploring independently, or relaxing as if deep in thought?

Next, observe the dog as you interact with her. Is she interested in you or relatively indifferent? Does she try to engage you in active play and cuddle with you, or does she try to avoid you? Does she readily accept petting, or does she shy away? Does she jump all over you, or does she stand nicely, waiting to see what you do next?

Observing these behaviors takes time and effort, so don't expect to be able to immediately adopt a dog after your first meeting, especially if you have any reservations about the dog's temperament. Spend several "get acquainted" sessions with the dog to gain a more accurate feel for her individual personality. If you know your dog's breed or can guess what breeds may have contributed to her mix, you can research the typical temperaments for which each breed is known and compare them to the way your potential pet acts.

Although every dog has a unique personality, a few red flags can signal temperament problems that can become difficult to manage in a pet situation. As you watch how a candidate for adoption responds to the world, look for the following warning signs:

✔ **Extreme shyness:** A dog with a good pet temperament doesn't act fearful and refuse to let you touch her. Hiding, cowering, crying, and flinching at your touch are bad signs. Extremely shy dogs may live stressful lives, suffer from ill health, and never really bond with their owners. They can also bite out of fear.

✔ **Aggression:** A serious temperament flaw, aggression puts many dogs into the unadoptable category. Signs of aggression include teeth baring, growling, lunging, nipping, snapping, biting, and chasing. Aggression can be caused by extreme fear, an overdeveloped sense of dominance, a lack of trust for humans, past abuse, or a congenital bad temperament.

Avoid any dogs who show signs of aggression toward children or small pets. If you do decide to adopt a dog who shows aggressive tendencies, be prepared to provide plenty of targeted training with the help of a professional who specializes in overcoming aggressive behavior problems. Don't take on this type of project if you have children or if children frequently visit your house.

✔ **Hyperactivity:** Many dogs, especially puppies and adolescents, have high energy and require a lot of exercise and interaction. Such an energy level is normal. Dogs who are truly hyperactive usually are so high energy that they rarely calm down and are virtually uncontrollable. They have a hard time focusing on you, listening to you, or interacting with you even after you've spent several hours with them. Pet owners will have a hard time fulfilling their exercise needs or training them.

Discerning the difference between a high-energy dog and a hyperactive dog can be difficult at first. Some dogs are hyperactive in adolescence and calm down when they're older, but you probably won't be able to tell whether this situation will be true for your potential pet. Some breeds naturally are active, such as sporting dogs like Retrievers and Pointers and herding dogs like Border Collies and Shelties. Others got so little attention for so long that they simply are frantic to get any attention they can from you. Neither of these cases is a sign of a hyperactive temperament. So before you cross these dogs off your list, remember that many dogs just need a loving home, plenty of exercise, and some good old-fashioned attention.

These general observations can probably give you a basic sense of a dog's temperament, but you also need to hear what shelter or rescue workers have observed about the dog you're considering. They've probably interacted much longer and more intensively with the dog than you have and thus can offer you some good insights.

Go-getters, chill-outers, wait-and-seers

By observing the dog's temperament, you can begin to get a sense of the dog's personality. He may be outgoing or shy, self-confident or needy, active or sedentary, social or reserved. These various personality traits can help you determine whether you and the dog are a good match:

- ✔ **The go-getters:** These dogs are always on the move, always excited about the next new game, project, or travel opportunity. They relish the unfamiliar adventure. Go-getters love to hike, run, and play sports. Depending on the breed or breed combination, they enjoy engaging in high-energy dog sports like agility, flyball, canine freestyle, rally, dock jumping, earthdog, disk sports, water retrieving, tracking, and hunting tests. They're active and energetic, great matches for people who lead active, physical, athletic lifestyles.

- ✔ **The chill-outers:** Although dogs tend to be at their most active as puppies and adolescents, some individual dogs are more laid back. Like some people, they tend not to get riled up. Instead, they're typically adaptable and easygoing, and they prefer hanging out or cuddling with you on the couch to going for a 5-mile run. Sure, they need exercise and enjoy a rousing game of fetch the same as the next pooch, but they generally are less likely to run you ragged. This canine personality is perfect for the more sedentary, stay-at-home type of pet owner who wants a companion more than a four-legged dynamo who's bouncing off the walls from boredom.

✔ **The wait-and-seers:** These dogs like to hang back a little until they're sure about what's going on. Rather than plunging into the next new event, they're more hesitant. Whether pausing until they recognize something familiar or waiting for the go-ahead from their keeper, these dogs are more reserved. They don't typically dash up to a stranger with tail wagging. They may wait patiently or even stiffen and be on guard until they're more sure about the new person.

Guardian breeds, with their long history of serving as watchdogs to owner and property, especially tend to be wait-and-seers. Some toy dogs also react this way, perhaps out of a sense of self-preservation. (When you weigh 4 pounds, you have to be careful who you tangle with!) These cautious, reserved dogs make admirable and intelligent pets, and they're excellent companions for people who can spend time with them because they typically bond closely to one or two people. If well socialized, they can be trusted to act appropriately when around people, without nipping or growling when someone friendly tries to approach you or them.

Regardless of the dog's personality, look for a type of pet that you can deal with and relate to. Just as in human relationships, some personalities mesh well together; others clash. The dog-human team that meshes has a strong foundation for building a relationship.

Thinking about Health and Longevity

Dogs, like people, are living longer. New technology, better nutrition, and genetic testing of parents can help increase the life span of puppies. Indoor living, routine vet care, and canine laws (no more dogs running loose to be poisoned by garbage, squashed by cars, attacked by more powerful animals, or shot by angry neighbors) are helping us enjoy dogs longer. Many dogs live a dozen years.

It may seem odd to be asking about life expectancy before you even decide about a pup, but you can't change your mind after you've given your heart to a dog. Just as heart problems or high blood pressure and other diseases can run in family lines, certain canine problems can affect breeds or families (see next section). You can find a lot of information on doggie healthcare in Book II. Book V, on breeds, also contains some health-related information.

If you get your dog from a breeder, ask the ages of her oldest dogs. This information will give you an idea of how long you can expect yours to live.

Dogs never live long enough. Whenever we lose them, it's always too soon. But knowing their life expectancy prepares us better for the inevitable. As a

Book I

**Choosing
and
Bringing
Home a
Dog**

rule, most small breeds outlive larger ones (although teeny-tiny isn't necessarily better); giants have the shortest life span. Within a breed, however,
some lines can become canine centenarians.

Generally, old-age symptoms occur as follows:

   ✔ **Small:** Qualify as senior citizens at age 13 or 14

   ✔ **Medium:** Earn their AARC (retired canines) card at age 11

   ✔ **Large:** Usually slow down by age 10

   ✔ **Giant:** Often near retirement by age 7 or 8

Any dog can become ill or develop an anomaly, and it isn't always predictable. To increase your chances of having a healthy pet, research breeds you
like. Talk to a veterinarian about breed dispositions. Ask other owners. And
remember that many shelter dogs can live just as long as purebreds. The
bottom line: A knowledgeable buyer has a better chance of finding and raising a healthy pet.

Signs of a healthy dog

No matter what age, size, sex, or breed you're looking for, the health of the
dog you're considering is one of the most important factors to evaluate before
you adopt. Although many adopted dogs have minor health issues that are
easily resolved — a skin irritation, an ear infection, or minor arthritis —
sound health keeps basic vet bills at a minimum. If you adopt a dog with serious health problems such as chronic kidney trouble, heartworms, glaucoma,
or heart disease, the vet bill can quickly skyrocket. Maybe you're willing to
take on that expense for the sake of an ailing pet, but unless you're specifically prepared to adopt a dog with special medical needs, adopting a healthy
dog probably is one of your top priorities.

Fortunately, most shelters and rescue groups have dogs checked by veterinarians and treated for any health issues before making them available for
adoption. If you want to adopt a dog who has a minor health problem such as
ear mites or a skin rash, you can ask the shelter to have these issues treated
first. Generally, shelters may not have the resources for such treatment, but
if the shelter's vet overlooked something, it may be willing to take care of
the treatment for you. You can expect the shelter to have records of all vaccinations, dewormings, pest-control measures, tests, medications, and other
medical diagnoses or treatments that were administered during the dog's
stay at the shelter. In some cases, the dog's previous owner may be another
source of information, providing medical records or at least the name of the
vet who previously cared for the dog.

Beyond written documents, you can tell a great deal about a dog's health just by looking. When you evaluate a shelter or rescue dog, look for the signs of bright, vibrant health described in the following sections.

Bright eyes and bushy tails

When first examining a dog, look for a few obvious signs of good health, including the following:

- **Bright eyes:** Eyes really do need to be bright and clear, with no cloudiness or discharge. Dogs older than 5 or 6 years may have slight eye cloudiness caused by progressive hardening of the lenses; this cloudiness appears as a barely detectible blue in the pupils and eventually appears gray. Lens hardening is normal for older dogs, but milky, opaque lenses are a sign of cataracts that cause blindness and require expensive surgery. Some breeds —Poodles, Shih Tzu, Maltese, and other white or light-colored dogs — tend to have tear stains, which are not usually a sign of ill health; they can even be remedied with some special products. However, a thick, gooey discharge and redness or irritation in a dog's eyes may be a sign of an eye infection that requires medication.

- **Tight eyelids:** Eyelids should fit tightly around the eye and not hang loose, except in the case of loose-skinned, droopy-faced dogs like Bloodhounds and Bassett Hounds. Some dogs have *entropion,* a genetic condition in which the eyelid curls inward, irritating the cornea. A similar condition, called *ectropion,* causes the lower eyelid to curl outward, hanging and enabling debris to become trapped under the lid. These conditions are fixed with surgery, but they need to be addressed.

- **Discharge-free noses:** The dog's nose should be free of any discharge, and the dog should not be wheezing or coughing. These symptoms can signal a respiratory infection or other problems. A cold, wet nose isn't necessarily a barometer of good health — and a cold, wet, oozing nose is certainly *not* a sign of good health.

- **Polished ivories:** Take a look at those teeth. They should be white, clean, and mostly free of tartar buildup. If they aren't, you need to do something about it. Clean teeth are important because dental bacteria can travel through the bloodstream, infecting the dog's heart, causing heart disease, and decreasing life span. A vet can professionally clean teeth with a lot of tartar while the dog is under anesthesia. Generally, this procedure is safe, but anesthesia can be risky for some breeds and for older dogs (not as risky as letting periodontal disease progress). Dental cleaning also can get pricey.

- **Clean, infection-free ears:** Ear infections, usually caused by yeast or bacteria, are common in dogs, especially ones who have been wandering outside for extended periods and dogs with floppy ears. Even dogs with short, pricked ears can get ear infections because the ears are wide open to the introduction of bacteria. Another common ear problem is ear mites. Signs that a dog has an ear infection or mites include scratching, head shaking, and pawing at the ears. Ear infections must be treated by a vet but usually are easy to resolve.

Skin-tastic coats

A dog's coat — whether short, tight, smooth, long, flowing, glamorous, bristly, crispy, or wiry — is her crowning glory. The condition of her coat can also be an important indicator of her overall health. Many health problems manifest in the skin and coat.

Parasites like fleas, ticks, and mange mites can result in rashes, allergic reactions, and massive hair loss and sores, including red, inflamed, painful areas called *hot spots.* Parasites also can transmit serious and even fatal diseases. Skin infections — common in animals that are injured while wandering — can be caused by staph or other bacteria, or a wound that becomes infected. Likewise, immune system problems can cause dull coats, hair loss, and skin problems.

Any of the following skin-and-coat conditions can indicate a health problem that needs to be addressed:

- **Patches of missing hair:** Even small patches of missing hair can signal a skin infection that requires treatment. Large patches can indicate mange, caused by tiny skin mites.

- **Signs of fleas:** You may see tiny black specks — flea dirt — or the little brown hopping bugs themselves.

- **Ticks:** Ticks can be as tiny as pinheads or, when attached to the skin, can be swollen with blood to the size of acorns.

- **Signs of mites:** Mites are tiny black bugs — smaller than fleas — that you may not be able to see. Signs of mites include itching, ear irritation, red scaly patches, rashes, and hair loss. Demodex and Sarcoptic mites are microscopic. Cheylatella mites look like tiny white dander. You can see ear mites if you look closely down in the ear canal.

- **Hot spots — red, itchy, inflamed, weeping wounds caused by excessive scratching:** The most common cause of hot spots is allergic reaction to fleabites, food, or other environmental irritants, or an irritated or infected injury. Although they're usually not serious, hot spots are uncomfortable for the dog and can be difficult to resolve because the dog will keep scratching and licking the wound.

- **Dull, thin coat:** A dull coat can signal diseased skin. Keep in mind, however, that this symptom also can be a sign of something as normal as a seasonal coat change or post-delivery hair loss (in some breeds, the female loses much of her coat after having a litter of puppies). If coat changes signal a serious disease, such as hypothyroidism, a veterinarian must treat it.

✔ **Lumps or bumps in or underneath the skin:** These afflictions may be cysts or tumors, either simple to remove or cancerous.

The rear view

Just what is under that tail? Take a look. A dog's rear end should be clean and free of discharge, with no signs of irritation or infection. Dogs with worms sometimes have infected rears, and in some cases, tiny worms are visible around the anus. If you get a chance, take a peek at the dog's stool (just don't do it right before lunch); some worms are visible in the stool. The stool also should be firm. Loose, very dark, or bloody stool can signify a problem with worms or other intestinal conditions.

Puppies commonly are infected by parasitic worms in utero and, if not treated, can carry these worms into adulthood. Medication can resolve problems with worms. Likewise, newly admitted dogs commonly get temporary diarrhea, sometimes with mucus or blood in it, caused by the stress of caging, new noises, loss of family, and dietary changes. This condition usually resolves itself in the first week.

If you see abnormal stool in the cage, tell the staff and ask how long the dog has been in the shelter. If he's been there longer than a week, ask if a parasite check with a microscope has been done and if the dog has been dewormed.

The great big world: How the dog interacts

A dog's temperament is crucial in determining health. Dogs who are shy, hesitant, guarded, cowering, or growling and aggressive may actually be in pain or discomfort because of an undetected health problem. Temperament also is an indicator of personality (see the earlier section on temperament), but don't overlook the possibility that poor health is causing any behavior problem you see.

Although any of the following signs can simply be related to the stress of the environment or the dog's situation, these factors can look like temperament problems but actually indicate a health problem:

✔ Cowering or exhibiting extreme shyness, hesitation, or a reluctance to be touched

✔ Backing away, hiding, or avoiding people and other dogs

✔ Whining, whimpering, crying, or appearing agitated

✔ Scratching constantly

✔ Circling, pacing, panting, or displaying other nervous behavior

✔ Drooling excessively, especially accompanied by panting

✔ Growling, nipping, or showing other signs of aggression (No dog behaving aggressively should be offered for adoption, so alert shelter workers if you notice signs of aggression.)

Book I

Choosing
and
Bringing
Home a
Dog

Picking Your Perfect Puppy

You can't wait to get through all the paperwork. You don't want to read the information you've been given. You just want your puppy — now. Well, you'll soon have all the time in the world to make a fuss. Keep your enthusiasm in check just a little longer.

Before you bring home the puppy who'll share your life, take a second to confirm that you've covered your bases. Be sure you're dealing with a reputable source — a good shelter or a reputable breeder. You don't want to fall in love with a puppy who has health and temperament problems. Before making your final choice, review these good-puppy criteria:

✔ Be sure you're getting your puppy at the right age — between her 7-week and 8-week birthdays. Some breeders, especially ones with toy breeds, insist on holding their puppies longer because they're small and delicate. That's fine, but only if the breeder has continued to socialize the puppy with people. You want a puppy who can get along with other dogs, but you don't want one who's too dog oriented to bond well with you. Age is not as big a concern with a shelter puppy, who has probably been well handled by staff and volunteers.

✔ Look for a puppy who has been raised as a pet — in the kitchen, ideally. You want a puppy who has heard the normal sounds of living with people from the day she was born — talking, laughter, arguments, the TV, music, and the sound of the dishwasher. Health screenings and good breeding are very important, but so is socialization. Don't buy a puppy from someone who has raised her in a kennel, barn, or basement. If you don't know how the puppy has been raised, check out her temperament (see the upcoming "Puppy testing" section).

✔ Check for signs of good health. Your puppy should see a vet within 24 hours — make a health check a condition of adoption — but you probably can spot obvious signs of disease on your own. Your puppy should be plump and glossy, with eyes, nose, and ears free of any discharge. She should seem upbeat and happy, not listless.

Is a Christmas puppy a good idea?

No. Sure, the image of a beribboned puppy and delighted children on Christmas morning is both endearing and enduring. But humane societies, trainers, veterinarians, and reputable breeders say that Christmas morning is just about the worst time to introduce a puppy to the family. To parents with camera at hand, the scene *seems* worth the trouble of an energetic ball of fluff rolling around on one of the year's most hectic days, but it probably isn't.

Getting a Christmas puppy is okay — if you get one before or after Christmas. Introducing a puppy on Christmas Day is stressful for all concerned: The puppy needs your attention — but so does everything else.

Even if you get your pup before or after the actual holiday, you have some challenges. The first may be finding the right puppy. Many shelters and reputable breeders don't place puppies right before Christmas because they believe that the time is just too high risk. That leaves you with less-than-ideal sources for your pet.

And consider the problem of socializing and training a puppy in the dead of winter, if snow visits your corner of the universe in December. By the time the snow starts to melt, you could have a half-grown canine terror on your hands.

Giving up that Norman Rockwell moment when your children discover that St. Nick has answered their pleas for a puppy is difficult. But if you want a better chance of still having that pet as a well-loved member of the family at future Christmases, consider this option: Wrap a collar and leash and a dog book for the children and put that under the tree — promise your children that their puppy had to wait to be born but will be with them as soon as she can.

If you still want to get the puppy around a holiday, Easter is better for starting out a puppy. Your camera works just as well then, your children will be just as happy, and your puppy will have a better chance of getting the attention she needs.

If you have questions, ask the seller, and make sure that you're satisfied with the answers. Above all, don't let your enthusiasm override your common sense. It's hard to say no to a puppy, but sometimes you must.

Sometimes a single pup is born to a mother who died in childbirth. Should you avoid such a puppy? That depends on the breeder. A knowledgeable breeder does his best to make up for shortcomings, taking over the role of the mother and, later, giving the puppy exposure to other dogs. Single puppies are often sent to be "adopted" by dogs with puppies close to the same age or are at least given the opportunity to socialize with other puppies after weaning.

If this socialization has been done, you need not have any qualms about adopting such a puppy, but continue to look for as many opportunities as you can to expose your puppy to other dogs as she grows up.

Working with a breeder

If you've found a reputable breeder, you may not have much to do when it comes to choosing your puppy. You've let the breeder know if you prefer a male or a female and whether you want that puppy to be more than your pet — you're considering showing him, for example, or entering some other canine competition (more on that in Book IV, Chapter 6). Or maybe the litter has puppies of different colors and you have a strong preference. All these factors can narrow your choices dramatically (even when considering a large litter).

The breeder has been narrowing the choices, too. She's talked with you enough to get a feel for the kind of home you offer, whether you'd be too demanding for a shy puppy or too easy on a bossy one. In the end, you may have a choice between two or three puppies — or maybe just one fills the bill.

This process is about give and take, of course, and you may decide to broaden your selection criteria a little when faced with a squirmy litter of fat, healthy puppies. Suddenly, a black Lab may seem perfect when before only a yellow one would do. The breeder, too, should be open to discussion. Just remember that she has a better idea of the personalities of her puppies — she knows her dogs, after all, and has been living with these pups for weeks. If she suggests that the bold puppy who's crawling all over your son may not be the best bet for your family, believe her — she probably learned her lesson from an unhappy family in the past.

Although it's a pretty good bet that you'll have plenty of puppies to choose from in a litter of Great Danes, that may not be the case if you're dealing with a toy breed, in which small litters are the norm. You may want to hedge your bets a little by dealing with more than one breeder. The breeder may already have that in mind: Good breeders are active locally and likely will know who else has a litter that may suit you if theirs does not. Just ask.

Puppy testing

What if you aren't dealing with a breeder, you're not selective about gender, and you couldn't care less about your puppy's color or markings? What if you're offered the pick of any pup you want, not just from one litter, but from a whole shelter? How can you decide?

You test the personalities of your prospective pet. Remember that even though you can find a good puppy anywhere, making the most of any help offered is a good idea. Good breeders and good shelters test their puppies, and many shelters offer adoption counseling. (If you're dealing with one that doesn't, what else isn't top rate?)

Puppy-testing methods vary widely, but the general purpose of testing is the same. The goal is to determine the following:

- ✔ **A puppy's level of dominance:** How bossy or shy is she? Although a lot of people are inclined to pick the boldest pup of a litter — because she seems to pick them — she's probably not the best choice for most homes. She may be just the ticket for someone with a great deal of dog-training experience who intends to compete with the dog, but for an average home, a less dominant dog is a better choice. Avoiding the shyest, least dominant puppy ("because she needs us!") is best, too.

- ✔ **A puppy's level of interest in people:** Some puppies are more dog oriented or don't care much about anything at all. A puppy who's not curious and interested in people, perhaps because of little or no social-ization, isn't a good prospect as a pet. You want a pup who wants to be with you.

- ✔ **A puppy's trainability:** The goal here is a puppy with the ability to concentrate — as much as any baby can — and absorb information. Avoid a puppy who is so busy bouncing off the walls that she can't give you even a moment's attention.

Take each of the puppies you're thinking about to a safe, secure area away from littermates. Observe how the puppy reacts to the change — tentative exploration is okay, but beware the puppy who's so terrified that she won't move. Also look for how busy a puppy is: Playfulness is fine, but full-out go-go-go may be a little too much.

Ideally, you can compare your observations with the observations of others who have looked at these puppies, such as the volunteers and staff at the shelters or the breeder.

Try to see the litter you're considering more than once. If all the puppies seem lethargic, ask the breeder if you've caught them just after eating. Puppies have two speeds, after all: completely on and completely off!

Keep in mind that the puppy who's probably best for you — after you find the right breed or breed type, locate the right source, and decide between male and female — is "medium" in personality. She may not be the smartest in the litter, but she may be more interested in your point of view than the one who is the smartest. She's got moxie, but not so much that she'll drive you crazy. She's willing to try new things — she's no shrinking violet — but she'll like the new things better if you're with her

Although a particular breeder may always test his puppies at a particular age — 6 weeks, say — you may not have this luxury. Anything in the range of 5 to 12 weeks is okay, but if you're testing puppies in their 8th week, they may be a little skittish because at this age they're a little leery of new things. Testing before or after this stage is a better idea.

You can size up a puppy's personality in several ways, but these exercises are easy for anyone to do:

- ✔ **Is she interested in people?** Put the puppy down facing you. Walk a few steps away, bend over, and call to her. (Bending over makes you less intimidating.) If the puppy seems a little tentative, crouch and open your arms. You're not ordering the pup — she doesn't know what you want, after all. You're trying to see how attracted she is to a nice person. So be nice. Call gently, click your tongue, rattle your keys. The medium puppy you want will probably trot over happily, perhaps after a slight hesitation. The bossy puppy may come over and nip at you, and the shy one may not move except to shiver in terror. The one who doesn't care a bit about people may go investigate a bug in the corner of the room.

- ✔ **Does she accept authority?** Gently roll the puppy onto her back and hold her there with your hand. The medium pup you're looking for will fuss a little, settle down, and maybe even lick your hand. Bossy pups usually keep struggling, and the shyest ones generally freeze in terror.

- ✔ **How does she respond to praise and petting?** Praise and petting are integral parts of training and communicating with your dog, so finding a puppy who wants affection enough to earn it is important. Talk to the puppy lovingly and stroke her, but let her decide whether she stays with you — don't hold her. The medium puppy will probably lick your hands and be glad to stay with you. Rolling over is okay, and don't be surprised if she urinates a little — called submissive urination, this gesture is kind of a canine compliment, a recognition that you're top dog. A puppy who bites hard is probably dominant and unsocialized, and the one who wants nothing to do with you probably isn't people oriented enough. Also stay away from the pup who's terrified of being touched.

Listen to your head, not your heart. Doing so is really, really hard when you're in a shelter and thinking the puppy you don't pick isn't going to get picked at all. Don't play the guilt game. Pick a puppy with a temperament that likely will produce a good pet. You're still saving a life in the case of a shelter puppy, still providing a good home in the case of any puppy. Keep that in mind and pick the best puppy you can.

You may be tempted to take *two* puppies home, with the grand idea that adopting littermates will keep them from being too lonely while you're at work and will give them something to do besides pester you. Give this idea a *lot* of thought. Raising two puppies together means twice the work, twice the craziness, and twice the mess. Most people barely have time to properly socialize and train one puppy, much less two. Plus, two puppies raised together may remain more bonded to each other than they are to you.

If you want two dogs, consider waiting until your puppy is grown to add another puppy. Adding a grown dog at the same time you add a puppy may be okay, but still, puppies are such work that you're better off getting your little one squared away before you add to your pack.

One of the best ways to start this special relationship properly is to take time off work when your first get your puppy. Call it *mutternity leave,* if you like. A week — two is even better — gives you time to get housetraining off to a great start and enjoy your puppy while easing the transition between life with her littermates and life with you. For more on early puppy training, see Book IV.

Bringing Home a Puppy

The day your puppy comes home is a big step for both of you. He's leaving his littermates and throwing his lot in with yours. You're taking on the huge responsibility of raising a dog. You want the transition to be as smooth as possible, yet you want to make sure that from that very first day, you're laying the groundwork for a wonderful life together. Repeat the following:

I will never let my puppy do anything I wouldn't let him do as a grown dog.

You're ready to be a full-fledged puppy parent now, heaven help you. When you go to pick up your puppy, bring towels, both old bathroom ones and the paper kind. Chances are, your puppy will get carsick. (He won't necessarily be carsick his whole life, though.) Don't go alone, either. If you're a single person, have a friend drive so you can hold your puppy. Have a spouse or kids? Take 'em. This moment is one you'll want to remember.

But don't let your children fight over the puppy. He's not a football. One person can hold him, on a towel, for the ride. (Maybe draw lots and make it up to the other kids later.) Remember that you want to lay the groundwork for your puppy from the beginning. Do so with your children, too, by insisting on gentle, respectful handling. If the puppy throws up or makes any other kind of mess, don't make a fuss. Change to a clean towel, and clean it all up when you get home. When you get home, take your puppy outside and praise him for relieving himself, if he does.

The name game

Naming a dog has to be one of the most delightful parts of getting one. It seems not a year goes by without a new book of dog names being published, including ones that specialize, such as a book on Irish names.

Avoid names that sound like common obedience commands, like Sitka or Stacy. Keep names short — one or two syllables — and easy to pronounce. Using names that are not traditionally for people reinforces the fact that a dog is a dog, after all. Name books are a good start, but don't forget atlases or special dictionaries such as foreign dictionaries or books of baseball, railroad, gardening, or music terms.

Make your puppy love her name as much as you do by making sure that it has a positive association. Never scream your puppy's name at her or use it in punishment. The late dog trainer Job Michael Evans used to recommend making up a song with your dog's name in it and singing the song to her. Commercial jingles are wonderful for this, he said, because they're catchy and you can put the pet's name in where the product is mentioned. Yes, it's silly. But try it anyway.

The name your dog hears — her everyday name — is what fanciers term a call name: That is, it's what you *call* your dog. If you have a purebred dog, she'll have a registered name, too. You get 28 letters and spaces with the American Kennel Club to come up with a registered name for your pet. If you choose a name someone else has already chosen, the AKC issues it along with a number to distinguish your dog's name from the others, so unless you want your Collie to be the AKC's Lassie 897,042, use all those spaces to come up with a middle name or two, something sure to be unique.

Puppy's first night

Your puppy will probably be so overwhelmed by the new sights, sounds, smells, and attention that he won't much miss his littermates and his old home. Everyone will want to hold the puppy and play with him; that's fine, but remember that he's still a baby and gets worn out quickly. He needs to sleep, but he may not eat on that first day. He has a lot to get used to — don't worry about it much. Let him explore.

Puppies aren't stuffed toys, and you must help your children realize that. Small children — especially kids under 5— can't really help being a little rough with puppies (and dogs) and must be carefully supervised to ensure that neither hurts the other.

Where should your puppy sleep? Dogs can sleep in the bedroom — not on your bed, but in their own bed or in a crate. Allowing the dog to sleep in the bedroom is especially important in households where a dog is left alone for hours at a time when the family is at work and at school. Letting your dog sleep in your bedroom — or in your child's bedroom — counts for time together, even though you're all asleep. It can go a long way toward building and maintaining a strong bond, assuring your pet that he's an important member of the pack.

If you want your dog to sleep in the service porch, that's your business. But please don't start on the first couple nights after you bring your puppy home. He needs you now. Those first couple nights are tough on a puppy. The reassuring warmth of his littermates is gone, and everything has changed. He's going to have a lot to say about this situation, so be prepared. He will fuss less if he's in your presence, if he can be reassured by your smell and the sound of your breathing.

Set up the crate next to your bed and prepare it with a soft blanket to sleep on and a chew toy or two. Tell him "Crate" firmly, put him inside, and close the door. Then open a book, because you won't be sleeping for awhile. (For more on the use of crates in puppy raising, see Book IV.)

Endure the cries and whines as best you can, but don't punish your puppy, and don't take him out when he's carrying on — you'll teach him that all he needs to do is fuss to get what he wants. He'll probably settle down and then wake once or twice in the middle of the night. Take him out to relieve himself — and praise him for doing so — and then put him back in his crate.

In a day or two, the worst of the heartbreaking crying will be over.

Chapter 4

Looking for Love in All the Right Places

*Y*ou can find love in three places: right in front of your eyes, farther afield but within driving distance, or on the other side of the world. The natural starting point is to look within your reach, but that isn't always the best place, nor is it always successful. With some research, perseverance, and patience, you're sure to find the perfect dog.

Don't close your mind to long-distance buying, because it can be worth the effort. When you're adding another member to your family, you need to pick carefully. Don't let a little inconvenience keep you from getting the right dog. After all, you'll be spending a lot of time, energy, and money on her in the years to come. This chapter introduces you to several means of and places for finding your new dog, as well as other issues to consider as you're looking for the perfect dog.

Searching at Shows

If you decide that you want a purebred registered dog, attending a dog show is a good idea. Watch the prestigious Westminster Kennel Club show, which is telecast annually in February, to see an overview of all AKC breeds. One (or more) is sure to appeal to you. Shows offer classes for all recognized breeds, plus breeds that are working toward recognition. Magazines and local clubs furnish information on dates and sites of shows.

Plan to spend a full day to observe several breeds. Catalogs are available, providing owner information and schedules for each breed. Watch the breeds you're considering both in and out of the rings, and study behavior and personality. Talk to fanciers and mention your interest in the breed.

Talking with exhibitors

When exhibitors are finished showing and able to relax, they're pleased to talk about their dogs and willing to answer your questions. Asking just before they walk into the ring, while they're nervously concentrating on their three minutes in the limelight (especially if you muss up the strategically placed hairs of their dog), is liable to invite a snap — from the handler!

When you have a chance to talk to exhibitors, remember that most of them are breeders. Be prepared for a rosy picture — they're enchanted with their chosen breeds. But they are truly a wealth of information. If you really want to know whether a particular breed sheds or can run a marathon with you, ask.

Benefiting from their experience

Show breeders usually have dedicated themselves to one or two breeds. Their knowledge is helpful, so you can gain from their experiences instead of having to get answers by guess and by golly. Check out the AKC's Web site at www.akc.org to find breeders in your area (plus a whole lot of other useful information). Let your fingers do the searching!

Although show breeders enjoy showing their dogs, most of their puppies are sold as companions, for a couple reasons. First, more people are seeking pets than show dogs. Second, even the best-bred litter usually has a few puppies that will do better as pets than as show-ring stars. But most of all, breeders want loving homes for all their puppies, whether they're pets or show prospects.

Checking Out the Club Scene

Many of the people who belong to dog clubs are breeders. National (often called parent clubs), regional, and local kennel clubs offer additional search avenues in your quest for a new dog. Some clubs are limited to a single breed and are known as specialty clubs. Others are all-breed clubs (also local). Similar group clubs serve breeds within groups, such as all terriers or all sighthounds. And to add further confusion, all-breed clubs rarely have all possible breeds represented within their respective memberships; they just play host to shows that are open to all breeds, unlike specialty clubs, which sponsor shows for only one breed.

If you want to see a lot of one breed, attend a specialty show. If you want to see a few dogs of several breeds, go to an all-breed show.

Regardless of appellation or location, almost anyone active in a dog club can refer you to breeders — if they don't happen to breed the kind of dog you want, they'll likely be able to refer you to someone who does. Networking counts here!

And don't forget obedience clubs and other performance event organizations. People who love dogs know scads of other people who love and breed dogs — dogs of a feather pack together.

Clubs may be listed in the phone book, but many have only small treasuries and, therefore, don't have phones. Extend your search through a veterinarian or the Better Business Bureau, or ask someone you know who has attended a training class.

Researching Off- and Online

Most people think of starting their search with the local newspaper. You can easily find popular breeds in the classifieds. As in any other source, advertisers can be either reputable, knowledgeable breeders or riffraff. Breeders also advertise in dog magazines. You can probably find several on your local newsstand: *AKC Gazette, Dog Fancy, Dog World, Dogs USA,* and *Puppies USA.* You can search the Internet for other titles. Few, if any, newspapers or magazines require credentials, so it's up to you, the buyer, to determine where to buy your dog.

When you've settled on one or two breeds, read everything you can find on them (especially books on individual breeds) to gather various viewpoints. Concentrating on chapters that cover character can help you see whether a given breed is really the dog for you. Seek out live examples of the breed so that you can view and interact with them in the flesh.

If you're even semi-computer-savvy, a world of information is right at your fingertips. If you're not a whiz, a friend or a librarian may take pity and help you do a search and print a few pages. You can find information on almost every breed in cyberspace. Many breeds have their own Web sites, as do individual breeders. National and local clubs are listed as well and often feature breeder lists. To expand your classifieds search regionally or nationally, don't forget Craig's List (www.craigslist.org).

Nobody can guarantee that the people listed on Web sites are the kind you want to have as birth parents of your soon-to-be-adopted pup. Only you can do that by asking discerning questions. The section on questions to ask a breeder (later in this chapter) can help you get the information you need.

Bonding with a Breeder

No matter how you locate a breeder — at a show, through a club, or over the Internet — buying a puppy from a conscientious breeder is the best way to ensure that you will get the right support and that your new addition will be healthy and happy. So how on earth do you tell the difference between a good breeder and a bad one? Visit and observe. Look for subtle as well as obvious signs of love and dedication. If the place smells so bad that it brings tears to your eyes, leave. Go with your gut feeling. Ask yourself whether you'd trust this person enough to buy a used car from him. If you wouldn't buy an inanimate object, how can you take a chance on a living creature?

Recognizing a good breeder

When the breeder meets you at the door wearing a sweatshirt that reads "Havanese Heaven" and dog-tag earrings, you know she's cuckoo about her breed. The 3-foot stack of dog magazines, the shelves of books and bric-a-brac, and the dog bowls nested beside the kitchen sink are other obvious signs. You *want* a breeder to be crazy about her dogs — it's a good indication that she'd do anything and everything to ensure their well-being.

You can discern more subtle signs of devotion when the breeder speaks with enthusiasm about her breed. Still, she should demonstrate that she understands your need to be realistic about any drawbacks of the breed — size, grooming, shedding, or attraction to mud puddles. Their idiosyncrasies may

Book I

Choosing
and
Bringing
Home a
Dog

endear dogs of her breed to her; in fact, she may even laugh about the day
the puppy puked in the preacher's Panama hat.

But a good breeder is a valuable source of information. She knows the history of the breed and what physical problems occasionally occur. She's likely
to introduce you to the adults in her household first so that you know what
you're in for. Puppies are always adorable. A good breeder will

- ✔ Encourage you to train your pup.
- ✔ Suggest that you join a local dog club.
- ✔ Ask you to keep in touch.
- ✔ Offer instructions on feeding, vet care, and grooming.
- ✔ Give you spay/neuter requirements for a pet, or show and health documentation if you plan to breed your dog.
- ✔ Request that you notify her if you ever need to place your dog.

Notice whether the dogs look at the breeder adoringly and whether she
strokes them almost subconsciously when talking to you. A physically sound
dog's eyes shine, the weight is good, and the coat appears to be healthy
(albeit a mite ragged, in the case of the mother). By evaluating the dogs, you
can tell what kind of care they've received.

Breeders want their puppies to be happy, and the best way to ensure that is
for new owners to be happy, too.

Knowing what questions to ask a breeder

Don't stop with just "How much?" Although we all have to consider expense,
money should *not* be the most important consideration when choosing a dog.
The dog's health and the breeder's support and ethics should be high on
your list of priorities. Ask these questions:

- ✔ How long have you been involved with the breed?
- ✔ Why do you love this breed?
- ✔ Why do you breed dogs?
- ✔ How often do you breed? When do you expect your next litter?
- ✔ May I see the *dam* (mom) and photos of the *sire* (dad) and other relatives?
- ✔ Can I see where you raise the pups?

- ✔ What defects occur in this breed? Have you produced any of these? (If so, how many? A low percentage is good. Any breeder of more than two litters is bound to have had some problems.)

- ✔ Are the parents certified to be healthy? (Ask to see certifications.)

- ✔ Do you belong to any clubs? (Clubs often have codes of ethics.)

- ✔ Can I see the pedigree? (Look for titles within the first two generations — a sign of soundness and dedication.)

- ✔ Do you pick the puppy or do I? (He'll want to match personalities.)

- ✔ What is the medical history of the pups? (Usually the pups will have had one or two inoculations, a fecal examination, and possible deworming.)

- ✔ What does the guarantee cover? (Ask to see the contract.)

- ✔ What is the average life span of the breed?

Families with children want to ask whether the pups have been kid-proofed. Even childless people usually have friends or family whose youngsters visit. And families with one or two well-behaved children often have a half-dozen others running in and out the door, sometimes not as quiet and mannerly. Pups need be exposed to household noises, screeching kids, and wrestling mania if those sounds are to be part of their future life.

Answering the breeder's questions

A bad breeder doesn't care what you're going to do with the dog, as long as your check clears. A good breeder genuinely loves her pups and wants to make sure that they all have a good lifelong home. Expect good breeders to ask you the following questions:

- ✔ What is your attraction to this breed?

- ✔ Have you thought about the pros and cons of owning a dog?

- ✔ Do you have children — if so, what ages?

- ✔ Have you owned dogs before? How did they die?

- ✔ Will this dog live inside? (Few breeders want to sell to someone who plans to tie a dog outside 24/7.)

- ✔ How do you plan to confine your dog? (The breeder will want you to have a fence or to walk the dog on leash.)

- ✔ Do you realize the expense of raising a dog?

✔ Do you understand that pet ownership is a commitment of many years?

✔ Will you contact me if anything ever occurs that means you must place the dog?

Now, are you ready to buy the pup? Is this place the right one? Think, because this will be your final answer.

Ironically, popularity often sounds a breed's death knell. Opportunists looking for a quick buck leap into dog breeding to satisfy the desires of pet buyers. Without knowledge of genetics and good breeding practices, the mass-produced misfits are plagued with health and temperament problems. These junkyard dawgs are lost causes when the wind changes direction. To avoid buying trouble, be sure to deal with a reputable breeder.

Recognizing that breeding makes no cents

When you get a dog from a reputable breeder, you can be confident that the dog's best interest has always been at heart. Most breeders breed dogs because they love them, not because they're trying to make a quick buck. An average litter of medium-sized dogs produces about five or six pups. Many breeders plan a litter to keep one pup for themselves and/or provide one for a previous buyer. That leaves four or five for sale. Breeder expenses for raising a litter in a caring, nourishing, and healthy environment include the following:

✔ Genetic testing for the dam

✔ Prebreeding tests for the dam

✔ Travel expenses or shipping to the sire

✔ Stud fees

✔ Puppy food and extra food for the dam

✔ Advertising

✔ Registrations

✔ Long-distance phone calls to prospective buyers (Many breeders also send photos or videos and educational material to prospects.)

✔ Pedigrees

✔ Initial exams and vaccinations for the pups

✔ Puppy-care packages to go home with the adoptive parents

✔ Replacement or refund guarantees

In/line/out: Breeding programs

Geneticists describe *inbreeding* as being farther reaching than one generation, and *outcrossing* as breeding two different breeds (such as Schnauzers and Beagles). But because you'll be dealing with breeders instead of scientists, we use the more familiar breeders' terms.

In breeder lingo, *inbreeding* means mating closely related animals — in other words, sister to brother, mother to son, father to daughter. The term *linebreeding* is used for litters produced with a common ancestor (usually within the first three generations). To breeders, *outcrossing* occurs when a pedigree (the family tree) contains no (or distant) common ancestors.

Contrary to popular opinion, inbreeding of animals is no more harmful than any other method of breeding them. Yes, any bad traits can be doubled, but so can the good ones. The keys to success are mating two animals without serious faults and choosing dogs who compensate for each other's less-than-perfect characteristics.

Many breeders employ linebreeding as their method of choice, with judicious use of inbreeding and outcrossing when needed. For instance, a kennel that has used linebreeding successfully for a number of years may find that coat texture has become softer than desired and pigmentation occasionally fades. The breeder looks for an unrelated (preferably linebred) stud who is particularly strong in the characteristics the breeder's stock is lacking. The best *progeny* (offspring that exhibit the desired attributes) from that litter eventually are bred back into the kennel's line.

As a buyer, your charge is not to worry what method was used, but rather to find a litter with healthy, sturdy parents and grandparents. Those two generations have the greatest influence on the puppies.

Diggin' That Doggie in the Window

Many pet stores have stopped selling dogs and cats, preferring to deal with inanimate merchandise that doesn't require the care that live animals do. To encourage placements, some of the largest chains conduct "adoption days," when dogs from local shelters are brought into the store. The wannabe pets are tidied up and often sport bandanas around their necks to add to their appeal. Volunteers may teach the dogs basic manners or maybe a few tricks, putting them through their repertoire for visitors.

Identifying a conscientious pet store

A few pet stores, however, continue to sell puppies that are obtained from various sources — either a local owner who was unable to place the puppies or a broker for a larger commercial enterprise. Although puppies are hard to resist and seem to magnetically attract attention, be sure that the store where you shop has a caring staff with adequate time to spend holding or playing with the puppies. Puppyhood is the crucial age for developing social skills.

Pet store prices are usually more than a breeder's price, and the puppies are more often sick.

Getting the best from a pet store

If you decide to buy from a pet store, be sure to ask the same questions you would if you were buying a pup from a breeder (listed earlier in the chapter). Try to think with your mind rather than your heart. Everyone's first impulse is, "Aw, let's buy him." You must do a few things before cuddling the pup, though (remember, cuddling is a surefire sales gimmick):

- ✔ Ask to see the puppy's registration form and health certifications for the parents.
- ✔ Check the guarantee.
- ✔ Obtain copies of all paperwork stating that the pup is in good health, has been checked for parasites, and has received his initial inoculations.
- ✔ Ask for the breeder's contact information. Call the breeder to ask pertinent questions.

Don't buy a puppy that is younger than 8 weeks of age. For one thing, doing so is illegal in most states. For another, puppies need to be with their littermates to develop bite inhibition and social skills. Younger puppies have less control of their bowel and bladder functions and are more difficult to housetrain. Ask the pet store how long the puppy has been there. A pup may be 8 weeks old but was taken away from his mother and littermates two weeks before, which is problematic from the standpoint of social skills.

If you buy a dog from a pet store, make a veterinary appointment ASAP — within 24 hours. Store refund or replacement policies are often in effect only within 24 to 48 hours of the purchase. Returning an ill puppy is not always easy emotionally, but don't set yourself up for far greater heartbreak by taking a sickly pup under your wing.

Book I

Choosing
and
Bringing
Home a
Dog

Watching out for unchecked commercialism

Buyers want a puppy who's been raised with love. People who love their dogs raise them with kindness and the best care they can give. It's nearly impossible to give adequate care, let alone loving attention, to 50 or more animals. Yet one commercial breeder boasts of supplying semis full of puppies to stores — at a rate of 900 a week! If an owner with 50 dogs spends 12 hours a day with his dogs, that still is only 14 minutes per dog, which isn't enough.

You want to buy a dog from someone who understands the breed and can help you with any questions or problems that may arise. You want a puppy who's been raised in clean conditions, not in crates or small cages, sleeping among urine and excrement. You want a pup who knows that a raised hand means it's going to be kissed and cuddled, not smacked or poked.

Adopting an Orphan

Some shelters have the same rigorous requirements that breeders do. They may not place certain dogs in homes with small children, or they may require a fenced yard. They want the animal to have a second chance at a great home. Ask if you can bring other family pets to the shelter for a preadoption visit to see whether the current and future buddies tolerate each other. A few shelters require a 24-hour waiting period to ensure that the adopter is not acting on a whim and is sincere about wanting the animal.

Adoptive families need to ask whether any history is known about the dog. Some dogs are surrendered by previous owners. Reasons can vary from a move or divorce to a behavior that is impossible for one family to tolerate yet is considered a bonus to another. If the dog has been in the shelter for more than a few days (most strays are kept long enough to be vet-checked and to allow the lost owner a chance to be found), managers and employees will be able to provide you with helpful information. They've probably observed whether the dog barks a lot or is friendly, timid, or trained.

Most people want a dog who is friendly and calm, yet playful. Choose one who sparkles with good health. Most shelter dogs have something negative in their history, even dogs who were surrendered unwillingly because of the owner's poor health or circumstances. A dog who appears unsure of herself in a shelter can bloom with confidence after a week or so of doting love and kindness. But one who is bouncing off the walls in unfamiliar surroundings usually requires someone who is at least as energetic and determined as the dog. Either can reward you with great joy if you choose with care.

Shelters have various adoption fees and procedures. Fees are often $50 to $75, which may include a rebate when the pet is spayed or neutered — they don't want to place one animal only to receive eight in its place. Some shelters participate in early spay/neuter programs so that dogs are already altered ("fixed") before they are adopted. Others offer referrals to clinics that perform the surgery at a reduced fee. The more responsible shelters follow up on adoptions, making sure that the dog is altered and in a good home. Shelters occasionally have lists of local clubs or breeders who are willing to provide you with tips about your breed.

Buying from Afar

How do you buy a puppy 1,000 miles away? It happens all the time. But if you cannot see the pups personally, breeders should be willing to send you pictures of the parents and pups. With today's technology, they may send pictures and video over the Internet. Trusting that the breeder has good ethics is especially important when buying sight unseen.

Getting the ball rolling

Initial contacts come through e-mail or phone calls. Once in a while, the courtship is conducted through letters (although, frankly, the response to a letter is usually much slower and sometimes nonexistent). Ask whether the breeder has a litter or plans one in the near future. You'll have dozens of questions to ask the breeder, and don't be surprised when you receive just as many. (See the sections on questions to ask and answer earlier in this chapter.)

When you feel a connection with this person you haven't met, you'll probably talk many times before Baby comes bouncing into your home. Preliminary mailings usually include photos of the sire and dam, their health clearances, pictures of past puppies, and information about kennels. You may also get info about the breed and guidelines on teaching manners, crate training, housetraining, and more.

While you're waiting for a litter, or while you're still trying to narrow your choices, ask the breeder to send photos or videos of the extended family and puppies as they grow. It's sure to either help you make up your mind or endure the waiting period, depending on your situation.

Making travel plans

Many buyers are willing to drive any distance within six to eight hours to avoid shipping. Beyond 500 miles, unless you're into long, long drives, your puppy likely will be shipped to you. Flying to the breeder and bringing your puppy back as under-the-seat baggage is the best way — unless, of course, you're buying a Newfoundland, which would have to travel in the cargo hold. Medium-sized or smaller breeds fit well.

Otherwise, the next best way to fly your puppy home is to have her marked "priority" or "counter-to-counter," meaning she'll be the last loaded into baggage and the first off. Make sure that you book a direct flight, even if you have to drive to a larger airport, so that your puppy doesn't have to change planes. Breeders know all the best ways of handling transportation — consult them on the details. They want to ensure that their precious bundle of joy arrives safely in your hands.

Adopting a Rescue or Ricochet Dog

Maybe canine blue blood or registry doesn't mean anything to you. If that's the case, many delightful dogs are available through purebred rescue organizations and animal shelters, both staffed with dedicated volunteers who do their darnedest to help canine throwaways. Most rescue organizations focus on helping a breed of choice.

Animal shelters, on the other hand, draw no such lines. Big/small, young/old, pure/mixed — they're all the same in their eyes: homeless dogs.

Dogs may end up homeless for many reasons:

- ✔ Dogs are credited with helping their people to be healthier in mind and body. Unfortunately, it doesn't mean a person will live forever, and sometimes an owner dies.
- ✔ Broken homes are a dismal part of today's statistics, and when they occur, the pet can wind up with no home at all.
- ✔ People may become incapacitated and can no longer take care of a dog.
- ✔ A dog may accidentally escape and not be reclaimed.
- ✔ A move can mean that an owner cannot take an animal along.

Book I

Choosing
and
Bringing
Home a
Dog

---

101 unwanted Dalmatians

The popularity of the Dalmatian soared to great heights following Disney's feature films and then plunged to *Titanic* depths when buyers found that these cute little spotted pups grew up and actually behaved like real dogs rather than cartoons. Although the Dalmatian Club of America strove mightily to warn people that no dog is appropriate for everyone, many Dalmatian owners decided that their ship was coming in and this was the time to set sail into Breeders' Land.

Dalmatian pups sold like popcorn at the movies and later were discarded like the empty boxes. Greasy cardboard is easily cleaned up . . . not so for living creatures. Dalmatian rescue agencies found themselves swamped with adolescent Spots. You can check out some of these Dalmatians at `www.thedca.org/rescue.html`.

Face it, people (especially people who don't read this book) make mistakes and form bad decisions about pet ownership. Lifestyles change, and sometimes owners realize that, as much as they love their dogs, their pets need more attention than they can give at particular stages of their respective lives. So for all sorts of reasons, dogs can become homeless.

Some buyers think that they want to start with a puppy so they can mold his character and train him to be the kind of dog they want to live with — or, at least, claim his bad habits as their own creation. However, not everyone wants the "blessings" of puppyhood, so they consider a recycled adult.

Elderly dog lovers often think they're no longer capable of training or keeping up with an energetic young pup. Sometimes they also think restricting a young dog to a more sedate, leisurely lifestyle isn't fair. And occasionally, senior citizens fear their dog will wind up an orphan if Father Time sounds the quitting whistle for them. Thus, an elderly dog can be just the right soul mate for the winter of both their lives.

However, not all homeless dogs are adults — sometimes baskets of foundlings are left at the doorsteps of shelters — although most surrendered dogs are at least several months old. The saddest of all these victims of society are the older dogs, with their grayed muzzles and bewildered eyes, not understanding why they've become *canina non grata*.

The greatest numbers of homeless dogs are dogs reaching puberty, at approximately 1 year of age. At that age, the cuteness of puppyhood is starting to wear off and the novelty of dog ownership is becoming a chore. Longhaired dogs are at their worst coat stage, with mats forming by the minute. Hormones are surging in those dogs who still are intact, and like human teenagers, they sometimes act out their bodily urges and mental anguishes. But dogs can find themselves in need of a home at virtually any age.

Rescues: Giving a Home to the Hopeless

Sadly, too many dogs find their way to animal shelters and Humane Societies. However, networks of dedicated dog lovers (some are breeders) do all they can to rescue as many of these hapless pooches as possible and place them in new homes.

Most breeders love all dogs, particularly their own chosen breeds. Breeders who are active in rescue check out strays or dogs who have been surrendered at Humane Societies. Rescuers examine them to determine whether the dog can be placed or whether she has unsolvable mental or physical problems. Almost all national parent clubs support rescue organizations for their breeds.

Rescue organizations don't want repeat offenders. They'd just as soon place the dogs in the right home to begin with. They'll ask as many questions as breeders and make certain demands on the adopters. In fact, they may even be more particular because they know the dog already has been subjected to abuse, neglect, or abandonment and they want to avoid further trauma for the dog.

Rescue associations will conduct follow-up visits and interviews to make sure that the dog (and you) are adjusting to each other. Because they know the breed so well, they'll be available to give advice when you need it.

These organizations stay afloat mainly through donations given by grateful adopting families and from club members devoted to helping their breed. Rescuers are not paid for their efforts and, in fact, often donate their expenses as well as their time.

Understanding how rescue systems work

A national coordinator solicits help from club members or regional assistants (sometimes even calling upon experts in other breeds) to identify the dog as a purebred. Foster homes are found; healthcare is provided. Almost without exception, the dogs are spayed or neutered if they are intact. They're debugged and dewormed.

Some individuals — like Beardie lovers — help out Neardies when possible. (A Neardie is a dog with a lot of Beardie in him — he's nearly a Beardie.)

During foster care, the dogs' hungry tummies are filled with good food, and they're also nourished mentally with the love and attention they hunger for. They gain weight and regain health. Matted dogs often must be shaved or shorn. It can be humorous to watch a formerly filthy, dejected beastie strut in style after a session with a groomer.

Want to "try on" a breed? Volunteer to foster a dog until a home can be found (or the dog becomes your permanent resident).

Foster families carefully observe their charges for behavioral and temperament problems. Breed rescues operate on a shoestring and can't afford to be sued for placing a vicious animal. Nor do the volunteers want anyone to be injured. But what one family can't tolerate may be exactly what another person is looking for. Matching the dog to the family is of prime concern. Dogs who are too rowdy for young children or elderly people often fit the bill for a family with teenagers. Timid dogs are happy to curl up in the lap of a quiet adult.

When the dogs' bodies and minds are healed, the adoption process begins. Transportation can be provided, through an "aboveground railroad," shuttled by dog lovers across the country, if need be, to a new home.

Recognizing who gets rescued

The lucky breeds have waiting lists for rescues. With more populous breeds, however, dog lovers make desperate efforts to save all they can, but knowing so many dogs' lives are lost is disheartening, even though those dogs have done nothing wrong except be in the wrong place at the wrong time. Dedicated rescuers struggle on, saving one dog at a time, as in the story about the little boy who saved one starfish by placing it back in the ocean. He knew he couldn't save them all, but he could save *that* one.

Rescue organizations can be located through the national clubs of the various breeds, which you can find by contacting one of the registering bodies, such as the AKC or UKC. Several breed rescues have Web sites that you can easily access by using your favorite Internet search engine.

Rehoming Ricochet Dogs

Breeders want one thing above all: a forever, loving home for each of their puppies. Sadly, it doesn't always work out that way. No matter how much effort a breeder puts into interviewing buyers and finding the right homes, occasionally the unexpected happens.

Ricochet dogs are dogs whom owners return to the breeder for whatever reason. Placing these ricochet dogs in new homes is called *rehoming*. Conscientious breeders who love their dogs always welcome their pups back — at any age — if they ever need to be placed again. In fact, they usually stipulate this requirement in the sales contract.

Breeders hate to make mistakes in matchmaking, and they hate that the dog must adjust to returning to his birthplace and again to a new (and, hopefully, permanent) home. But taking these dogs back is one of the obligations breeders assume when they bring puppies into the world.

A breeder generally hears the words "I can't keep him" with a sinking feeling in the abdominal pit. Yet no matter how a responsible breeder has to shuffle other dogs or her own life, her immediate response is, "Bring him back." She sets another place at the table and throws another burger on the barbie.

Ricochet dogs may be any age. If they're elderly, they usually join the pack in the home where they were born. If they're sickly, the breeder may have to bite the bullet and face the difficult choice of euthanasia.

Most, however, are rehomed through the breeder's waiting list and rescue network — which have been expanded and made even swifter by the Internet. Many breeds have electronic lists that their breed lovers can subscribe to, and word passes quickly.

One advantage of obtaining a ricochet dog from a breeder is being able to ascertain the health of the parents and having access to health records. The breeder's knowledge of the dog's ancestors also is helpful.

Owners and breeders need to prepare for the unexpected and plan in advance for what-if scenarios. Never collect or produce more dogs than you (or a relative or friend) can comfortably house, at least temporarily.

Finding Restful Homes for Retirees

Breeders have busy lives. They also usually have a menagerie of puppies, young show prospects, brood matrons, stud dogs, and golden oldies. Sadly, Grams and Gramps may receive the least attention, just because their needs aren't as immediate. Old dogs usually fit in well. They're used to routines and often are content with snoozing on the couch.

Because former stars of the show ring and whelping box are less demanding, they're fed, watered, vetted, and petted, but they're only one of the pack. Although heart-wrenching, some owners think their oldies deserve individual attention and that placement in a one- or two-pet home is better for the dog, so they're willing to place them in new homes.

Book I

Choosing
and
Bringing
Home a
Dog

Mixed breeds offer many charms

One advocate of mixed breeds says, "I want one of these and one of these and one of those . . . and I think that's why I end up with mixes. That way you get them all, one way or another. I say that's part of the charm of a mixed breed: You don't know exactly what you're getting, it's unique, and you'll never again have one just like that."

Many buyers have a breed or two or ten in mind. But if you simply want a pet who will love you, you may find the perfect dog waiting for you at a pound, shelter, or Humane Society. As many as 25 percent of shelter inmates may be pure-bred, but the other 75 percent — mixes — need homes, too. Just choose carefully. Dog lovers want to empty shelters, not fill them.

Not all retired dogs are old. Many are middle aged but have retired from a breeding program. Males can stand at stud for several years, but females often are spayed after three or four litters (at about the age of 5 or 6). Thus, most retirees are females.

Retirees can be great choices for people who are too busy to train puppies (or who've been there, done that, and don't want to do it again). Many of these animals are former show dogs and thus are well-trained, outstanding examples of the breed.

Sorting through Shelter Stats

The world would be a perfect place if everyone, human or canine, had a loving home. Sadly, until all breeders carefully plan litters and judiciously place puppies, and all buyers choose wisely, shelters will always overflow with unwanted dogs. While some of these homeless dogs are purebreds, many others are mixed breeds.

Shelter statistics indicate that adopters most often choose small or medium-sized, fluffy, purebred puppies. So a larger, short-haired, mixed-breed adult has the least chance of being adopted. Yet such a dog just may be the perfect one for you.

Some dogs are known to be half of one breed and half of another. Others are so obviously indiscernible that they're called *Heinz 57* because many variet-ies of dogs may be adding their genes to the mix. If the ancestry is known, some guesstimate may point to the instincts and proclivities of the individ-ual. Maybe she'll be a good retriever like her Chessie mom and aristocratic like her Pekingese dad. Then again, maybe she'll just join you in the bathtub and under the hair dryer now and then.

Considering Pup's Early Environment

When you're trying to decide on a canine companion, consider not only his future with you, but also the environment of the dog's puppyhood. When you can, watch how the breeder interacts with the litter. If the pups greet him with glee, eagerly welcoming pats and attention, they've been handled with love and are well socialized. Eyes sparkle with health and fur shines (though they may have just somersaulted through a puddle on the way to meet you).

Some owners tuck the *whelping box* (where pups usually spend their first four to five weeks) in a corner of a room. Not everyone, however, has space for this arrangement. The nursery may have been in a simple unadorned kennel, basement, or garage, but it needs to be clean, comfortable, and visited by people several times a day.

Breeders can't acclimate pups to every noise, creature, or contraption that they'll meet in life. However, exposing pups to a loud radio, slamming doors, and a dropped pot now and then can alleviate future trauma. Baths, collars, car rides, and nail clipping need to be part of a pup's background by the time he's ready to depart the nest.

When searching for your pup, ask about health. Individual lines differ, but in most cases, health clearances are for the parents rather than the puppies. So don't expect your pup to have certificates of health. A few tests, such as heart and juvenile cataract exams, can be conducted in puppyhood. Talk to a veterinarian about what to look for in your chosen breed. See the chapters in Book II for a lot more on health concerns.

Timing Your Adoption

Good breeders won't permit a pup to go home with a new owner on a child's birthday or a major holiday, particularly at Christmas — with rare exceptions (such as to homes with one or two adults planning a quiet celebration in front of the fireplace). Holidays are hectic enough, with parties to attend, visitors popping in, shopping to finish, and popcorn to string. Pups are likely to be underfoot, putting an extra demand on time. If you want to surprise the kids with a pup, plan ahead by asking the breeder for a picture of the pup (or the parents). Wrap a bowl, brush, leash and collar, and box of dog biscuits. Buy books about the breed, training, and even puppy names.

Getting a dog from a neighbor or colleague

Neighbors, co-workers, and acquaintances whose dogs have puppies can suddenly become your best friends. If the litter is unplanned (except by the two guilty parties), the owners may be desperate to place the little critters who eat and eliminate copious amounts of food. People who give away pups for little or nothing aren't motivated to invest a lot in their care. Anyone can be a breeder — not everyone is a *good* breeder.

Unfortunately, breeders can't arrange litters during the prime times for buyers. Pups are born throughout the year (in fact, usually during the most inconvenient times). Begin your calls several months before you're ready because finding the perfect pup often takes a few weeks or months. If you want a pup in the summer, start calling in the winter. Litters are often reserved before they're born or shortly afterward.

When You're the Matchmaker: Stray Dogs

Occasionally, you don't choose the dog; the dog chooses you. One morning you open the door and there, smiling his way smack into your heart, is your new dog. Or you're driving down the road and run into (but not run over, as long as his guardian angels are watching out for him) the saddest story in dogdom: a dog who has been abandoned and is hopelessly searching every face in every car for his erstwhile loved one.

If you give your heart and your home to a stray, whether purebred or mongrel, you're performing a good deed, serving as a lifesaver for the dog, who'd otherwise likely end up as a pound stat or roadkill. Adopting a foundling also is a good deed for society because your dog won't be a canine criminal, chasing and destroying farm stock. The rescued foundling won't bite-and-run, dirty the streets, strew garbage, or haplessly spawn more happenstance homeless canines.

Some homeless dogs are on the streets through no fault of their own. Others are there because of behavior problems or uncurbed instincts that urge them to *Run! Chase! Bark!* Their previous owners hadn't bothered to channel those instincts or found it difficult to do so. Although most animals (again, like their human counterparts) are on good behavior while settling in, once settled, they show their true habits. Within a matter of days — or surely weeks — of adopting a stray, you may have to decide whether the conduct is something you can live with or whether it's something you're willing to work with and train into acceptable behavior.

If you decide you cannot live with a particular problem, take the dog to a shelter. Be truthful about the particular bugaboo. If the person to whom the dog is surrendered has an idea of what the annoying behavior is, placing the dog in a suitable home or retraining it still may be possible. Don't replay the abandonment story the dog has already suffered once. The final chapter of that book always is a sad one.

Although taking in a stray dog is the least expensive way to obtain a pet, it bears mentioning that because Fido doesn't come bearing medical records, he'll need a complete work-up at the vet's office.

Whether the story has a happy ending for you, however, only time will tell. When you're unsure of the environmental circumstances and genetic influences molding your dog's temperament, you're groping in the dark, unable to see what's ahead. If that's what your heart tells you to do and you're prepared to face and conquer problems, bless you. But if you think that taking in a stray is an inexpensive way to obtain a pet, it does neither you nor the dog any good to rerun this scenario.

Chapter 5

Helping Your Adopted Dog Make the Homecoming Transition

Congratulations, you've found the dog for you! But wait . . . don't bring him home just yet. You have some preparation work to do.

Fortunately, you can make a big difference in how well your new dog adjusts to his new surroundings by making use of a few targeted strategies. On his first day home, your new best friend may not believe that he's finally in his forever home — and with his own cozy bed and shiny new food bowl and everything. He may be a bit nervous, even scared, when he first comes home with you, despite the fancy new collar and deluxe chew toys. Lucky for you, this chapter tells you exactly what to do to ensure that your new four-legged friend's homecoming is a happy one.

Preparing Your Pad

If you don't already have a dog, you need to do some pooch-proofing before you bring your new friend home — to keep your new dog and your old possessions safe. Pooch-proofing is important for exploring, chewing, mischievous puppies and for adult dogs who haven't quite learned what is unacceptable in your home. These precautions are particularly important for dogs who never spent much time indoors until now. Although an adult dog may not even consider gnawing on the legs of the kitchen chair, eating your shoes, or rooting through the garbage, you won't know for sure until you bring her home. Better to pooch-proof, just in case.

You also need some stuff to keep your dog healthy, well exercised, and amused. If you're someone who likes shopping, this part of bringing home your new dog is fun.

Puppy-proofing first, even for adult dogs

Before bringing a dog into your home, you need to come to terms with the many things that a short four-legged animal can get into. Any dog in a new environment is bound to explore, and some dogs explore more — shall we say — *enthusiastically* than others. Puppies, in particular, explore the world with their noses and mouths, and that may mean chomping on choking hazards, chewing through electrical cords, and munching on your favorite possessions. Energetic puppies and older dogs unaccustomed to being inside also are at risk of falling, having things fall on them, and getting stuck in the strangest places. Some of these situations can be dangerous for the puppy, such as getting stuck inside a recliner or underneath a car in the garage.

Your home doesn't *have* to be a house of hazards for your new dog. You just need to take some precautions first. On the other hand, just because you have a new dog doesn't mean that you have to resort to installing vinyl flooring and covering all your furniture with sheets. You do, however, need to look around and eliminate potential hazards. Watch for the following when pooch-proofing:

- **Choking hazards:** Look at all your floors. Do you find paper clips, bits of paper or string, rubber bands, or other objects a young puppy may find tempting enough to sample? Pick them up; they're choking hazards.

- **Unsteady objects:** What if you knocked the base of that side table with your wagging rear end? Would that lamp fall on your head? Can big puppy paws reach the edge of that coffee table and knock off all those breakable knickknacks? Either make those unsteady objects steady enough to withstand the onslaught of your new dog or move them.

✔ **Strangulation hazards:** Does the dangling curtain fringe beckon, begging your pup to grab it with his teeth and give it a good shake? Are the mini-blind cords hanging within reach of dog necks? Find a way to remove these potential strangulation hazards from your dog's reach by taping them down, tying them out of reach, or removing them altogether.

✔ **Electrocution hazards:** Can you imagine what those sharp little puppy teeth can do to an electrical cord? Yep, you're right. A puppy can bite through a cord in seconds, causing severe burns and electrocution. Make sure that you tape down cords or put them behind furniture so your puppy isn't tempted by an electrocution hazard.

✔ **Tempting trash:** Is the garbage can, with its luscious aromas, standing open for your dog to topple? The tempting trash from some garbage can really harm a who may be used to scrounging for meals. Some particularly hazardous examples are tasty but dangerous cooked bones that can splinter in your dog's intestine, rotten food, and choking hazards such as milk bottle caps, used dental floss, and metal soft-drink tabs.

✔ **Poisons:** Did you know that anything that can poison a human toddler can also poison a dog? Put safety locks on cabinets that are within the reach of your new dog, particularly the ones that contain poisonous household chemicals like cleaners, pest poisons, medications, and even toiletries like shampoo, lotion, and sunscreen. (For what to do if you suspect your dog has been poisoned, see Book II, Chapter 3.)

✔ **Your prized possessions:** Dogs love and need to chew on things. For puppies, chewing feels good during teething, and some mouthy breeds like Sporting breeds, Hounds, and Terriers chew throughout their lives. However, dogs don't know that your child's favorite stuffed bunny or expensive piece of sports equipment is any different than a fleece stuffed toy or rubber chewie. An adopted dog who never was taught the difference between dog toys and human things may have a hard time telling the difference, so put your *prized possessions* away!

Most puppy-proofing is a matter of common sense and can be essentially summarized in one Golden Rule of puppy proofing: *If you don't want your dog to chew it, put it out of reach.*

A lot of dog owners discover this lesson the hard way. If you leave things like toys, clothes, slippers, new shoes, wallets, or plates of after-school snacks out where your dog can get at them, don't blame your dog for thinking he can help himself. Only an impressively self-controlled canine can resist these things when nobody is watching. This threat is an excellent motivation for children to keep their rooms clean — or at least close their bedroom doors so the puppy can't get in. Otherwise, they risk chewed up and ruined toys and laundry. Dogs especially love to chew holes in underwear and socks.

Avoiding poisons

Many items that are poisonous to humans are also poisonous to dogs, but dogs can react — sometimes severely — to substances that are completely benign for humans, such as chocolate and onions. The following foods, plants, medications, and poisons are particularly dangerous for dogs. Don't let your dog ingest any of the following:

✔ **Chocolate:** Dogs can react severely to both the caffeine and the theobromine in chocolate.

✔ **Raisins or grapes:** Some dogs suffer acute kidney failure and death caused by these foods, even in small amounts.

✔ **Onions:** Onions can cause severe anemia in some dogs.

✔ **Prescription and nonprescription medications for humans:** Many human medications are very dangerous for pets. For example, acetaminophen, the active ingredient in Tylenol, can cause liver failure and the destruction of red blood cells (cats are even more sensitive to acetaminophen than dogs). It's just a good idea to avoid giving your dog any medication intended for humans unless your vet has advised you to do so.

✔ **Antifreeze:** A few drops of antifreeze can kill a dog. Unfortunately, antifreeze tastes and smells appealing to dogs, so watch for stains in your garage or driveway.

✔ **House and garden flowers, ferns, shrubs, and other plants:** Check out the ASPCA Animal Poison Control Center's Web site, which lists many common plants that can be poisonous to pets. Find it at `www.aspca.org/pet-care/poison-control/plants/`.

Dog destruction doesn't just apply to your furniture and wearables. It also applies to your food. Dogs of any age are incredibly clever when they smell something delicious. Adopted dogs may have spent some serious time scrounging for every piece of food they could find and going for long periods of time without any food at all before they came to live with you. These dogs can become extra clever at scoring tidbits, so you always have to be one step ahead of them. Don't leave your dinner on any counter low enough to be within a dog's lunging reach.

Supervision is a key element to puppy-proofing. Although you may not be used to keeping an eye out for what your puppy is doing at all times, doing so is essential for your dog's safety, not to mention a crucial part of housetraining.

Gathering essential doggy accoutrements

Dogs get by perfectly well with only a few basics, but you may want to consider a few luxury items, too. ***Note:*** Chew toys are *not* luxury items; they're a necessity, especially for puppies.

The basics

Dogs don't require thousands of accessories, and you certainly don't need to spend a fortune to equip your dog. However, to be able to manage and train your dog successfully, you need some basic tools that your friendly local pet store should be able to supply.

- ✔ **Identification tags:** ID tags are the most important dog accessory you can buy. Engraved with your dog's name and your address and phone number, an ID tag can be your dog's ticket home if she ever gets lost. A pet tag is important even if your dog has a microchip implanted from the shelter or the vet. Anyone can find your dog when it strays, but that doesn't mean anyone can or will take your dog to a shelter or vet to scan for the microchip. An identification tag on the collar makes finding the animal's owner easy. Put it on your dog and never take it off. Check periodically that it's still there — ID tags have a way of getting lost.

- ✔ **Buckle collar and 6-foot leash:** Choose nylon or leather with a metal or plastic buckle, decorated or simple. For some small breeds or dogs who pull a lot, consider a harness in addition to a collar, but make sure that you still can include identification tags.

- ✔ **Crate or kennel:** Choose a crate or kennel that is big enough for your adult dog. A *crate* is a plastic carrier with a wire front. Crates are sometimes called kennels, but *kennel* also refers to a wire cage. Your dog needs to be able to stand up, turn around, and lie down comfortably inside. If you have a puppy that will grow quite a bit, buy a crate or kennel to fit the dog's adult size (if you know what it will be) and temporarily block off part of the crate to make it smaller. Otherwise, the puppy may use one end for a bed and the other end for a bathroom. The crate or kennel is absolutely essential for housetraining (see Book IV, Chapter 1 for more on housetraining) and general management, because it becomes your dog's beloved den (see the section "Showing your dog to her den" later in this chapter), and she will love it even more than you do. If you travel a great deal, look for a crate or kennel that can be buckled into the backseat of your car or van.

- ✔ **Dog seat belt:** No, this device is not a luxury, but rather an important safety item. If your dog's kennel is too large to fit in the backseat or to buckle in, look for one of several different high-quality dog seat belts that attach to your car seat belt. Dog seat belts keep you and your pet safe in the car. When she's wearing a seat belt, your dog can't jump on you, distract you while you're driving, or injure anyone else in the car in the case of an accident. With this device, you can *all* buckle up safely.

- ✔ **Food and water bowls:** Metal and ceramic are easy to clean and unlikely to harbor bacteria, and they're not tempting to chew.

- ✔ **A high-quality dog food:** Check out Book II, Chapter 1 for more information about choosing a good food.

- **Assorted brushes, depending on your dog's coat:** A natural-bristle brush can be used for short- and medium-coated dogs, and wire-pin and slicker brushes work for long- or fluffy-coated dogs. Bristle brushes are good for regular maintenance brushing, while pin brushes are good for double-coated dogs because they brush down to the skin. Slicker brushes are great for pulling out excess undercoat during periods of heavy shedding.

- **Shampoo made just for dogs:** You'll also want conditioner for long-coated dogs.

- **A nail clipper made for dogs:** This tool comes in sizes (the label says whether the clipper is for small, medium, or large dogs).

- **Pest-control products to prevent fleas, ticks, and heartworms:** The best ones come from your veterinarian (for more on pest control, see Book II, Chapter 2).

- **Chew toys:** Puppies need to have acceptable things to chew so they don't chew your things. Chew toys include hard rubber teethers and edible chew toys like rawhide, pig's ears, hooves, and jerky treats.

  Some vets advise against certain edible chew toys, like rawhide, for some dogs, because they can pose a choking hazard or upset a stomach. If you aren't sure which edible toys are safe for your dog, talk to your vet.

- **Interactive toys for bonding time:** Whether you throw a tennis ball or a Frisbee or play tug of war with a rope toy, be sure to get a few toys that you and your dog can play with together. These toys give you great ways to play with your dog in the doggy way that she enjoys.

Beyond the basics

Some doggy accoutrements are necessities for certain dogs and luxury items are for others. Dog litter boxes, ramps and stairs, and special grooming supplies are among the more common ones.

Dog litter boxes are good for pet owners who can't easily take their little dogs outside, people with mobility issues, or pet owners who live in high-rise apartments in the city. Dog litter boxes are sized for different dogs and come with pelleted paper litter-box filler that absorbs moisture. When litter-box training your dog, you need to change the litter after each use. Another option is framed squares of sod or artificial turf so your dog gets the feel of going on the grass even while he's inside.

Coat conditioner and coat spray are essential for long-coated dogs. A square of velvet or a chamois to polish short coats is a nice addition. Some dogs look better when washed with special shampoos made to brighten white coats, darken dark coats, or soothe sensitive skin. Dogs with allergies or fleas may need special shampoos that help them resolve their health issues. Some companies make lines of dog spa products with natural botanicals. You can even buy doggy cologne to keep your pooch sweet smelling.

Ramps and stairs are good for dogs with sensitive spines, like Dachshunds, or senior dogs with arthritis who have trouble jumping up and down from couches, beds, and cars. You can buy beautiful padded ramps and stairs for inside, or more utilitarian versions for cars and even for swimming pools and boats to help your little swimmer get out of the water more easily. This item may actually be an important safety device if you have a swimming pool and your dog can't easily get out of it. In that case, consider it a must-have.

Book I, Chapter 6 has a lot more on doggie stuff you may want to buy.

Book I

Choosing and Bringing Home a Dog

Welcoming Doggy Home

When the house is prepared and well stocked, you can load up your adopted dog into the car (don't forget a dog seat belt or crate!), drive home, pull into the driveway, coax him out of the car, and then . . . wouldn't it be nice if your new adopted dog bounded happily into the house, engaged in a quick game of fetch, sniffed and licked the family, and then curled up in his doggy bed for a nap, happy tail a-waggin'?

Even though such scenarios have been known to happen, they're not common. The more likely reaction you can expect from your adopted dog is that she will be a little nervous, maybe a little scared, probably curious, and maybe so excited that she can hardly contain herself — literally. She may even experience a few more serious adjustment problems.

The trick to helping your dog make a smooth and quick transition to her new home is immediately establishing routines and sticking to them. Dogs pick up quickly on the rules of a new place, so the sooner they get that information from you, the sooner they can adjust to their new situations. Keep initial introductions calm and limited. Don't mob your new dog with people, toys, games, treats, and attention all at once. Dogs react to the moods and actions of the people around them, so if you want a calm, relaxed dog, then try to act calm and relaxed. If you act anxious, worried, or excitable, your dog picks up on your cues. If your dog thinks you have the situation fully and confidently in hand, she can relax a little bit and not have to worry about trying to manage things herself.

In most cases, calm behavior and a comfortable routine win out, quickly sending your adopted dog the message that all is right with the world again.

Dog, meet potty spot

Taking care of business is the first thing to do when you get home with your adopted dog — and by "business," we mean the business of housetraining. Regardless of your dog's age, adults and puppies need to know where they are allowed to fulfill their, um . . . elimination requirements. Housetraining problems are among the chief reasons people give up their dogs to animal shelters, so managing this issue right from the start is super important.

Choosing a potty spot

Before bringing your new pet home, you need to know in advance where you want him to go. If you have a yard, great. But you also need to pick a spot in the yard that will be most convenient, a spot where people aren't likely to walk through. Secluded locations are better than spots right near the sidewalk or street. Some dogs don't care where they go, but others may feel vulnerable and don't want to do their business with cars whizzing by on the other side of the fence or other dogs wandering past with their owners and barking.

If you want to paper-train or litter-box-train your pet, the spot where you place the receptacle must be ready to go before your new dog comes home. Place it in an area that's away from high foot traffic and easy to clean, such as on a linoleum or tile floor and far from your dog's sleeping area. Dogs don't like to eliminate near where they sleep.

Telling your dog where to go

As soon as you get home, you may be tempted to take off your dog's leash and let her explore the house. Wait! Don't unclip that leash from that collar just yet. First, take your dog to the place where you want her to eliminate, either in the yard or in the area of the house you've chosen. Keeping that leash on, have your dog sniff, circle, and check out the spot, but stay where you are until she relieves herself. Although this process can take a long time, wait. If you know that your dog recently relieved herself and simply doesn't need to go, skip to the next section about introducing your dog to her den. You can go back and try this step again and again. And again. You'll find repetition of this step a worthwhile endeavor.

Rewarding a job well done

When your dog does go in the right spot, say hooray! Praise him, pet him, and call him a very good dog because he just did something very good. He went where you wanted him to go, and that's a big step for a new dog in a new home. Make sure that he knows he has pleased you.

Then if you have a fenced yard, you can let him off the leash to explore on his own. If you don't have a fence, lead him around the yard on the leash and let him sniff, check out the perimeter, and figure out what's what. Finally, bring him in the house. Or if your dog's potty spot is inside and you're already in the house, you can give him a chance to explore the rest of the house now.

Book I

Choosing and Bringing Home a Dog

Showing your dog to her den

Now is the time to grab some treats, because you're about to introduce your dog to her new best friend — aside from you, of course. Dogs are naturally den animals and like a safe place to call their own. One of your most powerful tools for helping your dog feel safe and comfortable in her new home is the dog den.

Whether you choose to use a plastic crate (see Figure 5-1), a wire kennel, or a portable wire enclosure — sometimes called an *exercise pen* or X-pen — your dog needs somewhere to feel safe. Crates and kennels with latching doors can help with housetraining and travel, but if your dog already is house-trained and not destructive, you may not need to latch the door just yet. If the kennel is all wire, cover it with a blanket, leaving only the front open. Dogs feel safest when they can rest without feeling the need to watch their backs. Your dog probably wants to be near you, so situate the den in a room where your dog can at least hear, if not see you, when she's resting.

Figure 5-1: One good choice for a "den" is a plastic crate with solid sides and a door that opens and closes.

To attract your dog's interest, make sure that the den is comfortable and soft, and then open the door. Get your dog's attention with a treat, or lead her to the den by her leash. Then toss a few treats into the den and step back. Don't force your dog to go inside the den, and don't shut the door after her if she does go in on her own. Leave the den open so she can explore. If she goes in to get the treat, praise her, but stay back. Let her know her den is a safe spot, not jail, and that even you won't grab at her while she's in there. Talk softly and pleasantly to your dog as she explores her new den. Hide treats inside the den periodically so your dog gets the message that she is likely to find something delicious inside that safe, comfy spot.

And what if your dog doesn't take to the den right away? Young puppies can quickly learn to accept the den but can endure being in it only a few minutes at a time at first. Even if your pup is whining and crying, don't make a big deal about it, or you risk increasing her anxiety. Put her in the den, shut the door, stay nearby, talk casually but reassuringly to the dog, and then let her out again. Increase the amount of time your dog spends in the den just a few minutes at a time over a period of a few days. Pretty soon, your puppy will get used to the routine and recognize the den as something safe and predictable.

In the case of an older adopted dog who has neither been in a crate before nor had any bad experiences with the crate, *not* forcing the issue is an important attitude for you to take. Just leave the den door open and let your dog adjust at her own rate. If the dog is truly fearful of the crate, keep working to make the den an inviting place without putting any pressure on her.

If your dog's first experiences with her den — and with the entire house and yard — are filled with positive associations like pleasant, calm interaction and plenty of yummy treats, you set the stage for a happy home.

You can let your dog rest in her den awhile or you can move on to introduce her to her new family, if she's ready.

Introducing people

The more people your dog meets in a pleasant and positive environment, the better socialized he becomes. First of all, he needs to get to know you, his new favorite person. Next, he needs to meet the other people who live in your house. Finally, he needs to meet all kinds of other people, too.

Dogs who are familiar with many different people of different ages, sizes, hair types, colors, and mobilities become better judges of character than dogs who rarely see anyone beyond the people who live in the house. Dogs are social animals, and they find people fascinating. The more they know about the curious existence of their two-legged caretakers, the better they get along living in a human world. (The next section covers a lot more about socializing.)

Meeting the parents

Your dog first must get to know you and the other adults in your household. These introductions need to be positive, friendly, and not too overwhelming. Your dog is learning about you as you take her around the house and yard, showing her this new environment, but you also need to spend some time focusing on your dog on that first day:

Book I

Choosing and Bringing Home a Dog

- ✔ Sitting on the floor with your dog
- ✔ Letting your dog sniff you
- ✔ Petting your dog
- ✔ Talking to your dog
- ✔ Showing your dog some toys

See what happens when you throw a ball for your dog. Will she chase it? Retrieve it? Or ignore it? Try to figure out what your dog likes and doesn't like, what interests her or makes her nervous. The more you find out about your dog, the more she will also learn about you.

When introducing your dog to other adults, one person at a time is plenty for your dog to take in. Have your dog sniff and investigate the other adults in the house, and have the other adults give your adopted dog treats and gentle petting. Take cues from your dog. If she seems overwhelmed or nervous, take it slow, or save introductions for later. If she seems interested to meet everyone, give him that interaction time.

Lapping up the kid time

Kids love dogs and get pretty excited about a new dog in the house. Dogs love kids, too — most of the time. Before you're completely familiar with your new adopted dog, however, prepare your child for how to interact with a new dog and carefully supervise all child-dog interactions. For that first introduction, clip on your dog's leash.

Before bringing home an adopted dog, children need to know that this newest four-legged family member may be nervous, overly excited, or even scared. Loud, quick-moving children can intimidate a dog, especially one that isn't familiar with children. Explain to your children that first impressions are important, and if the new dog's first impression of them is one of fear, then the new dog may not want to play with the children. Children need to approach a new dog quietly, slowly, and with soft gentle voices.

Likewise, children need to play with a new dog (or any small dog or puppy) while sitting with her on the floor instead of trying to pick up the puppy and carry her around. Have the child sit, and then let the dog approach the child while the dog is on a leash held by a responsible adult. Keep control over the dog so she doesn't jump on the child, and make sure that the child handles the dog gently. Depending on their age, you can let children feed the dog treats or offer her a new toy, but only under strict adult supervision. You don't want your new dog bullying your child to get the treats. With your help, the child needs to be in control of when the dog gets the treat. This kind of positive first meeting sends a message to your dog that short little humans are just as nice and safe and rewarding as the taller ones. Your dog can become your child's best buddy, but maintaining control over the situation is important so the relationship starts off on the right paw.

If your dog reacts too roughly or even fearfully or aggressively toward a child, take the matter seriously and don't let child and dog interact unsupervised, ever, until the matter is fully resolved. Consult a professional trainer or behaviorist for advice. See Book IV, Chapter 2 for more information about handling behavior problems in adopted dogs. Take aggressive behavior seriously and tackle the problem immediately. Aggression doesn't just go away on its own. Don't risk any child's safety.

Relying on friends to help socialize your dog: The welcome-home party

Even if you have a big family, meeting other people is important for your new dog. It can happen on walks through the neighborhood or trips in the car, but another great way to socialize your dog with all kinds of people is to have a dog party. Ask a variety of friends over for snacks and playtime with your new dog.

Throwing a party doesn't mean that you just let your friends mob your adopted dog. Remember that all your dog's initial interactions with people need to be calm and positive. Give your friends treats to give your dog. Have them approach her one at a time for petting and play. As everyone gives your dog focused and happy attention, your dog gets the impression that people are just great to be around and well worth pleasing.

Before socializing your dog, make sure that she doesn't have any aggression issues, such as snapping to protect food, or fear issues, such as anxiety around certain kinds of people. Putting your dog in situations in which she feels nervous, cornered, or surrounded by too many people before she's ready can actually make her more fearful or anxious. You're the best judge for determining whether your dog is ready for this kind of stimulation and socialization. If you aren't sure, try inviting friends over one at a time for awhile to find out how your dog reacts. And keep the treats coming.

Introducing other pets

Meeting the humans in the house is one thing; introducing other pets is something else. Some dogs get along just fine with other dogs, but others have issues with perceived competitors. Some dogs don't think twice about cats, but others follow the cartoon stereotype and see cats as prey animals and great chase opportunities. Small animals and birds can look a lot like prey animals, too.

Some cats, in turn, are not accepting and are downright nasty about canines intruding on their happy homes. Your task: Carefully introduce your new dog to other pets in the household, to prevent conflict and to subvert potential tragedy. Doing so can take some time, and some animals don't adjust to their new siblings for weeks or even months. Take it slow, be diplomatic, and supervise all interactions until everyone can be reliably trusted.

Book I

Choosing and Bringing Home a Dog

Dogs meet dog

Most dogs tend to relate to each other in a hierarchical system of leaders and followers, and most dogs tend to be at least somewhat territorial. If you already have a dog who's used to being the only dog in the house, he probably will see another dog as an interloper and want to make darned sure that the new dog knows his place.

A new dog on new turf may defer to the previous resident dog. On the other hand, expect no guarantees of a conflict-free meeting. Dogs learn crucial dog-to-dog communication skills when they are still with their littermates between 3 and 6 weeks of age. Puppies who are deprived of this time together may not understand how to communicate well with other dogs. Like people, some dogs just tend to have stronger personalities and try to be the leader. If you put two such dogs together, you can have squabbles.

You can reduce the likelihood of a brawl by taking some or all of these steps:

- ✔ Adopt a female dog if you already have a male dog, or vice versa. Male and female dogs together are less likely to fight than dogs of the same gender. Spayed or neutered dogs get along better, too.

- ✔ Introduce the dogs first on neutral territory, such as at the shelter or the home of a friend.

- ✔ Remember that the first dog may see your home as his territory and feel threatened that another dog is on his turf. Supervise all interactions until the dogs accept each other.

- ✔ Be patient. Dogs may take a few hours to become fast friends, but some dogs may never get along very well. The relationship probably will improve with time, but it can take weeks or even months.

- ✔ Keep both dogs on their leashes, with each handled by a separate adult. You must be a strong presence and maintain control. When both dogs think a third party is in control of the situation, they may feel less anxious, fearful, or defensive.

- ✔ Let both dogs spend some extended time getting acquainted on either side of a baby gate (see Figure 5-2), screen door, or other barrier that neither is able to jump over. Doing so can help dogs gain interest in each other without the threat of one dog invading the other's space.

- ✔ Give each dog his own space, his own den, and room to run away to in case of a confrontation. A brand-new kennel or crate isn't automatically the resident dog's property, so it gives the new dog a place to feel safe. Keep the door open so the new dog can go in whenever he needs a safe spot, but keep the resident dog out of the new dog's den.

✔ Give both dogs plenty of attention and separate training time, especially your resident dog, who may be feeling neglected. Make sure he knows you aren't replacing him!

✔ Take it slow. Not everybody wants a new sibling. Let both dogs take time getting to know each other, and supervise all interactions until they work out their new relationship.

Figure 5-2:
A baby gate can help your new dog and your resident dog get acquainted.

 If your two dogs get into a fight, don't stick your hand in the middle, because you can get hurt doing so. Keep a squirt gun or a spray bottle filled with water handy and distract the dogs with a spritz — or make a loud noise, like shaking a can of pennies or pebbles. As soon as they stop fighting for a moment, separate them immediately and put each in his or her respective den or separate room to cool off.

 If you can't seem to resolve the issue, call a local dog trainer who uses positive reinforcement. A trainer can work with you and your dogs, giving you some strategies tailored for your individual situation.

Introducing kitty

Some dogs get along just great with cats. Honest! In many cases, though, dogs who aren't raised with cats see them as something to chase. Conversely, dogs who are raised with cats may let their guards down in front of a claw-wielding whirlwind, so be careful in that case, too. A new puppy probably can learn to accept your cat as a member of the family. An adult dog who has lived with cats successfully before also will probably be okay.

A shelter or rescue worker may be able to provide information about the dog's history. An adult dog who isn't familiar with cats may pose a problem.

When introducing a dog and a cat, both need protection. Be sure that your cat's claws are trimmed, to prevent serious injury to your dog, whose eyes are especially vulnerable. And make sure that your cat has safe places to escape if the dog attempts to give chase. Finally, supervise all interactions until you're sure that both pets can be trusted.

Some people keep their dogs and cats separated, giving each one a separate level of the house or individual room, but doing so can be complicated and a slip-up can cause disaster. Regular obedience training can help you and your dog communicate so that your dog understands what is and is not allowed in your home — and that includes cat chasing. A few dogs never are able to live peacefully with cats. If that happens to you, you may need to consider returning your new pet to the shelter or rescue group in favor of a dog who does get along with cats. Naturally, returning to the shelter is stressful for the dog, so never rush into an adoption without a good chance that your new dog will fit into your home situation.

Small animals: Friends, not doggy snacks

Some dogs have strong instincts for chasing and killing small animals. Terriers, for example, have been bred for centuries to strengthen their instincts for going after vermin — that's why they're called *ratters*. If you have hamsters, gerbils, rats, mice, guinea pigs, ferrets, or rabbits as pets, your dog may feel a compulsion to get to them, so you must be extra careful to keep these small creatures safe. Introduce them carefully, or keep the small animal in a place where the dog won't see it, and never leave small animals or birds alone with dogs, for the safety of both — a dog can kill a small bird, but to a small dog, a large parrot is a formidable foe. Make sure that bird cages are out of reach and inaccessible to your dog.

Book I

Choosing
and
Bringing
Home a
Dog

Downtime

Your dog now has had a bathroom break (or two), seen his den, met the family and other pets, and done some power sniffing around his new digs. That's a big day for a dog! Before you launch into a training session, a walk around the neighborhood, or any further family chaos, give your dog some downtime.

Remember that doggy den? Take your dog back to his special safe place, throw in some treats, and let him go inside. If he won't, herd him gently inside and close the door. Praise him and talk gently and positively, and then without making a big deal about it, let him have a rest.

Your dog may whine, cry, or whimper pathetically, but never fear, you don't have to leave him in there for hours. Instead, leave him in the den for 15 to 20 minutes. He may settle down and take a nap, or he may just watch you for awhile. If he seems nervous, you can stay in the same room, but don't pay any attention to him. This time is specifically for your dog to be by himself, and your sympathetic attentions will only make him worry. Remind yourself that you aren't ignoring your dog. You're teaching him self-sufficiency and confidence, and you're teaching him that when he is in his den, his time is his own and nobody will bother him.

After a short rest period, let your dog out of the den again. Then take him right back to that potty spot outside, on his leash, until he does his business. Then get on with whatever activities you have planned next. Repeat these short, positive, unemotional den-rest sessions throughout the day; your dog will quickly learn to appreciate and even look forward to them. Pretty soon, he may go on in there all by himself.

When night falls, tuck your dog into his den until morning, close the door to keep him safely inside, and prepare to endure a night or two of crying and whining. Your new puppy, or even an adult dog, may not understand at first that this is time for sleeping and that he can come out again in the morning, but after a few nights, he'll get the routine. Remember how much dogs depend on routine? Young puppies probably need a bathroom break during the night, once or maybe twice, but don't get up every time the puppy cries to commiserate. Send the message instead that this is how it works and everybody likes it that way. Soon your puppy will like it that way, too.

For adult dogs who truly resist the crate, set up a comfy bed beside yours so your dog knows that you're nearby (be sure to close your bedroom door so the dog isn't free to roam while you sleep). Your new adopted dog needs a sense of security, and night is one opportunity to reinforce that. The first few nights can be trying on any new pet owner, but just think of how the adopted dog feels. Most dogs adjust very quickly and sleep through the night sooner than a human baby would. Plan on a nap tomorrow, and be patient. In a week, chances are those nighttime woes will be a distant memory.

Socialization and civility in the puppy world

A puppy is hard-wired with a prime socialization window. During this window, between 8 to 12 weeks, her brain is developing and she's receptive to new experiences. She's constantly looking to you for your interpretation of these experiences. Now is the time to introduce her to everything she will encounter throughout her life, from objects and people to noises and other animals.

Even though some of your early excursions may be restricted until your puppy is fully inoculated, make every effort to expose her to a variety of stimulants so that she'll be more relaxed when she's presented with something new.

If your puppy is older than 12 weeks, don't despair. Even though your puppy has passed her impression window, she's still open to your example when she gets overwhelmed or excited. A noticeably defensive or wary reaction simply indicates that your puppy has no conscious memory of such an occurrence and isn't sure how to act. In these circumstances, your reactions to both the situation and the puppy are important. Placating, soothing, or corrective responses actually intensify a puppy's reactions by focusing attention on the inappropriate behavior.

Calming Your Puppy Based on Her Age

Puppies, like children, go through developmental stages, and each stage brings with it a new perspective. In the earliest stages, everything is new, and your puppy's trust in you is innocent and faithful. As she ages, however, she's prone to challenge and question your opinion while still being unsure of life's variety. Maturing puppies, especially ones going through adolescence and puberty, have their own set of opinions and must be consistently persuaded to mind you. You'll need a creative approach to socialization.

Acclimating a young pup (8 to 12 weeks)

When he's very young, your puppy will mirror your reaction in all new situations. If you're nervous, he will be, too. If you get excited, uncomfortable, or edgy, he'll follow suit. Expose your puppy to new experiences under controlled circumstances so you'll be centered and prepared to deal with your puppy's reaction.

Young puppies generally react to new situations in one of four ways:

✔ **Fearfully:** Noted by a hesitant body posture, these puppies pull back or scurry to leave the environment. Often they scratch to be held or acknowledged.

- ✔ **Calmly:** These pups are patiently observant and have a relaxed body posture and mild curiosity.

- ✔ **Actively:** Because they're very interactive, these puppies explore the new stimulation with gusto and may be hard to calm down or refocus.

- ✔ **Defensively:** Puppies who act defensively may back up, hold still, or run forward. Or they may do all three maneuvers and bark or vocalize their feelings in some way. Their ears may be flattened against their heads, and they may hide behind your legs or try to climb up into your arms or lap.

Any attention given to a puppy reinforces his reaction, which is fine *if and only if* your puppy is reacting calmly. Other responses need redirecting. Read on to find out how.

Fear is a common response that shows your puppy doesn't like to make interpretations alone. Because of your pup's dependence, new situations demand your guidance and direction.

Don't coddle your puppy if she has a fearful reaction, because your immediate attention indicates submission, not leadership. Your lowered body posture and high-pitched tone convey the message that you're afraid, too. A better response on your part is to stand tall, either ignoring your puppy or kneeling at her side. *Brace* her by clipping your thumb under her collar and holding her in a sitting position. Above all else, though, you need to remain calm and assured: Your puppy will be impressed by your confidence.

A relaxed reaction is a good sign that your puppy will take everything in stride. Some puppies are so relaxed, however, that they don't register the distraction you're introducing, such as a uniformed police officer. If this scenario sounds familiar, use treats to bring your puppy's attention to the situation at hand.

Many puppies love life — a lot. To them, new experiences hold endless possibilities. Even at a young age, passion emanates from everything they do. The goal in new situations and introductions isn't to bring these pups out of their shells. Instead, the goal is to successfully contain their excitement. To displace their enthusiasm, use toys and the bracing technique.

An early defensive reaction (before 12 weeks) should be noted and taken seriously. If the tips in this book don't lessen your puppy's intensity, hire a professional. The onset of adolescence, with the release of adult hormones, will only intensify an aggressive response. Deal with such behavior immediately.

If your puppy has an intense reaction (one that's fearful, overexcited, or defensive) to a new situation or person, determine her Red Zone: the distance from the stimulus where she can stand comfortably. Stand just outside this zone and handle your puppy calmly by using commands, toys, or treats to keep her focus.

Book I

Choosing
and
Bringing
Home a
Dog

Catching up an older pup (12 weeks and older)

A puppy past the critical socialization time may have a more pronounced reaction to new situations, especially if he has no similar experience in his memory bank. For example, an older puppy who hasn't navigated a stairway or hardwood floor may be terrified at the prospect. How you handle such a situation determines his future attitude. A dog who is fearful of specific things will be more leery of new situations throughout his life.

Discover your puppy's body language and take it very seriously. Focus on his eyes, body position, tail, and mouth. Even though he can't talk in words, your puppy will tell you everything if you listen with your eyes. Check out Table 5-1 for guidance.

Table 5-1	**Reading Your Puppy's Body Language**				
Body Part	**Fearful**	**Undecided**	**Relaxed**	**Active**	**Defensive**
Eyes	Squinting, darting, unfocused	Focused or shifting	Focused	Attentive, focused	Glaring, hard
Body	Low, arched, pulled back and down	Shifting from forward to pulled back, approaching but then immediately avoiding the person	Relaxed	Comfortable posture, moving side to side	Pitched forward, stone still, tense
Tail	Tucked under belly, wagging low	Tucked under belly, arched slightly over back, fluctuating between the two	Still, gently swinging above rump	High, wagging enthusiastically	Still above rump or arched above back in a tight, repetitive wag
Mouth	Pulled back, often in a semismile	Terse, trembling	Normal	Panting, normal, may be parted in a vocalization	Tight, unflinching, may be parted in a growl or vocalization

Turn your "can't do" puppy into a "can do" dog by being the example you want him to follow. When your puppy's response is pronounced, stay very calm. Keep your eyes focused on the situation at hand (not on your puppy) and interact with the stimulus — be it a person, situation, or object — in the manner you want him to mirror.

If you look at your puppy, or even glance back at him, he may misconstrue your posture and visual confirmation as insecurity. For example, think of playing on a team: The captain wouldn't shout a direction and then look to the players for confirmation. The same rules apply with your pup. When directing your puppy, stand confident and focus on the situation at hand.

Teaching Your Puppy to Be Accepting of All People

Regardless of your puppy's age, three variables determine her ability to relate to others around her:

- ✔ Breed influences
- ✔ Socialization experience
- ✔ Your example

Even though your puppy's breed drives are predetermined, you can vastly shape the future through socialization and positive modeling.

Socializing your young puppy (8 to 12 weeks)

A young puppy will look to you to interpret everything in his life. How you interact with and greet people from all walks of life is his greatest example. Disciplinary issues evolve when too much excitement is present during greetings. These issues evolve because your puppy interprets this excitement as hyperactive play, and though it can be fun initially, it gets old fast.

A better plan is to actually have a plan. Expose and introduce your puppy to as many new people as time allows. You should follow the same routine whether the person is 9 or 90, in a tux or dressed down, uniformed, or in costume. The wider the variety, the better.

Mothers are right when they say good manners start at home. When greeting your puppy, be very casual. Even though you may be beside yourself with delight, stay calm and interact with your puppy only when he's calm, too.

Condition your puppy to a leash and collar, and keep these items on him when meeting new people. Use them to guide him, as if you're holding a young child's hand. When possible, ask people to ignore any extreme reactions, from hyperactivity to fear or defensiveness. Simply put, when he reacts extremely, act as if your puppy isn't even there. When applied for a few minutes, this approach will de-escalate any concern and will condition your puppy to look to and reflect your reaction.

After the new person is an established presence, which takes about one to five minutes, kneel down next to your puppy, *brace* him by clipping your thumb under him collar, and hold him in a sitting position (see Figure 5-3). Repeat "Say hello" as the person pats your puppy.

Figure 5-3: Bracing reassures your young puppy when meeting unfamiliar people.

If your puppy is fearful or tense, ask the person to shake a treat cup and treat him, to create a new and more positive outlook.

Shaping up older puppies

Is your older pup out of control or poorly conditioned to greeting new people? Don't give it another thought. She may become hyper when the doorbell rings, react defensively to men in uniform, or act warily around toddlers, but you can reshape her focus with patience, ingenuity, and calm consistency.

When left unchecked, such behavior may result in a dog who's permanently wary of children or defensive with the delivery man. Consider living with this erratic behavior for ten or more years — it won't be fun. However, you have the power to reshape your future.

Remember the following three key points, regardless of her preestablished habits, when introducing your puppy to new situations and people:

- ✔ Whoever is in front is in charge.
- ✔ A confident and calm body posture conveys confidence and self-assurance.
- ✔ A steady voice will be followed.

No matter what your puppy's behavior is, it developed in large part because of your attention. Puppies repeat anything that ensures interaction — they don't care whether it's negative or positive interaction. If your pup is hyper, you likely tried to calm her by grabbing her fur, pushing her, or holding her. When a defensive or wary reaction results in a soothing and high-pitched "It's okay," the translation is that of mutual concern. What this puppy needs is a human example of confidence, which is conveyed with clear direction and a calm, upright body posture.

To resolve this greeting dilemma and recondition your pup, do the following:

- ✔ Create a greeting station in sight of, but at least 6 feet behind, the greeting door.
- ✔ Secure a short 2-foot leash to the area and repeat "Back" as you lead your puppy and attach her before opening the door.
- ✔ Ignore your puppy until she has fully calmed down.

Though it may be difficult to ignore her initial vocalizations and spasms, it won't take long for her to discover that a relaxed posture gets immediate attention.

Encourage everyone in your home to respond in kind: No one gives the pup attention until she's considerably calmer. You can leave a bone or toy at her greeting station to help her displace her excitement or frustration.

If your puppy is defensive or fearful, put a head collar on her. This head collar automatically relaxes your puppy because the weight placed over her nose and behind her head stimulates the same pressure points her mother would use to calm her. Book I, Chapter 6 discusses collars in more detail.

Also, to help her become used to new situations and people, take your puppy out and socialize her with as many new people as you can find. Teach and use the directions "Let's go," "Stay," "Down," "Wait," and "Back," as described in several chapters of Book IV. These commands teach your pup the following:

- ✔ **Let's go:** Instructs your puppy to walk behind you and watch for your direction.

> ✔ **Stay:** Stresses impulse control and focus. Precede this direction with a "Sit" or "Down" command.
>
> ✔ **Under:** Directs your puppy to lie under your legs or under a table. These safe places reinforce that you're her guardian and protector.
>
> ✔ **Wait:** Instructs your puppy to stop in her tracks and look to you before proceeding.
>
> ✔ **Back:** Directs your puppy to get behind you and reminds her that you're in charge.

Book I

Choosing and Bringing Home a Dog

If your puppy is wary of a person, ask him to ignore the puppy and to avoid all eye contact. Eye contact is often interpreted as predatory or confrontational and will often intensify your puppy's reaction.

Introducing your puppy to people of all shapes and sizes

Getting your puppy comfortable with life needs to start with introducing him to the variety of people he'll meet in his lifetime. Each person has a unique look and smell. So that your puppy doesn't mature into a dog who singles anyone out, you need to socialize him early on with the whole spectrum. Check out Table 5-2 for guidance.

The use of a creamy spread (such as peanut butter, tofu, cheese, or yogurt) encourages a gentle interaction. Infrequent use means that your puppy will be enamored with any situation that produces this delight.

Table 5-2			Meeting New People		
Human	*Directions*	*Leash*	*Position*	*Treat Location*	*Comments*
Baby	"Gentle" and "Stay."	Yes, if excitable.	Braced to prevent jumping.	On the floor, or put a creamy spread on the baby's shoe.	Using a creamy spread on the baby's shoe directs your puppy to this body part. Say "Ep, ep" to discourage facial interaction.

(continued)

Table 5-2 *(continued)*

Human	Directions	Leash	Position	Treat Location	Comments
Child	"Sit," "Down," "Back," "Stay," "Gentle," "Follow," and "Say hello."	Yes. Consider two so the child can direct if the dog is trustworthy.	Braced or "Back" behind your feet.	Ideally, the child gives the pup a treat. It can also be thrown if your puppy is wild or wary.	A creamy spread in a tube or on a long spoon can be extended to a calm puppy in a "Sit" or "Down" position. Teach your puppy a trick (see Book IV) to encourage a happy interaction.
Opposite sex	"Follow," "Stay," and "Say hello."	Only as needed in public or if your puppy has an extreme reaction.	Braced or at your side if your puppy's reaction is inappro-priate.	The other person gives the treat unless your puppy is wary. Then the treat can be tossed or given by you close to the other person.	Be calm and comfortable, not unnaturally excited or affectionate. Puppies sense feigned affection and find it odd and unconvincing.
Costume	"Back," "Stay," and "Under."	Absolutely. Costumes are scary for pup-pies, and the leash gives you the ability to "hold your puppy's hand."	Braced in the "Stay" position. Kneel in front and hold him steadily. Don't pet him until he's calm.	Yes, initially.	Wear the costume yourself. Place it on the floor and surround it with treats. Allow your puppy to watch you put it on.

Human	*Directions*	*Leash*	*Position*	*Treat Location*	*Comments*
Unfamiliar ethnicities	"Back," "Stay," and "Say hello."	In public and when unmanageable within the home. Otherwise, no.	Braced during a greeting. Use a ball or toy to encourage a normal response.	Yes, when meeting the person directly. Otherwise, no.	Dogs aren't racist, but some will notice variations in skin color. Seek out different environments to expose your dog to.
Shapes and sizes	"Back," "Stay," "Follow," and "Say hello."	Use a dragging leash and hold the leash if your dog is startled or reactive.	Braced during a greeting. Use a ball or toy to encourage a normal response.	Yes, when meeting the person directly. Otherwise, no.	A trip to town will expose your pup to a variety of body shapes and sizes.
Uniforms	"Follow," "Stay," and "Say hello."	Leash initially and always in public.	Walk by nonchalantly and say "Follow." Brace if unsettled. Use "Stay" direction to stabilize reaction.	Use treats to encourage your puppy's focus on you when this person is present.	Wear a hat or costume if your dog is overtly reactive. Expose early and often, especially to delivery people.
Sporting Equipment	"Stay" and "Sniff it."	Yes	Discover your puppy's Red Zone (discussed earlier). Observe at a distance and gradually bring your puppy closer.	Use treats or a toy to encourage your puppy's focus.	Lay the equipment on the floor and encourage your puppy to "Sniff it" as you explore together.

(continued)

Table 5-2 *(continued)*

Human	Directions	Leash	Position	Treat Location	Comments
People holding equipment	"Stay" and "Sniff it."	Yes, unless you're holding the equipment.	Discover your puppy's Red Zone (discussed earlier). Observe at a distance and gradually bring your puppy closer.	Use treats or a toy to encourage your puppy's focus.	Lay the equipment on the floor or hold it yourself. When you see another person holding equipment, do treat exercises at a distance.

Conditioning Your Puppy to Life's Surprises

Socializing your puppy to all of life's surprises is just as important as training her during the first year. Though a puppy may do a four-star "Stay" in your living room, if she falls to pieces after you hit the road, you won't be able to take her anywhere. And your puppy has so much more in store for her than a variety of different people. Exposing your puppy to all of life's surprises will encourage calm acceptance and healthy curiosity to anything new the two of you may encounter.

Other animals

A 1-year-old Terrier-Whippet mix was rescued from New Orleans after Hurricane Katrina. Not only was snow a new concept to her, but squirrels were riveting. Sweet and demure, she spun 180 degrees when facing the prospect of chasing a yard full of busy, gray tidbits. Three directions were needed for this pup: "Back," "Sit-stay," and "Wait." Impulse control was the order of the day.

Book I

Choosing
and
Bringing
Home a
Dog

Whether your pup is young or old, he must learn impulse control when he notices other animals in his surroundings. When you notice a critter before your puppy does, instruct him by saying "Back" and guide him to your side. Then kneel down facing the critter and use the command "Sit-stay" to encourage your pup's containment. If your puppy's radar alerts first, however, you'll notice it in his ears, which will be erect and riveted. He'll orient himself toward the distraction. When he does, direct "Back" and kneel down to brace him. Finally, instruct "Stay."

As your puppy's impulse control matures, encourage him to follow you by using the "Follow" direction. You can discourage any interest with a quick tug of the leash. Praise and treat him for resisting the temptation.

Weather patterns

Your puppy's first thunderstorm may be a memorable event. The best thing you can do is absolutely nothing. Emotional reassurance on your part will get misconstrued as mutual fear, and your puppy could quickly develop a phobic reaction to the situation. By staying calm, reading a book, or laying low, you're setting an example of how to act in a storm. Also consider taping a storm and playing it at low levels during play or feeding until your puppy is conditioned to the sound.

If your puppy has already developed a fearful reaction to storms, fit her for a head collar and guide her on the lead through each storm, acting as though nothing is happening. When possible, stay on the ground floor, offering your puppy nothing more than a flavorful bone. Pay attention to her only when she's relaxed. Her reactivity will improve in time. Speak to your veterinarian about medication if the lead training doesn't work.

Some puppies don't like going outside in the rain, and others don't ever want to come in. Even though your puppy is unlikely to change her mind about the rain, you can try winning her over by leaving her inside as you play outside in the rain — but make sure that you play where she can watch. If you have no luck, it's time to get a big golf umbrella and plan quick outings with your pup.

Snow and cold present another issue, especially for tiny or thin-coated breeds. When the temperature drops, your puppy's muscles contract. This contraction includes your puppy's bladder muscles, which makes elimination difficult, if not impossible. Consider a puppy coat and, dare we say it, booties, when faced with cold weather. If your puppy is small, consider teaching her to go on paper exclusively or in addition to eliminating outside. If you don't like the papers inside your home, consider putting them in the hallway or garage and using them only when the weather's bad.

Objects

You're walking down the road, whistling and strolling happily along, when suddenly you notice three gigantic black garbage bags wafting in the wind. You visually assess the situation and are quickly done with the thought process. It's not, however, so easy for your puppy. Puppies assess new objects with their noses and can't emotionally settle until they've had a good sniff. Whenever possible, approach the situation like a grown dog. Doing so will provide a confident, assured example for your puppy to follow.

Let the leash go slack when safe and hold the end as you approach the object. Kneel or bend down to your puppy's level and pretend to sniff the object confidently. Wait patiently as your puppy assesses your reaction. When he approaches, speak calmly, petting him and tucking him into your side when he's comfortable.

If you can't approach the object, simply kneel at your pup's side and brace him as you remind him to "Stay" and then "Follow."

Various noises

Included on a good list of important noises to socialize your puppy may be fireworks, trucks, construction noises, vacuum cleaners, washing machines, sirens, and a baby's cries. Each time you approach a loud situation or set one up, kneel and brace your puppy. If she is startled, back up until she's more at ease and then repeat the handling technique. When she can comfortably face the distraction, calmly instruct her to "Stay." Gradually move closer, and eventually the instruction to "Follow" may be enough to assure her because she has integrated the noise into her stimulus memory bank.

If your puppy has a more startled reaction, or if your puppy is older and unfamiliar with a noise or situation, you need to craft your approach to limit the intensity. If your pup looks like she may attack or run from a distraction, she's clearly in a state of panic. Retreat from the situation immediately and figure out your puppy's Red Zone. Work on treat- and toy-based lessons, brace her, and gradually move closer to the distraction.

If a specific sound is unsettling to your puppy, tape-record it. Play it at gradually increasing volumes while your puppy is playing or eating. If she's still startled by the noise, lower the volume and play it in a distant room.

Places

You'll have to wait until your puppy is inoculated to go on field trips. However, when your vet gives you the green light, go, go, go! Away from his home turf, surrounded by the unknown, your puppy will suddenly grow hyper with impulsive excitement, fearful, or defensive. Each reaction gives you the perfect opportunity to step in and direct him.

Regardless of your puppy's response, use the directions "Let's go," "Stay," and "Wait" as you navigate new places together. By doing so, your direction and posture says to your pup, "I'm the leader, follow me!"

In addition, bring a familiar bed or mat for your puppy to ride on in the car and to sit on when you expect him to be still. If you're going to an outdoor restaurant, the vet, or school, bring his mat along and direct him to it. His mat will act like a security blanket, making him feel relieved, happy, and safe.

Quieting an excitable response

Freaking out with excitement is a common response to a new place for some puppies. Fit this type of pup with a head collar and brace her frequently. If she's motivated by food, use it to focus her attention. Stay very calm and be the example you want her to follow. Brace her securely before people approach you.

You'll have to work hard to teach this type of pup not to jump. If she rolls onto her belly during a greeting, say "Belly up" to encourage that response.

Correcting a fearful reaction

A fearful puppy needs a guardian and protector to step up and direct him: Here's your curtain call. Avoid the temptation to bend and soothe your puppy. Instead, use a head collar to guide him — a neck collar can intensify fears because it may feel as if it's choking him. Brace him when he's most distressed, and stave off admirers until he's more sure footed. When it's time for introductions, bring yummy treats and be generous.

Chilling out a defensive reaction

A defensive puppy takes life a little too seriously. Socializing her is necessary to calm her intensity. Put a head collar on her and sit on the outskirts of a given activity or social setting. Teach your puppy the term "Back" to mean "Stay behind me because I'm in charge." Repeat "Stay" when necessary, and remind her to "Follow." Over time, your pup's resolve will melt. Make a commitment now to socialize the paw off this puppy. Just remember that it may take many outings to mellow her caution to where she'll become more pleasant to have around.

Chapter 6

All the Right Stuff

A dog can get by without much in the way of material belongings, and a great many of them do. A collar. A leash. A container for water and one for food. A warm, dry place to sleep. Something to play with or chew on.

Add love, training, and attention to the list, and, in truth, a dog doesn't need much more. But, oh, how we love to spend money on our dogs! Selling pet supplies is a multibillion-dollar industry, with so much money spent on dog-related furniture, food, and toys that it seems the only difference between having a kid and having a dog is that you don't need a college fund for the latter. That, and no matter how many things you buy your dog, she never gets spoiled.

Your dog couldn't care less if the collar you buy her is diamond encrusted. A crystal bowl or a stainless steel one — it really doesn't matter to her, as long as you put food in it. And you can color-coordinate her leash to match her collar and the interior of your SUV all you want, but it won't impress her. Most of the dog-accessories decisions you face you make to please yourself. And that's fine, as long as you meet your dog's needs with gear that is well made, practical, and appropriate for her size and temperament.

At the most basic level, your dog needs food and shelter. That's about the most any dog could ever have hoped for during the thousands of years humans and dogs have worked and lived together as companions and workmates. Everything you add to those basics is designed to make your dog's life — and your own — safer, more convenient, and more enjoyable.

For information on canine nutrition and what food to buy your dog, see Chapter 1 in Book II. Keeping your dog well groomed — including the tools you need to buy to accomplish the deed — is covered in depth in Chapter 1 of Book III.

Outdoor Accessories: Fences, Dog Runs, and Barriers

You have a responsibility to provide a safe, dry place for your dog, one that's cool in the summer and warm in the winter; keeps him from roaming the neighborhood; and protects him from cars, thieves, and assorted sickos. Those requirements are the basics, but you'll have a much better relationship with your dog — and he'll be much happier — if you take him out of the doghouse and into your house.

What's the point of keeping a completely outdoor dog as a pet? Protection? Fat lot of good that big dog will do you outside when burglars are inside your house. Companionship? You work all day and then come home, feed the outdoor dog, and maybe play with him a little. Then you go in and watch TV, and he sits outside alone.

Although some dogs handle the outdoors better than others, they still can cause a lot of problems. They bark day and night out of boredom and loneliness. They dig. They chew the siding off your house. They can teach themselves to be overzealously protective, to the point of dangerousness.

Some people who own outdoor dogs didn't start out intending for them to live outside. Maybe the dog never was fully housetrained or was never taught to not jump on guests. Perhaps he doesn't know how to behave himself around children. Perhaps he's destructive, and you figure that it's better if he eats the picnic table rather than the coffee table. Perhaps he smells horribly rank.

All those problems are fixable. Training solves behavior problems, and smell problems — well, that's why we have baths. Grooming tips are covered in the chapters in Book III; behavior problems are explained in Chapters 1 through 3 in Book IV.

You owe it to your dog, your family, and your neighbors to do what you can to avoid leaving your dog outside all the time.

If you *must* leave your dog outside, you *must* do your best to bring a little joy into your lonely dog's life with time and outings to strengthen the bond between you. Don't just throw some food out in the yard and forget him. That qualifies as abuse and could get you in trouble when neighbors complain to the authorities.

Book I

Choosing
and
Bringing
Home a
Dog

The dangers of chains

In many parts of the country, fenced yards are uncommon, so many people keep their dogs on chains. Tethering a dog for a short while is okay in a pinch — never with a choke collar, though — but a tethered existence is not a good one. And a chained dog should never be left unattended. In hot weather, staying outdoors can be even more dangerous, and even lethal, for a dog.

Dogs who spend their lives on chains are more likely to become dangerous, biting anyone who comes onto their turf, because they feel lonely and vulnerable. In fact, the profile of the average dog involved in a vicious bite incident is a young unneutered male on a chain.

In some cases, dogs have tried to jump a fence, didn't have enough chain to clear it, and ended up hanging themselves from their collar on the other side of the fence. Dogs have also wrapped their chains around trees and died because they were desperately searching for water on hot days.

If you don't have a fenced yard and you refuse to let the dog inside, then you really shouldn't get a dog. If you do anyway, walking your dog a lot and installing a kennel run and a doghouse (covered elsewhere in this chapter) for him is far better than just putting him outside on a chain.

Good fences make good dogs

Unless you're an apartment dweller, your dog will probably spend a certain amount of time in your fenced backyard, ranging from a few minutes a day to do her business to perhaps the hours while you're at work. You want to make her time outdoors as pleasant and safe as possible.

The ideal setup is a fenced yard away from the street. Solid 6-foot fencing is best to protect your pet from the view of people who might tease or steal her and to give her fewer reasons to bark. If you're a gardener, consider allocating part of the yard for your dog and keeping the rest of it off limits unless you're with her. One creative person designed a yard with a U-shaped area around the outside for the Airedale and an interior courtyard that was kept safe from his big paws.

Kennel runs

Kennel runs also work fine for keeping dogs out of trouble when you're not with them. A kennel run is an longish enclosed area that the dog has access to. Keep it well protected from heat, cold, and wind; keep fresh water and toys always available; and be sure that your dog spends only a short amount of time in the run. Remember, a 10 x 6-foot run is a safe place to spend a few hours, but it's no place to spend a life. You can build or buy a kennel run. Many online retailers sell materials for kennel runs and kits.

Electric fences

Electronic boundary systems that use shock collars to teach dogs the property lines can be useful in some situations, but they have some serious limitations. First, some dogs choose to go ahead and be shocked if the temptation on the other side is great enough, but once out, they avoid taking another hit to get home.

Also, an electronic boundary system does not protect your pet from animals or people who enter your property, so your dog can easily be attacked, poisoned, or stolen. And it does not protect people from your pet. Children can be bitten after coming into the territory of a dog behind an electric boundary system. A solid fence can spare children the injury — and also save a dog's life, because a dog who bites a child will be put down.

Good fences make good neighbors. Sturdy, solid-wood fences also make good dogs.

Entrances and exits

Two products that make the ins and outs a little easier to handle are dog doors and baby gates:

- ✔ **Dog doors:** Most dog doors consist of a flap of metal or plastic that a pet can push with his nose or paws to open. They are great for anyone who doesn't want to get up every time the dog scratches or whines at the door, and even better for people who leave a dog alone all day and want to provide access to the outdoors while they're gone. Dog doors can be set up between house and yard, or between a garage and a yard. Some people build chutes with dog doors at both ends to cut down on drafts.

  For the sake of security, have your door installed where your pet's comings and goings aren't so noticeable, and close and lock it when it's not needed, such as when you're on vacation. Do remember, though, that a dog door — especially a large one — always carries a certain degree of risk. A young burglar, or a thin one, can gain access to your house through the flap.

  You can also install a dog door through an exterior wall rather than a door, though you'll need the help of a contractor.

- ✔ **Baby gates:** These portable, removable barriers are available in pet-supply catalogs and anywhere children's things are sold. You can use them to limit a pet's access to certain parts of the house.

You can use the two products in combination to provide a safe and secure place for your pet when you're away from home: Baby gates can keep the dog in the kitchen, for example, and a dog door can allow him to go to the part of the yard that he's allowed in when you're not with him.

Doghouses: Protection from the elements

If your dog spends much time outside — while you're at work, perhaps — she needs shelter from heat and cold. One of the easiest ways to provide this shelter is to give her a doghouse. Your choices are pretty much wood or high-impact plastic.

No matter what material you choose, a doghouse should fit your pet snugly — she should be able to stand up and turn around, but not much more. Dogs have liked them for thousands of years. Providing your dog with a house that's too large also makes it hard for her to stay warm inside it with just body heat. The doghouse should have an entrance that's off-center so the dog can curl up in one end for warmth. A removable roof is helpful for easy cleaning, and the doorway should have a flap over it to keep out drafts.

Building a doghouse is an easy weekend project for anyone with basic carpentry skills; you can find plans at libraries or building-supply stores. You can also buy complete wooden doghouses and kits, including some that are extremely fancy and designed to match your home's architecture — Cape Cod, Georgian, ranch style, and so on. It can be a great project for the kids to help with, too. Several manufacturers offer doghouses of molded, high-impact plastic that, in some ways, are superior to traditional wooden ones. They clean easily, do not retain smells, and offer no place for fleas to breed — as long as you keep the bedding fresh (more on bedding in the next section).

Where you place the doghouse has a lot to do with how comfortable your dog is when she's in it. In winter, place it in a spot that's protected from the wind. In summer, definitely place it in the shade. Obviously, finding a place that satisfies both criteria is preferable so that you don't have to move it.

Indoor Comforts: Crates and Beds

Indoor dogs need a place to sleep, too. Opinions on this topic are various and passionate, but unless your dog has impeccable manners and respects your authority, he probably shouldn't be on your bed — it gives him the wrong idea concerning who's the top dog in your family. Don't feel sorry for him, though: More beautiful and comfortable beds are available today than ever before, to fit every dog, every budget, and every decor.

Reaching for crateness

One possibility for a bed is a crate (see Figure 6-1), probably the most versatile piece of dog gear ever made. Once used primarily for transporting dogs on airplanes, the crate in all its varieties — open mesh, solid metal, or high-impact plastic — is now widely used and recognized as one of the best tools for making living with your pet easier. A crate is also one of the easiest and fastest ways to housetrain a puppy or dog (housetraining is covered in Chapter 1 in Book IV), and it's also a decent whelping box, if you ever choose to breed your pet. With some modifications to cut down on the drafts, it even makes a decent doghouse.

Figure 6-1:
A dog crate is an extremely versatile piece of canine equipment.

If your dog misbehaves, the crate is a good place to put him for a "timeout." If for any reason you don't want him underfoot — a guest with allergies, a contractor marching in and out — the crate is a godsend. But be careful — don't make him associate the crate too much with punishment.

The crate is also perfect for its original purpose: transporting your pet. A loose dog in the car can be an annoyance, even a danger. Everyone is safer when you use a crate. In an automobile accident, a loose dog is as vulnerable as an unbelted human. And talk about safety! Crates are tough, so much so that a crated dog once survived an airline crash with near-total human casualties. And when traveling with your pet, you'll find that showing up with a crate will endear you to hotel owners, some of whom can be sweet-talked into lifting "no dog" rules if they know your dog will be crated in the room instead of chewing up the bedspread.

Dogs who are accustomed to crates love them. It's a room of their own, cozy and secure, and many dogs seek out their crates voluntarily. Always-open crates can serve as an unconventional end table in the den, and you will often find your dog snoozing inside, by choice. To increase comfort, you can buy pads to fit the floor of crates. You can also make your own without too much difficulty by tucking a washable blanket inside — or you can just leave them empty, especially in warmer weather.

Need yet another reason to buy a crate? In times of disaster — floods, earthquakes, hurricanes — a crate can save your pet's life by keeping him secure and providing you with alternatives if you have to evacuate your home. The cages of veterinary hospitals and animal shelters adjacent to a disaster area fill up quickly, but there's always room for the pet who brings his own shelter.

Consider what you'll be using a crate for before you buy one. If you ever intend to ship your dog by air, be aware that not all crates are intended for this purpose. Some are designed for light use — housetraining puppies in the home, for example — whereas others are designed for car travel, a medium-grade use.

If you intend to use a crate for housetraining, as a bed, for travel, for occasional confinement, and possibly for a whelping box, you're better off buying a top-quality crate of high-impact molded plastic, approved for air travel.

Buy a crate to fit the size your puppy will be when grown. He should be able to stand, turn around, and lie down comfortably. When housetraining a puppy, make the crate smaller by using a panel. As an alternative, borrow a puppy-sized crate from a friend or the puppy's breeder.

A crate is a big-ticket item, so shop aggressively. Underutilized sources include garage sales and classified ads.

Letting sleeping dogs lie . . . in their own bed

Although a crate can be used for almost anything, it's not the only choice when it comes to a bed. Dog beds keep floors and carpets cleaner, provide a cushion that makes all dogs more comfortable (especially older or arthritic ones), and allow you to live without guilt for keeping your dog off your bed.

Every dog needs a bed, even if it's just an old blanket. Two of the most popular varieties include

- ✔ **Oval cuddlers** designed for dogs to curl up in, lined with plush or polyester sheepskin
- ✔ **Stuffed cushions** that resemble 1960s beanbag chairs, albeit in more muted colors

The most important point to remember when picking out a bed (see Figure 6-2) is that it must be washable, or at least have a removable, washable cover. You'll almost certainly have a problem with fur, smells, and fleas if you don't wash pet bedding on a regular basis — weekly is ideal.

Figure 6-2:
Make sure that your dog bed is machine washable or you'll be buying many of them.

Photo courtesy of Gina Spadafori.

Washability is why carpet remnants are not recommended. You just can't keep them fresh and clean smelling, and they're like a welcome mat for fleas.

Some of the handsomest and sturdiest beds are available on the Web and by mail order, in a wider range of colors and sizes than you may be able to find locally. Doctors Foster and Smith, a pet-supply firm in Wisconsin, has some of the nicest (www.drsfostersmith.com). Another great source is L.L. Bean (www.LLBean.com).

You can also find great beds at dog shows, and some of these beds are *only* sold at dog shows.

Canine Tableware

In dog dishes, too, you have a lot of options, from using an old pot to buying a hand-thrown ceramic bowl with your dog's name painted on it. Dishes designed to store up to a couple days' worth of food or water are available, as are paper bowls good for one meal only (the latter most commonly used at boarding kennels and veterinary hospitals).

Usually the best choices are dishes of molded, high-impact plastic or stainless steel that resist chewing or scratching and can be sterilized in the dishwasher. These dishes — stainless steel, especially — retain their good looks, handle any abuse a dog can dish out, and last forever. Dishes that damage easily are hard to keep clean and invite the buildup of food and bacteria in the dents and scratches. Some dogs also have a sensitivity to flimsy plastic bowls.

For dogs with long, silky ears — like Cocker Spaniels — look for bowls with a narrow opening and high, sloped sides to keep that fur out of the food. If your dog is a ravenous eater, a bowl with a rubber or otherwise nonskid base will help keep the dish from ending up under the cabinets.

Some people are a little squeamish about putting dog dishes in the dishwasher, but, if your dishwasher's doing its job right, the water will be hot enough to render everything in it clean enough for *you* to eat out of.

The "dog prewash" can save water and perhaps even extend the life of your dishwasher. Don't allow your dog to beg while people are eating, but your dog can help with after-meal cleanup by licking the plates clean before you load them in the dishwasher.

Although you should pick up your dog's food dishes after meals, wash them, and put them away, you need to keep water dishes full and available at all times. Here, too, stainless steel is your best choice. Dishes with reservoirs are fine, but they're hard to keep clean. And unless your dog needs a lot of water, these products get mucky before the water needs to be refilled.

For outside water, the Lixit, available in any pet-supply store or catalog, has long been a popular device. Attached to an outside faucet, it releases fresh water when the dog licks or nuzzles the trigger, and stops the flow when the dog is finished. It needs to be installed in a shaded area, however, because the metal can become frying-pan hot if exposed to full summer sun.

All water sources need to be sheltered from both heat and freezing cold, or they won't be available to your dog at all times — a potentially deadly situation in extreme weather. A couple blocks of ice — you can make them by putting water-filled margarine tubs in your freezer — will keep a shaded water supply cool for hours. Heated bowls are available to keep water from freezing, as are special devices designed to fit into buckets to do the same thing.

If you and your dog are constantly on the go, look into a more portable water source. Several different kinds of traveling bowls are designed to reduce splashing, and some collapsible products can be put away in a space as small as a fanny pack. You can also use a squeeze-type bottle like bicyclists use — your dog will quickly learn to catch the flow. You may want to mark it with indelible ink so everyone knows it's dog water.

With a little kitchen remodeling, you can have low pull-out drawers reveal recessed dog dishes — stainless steel pop-outs, for easy cleaning — and secure storage for kibble.

Collars and Leashes

Fashion aside, collars, harnesses, halters, and leashes perform a very vital function: They help you train your dog and allow you to keep her out of trouble in public. Collars also protect your dog when you can't, by carrying identification that will get her home if she ever slips away from you.

When buying a collar — buckled or quick-snap — for regular wear, measure the circumference of your dog's neck a couple inches down from your dog's head and then add 2 inches. For tiny dogs, add 1 inch. When trying on collars, you should be able to fit two fingers snugly between collar and neck, or one finger on a small dog. The goal is to have a collar snug enough so your dog can't back up and out of the collar, but loose enough for comfort.

The everyday collar

A regular dog collar is an essential purchase for your dog, but if he's wearing the wrong collar at the wrong time, he could end up hurt or even dead. Understanding some key points before you go shopping is important.

Your pet's everyday collar, the one you put the tags on, should be a buckled collar, either flat or rolled, made of nylon web or leather. Either a flat collar or a rolled collar works fine on dogs with short or medium fur, but rolled collars are preferable on dogs with long, thick fur at the neck, such as Collies.

Nylon web collars are probably to be preferred. Some dogs are more apt to chew off the leather collar of another family dog, but nylon is much tougher. Nylon collars also come in an incredible variety of colors and patterns. As long as the collar is well made, though, both nylon and leather will last for years. Quick-snap closures have become popular, especially on flat nylon web collars. And it's easy to see why: Press in at the edges, and the collar's off easily for baths and changing tags. Press the tips together and, snap, it's on again. For most dogs, these collars present no problems. Because they are so simply adjusted, they're ideal for growing puppies. Some trainers think buckled collars are more secure for large, strong, and impulsive dogs, but a high-quality quick-snap collar should be just as sturdy.

Some people may think that elegant canine collars are a recent development, but it's simply not true. Owners who can afford it have always put ritzy collars around the necks of their prized canine companions — gold, silver, pearls, and gems have been part of the society dog's wardrobe for centuries.

Some of the loveliest collars imaginable crop up in specialty Web sites, catalogs, and pet boutiques, for prices that would keep some dogs in kibble for months. Want one? If you can afford it, why not? Just make sure to make a matching donation to your local shelter so the guilt doesn't get you down.

Training collars

A properly fitted buckle or quick-snap collar — with tags and a license — is all a puppy needs for the first few months of her life and maybe all that she ever needs (see Figure 6-3). But most dogs need a collar for training, or for you to be able to control yours better on a leash.

The most commonly used — and misused — training collar is the slip, or choke, collar. This collar is a length of chain — sometimes nylon — with rings at both ends. To use it, you drop the length of chain or nylon through the end (stationary) ring and then slip the resulting loop over your dog's head. The leash is normally attached to the moving ring, called the *live* ring — not the stationary one, called the dead ring (see Chapter 3 in Book IV for how to train your dog with a training collar).

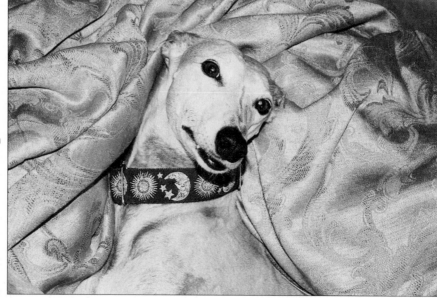

Figure 6-3:
Choice in
collars has
never been
greater,
with some
seeming
almost
works of art.

Beauty/Photograph courtesy of www.greyhoundgang.com.

The most important cautions to know about a slip collar is that it must never, *ever* be your dog's everyday collar, and you must always remove it when you're finished training or walking your dog. The moving (live) ring of the collar can get caught on just about anything — even the eyetooth of another dog in play. When caught, a dog's natural reaction is to pull away, a move that tightens the collar, which panics the dog into pulling away more. Even if you're there, you may not have the strength to rescue a terrified dog in this situation — and even if you do have the strength, you may be badly bitten while trying. Many dogs have died from misuse of this common piece of training equipment, and near misses are even more common.

You can call it a choke collar if you want, but know this: Choke collars do not actually choke. If you're choking your dog, you're using it wrong. That's not training, it's cruelty, however unintentional. Be sure that the leash is attached to the moving ring on the chain, not the stationary one. The moving part of the training collar should go over the dog's head, not under it. When positioned properly, the collar tightens when you pull on the leash and releases when you slack off. If the moving part of the collar is under the dog's head, when you tighten, the collar tightens but doesn't release when the pressure's off.

How can you get it right? With the dog sitting on your left, hold the collar in a P shape, with the loop away from you and the bottom of the P on top. Slip it over your dog's head, and it will be in perfect position.

The slip collar is by far the most common collar for training and control, but a few others also are used:

- **Partial slip collars** can be a hybrid between a flat collar and a slip collar, part flat nylon, part chain, or all chain. They are designed to limit the choking action of a slip collar — they tighten, but only so much. Some trainers use them all the time; others recommend them for people who have an exceptionally difficult time with the release of the slip collar's snap-and-release motion.

- **Pinch or prong collars** are more popular than ever because they are an efficient way of dealing with large dogs with especially well-muscled necks, like Rottweilers. As with a partial slip collar, they can be tightened only so far, but, unlike the partial, they have blunt metal prongs evenly spaced along the inside of the length of the collar. When the collar tightens, these blunt prongs press firmly — but not cruelly — into the flesh of the dog's neck.

  These collars are very controversial, in part because of their cruel appearance, which is probably why some people like them: They look macho. Pinch collars should not be a first-choice training collar, but in the hands of a knowledgeable trainer, they can help with a powerful dog.

- **Head halters** are another device with a public-relations problem, this time completely unwarranted. The problem: They look like muzzles. In fact, they operate on the same principle that has worked for years with horses: Where the head goes, the body follows. The leash is attached to a ring under the jaw, and when pulled, pressure is placed around the muzzle and around the neck — both important in canine body language.

  Properly fitted and used, a head halter can make even a large, powerful dog controllable enough to be walked by a child — but, then, so can a proper course of training.

- **Electric collars** give a shock either automatically, such as when a dog barks, or manually, at the push of a button. They are widely used in training dogs for hunting and field work, and for correcting some serious behavior problems. Although electric collars are widely available in pet-supply stores and catalogs, pet owners should use them only with the guidance of experienced trainers. Without a thorough knowledge of training theory and a perfect sense of timing, this training tool is more cruel than effective.

- **Harnesses** for walking a dog are best left on little dogs because they offer nothing in the way of control and give up a great deal in the way of leverage. Some small breeds — such as Toy Poodles — have a tendency toward collapsing tracheas, in which the rings of cartilage in the neck collapse temporarily when the dog gets excited. These dogs are ideal candidates for harnesses, to relieve the pressure on their necks from pulling. (Again, you can train your dog not to pull, but people with tiny breeds don't really have to, so they rarely do.)

Your veterinarian may suggest a harness if your dog is of a breed known for neck or back problems, or if your dog has had a neck trauma or surgery.

A couple harnesses on the market do offer some control, tightening around the dog's chest as he pulls. These harnesses are an option even for larger dogs.

Some harnesses are made for dog sports — for tracking or for pulling sleds or wagons.

ID tags and microchips

Your young daughter leaves the front door open, or the wind blows down the fence: A lost dog can happen to the most conscientious of families. For this reason, your dog's collar should have tags.

A dog's collar should always have an ID tag with your phone number, and a rabies vaccination tag from your vet. When you move, get a new ID tag first thing. Also check the tags frequently, to ensure that the information is still readable. Even better is to subscribe to a 24-hours-a-day, 7-days-a-week tracking service, like 1-800-HELP4PETS, which not only reunites you with your dog if she becomes lost, but also arranges for boarding or medical care if you cannot be immediately found.

You can ID your dog in other ways, of course. Tattooing, with your driver's license number or another traceable number (like a registry number from the American or Canadian Kennel Clubs) has been popular for years. Microchipping has come on strong in the last decade. The microchip is permanent identification no bigger than a grain of rice. Your veterinarian embeds the microchip under the skin over your pet's shoulder blades, using a large needle. (But don't worry: One yip is about all you'll hear, and then it's done.)

Microchips used to be of dubious value for returning lost pets, because one company's chips couldn't be read by another company's scanner, and shelters couldn't (and wouldn't) cope with competing systems. That has changed, with manufacturers moving toward one industry standard and with the entry of the American Kennel Club as a registry of microchipped animals in the United States and Canada — for any animals, not just AKC-registered purebred dogs. Having your pet chipped by your veterinarian costs anything from $40 to $100, but it's a good investment in your dog's safety.

If you're planning to have your canine companion microchipped, find out what, if any, chip scanners the shelters in your area use, and make sure that your pet is implanted with a chip that can be read by using that brand of scanner. Also register your pet with AKC Companion Animal Recovery (800-252-7894), which offers 24-hour match-up service, 365 days a year. Although the service was set up in conjunction with one manufacturer, you can register the number of any chip — or tattoo — you use. If someone calls to report finding your pet, the service will release your number so you can be reunited quickly.

Leashes

Choices aren't as varied in leashes (also called *leads*) as in collars. You can find a lot more colors and designs these days, but the same basic choices remain: leather, nylon, or chain.

You can use anything you want when your dog is trained, but until you reach that point, the standard 6-foot leather leash is your best choice. Nylon is a very close second, but it's not as easy to grip as leather and can give you burns if your dog takes off suddenly and whips the leash through your hands.

Chain is horrible to train with: It'll cut your hands to pieces, and your dog will confuse the noise of the leash with the noise of the collar.

Several lengths are available, from a 1-foot traffic lead that's useful for moving a large dog quickly from one place to another, to long leads for training or to give a dog a little more room to roam without unleashing him. For walking or training, the 6-foot lead is still best: It lets you give your dog some freedom while still giving you plenty of control. It's also the length spelled out in most leash laws.

Leashes are sold in ¼-inch, 3/8-inch, 1/2-inch, 5/8-inch, 3/4-inch, and 1-inch widths, with the two middle sizes the most commonly used in obedience training because they're easier to grip than the other sizes. The weakest parts of a leash are where the snap attaches and the handle is formed. Look for sturdy stitching or, in leather leads, one-piece construction.

One of the most popular leashes is the reel-type flexible extension-type lead that offers a dog up to 32 feet of freedom, yet allows the owner to stop it from extending by pressing a button on the plastic handle. Although it's not meant to help you teach dogs to walk without pulling, owners commonly use it to teach dogs to come when called. This type of leash is great for travel, too, and for dogs who can't be trusted off-leash but still need to stretch their legs.

These leads, widely available in different sizes and lengths, are wonderful for letting a dog sniff around in areas where it's not safe or where you're not allowed to let her off-leash. "Flexis" aren't designed to give you control over your dog, especially if he's large and strong. It's easy to lose your grip if the dog hits the end of the line running. For these reasons, don't use a flexible lead in areas where it would be dangerous if your dog got loose.

The Wonderful World of Toys

Every dog needs toys. They keep your pet occupied and amused when you cannot, and they provide you with another avenue for interacting and bonding. Toys give your pet something to chew on besides your toes (or shoes, furniture, or books), and they are absolutely essential to puppy raising, because puppies feel better when their teeth are cutting through. Of course, toys are also fun to choose and buy. A couple cautions in the toy area are warranted, but not many.

Chewies

The kind of chewie toys you buy has everything to do with the size of your dog and how aggressive a chewer she is. Some of the toughest chew toys on the market are made by Nylabone, in a variety of sizes, shapes, and colors.

The king of chew toys is the Kong, a hard rubber toy that looks a little like the Michelin Tire man. Kongs have hollow centers that you can fill with peanut butter or another kind of treat, which gives dogs plenty of interesting activity as they try to get all the treat material out. Not only are Kongs almost impossible to destroy, but they also bounce in a sprightly manner, in unpredictable directions.

Chewies designed to remove plaque and stimulate gums are also popular. They have nubs along their length, or indentations designed to be filled with canine toothpaste.

Rope chews — some of them adorned with hooves at the ends or rubber balls in the middle — are popular, but some trainers think they're too much like things you don't want your pet to chew on, like carpet fringes and curtains.

Monitor your pet's chew toys. When they're worn or chewed to the point they can be swallowed, replace them.

Squeakies

Puppies and dogs alike love toys of either plush or vinyl that make a noise when squeezed. However, they can turn into a very expensive proposition if you own a dog who isn't happy until the squeaker is dead.

One of the nicest and sturdiest plush toys is the Vermont Chewman, solidly made of thick, fake lambskin and available in catalogs and pet-supply stores.

Fetchies

Fetch is an outstanding way to exercise your dog while reminding him of your role as pack leader. Many people use flying discs for this sport, and although it's great fun, be aware that some dogs have been injured while leaping after flying disks, to the point of needing surgery on their knees and backs.

Tennis balls are another common toy with built-in risks. It may seem safe, but never let your dog chew on a tennis ball or play with one unattended. Some dogs have died after a tennis ball, compressed by powerful jaws, popped into the throat and cut off the air supply.

Does that mean you should avoid playing with flying discs or tennis balls? No, but use some common sense. With flying discs, avoid the acrobatics that wow spectators at half-time shows but have your dog leaping, twisting, and landing hard. Work on low throws in front of your dog, to encourage him to run but not to jump. And use floppy ones made of fabric or rubber, not plastic. Tennis balls are fine for fetch, but put them away when the game's over.

You can, of course, buy solid rubber balls. And for water retrieving — a great exercise for the dog who enjoys swimming — Kong makes a floating variety with a rope handle that's easy to throw a long way on land or in water.

If you buy a toy that invites tug-of-war games, it's fine to let your pet pull against another dog. But never play tug of -war with your dog, and make sure that your children don't, either. What seems like an innocent game could be a setup for tragedy. Tug of war can teach your dog to be dominant. Consider this scenario: You play with your dog, pulling against her in a battle of dominance, however playful in appearance. You get bored, the phone rings, and you drop your end. You think: Game's over. Your dog thinks: *I win* — exactly the opposite of the message your dog should get, and one that may lead to other dominance challenges.

Green Dog Accessories

These days, more people are going green when it comes to food, cars, clothing, and even beauty products. We're also beginning to understand the benefits of choosing products that have a lower impact on the environment. So if organic foods and chemical-free shampoos are healthier for us, why shouldn't we try to provide the same for our dogs? Fortunately, you don't have to look very hard to find green pet products in the marketplace. Internet and specialty shops abound, and many conventional pet supply stores have a selection of eco-friendly products.

You'll likely come across the following hot topics in your eco-quest:

- ✔ **Organic:** Foods, textiles, and other products that are organic are considered better for our bodies and for the planet because they are grown or raised without synthetic fertilizers, pesticides, chemicals, or hormones.

- ✔ **Sustainable:** Reducing our impact on the earth's resources is the main idea behind sustainability. As a dog owner, you can make lifestyle and consumer choices to limit your use of resources.

- ✔ **Recycled:** The mantra "Reduce, reuse, and recycle" applies to pets, too. Pet toys, beds, and other items can be manufactured from recycled products, reducing the load on landfills.

So save the planet and start shopping — and be sure to bring your canvas shopping bags.

Bedding with eco-benefits

Dogs may be Man's best friend, but few bonds are stronger than the one between a dog and his bed. Given how many hours a dog will spend sleeping, comfort is a key factor. For eco-minded owners, however, comfort is only one consideration when choosing a bed.

A growing number of manufacturers now produce environmentally friendly beds for pets. Whether it's a cuddler, cushion, blanket, or sleeping mat, these cozy products are made with your pet's and the planet's health in mind. People who lean toward the green side of dog ownership can choose from washable covers of naturally dyed organic cotton and hemp, as well as recycled fabrics. You'll rest easy knowing your beloved dog has a chemical-free spot for snoozing. Think eco can't be stylish? Think again. You can find colorful, classic, and hip designs for these earth-friendly beds.

To keep your puppy properly cushioned, many green beds are packed with soft and durable IntelliLoft stuffing, made of 100 percent shredded recycled plastic bottles. How's that for eco-friendly?

Toys you can be proud of

Toys are great fun, especially when they're made of materials that won't harm your pet. To make playtime a safe time for your pet, consider toys that are free of pesticides and chemicals.

Book I

Choosing
and
Bringing
Home a
Dog

- **Plush toys:** Look for organic fabrics and recycled stuffings such as IntelliLoft; natural dyes are also good.
- **Chew and fetch toys:** Seek out lead-free and latex-free chewies; toys made from nontoxic Zogoflex are supertough, buoyant, and pliable, and are designed to be recycled. Instead of spending money on average toys, choose durable, natural rubber toys that can stand up to serious play.

Eco-leashes and collars

So you want to spread the good news about being an environmentally responsible dog owner? Well, put on your pup's eco-friendly collar and leash, and go for a walk. While you're out strolling, you can explain to your friends and neighbors that most pet collars are made of nylon, a product of petroleum. Explain that both your dog and the environment benefit when you choose to buy collars, leashes, and harnesses made of durable natural fibers like hemp, cotton, grosgrain ribbon, and leather. Mention that these earth-friendly accessories come in an impressive variety of colors and designs.

Green duds

If you're an environmentalist who's into canine fashion, you're in luck. You should have no problem finding doggie duds made from natural materials and fibers. Shop for earth-friendly sweaters, coats, hoodies, and rain gear designed with your style in mind.

Green suds

At some point, your pooch will need some primping, and now you can tackle your grooming tasks with an arsenal of effective green products. From shampoos to sprays, you'll find a wide range of canine beauty supplies that are natural, gentle, hypoallergenic, and biodegradable; look for products without alcohol, artificial dyes, sulfates, chemicals, detergents, or harsh fragrances.

When it's your house that's a mess and not your pet, take care of the problem with eco-friendly cleaners and stain and odor removers; they do the job without leaving harmful chemicals behind. As an added benefit, many of these products come in recycled packaging.

Chapter 7

Understanding Your New Roommate's View of the World

*T*he greatest gift you can give your dog is a stress-free existence. Structure your dog's world so that he feels safe. Provide for his needs, anticipating them before he does, and incorporate as much playtime into your daily routine as you can. A young puppy doesn't understand the word "no" or develop impulse control before he's 6 to 8 months old, so put your expectations and frustrations on the back burner until you can channel both into useful communication. Puppyhood, like childhood, is short — let your puppy enjoy his to the fullest.

You have to understand the world from a dog's perspective. Though his curiosity may result in behaviors that you find aggravating, don't take any of his antics personally. Getting angry at a new dog is as silly and ineffective as yelling at a 6-month-old child. Not only will you not get through to him, but you'll also frighten him. You, the very person he should feel most safe turning to, will be scaring and confusing him. This routine is neither educational nor good for long-term bonding. Look for a better way to navigate through this time — a much better way.

In this chapter, you put yourself in your dog's paws and understand just how he views your world and life together.

Because most adopted dogs are puppies, this chapter puts a lot of emphasis on puppies, but you'll find useful information about older dogs as well.

Recognizing the Eight Stages of Dog Development

You may be dreaming of an agility champion, but setting your dog on course before she's housetrained is like pressuring a toddler to balance your checkbook. As with children, your puppy's mind will develop along a predictable course; you have to be patient. Knowing this fact helps you understand what to expect, what to teach your puppy, and what milestones will define your expectations and bolster your success.

Infancy (8 to 12 weeks)

Life for a young puppy centers on five basic needs: eating, drinking, sleeping, eliminating, and playing. Even though your puppy is capable of learning, don't expect too much at this stage. You should be feeding your puppy three to four times a day, taking him out constantly, and letting him sleep when he wants to. Your puppy will learn best when you incorporate training into playtime. Show him the basic stuff: Hang out with him, use his name, talk to him, and introduce the leash. Discipline will only frighten your puppy and erode your relationship: He's simply too young to comprehend it. Have fun and take lots of photos, because your puppy will be all grown up before you know it.

The terrible twos (12 to 16 weeks)

As your puppy matures, you'll notice her personality developing. She'll get a bit bolder and braver and harder to impress. By 12 weeks, a puppy's brain is fully developed and she's ready to learn. She's old enough to understand and remember your direction, but she's still too young to take matters into her own paws.

Puppies at this stage are starting to learn things, whether they're guided or not. If you don't train your puppy, she'll train you.

The budding adolescent (16 to 24 weeks)

Suddenly, you may notice that a strange dog, who looks rather like your puppy did, is taking over your house. Welcome to adolescence. Be prepared and consider yourself warned: You're about to enter the bratty zone. Try not to panic — as much as you may want to hide under the couch for the next three months, don't! Now is the best time to start training. Because this stage lasts about eight weeks, break down lessons week by week. Breaking down lessons helps your puppy feel successful and allows him to master each exercise before you apply it in his day-to-day world. This concept is similar to letting children master the alphabet before expecting them to spell.

Puppy puberty (6 to 9 months)

Puppies at this stage go through a major transformation called growing up. You remember growing up, don't you? With all its hormones, rebellion, confusion, and curiosity? Well, it's never a pretty sight. On top of these typical growing pains is the awakening of breed-specific instincts that tell herders to herd, hunters to hunt, guarders to guard, and pullers to pull. This stage is utter canine chaos, and all while they're still cutting their baby teeth! You now have this puppy/dog who's full of hormones, high spirits, and anxiety. It's no wonder she may give you the puppy equivalent of a teenage eye roll when you give her a command.

The trying teen (9 to 12 months)

Your first milestone is in front of you, but it's not over yet. A puppy at this stage usually calms down and manages better on his own. He'll chew his bone quietly, potty where he ought to, and listen most of the time. Okay, sometimes he'll still ignore you. Puppies at this stage want to behave, but their teenage genes are relentlessly telling them to make one more glorious attempt for Top Dog status.

This stage often brings with it a subtle campaign of defiance. You may not think a sloppy, sideways sit is a very big deal, but your dog makes a little mental check mark every time you let him get away with something. You can't relax your efforts just yet!

The young adult (12 to 24 months)

At this age, your dog begins to hit her stride. If a dog isn't spayed or neutered by now, this time is when the breeding age begins. The puppy personality is gone, replaced by a (hopefully) calmer manner and more stable, predictable personality.

Or not. About the time a pup reaches physical maturity is also when many owners first realize they've taken on more than they can handle and recognize that they ended up with a dog who's too big, too active, or too dominant for them. Puppies grow up fast, and too many people put off until tomorrow the socializing and training they should have done yesterday. These birds now come home to roost. However, lots of these overgrown puppies just need a little work — some basic obedience and problem.

All young adults are bound to be a little more high spirited and distractible than a mature adult of 2 or more. These dogs still have a bit of growing up to do.

The adult dog (2 to 8 years)

This is it, the long stretch of time you will remember best when you reflect years hence. Dogs who mature into adulthood are in their prime years. If all has gone well, you have a nearly flawless dog here, calm and sensible, benefiting from that obedience training you instilled. Of course, you may also have a dog who's settled into some bad habits. Of course, he couldn't have gotten that from you, right?

The senior dog (8 years and older)

Depending on the breed, these years will be either a slow process of dignified deterioration or a rapid slide into old age. Of course it's sad to see dogs age, as it's sad to see humans age. Senior dogs are troopers, though. Older dogs are more docile and less destructive, and require less exercise than young ones. They are often wise and quiet, and can seem downright philosophical. A senior dog reminds you every day how loyal your friend has been for so long. Sure, she needs more loving care than ever, and health problems escalate, but you will be glad to give it in return for the affection you've received all this time.

Understanding Your Puppy's Basic Needs

Your puppy is a lot like a human baby. Okay, sure, your pup may have a furry coat, a curly tail, and a full set of teeth, but many of the differences stop there. Like a child, your puppy has basic needs and an instinct to satisfy them. A baby communicates his helpless neediness through crying. It's a guardian's role to interpret the cry and satisfy the need. In essence, a cry indicates that the baby lacks the ability to associate a specific need with a bodily sensation. When he's hungry, his belly hurts. When he's tired, his brain shuts down. When he's thirsty, his throat constricts. If these needs aren't satisfied, he gets anxious. When a loving caregiver routinely satisfies his needs, without stress, discipline, or confusion, he develops a strong bond with that person.

The same holds true for puppies. Like babies, they have five basic needs: eat, drink, sleep, potty, and play. Unlike babies, many puppies don't cry when their needs aren't met. Instead, they start nipping and, if directed, may bark and become frantic and fidgety. The behaviors are different, but the concept is the same. Both are easily overwhelmed when their bodies make demands. If initial nips are met with harsh discipline, the puppy may develop defense reactions, such as aggression or barking back.

You can help your puppy identify his needs by pairing directions with routines. Whereas a child develops language and a more civilized approach to communicating her requests, your puppy will develop his own system of communicating by prompting the routine. Read about puppy needs in the upcoming sections, and use Table 7-1 to create your own routines — your puppy will be ringing the bell to go outside in no time!

Whoever satisfies a need is held in high regard. Though it may take some time for your puppy to "pay you back" with his love and devotion, each passing day brings you closer to that ultimate connection. Need by need, your bond will grow.

Table 7-1	Needs Chart	
Your Puppy's Need	*The Word or Phrase You Say*	*The Routine You Follow*
Eating	"Hungry" or "Eat"	Schedule feeding times. Place the bowl in the same spot and encourage your puppy to sit before feeding.
Drinking	"Water"	Keep the bowl in the same spot. Encourage him to sit before drinking.
Going potty	"Outside," "Papers," "Go potty," or "Get busy"	Encourage your puppy to nose/paw a bell to signal this need. Follow the same route to the same potty spot. Restrict attention until your puppy goes.
Sleeping	"On your mat," "In your crate," or "Time for bed"	Designate one spot in each shared room. Take your pup to his mat or bed, provide a chew toy, and secure if necessary.
Playing	"Bone," "Ball," "Toy," or "Go play!"	Establish a play area inside and outside the house. Make sure all four paws are on the floor before you toss a toy or give a bone.

Eating

Puppies are happiest when a predictable routine has been set. A hungry puppy is understandably upset and may show you by eating anything — even the difficult-to-digest things such as tissues, remote controls, or walls. Schedule feeding times and stick to them as closely as possible. If you notice your puppy getting nippy or difficult, check your watch. The behavior could be a result of hunger tension. See Table 7-2 for guidance when setting up feeding times.

Table 7-2	Your Puppy's Feeding Schedule			
Age	*Morning Meal (7 a.m.)*	*Midday Meal (11:30 a.m.)*	*Afternoon Meal (4 p.m.)*	*Late Evening Meal*
8 to 10 weeks	*	*	*	*
10 weeks to 4 months	*	*	*	
4 to 6 months	*		*	

A young puppy has a high metabolism and should have more frequent meals. Schedule three to four meals throughout the day, slowly phasing out meals as your puppy matures. At some point after your puppy reaches 6 months, you may drop to one meal.

Whoever feeds your puppy should follow the same organized routine that you do. Puppies (like kids) are happiest when they know exactly what will happen next.

Drinking

Puppies need a lot of water, especially when the weather is hot or when chewing and playing. Even though it's important to allow them access to water when their system demands it, it's equally important to monitor their drinking habits. Bladder muscles are the last to develop, so what goes in, comes out quickly. Dogs can hold their urine for a long time — puppies can't.

Establish a drinking station for your puppy and keep her dish there whether it's empty or full. Give your puppy water with her meals; after playing, chewing, or napping; or as you're on your way to her potty area.

Book I

**Choosing
and
Bringing
Home a
Dog**

If you're forgetful, it's better to fill his dish and leave it out for her throughout the day. Though it may delay your housetraining, it's better than having her go thirsty.

Restrict water after 7:30 p.m., unless you want to be up all night taking your puppy outside. If your puppy clearly needs a drink, either give her a small amount (no more than a cup for a large dog or a quarter cup for a small fry) or offer a couple ice cubes.

Sleeping

We all love a good sleep, and you'll find that your puppy is no exception. Create a quiet space where your puppy can escape the daily hubbub and catch 40 winks whenever he needs too. Make it clear to friends and family that this area — perhaps a crate, bed, room, or pen — is off limits to people when your puppy needs to nap. An overtired puppy is impossible to deal with. Like a child, a puppy will simply melt down. In fact, when pushed, his mouthy, testy behavior may turn into snappy aggression. Don't correct, worry, or admonish him. Have pity instead — he's exhausted.

Like kids, some puppies have a hard time putting themselves to sleep, especially when excitement levels are high. If you have kids, ask them to baby him by staying quiet until he's sleeping. Each time he seems tired, escort him to his resting area while saying a cue word like "Bed." Eventually, he'll go to this area on his own when he's tired.

Going potty

Housetraining can't be summed up any better than with the wonderful maxim, "Whatever goes in must come out." Your puppy's biological clock will have her eliminating on demand. When her bladder or bowels are pressed, she'll let loose whether she's outside or on the papers — or on the rug, if you're not watching.

If your puppy is coming straight from Mom, she may have paved the way for you by urging her puppy to leave the "nest" when eliminating. This stage occurs between 7 and 8 weeks. If Mom was too relaxed or you picked up your puppy before this stage, the puppy will rely on you to clean up after her, a message of total care and devotion.

Your goals are to teach your puppy where to go and how to let you know if an obstacle (such as a door) is stopping her from getting there. Fortunately, you'll find this task easy after you commit to a routine and relax your expectations. Tension or expressed frustration is confusing; your puppy won't learn quickly and may grow increasingly afraid of you. Your puppy needs a schedule, a routine, and a consistent pattern — all of which are within your grasp.

For a lot more on housetraining, see Book IV, Chapter 1.

Playing

The urge to play and express himself energetically is one of the most natural responses in your puppy's repertoire. As with children, play and lighthearted interactions can be fabulous instructional tools and can be used exclusively during your first few months together.

How you play with your young puppy determines your long-term relationship. Rough, confrontational games, such as wrestling or tug of war, communicate confrontation, which can be detrimental to your relationship. A confronted puppy will be more likely to challenge you and ignore your direction. Games such as the two-ball toss, soccer, and name games instill cooperation and a fun-loving attitude — this puppy won't ever want to leave your side.

Speaking Doglish and Presenting Yourself As Top Dog

Dogs have a lot of team spirit. Many people refer to this as their *pack instinct,* but the concept of teams also works. Team consciousness and the canine psyche have a lot in common. Teams focus on winning, with each player working for it, wanting it, thinking about it, and striving for it. Dogs live their entire lives, every waking moment, by this same team structure. Instead of "winning," however, their mantra is bonding and survival. To your dog, you and your family are her team.

Some other, less obvious factors also determine a team's success: cooperation, structure, and mutual respect. Without these factors, even a group of phenomenal players would produce only chaos. A good team is organized so that all members know who's in charge and what's expected of each of them. And if one of them gets in trouble or gets hurt, that member can trust that another teammate will help out.

For your dog to feel secure and safe, she needs to know who's in charge, and it's your job to teach her what you expect. In dog land, teams are organized in a hierarchy, so you must teach your four-legged friend that two-legged team members are the ones in charge — the captains of the team. If you have more than one person in your household, teaching this concept requires some cooperation on everyone's part, but it's important if you want your puppy to mature into a dog who respects everybody.

If you don't organize the team hierarchy, your dog will, and that can be a real nightmare. If your dog has the personality to lead, you'll find yourself living in a very expensive doghouse under dog rule. If your dog doesn't have the personality to lead but feels like she has to because no one else is, you'll end up with perhaps an even bigger headache, because dogs in this state are very hyper and confused.

So how do you organize your team and teach your dog the rules? You have to understand what motivates your dog's behavior, and you have to master her communication skills. But you have one small problem: Your puppy doesn't understand English. Like a human plopped into a foreign country where no one speaks her language, your puppy will feel lost in translation. To be the best teacher, you need to be fluent in *Doglish,* the language of dogs. Give your family or friends a lesson, too, and encourage consistency.

Doglish consists of three elements:

- ✔ Eye contact
- ✔ Body language
- ✔ Tone

In Doglish, words, feelings, and lengthy explanations don't count. Complex reasoning in English is impossible for your puppy to follow. The following sections break down the three elements of Doglish so that you can put them into practice ASAP.

Figuring out Doglish may seem like hard work, but watching the techniques in action is quite fascinating. Your dog will respond to you more willingly if you make the effort to understand and use her language. With an ounce of effort, a little time, and some structure, you can earn your dog's respect, cooperation, and trust. Plus, you'll have a teammate who will be at your side when the cards are down. You can't beat that bargain.

Eye contact: Attention = affirmation

Are you constantly making eye contact with your dog in stressful situations (someone's at the door and he's barking like a madman, or maybe he's stealing the dishrag)? Are you having trouble encouraging your pup to pay attention to you? Well, guess what? By making constant eye contact, your dog thinks you're depending on him to be the leader. He thinks you want him to make all the judgment calls. Before you can figure out how to handle these situations, you have to understand that, to train your dog, you must encourage him to look to *you* for direction.

When you make eye contact with your dog, you reinforce whatever behavior he's actively engaged in. Look your well-behaved dog in the eye and guess what you get? You got it: a well-behaved dog. However, if you make eye contact while he's running around the house with a wet wash rag flopping from his mouth, you'll reinforce that behavior because you're giving him the attention he so desperately wants. He wants you to look at him, so if you do so while he's eating your favorite album, he learns to do that.

Think of your dog's energy on a scale from 1 to 10, with 1 being sleep and 10 being hyperexcited play. Between 2 and 8 is the focused, civil, happy zone, which includes all the endearing behaviors you love, such as relaxing during a heartfelt pat, bringing a toy to you for play, and chewing on a bone while you're busy. Between 8 and 10 is the impulsive, unfocused zone, which contains all the behaviors that drive you crazy. Some of these behaviors include jumping, stealing, nipping, and running out of control.

By realizing that dogs repeat behaviors that result in attention, you can see that you get what you interact with. By redirecting wild energy and focusing on the good stuff, you know what you get? A perfect little angel. (Well, almost.)

The bottom line is this: Make eye contact only when your dog is calm (in the 1–8 zone).

Believe it or not, the 8–10 zone is no picnic for your canine, either. Even though he's rowdy and unfocused, this manic behavior is only a simple reaction to his misunderstanding of what you expect. Unfortunately, discipline doesn't help this situation because your dog may interpret it as confrontational play. Structure, positive reinforcement, and training help the most. (See Book IV, Chapters 2 and 3 for more on training.)

Body language: Stand up and stay calm

Body language is a funny thing. Imagine this: Your dog becomes excited and hyper when company arrives at the front door. Desperate to save face, you start shouting and pushing your dog as the company fends the two of you off with their coats. You try every possible command — "Sit, Boomer! Down! Off! Bad dog!" — but to no avail. The whole arrival scene is one big fiasco.

Body language is an integral part of Doglish. Play, tension, relaxation — they all have different postures. Your dog doesn't quite grasp the "I'm pushing you frantically because I'm unhappy with your greeting manners" concept. By dealing with the situation in this way, you're communicating differently than you think you are. In fact, by pushing and shouting, you're actually copying her body language, which reinforces her behavior.

As you blaze the training trail, remember these guidelines:

Book I

Choosing
and
Bringing
Home a
Dog

- ✔ Stand upright and relax when directing your dog. When giving your puppy direction or a command, throw your shoulders back and stand tall like a peacock. Tell your family and friends about this peacock position, and start strutting your stuff.

- ✔ Don't face off or chase your puppy when you're mad. She'll only think you're playing.

- ✔ When you're trying to quiet or direct your puppy, stay calm.

- ✔ Always remember that you set the example.

Can you ever get down and play or cuddle with your puppy or dog? Of course you can! Just don't play with your puppy when she's in a mischievous mood, or you're asking for trouble.

Tone: Using the three D's

If your dog thinks of you as another dog and you start yelling, he hears barking. Barking (yelling) interrupts behavior; it doesn't instruct. It also increases excitement. You may have a puppy who backs off from a situation when you yell (although he'll probably repeat the same behavior later). He's backing off because your yelling frightens him, not because he understands what you're yelling about. Yelling is just no good.

Commit three tones to memory — the three D's:

- ✔ **Delighted:** Use this tone when you want to praise your dog. It should soothe him, not excite him. Find a tone that makes your pup feel warm and proud inside.

- ✔ **Directive:** Use this tone for your commands. It should be clear and authoritative, not harsh or sweet. Give your commands *once* from the Peacock Position.

  If you bend over when giving your dog a command, don't be surprised if he doesn't listen. You're doing the doggy equivalent of a *play bow,* which is a posture that invites a game. When giving your dog directions, stand tall and proud like a peacock.

- ✔ **Discipline:** You may not be much of a disciplinarian, but you should have a few tones that tell your dog to back off or move on. The word you use doesn't matter as much as the tone. The tone should be shaming or disapproving, such as "How could you?" or "You'd better not touch that." Discipline has to do with timing and tone.

Teaching kids how to use the proper tone

If you have kids, you've probably noticed that sometimes they call out to the puppy in a very high-pitched tone, and sometimes they don't pronounce commands properly, either.

Until kids are 12 years old, you're better off focusing on what they're doing right rather than homing in on their imperfections. Simply overenunciate all your commands so that the kids figure out how to pronounce them properly and in an appropriate tone. If you overenunciate each command, your kids will notice the effects and start mimicking you. And when your kids copy your intonations, they transfer the control from you to them.

Don't repeat your commands. Saying "Sit, sit, sit, Boomer, sit! Sit! Sit!" sounds different from "Sit" — which is what Boomer is used to. If you want your dog to listen when you give the first command, make sure that you give it only once; then reinforce your expectations by positioning your dog. (When positioning in a sit, remember to gently squeeze the waist muscles and lift up on your dog's collar.)

Gimme, Gimme, Gimme: Puppies Want All the Attention

Imagine being a puppy, with humans just being big dogs milling all about, jabbering away in some nonsensical language, and providing virtually no instruction on what to do. When you lay a head in their lap or paw at them inquisitively, the human may shoo you off or lay a warm hand on your head, while often continuing to ignore your request for direction. The talking box on the wall and hand-held objects hold more interest for the humans than your interaction does. You hear noise and more noise. You catch sniffs that can't be explored or trailed. And you see sights that you're expected to ignore. Being a puppy in a human's world can be tough.

The power of positive attention

What do you do when you catch your puppy resting or chewing a bone quietly? "Nothing. It's a moment of peace." Well, it's those times when you ought to be showering your puppy with attention. Not wild, twist-and-shout, hoot-and-holler attention, but calm, soothing, loving attention. A soft, whispering praise is best mixed with a massagelike pat.

Your dog will repeat whatever action you pay attention to.

Dogs are drawn to positive energy fields. Think of yourself as her teacher and mentor. If you keep up the cheer, your dog won't want to be anywhere else.

Why negative attention doesn't work

Picture a very excited, jumping dog. You're trying to read the newspaper calmly, but he wants your attention. What do you think would happen if you tried to correct the dog by pushing him down and screaming "Off!"? In all likelihood, the dog would jump again. Do you know why? Because you just gave him attention. *Attention,* in a dog's mind, includes anything from dramatic body contact to a simple glance. Yes, even looking at your dog reinforces his behavior.

Though this phenomenon may sound far fetched at first, it's actually pretty elementary. Dogs think of you as another dog — really. Maybe a funny-looking dog with godlike powers, but a dog nonetheless. If they get excited and then *you* get excited, they think you're following their lead. By mimicking their energy level, you communicate that they must interpret new situations. The fact that you're upset with their behavior just doesn't register. Being upset is a human emotion. Excitement and body contact is the dog way. Even if you push your dog so hard that he stops and slinks away, your only accomplishment is scaring him. And who wants to train a pup through fear? You have a better way.

Consider another example: What happens if your dog grabs a sock and everyone in the household stops to chase him? Think you have a dog party? You bet. The dog is thinking "What fun!" as he dives behind the couch and under the table. Chasing a dog doesn't come across as discipline; it comes across as *prize envy* — "Whatever I have must be really good because everyone wants it!"

Dogs often interpret negative attention as confrontational play: "You're animated, you're loud, and you're fierce. Let's play rough!" Out-of-control negative attention reinforces the very behavior you're trying to change. To resolve these problems, be patient and read on.

Showing Your Pup How to Live in a Human World

If this training isn't coming naturally to you, don't be discouraged. To be a schoolteacher for children, you'd have to enroll in four to six years of college education. However, to teach your puppy, you only need to understand the concepts and exercises outlined in this book.

A lot goes into being a good dog trainer, and most of it's mental. Dogs, like humans, have spirits that you must understand and encourage in ways that make sense to the dog. Your dog has bestowed on you the highest honor, and it's one you'd never receive from a human: a lifetime commitment to respect your judgment and abide by your rules. You need only show her how.

To show your dog how to respect you and your rules, remember three key points that a good dog trainer does:

- Accepts and modifies his own personality
- Never blames the pup
- Recognizes the pup's unique personality

Recognize and modify your personality

Now's the time to analyze yourself. Take out a pen and paper, and write down three adjectives to describe your personality. What kind of person are you? Demanding? Sweet? Forgiving? Compulsive? Be honest. Then compare your personality with your pup's character.

If you discover that you're demanding, say, and your dog is sweet, someone's going to have to change. Making too many demands on a sweet dog will only frighten him, and he'll shut down or run away when training begins. If you're compulsive and you have a laid-back dog, you'll be laughed at. Have you ever seen a dog laugh at his owner? It's quite embarrassing. For you to be a good dog trainer, you must modify your expectations to better suit your dog's personality.

Never blame the pup

Believe it or not, puppies don't react out of spite. Your puppy's behavior is directly related to your own reactions, whether they're positive or negative.

So how do you handle unruly situations? The first step is to *stop blaming the dog.*

Never run at your puppy. Racing headlong toward a puppy is scary. Visualize someone two to four times your size barreling down on you. Talk about overwhelming. Your puppy may collapse in fear or run from you, but she won't take anything useful from the situation. Consider other options, such as using treats to reinforce good behavior.

Recognize the pup's unique personality

Yes, puppies have personalities, too. If you've had more than one pup in your lifetime, you know exactly what that means. Each dog is unique. And to train him, you must begin by understanding his personality.

No matter what his personality, your pup needs to interact and be understood. Dogs love to share their secret language with you, and they're content staying close to you as long as you include them in your daily activities.

Regardless of size or coat color, your dog is hardwired to act like . . . well, like a dog. He isn't a kitten, bunny, guinea pig, or child. His behavior is unique and predictable: He'll walk on four legs, sleep at night, and seek affection. These universal behaviors can give you a leg up in communicating with and training him.

If dogs ran the world

Only recently have people expected dogs to adjust to long periods of alone time. For most of the 20th century, no leash laws existed — hard to imagine, but true. Dogs were left out on the back porch during the day and often left to run free at night.

Long ago, most dogs weren't even considered pets. They were domesticated and bred to aid man in tasks that clearly advanced society, from herding sheep, to guarding property and towns, to hauling supplies in wagons or sleds.

The evolution of dogs as "pets" has come with the expectation that they put their working genes to rest (which isn't entirely possible), as well as a growing awareness of their psychological and emotional needs. Most dogs have retired from their genetic jobs.

Dogs so completely identify with their group or team that few would even know how to cope if left on their own. Ask various breeds what they'd do if they were suddenly put out on the street, and although you may get different answers, none would much enjoy their independence:

- **Golden Retriever:** Would scramble about for the nearest ball or stick and drop it eagerly at the nearest foot

- **Border Collie:** Would herd all the people within sight into a tight circle

- **Beagle:** Would sniff merrily through a crowd until someone started to follow

- **Jack Russell:** Would bark fanatically at a mysterious noise in the corner of a building until a crowd gathered

- **Cavalier King Charles Spaniel:** Would head for the nearest lap

- **Labrador Retriever:** Would race into the nearest restaurant, lie under the table, and wait eagerly for scraps to fall

Recognize your dog's behavior patterns, understand his communication style, and adjust your approach to teaching him how to behave. You need to talk Doglish and look at your current situation from his point of view. This chapter also helps you get a handle on everyday life immediately, from civilizing your dog's manners to deescalating mismanaged behaviors, such as hyperactivity, assertiveness, fear, and impulsivity.

Understanding How Hierarchy Differs from Democracy

Your dog looks to you and your family in much the same way she would seek inclusion in a group of dogs. She is a team player, as mentioned earlier. This truth places dogs, on a whole, above other species in their loyalty and focus for our direction. Defining her life's orientation to your group activity, she focuses on her position within your family, yet she reflects her position in hierarchical terms, *not* as part of a democracy. This defining difference between our two species must be fully embraced. Democracy is an ineffective model when civilizing a dog.

Either be the team leader and give your dog direction, or she will — out of her desire to keep the family or pack system working — take over the leadership role and train you.

In a group, someone must take charge and make the important decisions.

It's in their genes

Most people wouldn't ignore a toddler who looked at them with a confused expression, but those same people may overlook a similar expression coming from their dog. Because dogs are genetically programmed, especially when young, to look for direction, the opportunity to capitalize on their devotion is in the human's hands. When ignored, a dog often repeats whatever behavior got him attention previously, creating a hard-to-break cycle.

Teach your dog three directions that you can use whenever he looks to you for direction:

- ✔ Get your ball.
- ✔ Let's find your bone!
- ✔ Sit/settle down.

If your dog hasn't learned these directions, look carefully at the upcoming "Giving direction" section and then direct him to the object or into position. Praise his cooperation, even as you're helping him respond appropriately.

When your dog stares at you, he is often looking for guidance, but constant adoration makes your dog restless. Acting out soon follows, often in the form of house-soiling, destructive chewing, or stealing objects.

If your puppy has been assertive from the get-go, he's likely to have a more dominant, leadership-oriented personality. This puppy needs a consistent take-charge approach. If your dog develops these traits during adolescence or later, he has taken the leadership role only because you did not. You then need to change your behaviors to regain your status; although you need to be consistent, this dog will be grateful that you're taking over the demanding job. Being a leader is hard work!

Asserting benevolent authority

If you suspect that your dog is organizing your routines, you need to reorganize the hierarchy. Unless you want to be dog trained, the first step in the process is deciding that you want to do it and reassuring yourself that you can do it. Attitude is everything.

Your dog is preprogrammed to accept direction, so in many ways, you're already ahead of the game.

Defining your space

Dogs define their role based on social and spatial definition. If you walk around, step over, or move out of your dog's way, your message is loud and clear: Your mindful avoidance communicates your respect for your dog's authority. Stop right there and try the following exercises:

- ✔ **Teach your dog "Excuse me."** Your dog identifies your relationship based on spatial deference: Either you move out of her way or she moves out of yours. Teach her to respect your space immediately. If she's in your way, say, "Excuse me," and nudge her gently with your foot until she moves. If she cuts in front of you, walk straight into her until she shifts out of your way. Is she leaning against you excessively or inappropriately? Say, "Excuse me," and use your leg to push her off until she respects your personal space.

- ✔ **Condition your dog to lie on the sidelines.** Does your dog always position herself underfoot? Aside from being dangerous, her intrusion is a cry for attention. Provide her with a proper area in each room of your house and identify it with bedding and toys. If she's reluctant to stay there, check out the upcoming "Assign play stations in each room" section.

The two preceding exercises are important lessons in civility, and even more essential if you're living with a problem dog.

If you ask your dog to move and she growls at you, stop. This action is a sign that it's time to pick up the phone immediately and call for professional help. Actively aggressive behaviors require expertise that may go beyond the scope of this book — although you can read more about aggression in Book I, Chapter 1 and Book IV, Chapter 2

Encourage all your friends and family to take part in your efforts to civilize your dog. If your dog ignores any of them, step in to reinforce their directions. Your dog must learn to respect everyone.

Giving direction

Everyone knows that a small toddler needs lots of direction, interaction, and patience. Dogs do, too. The key difference is that children are programmed to communicate with words, whereas dogs are not, although they learn to respond to sound cues and hand signals. You need to teach your dog the proper response for a series of everyday directional cues. These six cues can get you and your dog started:

- **Name:** Help your dog create a positive association with his name. Call out your dog's name whenever you come home or to highlight a positive moment, such as when you're offering a treat, loving pats, or playtime with a favorite toy.

  Don't call your dog for unpleasant activities, such as isolation or unwanted grooming. If you do, he may hear "Come" and think "Run!" If "Come" has a reverse effect, stop using it. Use a treat cup and also check out the other training techniques in Part IV. Of course, you could just keep your dog on leash.

  Call your dog as you're walking away from him or when you're hidden from sight, to pique his interest. Shake a cup of treats while saying his name, to encourage his enthusiasm for listening and following you. Though initially he'll respond for the food, you'll eventually condition a positive cooperative habit. Ultimately, you can phase out food treats and replace them with praise and petting.

- **Ball and/or toy:** Often during the day, your dog may look to you for ideas. If you say nothing, his restlessness may lead to mischief. Instead, teach him these words. Each time you play with him or give him a chew, repeat a word like "Toy" or "Bone."

Book I

Choosing
and
Bringing
Home a
Dog

✔ **Sit/please:** A dog who sits politely is, in essence, saying "Please." Teach your dog to sit either by enticing him with a treat held near his nose and moved back over his head, or by placing pressure on his waist muscles with your thumb and forefinger as you put gentle upward pressure under his chin.

Teach your dog that he must sit before rewards, food, or attention.

✔ **Wait/okay:** This direction tells your dog to freeze and wait for your next cue. Use it at thresholds and curbs or when entering or exiting your home, a building, or your car. To teach it, either control your dog on a leash or hold him steady, pulling back as you say, "Wait"; then release him with "Okay."

✔ **Follow me:** This direction simply reminds your dog that you're the leader and will make all the directional decisions for both of you. More than a dominance gesture, your leadership efforts convey your willingness to be his guardian and protector.

✔ **Settle down:** This direction encourages your dog to relax. As often as possible, direct your dog to a mat or comfortable rug/bed and provide him with a displacement activity, such as a bone or toy, which will distract him and keep him from idly wandering about. You can use it both in your home or when traveling about. Whether your dog is restless at your dinner hour or quiet time, or you're waiting your turn at the veterinarian, this familiar direction will give your dog a sense of calm.

Don't be afraid to use a leash

You may be saying: "I want my dog to join me, but he's so unmanageable. We try, but after a short bit, we have no choice but to shut him away by himself again. If he'd learn to behave, he'd get a lot more freedom."

If the thought of letting your dog loose leaves you shaking in your shoes, you've probably gotten yourself caught in a vicious cycle. You may not realize that, ironically, the prolonged periods of isolation are resulting in your dog's impulsivity and mischief.

One solution is to use your leash indoors. Find an appropriate training collar (see Book IV, Chapter 3), and use a collar-and-leash ensemble to lead him through your home. Use the directions in this chapter to teach him his manners and socialize him to each room.

The leash is not a cruel device; think of it as akin to holding a child's hand. What's cruel and confusing is forced isolation. When your dog is cooperating, let him drag the leash behind him so that you can easily grab it, if needed, for additional control. When you're sure that his manners have improved and he's acting civilly, you can dispense with the leash — but not before you're certain that it's no longer needed.

Establishing your social status

Your dog is programmed to accept you and your family as if they were other dogs. She depends on the social structure you create to make her feel connected and safe. If you communicate direction to her and provide for her needs with consistency, she will look to you to interpret other situations as well. If your dog is unclear of what you want or you often get frustrated with her, she may perceive you as a moody adolescent dog rather than a leader. Even worse, your dog may decide that you're an unreliable or incompetent leader, which is bound to make her insecure and frustrate her. When this happens, later behavior problems are virtually guaranteed.

Practice the exercises in the following sections to reestablish your social status.

Assign play stations in each room

Your home is nothing more than a big den to your dog. How you establish routines indoors affects your relationship more than any activities or training programs you're involved in.

Think of providing your dog with a play station like offering a guest in your home a chair. Your dog doesn't know where to go in your house until you tell him; when you do, he'll feel welcome, calm, and included. If you don't, he'll likely misbehave, which provokes your negative attention. Because your negative reaction can be interpreted as a controlled or restrained confrontation, your dog may think his freedom is an invitation to play.

Give your dog a play station like this:

1. **Decide the rooms your dog is welcome in.**

   If you have to isolate him now but want him to share, say, the whole house or the downstairs area, take strides immediately toward this goal.

2. **Go into each room and select a spot on the floor (or a section of a chair/sofa) for your dog to call his own.**

   You may as well call this area a *play station.*

3. **Identify that location with a rug, a flat mat, or bedding, and place a few of your dog's favorite bones or toys on it.**

4. **Introduce your dog to his special area.**

   Bring him into the room on a leash if he's too fidgety and say, "Settle down," as you lead him to his play station. Sit with him and encourage him to focus on his things. Give him lots of attention and feed him treats.

Bring your dog with you to these places often. If he won't stay at his play station, make sure that he's had a good romp and time to potty, and then hold him still with a leash or secure a leash to something immovable.

Restraint at the door

From your dog's perspective, your main door is the mouth of her den. Whoever orchestrates comings and goings runs the show. If your dog barges through or reacts inappropriately when visitors arrive, she'll assume she's in charge.

In essence, you may be paying the mortgage or rent on a very elaborate dog house. Changing this situation is easy enough, but to do so, consistency is a must:

1. **Teach your dog to follow you in and out of the door.**

   Initially, manage her on a leash and teach her to properly respond to the directions "Wait" and then "Okay."

2. **Teach your dog a proper greeting ritual, remembering that good manners start at home.**

   Ignore your dog if she behaves in an overexcited or inappropriate manner when you or other family members arrive. If she has been confined alone in a crate, pen, or room, don't speak to her until she has calmed down or is chewing on a toy. After she has calmed down considerably, brace her as you greet her (see Figure 7-1), with your thumb clipped over the underside of her collar to prevent her from jumping up.

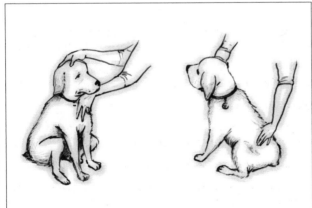

Figure 7-1:
Bracing a dog during greetings.

Create a greeting station 6–15 feet from the door. This location is the place where you'll send your dog before opening the door when company arrives. Teach your dog the term "Go back" ahead of time, leading her to the area and telling her "Wait" while you open and shut the door.

If your dog doesn't stay put when no one is present, she won't sit still when other people are. In this case, affix a leash to an immovable object. When you send her back from the door, secure her on the leash. Practice doing this routine when no one is there, and then with your family, and each time someone calls. Release your dog after you've welcomed the visitor, but only when she has calmed down.

The goal is for your dog to mirror and mimic your response to newcomers. Your dog isn't the leader — you are. You can shape her responses by establishing your authority in this way.

Was that out of spite?

Do you think your dog behaves poorly out of spite? Think again. Dogs repeat behavior that get them attention (good or bad) and often act out of anxiety when left alone, but they don't react out of spite.

Dogs aren't dishonest or mean. The conclusion that your dog is vengeful will do nothing for your relationship — such thoughts only result in bad energy in the home. Ask not what your dog is doing wrong, but what you may not be doing right.

Chapter 8

Fido and the Law

· ·

In This Chapter

▶ Understanding the basics of canine law

▶ Finding the laws that apply to you

▶ Playing by the rules

▶ Taking the bite out of dog bite law

▶ Preventing cruelty to dogs

· ·

We live in a litigious society. Whether or not you've been involved in a lawsuit, the law likely will somehow touch more than a few aspects of your life — including your canine companion. From federal laws to local ordinances, countless regulations exist to protect homeowners, neighbors, dogs, businesses, and more.

Of course, we all prefer to be on the right side of the law, but at some point you may find yourself faced with a legal conundrum. Maybe your dog barks from the minute you leave in the morning until you walk in the door for dinner — and the police are tired of getting calls from your frazzled neighbor. Perhaps your landlord has decided that your shepherd mix is a bit too big for his liking and he's terminated the lease on your apartment. Worst of all, maybe your dog bit a neighborhood child who came into your yard to get his wayward baseball.

This chapter fills you in on some common canine legal issues — licenses, leash laws, and noise ordinances. Other laws that have to do with animal welfare, such as animal hoarding or keeping a dog chained up or locked in a car, are also covered. A relatively new issue, that of breed-specific laws against "dangerous dogs," surfaces in the media from time to time and also merits discussion.

You shouldn't need a law degree to share your life with a dog, but some basic knowledge, as well as an added bit of research thrown in for good measure, can't hurt.

Discovering the Laws That Affect You

In most cases, local governments are in charge of basic animal regulations, such as leash laws and license requirements. Although these laws are similar from one city or region to the next, details may vary, so it's worth checking when you first get a dog or move to a new town.

So how do you find out about the laws related to your dog? Start local and work your way up. Begin with one or more of these approaches:

- ✔ Contact your local animal control agency or health department.
- ✔ Ask the city clerk for a written copy of the municipal code (city ordinances), including those having to do with dogs.
- ✔ Go to the library and look up the city codes and dog laws.
- ✔ Find the codes on the city's Web sites.

Depending on your situation, you may want to continue your research at the county level; do so by talking to the county clerk or visiting the county's Web site.

State law varies greatly, but many sites can help you monitor both current and pending legislation in your state.

The Dog Law Web site (www.doglaw.hugpug.com) offers helpful resources and information — tenant rights, traveling issues, dog bite liability — for the average pet owner. For issues related to pet welfare, try the research tool on the site of the Humane Society of the United States (www.hsus.org/legislation_laws/state_legislation/), which tells you where your state stands on laws about everything from tethering (keeping a dog tied up) to spaying and neutering. Another online service, the Animal Law Web Center (www.animallaw.info), run by the Michigan State University College of Law, is an invaluable source of legal materials geared toward nonlawyers. With a library of cases and statutes, and content categorized into more than 50 topics, the site is a user-friendly source of information on a wide variety of animal issues.

Though most of the laws that affect pet owners are at a local, county, or state level, federal legislation does cover issues such as animal welfare and fair treatment of disabled persons who use guide dogs (see the sidebar "Protecting service dogs").

Book I

Choosing
and
Bringing
Home a
Dog

Cracking the code

Most (but not all — Google is your friend) city and county Web site addresses follow these formats, simplifying the process of finding your local ordinances online:

✔ **County**: www.co.<county name>.<state postal code>.us (as with `www.co.monmouth.nj.us`)

✔ **City**: www.ci.<city name>.<state postal code>.us (as with `ww.ci.tulsa.ok.us`).

Making it official: Getting a dog license

Almost no matter where you live — town, city, or village — most dogs are required to have a license. Why, you ask? Licensing helps protect all of us from rabies, because dogs must have proof of the rabies vaccination before they can be licensed. Plus, the identification tags that go along with a license help get lost or stray dogs returned to their owners. Getting your dog licensed is a fairly simple process when you follow these steps:

1. Have your dog vaccinated for rabies (usually at around 4 months of age); get proof of the vaccination from your veterinarian.

2. Fill out the required application, typically with the city or town clerk. Have your proof of vaccination with you.

3. Pay the fee. Annual fees run about $10 to $20, but they are generally less for spayed and neutered dogs (bring proof from your vet). Some cities are now raising fees for unaltered animals, to encourage owners to spay and neuter. In most cases, fees are waived for guide and service dogs, as well as waived or reduced for the dogs of senior citizens and disabled persons.

4. Attach the license tag to your dog's collar; file the paper license with your legal paperwork.

5. Renew your dog's license when necessary; most agencies send renewal notices.

Of course, a license won't do much good if you don't renew it every year or you don't keep the tag on your dog at all times. Without a tag, an animal control officer may be forced to take your lost pup to the animal shelter.

Vaccinating your dog

Most veterinarians agree that certain vaccines are necessary, but laws and practices may vary, so check with your vet about the vaccination schedule she recommends. The most common vaccines are parvovirus, distemper, rabies, and adenovirus. Although the disease is rare, your dog will need a rabies vaccination to be licensed. Check with your town or city about vaccination requirements and any free or low-cost clinics that are offered.

Spaying and neutering

With millions of unwanted pets, and shelters and rescues overwhelmed, a logical solution is to encourage owners to spay and neuter. In fact, most states now require people who adopt dogs from a shelter to spay or neuter them, a measure that may have a limited effect on the problem but is a good move nonetheless.

But what about those unaltered dogs who are already breeding — intentionally or accidentally — in the general dog population? A few cities are taking a more drastic approach, requiring spaying or neutering of all pets unless the owner buys a special breeding permit each year. The tactic is controversial among some people, but it may help reduce the number of unwanted pets in this country.

Protecting service dogs

Service animals are dogs who are trained to perform tasks for people with disabilities — guiding the blind, alerting the deaf, pulling wheelchairs, or performing other special tasks. Because service animals are working animals, not pets, they have special rights in the world of canine law.

Although a restaurant won't likely welcome the typical dog, under the Americans with Disabilities Act (ADA), a federal law, "businesses and organizations that serve the public must allow people with disabilities to bring their service animals into all areas of the facility where customers are normally allowed to go." This applies to restaurants, schools, hotels, taxis, grocery and other stores, hospitals, theaters, health clubs, parks, and even zoos.

Other special considerations are also made under the ADA, including allowing service dogs to live in housing with "no pets" policies. In addition, in many cases, local ordinances about licensing and even pooper-scooping don't apply to assistance dogs.

Staying Out of Trouble

A bit of common sense goes a long way when it comes to keeping you and your pup out of trouble. Nuisance laws — those laws that prohibit constant barking and require that owners clean up after their dogs — are among the most common you'll come across. To reduce your dog's chance of being a nuisance, do the following:

✔ **Use a leash and put up a fence.** If your dog is safely secured in your yard or on a leash, he can't bother anyone or harm someone's property. The day you make an exception may be the day your pooch decides to dig up your neighbor's flower garden.

✔ **Spay or neuter your dog.** Your dog may behave better and wander less. Careful breeding programs are one thing; random neighborhood couplings are another. See the earlier section, "Spaying and neutering."

✔ **Socialize early and often.** From an early age, expose your dog to lots of people — children, too. Your friends, family, and neighbors will appreciate not being nibbled on, barked at, or jumped on.

✔ **Try training.** Even if you don't have any aspirations of owning an obedience champion, training your dog to walk on a leash and follow the basic commands of Sit, Lie Down, and Stay may mean the difference between a well-behaved dog and one who can't be trusted with company.

✔ **Leave no trace.** Always pick up what your dog leaves behind. Grab a plastic grocery bag or use a fancy sack — just pick up the poop and dispose of it properly.

✔ **Prove that your dog is good.** The American Kennel Club offers a certification program designed to reward dogs "who have good manners at home and in the community." See Chapter 2 of Book IV for more on doggie manners.

Read on to find out more about the legal implications of the common nuisance laws.

Taking care of business: The scoop on poop

Like everyone, dogs poop — it's a fact of life. But it wasn't until more of us starting living in cities with our dogs that the canine byproduct became a real problem. It doesn't take long for a sidewalk to become littered with dog feces when owners don't pick up after their pooches. And no one — *no one* — enjoys stepping on the stuff.

In the 1930s, New York City was an early battleground in the war against doggie doo. "Please Curb Your Dog" signs were minimally effective, but in 1978, New York State's Canine Waste Law (commonly called the "pooper-scooper law") went into effect; the law called for the removal of canine waste in any city with a population of 400,000 or more. Since then, cities and towns of all sizes have followed suit.

Still don't feel like picking up after your dog? Expect to pay a fine of anywhere between $25 and $100.

Leash laws

It would seem that laws about leashes have to be among the simplest on the books, simply because it makes good sense for dogs be leashed when they're off their owner's property. Not so. Although many of us assume that all states have a mandatory leash law, it's not likely to be the case. To complicate matters, some municipalities have leash laws and some don't, so it's important to look into your local regulations.

Check out www.animallaw.info/articles/ovusdogleashlaws.htm for a break-down of the states' widely varying leash laws.

A typical leash law requires dogs to be leashed and under control when they're off their owner's property. This means that the days of letting a dog run loose in the neighborhood are over, and your dog should be walked on a leash even if you're confident that she's completely off-leash trained. Unleashed dogs can get loose and run the risk of being hit by a car or picked up and taken to an animal shelter; owners are liable for fines, as well as any legal actions — say, if a loose dog bites someone.

Try to find a local dog park for a safe place to let your dog run free. Like playgrounds for pooches, dog parks are popping up in communities throughout the country.

Noise ordinances

Anyone who's had to put up with a barking dog for more than a few minutes can attest to the level of piercing annoyance it causes. It's not a surprise that noise complaints are among the most common lodged against dogs and their owners. Though such complaints are usually resolved between individuals and rarely end up in a courtroom, laws help protect neighbors from the headaches and sleepless nights caused by a chronic barker.

Book I

Choosing
and
Bringing
Home a
Dog

Resolving disputes: Giving peace a chance

If you end up in the middle of a neighborly dispute about a dog (yours or the neighbor's), first try to talk through the problem. Even if it doesn't work and you end up in a court of law, you'll know you tried to be civil. Consider some tips:

✔ Try it in writing — write a friendly note to set up a meeting and get the ball rolling.

✔ Be calm and listen.

✔ Don't threaten to call the police or a lawyer.

✔ Offer solutions and listen to those offered to you.

✔ Agree on a plan and then schedule a date to meet again for a progress check.

If you can't resolve the issue, you may have to bring in some help — a mediator, perhaps. Of course, if all else fails, you may need to do your research to find out your legal rights.

In many cases, specific state laws or local ordinances cover the problem of barking dogs. When a law isn't specifically geared at dog noise, a general noise ordinance usually does the trick; most local noise ordinances designate quiet hours from 10 p.m. to 7 a.m., so anyone allowing their dog to bark, howl, or whine during those hours can be charged with disturbing the peace.

When a barking dog becomes a real problem, it's best for everyone (you, the neighbor, and the police) to resolve matters without involving the police or animal control. See the nearby sidebar, "Resolving disputes: Giving peace a chance," for tips. When all else fails, though, you may have to check your local and state laws and pursue a legal avenue.

Biting

Although the majority of dogs are harmless, the statistics for dog bites are startling. The Centers for Disease Control and Prevention estimate that 4.7 million people are bitten by dogs each year, with about 800,000 — half of them children — requiring medical attention.

Regardless of breed or prior history, even the friendliest dog may bite. A bite is a bite, whether the dog was provoked, afraid, hurt, acting on a natural instinct to be protective, or even being playful. In short, people win. And under many laws, owners may be held financially liable when their dog hurts someone. This is no small matter. According to the Insurance Information Institute, the average cost of a dog bite claim was $24,461 in 2008.

Laws vary, so it's a good idea to determine the type of dog bite law imposed in your state. About two thirds of the states have what is known as a *strict liability statute,* which makes the owner liable for any personal injury caused by a dog, regardless of the owner's knowledge of viciousness. This means that a victim has a valid case against the owner even if a dog has never bitten anyone. Some exclusions may apply, such as some that pertain to whether a dog was provoked or questions on whose property the bite occurred. Go to www.animallaw.info/articles/qvusdogbiteslstatutes.htm to see specifics about each state's statute.

Some states follow the common-law doctrine of the "one bite" rule, which basically means that a dog owner can be held liable for any injury if he had knowledge of any vicious tendencies. However, an owner may be deemed liable after a dog has bitten the first time or if the victim can prove negligence (a fence wasn't high enough to secure a dog, for example). Many states have switched from this law to the strict liability statute.

In many states, cases that involve breeds considered "dangerous" — mainly the Pit Bullish breeds — are handled differently. Often these dogs are bred or trained to be aggressive. For more on the issue of breed-specific law, see the section "Regulating Dangerous Dogs."

Keeping in mind that any dog may bite, you can take measures to help prevent a bite from happening:

- ✔ Never let your dog run loose. Secure fencing and leashing are critical.
- ✔ Socialize and train your dog from an early age.
- ✔ Spay and neuter your dog to help reduce aggressiveness.
- ✔ Carefully monitor contact with children — insist on considerate behavior, and never leave a dog alone with a child.

Regulating Dangerous Dogs

Even the sweetest dogs can snap (literally and figuratively) under certain circumstances, but individual dogs who do bite someone or display dangerous tendencies are, from then on, considered "dangerous" or "vicious," according to some laws. Although most dangerous dog laws are found at the local level, a number of states are now adopting versions of such laws.

Many believe that dangerous dog laws help protect people from dogs who have been deemed vicious. However, some cities and states have taken the next step and adopted breed-specific laws, which some people feel unfairly target breeds such as Pit Bulls and Rottweilers; in fact, some breed-specific laws even ban these breeds.

Dangerous dog laws and breed-specific laws require owners to take special precautions to protect others from harm. The following are some examples of restrictions placed on dangerous dogs and breeds and their owners:

✔ The dog must be locked in a secure, confined area.

✔ The dog must be muzzled in public.

✔ The dog must be identified with a microchip or tattoo.

✔ The owner must have the dog sterilized.

✔ The owner must purchase a special license or permit from the town, city, or county.

✔ The owner must purchase more liability insurance.

✔ The owner must post "Beware of Dog" signs.

✔ The owner must pay fines or face jail sentences if proven to have deliberately created a dangerous dog.

Opponents of breed-specific laws believe that these regulations disregard the individual nature of dogs. Temperaments vary within any breed — a doe-eyed Cocker Spaniel may be more ferocious than a steel-jawed American Staffordshire Terrier, for example. And most individuals within a breed, even those breeds originally developed for dog fighting, are not dangerous. All dogs are influenced by factors such as breeding, training, and socialization, leaving dog advocates and lawmakers with a complicated issue. These laws likely will continue to evolve as time and debate goes on.

Preventing Canine Cruelty

What is the definition of animal cruelty? Because the legal explanation differs from state to state, even animal welfare advocates struggle with the question. Animal cruelty generally means causing unjustified injury or death to an animal, but the exact meaning depends on individual laws.

Although no federal anticruelty law is on the books, every state in the nation has an animal anticruelty statute that applies to dogs. These state laws penalize two types of actions:

- ✔ **Intentional acts:** Hitting, burning, maiming, or killing a dog
- ✔ **Failure to act:** Situations of neglect in which food, water, veterinary care, and shelter are not provided to a dog

The laws vary greatly, however, with some much stronger and more encompassing than others. The Humane Society of the United States features a way you can review your state's animal cruelty laws: `www.hsus.org/acf/cruelty/publiced/animal_cruelty_laws_by_state.html`. The organization also offers information on some of the common issues related to dog welfare.

Breaking free from the chains

A truly sad and unfortunate sight is that of a dog chained to a stake in a patch of dirt in the middle of someone's backyard. The dog is lonely, bored, frustrated, frightened, and maybe even thirsty and hungry.

Tethering — tying or chaining a dog to a stationary object for an extended period of time — is inhumane and can cause serious problems, such as aggression and psychological damage. Tethered dogs also suffer from biting insects, extreme temperatures, and sun exposure; tragically, many dogs have been strangled to death by tethers.

Fortunately, tethering is becoming increasingly recognized as an unnecessary act of animal cruelty. In fact, according to the Humane Society, more than 100 communities in more than 30 states have passed laws that regulate the practice of tethering animals. Other communities allow tethering for only limited periods of time.

If dogs are to be left outside during the day, they need a securely fenced outdoor pen or other space that has a shelter to protect them from the elements. And all dogs should be taken indoors at night. The only object your dog should be attached to is the leash you use on his daily walks.

Dogs in vehicles

Cars and dogs have a love-hate relationship: Dogs love to chase cars and ride with their noses poked out of car windows; unfortunately, they are too often injured or killed in or by cars. Dog lovers have worked hard to get anticruelty laws passed to protect pooches when it comes to automobiles:

Book I

Choosing
and
Bringing
Home a
Dog

✔ **Parked cars:** An enclosed car can heat up fast on a warm, sunny day, with the temperature exceeding 100 degrees Fahrenheit in just minutes. Don't be fooled into thinking that your dog will be fine if you park in the shade or crack a window or two. Anticruelty statutes and laws forbid owners from leaving a dog in a parked vehicle without adequate ventilation.

✔ **Pickup trucks:** Approximately 100,000 dogs a year are killed in the United States because they jump or are thrown from the open back of a pickup truck. Many local governments and some states — California to name one — have adopted laws that require dogs to be in cages or otherwise secured in truck beds.

Setting limits on numbers

To protect both animals and residents, some communities have put into place ordinances that restrict the number of dogs residents can have, usually to two or three per household. Many times these laws are created to cut down on the problems of noise and odor that can be caused by high concentrations of canines. In some cities, owners can pay for a special permit that allows them to keep more dogs.

Animal hoarders, people who collect animals beyond their ability to provide for the animals' needs, are at the extreme end of the spectrum — but of special concern to anticruelty organizations. These are the cases that occasionally surface in the media; the abuse typically differs from other types of cruelty because the hoarders themselves can't or don't see the problem, many times because they are suffering from some sort of psychological issue such as obsessive-compulsive disorder.

Book II
Dog Nutrition and Health

The 5th Wave   By Rich Tennant

@RICHTENNANT

"Well, someone's starting to show his age. Look at how Rusty has to hold his chew-toy at arm's length now to see which one he's got."

In this book . . .

Once you have a dog, you had better find out how to feed him right and keep him healthy. These chapters deal with nutritional, medical, exercise, and other health issues. There's also a chapter on caring for an aging dog, and one that introduces the topic of starting your own breeding program.

Chapter 1

The Scoop on Dog Food

In This Chapter

▶ Knowing how much protein, carbohydrates, and fats your dog needs

▶ Making sure that your dog is getting the right amount of vitamins and minerals

▶ Getting an inside look at how your dog's food is made

▶ Checking out organic options

Dogs are carnivores — meat eaters. Their teeth are shaped for biting, tearing, and grinding flesh and bones, and their intestinal tracts are short, with enzymes that are good for digesting proteins (but not very good at breaking down and absorbing plant material). So it only makes sense that your dog's diet should be meat based.

Dogs are also opportunists, which means they'll eat whatever comes their way, including the trash in your kitchen and the grass in your yard. They do gain nutritional benefits from vegetables, fruits, and grains, but they need meat in their diets as their main source of nutrition.

This chapter covers the eight building blocks of nutrition. All these building blocks are required in a well-balanced diet, regardless of the dog. But the *amounts* of these nutritional elements that each dog needs depends on that dog's unique situation — puppies and adults need different amounts, as do spayed and pregnant females, and active and inactive dogs.

Proteins

Proteins are the most critical component of food for your canine carnivore. They are also the most abundant component of your dog's body. Your dog needs proteins to produce hair, nails, tendons, cartilage, and all the connective tissues that support the rest of the tissues and organs in her body. Adequate protein is important for your dog's growth and proper development, her muscle development and strength, a functioning immune system, the production of functioning hormones, the proper volume of blood, injury repair and prevention, and much, much more (see Figure 1-1).

Figure 1-1:
This dog, Fate, arrived at a shelter in terrible condition, but after two months of proper nutrition, her coat is rich and glistening.

Your dog's body can also use proteins to produce energy, if necessary. Fats and carbohydrates are much more readily available sources of energy, but dogs can break down proteins and convert them to energy when necessary, such as when food supply is low.

Proteins are made up of amino acids linked in a chain. When your dog eats protein, enzymes that the pancreas secretes into the intestines break them down into shorter chains of amino acids called *polypeptides*, which are small enough for the intestines to absorb. A dog's body makes 20 different amino acids — some are *essential amino acids* and others are *nonessential amino acids*. As the name implies, your dog requires essential amino acids in his food. Food that contains all the essential amino acids is called a *complete protein source*. The nonessential amino acids are . . . drum roll, please . . . not essential; if your dog doesn't get them in his diet, he can convert other amino acids into those that he's missing.

Your dog can get proteins from both animal and plant sources. But only animal-source proteins are complete protein sources, and not all of them are complete. Examples of complete protein sources that come from animals are eggs, whole milk, and lean meat. Grains are another important source of proteins in dog foods, but they are incomplete protein sources because they don't contain some of the essential amino acids your dog needs. Plant protein sources frequently used in dog foods include soybeans, wheat, and corn.

Your dog's major source of protein should be animal products, not grain. Don't buy a dog food in which soybean meal, soy flour, or corn gluten meal is the primary, or even the secondary, source of protein (see the section "Reading a Dog Food Label" later in this chapter for more on this). Dogs don't have the enzymes to use grains properly as main sources of protein.

The American Association of Feed Control Officials (AAFCO) is the organization that sets guidelines for the types and amounts of nutrients dogs need in their foods. The AAFCO has determined that foods for adult dogs should contain no less than 18 percent protein, and that foods for lactating females or puppies should have a minimum of 22 percent protein. Military or police dogs, mushing dogs, and other dogs who work hard every day or who are under stress may need more. Dogs recuperating from injuries or surgery may need more protein as well, to repair muscles, tendons, and ligaments.

Book II

Dog Nutrition and Health

Not all complete protein sources are created equal. A cow's hoof and a filet mignon may both have all the essential and nonessential amino acids, but your dog can get the amino acids he needs more easily from the filet mignon than from the cow's hoof. Some proteins are just more digestible than others. So how do we know which protein sources are digestible and which aren't? Nutritionists measure the amount of protein in a food, feed it to dogs, and then measure the amount of protein in the dogs' feces. The difference between how much was in the food to begin with and how much the dog excretes reveals how much of it the dog absorbed, and that is the digestible protein. A protein isn't very useful to your dog if it ends up on your lawnrather than in his body. Hair and feathers are a cheap source of protein, too — but they're indigestible. On the other hand, eggs are highly digestible but expensive. Not surprisingly, the more digestible the protein, the more expensive the dog food. As with many things in life, you get what you pay for.

Beware of foods that advertise over 90 percent digestibility. The highest-quality dog foods are 82–86 percent digestible, whereas economy foods (inexpensive brands you get in grocery stores) are around 75 percent. The percent digestibility of a dog food is not stated on the label, but most dog food manufacturers provide that information on request.

If your dog's feces are voluminous, it may be a sign that his food isn't highly digestible.

A brief history of dog food

Before the late 19th century, there was no such thing as prepared dog food. Lucky dogs owned by the well-to-do ate the leftovers from their owners' dinners, and street dogs aplenty canvassed the alleys, scrounging in the trash. In the 1870s, a time when transportation literally used horse power, a European entrepreneur devised a unique way to solve the problem of what to do with the carcasses of the many horses that died every day in the cities: He decided to package and sell the horse meat as dog food. The idea caught on, particularly among the wealthy, who appreciated the convenience of having a ready-made food for their dogs.

The first commercial dog foods in North America were made by Ralston-Purina in 1926. The foods were tested on dogs that the company kept in large kennels on the property near St. Louis, Missouri. Ralston-Purina dog food was given the ultimate test when it was fed to the sled dogs on Admiral Byrd's expedition to Antarctica in 1933. Although this was a punishing test for a dog food, it also was an early precursor to the celebrity endorsements that are a major part of the advertising budgets for many large companies today.

In the decade after World War II, the idea of prepared dog food really caught on. The economy was booming and people didn't mind spending a little money for the convenience of having a ready-made dog food for their canine companions. Besides, the companies producing these dog foods were performing studies on the nutritional needs of dogs, and their foods were billed as containing everything a healthy dog needed.

At that time, most dog foods were canned. This method of preserving food was familiar to Americans, who enjoyed the convenience of canned human foods that could be stored for months or even years on their shelves. In 1956, dog food companies began to utilize the *extrusion process,* in which nutrients in dried form are mixed with water and steam- and pressure-forced through an opening; the extruded material then is cut into small pieces. The food pieces are cooled, coated with vitamins and other components that are lost in the process of heating, flavored, and packaged.

Dry dog food allowed the consumer to more easily carry large amounts of dog food home from the grocery store. In addition, people found pouring food from a bag more convenient than opening a metal can. Plus, dry foods were advertised as helping keep dogs' teeth cleaner. As a result, since the late 1960s, the majority of dogs have been fed dry dog food, although canned food is still widely used, especially for smaller dogs.

In the early 1970s, the National Research Council (NRC) published the first recommendations listing the minimal nutritional requirements of dogs. Dog food companies now had a standard by which they could measure the nutritional value of their foods and parameters by which they could claim their foods to be complete and balanced. (The term *complete* indicated that all the required nutrients were present in their foods, and *balanced* indicated that these nutrients were in the correct proportions.) The NRC nutrient requirements for dog foods were supplanted in 1992 by nutrient profiles established by the American Association of Feed Control Officials (AAFCO). Throughout the late 20th century, as the dog population continued to grow, so did the dog food industry. By 1999, the pet food industry was an $11-billion-a-year industry — and very competitive. Today dog foods are advertised and marketed every bit as competitively as human foods, highlighting the importance of being aware of what you're buying.

Fats

Fats are the major source of energy for dogs. Dogs who live outdoors in the cold need more fat to supply them with the energy to keep warm. And police dogs and working dogs need enough fat so they don't have to get their energy from carbohydrate or protein supplies.

But fats do more than provide your dog with energy. They also help keep skin and foot pads supple and coats healthy. Supplying an allergic dog with the proper amount and type of fats can make a huge difference in how much she scratches. Fats also carry fat-soluble vitamins into the body from the intestines. These vitamins are essential for health, and the only way your dog can absorb them is if she eats enough fat to carry them into her body. Plus, just as with our own food, fat makes a dog's food tastier, which can be important in helping dogs who are ill to eat enough.

Fatty acids are the major component of fat. Dogs really need only omega-6 fatty acid (*linoleic acid*), because they can't make it on their own. Linoleic acid keeps your dog's skin supple and pliable, and her pads and nose leather flexible. Dogs lacking linoleic acid have scruffy, dry coats and dry, cracked pads. Luckily, dogs don't need a lot of linoleic acid. Good sources are beef, pork, chicken, and the oils from corn, safflower, and soybeans.

Omega-3 fatty acids can also help dogs with allergies by controlling the inflammatory responses in their skin. Omega-3s can improve dry skin and decrease stiffness from arthritis. But omega-6 and omega-3 fatty acids have some opposing functions, so you need to be sure that your dog is getting a balance between these two components. Shoot for a ratio of omega-6 to omega-3 fatty acids of about 5 to 1. Your dog is better off if her food has the correct ratio of omega-6 to omega-3 fatty acids than if you try to provide it in supplement form. Look for dog foods that have safflower oil or corn oil for omega-6 fatty acids, and fish oil or fish meal for omega-3 fatty acids.

The ratio of omega-6 to omega-3 fatty acids is listed on the bags of some of the better-quality foods, so if your dog is having skin problems, opt for a higher-quality food — and one with the correct ratio of omega-6 to omega-3.

Although your dog needs fat in her diet, too much fat can contribute to obesity, the number one nutritional problem in dogs. Excessive fat can also slow the digestive process and may cause nausea, diarrhea, and vomiting. High-fat diets also play a role in the development of *pancreatitis,* an inflammation of the pancreas that can result in very severe vomiting and sometimes even death. So you need to control the fat levels in your dog's diet. Feeding a high-quality dog food (and not giving lots of extras), watching your dog's weight, and making sure that she gets enough exercise is the best way of ensuring that she won't become obese. On the other hand, that doesn't mean a *low*-fat diet is good for dogs. Too little fat can lead to dry, flaky skin; dry, cracked pads; and a dull coat.

Be sure to read the dog food label before choosing a diet for your dog and observe your dog's response to the food. If you don't like the appearance of your dog's coat and skin on one diet, try a different one.

Carbohydrates

Every cell in your dog's body needs a continuous supply of carbohydrates, particularly in the form of glucose, to function properly. In fact, it is so important for cells to have glucose that the body produces the hormone *insulin* to drive glucose into the cells. Glucose is especially important for your dog's brain and muscles. Carbohydrates also assist in the digestion of other nutrients, especially fats. Your dog's carbohydrate requirements vary according to his level of activity, health, and overall energy needs.

Carbohydrates come in three basic forms: sugars, starches, and cellulose. Sugars and starches are *simple carbohydrates* because they are readily available as glucose or can be broken down into glucose. Good sources of simple carbohydrates are rice, oatmeal, corn, and wheat. Simple carbohydrates are easy for your dog to digest when properly cooked; they also add texture to the food, making it more palatable. Cellulose, the main carbohydrate found in the stems and leaves of plants, is a *complex carbohydrate.* Dogs don't have the enzymes to digest cellulose (most animals don't), but it serves as *fiber,* helping regulate water in the large intestine and aiding formation and elimination of feces.

The best foods use the carbohydrates that come in grains; sugar need not be added to food, although some manufacturers do this to make it taste better. The AAFCO has no recommended minimum or maximum levels of carbohydrates in dog foods. Carbs make up the remainder of the bulk of the food after fats, proteins, fiber, and vitamins and minerals have been added.

Fiber

Fiber is an important component of dog food. It provides bulk to the food and helps the intestinal contents absorb water, which results in formed stools that are readily expelled. If a food has too little fiber, the dog may have loose stools, because there is nothing to help the stools form. If a food has too much fiber, it will pass much more quickly through the gastrointestinal system, making digestion less efficient and the stools hard and compacted.

Beet pulp is an excellent source of fiber. It is the dried residue from sugar beets, which first have been cleaned and freed of crowns, leaves, and sand, and then used to extract sugar for human foods. Dried tomato pomace is another good source of fiber. It is the dried mixture of tomato skins, pulp, and crushed seeds, a byproduct of the manufacture of tomato products.

Most dog foods contain between 3 and 6 percent fiber. Weight-reduction diets may have between 8 and 25 percent fiber.

Water

Water is the most plentiful molecule in your dog's body (your dog's body is two-thirds water) and is essential for every function, from digesting food to dashing across the yard. In the gastrointestinal tract, water dissolves nutrients to prepare them for digestion and helps transport the nutrients across the intestinal wall.

Your dog loses water by several routes, through salivation and respiration, and in urine and feces. If your dog loses more water than she takes in, she will suffer from dehydration, which, if severe and untreated, can be fatal.

Every dog should have access to clean, fresh water at all times.

Book II

Dog Nutrition and Health

Enzymes

Enzymes play a role, often in conjunction with vitamins, in just about every body reaction. They are like the keys that unlock the doors to chemical reactions. Each enzyme is the catalyst for one specific reaction, which is why so many different enzymes exist. The pancreas secretes several kinds of enzymes that assist in digestion. In addition to enzymes secreted by the pancreas, enzymes are present in fresh foods.

In most dogs, the pancreas produces sufficient enzymes for digestion. However, in some dogs, pancreatic function is not optimal. Older dogs frequently have trouble fully breaking down their foods for optimal absorption of nutrients, as do dogs with pancreatitis (inflammation of the pancreas) or pancreatic cancer.

Vitamins

Dogs require 14 different vitamins. With only a few exceptions, dogs don't make the vitamins themselves, which means they must get these vitamins in their food. Vitamins participate in numerous chemical reactions that help to release the needed nutrients from food and help the dog's body put those nutrients to use. Vitamins can be either water soluble or fat soluble.

Water-soluble vitamins

Water-soluble vitamins have to be supplied on a daily basis, because they are continually broken down and excreted. They include the following:

- **Thiamin (vitamin B1):** Promotes a good appetite and normal growth. Required for energy production.

- **Riboflavin (vitamin B2):** Promotes growth.

- **Pyridoxine (vitamin B6):** Aids in the metabolism of proteins and the formation of red blood cells.

- **Pantothenic acid:** Required for energy and for protein metabolism.

- **Niacin:** Exists in many enzymes that process carbohydrates, proteins, and fats.

- **Vitamin B12:** Necessary for DNA synthesis and intestinal function.

- **Folic acid:** Works together with vitamin B12 and in many of the body's chemical reactions.

- **Biotin:** Acts as a component of several important enzyme systems.

- **Choline:** Required for proper transmission of nerve impulses and for utilization of sulfur-containing amino acids.

- **Vitamin C:** Participates in the formation of bones, teeth, and soft tissue.

The daily requirements for each of these vitamins are supplied in premium dog foods. Generally, an excess of these water-soluble vitamins is harmless because they are excreted in the urine. As long as your dog is eating a high-quality complete and balanced commercial diet and is healthy, you don't need to worry about supplementing her diet with water-soluble vitamins.

Fat-soluble vitamins

Fat-soluble vitamins don't have to be supplied in the food every day because excess levels are stored in a dog's body's fat. Long-term storage means that they can accumulate to toxic levels, but this is very rare. Your dog needs the following fat-soluble vitamins:

- **Vitamin A:** Necessary for proper vision, especially night vision. Important in bone growth, reproduction, and maintenance of tissues such as the lungs, intestines, and skin.

- **Vitamin D:** Critical to the dog's ability to use calcium and phosphorus for bone and cartilage growth and maintenance.

✔ **Vitamin E:** An antioxidant that protects the cells (and dog food) from oxidative damage. Important for muscular and reproductive function.

✔ **Vitamin K:** Essential for normal blood clotting.

Minerals

Minerals are present in small amounts in the tissues of all living things. Teeth, bones, muscles, and nerves have especially high mineral content. Although the AAFCO provides guidelines for the minimum amounts of minerals necessary for canine growth and development, each dog's mineral requirements depend on the current nutritional state. For example, if a dog is iron deficient, he will need and absorb more iron from the intestinal tract. Working dogs and ill or stressed dogs may also have higher requirements.

Minerals can be divided into two groups: major minerals and trace minerals. The major minerals are required in gram amounts each day, whereas the trace minerals are required in milligram or microgram amounts per day. Of the trace minerals, several are known to be required for canine health, and the roles of others are less understood.

Your dog's body needs to maintain a delicate balance between the various major and trace minerals. For several trace minerals, the line between the required amount and toxic levels is a thin one. So supplementing an already balanced dog food with minerals can create more problems than it solves.

Table 1-1 lists the different minerals your dog needs and which foods are good sources of these minerals.

Table 1-1	Sources of Minerals
Mineral	*Source*
Calcium	Dairy products, poultry, meat bone
Phosphorus	Meat, poultry, fish
Magnesium	Soybeans, corn, cereal grains, bone meals
Sulfur	Meat, poultry, fish
Iron	Organ meats
Copper	Organ meats
Zinc	Beef liver, dark poultry meat, milk, egg yolks, legumes
Manganese	Meat, poultry, fish
Iodine	Fish, beef, liver
Selenium	Grains, meat, poultry
Cobalt	Fish, dairy products

Major minerals

The four major minerals are calcium, phosphorus, magnesium, and sulfur. Calcium and phosphorus are the most important minerals in all dogs' diets, especially in the diets of growing puppies. Calcium is needed for muscle contraction, nerve transmission, and blood coagulation. It is also required to activate numerous enzymes that affect virtually every process in the cell. Phosphorus plays a part in nearly all chemical reactions in your dog's body. Both strengthen your dog's bones and teeth.

Although the ratio of calcium to phosphorus in a dog food is important, the total amount of calcium ingested may be more important. Excess calcium is thought to contribute to the development of hip and elbow dysplasia, *osteochondrosis dissecans* (degeneration of the joint cartilage), and other bone and joint problems. Calcium deficiencies frequently occur in dogs who are fed all-meat diets. A severe deficiency of calcium can cause rickets and bone malformations. A moderate deficiency can cause muscle cramps, impaired growth, and joint pain.

As of this writing, all premium-quality adult maintenance dog foods produced by major manufacturers have enough calcium to support the healthy growth of puppies, including those of giant breeds. Resist the urge to provide extra supplementation of vitamins and minerals, particularly those containing calcium, to your growing puppy on a premium dog food.

Never add bone meal to a complete and balanced diet. Not only are you likely to alter the critical calcium to phosphorus ratio, but you also risk decreasing your dog's ability to absorb and utilize many of the other minerals he needs.

Magnesium is essential for many enzymatic reactions. It also helps promote the absorption and metabolism of many other vitamins and minerals, including vitamins C and E, calcium, and phosphorus. As with calcium and phosphorus, magnesium is important in bone growth and development. In fact, 70 percent of the magnesium in your dog's body is in his bones. Magnesium is rarely deficient in complete and balanced diets. However, its absorption can be impaired when the diet is too high in calcium and phosphorus.

Your dog needs sulfur for the synthesis of a variety of components in his body, most notably proteins. Sulfur is also an important constituent of joint fluid and cartilage and, thus, is important for proper joint health.

Trace minerals

Your dog needs only very small amounts of trace minerals in her diet. Trace minerals are found in meat and grains and are provided as a supplement in complete and balanced premium dog foods. A balanced diet is still the best source for all the vitamins and minerals required for optimum health.

The trace minerals include the following:

- ✔ **Iron:** Iron is present in every cell in the body. It is particularly important, along with protein and copper, for the production of red blood cells, which are responsible for transporting oxygen from the lungs to every part of the body. Dogs with iron deficiency develop anemia. But remember, iron is needed in only small amounts, so it is important that you not supplement with iron unless you have a prescription.

- ✔ **Zinc:** Zinc is important in the metabolism of several vitamins, particularly the B vitamins. It is also a component of several enzymes needed for digestion and metabolism, and it promotes healing as well. Your dog needs zinc for proper coat health. Some breeds of dogs, particularly the northern breeds such as Siberian Huskies, appear to have problems with absorption and/or utilization of zinc. These dogs develop poor coats and dry, scaly skin with sores (particularly on the nose and mouth) and stiff joints unless they are supplemented with zinc.

- ✔ **Copper:** Copper is a trace mineral that has many different functions. It is needed for the production of blood and for the proper absorption of iron. It is also involved in the production of *connective tissue* (the cells and extracellular proteins that form the background structure of most tissues) and in healing. Copper is found in fish, liver, and various grains. The amount of copper in a grain is related to the level of copper in the soil where the grain was grown. A copper deficiency can result in anemia and skeletal abnormalities. Some breeds of dogs, such as Bedlington Terriers and Doberman Pinschers, can have a genetic problem that interferes with the metabolism of copper. In these dogs, copper is stored in the liver to toxic levels, resulting in hepatitis.

- ✔ **Iodine:** Iodine is critical for the proper functioning of the thyroid gland, which regulates the body's metabolism and energy levels and promotes growth. Iodine is found in high levels in fish. It is added to most dog foods to make the levels sufficient for canine health.

- ✔ **Selenium:** Selenium works with vitamin E to prevent oxidative damage to cells. It is needed in only minute amounts in the diet. Meats and cereal grains are good sources of selenium. In dogs, an excess of selenium results in death of the heart muscles, as well as damage to the liver and kidney. Deficiency results in degeneration of heart and skeletal muscles.

- ✔ **Manganese:** Manganese is a component of many different enzyme systems in the body. Most important, it activates enzymes that regulate nutrient metabolism. It is found in legumes and whole-grain cereals; animal-based ingredients are not a good source of manganese.

- ✔ **Cobalt:** Cobalt is a part of vitamin B12, which is an essential vitamin. Cobalt does not appear to have any function independent of vitamin B12.

Book II

Dog Nutrition and Health

In addition to these trace minerals, other trace minerals known to be important in laboratory animals but with an unclear role in dogs include molybdenum, cadmium, arsenic, silver, nickel, lead, vanadium, and tin.

As scientists discover more about the nutritional needs of dogs, they are beginning to recognize that our canine companions may need different nutrient levels for optimal health than they need just to prevent deficiencies. Be sure to discuss nutritional questions with your veterinarian — and take a vet's advice over anyone selling dog food, because stores may push the brands that give them a bigger profit margin. And if you have a question about a specific dog food, call the manufacturer.

How dog food is made

How do some cows or chickens and a pile of grains turn into your dog's dinner? First the animals are slaughtered and the body parts not used for human consumption are put into bins according to which parts of the body they do or do not contain. These are either shipped directly to the dog food manufacturer or are rendered and the meal (what remains after the fats are removed) is shipped to the manufacturer. Similarly, either grains or the meal (what remains after the oils have been extracted for use in human foods) may be shipped to the dog food manufacturer. If whole grains are sent, the manufacturer grinds and separates the grains into their different components. For example, wheat may be separated into wheat flour, wheat germ meal, wheat bran, and wheat middlings.

The ingredients are then mixed in proper proportions and added to the *extruder,* a large tube containing a screw that mixes the ingredients with steam and water under pressure, and then squirts out the mixture through holes at the end, like a pasta maker squeezes out spaghetti. A knife cuts the ribbon into small pieces, which are then moved along a conveyor belt through a dryer/cooler until the right amount of moisture remains. The food is then coated with fat, vitamins, and flavorings.

The high temperature at which dry dog foods are processed breaks down proteins and may change their structure and quality. In addition, the heat destroys any enzymes that were in the food components. Vitamins that have been destroyed during processing have to be sprayed back onto the food after it cools. But whether the components that are added back are really the same as those that were present in the unprocessed food components is unclear, and this is why some people prepare foods for their dogs at home. As a trade-off, however, processed dog food is virtually sterile. None of the common bacteria present on beef and poultry, such as *salmonella* and *E. coli,* remain after the food is processed.

Semi-moist foods are not dried as much, and they have more preservatives and sugar added. Canned dog foods are heated but not sent through an extruder. Thus, they tend to retain more of the natural proteins, fats, vitamins, and enzymes.

The Main Types of Dog Food

If you're like most people, when you look at the shelves of dog food in the store, you're bewildered by the choices available: puppy foods and senior foods, foods for large dogs and small dogs, diet foods for pudgy pooches, foods that claim to be all natural, foods that promise to improve your dog's coat, foods that make their own gravy, and foods shaped like little bones.

How can you possibly pick the best food for your furry friend that will give him all the nutrients he needs and help him live a long and healthy life? Worry not. The following sections help you make better choices when buying dog food.

Book II

Dog Nutrition and Health

Many different forms of dog food are available today. *Dry food* usually contains less than 10 percent water, *semi-moist foods* contain 25 to 40 percent water, and canned food contains 75 to 80 percent water.

You may also have heard the terms *premium* or *super-premium* to describe dog foods, but these terms don't have a legal definition — they can be used by anyone. *Premium* is a term frequently used to describe high-quality dog foods generally sold in pet supply stores rather than grocery stores. *Super-premium* generally refers to the highest-quality foods that are prepared using the best ingredients available. Likewise, no legal definitions govern the terms *gourmet* or *natural* when referring to dog food.

Most veterinary nutritionists agree that semi-moist dog foods offer very little nutritional value. These foods contain dyes and other nonessential additives so that they can be shaped into little bones, steaks, or other shapes. The additives may make the food visually appealing to the consumer, but dogs don't care what their food looks like. Semi-moist foods also are preserved with sugar, which contributes to obesity and periodontal disease in dogs.

Avoid foods that don't have complete nutritional information on the label (see the "Reading a Dog Food Label" section of this chapter for more information). Foods that are produced and sold within the same state aren't required to have complete nutritional information the way foods that are sold across state lines are. These foods may be nutritionally sound, but without complete information, you can't be sure. Also steer clear of dog foods that haven't been tested in feeding trials with real live dogs.

Who's in charge around here?

Several watchdog groups oversee various parts of the dog food manufacturing and marketing process. Take a look at this rundown of the regulatory agencies and what they do:

✔ **The Association of American Feed Control Officials (AAFCO):** The AAFCO consists of animal food officials from the United States and Canada who have joined to develop minimum standards for dog foods (and other animal foods as well). The AAFCO publishes standardized nutritional guidelines for dog foods, which most dog food manufacturers use as their nutritional standard. The AAFCO has also established specific guidelines for what should and should not be included on dog food labels. Although the AAFCO does not have any powers mandated by law, reputable dog food companies willingly comply with its guidelines — which allows them to state on their dog food labels that they meet or surpass AAFCO guidelines. Visit its Web site at www.aafco.org.

✔ **Pet Food Institute (PFI):** PFI has been around since 1958 and is the national trade association for pet food manufacturers. It monitors legislation that affects the pet food industry and lobbies for the interests of pet food manufacturers before federal legislative bodies, such as the Food and Drug Administration (FDA), the U.S. Department of Agriculture, the Federal Trade Commission (FTC), the AAFCO, and Congress. As a way of self-policing, PFI has established the Nutrition Assurance Program, which provides specific guidelines for the feeding trials that are used to test the nutritional quality of dog foods. Dog food companies that have complied with these guidelines in their food trials can state on the label that their food provides complete and balanced nutrition according to AAFCO procedures. For more information, visit its Web site at www.petfoodinstitute.org.

✔ **National Research Council (NRC):** The National Research Council's Committee on Animal Nutrition was the first group to establish minimal requirements for canine nutrition. First published in 1974, the minimal requirements are similar to the recommended daily allowances (RDAs) you see on packages of human foods. The NRC requirements for dogs were updated in 2001, based on a comprehensive review of the scientific literature on canine nutrition. The Canine Nutrition Expert Subcommittee of the AAFCO currently recommends that dog foods use its nutrient profiles rather than those of the NRC. However, the NRC provides an important and independent source of information for the consumer on the nutritional requirements of dogs. Access the NRC at www.nas.edu/nrc/.

Reading a Dog Food Label

The first place you need to look when trying to decide on a food for your furry friend is the label on the bag, box, or can. Reading a dog food label isn't very different from reading the one on your cereal box. A certain amount of nutritional information must be included on the label, but a certain amount of leeway exists in how the dog food company presents it.

Divide the label into two parts: the *product display panel* (on the front of the package) and the information panel (usually on the back).

The product display panel

The product display panel is the place where the dog food company hopes to catch your eye. So it makes sense that it appears on the front of the package. You'll typically find a few key pieces of information on the product display panel, primarily the dog food company name, the product identity, the product use (whether it's dog food or cat food, for example), and the net weight of the package. You may also find a banner statement, which is where the dog food company makes claims about the quality of the food.

Product identity

The product identity section states the name of the product, such as Big Bart's Beefy Dinner.

Any terminology regarding the meat or meat flavor used in the product identity statement has to comply with a list of specific definitions. Consider some examples of common phrases and the standards that need to be met before the dog food company can use the phrase:

- **Beef for dogs:** The food must contain 95 percent beef by weight.
- **Beef dog food:** The food must contain 70 percent beef by weight.
- **Beef dinner, beef entrée, or beef platter:** The food must contain 25 percent beef by weight.
- **Dog food with beef:** The food needs to contain only 3 percent beef.
- **Beef-flavored:** The food doesn't need to contain any beef; it just needs to taste like beef (using artificial flavors).

The same rules for terminology apply to any meat source in dog food, such as chicken, lamb, and so on.

Product use

The product use statement just indicates which animal the food is formulated for (dogs or cats, for example).

Net weight

The product display panel includes the net weight of the package contents.

Just as with human foods, dog food manufacturers frequently change the size of containers without changing the price. For example, a can that looks to be a standard 6-ounce size may actually contain 5.5 ounces, but at the same price. Be sure to read the label carefully.

Banner statement

The front of the package may also have a *banner statement,* which is where the manufacturer makes specific claims about the dog food. The AAFCO regulates the content of banner statements. For example, if a label says that dogs prefer the taste of that food, it must also tell you what other dog foods were tested to arrive at that conclusion. An example of a correctly worded statement regarding preferred taste would be, "Preferred by dogs over the leading premium brand."

Rules also govern what defines a *light/lite, low-calorie,* or *less fat* dog food. If a manufacturer states that its food is *light* or *low-calorie,* that food must have 15 percent fewer calories than the average of other dog foods in the same category. If the manufacturer claims that a certain dog food has *less* of a component, the claim must state how much less and tell the consumer less than what. For example, a dog food claiming to have *less fat* must state the percentage reduction in fat (on the basis of weight, not volume) and must state that this is less fat than other dog foods in the same category (dry, semi-moist, or canned, for example).

Dog foods using the terms *lean* or *low-fat* must meet yet another set of standards. They must have a maximum fat content that is 30 percent less than the industry average for dog foods. In addition to the required statement listing the minimum amount of fat in the food (see the "Guaranteed analysis" section later in this chapter), these foods must state the maximum amount of fat, because these diets are used for weight loss.

The information panel

The information panel is where the manufacturer tells you the nitty-gritty details of what's in the food. You'll usually find it on the back of the package. The information panel should provide a guaranteed analysis of what's in the food, an ingredients list, a nutritional adequacy statement, feeding guidelines, and the manufacturer's contact information.

Guaranteed analysis

Legally, dog food labels are required to state only the minimum levels of protein and fat and the maximum levels of moisture and fiber in the food. These are only minimums and maximums, so keep in mind that the dog food may have more than the minimum amounts or less than the maximum amounts of components stated on the label.

If your dog is ill, small differences in the amount of these important nutrients may make a difference in her health. If you have any questions about your dog's food and whether you're giving her what she needs, talk with your vet.

The AAFCO nutrient profiles for dog foods let you know the minimum requirements for protein and fat for both adult dogs and puppies. But the AAFCO protein and fat levels are listed on a dry-weight basis, whereas the proteins and fats on a dog food label are listed on an as-is basis, which includes water. This difference can lead to some confusion when you try to determine whether a given dog food has the levels of nutrients your dog needs. It can also be confusing when you compare one dog food to another, because each dog food may have a different level of moisture (which affects how much of the nutrient is actually there on a dry-weight basis).

To make accurate comparisons between two foods, you need to do some math, so get out your calculator and follow these steps (protein is the example, but you can do the same equation for other nutrients as well):

1. **Find the percentage of protein in the dog food.**

2. **Find the percentage of moisture in the dog food.**

3. **Subtract the percentage of moisture from 100 to get the percentage of dry.**

4. **Divide the number from Step 1 by the number in Step 3 and multiply by 100.**

   This gives you the percentage of protein on a dry-weight basis.

For example, if you're looking at the label of a dry dog food (see Figure 1-2) and it says that the food contains 26 percent protein and 10 percent moisture, subtract that 10 percent moisture from 100, which gives you 90 percent dry. Then divide the 26 percent protein by 90 percent dry and multiply by 100; you get 29 percent protein on a dry-weight basis.

Book II

Dog Nutrition and Health

Figure 1-2:
A dog food label can tell you how much protein is in there, but you need to do a little math.

Ingredients: Chicken, Corn Meal, Chicken By-Product Meal, Ground Grain Sorghum, Ground Whole Grain Barley, Chicken Meal, Chicken Fat (preserved with mixed Tocopherols, a source of Vitamin E, and Citric Acid), Dried Beet Pulp (sugar removed), Natural Chicken Flavor, Dried Egg Product, Brewers Dried Yeast, Potassium Chloride, Salt, Choline Chloride, Calcium Carbonate, DL-Methionine, Ferrous Sulfate, Vitamin E Supplement, Zinc Oxide, Ascorbic Acid (source of Vitamin C), Dicalcium Phosphate, Manganese Sulfate, Copper Sulfate, Manganese Oxide, Vitamin B_{12} Supplement, Vitamin A Acetate, Calcium Pantothenate, Biotin, Lecithin, Rosemary Extract, Thiamine Mononitrate (source of Vitamin B_1), Niacin, Riboflavin Supplement (source of Vitamin B_2), Pyridoxine Hydrochloride (source of Vitamin B_6), Inositol, Vitamin D_3 Supplement, Potassium Iodide, Folic Acid, Cobalt Carbonate.

Guaranteed Analysis:
Crude Protein not less than 26.0%
Crude Fat not less than 14.0%
Crude Fiber not more than................. 4.0%
Moisture not more than 10.0%

Animal feeding tests using Association of American Feed Control Official's procedures substantiate that this product provides complete and balanced nutrition for adult dogs.

If you're looking at the label of a canned dog food, the formula is exactly the same, but you'll find significantly different results. If the label says that the food contains 9 percent protein and 80 percent moisture, subtract that 80 percent moisture from 100, to get 20 percent dry. Then divide the 9 percent protein by 20 percent dry and multiply by 100; you get 45 percent protein on a dry-weight basis.

So what does all this math tell you? If you just compared the labels of the food, you would have thought that the dry food had more protein (because the dry food label said the food contained 26 percent protein and the canned food contained only 9 percent). But when you do the math, you discover that the canned food actually has 45 percent protein (on a dry-weight basis), compared to 29 percent in the dry food.

If all this math seems to be more trouble than it's worth, here's a quick rule of thumb to help you compare dry and canned foods. For a dry food, to determine the level of protein, fat, or fiber on a dry-weight basis, add 10 percent to the level that is listed on the label. For a canned food, multiply the amount of protein, fat, or fiber by four. This timesaving tip makes it easier to compare while you're standing in the store aisle.

As this exercise shows, canned foods typically have much more protein than dry foods. A major reason for this is that grains are needed in dry foods to help them hold their shape after extrusion. Canned and dry foods made by the same manufacturer usually have very different percentages of protein.

Ingredients list

Dog food manufacturers are required to list the ingredients in each dog food in descending order by amount, on a dry-weight basis (refer to Figure 1-2 for an example). The label must list every ingredient. A dog food company can actually have a grain as the most abundant ingredient in its food while making it *look* like the most abundant ingredient is a meat. Take a look at how they do it: Say that the Chow Hound dog food company is making dog food using wheat as the main ingredient and poultry byproduct meal as its second-most-common ingredient. Instead of just listing *wheat,* the company can break down wheat so that it's listed on the label as *wheat flour, wheat germ meal, wheat bran,* and *wheat middlings.* This allows the company to list *poultry byproduct meal* first, because the food has more poultry by-product than it does wheat flour, wheat germ meal, wheat bran, or wheat middlings. The four wheat ingredients can be put lower on the list, making the wheat seem like a less important and less abundant ingredient. Scan down the list of ingredients, and if the second, third, fourth, and fifth ingredients on the list are all something other than meat, your dog may be getting more of that than meat.

In general, a good-quality dog food has two quality animal protein sources listed in the first few ingredients. Look for a food that also has two different sources of fat in the ingredients list, for adequate energy and to provide all essential fatty acids (see earlier in this chapter for more on fats).

Dog food companies frequently change the composition of their dog foods, so the label on the food you purchased yesterday may not be the same today. Keep the ingredients list from your current dog food label in your wallet and periodically check it against the labels on the dog foods you're buying, just to make sure that you're buying what you thought you were.

Vocabulary 101

If you're confused by some of the lingo on dog food bags, you're not alone. Some of the definitions for the food terms you'll see in the ingredients list include the following:

- **Animal byproduct meal:** Rendered animal tissues that don't fit any of the other ingredient definitions. It still can't contain hair, horns, hoofs, hide trimmings, manure, or intestinal contents or extraneous materials.

- **Byproducts:** Non-human-grade proteins obtained from animal carcasses. They can vary greatly in their digestibility, and the consumer has no way to determine their digestibility.

- **Meat:** The clean flesh of slaughtered cattle, swine, sheep, or goats. It must come from muscle, tongue, diaphragm, heart, or esophagus.

- **Meat and bone meal:** Rendered mammal tissues, including bone. Other than that, it is similar to meat meal.

- **Meat byproducts:** Fresh, nonrendered, clean parts of slaughtered mammals. It does not include meat but does include lungs, spleens, kidneys, brains, livers, blood, bones, fat, stomachs, and intestines. It cannot include hair, horns, teeth, or hoofs.

- **Meat meal:** A rendered meal made from animal tissues. It cannot contain blood, hair, hoofs, horns, hide trimmings, manure, or intestinal contents or extraneous materials. It may not contain more than 14 percent indigestible materials. Lamb meal is made from lamb parts. Meat meal is made from cattle, swine, sheep, or goats.

- **Poultry (or chicken or turkey) byproduct meal:** Ground, rendered, clean parts of the carcass of slaughtered poultry, such as necks, feet, undeveloped eggs, and intestines. It cannot contain beaks or feathers.

- **Poultry (or chicken or turkey) byproducts:** Nonrendered clean parts of slaughtered poultry, such as heads, feet, and guts. It must not contain feces or foreign matter.

TECHNICAL STUFF

Preservatives and antioxidants in your dog's food

Antioxidants are preservatives that are added to foods to help protect the fats, oils, and fat-soluble compounds such as vitamins from breaking down. Unsaturated fats readily mix with oxygen in the air and become rancid. Rancid fats are not just a problem because they smell bad; they also cause the food to lose its flavor and texture. More important, rancid fats can affect a dog's health. When a dog eats rancid fats, he may end up suffering from a relative deficiency of vitamin E, a natural antioxidant that the body uses to combat rancid fat.

Because all dog foods contain *some* unsaturated fats, they all require some sort of antioxidant preservative. Many foods are preserved with preservatives, including BHA, BHT, and ethoxyquin. Ethoxyquin has been especially controversial, because concerns arose that it caused cancer. However, studies in dogs and puppies have not shown an increase in cancer from ethoxyquin. Still, due to consumer preferences for natural ingredients, most dog foods are now preserved with vitamin E and

vitamin C. Ironically, the vitamin E and vitamin C that are used in dog food are man made, too — so they're not exactly "natural."

If you're feeding a dog food that has been preserved with vitamins E and C, be sure that the food is less than six months old when you give it to your dog. Most manufacturers use a production code that indicates the date and even time when the food was made, along with the plant that manufactured it. Others use a *best used by* code, which indicates the time by which the food should be consumed. To determine how fresh your dog's food is, call the manufacturer and ask them to explain their code. They will tell you what each number and letter means.

Finally, a food's antioxidant powers are depleted more rapidly during hot, humid weather, so in the warm summer months, use food that is less than six months old. Always store your dog's food in a cool, dry place, and don't buy more than a month's supply at a time.

Nutritional adequacy statement

Dog food manufacturers can determine the nutritional adequacy of dog foods in two ways. The best way is for the dog food manufacturer to conduct *feeding trials,* in which it feeds its foods to real, live dogs and sees whether they like to eat it, whether they gain weight at the proper rate, and whether their blood and bodies have the right composition of proteins and fats. AAFCO requirements state that dogs in feeding trials must be fed the dog food for at least six months. If a dog food has been tested in feeding trials, the label will say so, usually in a statement like, "Animal feeding tests using Association of American Feed Control Officials' procedures substantiate that this food provides complete and balanced nutrition for maintenance." Try to choose a food that makes this kind of claim on its package.

Dog food manufacturers can also sell dog foods that have been formulated according to the AAFCO nutritional profiles for dogs but have not been tested on dogs in feeding trials. To make a formulated food, the manufacturer adds an amount of protein that is at least 18 percent for adult dogs, an amount of fat that is at least 5 percent for adult dogs, and the required amounts of all the other required nutrients. If you feed your dog a food that has been formulated but not tested on dogs, your dog essentially becomes the test subject. Examples abound of formulated dog foods that looked good on paper but, when fed to dogs, resulted in nutritional deficiencies. Stay away from foods that have not been tested in dogs.

However, the regulations regarding feeding trials for dogs have a loophole. After a dog food manufacturer has proven by feeding trials that a given food is nutritionally adequate, the manufacturer may state that formulated foods have been tested by feeding trials, as long as the formulated foods are in the same *family*. Unfortunately, no guidelines spell out the definition of a *family* of dog foods. We are left to trust the manufacturer's word.

Feeding guidelines

Every dog food label must have recommendations regarding how much to feed dogs of different sizes. However, the feeding guidelines on the label usually *overestimate* the amount of food a typical dog needs to eat every day. Cynics say that this is a ploy the dog food manufacturers use to sell more food. The dog food manufacturers indicate that these guidelines are based on calculations of what typical dogs in their feeding trials needed to satisfy their energy requirements. The dogs in these feeding trials are unaltered (not spayed or neutered) and get a great deal of exercise, and few dogs fit the same mold; most need much less food than the amount listed on the bag. (For more information, see the section "Figuring Out How Much to Feed Your Dog" later in this chapter.)

Manufacturer's contact information

Manufacturers are required to list the address and telephone number of their customer service departments on every dog food label. In addition, many dog foods now also provide Web site addresses.

The customer service departments of dog food manufacturers are usually very helpful. If they don't know the answer to a question, they will hunt it down and call you back. If you call a company and they can't or won't provide the information that you need, don't feed that food to your dog.

Book II

Dog Nutrition and Health

Figuring Out How Much to Feed Your Dog

How do you decide how much food to put in the bowl? If you're just starting to feed a new food, and the label tells you how many calories the food contains, you may want to start with the information in Table 1-2, which lists the calorie requirements of dogs depending on the dog's weight and activity level. For the purposes of the table, an *inactive* dog is one who rarely gets more than a jaunt around the yard, a *moderately active* dog is one who gets 15 to 30 minutes of continuous exercise every day, and a *highly active* dog is one who gets at least several hours of exercise every day.

If the label doesn't provide information on the caloric content of the food, you have to use the manufacturer's recommendations as a starting point. Start by feeding 25 percent *less* than the manufacturer recommends and then increase or decrease the amount as necessary.

Table 1-2	Caloric Requirements of Dogs		
	Caloric Requirements (Based on Activity Level)[1]		
Dog's Weight (In Pounds)	*Inactive*	*Moderately Active*	*Highly Active*
10	234	303	441
20	373	483	702
30	489	633	921
40	593	768	1117
50	689	892	1297
60	779	1008	1466
70	863	1117	1625
80	944	1222	1777
90	1022	1322	1923
100	1097	1419	2064

[1]*Figures represent the average number of calories required daily to maintain the dog's weight.*

The figures in Table 1-2 include treats and snacks.

As dogs exercise more, they need more calories to maintain their weight. But as dogs get larger, they require relatively fewer calories to maintain their weight. This is because larger dogs generally have slower metabolisms than smaller dogs. Age can affect caloric requirements, too. As a dog goes from 1 to 7 years of age, her energy requirements drop by an incredible 24 percent.

Dogs' metabolisms vary so greatly that the best way to know exactly how many calories your dog needs each day is by trial and error. Feed the amount of food that will maintain your dog's weight. If she loses weight, feed more. If she gains, feed less.

Choosing the Best Food for Your Dog

How do you make that final decision? As a general rule, start by feeding a name-brand, good-quality, commercial balanced diet that has been tested by feeding trials in dogs. Put more trust in companies that have been around a while, because they have their own internal quality controls in addition to those imposed by the regulatory agencies.

Sorry, but the best-quality foods are not the cheapest. However, the reverse isn't necessarily true: Paying a lot for your dog food doesn't *guarantee* its quality. As you search for the best food, don't hesitate to experiment. Be a good observer. Talk to your veterinarian and other dog people, such as your breeder. Over time, you will gather more information and be able to make better decisions based on fact as well as experience.

When you have selected a quality food for your furry friend, your job isn't done. You still need to keep close track of your dog's response to the food. Watch his body condition. Your canine companion should maintain a correct weight on his new food. If he gains some weight but looks and acts healthy and full of energy, it may be that the nutrients in the new food are more digestible than those of the previous food, so you don't need to feed as much. If your dog loses weight on his new food, start looking for another. Your dog's coat should grow and glisten on his new food, and his skin should be pink and supple, with no sores. A dog's coat is often a reflection of his general health, although it isn't the only monitor to use. For example, during the spring in temperate climates, most dogs' coats look dry as they shed their heavy winter garb for a lighter spring coat.

One of the best criteria you can use to monitor your dog on a new food is to observe his stools. Stool quality is determined by the ingredients in the food, the relative amounts of different ingredients, the type and amount of fiber, and the digestibility of the ingredients. Small, firm stools indicate a food that is highly digestible. However, your dog should not be constipated or straining to defecate. Large stools, particularly if they are somewhat loose, may indicate a food with less digestible nutrients and/or a high fiber content. Your dog's stools will vary from day to day. But if your dog often has small, hard stools, consider changing to another food. Those stools may be easy to pick up, but they may also mean that your dog is chronically constipated.

Monitor your dog's attitude and energy level. If you feed your dog a good-quality food, he will have lots of get-up-and-go. He will have the energy and endurance to play all you want. Most of all, he will have that joy for life that we all appreciate in our canine companions.

What's the best dog food for your dollar? Most people find that they save money by buying good-quality, premium foods for their dogs — the kind of food sold at pet supply stores rather than grocery stores. This is because dogs need to eat much less of a good-quality food to take in their required nutrients. In addition, dogs on high-quality foods probably have fewer health problems, and when they do, they heal faster. The icing on the cake is easier cleanup in the yard.

Paying Attention to How You Feed Your Dog

Many people *free-feed* their dogs, which is the practice of keeping a dog's bowl full and letting him eat whenever he wants. Although this may seem like an easy approach to feeding, free-feeding isn't a good idea, for many reasons:

✔ **Dogs who are free-fed are more likely to be overweight.** This may not have been true in the past, but with today's highly palatable foods, your dog will enjoy eating long past the point at which she's full. She will likely take in more calories than she needs and carry the fat to prove it.

✔ **You can't tell exactly how much your dog is eating.** In fact, you may not recognize that your dog is ill until you suddenly notice you haven't been adding much food to her bowl in the past few days. Food intake is one of the best indicators of health, so you should always be in a position to monitor your dog's intake accurately.

✔ **Medicating dogs who are free-fed is more difficult.** If you have to give your dog pills, such as heartworm preventive, and your dog is free-fed, you will have to make sure that you pop it down her throat and she swallows it. However, if she gets fed two square meals a day, you can just add the pill to her food and it will go right down the hatch!

✔ **Free-feeding is difficult in multidog households.** Frequently, one dog hogs the food and gains weight, while the other dog is deprived of the food and loses weight. Plus, free-feeding is impossible if your dogs require different kinds of food.

So how many times a day should you feed your dog? Feed puppies four times a day until they are 3 months of age, when you can move them to feedings three times a day. At 6 months of age, dogs can be fed twice a day, and this is probably the best feeding schedule for a dog to stay on for life. Some dogs are fed just once a day and get along fine. Occasionally, however, dogs who are fed once a day vomit a little fluid or bile 12 to 18 hours after their last meal. If they are fed twice a day, this problem goes away.

Book II

Dog Nutrition and Health

No two dogs are exactly the same. They have different metabolic rates, they have different metabolisms, and they may need to eat different diets. If you have more than one dog, it may be more convenient to feed all your dogs the same food, but make sure that you monitor each dog's response to the diet you are feeding and change the food if an individual dog needs it.

Give your dog a quiet place to eat. If other dogs live in the house, don't feed them from the same bowl. Feed them at a distance from each other so they don't feel threatened that the other dog will steal their food. The best solution is to feed your dog in a crate so she can enjoy his meal in the privacy of her den. When you put the bowl down, give your dog 15 minutes to eat. If she hasn't finished in that time, either you are feeding her too much or she isn't motivated to eat. By removing the bowl, you can be assured that she will be much more motivated to eat at the next meal. Don't be held hostage by a picky dog. If you try to encourage her to eat by talking nicely to her and giving her delectable treats, she will soon up the ante, demanding better and better treats until she's not consuming her dog food at all.

Many veterinary nutritionists believe that we should be rotating our dogs' diets — feeding them one food for three to six months, and then switching to another diet. They theorize that abnormal proteins may be formed during the processing of food or that individual foods may have undetectable deficiencies or small differences in the availability of certain nutrients. By rotating your dog to a new food every three to six months, you prevent too much exposure to the abnormality in any given food.

People food is okay in small amounts

Giving your dog fresh vegetables and even some fresh fruit on a regular basis is a good idea. Wolves (from which our dogs are descended) eat the greens and grains from their prey's stomach, and also eat grasses and berries at times. Dogs enjoy fresh vegetables and benefit from the vitamins and fiber they provide. The only vegetable to stay away from is raw onions (some say cooked onions are fine, but some say they aren't).

Feed your dog the leftovers from your preparations for dinner, in addition to other vegetables, especially the meats and vegetables. That way,

both you and your dog benefit. Just make sure that vegetables aren't the major component of your dog's food.

If you give the vegetables in large pieces, they provide mostly fiber because dogs don't have the enzymes to digest *cellulose,* the major component of the cell walls of plants. However, if you put the vegetables through a juicer or a super-blender that breaks down the cell walls and turns the vegetables to mush, your dog will also benefit from the nutritional content of the vegetable.

Organic Options for Feeding Your Dog

Maybe you're going organic with your own diet. Or your dog suffers from allergies and you've heard organic food may help. Perhaps you just want your dog to eat as well as you do. Whatever your reason for exploring organic options for your dog, you're wise to do a bit of research before making a switch. Of course, as with any decision related to diet and your dog's health, check with your veterinarian before making any changes.

Sales of organic dog foods — foods grown without pesticides, preservatives, hormones, and antibiotics — are on the rise, up 48 percent from 2007 to 2008, according to the Organic Trade Association, which monitors organic market trends. Though organics still make up only a small fraction of domestic pet food sales, eco-conscious consumers are finding it easier to purchase the products they need. You can find brands such as Newman's Own Organics and Natura Pet Products in many pet supply stores.

Often the reason behind a switch to organic begins with some sort of health issue. Skin conditions and allergies can be especially troublesome for some breeds. When sprays, dips, shampoos, medications, and even dietary changes don't work, some owners turn to organic foods for success. Organic foods are free from the artificial dyes and chemical additives that can trigger a dog's allergies.

Food for thought: Organic versus natural

Deciphering food labels can feel like a chore, but it's a chore worth doing when you're serious about good health. A particularly confusing labeling distinction — and one that applies to food for humans and canines alike — is the one between *organic* and *natural.* Don't be misled — organic and natural are not the same. Organic foods must be certified as organic by the U.S. Department of Agriculture — that is, produced and processed without chemical pesticides, synthetic fertilizers, hormones, and antibiotics. Although natural foods are free of food coloring and chemical additives, they are not organic. So although natural foods have some benefits, they are not held to the same higher standard as organic foods.

In more serious cases, owners of dogs with cancer switch to packaged organic foods (kibble, canned food, treats), believing that organic food may give a sick dog ammunition for fighting the disease. Some people go as far as cooking meals for their dogs, although a veterinarian should first approve this type of diet.

So what are some advantages and disadvantages of organic dog foods? Take a look. As for the advantages, organic dog food

- ✔ Is produced without chemicals, steroids, or artificial colors and flavors.
- ✔ Contains better grades of grains and proteins to help with digestive issues such as gas or diarrhea.
- ✔ Has no bulk fillers, making food easier to digest. It may also help manage weight.
- ✔ May help with allergies and skin ailments.
- ✔ May help boost immunity, helping your dog ward off ailments.

Disadvantages include the following: Organic dog food

- ✔ Isn't as widely distributed as conventional dog food.
- ✔ Is more expensive than nonorganic dog food. (The same situation is true of organic food for humans.)
- ✔ Has not been proven through scientific evidence to help your dog live a longer or healthier life.

Weigh these pros and cons, and think about what is best for your dog.

Chapter 2

Vaccinations and Common Health Issues

In This Chapter

▶ Keeping your dog safe from viruses, bacteria, and parasites

▶ Protecting yourself and your family from the bugs that like your dog

Scientists know of millions of species of viruses, bacteria, fungi, and parasites — and they discover new ones every day. Although this chapter discusses bugs that are problematic to dogs, most microorganisms don't cause disease. They live in the soil and infect plants, animals, and even humans, but you can't even tell they're there unless you look.

In fact, microscopic critters are an important part of the circle of life. Without bacteria and fungi to decompose organic matter, humans would long ago have been buried in debris. Without the bacteria that digest plant material in the stomachs of cows, you'd have no milk or beef. Without the bacteria that inhabit your body, you would soon die of infection. Yes, ironically, beneficial bacteria even protect you from infection by their nasty relatives.

The bugs discussed in this chapter are the rare ones that infect dogs and cause *systemic diseases* (ones that affect the entire body).

Vaccinating against Viruses

Viruses are the smallest bugs scientists know of. You can fit 25 million viruses on the period at the end of this sentence. Viruses must grow inside a host cell; they can't replicate on their own. Although this fact may seem like it would be a disadvantage to a virus, it's exactly what makes viral infections so hard to fight. After all, how do you kill a virus that's living in a cell without killing the cell itself? Because of this problem, very few drugs effectively treat viral infections, and many of the existing antiviral drugs are quite toxic.

The key to fighting a viral infection, therefore, is to make sure that your dog never gets infected, and the best way to accomplish this is to vaccinate him. Most of the vaccines given to dogs are designed to prevent viral infections: rabies, distemper, parvovirus, parainfluenza, and adenovirus (and kennel cough, though that can also be caused by bacteria). The following sections provide a little bit of information about the worst of the bad bugs. When you know what they can do to your furry friend, you'll never want to get behind on his vaccinations. As always, talk to your vet about which vaccinations your dog may benefit from.

Rabies

This viral infection is the most important infectious agent that you should vaccinate your dog against. Rabies vaccinations are so important, in fact, that in North America, it is illegal to have a dog who is not vaccinated for rabies. In most states, a dog who has bitten a person and is not vaccinated for rabies can be impounded and perhaps destroyed. Why does the government care whether your dog gets rabies? It's simple: Rabies can be transmitted to humans by the saliva of an infected dog, through either a bite wound or a cut. When a person becomes ill with rabies, it is generally fatal if not treated within two weeks of the injury.

If you want to see the incredible (and justified) fear people had of rabid dogs in the days before the rabies vaccine was developed, watch the film *To Kill a Mockingbird*. In that movie, a rabid dog stumbles down a residential street while people hide in their homes, watching it and hoping that someone will have the courage to confront the dog and shoot it.

Rabies usually infects an animal (or human) through a wound such as a bite. When the virus enters the body, it moves to a nerve and then travels up the nerve to the spinal cord and brain, where the virus replicates and kills brain cells. The victim then begins to act in bizarre ways: Dogs may become very hyperactive and aggressive, or they may become weak and unresponsive. Death occurs in days, weeks, or months, depending on how far the virus has to travel through an animal to get to the central nervous system.

Luckily, vaccination of dogs against rabies is virtually 100 percent effective, and humans can share home and hearth with their canine companions without concern. Rarely anyone in a developed country contracts rabies today. However, in less developed countries, such as India, 50,000 people (mainly children) still die every year from rabies.

Puppies should be vaccinated against rabies for the first time after 12 weeks of age and then again at 1 year of age. After that, they should be vaccinated yearly or every three years, depending on state laws and the type of vaccine used. When your dog is vaccinated, you receive a vaccination certificate and a rabies tag. Always make sure that your dog wears her rabies tag, and keep the rabies vaccination certificate in a safe place where you can easily find it. If your dog escapes and bites someone, her rabies tag (and your vaccination certificate) will provide proof to animal control officers, veterinarians, and physicians that the dog was vaccinated. This documentation will prevent the unfortunate person from having to undergo *post-exposure prophylaxis,* a series of rabies shots designed to stop the virus in its path through the body to the brain.

Many species of wild animals throughout North America can live normal lives while being infected with rabies. The most common species are foxes, raccoons, skunks, and bats, but other animals can be infected, too. In many species, including skunks and raccoons, the virus can be present at high levels in the saliva and blood without even causing the animal to become ill. For this reason, it is never a good idea to keep these wild animals as pets; in some states and provinces, doing so is illegal. The risk of exposing humans to rabies is just too high.

Never touch a dog, cat, or any wild animal who is staggering, acting aggressively, or otherwise behaving bizarrely. If such an animal bites you — or if *any* animal you don't know bites you — get medical attention immediately. Never touch a wild animal that approaches you. Wild animals should have a natural fear of humans. If they don't, it may be because they are suffering from rabies.

Book II

Dog Nutrition and Health

Canine parvovirus

Canine parvovirus enteritis was first identified in the late 1970s, when it swept through dog populations worldwide, killing thousands. The veterinary community worked tirelessly to determine the most effective ways to treat the condition, identify the virus, and produce a vaccine. An effective vaccine was developed and put into use within three years, quickly reducing the number of deaths.

Parvovirus attacks and kills the cells that line the small intestine. As a result, the dog cannot absorb the fluids in the intestine and the dog develops diarrhea, often with blood. Dogs with parvovirus often vomit because of the upset in their digestion. Some people say that they can smell a particular odor in parvovirus-infected puppies. Mildly affected dogs may recover in a few days, but severely affected dogs become depressed and dehydrated, and can die within a day or two. The severity of the parvovirus infection depends on the dog's immunity to the virus. Dogs with inadequate immunity, especially puppies, still continue to die of parvovirus enteritis despite treatment. If your dog has diarrhea for more than 24 hours or has diarrhea with blood in the stool, seek veterinary attention.

Unfortunately, parvovirus is here to stay and continues to kill puppies who have not been vaccinated. Worse, vaccinated puppies may still contract parvovirus even if they *are* vaccinated while they still have antibodies that they obtained from their mother's milk. Although every puppy gets antibodies in milk, and these antibodies are important to protect the puppy from infectious disease while the pup is very young, these maternal antibodies can also interfere with vaccination by neutralizing the viral proteins that are inoculated during the vaccination. Because puppies lose their maternal antibodies at different rates, it is difficult to know whether a young puppy still retains maternal antibodies at the time he's vaccinated. For this reason, vaccinating puppies against parvovirus several times during puppyhood is critical. The hope is that if maternal antibodies neutralized the first vaccine, the next vaccination will have the desired effect of stimulating the puppy to make his own antibodies.

Puppies should receive their first vaccinations against parvovirus at 5 to 7 weeks of age. They then should receive booster shots every three to four weeks until they have had at least three shots. Your veterinarian will provide you with a schedule for your puppy's vaccinations. Stick to the schedule as closely as possible. The virus is very stable in the environment and can survive for months on inanimate objects such as clothing and floors, making it even more important to vaccinate your dog against this virus.

Kennel cough

Kennel cough got its moniker for obvious reasons: Dogs commonly contract it from other dogs in kennels, and it causes coughing. Some vets are beginning to prefer the term canine cough, as your dog doesn't have to be in a kennel to contract it.

Kennel cough, also called *infectious tracheobronchitis,* can be caused by a single virus or a combination of viruses, particularly canine adenovirus-2 and canine parainfluenza virus. A bacterium called *Bordatella bronchiseptica* also can cause kennel cough alone or in combination with one or more of the viruses. Sometimes the viral infection impairs the normal defense systems of the lung, allowing bacteria to enter the lung, replicate, and cause pneumonia.

Dogs infected with kennel cough have a dry, hacking cough that often has a honking sound. At the end of a series of coughs, the dog may gag or retch so severely that it seems as if the dog will vomit. Indeed, sometimes the dog brings up a little frothy material at the end of the cough. The coughing worsens if the dog is exercised or becomes excited. Dogs may also have a watery discharge from the nose or eyes. Kennel cough itself lasts from seven to ten days, and dogs recover without treatment. If a dog contracts a secondary bacterial pneumonia, however, the results can be much more serious and, without treatment, can result in death.

The infection is highly transmissible between dogs and can spread like wildfire through dogs in a kennel or at a dog show (hence the *kennel* part of its name). Dogs are infectious before they show signs of coughing, and sometimes even after they have recovered, so it is hard to prevent transmission.

Book II

Dog Nutrition and Health

The best prevention for kennel cough is vaccination. Because several agents can cause this infection, vaccination is not foolproof, but vaccinated dogs who do become infected usually have milder symptoms. The most effective vaccination protects against parainfluenza virus and Bordatella, and is instilled into the nose of the dog. This vaccine consists of a live virus that has been modified so that it cannot cause severe disease. It can, however, cause a mild cough for a few days after vaccination, and can even be transmitted to other dogs during that time. Because of these side effects, however mild, most veterinarians suggest vaccination only for dogs who are at high risk for infection. This category includes dogs who regularly go to dog shows, are boarded at kennels, attend doggie daycare, or commonly have contact with other dogs.

If your dog has a persistent hacking cough for more than 24 hours, call your veterinarian instead of going to the clinic. The doctor then can decide over the telephone whether you should come to the clinic and risk transmitting this highly contagious infection to other dogs in the waiting room or hospital. If he decides it is a case of kennel cough, he may want to examine the dog, prescribe some cough suppressants, and advise you to have your coughing canine rest for seven to ten days until she is better. If your dog is not eating or is lethargic, she may have a secondary bacterial infection. Your veterinarian will want to examine her and will probably prescribe antibiotics or an injection and other supportive care.

Some evidence suggests that Bordatella can be transmitted from dogs to immunosuppressed individuals, such as people who are taking immuno-suppressive drugs after transplants or to fight cancer, or people suffering from AIDS. Keeping coughing dogs away from these individuals is probably best.

Distemper

Distemper is a vaccination success story. Once the scourge of the pooch population, now most people have never heard of a dog actually having this infection, because vaccination programs have been highly successful in reducing the incidence of the disease.

The canine distemper virus is particularly wily. The first thing it does after entering the body is spread in the blood to all the lymph nodes and kill the lymphocytes that reside there. *Lymphocytes* are the major cells for antiviral defense, so the infected dog becomes severely immunosuppressed (and at risk for many other illnesses). This action allows the virus to replicate in the lungs (and cause pneumonia) and the gastrointestinal tract (and cause diarrhea and dehydration), and even to enter the brain (and cause encephalitis, paralysis, and seizures). In addition, because the virus causes immuno-suppression, infected dogs frequently contract secondary bacterial and parasitic infections that can also be life threatening.

The first signs of distemper may be a discharge from the eyes accompanied by a fever. The dog may also be coughing, exhibit weight loss, suffer from diarrhea, and lack interest in food. The signs of distemper are so varied that any young puppy who is sick should be taken to the veterinarian for a definitive diagnosis. About 50 percent of adult dogs and 80 percent of puppies who contract distemper die, and dogs who do recover often retain lifelong debilitations such as seizures, blindness, and lameness.

As with most viral infections, treatment for distemper is limited. With supportive care, some dogs can pull through, but the key to beating this disease is to prevent infection by vaccination. Inoculating puppies when they are still very young is important and effective.

Battling Bacteria

Bacteria are veritable giants in comparison to viruses. You can fit only 25,000 bacteria (as compared to 25 million viruses) on the period at the end of this sentence. Bacteria differ from viruses, in that they can live on their own and don't need a host cell to replicate.

Bacteria live in the soil, in plants, and in animals — including you. Although most species of bacteria are beneficial — or, at least, cause no harm — the following sections discuss a couple problems caused by some nasty bacteria.

Lyme disease

Lyme disease is a tick-borne bacterial disease that was first recognized in humans in Lyme, Connecticut, in 1975 and in dogs in 1984. The Lyme disease bacterium is transmitted to your dog by the tiny deer tick (shown in Figure 2-1) and probably, although less commonly, by other species of ticks, too. Deer ticks live on white-tailed deer and white-footed mice in the wild. They are very small — no larger than the head of a pin — making them hard to see, especially in a dog's thick coat. A dog's greatest chance of becoming infected is from May to September, when the ticks are most active, but transmission can also occur at other times. Up to 40 percent of the deer ticks in the northeast, mid-Atlantic, north-central and Pacific coast of the United States contain the bacterium that causes Lyme disease.

Book II

Dog Nutrition and Health

Figure 2-1: Left to right: a nymph (young tick) before it has attached, an engorged nymph, an adult before attaching, and an engorged adult deer tick. All can transmit Lyme disease.

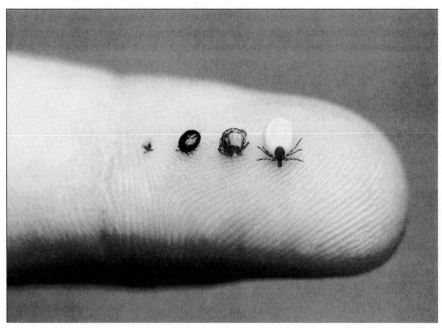

Photograph courtesy of Fred Dubbs

Although many dogs get infected with the Lyme bacterium, only a few develop Lyme disease. Typical acute infection results in swollen joints, lameness, and muscle pain. However, the bacterium can also cause vague symptoms such as fever, loss of appetite, and lethargy, which can make infection difficult to diagnose in a timely fashion.

If your dog is suddenly lame without evidence of trauma; has a hot, swollen joint; or has a fever, especially if you know he was recently bitten by a tick, take him to the veterinarian. The vet will perform a complete physical examination and will take blood to be tested for antibodies to the Lyme bacterium.

If Lyme disease is undiagnosed or left untreated, permanent damage to the joints can occur, and the bacterium also can spread to the heart and kidneys. Infected dogs should be treated with appropriate antibiotics as soon as possible.

Prevention of Lyme disease requires a two-pronged attack. Vaccines are available to protect your dog from infection. The vaccine is unique because it actually kills the bacterium inside the tick before it ever gets a chance to enter your dog. However, as with all vaccinations, side effects may result, so discuss the pros and cons of vaccination with your veterinarian. Vaccination probably is a good idea for dogs who live in areas where Lyme disease is more common and for dogs who are frequently outdoors, like the one shown in Figure 2-2.

Figure 2-2:
Dogs who work or play outdoors are exposed to ticks and are at higher risk for contracting tick-borne infections such as Lyme disease.

The second part of your Lyme disease prevention plan is to try to ensure that your dog doesn't become exposed to the Lyme bacillus. Apply a product that repels ticks before your dog goes out for an adventure in the wild outdoors. Use a product your veterinarian recommends — repellents purchased at pet stores and grocery stores frequently are not as effective. Examine your dog daily for ticks during the spring and summer months, and remove them gently. To remove a tick, use tweezers to grab the insect as close to your dog's skin as possible, and pull straight out, without squeezing or twisting.

Leptospirosis

Book II

Dog
Nutrition
and Health

Leptospirosis is another disease that, like distemper, used to be a major dog killer but has been very uncommon during the past three decades. We can thank effective vaccines for that. In the last three years, some unusual strains of leptospirosis were diagnosed in an increasing number of dogs. Veterinary scientists went to work and have now designed new vaccines to be effective against these canine killers.

Leptospirosis is caused by any one of about 200 different but related strains of bacteria. The bacteria infect many different species of wild and domesticated animals, including raccoons, skunks, opossums, and cattle. The infected animal sheds large numbers of bacteria in urine. Leptospira bacteria are specialists in water survival, so if the urine drains into standing water, these bugs can survive for a long time, just waiting for your dog to come along and have a drink. The bacterium then enters the blood stream and travels throughout the body to many tissues, where it replicates and causes damage. Leptospira particularly like to grow in the kidney and can cause severe renal failure in dogs. Of course, by replicating in the kidney, the bacteria has easy access to the urine so that it can be expelled to the environment and infect another unsuspecting animal. Pretty ingenious, huh?

The signs of disease in dogs include a sudden onset of fever or trembling, lethargy, nausea, jaundice, vomiting, and diarrhea. If the dog is not quickly treated with antibiotics, she may stop producing urine and hemorrhage into the lung and intestine. Luckily, with antibiotics and supportive care, most dogs recover, but complete recovery may take several weeks.

Leptospirosis also infects humans. Most people, just like dogs, get infected by exposure to urine from wildlife or farm animals. However, it's also possible for dogs to transmit the infection to their people. In areas where leptospirosis outbreaks are occurring, keep pets away from children's play areas, including sandboxes and wading pools.

Rickettsia: What a racket!

Rickettsia are poorly understood organisms that are intermediate in size, between viruses and bacteria. They live inside cells like viruses do, but they are susceptible to some of the antibiotics that kill bacteria. The two main rickettsial diseases of dogs are Ehrlichiosis and Rocky Mountain spotted fever. Both are carried by those diabolical disease-delivery units — ticks.

Ehrlichiosis and Rocky Mountain spotted fever are both characterized by fever, rashes, anemia, hemorrhages, and joint and muscle pain in dogs. If your dog is ill for more than 24 hours, particularly if you know a tick has bitten him, it's a good idea to have a veterinarian give him the once-over. Only a vet can differentiate between these two diseases, which can appear quite similar clinically. Blood tests are required to make a definitive diagnosis, and even they aren't foolproof. Treatment of rickettsial infections requires antibiotic treatment for six to eight weeks.

Fighting the Fungus among Us

There's a lot more to fungi than the fact that one of them provides a common pizza topping. Fungi inhabit soils throughout the world. Some inhabit the soil of the Mississippi Valley, the mid-Atlantic states, and southern Canada; others grow in soil contaminated with bird or bat excrement; and still others call the dry Southwestern soils home. Active dogs who spend a lot of time running outdoors (like the hunting dog in Figure 2-3), especially dogs who love to dig, risk becoming infected with fungal organisms that live in the soil. Usually a strong immune system will keep these bad bugs at bay. But if the dog is battling another infection or has a weak immune system, these organisms can get a foothold in the dog's body and cause serious disease.

These fungal agents cause arthritis, pneumonia, infections in bones, and signs of systemic infection such as fever, loss of appetite, and malaise. No vaccines are available for these organisms. If you live in an area where fungi are present, the best way to prevent infection is to keep your dog from digging, especially around the holes of burrowing animals where the fungi are especially abundant. Also keep your dog away from areas frequented by large numbers of bats or birds.

Figure 2-3:
Hunting
dogs like
Flyer are
exposed
to fungal
organisms
in the soil.

Preventing Parasites

Parasites are the ultimate opportunists, living on the skin, in the intestine and just about anywhere they can gain a foothold. Luckily, with today's excellent veterinary preventive medicine programs, dogs don't have to suffer parasitic infections. Parasite control is also important because some of them (roundworm and hookworm) can spread to humans.

Fleas

Fleas are the bane of a dog's existence. They make him itch, itch, itch. And the more a dog scratches, the itchier he seems to get. These irritating insects can cause itching in two different ways. First, they bite on a big chunk of skin and start sucking blood. They stay at one spot until they are full, or hop around, drinking at many different sites. Worse, they often bite in thin-skinned, sensitive areas such as near the ears, at the base of the tail, and in the groin area. Flea bites are irritating enough, but many dogs actually develop an allergic reaction to the saliva of the fleas and become extremely itchy all over, even with the bite of only one flea. Sometimes the allergy is so severe that a dog will chew at himself until he loses big patches of hair, bleeds, and ultimately develops thick, crusty skin, especially on his feet, at the base of his tail, and around his back legs.

If you see your dog scratching vigorously or biting aggressively at himself, it's time for a bug check. Start by looking around your dog's ears, at the base of his tail, and on his tummy. Part the hair and look for brown, flat, oval bugs about 1⁄8 inch long. Keep your eyes peeled, because a startled flea can jump quickly into the air and land several inches away. Frequently, you won't actually see a flea, but you can see flea dirt stuck in the dog's hairs. *Flea dirt* is a polite term for flea excrement, a crumbly black material that consists mainly of digested blood. You can identify flea dirt by placing a drop of water over the dirt, letting it soak up the water for a minute or two, and then smearing the dirt on a piece of white paper towel. A reddish smear confirms that it is, in fact, flea dirt.

If you identify a flea or flea dirt, leap into action. The only thing that will give your dog relief is ridding his body and your house of those pesky pests. You'll be delighted to know that the solution may entail giving your dog a hot bath with anti-flea shampoo, applying an anti-flea treatment between his shoulder blades, administering pills, vacuuming every inch of your apartment or house, and spraying along the floorboards with another anti-flea product. With the many safe anti-flea products available today, your dog no longer has reason to suffer.

Fleas are especially fond of cats, so if you share your digs with an animal of the feline persuasion, be sure to include her in your flea prevention and treatment protocol.

Ticks

Ticks are major pests not only because they can bite your dog and cause local skin irritation, but because they carry a host of other pesky germs that can make both you and your dog sick (including the already-discussed Lyme disease). Ticks live on long grasses and shrubs, and they have a sticky substance on their bodies that enables them to easily cling to the fur of passing animals such as your dog. They then crawl down the hair to the skin and latch on, taking a big bite. They suck blood for hours and even days until they are full to bursting. During this time, they can transmit whatever infectious organisms they happen to be carrying.

If you live in an area where ticks are prevalent (most of the United States, except the Southwest and Alaska), check your dog for ticks every day, at least during tick season — usually the spring and summer months, but sometimes later depending on warm weather. Carefully remove every tick you find (see the earlier coverage of Lyme disease).

If your dog enjoys the outdoors (and most dogs do), apply a product that prevents ticks from attaching to the skin. Be sure to get advice from your veterinarian on which product is best, because new products enter the market all the time. Also continue to check your dog from head to toe every time he comes in from outside. You're most likely to find ticks around your dog's face, eyes, and ears, although they really can be anywhere. Be sure to look inside the ears, too!

Worms

Dozens of kinds of worms can set up shop in your dog's body, often in the intestine. Puppies are especially susceptible to infections with worms, because some species of worms are transmitted from the mother before the puppy is even born. For this reason, deworming puppies is very important (see Book II, Chapter 4).

(see Book II, Chapter 4).

The general level of care for dogs these days is so high, however, that adult dogs rarely have problems with worms (with the exception of tapeworms). Nonetheless, it is a good idea to bring a fecal sample to your annual veterinary visit every year, just to be sure.

If you adopt a dog from a shelter or find a stray, be sure to have her checked for worms, because you won't know whether she has had adequate veterinary care from puppyhood.

Being Aware of Which Bugs Infect Humans

Just as we share our lives with dogs, we sometimes share our infections, too. Be aware of the potential transmission of organisms from dogs to humans, called *zoonosis,* so you can take preventive measures. The most important zoonotic disease in dogs is rabies, but dogs can unwittingly share many infectious organisms with us, including leptospirosis, roundworms, and hookworms.

Humans also can be infected by the canine roundworm *Toxocara canis.* If a human accidentally ingests Toxocara eggs, the eggs will hatch and larvae will migrate through the body, causing fever, rash, and cough. This condition is called *visceral larval migrans.* If the worm larvae migrate to the eye, they can cause blindness. Larvae can migrate through the spinal cord and brain, causing severe neurologic disease, too. These infections usually occur in children who live in conditions of poor sanitation. Toxocara eggs must mature in the environment for one to three weeks before they are infectious,

Book II

Dog Nutrition and Health

so humans don't become infected by handling dogs directly. They must contact eggs in the environment. Toxocara eggs are very hardy, however, and can survive in the environment for weeks or months.

Consider these tips to prevent human infection with Toxocara:

- Deworm all puppies, regardless of whether Toxocara eggs are detected in fecal samples, twice (21 days apart) during their initial vaccination period. Have the vet check multiple stool samples during puppy visits. Use a monthly heartworm prevention that deworms for roundworms.

- Do not allow children to play where dogs defecate.

- Always clean up after your dog in public places. And always wash hands with hot water before eating.

Several other infectious organisms can be transmitted from dogs to humans, but they infect only immunosuppressed humans, such as people undergoing cancer treatment or organ transplantation, and individuals with AIDS. If you are immunosuppressed and want to have a dog, your best bet is to get a clinically normal adult dog from a private family. If this is not possible, have a veterinarian give the prospective four-legged family member a thorough physical examination, complete with fecal and blood tests.

Intestinal parasites are dangerous. It's very important that people who own dogs understand this fact about common intestinal parasites — roundworms, hookworms, whipworms, tapeworms, and to a lesser degree coccidia. Always follow the advice of your vet regarding deworming, even if a stool sample is negative.

Chapter 3

Canine First Aid

Accidents happen to all of us, including our dogs. Although you can take some safety precautions to help your dog avoid these pitfalls, you can't guarantee that she'll never run into trouble. And that's where knowing first aid comes in handy. In this chapter, you get everything you need to know to care for your dog when she's injured or ill — from bites to breaks and everything in between. Read this chapter now, while your pooch is sleeping by your side. Don't wait until you need it.

Being Prepared for an Emergency

One of the best things you can do to help your dog in the event of an emergency is to be prepared before the emergency strikes. Administering first aid is very difficult — if not impossible — without a few essential supplies. And you can do a lot beforehand to get to know your dog so that when you're faced with an emergency, you're ready to do what's required.

Assembling a canine first-aid kit

Before you're faced with an emergency, assemble two first-aid kits for your dog — one for your car and one for home. Always keep the kits in the same place so you can get your hands on one right away in an emergency.

Your first-aid kit doesn't need to be big or expensive to be useful.

Getting the container ready

Find a water-resistant container that's large enough to carry everything without being cumbersome. Fishing tackle boxes work well because they have trays with dividers to keep things organized.

Put a large red cross and the words *first-aid kit* on each side of the container. Someone may need to locate and use it in an emergency, and labeling the kit clearly can be a big help. To the inside of the lid, tape a piece of paper with the following information in clear letters (do this for each dog):

✔ **Your name, address, e-mail, and telephone number.**

✔ **The breed, name, and date of birth of the dog.**

✔ **Any medical conditions your dog has and any regular medication.**

✔ **Names, addresses, and telephone numbers of emergency contact people, in case you are incapacitated.**

✔ **Name, address, and telephone number of your veterinarian.** Be sure to provide the contact information for your after-hours emergency clinic.

✔ **Contact information for the National Animal Poison Control Center.** You can reach the center at 888-426-4435, 24 hours a day, 365 days a year to inquire about the toxic potential of various household products and plants your dog may have found tasty. You also can get advice about emergency care for a dog who has gotten into a toxin. The cost per case is $60, which includes follow-up (including contacting your veterinarian, if you request), and is charged to a major credit card. To have the fee charged to your telephone bill (and avoid having to track down your credit card number in an emergency), dial 900-680-0000. For more information on the service, visit www.aspca.org.

✔ **A list of the contents of your first-aid kit.** For each of the drugs in the kit, have a note indicating the appropriate dose for each of your dogs. That way, you won't have to do any calculations in your head in a time of crisis. When preparing the kit, be sure to check the doses with your veterinarian.

The information in this list can be useful at home as well as on the road. In addition to taping this list on the inside lid of your first-aid kit, include the following for the kit that you keep in your car:

✔ **Your dog's rabies certificate:** Some states require that you have a rabies certificate at all times if you are traveling with a dog.

✔ **A photograph of each dog, with her name, tattoo, and microchip number:** This can help a rescuer identify each dog if you are incapacitated.

Keep these materials in a resealable plastic bag so they're all together.

Knowing what to put in the first-aid kit

Following is a list of the components of an all-purpose first-aid kit and a brief description of what each item is used for. You can find most of these items at your local pharmacy; you can get the rest from your vet or dog supply catalog.

With time and experience, you may add other items to the kit, because you may find yourself using the kit for yourself and other humans in need. You may also find that you don't need some of the items. Eventually, your first-aid kit will reflect you, your dogs, and your needs. But the following supplies are a good place to start:

Book II

Dog Nutrition and Health

- ✔ **ACE brand elastic bandage:** You can use this bandage to hold an ice pack to a dog's leg, to wrap (not too tightly!) a sprain temporarily until you can get veterinary assistance, or to secure an injured dog to a makeshift stretcher.

- ✔ **Adhesive tape:** Use tape to secure bandages and splints. Make sure that you have a large roll, and replace it when it gets close to running out.

- ✔ **Alcohol swabs:** Look for individually packaged swabs, which you can use to sterilize instruments or small areas of skin.

- ✔ **Aspirin (enteric coated):** Give 5 milligrams per pound every 12 hours to temporarily relieve pain. Many dogs vomit after taking regular aspirin, so be sure to get the enteric-coated variety, which is gentler on the stomach. Or get NSAID from your vet, specially formulated for dogs.

   Never substitute ibuprofen or acetaminophen for aspirin. Both of these substances can be toxic to dogs.

- ✔ **Bacitracin or Neosporin:** Apply this or another antibiotic ointment to cleaned wounds that are likely to become infected.

   Never use these ointments in the eye. Special antibacterial formulations are used for the eyes — but use them only with your veterinarian's recommendation.

- ✔ **Benadryl:** You can use Benadryl for insect bites or stings. Give your dog 1½ milligrams per pound, every eight hours.

- ✔ **Cohesive bandage:** Use this stretchy wrap to cover and secure gauze bandages. It clings to itself, so you don't need adhesive tape.

- ✔ **Cold pack:** Use a cold pack to prevent or reduce swelling after a sprain or strain, or to treat burns. Buy the kind that gets cold when you fold it in half.

- ✔ **Cotton squares:** You use these to clean and protect wounds. They're better for cleaning wounds than cotton balls because they don't shed fibers when you wipe them over sticky areas, such as where blood is drying.

- **First-aid instructions:** Photocopy the pages of this chapter that discuss first-aid treatments and store them in your first-aid kit. When you're trying to take care of a sick or injured dog, remembering all the details can be difficult.

- **Gauze bandage roll:** You use this wrap to bandage wounds and hold splints in place. Cut off a length of bandage and fold it up to cover a wound, or wrap the bandage around the leg to keep a cold pack in place or secure a splint.

- **Gloves (latex):** Any time you need to keep your hands protected or clean, wear a pair of latex gloves.

- **Green Soap or Hibitane:** You can use any gentle liquid antibacterial soap for cleaning skin and wounds. Betadine or iodine solution are good wound cleaning solutions.

- **Hydrogen peroxide:** Give your dog 1 to 3 teaspoons of hydrogen peroxide every ten minutes to induce vomiting. Don't give more than three doses ten minutes apart, and don't use it to clean wounds.

- **Imodium A-D:** Give your dog 1 milligram per 15 pounds once or twice a day to relieve diarrhea. May contain aspirin and irritate the stomach.

- **Lubricating jelly:** Use this item to lubricate a thermometer or to prevent gauze bandages from sticking to a wound. It also comes in individual packets.

- **Muzzle:** You can use a length of gauze bandage, a belt, or a soft rope to make an emergency muzzle. Even if your dog has never showed signs of aggression, if he is in pain or is frightened, he may snap at you or others.

- **Needle and thread:** For emergencies only! Use a needle and thread to stitch wounds (or — better — a surgical stapler purchased from your vet) when you know you won't be able to get veterinary help within six hours. Bear in mind that your dog will not like (or perhaps allow) you to suture him. Clean wounds before closing them.

- **NuSkin liquid bandage:** Use for small, clean, recent wounds.

- **Penlight flashlight:** Use a flashlight to look down your dog's ears or throat — anywhere you need extra light. You can also use it to check whether a dog's eyes respond to light, in case of an injury to the head.

- **Pepto-Bismol liquid:** Give 1 teaspoon per 25 pounds every 6 hours to relieve diarrhea and vomiting. The liquid form works faster than the tablet form. May contain aspirin and irritate the stomach.

- **Plastic bags (resealable):** These bags are handy for temporarily packaging items that are leaking, protecting open packages from drying, or collecting specimens such as fecal samples.

- **Razor blade (retractable) or blunt-ended scissors:** Use these items for cutting bandages and tape and for trimming the hair around a wound.

- **Safety pins:** Use pins to fasten bandages if you don't have tape.

✔ **Sterile saline solution:** Use to rinse out the eyes or to clean wounds.

✔ **Stockinet or bootie:** Put one on your dog to protect a bandage on a leg or foot.

✔ **Styptic powder:** Use to stop small areas of bleeding, such as when you accidentally clip your dog's nails too close.

✔ **Sun block:** Apply to your dog's nose or areas of light skin if your dog has a thin coat.

✔ **Syringe:** Use to flush a dog's eye with saline or to administer peroxide.

✔ **Thermometer (rectal):** Use a thermometer made for dogs. A dog's normal body temperature is between 100.5 and 102.8 degrees.

✔ **Tweezers (flat-ended):** You can use tweezers to remove foreign objects, such as ticks, thorns, and foxtails, from your dog's skin.

Book II

Dog Nutrition and Health

Keep a blanket in your car at all times. You can use it to warm a dog suffering from frostbite, to wrap a dog who is in shock, or as an emergency stretcher.

Label each item in your first-aid kit with its name and expiration date. Go through your kit before trips and every year, replacing medications that have expired or for which the labels have become hard to read, and replenishing supplies.

Knowing your dog before an emergency

Before an emergency happens, find out as much as you can about your dog's anatomy and her inner workings so that you will be prepared to examine her and make decisions quickly, when necessary. Become familiar with these techniques now, before emergency strikes.

Taking your dog's temperature

Know how to take your dog's temperature quickly and without causing stress. You'll need a rectal thermometer (a digital one is preferred), lubricating jelly, and a clean cloth:

1. **If it's not a digital thermometer, grip it tightly and shake it down until it registers below 98 degrees.**

2. **Dab some lubricating jelly onto the end of the thermometer.**

3. **With your dog standing or lying on his side, raise your dog's tail and insert the thermometer into the rectum with a slow, twisting motion.**

   Talk to your dog and praise him for remaining still. The first few times you do this, you may want to have someone give him a treat while you are inserting the thermometer, to keep his mind occupied.

4. After one minute, remove the thermometer slowly, wipe it with a clean cloth, and read the temperature.

A dog's normal temperature ranges from 100.5 to 102.8 degrees. The temperature can rise significantly after exercise, but it should return to normal within 20 minutes.

New electronic thermometers on the market allow you to take a person's temperature by placing a plastic probe just inside the ear canal. Before you use one on your dog, ask your vet whether your model will work on dogs.

Counting your dog's breathing rate

Become familiar with your dog's breathing. Count how many times a minute she breathes while she's resting and compare it to her breathing rate after she exercises. Most dogs have a resting breathing rate of 15 to 30 breaths per minute. The breathing rate may rise when a dog is in pain or has a fever.

Checking your dog's pulse

When you check your dog's pulse, locate the *femoral artery,* which lies just below the skin on the inside of the leg, between two large muscles where the leg joins the body. With your dog standing, reach around in front of the rear leg where it joins his body, and slide your fingers into the groin area. You will feel the artery pumping each time the heart contracts. When you have found the artery with your dog standing, try it with your dog lying on his side. Count how many pulses you feel in 15 seconds, and multiply by 4 to get the number of beats per minute.

Become familiar with your dog's pulse rate and how his pulse feels when he is relaxed, as well as after exercise. Dogs normally have a pulse between 70 and 120 beats per minute. In puppies, the pulse ranges from 120 to 160 beats per minute.

Examining your dog's gums

Lift your dog's lip and look at the color of the gums above an upper canine tooth — the gums should be pink. Press on the gums with your finger. When you remove your finger, the gums should briefly look white but should return to their pink color within two seconds. This is the capillary refill test.

If the gums are blue, the dog lacks oxygen. If they are white, the dog has lost blood, either internally or externally. If the gums are purple or gray and there is a slow capillary refill, the dog is probably in shock. If they are bright red, she may be fighting a systemic infection or may have been exposed to a toxin. Sometimes normal dogs have black-pigmented gums, which can make assessment more difficult. For these dogs, you need to examine the pink tissue on the inside of the lower eyelid by gently pulling down the eyelid. In this case, you can only observe the color of the tissue — you can't perform the capillary refill test — but the colors in the preceding paragraph apply.

Knowing What to Do in an Emergency

Just as you need to have a first-aid kit assembled and know how to check your dog's vital signs, you need to be aware of what to do in the case of an emergency. The following sections cover how to help an injured dog, how to give CPR, and how to treat common injuries and problems.

Approaching an accident scene

When you come upon an accident scene in which a dog has been injured, always be sure that *you* are safe before you try to help the dog. Every year people are killed on roads and highways because they put their own lives at risk to assist injured dogs or other animals. If the dog is in an unsafe area, secure the area and move the dog to a safe place *before* assessing her.

If other people are nearby, try to organize them to be a help rather than a hindrance:

- ✔ Ask a few people to keep passersby away from the dog.
- ✔ Ask one person to call a local veterinary clinic.
- ✔ Have another person arrange to transport the dog.
- ✔ You may also have someone assist you in performing CPR and have another person apply pressure to any wounds.

Handling an injured dog

Whenever you approach an injured dog, always start by protecting yourself from being bitten. If your dog is in severe pain and is afraid, even your best friend may bite the hand that feeds him. You can make a temporary muzzle out of a length of bandage, belt, shoelace, or pantyhose. If it turns out the muzzle wasn't necessary, your dog will forgive you for having used one. If it was necessary, you'll be glad you had the foresight to protect yourself.

To apply a muzzle, follow these steps:

1. **Approach the dog slowly, using a soothing tone of voice.**
2. **Bring the bandage (or other material) up under the dog's chin about halfway between the leather of the nose and his eyes.**
3. **Tie the two ends in one loop on top of the dog's nose.**
4. **Bring the bandage back under the dog's chin and tie another single knot under the chin.**

5. **Bring the two ends of the bandage to the back of your dog's neck behind his ears and tie them in a bow.**

6. **Tie the loops of the bow into another single knot to keep the muzzle securely fastened.**

The muzzle should be fairly tight, enough that your dog cannot open his mouth, but not so tight that it impedes breathing.

Examining an injured dog

When your dog is injured or ill, your primary job is to remain calm and be deliberate in your actions. Try to keep your voice from revealing the fear you may feel inside. Use the A-B-C checklist outlined in the following sections whenever you come upon a scene in which a dog is seriously injured and appears to be unconscious or in shock. Even if the dog has a bleeding wound, carry out this preliminary assessment first. Respiratory and circulatory problems usually are more life threatening than wounds. When you are certain the dog is breathing and is not in circulatory collapse, you can deal with the wound.

Airway

If the dog is unconscious and has no apparent neck or back injuries (excluding bleeding wounds), tilt her head back slightly, open her mouth, and look inside for any objects that may be impeding airflow. Gently pull her tongue forward (holding the tongue is easier if you grab it with gauze or cloth) and check for objects that may be deeper down the throat. Pulling the tongue forward also opens the airway, making breathing easier.

Breathing

Check for the rise and fall of the chest that indicates the dog is breathing. If the dog is not breathing and the airways are clear, begin rescue breathing immediately:

1. **Cup your hands around the muzzle and seal your lips around the edge of the leathery part of the dog's nose.**

2. **Breathe into the dog's nostrils for two seconds.**

3. **Watch for the dog's chest to rise, indicating that air is entering the lungs.**

4. **If the chest doesn't rise, check the airway again.**

   Repeat for a total of three breaths.

Give *gentle* puffs of breath (the amount depends on the dog's size). Your lungs are much bigger. Don't blow as though you're trying to inflate a balloon.

Circulation

Assess circulation by checking the pulse at the femoral artery. If you haven't practiced on your dog before, see the earlier section, "Checking your dog's pulse." A healthy dog's pulse is approximately 10 to 14 beats per 10 seconds and feels strong. (Smaller dogs have a more rapid pulse.) If the pulse is there but feels weak, the dog is probably in shock.

If you have trouble feeling the pulse in the groin, place your thumb and fingers on either side of the chest wall just behind the elbows to see if the heart is beating. If you detect no pulse or heartbeat, begin CPR immediately (see following section).

Examine the dog's gums to check circulation, too. If the gums are blue, the dog may not be getting enough oxygen. Be sure that you've checked the airway and cleared it of any foreign objects. If the dog has a weak or rapid pulse; shallow breathing; gray, purple, or pale gums; or glazed eyes, or if he exhibits weakness or collapses, he is in shock and you should make arrangements to get him to a veterinarian *as soon as possible*. In the meantime, keep him quiet, cover him with a blanket, and keep his head as low as the rest of his body. If the dog is not breathing or you cannot feel a pulse, begin CPR.

Book II

Dog Nutrition and Health

Administering CPR

If your dog is not breathing or doesn't have a pulse, follow these instructions to administer cardiopulmonary resuscitation (CPR):

1. **Position the dog on her side.**

2. **Clear the dog's mouth of any foreign matter (see Figure 3-1).**

3. **Hold the muzzle closed with your hands and give mouth-to-nose respiration at 12 to 15 breaths per minute (see Figure 3-2).**

   Watch for the chest to rise, to be sure that the air is getting into the lungs. If the chest doesn't rise, check again for anything that may be obstructing airflow.

Photograph courtesy of Angela Koeller.

Figure 3-1:
Before administering CPR, clear the dog's mouth of any foreign matter.

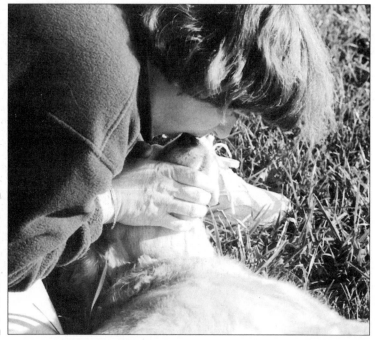

Figure 3-2:
Hold the muzzle closed and breathe into the nose 12 to 15 times a minute.

Photograph courtesy of Angela Koeller.

4. Begin chest compressions.

With a large dog, kneel at the dog's back. Push the dog's uppermost front leg forward, out of the way. Lay one hand over the other and compress the chest wall over the heart (right about where the dog's elbow would be with the leg at rest) with the heel of your hand (see Figure 3-3). Push gently, and then let go immediately. For a very small dog (one weighing less than 30 pounds), lay the dog on her right side, place your thumb and fingers on either side of the chest, and compress from both sides.

Regardless of the size of the dog, do 60 to 80 compressions per minute (approximately one compression a second). Don't compress the chest for more than a split second, or the heart won't have room to beat. If you're alone, give one breath and then five chest compressions. If you have help, one person can perform mouth-to-nose respiration while the other compresses the heart. In that case, give one breath for every three to four chest compressions.

Compress at approximately the speed of the beat from the Bee Gee's "Stayin' Alive" or Queen's "Another One Bites the Dust."

Book II

Dog Nutrition and Health

Figure 3-3: Place your hands over the heart and compress the chest 60 to 80 times per minute.

Photograph courtesy of Angela Koeller.

Giving first-aid treatment

When you're sure that an injured dog is breathing and has a pulse, you can start attending to his injuries. The following sections cover some common injuries and problems requiring first aid.

Knowing these first-aid techniques should help you in an emergency. But this is *first* aid — basic techniques to help you aid your dog *before you can get veterinary assistance*. First aid is *not* a substitute for the care and expertise of a veterinarian.

Allergic reactions

In addition to normal allergic reactions (like itching and sneezing), some dogs may experience more severe symptoms, including the following:

- ✔ **Hives or swelling of the muzzle:** Some dogs respond to an allergen with swelling of the face or bumps that appear over a large part of the trunk. You may also see the dog biting or licking at herself, or she may have red, weeping eyes. Apply a cold pack to the swollen area if it is small. If the swelling continues or covers a large area, administer Benadryl (at 1 to 1½ milligrams per pound) and contact your veterinarian. Check respiration periodically, because there may also be swelling of the throat, which can impair breathing.

- ✔ **Shock:** Signs of shock include weak or rapid pulse; shallow breathing; gray, purple, or pale gums; glazed eyes; weakness; or collapse. Lay the dog on her side and cover her with a blanket. Administer CPR, if necessary. Transport the dog to a veterinarian as soon as possible.

Bleeding

Blood from an artery is bright red and sprays from the vessel in time with each beat of the heart. A dog can lose a great deal of blood quickly if an artery is cut. Blood from a vein or from small vessels under the skin is burgundy in color and pours slowly or seeps from the wound.

To stop bleeding, apply pressure to the wound with a piece of gauze or cloth for several minutes. Even if the gauze is soaked with blood, don't lift it to see if the bleeding has stopped, because the gauze actually helps clot the blood. Just add extra layers of gauze. Depending on the area of the body and the size of the wound, it may take 10 to 15 minutes for bleeding to stop.

If ice is available, place it around the area of the wound to slow blood flow. When the bleeding has stopped, you can bandage the wound (see the "Wounds" section later in this chapter) and arrange to get the dog to a veterinarian.

Only use a tourniquet in extreme emergencies, because it can cut off necessary circulation to the area. See a vet immediately after use.

Broken bones

When your dog has a fracture, the goal is to stabilize her until a veterinarian can examine her and treat the injury. A broken bone is very painful. Fractures are sometimes obvious, such as when the leg is lying in an abnormal position or a piece of bone is poking through the skin. But sometimes a fracture may be present when the leg looks only swollen. If you try to move the bones, you may feel a grinding caused by the broken ends of the bone rubbing against each other.

If veterinary care is available, do not apply a splint. Carefully place the dog on a firm, level surface and take her to the clinic. If you are far from veterinary help, the leg should carefully be splinted before your dog is moved. The best splint is something rigid but padded, such as a board wrapped in a towel. The splint should be placed against the dog's limb, avoiding movement of the bones as much as possible. The leg and joints above and below the break should be taped or wrapped to the splint. (Do not bandage fractured ribs, spine, or pelvis.) Transport the dog to a veterinary clinic as soon as possible.

A *fracture* is a partial or complete break in a bone. Fractures are classified by severity, and the same classifications apply for both dogs and people:

- ✔ **Greenstick fracture:** The least serious fracture is the *greenstick fracture,* in which one side of the bone is broken but the other side is just bent. The two ends of the bone are not moved from their original positions. This type of fracture is seen more often in young, growing dogs because their bones are less brittle than those of adult dogs. A dog can walk (though gingerly) on a leg with a greenstick fracture; only X-ray can diagnose this kind of fracture.

- ✔ **Complete fracture:** A *complete fracture* is one in which the bone is broken through its width. Generally, the two ends of bone are moved from where they should be, because contractions of the muscle move the broken pieces of bone away from their original location. A complete fracture is more serious than a greenstick fracture; the damage to the bone is greater, and the surrounding muscles and maybe even ligaments and tendons are usually damaged. Complete fractures can be one of three types:

    - Simple, with just two pieces of bone

    - Comminuted, with many pieces of bone

    - Compound, with skin punctured by pieces of bone

Book II

Dog Nutrition and Health

No matter what kind of fracture it is, a veterinarian must return all the pieces of bone to their original location before healing can begin.

Burns

Dogs are most often burned when hot or *caustic* (strong acids or cleaning solutions such as lye) liquids are spilled on them. Burns may also result when a dog gets too close to a candle, a stove, or a fire. Some dogs can even get a blistering sunburn, especially on a sunny day after winter. Heating pads may cause burns.

Burns are classified by degrees, depending on their severity:

- ✔ **First degree:** The hair is singed and the skin may be reddened.
- ✔ **Second degree:** The hair is burned off and the skin is red and blistered.
- ✔ **Third degree:** The skin is black, brown, or white. If the third-degree burn is extensive, the dog may go into shock.

If a caustic liquid caused the burn, wipe or rinse off the liquid before treating the burn. For all burns, follow these treatment suggestions:

- ✔ **Minor burns (first and second degree):** If the burn occurred within the last hour, apply a cold pack for 20 to 30 minutes and then treat the burn as a superficial wound (see "Wounds" later in this chapter).
- ✔ **Severe burns (third degree):** If your dog permits, apply a cold pack or a cold, wet cloth to the area; cover the area gently with gauze; and take him to the veterinarian as soon as possible.

Never apply ointments or butter to severe burns, and never touch the skin or rub anything on it.

Choking and the canine Heimlich maneuver

Dogs are ever curious — and second only to their noses, they use their mouths to investigate new and interesting things. Dogs can choke on just about anything, but the most common offenders are small balls such as golf and squash balls, rawhide and bones, cellophane, and plastic children's toys. A dog who is choking makes retching motions and looks panicked, often pacing back and forth and pawing at her mouth. Her chest may be heaving, but she isn't making any airway noises.

If you suspect that your dog is choking, first examine her mouth. Pull the tongue forward and remove the foreign object, if possible. If you can't see the foreign object, use the canine Heimlich maneuver to try to dislodge the object:

✔ **For large dogs:** Stand behind your dog and place your arms around her body. Make a fist with one hand, and place the thumb of the hand with the fist against your dog's abdomen just where the sternum ends. With the other hand, grasp your fist and push upward and forward (toward the dog's shoulders), suddenly and forcefully (see Figure 3-4). Do this thrusting motion four or five times. Check the dog's airway again and clear any debris from the mouth. Repeat the chest thrusts, if necessary. If the dog is unconscious, clear the airway and perform rescue breathing.

✔ **For small dogs:** Hold the dog with her head up so that her spine is against your chest. Make a fist with one hand, and place it against your dog's abdomen just where the sternum ends (see Figure 3-5). Grasp the fist with your other hand, and give four or five rapid thrusts inward and upward. Check the dog's airway again and clear any debris from the mouth. Repeat the chest thrusts, if necessary. If the dog is unconscious, clear the airway and perform rescue breathing.

Book II

Dog Nutrition and Health

Figure 3-4:
To treat choking in a large dog, place your hands under your dog where the chest joins the abdomen and grasp your fist. Thrust upward and forward.

Photograph courtesy of Angela Koeller.

Figure 3-5:
To treat choking in a small dog, hold the dog against your chest and compress the lower ribcage with your fist several times.

Cold exposure

Hypothermia is a lowering of the dog's body temperature caused by cold exposure. Dogs don't suffer from hypothermia very often because they carry their fur coats with them everywhere they go. However, if a dog is wet or he has a very thin coat, he may get cold quite easily. A dog's first response when cold is to shiver. Later the dog may act lethargic and become unresponsive.

If you recognize that your dog has hypothermia, follow these suggestions:

- ✔ Move the dog to a warm environment and cover him with a blanket.
- ✔ Rub his body (not his legs) gently, to increase circulation.
- ✔ If he's wet, dry him with towels or a blow dryer on medium heat.
- ✔ Take your dog's temperature to monitor his recovery.
- ✔ Offer warm sugar water if the dog is conscious.

Do not apply heating pads or hot water bottles directly to your dog's skin.

If the dog begins to lick his paws or appears uncomfortable, he may have frostbite. Restrain him and place warm compresses on the affected area.

Diarrhea

If you have a dog long enough, you'll have to deal with diarrhea eventually. Diarrhea can be caused by a dog's propensity to eat garbage or rotten animals, by a viral, parasitic, or bacterial infection, or sometimes just by stress.

If your dog has diarrhea, withhold food for 24 hours in adults or 12 hours in puppies (younger than 6 months). Instead of giving water, offer the dog ice cubes so that she takes in the water slowly. Some vets don't recommend this, but you can administer Imodium A-D (1 milligram per 15 pounds once or twice a day) and/or Pepto-Bismol (1 teaspoon per 25 pounds every six hours) to help calm an upset stomach and stop diarrhea. For the next 72 hours, feed a bland diet (75 percent rice, 25 percent low-fat protein such as skinless chicken) in small but increasing amounts. Then shift to the dog's regular diet over the next two days.

Book II

Dog Nutrition and Health

If your dog has bloody diarrhea, is depressed and dull, or continues to have diarrhea for 24 hours while you are withholding food, take her to a veterinarian.

Drowning

Most dogs are excellent swimmers. Occasionally, however, a dog drowns because he gets caught in something underwater or gets overwhelmed by an undertow. Sometimes a dog who is an experienced swimmer drowns inexplicably. Some breeds have trouble swimming and may drown in shallow, safe water. Bulldogs, Pugs, and Pekingeses all have bodies that can make swimming difficult.

The first thing to do when you have brought the dog ashore is to empty the lungs of water. If the dog is small, elevate his rear end and water will drain out of the dog's mouth. If necessary, you can hold the dog upside down and swing him gently until the water is expelled. Pumping the chest and opening the mouth periodically may be helpful as well. If the dog is large, try to sling him over your shoulder so that the head, front legs, and chest hang down in front of you and the rear legs hang down your back. When the water is expelled, start rescue breathing. When the dog is breathing on his own, wrap him in a blanket and transport him to a veterinarian immediately.

Ear infections

Chronic ear infections are extremely uncomfortable to dogs and can ultimately affect hearing and balance. If your dog has ever had an ear infection, check her ears weekly and keep them clean — this is the best way to prevent infections and to recognize them quickly when they do occur.

To clean the ears, moisten a cotton swab with alcohol or hydrogen peroxide and clean the outer ear, making sure to clean around all the bumps inside the ear and down into the ear canal. Don't go farther into the canal than you can see — you don't want to risk breaking the eardrum. There are ear-cleaning solutions designed to break up wax and dry the ear canal. If the ear is truly infected it probably needs topical medicine to treat the specific type of infection — yeast or bacteria. If your dog has hair in her ear canal, pluck it to help with air circulation.

Electric shock

Occasionally, a dog (usually a puppy) bites down on an electric cord and suffers an electrical shock, often accompanied by burns. The dog may be unconscious and have burns around his mouth and on his tongue.

If you find your dog unconscious near an electrical cord, turn off the power to the socket *before* touching your dog. Examine the dog, using the A-B-C protocol described earlier in this chapter. Administer CPR if the dog is in shock or unconscious. When the dog is conscious, give first aid for burns and get him to your vet immediately.

Eyes

The eyes are very delicate and easily injured, especially in dogs who love to play in the great outdoors.

Dogs who run through fields may get dust or grasses in their eyes. The best solution is to wash the eye with sterile saline. Hold your dog's eye open and gently pour the saline over the surface of the eye. Using a penlight flashlight, examine the insides of the lids to be sure that you removed the offending particles. If repeated flushing doesn't help, get your dog to a veterinarian.

If a foreign body is penetrating the eye or the skin near the eye, do *not* touch it. Stop the dog from pawing at the eye by taping her hind legs together or using an Elizabethan collar (the "lampshade" — a wide cone-shaped collar that prevents the dog from being able to scratch her head). You can make a temporary collar by cutting a head-size hole in the bottom of a bucket and placing the bucket over her head, fastening it to the dog's collar. Then get your dog to a vet immediately.

Fishhooks

Every now and then, a dog playing near a fishing pond gets stuck with a fishhook left by a careless fisherman. As you can imagine, a fishhook can be very painful, particularly if the hook is in the foot and the dog has come running to you or tried to remove it with his mouth.

Start by calming the dog with gentle words and quiet motions. Getting your veterinarian to remove the hook is best, but if you have no access to a veterinarian, you can push the hook through the skin until the tip and barb come back out. Then cut off the hook and barb and back the rest of the hook out the way it came. Treat the hole as a wound (see "Wounds" later in this chapter).

If your dog swallows a fishhook, cut off most of the remaining fishing line, leaving approximately 12 inches dangling. *Do not* attempt to dislodge the fishhook by pulling on the line. Take your dog to a veterinarian immediately. Do not allow your dog to eat in the meantime.

Foxtails

Foxtail plants grow by roadsides and in fields throughout much of the United States. Dogs sometimes inhale or swallow their seeds in their exuberance outdoors. Foxtail seeds have a long, barbed appendage so that they can stick in the hair and even penetrate unbroken skin. When the seed is in your dog's body, it travels from place to place, damaging tissues and causing infections. If you live in an area with foxtails, always examine your dog's susceptible parts (nose, throat, armpits, and between the toes) thoroughly after she has been outdoors. Use tweezers to gently remove any foxtail seeds you find.

Heatstroke

The temperature doesn't have to be very high for a dog to suffer heatstroke. Working sled dogs in Alaska begin to suffer from the heat at 20 degrees because of their level of physical activity. Dogs are descended from wolves, animals who evolved in northern climes and, thus, have not developed natural mechanisms to fight the heat. As a result, they, like their wolf ancestors, don't have very good heat-control mechanisms. Breeds with flat faces, such as Bulldogs and Pugs, can suffer heatstroke even on mild days. Puppies also are more susceptible to heatstroke.

More dogs die of heatstroke in cars than any other way. Even on a mild day, the temperature in a car in the sun can rise to over 100 degrees in a matter of minutes. Every year, thousands of dogs die of heatstroke after being left in cars for "just a minute."

Never leave your dog in the car in the summer, even with the windows down. And never leave your dog in a yard without shade in the summer.

A dog suffering from heatstroke pants heavily and salivates excessively. His eyes may be glazed and he staggers or acts listless. The dog's pulse also feels rapid and weak.

Book II

Dog Nutrition and Health

If you suspect that your dog is suffering from heatstroke, you must act quickly. Move the dog to a cool area indoors, or at least to the shade. Submerge him in cool water (not ice water) and apply cold compresses to his head. Take his temperature to monitor his body's cooling. Keep him wet until his temperature reaches 103 degrees, and then remove him from the water and dry him off. Encourage but do not force him to drink water. Get him to the veterinarian as soon as possible.

Hot spots

Hot spots are localized areas of skin infection that are usually round, red, and warm to the touch. They can start very quickly and grow to several inches in diameter in a day or two. The infection is exacerbated by the dog's scratching or chewing.

The first thing to do if you identify a hot spot is to clip the hair away from the area, if possible. This is the best way to prevent the infection from spreading. Once or twice a day, wash the area thoroughly with liquid soap and apply an astringent. The best astringent is tea (green or black). Wet a tea bag and apply it to the area. Keep applying the astringent several times a day until the area is dry and covered with a scab — usually 24 to 36 hours. After the area is scabbed, let it heal, but watch it carefully, in case the infection begins to spread again. Keep the dog from scratching or biting at the area while it is healing; you may need to use an Elizabethan collar (see the "Eyes" section earlier in this chapter for more information). If you cannot get the hot spot under control in 36 hours, see your veterinarian, who may prescribe oral antibiotics and/or anti-inflammatory agents to treat it.

Insect bites

Many insects bite or sting, so becoming familiar with the ones that live in your area is a good idea. That way, you may be able to prevent your dog from exposure to these bugs.

Usually an insect bite appears as an area of swelling. If the bite is from a bee or a wasp, remove the stinger. If it is from a tick that is still attached, use tweezers to grasp the tick as close to the skin as possible and pull gently until it lets go (see Book II, Chapter 2 for more information on removing ticks). Apply a cold pack if the swelling is severe.

Poisoning

Many poisons lurk in houses, yards, and the environment, and their treatments can differ greatly.

If you suspect that your dog has been poisoned, contact your veterinarian immediately for instructions. If you cannot reach your veterinarian, call the National Animal Poison Control Center at 888-426-4435 for help.

If you know that your dog ingested the poison within the last hour, induce vomiting by pouring 1 to 3 teaspoons of hydrogen peroxide into his mouth between the cheek and the back teeth (or by squirting it with the first-aid syringe in your first-aid kit). If the dog hasn't vomited within ten minutes, repeat. Do not use hydrogen peroxide more than three times at ten-minute intervals.

Do *not* induce vomiting if the poison is unknown, corrosive, or a petroleum product, or if the animal is not completely conscious.

Wash the skin if the toxin can be absorbed through the skin.

Book II

**Dog
Nutrition
and Health**

Porcupine quills

Porcupines roam the woods on sunny days in the winter — and some curious canines just can't mind their own business. The result is usually a face full of painful porcupine quills. If you find your dog in this kind of a fix, first calm the dog as best you can (porcupine quills are very painful, and dogs tend to scratch and paw at their faces) and transport her to your veterinarian as soon as possible. The vet will anesthetize your dog and remove the quills while she is in Dreamland. If veterinary assistance is not available, muzzle the dog and have someone hold her while you pull the quills quickly straight out, *not* at an angle. Feel the skin for deeply embedded quills and look in the mouth for quills, too — a veterinarian should remove these quills.

Never remove quills from the eye. If your dog has a quill in her eye, calm her down (it is very painful) and tie her legs together to prevent her from pawing at the eye. Protect the eye until you can get her to a veterinarian.

Seizures

Seizures in dogs have many causes, from trauma, to tumors, to poisoning. In some dogs, seizures occur periodically for unknown reasons (in a condition called *idiopathic epilepsy*). Take action when a seizure occurs:

- Sit with your dog during the seizure, talking soothingly to him.
- Restrain him only if necessary to keep him from hurting himself. During the seizure, he will have uncontrollable movements and may defecate or urinate.
- Keep your dog quiet for 30 minutes after the seizure.
- If the seizure lasts longer than five minutes or recurs within two hours, take your dog to a veterinarian.

Do not attempt to pull the dog's tongue out or in any way get near the mouth, because severe bites can occur.

If your dog has a seizure, take him to a vet or (better yet) a veterinary neurologist for evaluation.

Snake bites

The most common poisonous snakes in North America are the rattlesnake, the cottonmouth, the coral snake, and the water moccasin. If poisonous snakes live near you, find how to identify them and stay away from them. Consider taking your dog to a snake-proofing session, where she will be taught to stay away from snakes. You can obtain information from your local dog club.

If your dog is bitten by a poisonous snake, do this:

1. **Restrain and calm your dog, to slow uptake of the venom.**

   Arrange for the dog to get to a veterinarian immediately.

2. **Allow the snake bite to bleed freely for 30 to 60 seconds, and then cleanse and disinfect the area.**

3. **Place gauze over the wound and apply pressure.**

   If the wound is on a leg, leave gauze over the wound and wrap the leg with cohesive bandage tightly, but not tight enough to cut off circulation.

4. **Take the dog to a veterinarian immediately.**

Do not cut into the wound caused by a snakebite. Do not apply suction to the wound. And do not apply a tourniquet.

If you and your dog hike frequently in snake-infested areas, talk to your veterinarian about whether you should carry an antivenin with you.

Spinal injury

If you suspect that your dog has suffered a spinal or neck injury, be very cautious about moving him, or you could further damage the spinal cord and cause permanent paralysis or even death.

Muzzle your dog and slide him gradually onto a flat surface such as a board or a piece of heavy cardboard. Secure the dog to the makeshift stretcher with wide strips of tape or an ACE brand bandage, and transport him to the veterinarian immediately.

Sprains and strains

A *sprain* is a stretched or torn ligament and a *strain* is a torn or overused tendon, but the results of both are swelling and inflammation in the area of damage.

The key to treating these injuries is to get ice onto the affected area immediately. Apply the ice for 20 minutes, remove the ice for 20 minutes, and then apply ice again for 20 minutes. The ice helps reduce the swelling and keeps further damage to a minimum.

Try bandaging the ice onto the affected area if your dog doesn't want to let you hold the ice on her body for that long.

Take your dog to a veterinarian if you suspect a fracture or if your dog doesn't bear some weight on the leg within an hour or two. The dog should rest for at least 48 hours after the injury — no running or playing, just short walks on a leash to go potty. If the dog is still limping after 48 hours, she should be seen by a veterinarian.

Book II

Dog Nutrition and Health

Wounds

In their enthusiastic love of life, dogs can get themselves into some fixes. They may run into tree branches or rub against sharp objects. They may even get in an occasional fight and end up a little worse for the wear. So knowing what to do for your walking wounded canine is important.

Wounds fall into two main categories: shallow and deep. Shallow wounds involve just the skin; deep wounds penetrate to the muscles and other tissues below the skin.

Shallow wounds

To treat a shallow wound, follow these steps:

1. **Wash your hands thoroughly.**

2. **Use cotton pads and mild antibacterial liquid soap to clean the wound thoroughly.**

3. **Rinse the wound with sterile saline solution.**

4. **Apply antibacterial ointment to the wound.**

5. **Cover the wound with gauze, wrap it with a bandage, and cover it with a cohesive bandage (but not so tight that you cut off circulation).**

   You can slip a stockinet or bootie over a foot and secure it with tape for extra protection.

6. **Periodically feel your dog's toes.**

   If they become swollen or cool to the touch, remove the bandage and reapply it after the swelling has diminished.

If the wound is small and clean, you can use NuSkin to glue the ends of the wound together. It works just like sutures.

Cuts that may require sutures should be examined by a veterinarian immediately. If a cut is more than about six hours old, it should not be sutured closed because it almost certainly is contaminated with bacteria from the environment. Suturing the wound closed would just trap the bacteria within the wound, resulting in infection and increased scarring. An older cut should be thoroughly cleaned and allowed to heal gradually as an open wound. If the wound is large, it may be partially sutured and a drain left in to help the infection escape.

Deep wounds

To treat a deep wound, do this:

1. **Stop the bleeding by applying pressure.**

2. **When the bleeding has stopped, bandage the wound and seek immediate veterinary treatment.**

If your dog becomes lost

First of all, you should have your dog "chipped" at the vet. An ID chip is a tiny electronic chip implanted under your dog's skin. When your dog is found and taken to the pound or a vet, staff members can scan the chip and get your contact info. Of course, your dog also should be wearing an ID tag with your name, phone number, and address. Some chips come with a tag that gives the chip number, which you can read over the phone to the dog pound when someone finds your dog.

Some people even make up some generic "Missing dog" posters ahead of time and keep them with emergency supplies. In the biggest type size you can, center the words LOST DOG, along with a clear picture of your dog. Beneath that, provide a description of your dog, including any identifying marks. Leave a space to add the phone number where you can be reached, along with any backup contacts, friends, relatives, neighbors, or your veterinarian. Print a hundred copies and keep them in a safe place.

A staple gun allows you to post your notices on anything wooden or cardboard in your neighborhood; keep a loaded staple gun with your supplies, along with thumbtacks and electrical tape.

If your dog becomes lost, post the flyers in your neighborhood and beyond, and distribute them at veterinary hospitals and shelters. While relying on the kindness of strangers is nice, offering a reward can make many strangers just a little bit kinder.

Chapter 4

Preventing and Treating Diseases: Working with Your Vet

*J*ust a few decades ago, to make it to adulthood, puppies had to avoid or successfully battle deadly diseases such as distemper, rabies, hepatitis, and leptospirosis. And fleas were a part of *every* dog's life — along with the scratching, infections, and allergies that accompany those irritating insects. But scientists and veterinarians have worked hard to develop vaccines that prevent canine infectious diseases and to design ways of keeping dogs healthy and prolonging their lives.

One of the most important things you can do to keep your dog healthy is to develop a relationship of mutual respect with a veterinarian. Knowing that you and your veterinarian are partners in maintaining your dog's health and in caring for your canine companion when he has problems can be a tremendous relief. This chapter gives suggestions on establishing this kind of relationship — from choosing a vet to making your dog feel good about going there. You also get some great ideas for tackling the often-expensive costs involved with keeping your dog healthy.

In this chapter, you also find out what you can do to prevent disease, and that often involves taking the dog to the veterinarian. Following these suggestions gives your dog a better chance of living a long and healthy life, which means more time for you to play fetch, teach him tricks, run with him, let him lick your face, and more.

Knowing What to Expect from the Annual Checkup

Taking your canine companion for a thorough veterinary checkup once a year is one of the most important things you can do for her. Even though your dog may seem to be the picture of health, a veterinarian often can detect early signs of disease or organ malfunction before your furry friend shows any outward signs of problems. Your veterinarian also can help you prevent common canine conditions, treat new problems early when treatment is most effective, or institute measures to prevent a condition from becoming worse.

Before your annual veterinary appointment, make notes of any changes in your dog's health or behavior. Jot down any questions you have about your dog's care. These notes will help you provide a complete description of your dog's health history so you can get answers to your questions — and so you're not left saying, "I know there was something I was going to ask, but I can't remember what it was." Bring a pen and paper to the appointment to take brief notes about your veterinarian's recommendations — they can be hard to remember later.

Take advantage of your veterinary appointments. Ask questions and be sure that you understand the answers. Use these meetings as an opportunity to work with your veterinarian to promote your dog's health and longevity. If your dog is found to be healthy at the annual checkup, don't feel you've wasted your time and money. Instead, count your blessings.

A thorough veterinary examination should contain all the components covered in the following sections.

Health history

The veterinarian should ask whether you have observed any changes in your dog's overall health. Now is your opportunity to ask questions and express any concerns you may have with respect to your dog's health or behavior. You may want to point out any skin lumps you've found, discuss changes in your dog's food or water intake, or ask about his urination or bowel habits.

If a specific problem has prompted your visit, bring a written history of the problem. If your dog has been vomiting periodically, for example, record the date the vomiting first began; how often your dog has vomited; when (in relation to eating) he vomited; and the amount, color, and texture of the vomited material.

Physical examination

Your veterinarian has been trained to perform a detailed physical examination of your dog. As he performs the examination, he is thinking about the dog's entire body and is trying to determine whether every organ system is functioning at its peak. The veterinarian should look in your dog's mouth, eyes, and ears, and he should run his hands over your dog's body, feeling for abnormalities in the size or shape of lymph nodes and abdominal organs. He should listen to your dog's heart and lungs with a stethoscope, take your dog's temperature, and weigh her.

Don't talk to your veterinarian or rub your dog while he's listening with his stethoscope. It makes it hard for the vet to hear your dog's lung and heart sounds.

Heartworm check

Heartworms are parasites that live in dogs' hearts and cause heart failure. Mosquitoes transmit larval heartworms from one dog to another by sucking the blood of an infected dog, and then regurgitating a little blood when they bite the next victim. Heartworm disease exists in most areas of the United States and in southernmost Canada. In some areas, such as the southeastern United States, a large percentage of dogs who do not regularly receive heartworm preventive medication are infected. Preventing this disease is critical because, when a dog becomes infected, treating adult worms in the heart requires intensive care and can be life threatening.

Several excellent products are available for preventing heartworm infection. Before a dog is placed on a heartworm preventive, however, a blood sample must be tested to make sure that the dog is not already infected. This simple test can be done in your veterinarian's office while you wait. In northern areas, where temperatures reach freezing, dogs need to take a heartworm preventive only during the spring, summer, and fall — after the test shows they aren't infected. Many vets recommend that dogs be given a heartworm preventive year-round.

Dogs on heartworm preventive should still be tested every year, just in case the medication was forgotten or was ineffective for some reason.

Most heartworm preventives are given monthly. The pills are so tasty that you can just drop one in your dog's food bowl and he'll gobble it up. A heartworm preventive can be given to a puppy with his first set of vaccinations. A heartworm test isn't necessary for a puppy under 3 months of age.

Book II

Dog Nutrition and Health

Blood chemistry, urinalysis, and vaccinations

If your veterinarian notices anything abnormal during his physical examination of your dog, he may take a blood and/or urine sample to perform biochemical tests. These tests can detect infections and malfunctions of the liver, kidney, pancreas, muscle, thyroid, and other organ systems.

Many vaccinations are administered annually, so having your dog vaccinated during the annual checkup makes sense. See Book II, Chapter 2 for more on vaccinating your dog.

Choosing the Right Vet for You and Your Dog

Choose a vet for your dog in the same way you choose a doctor for yourself. Just as you probably wouldn't have much luck choosing your physician from the Yellow Pages, you have better ways of finding a veterinarian than turning to the phone book.

Personal references from friends and acquaintances or your dog's breeder, if she lives nearby, can be very helpful in making your selection. Ask your friends whether their veterinarians have been able to make a diagnosis when their dogs haven't been well. If their dogs had surgery, find out whether the recovery was uneventful and complete. Also find out whether their veterinarians discussed the dogs' illnesses and treatments, and whether they answered questions thoroughly.

When you've compiled a short list of possible veterinarians, call and make an appointment to see each of them without your dog. Tell them you want to meet them, tour their clinics, and discuss your dog's care. Look for the following qualities when choosing a veterinarian for your dog:

  ✔ **Someone who can diagnose:** Your veterinarian should usually be able to give you a diagnosis after she has examined your dog and performed the necessary tests. She may not always come up with a single diagnosis, but she should have a list of possibilities and a plan for how to differentiate between those possibilities. And if your veterinarian doesn't know the diagnosis or can't answer the questions you have, she should at least be able to offer you an explanation of her thought processes and plans for further evaluation.

✔ **Someone you can communicate with easily:** Your veterinarian should be willing to answer your questions and should be able to explain, in terms you understand, both your dog's diagnosis and her recommendations for treatment and follow-up care. Your veterinarian should be willing to listen to you and shouldn't ignore your observations regarding your dog's health. She should work with you as a partner, as someone who can help her work to improve your dog's health.

✔ **Someone who works in a modern facility:** Your veterinarian should have a modern, clean facility with capable veterinary assistants and access to a diagnostic lab that can provide the results of most tests within 24 hours. She should have staff on the premises 24 hours a day to care for seriously ill dogs, or she should be able to move seriously ill dogs to a 24-hour emergency facility for overnight care and observation. Your veterinarian should be available during emergency hours or should be able to refer you to an emergency clinic for problems that occur at night or on weekends.

✔ **Someone who is willing to make referrals:** Your veterinarian should be willing to refer your dog to a specialist for further evaluation. She should not be threatened if you ask for a referral to obtain a second opinion about your dog's condition.

✔ **Someone who has specific interests and specialty training:** Every veterinary professional has areas of special interest. Perhaps your veterinarian is especially interested in working with dogs. Maybe she has a particular interest in your breed of dogs. Not all veterinarians enjoy or are equally talented at performing surgery. And that's okay. But because many dogs need surgery at some time in their lives, you need to know how comfortable your veterinarian is with surgery — what surgical procedures she performs and what kinds of cases she refers to a specialist. Ask her about the surgeons she refers to. Do the surgeons work in the same practice? If not, do they visit the practice to perform surgery, or would you have to transfer your dog elsewhere?

Book II

Dog Nutrition and Health

Don't wait until your dog is ill to find a vet; get the facts and start developing a working relationship with a veterinarian while your dog is healthy. When you visit a veterinary clinic, watch the staff. It always is a good sign when the receptionist and technical staff enjoy being with dogs and work well together.

Don't choose a veterinarian on the basis of the prices she charges for her services. Veterinarians have a great deal of time and money invested in their education, clinic, and equipment. A veterinary clinic has very high overhead because of the cost of maintaining assets and equipment (the building, the surgical and anesthetic equipment, an X-ray machine, ultrasound equipment, and so on), and the cost of top-notch personnel to care for your dog and to assist with surgery. A veterinarian who consistently charges less for her services than other vets in the same area is probably cutting corners somehow, perhaps in a way that can affect your dog's care. To get the best healthcare for your dog, expect to pay for it.

Above all, when choosing a vet, trust your instincts. If you feel uncomfortable talking freely with a particular veterinarian, if you are concerned about the care your animal receives, or if for some reason your dog takes a strong dislike to a particular vet, search for another veterinary partner.

Neutering Your Dog

Every year in the United States, millions of unwanted dogs — both mixed breed and purebred — are put to death. The reason: supply and demand. More puppies are born than there are lifetime homes available. Some unwanted litters are produced by accident (many dog owners don't realize their dogs can start having puppies by 5 or 6 months of age); some litters are just the result of well-intentioned but misinformed people. A common reason given by the people who fall into the latter category is that they want their children to see the "miracle of life" in person, by allowing their dog to have a litter of pups. But what they may not think about ahead of time is the fact that the birth of puppies is not always a beautiful experience, especially if a puppy or the bitch dies in the process.

If you want to teach your children a wonderful lesson about the animal population, teach them the importance of spaying and neutering pets, and take them to visit your local Humane Society or animal shelter so they can see firsthand how many dogs are in need of a good home.

Some people who buy purebred dogs believe they can recover the purchase price of their dog by breeding it — and maybe make a little pocket change at the same time. But this idea is a fallacy; the cost of providing for a litter of puppies until they find new homes can outweigh the purchase price of the dog. It often eats up most of the profit from the sale of a litter, too.

The bottom line? Having a litter consists of either weeks of intensity or a lifetime of responsibility. If you're ready for this, be sure to join your local breed club, where you'll find many other individuals who will be glad to help you with all the details of making puppies. If you aren't ready for the work involved, get your dog spayed or neutered. If you are really interested in breeding, take a look at Book II, Chapter 7.

The only way to be sure that your dog doesn't produce puppies is to get your female dog spayed or your male dog castrated. Failing to do so can lead to . . . well, you know. Intact male dogs and bitches in heat have an uncanny way of finding each other, and a breeding can occur in a snap.

Spaying involves removing both the uterus and the ovaries. *Castration* refers to removing a male dog's testicles. The term *neutering* is a general term to describe either spaying or castration (but you may hear the terms *neutering* and *castrating* used to mean the same thing — *neutering* certainly sounds less horrible).

In addition to preventing unwanted puppies, neutering your dog has many benefits:

✔ Female dogs who are spayed before their first heat cycle (which usually occurs between 6 and 9 months of age) have a significantly reduced chance of developing mammary (breast) cancer, compared to dogs who have had even one heat cycle.

✔ Spayed females can't develop *pyometra,* an infection of the uterus that can be quite severe and can even result in death.

✔ Spayed females tend to have more even temperaments and do not go through the hormone-induced mood swings that intact bitches sometimes have.

✔ Neutered dogs often are better behaved than their intact counterparts. Not only are they less likely to roam (visiting neighborhood females is a major reason for roaming), but they are also less likely to mark their territory by urinating in the house (testosterone is one of the major drives for this dominance-related activity). In addition, neutered male dogs are much less likely to be aggressive toward other male dogs. These behavior benefits are particularly true if you castrate your dog between the ages of 9 and 12 months, before he becomes sexually mature and develops bad habits.

✔ Neutering reduces the incidence of prostate problems often seen in older dogs.

✔ A neutered dog won't develop testicular cancer, a common cancer of older, intact male dogs.

Male dogs who lift their legs to urinate don't leave urine burns in the middle of the lawn because they usually urinate on trees, fence posts, and other vertical objects around the perimeter of the yard. If you prefer that your male dog lift his leg rather than squat to urinate, wait until this habit is well established before getting him neutered.

Many people think their dogs will get fat if they are spayed or castrated, but this isn't the case. Neutered dogs frequently don't need as much food as their intact compatriots, but a simple solution is useful if yours does: Don't feed him as much.

Book II

Dog Nutrition and Health

The gory details

Neutering a male dog involves surgically removing the testicles with a relatively simple operation. When you make an appointment to have your dog castrated, your veterinarian will ask you not to give your dog any food or water after 8 p.m. the night before the surgery. (Keeping your dog from eating or drinking decreases the likelihood of the dog regurgitating during surgery.) The veterinarian will anesthetize the dog and make a tiny incision in the skin just in front of the testicles. The testicles are then slid up under the skin and removed through this little slit. The skin is sutured with three to five sutures. Your dog is then allowed to wake from the anesthesia and to rest overnight — either at the veterinarian's office or at your home — after the surgery.

Spaying a female is more involved than neutering a male because it involves opening the abdomen. As with any general anesthetic, the veterinarian will ask you not to give your dog food or water after 8 p.m. the night before the surgery. After your dog is anesthetized, the veterinarian will make an incision in the center of her abdomen. He will find the uterus and ovaries and cut them out, first making sure that all the blood vessels are clamped off so

they don't bleed. In a young dog, the blood vessels are tiny and are easy to clamp off. After a female has been through a heat cycle, however, the vessels are larger and require special attention so they don't bleed. This is why spaying a dog after her first heat is usually more expensive. If a bitch is pregnant, the vessels are very large and are full of blood to feed the growing puppies; therefore, some veterinarians refuse to spay a pregnant bitch (sometimes requested to prevent the birth of puppies) because of the danger of postoperative bleeding. After removing the uterus and ovaries, the veterinarian sutures the abdominal incision and the dog wakes up. She then may stay overnight at the clinic to make sure that she rests and doesn't stress the incision in the early stages of healing.

For the first couple days after surgery (whether for castration or spaying), your dog should rest and should go outside only for the bathroom. For the next week, mild exercise such as on-leash walking is all right. About ten days after surgery, the veterinarian will check to make sure that the incision is healing properly and will remove the sutures (or check on self-dissolving sutures).

Depending on your locale and the veterinarian you select, castrating a male dog can cost between $100 and $150, and spaying a female dog costs between $150 and $200. This cost is an incredible bargain, given that the bill for a woman's hysterectomy costs upward of $10,000. For people on public assistance, people with lower incomes, and seniors on fixed incomes, spay/neuter clinics in most towns and cities can provide the service for a drastically reduced fee. These clinics usually are sponsored by animal shelters and veterinarians as part of an ongoing effort to control the local pet population. To find out when these clinics are held in your area, contact your local animal shelter. But costs can vary widely — always find out what services are included so you can compare apples to apples.

Helping Your Dog Enjoy His Trip to the Vet

You just love going to the doctor or dentist, don't you? Well, many dogs hate visiting the vet. And it's really not surprising, given the fact that their associations usually are negative.

Think how a routine veterinary checkup (see Figure 4-1) must appear to your dog. First, he has to wait in a small room full of dogs, cats, and other animals, most of whom are extremely fearful. Then he is led into a strange room and is placed on a cold, slippery table. Next, a stranger who smells like a mixture of soap, chemicals, and other animals touches him all over his body, looks in his mouth and ears, and sticks a cold glass thermometer up his rear end. To top it all off, the stranger usually pokes him with at least one needle, often more.

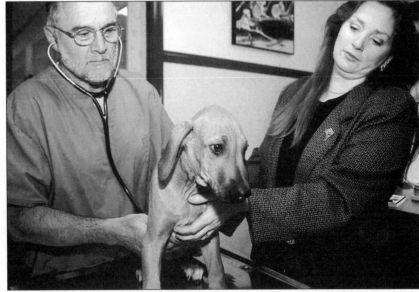

Figure 4-1: Visiting the vet can be difficult for many dogs, so find a vet who is kind and caring.

© Mary Bloom

You can take some steps to ensure that your dog's veterinary experiences are good ones. Consider these ways to prevent your dog from developing a fear of his trips to the vet:

- ✔ **Occasionally drop by the vet's office with your dog when you don't have an appointment.** Bring your dog into the office and have the receptionist give him a cookie or two. Chat for a while and then leave. This way, your dog will learn to view the vet's office as a fun place, instead of a place where he only gets poked and prodded.

- ✔ **Make sure that your dog gets experience riding in the car just for fun.** If he rides in the car only when he has to see the veterinarian, he soon will become fearful as soon as he gets in the car.

- ✔ **Schedule your veterinary appointments for a time when there are fewer dogs in the office, if you can.** This reduces the social stresses on your dog and reduces your time in the waiting room. If your dog is particularly worried while he's in the waiting room, stay with your dog in the car until the veterinarian is ready to meet with you (you can run in and let the office staff know you're in the parking lot and have them come get you when they're ready).

- ✔ **Bring an ample supply of treats with you.** Give your dog a treat for entering the door and another for sitting with you quietly. Train your dog in the basics of obedience — he'll feel more secure if he is asked to do something familiar (like "sit" and "stay") during this stressful period. During your office visit, ask the veterinarian to give your dog some treats periodically, especially just before she examines your dog or before she does something stressful such as inserting the thermometer.

- ✔ **Don't mistakenly praise your dog for being stressed.** Many people make the mistake of trying to comfort their dogs when they act fearful in the veterinary office. Your dog may interpret this attention as you praising him for his worry. You're better off ignoring him when he acts worried, and praising him and giving him treats for even small acts of boldness.

Start these preventive measures from the very first visit. Don't wait until your dog shows signs of fear.

Covering the Costs

If your dog gets sick, will you be able to pay the bill? Treating a simple infection can cost hundreds of dollars, and cancer treatment routinely costs thousands. Of course, you want to provide the best treatment possible for your furry friend, but top-notch veterinary care comes at a price. Before an accident or a sudden illness has you emptying your savings account or, even worse, opting for euthanasia because of a lack of funds, consider the alternatives in the following sections and see if one of these options is right for you.

Personal savings plans

The best way to make sure that you'll always have funds available to pay veterinary bills is to set up a canine cash reserve. If you deposit $30 to $50 a month in a savings account in your pet's name, you'll be surprised by how much you can save. In a year or two, you'll have enough to pay the bill for most serious illnesses. Save the spare change you collect at the end of the day, and you'll have all your dog's healthcare covered.

You can use your canine cash reserve to pay for *all* your veterinary bills, or you can set it aside for any expenses over a certain amount (such as $200). The money will continue to grow throughout your dog's life, and you will have a substantial sum accumulated when your dog is older (when she's more likely to require more expensive treatments).

The only disadvantage of this system is that you have to have the discipline to make it work.

Don't wait until the last minute to come up with funds to pay your dog's medical expenses. If you put $2 of change a day into a savings account, at the end of three years, you'll have saved more than $2,000 — enough to pay for your average catastrophic illness.

Pet insurance

Obtaining pet insurance is one way to ease veterinary sticker shock. Insurance companies charge annual premiums of between $150 and $300 for a healthy adult dog. Basic coverage for puppies is slightly less, and when your dog reaches 8 years of age, the cost of coverage rises incrementally as your dog gets older. Basic plans usually don't cover routine preventive care, although such coverage may be available for an extra charge. The basic plans are designed to cover a percentage of the veterinary charges for unexpected illnesses. They don't cover preexisting conditions or hereditary diseases. So if your dog has hip dysplasia, for example, surgical or medical treatment to ease his pain would not be covered. But if your furry friend were hit by a car or decided to eat a dish towel (yes, dogs have done that), the costs of veterinary care would be covered (after paying a deductible) up to a maximum amount for that condition.

Making sense of the deductions, maximums, exclusions, and other insurance lingo can be tough, so be sure to read the insurance company's literature carefully before signing on the dotted line. If you have any questions about what will and will not be covered, speak to an insurance company representative. Don't hesitate to ask whatever questions you have about the coverage you're considering. Think about some of the illnesses your dog (or one of your previous dogs) has suffered and ask what percentage of the charges would be covered. Using a real-life example will help you understand exactly how much you will be responsible for and determine whether the cost of the insurance is worth it.

If you keep good financial records, you can add up how much you spent on veterinary care during the last five years and calculate how much you typically spend on veterinary care every year. Take a look also at how much you have saved to deal with a catastrophic illness so that you can determine whether you may benefit from pet insurance.

Clinic-based HMOs

For a number of years, individual clinics have offered *well-care plans,* in which clients pay a monthly fee and receive discounts on routine care and preventive maintenance such as annual checkups, vaccinations, fecal exams, deworming, and heartworm checks. Some programs also offer member discounts on dental cleaning and surgical spaying or castrating.

Prepaid healthcare programs offer a way of spreading out (and perhaps reducing) the costs of routine veterinary care, but they generally do not cover hereditary diseases, preexisting conditions, or catastrophic illness. In addition, they cover your pet only for care provided in that specific practice. So if your pet gets ill while you're on vacation, or if he requires the care of a specialist not in that practice, you're on your own.

If you are considering taking advantage of a comprehensive preventive care program, do a little math to figure out whether it's right for you. Make a list of all the preventive care services you would normally avail yourself of in a year, and add up the cost of those services. Then compare that number with the cost for the services offered by the clinic's well-care plan. Clinic-based plans often provide a significant discount to clients who want to provide the most complete preventive care for their furry friends.

Pet-care credit companies

Several credit companies offer credit to cover unexpected veterinary fees. If your dog suddenly becomes ill or has an accident and you're short on funds, this option can save your dog's life. Unlike pet insurance, credit companies do not require you to sign up ahead of time (although your veterinarian must be registered with the company), and there are no exclusions or deductibles.

To take advantage of this service, you just fill out a credit application, which your veterinarian transmits to the lender. If the application is approved, your veterinarian is paid within 48 hours, and a payment schedule is established for repayment of your loan.

Of course, all this credit comes at a price. These companies generally charge 18 to 24 percent interest (similar to what you may pay in interest on a credit card debt), making them an expensive prospect if you have to make payments over a long period of time. Nonetheless, this option is available if the only other choice is euthanasia.

Another option, which gives you more power over the interest you pay, is to keep a major credit card with no balance, to ensure that you have enough money to pay for emergencies.

Book II

**Dog
Nutrition
and Health**

Chapter 5

Getting the Lead Out: Exercising Your Dog

*T*housands of years ago, for better or for worse, dogs linked up with humans (see Book I, Chapter 1 for more on this story). Overall, the marriage has been a great success for both parties. But one of the sacrifices most dogs have made is the ability to go outside and run free any time they want. Wolves often cover 100 miles a day while hunting and exploring; with most people leading very busy lives and working outside the home, dogs are lucky to do *one* mile on a leash every day, and most don't even get that.

Exercise offers tremendous physical and psychological benefits for your dog — and for you, too. With all the companionship your dog provides, she deserves to get the exercise she craves. This chapter tells you how to give your dog the hard body she has always wanted — even if you work all day, are disabled, or just plain don't have the energy.

Recognizing the Benefits of Exercise

Exercise provides immense physical and psychological benefits to dogs of all ages. Dogs who exercise regularly live longer, remain healthier, and are more active in their later years. With regular exercise, your dog will become stronger and more coordinated, and his muscles will become more powerful and ready to kick into action any time. Strong muscles stabilize the joints, slowing the progression of arthritis. Exercise strengthens the heart and the lungs as well, improving the delivery of oxygen and nutrients to tissues throughout the body. Exercise is also an excellent way to control your dog's weight; strong muscles are larger and utilize more calories while at rest than smaller muscles do.

Runners and other fitness buffs have long recognized the psychological benefits of exercise. It causes the brain to release *endorphins*, biochemical messengers within the brain that induce a feeling of euphoria and overall well-being. So exercise (and the good feeling it brings) can prevent a dog from developing problems such as *lick granulomas* (sores caused by repeated licking or chewing at the skin), destructive behaviors (chewing the corners of your new couch or digging up your tulip bulbs), restlessness, or excessive barking.

In fact, exercise is so important to a dog's psyche that it's the first line of treatment for most behavioral problems. Dog behaviorists claim that lack of exercise is a significant contributing factor in over 50 percent of all behavioral problems in dogs.

Despite all the benefits of exercise, most dogs in North America do not get enough. If your dog spends so much time lounging that he's starting to look like part of the furniture, it's time to get him on his feet and out of the house. Do it gradually, however. Just as you wouldn't head out the door to run a marathon without any training, you shouldn't expect your couch potato dog to be able to exercise for hours without building up to that level.

If your dog is seriously overweight (more than 20 percent heavier than his ideal weight), get the thumbs up from your veterinarian before you start him on a serious exercise program. Your vet should give your dog a physical examination, with special emphasis on the heart, lungs, and musculoskeletal system, to be sure that he's ready to up his activity level.

If you start your dog's exercise program slowly, increase the amount of exercise gradually, and use common sense, your dog faces only minimal risk of injury. To be safe, overweight dogs should not do much running with quick turns or jumping until they have slimmed down.

If your dog shows signs of fatigue such as excessive panting, grimacing, or scuffing the toes, ease up or stop altogether. Dogs who have a tendency to go until they drop definitely need guidance about when to stop.

To remain fit and content, a dog should get a minimum of 15 minutes of exercise a day and should have a longer exercise period two to three times a week. Be creative with your dog's exercise. This is a time when you and your dog can get to know each other better — make the most of it!

Try to provide a mix of both strength-training and endurance-training exercises. Like humans, dogs have a mixture of muscle fibers — some for strength and some for endurance. These fibers use energy differently and are called upon in different circumstances. Exercises such as retrieving and chasing, which involve many starts, stops, and turns, help build strength. Exercises such as trotting, in which the dog moves continuously for at least 20 minutes, build endurance. Dogs benefit most if you build both their strength *and* their endurance muscles.

If you are a fitness buff, be sure to not overexercise your dog. During sustained, repetitive physical activity, lactic acid builds up and breaks down muscle cells. Cells need 48 hours to repair themselves. So if you run with your dog beside you on a leash for more than 30 minutes, give your canine athlete a day off between runs to recover.

Being Creative with Your Dog's Exercise Routine

Does the word *exercise* evoke images in your mind of runners with sweaty shirts, glazed eyes, and sore feet? Don't worry, you can exercise your dog without sweating beside your panting pup over miles of hot pavement. You have at your disposal many more interesting and effective ways to give your dog the exercise she needs. With a little imagination, you can invent a variety of exercises and games that will build your dog's strength and endurance and that you'll both enjoy. Exercise takes a little time, but the payoff is enormous in terms of your dog's health and vitality, her confidence and behavior, and your relationship with her. Besides, who among us can't use a few moments of stress-free playtime during the day?

Inject a little variety into your playtimes. After all, too much of even a fun game gets boring. Play different kinds of games in different locales, at different times of the day, with different treats for rewards.

Instinctive activities

Often the activities that are the most fun for dogs (and their humans) are those that imitate the dog's natural drives and instincts. When your dog plays fetch, she imagines herself as a mighty hunter, chasing her prey and bringing it home to the pups. For dogs with herding instincts, such as Shelties and Collies, it's the chasing part that's fun, not the capture. They bring the ball back so they can chase it again. A pair of dogs often exercises each other, alternating between being the chaser and the chasee. Terriers and other dogs originally bred to hunt vermin love to play games with a killing theme. Nothing feels quite as good to a Terrier as chasing a stuffed toy, capturing it, and shaking it to break its neck.

 You can harness a dog's latent herding instinct by inventing chasing games. One fun game is to have your dog sit and stay in the middle of a soccer field, place yourself approximately three-quarters of the way to the goal, release your dog, and start running. See which one of you gets to the goal first. Be sure to handicap yourself, if necessary, so your dog wins about half the time.

 You also can recapitulate vermin-catching games for your Terrier. Drag a bone or a toy over the ground for 25 feet or so, and then bury it in an area of the garden that's okay to dig in. Watch your Terrier's face beam as you take him to the beginning of the scent trail and encourage him to "find the rat." To a Terrier, there's no delight quite like that of finding the prey and digging it out.

Walking

Many people derive great pleasure from a daily walk with the dog. For some, this means an early morning amble through the neighborhood, with the dew on the grass and the birds chattering in the trees. For others, it's a chance to put on the headphones, crank up the music, and forget the day's stresses. Most dogs enjoy walks because of their natural curiosity about the environment. They love to be surrounded by new sights and smells. You may find it kind of frustrating, however, to stop at each vertical object along the way so your dog can exchange pee-mail with the other dogs in the neighborhood.

 Always carry a plastic bag and pick up after your dog (and remind your dog walker or pet sitter to do so, too). Just slip your hand in the bag, grab the dog poop, and then turn the bag inside out over your hand and tie it in a knot. Find a trash can to deposit your package in, or throw it out when you get home. Your neighbors will appreciate your thoughtfulness and you will feel good knowing that you're doing your part to keep the neighborhood dog friendly. In many locales, this is not just a good idea — it's the law.

 Try a *waist leash,* a belt to which you can attach your dog's leash. Walking or running with your dog when your hands are free to swing at your sides is much easier than having to hang on to a leash the whole way.

Jogging and running

Jogging or running is probably the best way to ensure that both you and your dog are getting enough exercise. Most runners are consistent — they go on their daily runs regardless of weather or schedule. This consistency is best for your dog.

Running with your dog offers many benefits:

- ✔ It's excellent exercise.
- ✔ Your dog learns to stay at your side, regardless of distractions.
- ✔ If you run on a hard surface, your dog's nails don't have to be trimmed often (or at all) because the pavement will naturally file them for you.
- ✔ It's a great way of bonding with your dog.

Though you may run 3 miles or more when you exercise, don't start your dog at this rate. She needs to gradually build up tolerance to this distance. Start her at 1 mile and, over a period of two weeks, gradually increase her exercise tolerance to match yours.

Don't feed your dog within an hour before or after strenuous exercise. Some dogs are prone to *bloat* (a twisting of the stomach due to gaseous intake).

Skijoring

Skijoring — in which your dog pulls you over the snow on skis — is a great winter variation on taking a walk. If your dog gets a bit carried away or you are a cautious skier, you can also cross-country ski with your dog running beside you.

Running in deep snow is very strenuous, so reserve skijoring for dogs older than 2 years of age.

Some dogs get snowballs between the pads of their feet when they play in the snow. You can reduce this problem by trimming excess hair from the bottom of your dog's feet and between his toes. You also can apply petroleum jelly or cooking spray liberally to the skin between his toes before going outside. Another excellent fix is to have your dog wear booties, which are available at pet supply stores and through companies that sell products for mushing dogs. If your dog runs mainly on packed snow, get booties made of polar fleece. If he runs on mixed snow and gravel or pavement, get booties made of a tougher fabric, such as canvas or Cordura nylon. Booties can also be an excellent aid for the city dog who feels the sting of salt spread on the streets and sidewalks in the winter.

Fetch

Fetch is a favorite game of many dogs. Most people are fond of this game because they can play it while standing still. You can use many different fetch objects, from a simple stick to a ball or a disc. Some balls glow in the dark or have an internal flashing light, so you can even use them for a quick game of fetch when you get home from work on a dark winter night.

Bumpers (plastic cylinders that float and have a rope attached to one end) are a favorite fetch toy for many Retrievers, especially for retrieving on water. The rope makes them easier to throw, too. Many dogs like to chase flying discs as well. The way the disc floats in the air and changes directions is very exciting to the canine hunter.

Be careful when playing fetch with a flying disc. Throw the disc just above the ground so your dog doesn't have to leap up to catch it. Dogs can suffer severe injuries by twisting their backs or by landing on their rear legs when trying to catch a disc. Try to find a floppy one, made of rubber, to reduce the risk of hurting your dog's teeth.

If your dog isn't much of a retriever, she may enjoy playing soccer. Use a ball that is too large and too firm for her to pick up in her teeth. Kick it around the yard, encouraging her to chase it. She will eventually get the idea and learn to push the ball around the yard herself. Dogs can have a lot of fun playing with a large ball in the water, too. They use their noses to push the ball back and forth and try to capture it.

If you can't throw a ball very far and your dog is looking at you as if she wished she were owned by a baseball star, try using an aid to throw the ball farther. That way your dog will run farther for each fetch, making it more fun for her. Use a tennis racket or a bat to whack the ball as far as possible. Another great invention is the Chuckit, a plastic stick that cups a tennis ball at one end while you hold the other end and swing it. When you let it go, the ball flies up to 250 feet — much farther than if you used your arm. The Foxtail is another type of ball that is easy to throw long distances. This ball has a colorful nylon tail that flaps in the breeze as it trails the ball. If you use the tail to swing it before letting go, you can sling the Foxtail farther than you can throw it.

If your dog is a keen retriever, why not add a few twists to the old game of fetch? First throw the ball as far as you can. Then throw a short one. Then throw your dog a grounder; then toss the ball high into the air for your dog to catch. Praise her just for trying, and give her verbal praise and treats for extra-fast or talented retrieves. You also can make the game tougher by having your dog retrieve an object while running uphill. This increases the amount of weight she has to bear on her rear legs, thus increasing the amount of work the rear legs perform. This strengthens the rear leg muscles, which is especially important as the dog gets older.

Swimming

Swimming is one of the best forms of exercise for any dog. Because it's a non-weight-bearing activity, it strengthens the cardiovascular and muscular systems without stressing bones and joints. This is especially good for dogs with arthritis.

Many dogs, like the one in Figure 5-1, naturally enjoy swimming, and most can learn if they're given encouragement when they're young. The best way to teach a pup to swim is to start by putting on your boots and walking with him in a creek. Creeks have deeper and shallower parts, and eventually your pup will find himself swimming a short distance without even realizing it. If your adult dog is reluctant, get wet yourself and encourage him to join you in the fun. If he is hesitant to swim over his head, use the Hansel-and-Gretel principle: Walk slowly out to deeper waters, depositing dog treats as you go (Cheerios float very well) and offering encouragement. Often a dog's stomach will overcome his fears.

If your water-loving canine is going to swim in a pond, scout the area for broken glass, fishing lines, and other hazards first. If you find broken glass, seek out another place for your dog to swim, because there's likely to be more where that came from. If he bounds into the water and steps on broken glass, it can cut the tendons that run across the wrist just under the skin of his legs. Tendons are notoriously difficult to repair, and those particular tendons are critical for a dog to be able to walk and run without discomfort — you definitely don't want to risk it.

If you or a friend has a swimming pool and don't mind a little dog hair in the filter, letting your dog swim there is just fine. In fact, if you want your flabby dog to build a little muscle, you can put him on a leash and walk around the outside of the pool for 5 to 10 minutes while he swims beside you. Throw a few treats in the water every now and then to keep up his interest.

Figure 5-1:
The smile
on Tally's
face is all
the proof
you need to
know that
swimming
is one of
her favorite
activities.

Never let your dog swim in a pool without supervision. Every year, dogs drown in pools after becoming exhausted trying to find their way out, even when stairs are available. Plus, some breeds, such as Bulldogs, aren't built for swimming and can drown in shallow water. Be sure that you know your dog's limitations.

Biking

Having your dog run by your side as you bike is another great way for your dog to burn off excess energy.

If you decide to give biking a try, take several precautions, because you, and your dog, can easily be injured. First, acclimate your dog to your bicycle. Some dogs would rather chase bikes than run alongside them. Check out Book IV, Chapter 3 to teach your dog to heel, and then do the following:

1. **Have your dog heel with you as you push your bicycle.**

2. **When she's working well, get on your bike, but keep your feet on the ground to move it.**

3. **When your dog is walking nicely at your side, get on the bike and pedal slowly.**

4. Gradually increase the speed as your dog performs well, moving with you.

Make sure that your dog stays on the side of you that is away from the road. This will keep her from being hit by a car if she suddenly lunges outward. Try a device such as the Springer or K-9 Cruiser to attach your dog's leash to the bicycle, leaving your hands free (see Figure 5-2). It's a metal bar that attaches to the bike, with a hook on the other end to affix your dog's leash. This keeps your dog with you, while also keeping her a safe enough distance from the wheels. One incident with a squirrel running across your path should convince you of the benefits of these attachments.

No product available will keep your dog watching you instead of wanting to socialize with the neighbors' dogs as you go by. You might want to begin with walking and running before moving up to bike riding, to train your dog to remain with you regardless of your pace.

While you ride your bike or run on a hard surface, your dog is running on that surface barefoot! Without the benefit of booties, your dog might injure her pads. Try a pad conditioner (a cream you rub on your dog's pads) along with booties.

Book II

Dog Nutrition and Health

Figure 5-2:
Attach a device to your bike so that you don't have to hold on to a leash and try to maneuver the bike at the same time.

Photo courtesy of Todd Jackson.

Bicycling with an unleashed dog is dangerous. Even on country paths, a loose dog can chase wild animals such as rabbits or deer and become lost or injured. Use an attachment that connects your dog to your bicycle.

Hiking

Hiking is similar to walking, except you and your dog head out into the countryside, woods, or mountains. You may not be able to count on hiking every day, depending on where you live and what your schedule is like, but it can be a great addition to your dog's exercise routine.

Before you leave for your hike, make sure that you're familiar with the canine-related rules for the area. Most state parks require dogs to be leashed. Regardless of where you go, always have a leash with you in case your dog becomes unruly or more interested in chasing squirrels than in listening to you.

Pack a collapsible water bowl and a bottle of fresh water. When dogs exercise, they need to drink lots of water. Many lakes, streams, and rivers are contaminated with bacteria, so you want to make certain that your dog isn't drinking from them. If you give him a fresh water supply before, during, and after your hike, you shouldn't have to worry about him looking for water elsewhere. Carry a few treats with you so that every time your dog looks and/ or returns to you of his own accord, he gets a reward for doing so. This will tend to keep him closer to you and less likely to run after other hikers.

If you've been hiking for some time and your dog is just starting to go with you, you'll need to gradually increase his tolerance to the exercise. Dogs will keep going until they drop, so be aware of these signs that he's getting tired:

- ✔ Heavy panting
- ✔ Tendency to lie down whenever you pause
- ✔ Droopy eyes and ears
- ✔ A slow pace

Be sure to check his pads when you take a break. He doesn't have the benefit of hiking boots like you do, and you may be crossing rocky terrain that can easily slice his pads. Have a small first-aid pack handy (see Book II, Chapter 3), just in case.

Horse and hound

Horse and hound is great exercise for a dog. The species have been hunting together for millennia, so there's no reason why your dog can't learn how to respect the horse, watch the horse's leg movements, and listen to your requests at the same time. Dogs are great at multitasking, especially when it means a long run through fields and woods.

Before taking off in a run, acclimate your dog to horses. Horses are prey animals and dogs are predators, so you have to teach your dog to control her natural instincts and to listen to you from a distance. The guidelines in Book IV, Chapter 3 will help you train your dog so that horse and hound is fun and safe for both hound and horse.

Scheduling Time for Your New Dog

You got a dog to enrich your life. Your dog gives you joy and is something you look forward to each day — and you need to be the same for him. You have to make time for him — time for exercise, for specific feeding and relief schedules, and for an education.

When you make a schedule, stick to it. Dogs are creatures of habit. Knowing what's going to occur, and when, helps your dog adjust to his new life quickly.

Playtime

Walking along on a leash is great exercise, especially for an older dog, but younger dogs need more than this. And although training exercises do stimulate your dog's mind and make her tired, they don't totally exercise her body. Dogs need free play — off leash, preferably with other dogs, provided they haven't ever displayed any aggression to other canines.

A small dog often gets plenty of exercise racing around the house, but that isn't the preferred situation for a medium-sized or large dog. Having an 80-pound dog racing around an apartment or even a good-sized house can be quite disruptive — more so as she jumps over the couch, runs through the kitchen, and barrels over a trash can or two. Having any dog larger than 10 pounds means lots of exercise — outside, in all types of weather. A fenced yard helps, but your dog prefers to spend much of her exercise time interacting with you, such as going for long walks and playing fetch and chase games. Make time for this. Exercise is covered in more detail earlier in this chapter.

Feeding time

Dogs need to know when they're going to eat. Feed your dog in the same location every time so he knows where he'll be eating. This helps keep him from feeling that he can eat anywhere in your home. The feed dish should be in the kitchen, but not in a direct path with your cooking area. Under a desk, at one end of a kitchen island, and at the edge of the room are generally good places. Place the water dish near the feed dish.

Don't place the dog's dish near a trash can. He might think the can is part of his meals.

Stick to a feeding schedule to help your dog know that he'll be taken care of at a specific time. Feeding times depend greatly on your own work schedule, as well as the age of your dog. Let's say you work a regular 9-to-5 job. To give your dog time to exercise and relieve himself before and after work, try the following scheduling:

6 a.m.	Take him to his relief zone.
6:15 a.m.	Feed him.
6:30 to 7:00 a.m.	Take him to his relief zone and exercise him a bit before leaving for work.
5:30 to 6:00 p.m.	Take him to his relief zone.
6:15 p.m.	Feed him.
7 p.m.	Take him to his relief zone and exercise him a lot.

What if you work irregular hours? Try to still stick to some semblance of a schedule. You may not be able to offer consistent exercise times, but you do need to offer similar feeding times.

With their faster metabolism, puppies need to be fed more often than older dogs. Consider this sample feeding schedule for a dog younger than 5 months of age for someone who works the regular 9-to-5 job, keeping in mind that there *will* be an opportunity for the youngster to eat and exercise midday — whether you can come home at that time or have someone do it for you, it's a must.

6 a.m.	Take him to his relief zone.
6:15 a.m.	Feed him.
6:30 a.m.	Take him to his relief zone and exercise him a lot.
12 p.m.	Feed him.
12:15 p.m.	Take him to his relief zone and exercise him a lot.
6 p.m.	Feed him.
6:15 p.m.	Take him to his relief zone and exercise him a lot.

Dogs older than 5 months can safely be fed twice a day, as long as they don't have a medical condition that requires them to be fed smaller meals more often.

Potty time

Potty time goes hand in hand with feeding time, because when your dog eats has the most bearing on when your dog needs to go out (see the preceding section). If you want a housetrained dog, you have to adhere to a schedule. Make certain you either schedule her potty breaks into your day or arrange to have someone do it for you.

The younger the dog, the more often she has to potty. Keep this in mind when you choose a dog. Do you have the time to take her to her relief zone every couple hours or so? To housetrain a puppy (see Book IV, Chapter 1), you have to do so.

The more your pup exercises, the more often she needs to be taken to her relief zone.

Dogs older than the age of 4 months can hold themselves longer, but they still require relief more often than a dog older than 9 months of age. Take your 4- to 9-month-old dog out every three to four hours, to be on the safe side. After the age of 9 months, you can wait as long as six hours (or longer, if you have to), but that isn't kind to her on a daily basis.

Male dogs require more time to relieve themselves because they tend to urinate several times instead of letting their bladders empty all at once. They also have to relieve themselves more often throughout the day than most female dogs.

Knowing How Much Exercise Your Dog Needs

A dog's exercise requirements depend on many factors, including age, breed combination, and size. For example, dogs who have Herding blood need to run and exercise a lot every day because they were designed to help farmers, whereas dogs with Sporting blood generally don't need more than a couple good long games of fetch because their jobs traditionally involved aiding hunters in locating and returning game.

Puppies

Your puppy will go through several stages of development that affect his level of energy. Some studies suggest that a dog matures the equivalent of 21 human years within his first year of life and 5 years each year thereafter. If you consider the behavioral stages of people (and puppies), this is a good assumption. Imagine taking a child all the way from infancy to the legal drinking age in one year — that's what you do when you bring home a puppy.

Physically, the puppy grows from a little, short-legged, roly-poly, round-faced cutie into a dog with a sleek, more angular physique. After the first year, a dog doesn't change much physically.

Consider this overview of the kind of energy levels (and exercise requirements) you can expect from your pup in the first year of his life:

- **4 weeks to 3 months:** Between the ages of 4 weeks and 3 months, pups tend to sleep most of the time. They have short bursts of energy but they quickly tire out. A few minutes outside, and they're beat.

- **3 to 4 months:** When a pup is about 3 to 4 months old, his energy level changes a bit. He'll play more and for longer periods of time. This is when your pup begins testing his position in the pack — he'll display dominance when he plays with you or other dogs. He'll get into tug-of-war games in earnest. Fetch becomes a fantastic idea. Chasing butterflies is also very exciting. On average, a dog this age requires a half hour of exercise at least five times a day.

- **5 to 7 months:** At the age of 5 to 7 months, your puppy is at the peak of adolescence. This is the period when he needs more exercise than he will at any other time in his life. Not only will he be testing his pack position, but he'll be very easily distracted and want to do a zillion things at once (just like the typical teenager). An adolescent dog requires *at least* several hours of exercise each day, especially Herding, Sporting, or Terrier breeds. Your dog needs the freedom to run in a safely fenced area. Play with other dogs is the best means of blowing off steam. Though your pup will quickly tire during training sessions, these aren't enough to rid him of the zoomies.

- **8 to 10 months:** Between 8 and 10 months, your young dog will still be full of energy, but he's able to channel it a bit better. If you offer regular activities, he'll be happy to participate. He'll also begin showing signs of maturity, with a better understanding of house rules. He'll have more moments of lying at your feet than in the previous three months. An older adolescent dog still needs lots of exercise time — two to three hours each day. His exercise can be a combination of play with other dogs and a regulated activity such as a training session.

- **10 months to 1 year:** Between 10 and 12 months, your dog has become an adult. Don't worry — he'll still be playful and energetic. In fact, many dogs are energetic well into old age. If you give appropriate exercise outlets, you'll have a happy, healthy, easy-to-manage companion. Your dog will require a regular exercise regimen, but his activity can be more concentrated, such as training time, hiking, biking, or jogging. The zoomies are gone.

Growing dogs need lots of exercise. Confining them daily for extended periods of time is detrimental to their physical and mental development. Young dogs need to stretch their legs and minds as they mature. You need to discover the proper balance to train your dog in the house rules and allow him to "be a dog." Though you should confine him in a safe area when you can't be with him, be sure to observe him closely at play when you're home. Follow an exercise regimen with your dog. If you exercise *with* him, it can be great for bonding — and for your own health as well as his.

An exercise program for a puppy should not include strenuous exercises or long play periods. The *growth plates* (soft areas at each end of the bones) do not harden until a puppy is 10 to 14 months of age. These soft areas are susceptible to fractures, and even though the bone will heal, it is likely to grow unevenly, resulting in a deformity of the bone. Puppies also are more likely to injure themselves because of their lack of coordination and muscle strength. In addition, puppies are more susceptible to the stresses of heat and cold than are adult dogs.

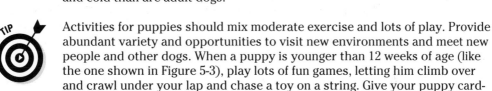

Activities for puppies should mix moderate exercise and lots of play. Provide abundant variety and opportunities to visit new environments and meet new people and other dogs. When a puppy is younger than 12 weeks of age (like the one shown in Figure 5-3), play lots of fun games, letting him climb over and crawl under your lap and chase a toy on a string. Give your puppy cardboard boxes, bricks, and other safe objects to step on and explore. At that age, you also can go for a five-minute walk or play in a shallow creek.

Puppies younger than 6 months of age need only moderate exercise. After 6 months of age, provide strengthening exercises such as games of fetch and chase, but don't add endurance exercises until those bones are fully mature (18 months for tiny dogs, 24 to 30 months for big dogs).

As your pup grows older, he'll be able to trot for greater distances and play for longer periods of time without needing a rest. Throughout adolescence, your puppy will have lots of energy and will want to be busy all the time. When his body reaches adult size, you may be fooled into thinking he has adult stamina. The trick at this stage is to give him abundant exercise, play lots of games, and give him many intellectual challenges — without overdoing it.

Book II

Dog Nutrition and Health

Figure 5-3:
This young
puppy plays
with her dad
every day.

Photograph courtesy of Marcia Halliday.

Adult dogs

How much exercise an adult dog needs depends largely on her breed. Even if you don't know exactly which breed(s) make up your dog's family tree, you can probably venture a good guess about which general breed groups she's a part of. For example, you can usually tell a Hound from a Terrier. If you're just not sure about your dog, your vet will probably be able to steer you in the right direction.

Table 5-1 shows recommendations for the amount of exercise different dogs need based on their breed group. If you know your dog has the genetics of one of these breed groups, you'll have a fairly good idea of how much exercise your dog needs.

Table 5-1	Breed Group Exercise Requirements	
Breed Group	*Energy Level*	*Minimum Hours of Exercise Per Day*
Sporting	High	3
Hound	Medium	2
Working	Medium	2

Breed Group	Energy Level	Minimum Hours of Exercise Per Day
Terrier	High	2
Toy	Medium to low	1
Non-Sporting	Varies greatly	1–3
Herding	Very high	4

Table 5-1 lists the *minimum* amount of exercise a dog needs every day. If you have a Hound and you want to exercise her more than one hour a day, your dog won't have any problems as long as you increase the amount of exercise gradually, just as you'd do for yourself. But if you have a Herding dog and you give her only an hour of exercise a day, the results could be disastrous. If you're not giving your dog enough exercise, she'll find all kinds of creative ways to burn calories on her own — by chewing and digging holes and doing all sorts of things that'll drive you crazy.

If you have a high-energy dog who needs three to four hours of exercise each day, don't panic. You can work this into your lifestyle in different ways. You don't have to take your dog on one long three- or four-hour run. In fact, it's healthier for your dog if you break up the exercise throughout the day. You can take her out for a long walk first thing in the morning, play tag or fetch with her in the afternoon, and take her for another long walk or training session in the evening. Let her blow off steam playing with other dogs.

Although allowing your dog to run in a large fenced area is nice, it isn't as fulfilling to your dog as taking her for a walk around the neighborhood or hiking in the woods. Your dog wants to exercise with *you*. If you can't do this on a regular basis, try having more than one dog — dogs will play with each other if you can't be there to participate. However, they still prefer to involve you in the games.

Dogs are athletes. They need to use their energy in a positive manner. Participating in activities with your dog fills this need while improving the bond you have.

Older dogs

As your dog gets older, his energy level won't be what it was when he was a pup. But he still needs exercise — not as much as when he was younger, but definitely a good hour per day.

The trick to exercising your older dog is to break up that hour throughout the day instead of trying to do it all at once. Most older dogs receive plenty of exercise through two to three 20-minute walks each day.

So how do you know if your dog is old? The concept of age is relative to the dog's breed mixture and size. Smaller dogs tend to live longer — they don't age as quickly as larger dogs. The giant breeds, such as Great Danes and Mastiffs, rarely live more than 9 years, on average. The Retriever and Setter breeds average 10 to 12 years. Large Hounds 10 years, smaller Hounds 12 to 14 years. Spaniel breeds often live 13 to 14 years, and Terrier breeds can live 14 to 16 years.

So the age of your dog depends largely on his size, not necessarily the breeds that constitute his genetics, although this generalization has many exceptions. For example, English Bulldogs, a mid-sized breed, don't live much beyond 10 years, while other mid-sized breeds, such as Cocker Spaniels, have a lifespan of more than 14 years.

Whether your dog just entered middle age or has become geriatric, he still needs exercise to remain healthy. As dogs age, arthritis and other physical ailments begin to degenerate their skeletal structure. Regular walks help maintain the muscle tone around their joints, improving their overall ability to move.

Trying Your Paws at Canine Sports

If training and competing with your dog appeals to you, you can get involved in one of many organized performance events in which dogs and handlers compete as a team through novice, intermediate, and advanced levels. You can even obtain championships in many of the performance events. Most canine performance sports are open to all breeds of dogs as well as mixed breeds. Several chapters in Book IV cover this fun part of dog ownership, but here we just provide an overview.

Agility is a very popular canine sport in which the handler must direct the dog over a course of jumps and obstacles within a certain amount of time (see Figure 5-4). Fast thinking and excellent teamwork are the keys to this sport.

Even if you never plan to compete, consider enrolling your dog in agility classes sponsored by a local dog club. The classes will give her some exercise, boost her confidence, and stimulate her mind while conveniently training her at the same time. (See Book IV, Chapter 5 for a lot more on agility training.)

Obedience trials test the ability of a dog to walk at heel on and off leash, to stand while being examined, and to come when called. At the higher levels, a dog must be able to differentiate between a dumbbell scented by the handler and eight others scented by a stranger. She also must be able to jump and retrieve, among performing other tests. In addition to being a fun sport, obedience training makes your dog easier to live with.

Figure 5-4:
This dog is
obviously
having fun
participating
in agility.

Photograph courtesy of Elinor Lerner.

Flyball is a popular sport in which a dog runs down a 50-foot mat, jumping over 4 jumps on the way, presses a pedal that releases a ball, catches the ball, and runs back over the jumps. Four dogs on a team race as a relay against another team of four dogs.

Dogs of specific breeds can also show off their particular instincts at events such as hunting tests for the Sporting breeds, herding tests for the Herding breeds, lure coursing trials for the sighthounds, and go-to-ground tests for the Terriers.

For more information about canine sports, go to www.dog-play.com. This Web site lists every type of canine sport you can imagine and has links to organizations that offer those sports. It is a veritable smorgasbord of canine-play Web sites.

Exercising Indoors

When the weather is bad or the days are short, you and your dog can still exercise together in the comfort of your home. Indoor exercises can strengthen your dog's muscles, improve coordination, and relieve some of the stress of being confined. Crawling strengthens the spinal and rear leg muscles, rolling over improves coordination, and waving one front leg strengthens the shoulder muscles. You can teach your dog exercises by using food to lure him into position and then encouraging him to try it on him own. Praise the dog every time he gets closer to doing what you want. You can also devise other exercises (see Figure 5-5). Check out *Dog Tricks For Dummies,* by Sarah Hodgson (Wiley), for more.

Doggie play groups in parks are a great way to let dogs exercise each other while the owners watch and chat. Just make sure that you monitor the dogs to be sure there isn't a canine bully in the group.

Try taping a long piece of Velcro (the side with the hooks) to the goal post at one end of a school's football field, and then stick 12 tennis balls to it. Take your dog to the other end of the field. Unfold your lawn chair and relax while your dog runs to get each tennis ball and brings it back. The possibilities are limited only by your imagination.

Always watch for signs that your dog is becoming fatigued. Don't depend on your dog to restrict his own activity when he is tired. Many dogs will literally exercise until they drop because they enjoy it so much. Signs of fatigue include stumbling, an anxious look, excessive panting, and widening of the end of the tongue.

Figure 5-5:
This Australian Shepherd has been taught to spin for exercise and stress relief.

Exercise for dogs with physical problems

Even if your dog has a physical condition such as hip dysplasia or arthritis, she still needs exercise. It's important to keep her muscles toned so they take over some of the work of the weakened joints. Moderation is the key here: a little bit of exercise every day. Don't let her be a weekend warrior by overdoing it on the weekend and spending the week on the couch.

As your dog gets older, be extra sensitive to signs that she is tiring when she's out playing. Continue to exercise her daily, but reduce the length and intensity of her exercise enough to prevent her from becoming fatigued.

Dogs with disabilities can play, too. Deaf dogs and blind dogs can play in familiar, safe areas. Deaf dogs enjoy toys that blink with lights, and blind dogs can retrieve toys that make continuous noise. Dogs who have had a leg amputated can get around almost as well as a dog with all four legs, and they will enjoy exercise just as much as other dogs.

Paying Attention to the Heat When You Exercise Your Dog

The ideal air temperature for a sedentary dog is 65 to 75 degrees with low humidity. At this temperature, a resting dog's body neither gains nor loses heat. The dog doesn't have to expend any energy to maintain his body temperature. (The normal body temperature for dogs is 100.5 to 102.8 degrees.)

Dogs have limited mechanisms for coping with overheating. Panting is their main mechanism for losing heat. Muscles in the tongue allow it to expand to approximately twice its normal size, increasing the surface area for heat exchange. In addition, blood vessels in the tongue dilate to bring more blood to the surface of the tongue to be cooled. Humidity inhibits the evaporation of moisture on your dog's tongue and in his mouth and lungs, contributing to potential heatstroke.

Although dogs don't have sweat glands like we humans do, they do perspire on the pads of their feet. If you walk your dog over a shiny floor on a warm day, you can see the imprint of each foot as he leaves a sweaty paw print on the smooth surface. Dogs also try to lower their body temperature by seeking cool places, by not eating (therefore producing less internal heat), and by reducing their activity level.

Be sensitive to the possibility of your dog becoming overheated. Human mechanisms for coping with heat are far superior to those of our dogs. So if *you're* uncomfortable, you can figure that your dog must be *very* uncomfortable. Your dog can't communicate verbally and tell you how warm he feels. Provide him with access to drinking water at all times, let him wallow in a pond or wading pool, or cool him by applying ice packs to his groin. If the temperature outside is hot, forget exercise and let your dog stay cool.

Signs of heatstroke include rapid, noisy breathing; a red, enlarged tongue; thick saliva; a body temperature above 106 degrees; staggering; and weakness. A dog with heatstroke should be wrapped in towels that have been soaked in cold water and transported to a veterinarian or emergency clinic as soon as possible. There he will be given further treatment, such as intravenous fluids and perhaps cool-water enemas, as well as treatment for shock, if necessary.

Giving Your Dog Things to Do While You're Away

Exercise is an important part of your dog's day, but if you're like most people, you're probably home for only a few hours every day. Providing activities for your dog while you're gone is a great way to help her get the exercise she needs.

Occupying busy paws

Always give your dog the opportunity to play with or chew a safe toy while he is alone. Several products on the market are designed to keep your pooch's paws busy while you're away (Book I, Chapter 6 offers lots of ideas).

Don't stay away too long. As a rule, dogs should never be left alone for more than ten hours at a time. Try to keep your absence from home to five or six hours, when possible. Puppies and some older dogs may need potty breaks every two to four hours.

One of the best objects to keep an active dog occupied is the Buster Cube, which is a tough plastic cube into which you pour a little dry dog food. Using a dial, you regulate the speed at which the pieces of food drop out of a hole in the cube. Your dog pushes the cube with his nose or turns it over with his feet. When the cube is positioned just right — voilà! — out drops a piece of food. When your dog realizes that this toy really is a food dispenser and that he is in control, he will keep working away at the cube until every last morsel is gone.

Note: The Buster Cube has two small disadvantages. First, some dogs move the cube around so aggressively that it bangs into the walls and the legs of nearby furniture. So it's best not to play this game in the room with Aunt Martha's valuable antiques. Second, this game involves food, and some dogs don't appreciate the assistance of other dogs in their quest. So the Buster Cube is best played alone or among (the rare) dogs who play cooperatively when food is involved.

Another way to keep your dog occupied during the day is to stuff the center cavity of a real bone with soft cheese or peanut butter (but not if your dog is a very strong chewer — he could bite off and swallow pieces of bone). You can even hide some broken cookies or pieces of kibble in the core of the bone. You can stuff other toys such as Kong toys with food and seal them with peanut butter or cream cheese. Getting to the good stuff can occupy your dog for many hours.

If your dog's personal area has a window looking out over a quiet place such as your backyard, place a couch or a safe table in front of it so he can watch the birds and other wildlife while you're away. It's usually better if your dog isn't able to see the activities on the street in *front* of your house, however, because if he sees the mail carrier bringing the mail to the house, for example, he may bark and carry on, sensing that he should guard the house in your absence. When the carrier leaves after delivering the mail, your dog becomes convinced that his barking has driven him away. If this scenario is repeated day after day, your dog may become quite aggressive toward the mail carrier — and others who come on the property, which is why tens of thousands of mail carriers and delivery people are bitten by dogs every year. Your dog doesn't need this kind of experience, and the mail carrier certainly doesn't, either.

A dog door can be a real boon for a dog who is home alone all day. Whenever he likes, he can go outside into his fenced-in yard, eliminate, catch some rays, chase a squirrel or two, and then go back in to sleep some more. Dog doors are especially helpful for older dogs who may have trouble holding their urine for a full day. If you use this convenience, however, your yard *must* be completely safe for your dog. He shouldn't be able to escape by climbing the fence or by digging under it. It's also best if your dog can't see the comings and goings of children and delivery people. A dog door works best if it is used in a quiet neighborhood and it opens to an enclosed kennel or to a secluded yard with a secure fence.

Doggie daycare

Doggie daycare is a booming industry because more people are away at work during the day, sometimes leaving their canine companions at home for long periods of time. If you want to give your furry friend an outlet for her energy

Book II

Dog Nutrition and Health

during the day, consider doggie daycare facilities, which offer a variety of services, including boarding, play groups, dog walking, obedience training, and even hiking or swimming.

The best way to find a reputable doggie daycare establishment is to ask dog-owning friends and neighbors if they know of any. If you come up empty, call a local dog club, a dog-training facility, or your veterinarian for a recommendation (assistants often moonlight as dogsitters).

When you've found a doggie daycare, inquire about the interview process. Good daycare facilities interview prospective clients and their dogs just as a children's daycare would. They want to know whether your dog is properly immunized against communicable diseases so she won't catch or spread any infections while she's there. They will also be interested in what activities your dog enjoys and whether she plays well with other dogs so she can participate in doggie play groups.

During your interview, find out what activities are available and how your dog's day will be structured. These important questions are worth asking:

- ✔ **Where will my dog stay when she is resting?** The kennel area should be clean and should have bedding and safe toys available for the dogs.
- ✔ **What does the owner do if dogs have tiffs over playthings?**
- ✔ **How does the owner handle a dog who is aggressive or dominating around others?**
- ✔ **How long do the dogs play each day, how much rest time do they have, and how much one-on-one interaction do they get with daycare personnel?**
- ✔ **What veterinary facilities does the facility use if one of the dogs has an accident or becomes ill?** Make sure that the owner has insurance to cover the facility.

As of this writing, no organizations oversee or accredit doggie daycare facilities. Be a good consumer and make sure that you get all your questions answered and lay to rest all your concerns before you enroll your canine family member.

Doggie daycare costs a little more than boarding a dog overnight in a kennel. It can be quite expensive if your dog attends every day, but it is an excellent solution for single people and busy families.

Dog walkers

Dog walking is a great way for your dog to get some activity while you're away. Dog walking also provides a great opportunity for neighborhood kids who have a love for animals and a desire to make a few bucks the old-fashioned way.

Depending on the size of your dog (which dictates how much he pulls when he sees a squirrel) and his level of obedience, a responsible child as young as 11 or 12 years old can be a good dog walker. Just make it clear to the young entrepreneur how he is to walk your dog — including which leash and collar to use, where he can go, how long he should walk him, and so on. Always post the phone number where you can be contacted, along with other emergency numbers such as another contact person and the telephone number of your regular and emergency veterinarians.

Book II

Dog Nutrition and Health

 If you hire a child to walk your dog, always meet with the child's parents first. They generally are involved in scheduling your dog's walk around the child's other after-school events. Their concern for the child's safety means they're keeping an eye on your dog, too.

 Adult or professional dog walkers are an excellent option, particularly if you have multiple dogs who may be too much for a child to handle. Many professional dog walkers are bonded and insured, giving you a little more security than you have with a neighborhood kid. Again, try to get a personal recommendation and have a thorough interview before you trust your dogs to a stranger.

 Don't hire a dog walker who walks several strange dogs together. This experience can be tremendously stressful to the dogs.

Pet sitters

Pet sitters can make a huge difference in your dog's life. They let your dog stay in her familiar environment when you have to be away for extended periods of time, making your absence much less stressful for your canine companion than a kennel full of strangers.

 The best way to find a dog sitter is to obtain a referral from someone who has used the dog sitter extensively and has been pleased with his work. You can also try the Web site for Pet Sitters International (www.petsit.com) to find a reliable and responsible pet sitter in your area. Or try your vet for a recommendation.

Always interview a new dog sitter before hiring him. Introduce your dog to him and make sure that they connect with each other. The dog sitter should not appear hesitant to handle your pooch, and your dog should accept his touch. He should appear genuinely interested in your dog and her welfare while you are away. He should ask specific questions about how you want your dog cared for. If you see any red flags, such as hesitance to interact with your dog or evidence of a short temper, the applicant probably isn't a good match for your dog.

Some dog sitters stay at your home while you're away; others visit three to four times a day for a predetermined amount of time to let your dog out, feed her, and walk or play with her. Either option can work well. Just be sure that you are comfortable with your decision.

Before your new pet sitter starts her first assignment, make an appointment for her to spend some time with you learning your dog's obedience commands and other house rules. If your dog always barges out of the door unless commanded to wait, have the pet sitter also make the dog wait, which will strengthen obedient behavior while you're away.

Be sure to leave complete written instructions for your dog sitter. They should include the following information:

- The address and telephone number where you can be reached

- The address and telephone number of an emergency contact near where you live

- Your veterinarian's name, address, and telephone number

- The name, address, and telephone number of an emergency veterinarian who is available after hours

- Complete feeding instructions (including the type of food, the amount, when and where your dog should be fed, and whether she needs to go out right away after she eats)

- Instructions for exercising your dog (including what activities she likes, for how long, and how often)

- Instructions for picking up the yard, if necessary

- Notes about any medication your dog needs

- Any other habits or needs specific to your dog

- Whether the dog sitter should answer the telephone or let it ring

Chapter 6

Caring for an Aging Dog

· ·

In This Chapter

▶ Easing the aging process

▶ Dealing with older-dog health concerns

▶ Letting go

▶ Getting help when you're grieving

▶ Providing for your pet in your will

· ·

*P*eople flip over puppies, but a well-loved older dog is also beautiful. An older dog has a nobleness about him, a look in the eyes that speaks of years of the special love only a pet can give — trusting, nonjudgmental, and unwaveringly true.

Your dog's health as he ages is not entirely in your control, but you can have a real impact on his attitude. When you see those first gray hairs appear on his muzzle, getting a little upset about them is natural. The normal life span of a dog isn't even remotely close to ours, after all, and those first signs of aging remind us that the years between a puppy's first gasp and the last sighing breath of a dying dog are not really that far apart.

But consider the following: Unless the guesses and assumptions of science are wrong, your dog doesn't know he's getting older. His gray hairs do not concern him, nor does he worry about the other visible effects of time, including the thickening of his body and the thinning of his limbs. He doesn't count the number of times he can fetch a ball before tiring and compare that to his performance when he was a young dog in his prime. He doesn't know that his time is growing shorter and that he'll get weaker or grow blind, perhaps, or deaf. He doesn't know that he'll die someday.

You know all of that, but this information is a secret best kept to yourself. Your dog takes his cues from you, and when you're upbeat, encouraging, and loving, he'll be at his best no matter what his age. Keep your aging dog fit and healthy, and don't exclude him from your activities. This time can be a special one for both of you, and it's up to you to make the most of it.

Special Care for Canine Seniors

Next to you, your dog's best friend as she ages should be her veterinarian. Preventive care is not only more cost-effective than crisis care, but it's the only way to catch problems before they lessen the quality of your dog's life.

Maybe you've had such a healthy dog that you've rarely taken her to the veterinarian. Take her in for a thorough senior-dog physical anyway when she hits 8 or so (as early as 6 for giant breeds, as late as 10 for tiny ones), including whatever tests your veterinarian recommends — blood, urine, and so on. The information these tests provide can spot treatable problems early and provide baseline information against which your veterinarian can compare new data as problems develop.

This rapport with your vet is never more important than when you're guiding your pet through her senior years.

Nutrition

Your dog's nutritional needs change as he gets older, and so, in most cases, should his food. If you have been satisfied with a particular food, you may be able to switch to the brand's formulation for older dogs. If not, your veterinarian may be able to suggest something suitable.

The biggest food-related problem for older dogs is obesity, which puts pressure on joints and internal organs that aren't able to withstand the pressure. If your pet is portly, talk to your veterinarian about safe ways to trim him down slowly.

Unlike us, dogs have no control over how much they eat: Your dog's weight depends on your self-control, not his.

Dogs with chronic health problems may end up on a special diet available only through your veterinarian. These diets — which come in both canned and dry varieties — are formulated to address your pet's particular health needs. Some pets may not like them, especially compared to the fat- and treat-based diet they were on before, but don't sabotage your pet's care by adding goodies to the mix. A simple strained broth made from boiling chicken bones with a crushed garlic clove or two — no added salt — may make the diet more palatable. Check with your veterinarian, though, before adding anything else to a prescription diet.

For the rundown on dog food — what's in it, what your dog needs, and how to choose — see Book I, Chapter 2.

Book II

Dog
Nutrition
and Health

Putting junior in his place

If you have an older dog and a younger one, the competition between them can be frustrating to the older dog. Here's an exercise that lets the older dog win and improves the obedience of the younger:

After your younger dog has chased a few balls to get rid of his excess energy, put him in a "down-stay" (make him lie down and tell him to stay — see Book IV, Chapter 3). If you've never tried this exercise under such tempting conditions, leave his leash on and then stand on it. Repeat the "stay" command and then throw the ball — a short throw — for your senior dog. Let him get the ball a few times, and then release the younger dog and praise him. Then tell them both they're wonderful.

Exercise

"Use it or lose it" is true for both humans and dogs. No matter what her age, exercise keeps your dog's body in good condition and brightens her outlook.

The secret as dogs age is increasing the frequency and diminishing the intensity. Instead of taking your dog to the park once a week to chase tennis balls until she's exhausted, take her for a daily walk. When you throw a tennis ball, keep it low to avoid leaps, twists, and hard landings, and consider walking to the park and back rather than driving. Warm-ups and cool-downs are more important for older dogs, whose bodies aren't as able to withstand the pounding a younger dog endures without pause. Inactivity punctuated by bouts of overexertion isn't good for any dog, but for the older dog it can be painful or even dangerous.

Despite your best intentions, sometimes an older pet will make like a puppy and play hard. The next morning, she'll surely feel it. Give her buffered aspirin, 5 milligrams per pound of body weight, every 12 hours. If the stiffness lasts for more than a day, consult your veterinarian. If your dog is on other medications, check with your veterinarian first.

Walking is good exercise for older pets; supervised swimming is another if you have a dog who enjoys it. (Choose a lake or pool rather than a river, and keep her close to the bank.) Keep her moving every day. Push her a little on the distance and the time, or at least try to maintain what you've got going, but don't overextend her — let her set the pace.

Think about games she can do just as well — or better — than when she was younger, such as Sniff Out the Hidden Toy. In my house, senior dog Andy no longer chases tennis balls at a gallop. Put your dog on "stay," show her a toy, and hide it for her to find.

Very few dogs, even young ones, get enough exercise to keep their nails short without trimming; senior dogs certainly don't. Arthritis and muscle stiffness make moving around hard enough for older dogs; overgrown nails make things worse, and they're something that you have the power to fix — so do it. (See Book III, Chapter 3 for tips on how to keep nails short.)

Dentistry

One of the most important recent advances in the care of older dogs is in the care of their mouths: Canine dentistry is an area of preventive care that you ignore at your pet's peril. (See Book III, Chapter 3 for a full discussion of dog dental care.) Start teeth brushing when a dog is a puppy — an older dog may never allow you to brush his teeth for the first time.

Preventive care involves brushing your older dog's teeth — two or three times a week is fine — using gauze wrapped around your finger or a toothbrush, whichever your pet tolerates best. Toothpastes made just for dogs are available, with flavors that appeal to the canine palate and ingredients that can be swallowed. Because dogs can't spit and rinse, people toothpaste and baking soda, which is high in sodium, aren't recommended.

Before you start your at-home regimen, your pet will likely need some help from your veterinarian. A complete dental work-up under anesthesia takes 45 minutes to an hour and involves not only cleaning and polishing the teeth, but also treating broken or rotting teeth, cavities, abscesses, and periodontal disease. This procedure is especially important if you've neglected your pet's mouth: Brushing prevents plaque from forming, but it won't help much with the muck that has already built up — and it won't fix bad teeth or infections.

Dental care is very important in older dogs, especially small ones, who tend to have mouths crowded with teeth. Neglected mouths can make eating painful. Infections are a problem, too, and the adverse effect of bacteria from chronic mouth infections takes a toll on your pet's internal organs and can overwhelm his immune system. Bacteria can even travel through the bloodstream from your dog's mouth to his heart and infect his heart valves.

The benefits of such care extend to more than the elimination of bad breath in an older dog: When your pet is no longer fighting infections and pain, his spirits lift along with his health, all of which can spark his appetite.

Some Common Age-Related Health Problems

Although every dog is an individual, a few age-related maladies seem to strike many of them. You should, of course, discuss how they affect your dog and the best approach to treating them with your veterinarian. But knowing a little bit about what you're dealing with before you go in is helpful.

Decline of the senses

Deaf and blind dogs do just fine, as long as you do your part to keep them out of any danger their disabilities may cause. Blindness, in particular, is a problem dogs adjust to with an ease that stuns their owners. But consider the following: Dogs don't have to read the newspaper, they don't care about TV, and they count on you to read the ingredients label on a bag of kibble. Sight isn't their primary sense anyway — they put much greater stock in their senses of smell and hearing. After they learn the layout of the land, they rarely bump into things (as long as you don't keep moving the furniture).

Handicapped pets should never be allowed off-leash on walks, because they can't see danger and cannot hear your warnings.

How do you know if your dog is really blind? Lunge at his face menacingly with your finger (don't make contact!). If he doesn't blink, he's blind.

Even if your older dog is blind (or deaf — check by clapping your hands behind his head), you may be able to do something. Ask your veterinarian for a referral to a specialist such as a veterinary ophthalmologist. Problems such as cataracts may be treatable with medications and surgery.

Incontinence

Many dog owners start wondering why their older dogs are no longer house-trained — and how to get them back on track. The first rule of any sudden-onset behavior problem is to make sure that it's not a health problem, and it could well be a health problem if an older dog is suddenly urinating in the house. Your pet could have an infection or, if she's an older, spayed female, she may be suffering from the loss of muscle tone related to a decrease in her hormone levels. Both are treatable; see your veterinarian.

At a certain age, a little dribbling of urine is practically inevitable, especially while your older dog is sleeping. You may want to place old rubber-backed bathmats in her favorite sleeping area. They catch the dribble and are easily washable, keeping odor and dampness — and flea eggs — under control. Living with pets, like living with children, can be one big mess.

Lumps and bumps

Benign fatty tumors are common in older dogs, and the vast majority are nothing to worry about. Benign tumors are round and soft, with well-defined edges. You can usually get your fingers nearly around them, and they don't seem well anchored. Showing them to your veterinarian for a more complete evaluation is important, and you should inform her of any changes in size or shape, especially if they happen rapidly. Your veterinarian may be concerned enough about the size, appearance, or location of a mass to suggest its removal and a biopsy; most bumps, however, are left alone. The best time to check for lumps and bumps? During regular grooming — weekly, at least. Run your hand over every inch of your dog, and don't forget to talk sweetly — he'll think it's petting.

Some breeds — Boxers, for one — are much more prone to cancer, and you should be more aggressive in investigating lumps and bumps. Work with your veterinarian closely to catch any problems early.

Stiffness

Your veterinarian can help you determine whether the stiffness is because of temporary muscle soreness — say, from overdoing it — or the onset of arthritis. Many dogs feel worse in cold weather and first thing in the morning. Arthritis is common in older dogs, and although no cure exists, treatments are available that can make your pet comfortable. Your veterinarian may prescribe buffered aspirin, food supplements, or anti-inflammatory medications, all of which your pet may need to take for the rest of her life. For your part, you need to be sure that your pet is not overweight and is kept consistently, but not strenuously, active.

Nonsteroidal anti-inflammatories — the best known is Rimadyl — have made life bearable for tens of thousands of older dogs, but they are not without risk. Rimadyl has been implicated in the deaths of many dogs — Labradors, especially, seem to be vulnerable. Don't let these tragedies dissuade you from considering a medication that can work wonders, but do press your veterinarian to explain all the risks and benefits so you can make the best decision for your pet.

Older dog and new puppy

All the trials of old age can make a dog downright cranky and make some people long to have a puppy in the house. Of course, you want to be sure that your older dog enjoys the change, or at least tolerates it. So should you add a puppy to an older dog's life?

That depends. For some older dogs, a puppy is a big boost to the senior's enthusiasm. For others, a puppy's energy and attention are enough to make an older dog want to leave home. You must determine which of these attitudes your older dog has.

In general, older dogs who are still fit and full of life probably get the most out of an addition to the household; elderly or severely debilitated dogs enjoy it least. No matter what your dog's age, try to keep tabs on the interaction until you're sure how things are progressing. Don't let your older dog overextend himself, and put the puppy in his crate or behind a baby gate to give your oldster a break from time to time. Finally, save some exclusive energy and time for dog number 1: Spend time together, just the two of you, so he realizes he is still very much loved.

Book II

Dog Nutrition and Health

Some dogs lose strength in their hindquarters as they age or become paralyzed because of a spinal injury. This condition need not mean euthanasia. A company called K-9 Carts manufactures wheeled devices that allow a dog to be mobile again (see www.k9-carts.com).

Reasonable Accommodations

The number of ways you can give your oldster a break is limited only by your imagination. Consider a few tips to get you thinking:

- **Beds:** Think soft. Think cushioned. Think low. Think heated. Your dog will thank you for all these thoughts, especially in cold weather.

- **Clothes:** Canine clothing isn't just for Poodles anymore. Older dogs, like older people, have a harder time maintaining their body temperature. This problem is even more pronounced in slender, short-coated breeds like the Greyhound or Whippet. So check out the sweater selection at your local pet-supply store, or consider altering one of your own for the task.

- **Dishes:** Raised food and water dishes are a kindness to tall dogs of any age, but they are especially easy on the back of an oldster. You can find them at pet-supply stores or you can make your own.

- **Ramps and steps:** If your dogs are allowed on the couch and the bed, you should be able to find or build something to help the dog who can no longer make it in one jump.

Anesthesia: Weighing the risks

As common as anesthesia is in veterinary medicine, many misconceptions exist about its use where older animals are concerned. Veterinary findings no longer support the idea that the risk of anesthesia outweighs the importance of preventive veterinary care.

The risks can be greatly minimized by a few basic tests, including a laboratory evaluation of blood and urine, a chest X-ray, and possibly an electrocardiogram. Although these tests admittedly add to the cost of a procedure, they allow your veterinarian to provide the life-enhancing and life-extending benefits of preventive care to the pets who need them most.

Your veterinarian may also recommend IV or subcutaneous fluids while your pet is under anesthesia, and, for dental procedures, pre- and post-surgical antibiotics.

No discussion of anesthetic danger can be complete without a few words on your responsibilities where anesthesia is concerned:

✔ Follow your veterinarian's instructions on preparing your pet for surgery. If no food is specified, make sure that you deliver a pet with an empty stomach. Following this one piece of advice is one of the easiest and most basic ways to reduce risk. Under anesthesia, a dog can regurgitate and inhale the contents of a full stomach into her lungs.

✔ Be prepared to provide special home care for your pet after surgery. Releasing animals before the preanesthetic sedation wears off is common practice. Such animals must be kept safe from hot or cold environments because their reflexes are reduced. If you don't feel comfortable caring for a sedated pet, arrange for your veterinarian to extend the care.

✔ Don't hesitate to ask questions. Make sure that you understand what the procedures are and what to expect. For example, pets commonly have a cough after anesthesia because the tube used to deliver the gas may cause some irritation. If the cough does not clear up in a couple days, call your veterinarian.

No matter what the age of the pet, chances are very high that the anesthetic will present no problem if both you and your veterinarian work to minimize the risks.

Knowing When It's Time to Let Go

Euthanasia, the technical term for putting a person or animal to sleep for humane reasons, is one of the hardest decisions you will ever make, and it doesn't get any easier, no matter how many times over the years you face it. Your veterinarian can offer advice, and your friends can offer support, but no one can make the decision for you. When you live with an elderly or terminally ill pet, you look in her eyes every morning and ask yourself, "Is this the day?"

Some owners don't wait until their pet's discomfort becomes pain and choose euthanasia much sooner than others would. Some owners use an animal's appetite as the guide — when an old or ill animal is no longer interested in eating, they reason, he's not interested in anything at all. And some owners wait until there's absolutely no doubt the time is at hand.

What about the remains?

You can handle your pet's remains in many ways, and doing so is easier if you make your decisions beforehand. The choices include having your municipal animal-control department pick up the body, burying the pet in your backyard or at another site (where it's legal and with the land owner's permission, of course), arranging for cremation, or contracting with a pet cemetery for full services and burial. Some people even choose to have their pets preserved like hunting trophies, or have a part of them cryogenically saved for cloning later. Again, no choice is wrong. Whatever feels right to you and comforts you best is what you should do.

The next topic is difficult, but you must consider it. If your pet dies unexpectedly or while under the care of your veterinarian and there's is any question about the cause of death or your veterinarian believes lessons can be learned by performing a postmortem examination, you should agree. This procedure may not help your dog, but it may help hundreds or thousands of others. What better way to demonstrate your love for dogs than to assist in the advancement of care for other pets with similar health problems?

Each guideline can be the right one, for some dogs and some owners at certain times. You do the best you can, and then you try to put the decision behind you and deal with the grief. Ironically, the incredible advances in veterinary medicine in the past couple decades have made the decisions even more difficult for many people. Not too long ago, the best you could do for a seriously ill pet was to make her comfortable until that wasn't possible anymore. Nowadays, nearly every advantage of human medicine — from chemotherapy to pacemakers — is available to our pets.

If you can afford such extensive care and have a realistic expectation that it will improve your pet's life — rather than simply prolong it — then it is an option that you should pursue. But let nothing push you into making a decision based on guilt or wishful thinking.

Euthanasia is a kindness extended to a treasured pet, a decision we make at a great cost to ourselves. It is a final act of love, nothing less.

Evaluating euthanasia options

As performed by a veterinarian, euthanasia is a quick and peaceful process. The animal is unconscious within seconds and dead within less than a minute; the euphemism "put to sleep" is actually a perfect description. People who attend the procedure usually come away reassured that their pet felt no fear or pain.

You're not alone

You may find talking to others about your pet's death helpful. Ask your veterinarian about pet-loss support groups. Almost unheard of a few decades ago, such groups are available in many communities today. You may also want to see a counselor.

Veterinary schools and colleges have been among the leaders in creating programs to help pet lovers deal with loss. A handful now operate pet-loss hot lines staffed by veterinary students trained to answer questions, offer materials that may help you (including guidelines for helping children with loss), and just plain listen. These programs are wonderful, and they're free for the cost of the call. (If you call during off hours, they call you back, collect.)

The American Veterinary Medical Association (AVMA) lists many pet-loss hotlines at `www.avma.org/careforanimals/animated journeys/goodbyefriend/pl hotlines.asp`.

Some people stay with a pet at the end, and some don't, but no decision you make regarding the last few minutes of an animal's life will change the love you shared for the years before those final moments. If you want to be there, then by all means stay. But leaving euthanasia to your veterinarian is no less a humane and loving gesture.

Call ahead to set the appointment, and make it clear to the receptionist what you're coming for. (The tone of your voice will probably tip her off, anyway.) That way, the practice can ensure that you don't have to sit in the waiting room but can instead be immediately ushered into an exam room, if you choose to remain with your dog. Your veterinarian will do his best to answer all your questions and make you comfortable with everything before proceeding. He may clip the fur on your dog's foreleg to have easier and quicker access to the vein for the injection of the euthanizing agent; he may also choose to presedate your pet.

Crying is normal, and your veterinarian will understand. So, too, will your dog.

You may want to hold your hand near your dog's nose so the last sniff will be of you. You may want to spend a few minutes with your pet afterward, and your veterinarian will understand that as well, and will give you all the time you need alone to begin the process of coming to grips with your loss.

You may be more comfortable with having your pet euthanized at home. If this is what you want, discuss the matter with your veterinarian directly. Many vets extend this special service to long-time clients. If yours doesn't, you may alternatively consider making arrangements with a mobile veterinarian.

Several manufacturers offer markers for your yard to memorialize your pet; they are often advertised in the back of magazines like *Dog Fancy*. Other choices include large rocks or slabs of stone, or a tree or rose bush. Even if you choose not to have your pet's body or ashes returned, placing a memorial in a special spot may soothe you.

Another way to celebrate the memory of your dog is to make a donation to your local humane society, regional school of veterinary medicine, or other favorite animal charity. A donation in a beloved pet's name is a wonderful act to do for a friend who has lost a pet as well.

Book II

Dog Nutrition and Health

Dealing with loss

Many people are surprised at the powerful emotions that erupt after a pet's death, and they are embarrassed by their grief. Remembering that pets have meaning in our lives beyond the love we feel for the animal alone may help. Often we don't realize that we are grieving not only for the pet we loved, but also for the special time the animal represented.

Taking care of yourself is important at this difficult time. Some people — the "it's just an animal" crowd — will not understand your feelings and may even shrug off your grief as foolish. The company of other animal lovers is very important. Seek them out to share your feelings. In some areas, pet-loss support groups may be available. Search the Internet for **pet loss** to come up with sites that can help. And don't forget the AVMA pet-loss hotlines available at the link given in the nearby sidebar, "You're not alone."

A difficult time, to be sure, but in time, the memories become a source of pleasure, not pain. Coming to terms with grief has no set timetable, but it happens.

A handful of books and one really fine video may help you help your child with the loss of a pet. From Fred Rogers (yes, Mr. Rogers of the Neighborhood) comes the book *When a Pet Dies* (Putnam) and the video

Death of a Goldfish. Rachel Biale's *My Pet Died* (Tricycle Press) not only helps children cope better by giving them pages to fill in, but also offers parents advice in special pages that can be torn out. Finally, Judith Viorst's *The Tenth Good Thing About Barney* (Aladdin) is a book that experts in pet loss have been recommending for years.

What If You Go First?

First things first: You can't leave your estate to your dog, because in the eyes of the law, an animal is an "it," with little more legal status than a chair. Nor can you set up a trust for your pet, for the same reason. The beneficiary of a trust must be a bona fide human being, and the fact that you think of your dog as a person doesn't really matter, because the courts don't.

Of course, you should discuss this matter with your attorney, but talking it over with your friends and family is even more important, because you must find one of them to care for your pet after you're gone. You must state that you're leaving your dog to that person, along with enough money to provide for the animal's care for life. You have no real control over the outcome, which is why you need to choose someone you trust and then hope for your dog's sake that things turn out okay.

No one likes to think about dying. But you have a responsibility to loved ones you leave behind, and that includes your pets. Talk to your friends, your family, and even your veterinarian. Call an attorney. Don't rely on the kindness of strangers to care for your pet if something happens to you. Your dog deserves better than that.

The Association of the Bar of New York City offers an online guide called "Providing for Your Pets in the Event of Your Death or Hospitalization" at www.nycbar.org/Publications/pub-provforpet.htm. And if you want to read more about caring for your senior dog, pick up a copy of *Senior Dogs For Dummies* by Susan McCullough (Wiley).

Chapter 7

Dog Breeding 101

. . . .

. . . .

Somebody has to breed dogs, or there wouldn't be any. Good breeders have always existed, and with any luck they always will. They care about their breed and the dogs they produce. They put years of study and effort into breeding dogs who are healthy and temperamentally sound — dogs who closely match the standards for their breed.

Unfortunately, these breeders are the minority. All is not right in the dog world, and it hasn't been for a long, long time. Consider these problems:

✔ Too many dogs are dying for want of a home — and not just mixed breeds, either. Shelters and rescue groups deal with plenty of purebreds.

✔ Too many dogs have health problems that can be eliminated through conscientious breeding.

✔ Too many dogs have inherited personality problems, such as aggression or shyness or even yapping.

✔ Too many dogs have personality problems caused by improper handling in the first weeks of their lives.

People who shouldn't be breeding dogs cause these problems. If you feel drawn to breeding and care about dogs — your dog and all dogs — consider breeding very carefully. Educate yourself about your breed and the congenital health and temperament problems within the breed. Develop a plan for breeding and a plan — as well as a fund — for dealing with emergencies. Think about the time you need to devote to helping the puppies be born, caring for them, and socializing them. Also remember that you need to know how to find good homes for them. You *can* be a good breeder, but you have to work at it. You can't take any shortcuts.

Be prepared to deal with the puppies you can't sell and the puppies that may be returned to you. They are your responsibility, too. If you can't say that you will do everything that a reputable breeder does, then you need to spay or neuter your dog.

Neutering, or at least making a decision not to breed your pet, is in the best interest of your dog and all dogs. It also makes your life easier. *Spaying* and *neutering* are the everyday terms for the surgical sterilization of a pet — spaying for the female, neutering for the male. The term *neutering* — or *altering* — is also used to describe both procedures. See Chapter 4 in Book II for more on these procedures.

What if you meant to spay your dog and you come home to find her mating with the dog from three doors down? She doesn't have to carry the litter to term. Spaying can be done on a pregnant dog, and the sooner the better.

The point here is that you need a deep understanding of both dogs and the responsibilities of breeding them before you even consider getting into breeding. Pilots don't jump into the cockpit and fly off into the wild blue yonder before they've completed the requisite courses and passed all the tests. Nor does the surgeon learn what's required by hacking away at a patient's liver. No one is allowed to assume those responsible positions without the extensive study that prepares them to do so.

Unfortunately, no courses of study or tests of knowledge are required of people who breed dogs. They just buy a female and, bang, they're out of the starting gate. Uneducated and irresponsible breeders sell, give away, or simply abandon their mistakes with no thought given to what the result of their carelessness will be. Unsuspecting dog lovers are saddled with thousands of dollars in veterinary bills and chronically ill dogs because the people who bred the dog had absolutely no idea what they were doing. Nor, obviously, did they care.

If an investigation were done, probably very few instances of dogs maliciously attacking children could be attributed to dogs coming from responsible breeders. Some dogs have a more aggressive nature than others, and breeders who own and appreciate these dogs go to great lengths to make sure that their dogs go only to homes where they will be properly trained and supervised.

Bottom line: You won't be able to produce worthy dogs of any breed unless you know what constitutes a top specimen. Even when you've mastered that part of your education, it's only the beginning. This chapter is intended to give you an overview of how dog breeding works, but reading it does not qualify you to breed dogs. If you're really intent on breeding dogs, you need more than this chapter before you begin. A good place to start is *Breeding Dogs For Dummies,* by Richard G. Beauchamp (Wiley).

But even if you becomes a master of the reading material on dog breeding, is mastering the tried-and-true methods a guarantee of any kind? Not at all. They are only the *best-known* methods, and they seem to work when intelligently applied. The only guarantee involved is that a person who embarks on a breeding program without sound knowledge is bound to meet with more failure than success. And if failure were the worst of it, these people would only have themselves to blame. In breeding dogs irresponsibly, you perpetuate your mistakes on an unknowing and unsuspecting public.

Breeders can increase their chances of producing dogs that live up to the standard of their breed in certain ways, and they can follow certain methods to avoid the pitfalls nearly every breed is susceptible to. This chapter gives you an introduction on how to take advantage of them.

What to Expect If You Decide to Breed

Breeding a dog takes time and money, especially for the owner of the female. Your dog and the dog you breed her to need to be certified clear of inherited problems such as hip dysplasia, deafness, and inherited eye diseases. Both dogs need to be tested for venereal diseases, be current on their vaccinations, be free of parasites, and be taking an heartworm-preventive medication. This clean bill of health costs money — easily into the hundreds of dollars.

When the male dog has all his health clearances, his job is easy. He gets to the party early and leaves the scene early. But after the coupling, the female's job has just started. Her owner bears most of the costs, starting with the stud fee. But even before you can pay that, you have to find a stud dog. You're not likely to find a suitable mate around the corner, or even in your town, which means you have to spend more money on transporting a dog.

Your dog will need high-quality food in significantly larger amounts than usual and possibly supplements, if your veterinarian recommends them, for the last few weeks of her pregnancy and the entire time she's nursing. If the litter is too much for her, you'll be hand-raising at least some of the puppies, and maybe all of them if she becomes unable to nurse. Above all, you have to be prepared to deal with a long list of medical emergencies that can threaten the life of both mother and puppies and can result in very large veterinary bills.

If your breed requires tail docking (trimming the length) or dewclaw removal (surgical removal of the vestigial "thumb"), you'll need to pay for that, along with vaccinations and other health needs. And you'll be paying for puppy food for the last three or four weeks you have the puppies (after they've been weaned). That's assuming you can sell the puppies promptly — sometimes you can't.

You'll have to take time off work when your dog's whelping, or giving birth, and you should take still more time off to socialize your pups to ensure that they become good pets for the people you sell them to. You need to expose your puppies to children, men, women, cats, and the normal noises of a human household. A litter of puppies is a constant mess-making machine: Your washing machine will be going around the clock, and you'll be begging your neighbors for their old newspapers and towels within a week.

You'll need a whelping box and hot-water bottles or a special heating element or lamp to keep puppies warm when they're young, because they can't regulate their own temperature well. When they're up on those pudgy little legs, you'll need an exercise pen to keep them safe and away from the many, many things those puppy teeth can decimate.

What if you can't get the price you want for your puppies? The popularity of fad breeds means that, before long, too many puppies are around and prices fall accordingly. You may be playing Let's Make a Deal with the last ones, or even giving them away. It's not unheard of for desperate first-time breeders to drop off the remains of a litter at a shelter.

Ask a reputable breeder to help you determine what producing a high-quality litter costs. Chances are, you'll find even more things in the expense column than are listed here — things such as ultrasounds to verify pregnancies or the cesarean deliveries that are common in some breeds. Litter announcements and advertising cost money, too, and hardly a breeder alive hasn't dealt with a disaster that has wiped out an entire litter of dreams and left nothing behind but huge veterinary expenses.

Are you *still* interesting in breeding dogs? If so, read on.

A Dog-Breeding Primer

The business of dog breeding hasn't changed much over the years: You breed the best to the best, and hope for the best. The ways of determining quality have changed a great deal, though, and will change even more as health screenings move to the chromosome level in the future.

Such progress would likely make the traditional owner of a working sheep or hunting dog shake his head. In the old days, if a dog didn't earn its keep, it didn't live long enough to breed. In some circles today, that's still the bottom line, although more — but not all — of the less-gifted career dogs today find homes as pets, be they Greyhounds, Beagles, or Border Collies.

The importance of quality

Because few breeders work their dogs as a shepherd does his, they rely on other factors to determine which animals they should breed. They show dogs to have judges evaluate their *conformation* — a measure of how closely they conform to the blueprint for the breed, called the *standard*. Breeders may test their dogs' working or hunting instincts in competitions that re-create the conditions of the real thing. They certainly have them tested for hereditary defects and consider temperament before breeding. High-quality dogs are produced through this selective process. For more on canine competitions, see Chapter 6 in Book IV.

You want to breed your dog to the best stud dog you can find, and that means the best stud dog for your *particular* dog — one who is a good match for her pedigree, her conformation, and her temperament. The person who can best help you find such a dog is an experienced, reputable breeder with knowledge of your dog's breed in general and her pedigree lines in particular. A better deal still is if you can convince this experienced breeder to mentor you through the mating, pregnancy, delivery, raising, and placing of the puppies. Everyone has to start somewhere, and good breeders know this.

If your dog is not of reasonable conformation, such a person may not want to work with you or allow a stud dog to breed with your female. It doesn't hurt to ask, though, because breeding your dog to a quality stud dog is a much better way to go than breeding her to one that your neighbor, cousin, or co-worker owns. The latter may be your only option, however, if your dog is not of a quality that should be bred. This verdict means, of course, that you shouldn't breed her.

Book II

Dog Nutrition and Health

Heat, mating, and gestation

Your dog should be at least two years old before you consider breeding her, because she needs to be more than a puppy herself to be a good mother to her babies. She should be in good health to withstand the rigors of pregnancy, whelping, and nursing. Her vaccinations should be current, and she should be clear of parasites and should be taking heartworm-preventive medicine. Tests for genetic defects in her breed should have come back clear, as should a test for brucellosis, a disease passed through mating that causes sterility in dogs. In other words, you need to be see your veterinarian.

The stud dog, too, must meet these criteria, and you should already have chosen him before your dog is ready for breeding. Females are usually sent to the stud for breeding. Some are shipped thousands of miles for just the right match.

Some breedings take place without the dogs ever so much as sniffing each other, thanks to frozen semen and artificial insemination. Some stud dogs have even sired litters after their demise! If the stud dog that suits your dog is too far away, discuss this option with the owner of the dog and with your veterinarian. This procedure is increasingly common, and the puppies are eligible for full registration with the American Kennel Club (AKC) and other organizations.

A female comes into season (or heat) for approximately 21 to 30 days every 5 to 7 months. Her heat begins at the first sign of bleeding and ends when she loses interest in breeding. The female does not become interested in breeding until a week or so after her season begins. Although your veterinarian can pinpoint when she is most likely to be successfully bred, the dog has a pretty good idea herself, flirting with the males and standing with her tail up in her best canine come-hither gesture.

The males don't need that much encouragement. Her smell from the first day of her season has been driving them wild, and the only thing that has kept them from mating with her sooner has been her refusal to allow it.

As soon as the first signs of season appear, you should finalize arrangements with the stud dog's owner and send your dog to the stud so she can be there when she's ready to breed.

An experienced breeder can best handle your dog at this point. She allows the dogs to become comfortable with one another and, when the female is interested, does what it takes to get the job done, including holding the female for the male and even inserting the male's penis into the female if the stud is inexperienced. Far from being embarrassed about such things, the experienced breeder considers it just another job that must be done to produce puppies.

The male starts to ejaculate soon after he starts thrusting, but the most sperm-rich semen is released after the action appears to have stopped and the so-called *tie* begins. The base of the canine penis swells while inside the female, locking the dogs together to give the sperm a chance to impregnate — and keeping competitors at bay. After the tie begins, the male turns away from the female so that the two are positioned rump to rump. This stage can last for more than a half hour before the swelling goes down and the dogs break apart.

If it lasts for more than two hours, call your veterinarian.

Whelping

Pregnancy ranges from 58 to 70 days, during which you should follow your veterinarian's instructions on prenatal care. A couple of weeks before her due date, you should prepare a whelping box — a place for her to have her puppies, placed in an out-of-the-way corner of your home. For large breeds, a plastic kiddy pool lined with layers and layers of newsprint works well; smaller breeds may use the bottom half of a shipping crate. The most important characteristic in a whelping box is that it can be easily cleaned.

Printed newspapers are messy, so try to get unprinted newsprint. Your local newspaper may sell — or give away — the ends of the giant newsprint rolls that go onto the presses.

Book II

Dog Nutrition and Health

Final preparations for long-coated breeds include clipping the hair on her hind end very short, to keep puppies from getting caught, and on her belly to make the nipple area neater. (Don't worry about how awful she looks; she'll lose even more fur on her own before it's all over and look even more dreadful.)

Talk to your veterinarian one last time about what to expect. Ideally, if you've been working with an experienced breeder, he'll be there to help you as your dog starts labor. He may suggest an ultrasound or X-ray to aid in predicting the size of the litter and identifying any potential problems with the delivery.

A day before the big date, your dog will probably lose her appetite and become more restless. She may dig in laundry piles; show her to her whelping box instead — you may need to be persistent, but she should have her litter where you can care for them best. Take her temperature: A dip to 99 degrees shows that labor is near. Make sure that you know where your veterinarian — or the closest emergency clinic — is and cancel all your plans, because the time is near.

Take the puppies and their mother to the veterinarian within the first day after the birth to make sure that everything's okay with them all. If dewclaws are to be removed and tails docked, discuss these procedures with your veterinarian right away — these minor surgeries need to be done before the age of 3 days. While experienced breeders often complete these procedures themselves, a novice breeder should not even attempt it — have your veterinarian take care of it.

Another job in those first few days: paperwork. Send in litter registration so that you get individual registration forms back in plenty of time to provide to puppy buyers. Contact the registry for more information on what's required.

The Principles of Breeding Dogs

Every foundation animal you buy, whether male or female, toy breed or giant, is the result of some kind of a breeding program. Breeding programs run the gamut from intelligent and conscientious to haphazard and irresponsible. Your stock should be a result of the former, and by this time you should understand why stock from a quality program is so important.

Every good breeder approaches her mission in a slightly different manner. You'll find that, more often than not, experienced and successful breeders are adamantly dedicated to their own method. It shouldn't come as any surprise that their dedication to a particular approach is a result of that approach having worked for them over the years.

Interestingly, all the various theories and breeding strategies can be categorized into three basic controlled breeding programs, which derive their names from the degree of relationship between the two dogs mated:

- **Inbreeding:** Breeding within the immediate family
- **Linebreeding:** Breeding among more-remotely-related family members
- **Outcrossing:** Breeding from the same breed but with no common ancestors within five generations

Inbreeding

Inbreeding is, as many geneticists have proclaimed, a powerful two-edged sword.

Don't attempt inbreeding if you don't have in-depth knowledge of all the good and bad points of the individuals who stand behind the two animals being mated. Inbreeding can intensify desirable characteristics to the degree that the resulting offspring are highly dependable for producing the desirable qualities. However, inbreeding can also call forth catastrophic consequences.

Inbreeding increases the chance that a gene obtained from the one parent will duplicate (match) one obtained from the other. This is the case for everything — both what is desirable and what is undesirable. Often, harmful and sometimes lethal genes float around in the pedigrees of dogs within a breed.

Knowledgeable breeders are apt to know if and where these genes exist. They use the utmost care in bringing together animals in any mating that may reproduce these abnormalities. In some circumstances, experienced breeders intentionally make breedings that risk such results, but they always have specific reasons for doing so. Only carefully selected individuals from those matings are retained for breeding; all others are neutered and eliminated from the gene pool.

Inbreeding can be scientifically defined as the mating of individuals more closely related than the average of the population that they come from. In other words, what may be considered inbreeding in a new breed with a small gene pool may not be considered inbreeding in a long-established breed that has hundreds, if not thousands, of dogs in the gene pool to draw upon.

In layman's terms, and for our purposes here, inbreeding is best explained as the mating of two *directly* related animals. Most dog breeders consider the following as inbreeding:

- ✔ Father bred to daughter
- ✔ Son bred to mother
- ✔ Full brother bred to full sister

One frequently hears people who are not familiar with intelligent breeding practices blame inbreeding for producing the health or temperament problems that exist in popular breeds. This assertion is seldom, if ever, true. Inbreeding isn't the main cause of a preponderance of health problems in a breed. People who lack knowledge of a breed's background do, however, create problems of this nature. If two dogs, closely related or not, who have a debilitating problem are mated, the chances of all the offspring having the problem obviously will be very high. Moreover, if the two animals who are mated are themselves free of the problem, but the problem runs rampant in the genetic makeup of their immediate ancestors, the chances of their passing it along are, for all intents and purposes, just as high as if they were afflicted themselves.

Linebreeding

Scientifically speaking, linebreeding and inbreeding are the same. The intensity is all that differs. In other words, if inbreeding increases the chance that a gene obtained from the one parent will duplicate (match) one obtained from the other, linebreeding reduces but does not eliminate those chances.

Although inexperienced breeders should not attempt inbreeding, intelligent breeders are also aware that a pedigree made up of dogs who are related only by breed won't ever provide any consistency or lock in any of the good traits that are necessary to maintain. Furthermore, it's doubtful that even the accidental outstanding individuals can be relied upon to reproduce themselves.

Linebreeding, then, is the best way to concentrate the qualities possessed by certain outstanding animals in the pedigree without running the risks of inbreeding. The certainty of getting what is desired is not as great through linebreeding as it is through inbreeding, but neither is the risk of intensifying highly undesirable traits.

Outcrossing

When no common ancestors appear within five generations of the two individuals being mated, the breeding is generally considered an outcross. True outcrosses are somewhat unlikely if breeders are working within popular bloodlines — *popular* meaning the bloodlines that are producing the kinds of dogs who are winning at the dog shows.

Outcrossing is the opposite of inbreeding. This method of breeding mates individuals of the same breed who, for all intents and purposes, are not related. This approach is less likely to fix faults in the offspring, but neither can it concentrate specific qualities with any certainty.

A certain look or style within a breed will become popular because it does well at the shows. Usually this style will emanate from a successful breeder's line or be stamped by an especially dominant stud dog. Other breeders will invariably attempt to incorporate that winning look into their own line. They do so either by dipping lightly into the winning line by making a single breeding to it, or by heavily reshaping their breeding program around the line that is producing the winning look. As a consequence, the breed as it is popularly seen becomes influenced to a greater or lesser degree by a few dogs from the source that began the trend. Eventually, hardly a dog in sight doesn't have at least a touch of the popular line somewhere, thereby making a true outcross breeding very rare.

Choosing Your Own Style

So which is the best way to go: linebreeding, inbreeding, or outcrossing? The following sections offer some thoughts.

The conservative breeder

Some breeders have a very clear-cut interpretation of the standard and stay within the lines that will produce that look and temperament, regardless of trends. Fads come and go, but these breeders stand by their linebreeding program that produces what they believe is correct and refuse to change hats even when that refusal slows the accumulation of those coveted blue ribbons.

Sticking by your line isn't always an easy thing to do. The trends can become so all encompassing that your dog becomes what you may call *odd man out* — the only dog in the lineup that looks different. It takes the knowledgeable judge who has the courage of his own convictions to decide which style is really right for the breed and to reward it accordingly. These diehard breeders often weather the storms of unpopularity and are there waiting when the winds of change calm down. In a good many cases, these kennels prove to be where newer breeders find the foundation stock that sets them in the right direction.

Keeping an eye on the prize

Other breeders keep abreast of trends within a breed and adapt their lines to keep pace. They are attracted to the qualities of the dog of the hour and use him, or the bloodline that produced him, in their own breeding program. These same individuals often have an eye for those winning qualities and are able to pick the dog most likely to succeed from their own litters. Soon they are out and winning with dogs sporting the new look.

Usually a significant amount of outcrossing is involved in breeding programs of this kind. Reliability is not the long suit of the line. Outcrossing can be a hit-and-miss affair, but breeders who subscribe to this approach seem entirely satisfied with those occasional hits that come along, because often they're big hits and account for highly successful win records.

Outcrossing for elusive qualities

Outcross breeding isn't done only to follow a fad or trend. When properly employed, outcrosses can bring qualities to a breeder's line that she sorely needs. Many intelligent breeders resort to occasional outcross breedings for very sound reasons. At times, a breeder's line will generally satisfy the breed standard in all respects but one or two — say, for example, pigment and eye color. The breeder finds that, try as she might, those qualities remain elusive within the line.

The logical thing to do, then, is to seek out another line (one known to consistently produce good pigment and eye color) and make a breeding, or sometimes two, into that line. Often this breeding requires outcrossing into another line that doesn't bear a close relationship to one's own. The method is more apt to succeed if the outcross line is closely linebred, because the chances of its being dominant for the desired qualities are higher. The dog whose appearance (also called *phenotype*) is not backed up by a concentration of the genes for that quality (*genotype*) may not be strong enough to pass along that quality to another, stronger line.

Sex-linked characteristics: Finding the formula

In addition to inbreeding, linebreeding, and outcrossing, breeders have to factor in another approach. In some cases, the sexes of the individual dogs who are used have a great bearing on which characteristics are passed along. These traits are called *sex-linked characteristics*.

In some cases, for example, the male is best at bringing in the quality you need from another line. In other instances, the female is more apt to give you what you want. It's almost as if Mother Nature is taunting you by giving you part but not all of the equation. Then it's up to you to find the missing piece and come up with the right answers.

Breeders who set out to improve their line or correct faults, instead of simply accepting them as part of the territory, may need generations of dogs to do so. In the end, however, the persevering breeder usually accomplishes this goal.

Getting an animal good enough to show is one thing. Getting one good enough to carry on your breeding program or to take the breed one step farther along the line of progress takes time and perseverance, and often leads to great disappointment. However, the dogs who carry breeds to greater heights in the show ring, in competitive events, and as producers are usually the result of someone's willingness to deal with all these setbacks.

Start with the Bitches

Absolutely nothing is more important to your breeding program than starting with a well-bred female of representative quality.

And now is as good a time as any to start using the term *bitch* rather than *female*. Everyone you deal with in the dog world refers to the two canine sexes as dogs (males) and bitches (females). If you want to work your way through elementary levels of your education in dog breeding, you may as well start using the terminology the pros use. And if you're waiting for a pun or joke about this lingo, well, in this particular instance you're going to be disappointed.

Why you don't need to keep males

The hobby breeder who's interested only in establishing a breeding program and setting a distinctive, yet representative, style needs to house only bitches. It's absolutely pointless — in fact, counterproductive — for any beginning breeder to house males.

The male will seldom, if ever, be used on the mother who produced him or on his sisters or his daughters. (As already mentioned, on a rare occasion a very experienced breeder will resort to this kind of inbreeding, but only in special, well-thought-out circumstances.) If you can't use him on any of the dogs in your own breeding program, what would be the reason for keeping him there?

If it's for those thousands of dollars you think you'll make on stud services, think again. Breeding dogs for profitable stud purposes is a highly specialized activity, best pursued after many years of successful dog breeding. To properly use a male, you have to go out and purchase the right female to breed to him. Doing so puts you right back at square one, with nothing to do but repeat the breeding over and over again. You'll have lots of offspring, but nothing to help you carry on a breeding program. All the dogs will be bred exactly the same — too closely to breed to each other.

The pointlessness of keeping a male becomes even more obvious when you stop to realize that you have access to any top-producing male in the country. And you can use a different male with each breeding.

The importance of foundation bitches

Successful breeders around the world agree on two things: First, beginners must go to a successful breeder for their foundation stock. Second, it's critical for the beginning breeder to buy the best possible daughter they can afford from the breed's best-producing *dam* (the term for a bitch used in breeding).

You may ask why these knowledgeable people have advised buying *a daughter* of a top-producing dam rather than the dam herself. To quote Norma Hamilton, a world-renowned breeder of the Quailmoor Irish Setters of Australia: "Only the person who has taken total leave of their senses would ever part with the great producing bitch herself. It would be like giving away your sails and then showing up to compete in the America's Cup."

Without a doubt, your bitch is the cornerstone — the very foundation — of everything you will do as a breeder. Don't even *think* of economizing in this respect.

Successful breeders also seem to agree that the foundation bitch doesn't have to be what could be described as a "glamour girl" — one who has won yards of blue ribbons. Records seem to indicate that as long as her bloodline credentials are impeccable, and she's well made and sound in all respects, her chances of being a noteworthy producer are very good.

If you can possibly arrange to do so, purchase *two* daughters of the producing bitch. They could be litter sisters or even half-sisters with different sires. There's no better way to assure yourself of establishing a tidy little producing nucleus than through obtaining high-quality sisters. The possibilities of breeding them out and then returning to your own line with the offspring are endless.

Having both quality male and female offspring emerge from even your earliest breedings isn't entirely unusual. But again, it's not necessary or advisable to keep any of the males in-house, no matter how good they are.

When you breed a fine male

When and if you do breed that great male, have no fear — you'll be able to make all sorts of breeding arrangements so that you will have access to him down the line when and if you have a bitch who's appropriate to breed to him. Don't sit up nights worrying about what to do if that one-in-a-million male comes along. And that's what the chances are of your producing him in your first litters — one in a million, if that high.

You'll have a line from here to Timbuktu waiting at your door if you have a top, show-quality male to place, with *top* meaning the very best. Trying to place the average, just-good-enough-to-become-a-champion male is not so easy. Average is easy to come by; tops is not. Furthermore, a male of only average quality is not one that others will seek out for breeding, nor should he be. The bull's-eye is the only thing you're aiming for.

Moving Outward: Making Partnerships

Working with bloodlines that seem to click, after a time you may find that you are coming up with a considerable percentage of high-quality, intelligently linebred bitches. In fact, you may be coming up with a few more than you can house properly but are afraid to let go entirely.

Breeding partnerships in Russia

No greater proof exists of the value of breeding partnerships than the breeders in Russia. Restricted by 70 years of communist domination, purebred dog breeders networked their breeding programs between partnerships of sometimes five, six, and seven breeders, many of them living in apartment complexes. All of them were severely handicapped by the lack of funds and the lack of nutritional supplements for their dogs. Even so, when the Iron Curtain was lifted, quality sprang forth as if from an underground stream.

You now face the small-breeder's dilemma: deciding which to keep — the females who have proven they can produce for you or the females who have been produced and are one step farther along in your quest for improvement?

One solution is partnership. Working closely with a partner, even the most limited breeder can create miracles. Naturally, the partners must have basically similar goals in mind and agree on what constitutes the essence of the breed. Both partners must also be dedicated to setting type and maintaining it. And neither should be unduly influenced by win records or fads and fancies. The partnership is a marriage of sorts. Be sure to pick someone with whom you're compatible.

A good many, if not *most* of Great Britain's great show-winning dog exports to America were dogs whelped in the most modest of homes — in the kitchen behind the stove, so to speak. The dogs shared living quarters with their owners, and their exercise came from being put out in the garden several times a day and from taking walks around the block with dad or the kids.

It's not how elaborately the dogs are kept — it's how good they are that counts.

Establishing and maintaining type in this day and age isn't easy. But then, it never really was, except perhaps for the few breeders blessed with the means to maintain those super kennels of the past. Can it be done today? Of course it can.

Small hobby breeders all over the world limit themselves to one litter a year or less. These small but important breeders are counted among the most influential in their respective breeds. Their influence didn't come about in a day, a week, or a year. It took time.

So You Have Puppies: Now What?

If you want to increase the chances of raising your puppies right — and be reassured that your puppies are "normal" — knowing how puppies mature is helpful. As with children, growth stages each have their wonders and their challenges. The stages pass too quickly, so to get the most out of the puppy experience, clear your calendar of nondog activities and keep your eyes open.

All puppies look much the same when they're born. You find size and marking differences, but they each come into this world looking something like a sausage, with tiny ears, tiny legs, and tightly closed eyes. Things start to change before long.

Although people have raised puppies for thousands of years, most of what we know about how people can influence a puppy's development — and about developmental stages in puppies — goes back only around 50 years, starting with the work of John Paul Scott and John L. Fuller in the 1950s. From their "school for dogs" in Bar Harbor, Maine, came the basis of what trainers and breeders have been using to get the most out of dogs ever since. *Animal Behavior* (John Paul Scott, University of Chicago Press) is a fascinating, if dated, place to start a study of dog behavior. Fuller and Scott teamed up with *Genetics and the Social Behavior of Dogs,* also from the University of Chicago Press. Although they're out of print, many libraries have these books, and a good secondhand bookseller should be able to find copies without too much trouble.

You can find more recent — and less academic — treatment of the subject in many subsequent books. Examples include Carol Lea Benjamin's *Mother Knows Best: The Natural Way To Train Your Dog* (Howell Book House); *How To Raise a Puppy You Can Live With,* by Clarice Rutherford and veterinarian David H. Neil (Alpine Press); and *The Art of Raising a Puppy,* by the Monks of the New Skete Monastery (Little, Brown).

Whelping and emergencies

Most dogs are natural whelpers and may not need your help at all. Many a dog owner has fallen asleep waiting for the big event only to wake up to a box full of puppies born, cleaned up, and nursing. If your dog isn't quite so efficient, you have to release the puppies from their amniotic sacs within 30 seconds or so and help them to breathe on their own. Clean the fluid from their mouths and noses by supporting their heads and swinging them between your legs, stopping sharply. You can also remove fluid with a bulb syringe. Rub the puppy with a clean towel and put her on a nipple. Above all, keep the puppies warm.

If the mother doesn't sever the umbilical cord, you may need to do that, too: Tie it off about an inch from the puppy with a thread soaked in alcohol and then snip with clean scissors. Dab the ends with Betadine to combat infection.

While many experienced breeders are sometimes as capable as any veterinarian when it comes to saving puppies, the novice breeder should not hesitate to get veterinary help quickly. You must take your dam to the veterinarian when any of the following occurs:

- ✔ She fails to enter labor 24 to 36 hours after her temperature dips to 99 degrees.

- ✔ She's in labor, and more than four hours lapse with no puppy being born, especially if a dark green fluid passes.

- ✔ She seems very uncomfortable and is panting heavily.

- ✔ A puppy gets stuck while being delivered.

- ✔ She has a puppy, and 30 minutes pass without another puppy being born, yet she's having strong contractions.

- ✔ If she doesn't expel an afterbirth, or placenta, for each puppy. Retained afterbirths can trigger infections.

If in doubt about anything, call your vet. Your dam may need more help than you can give her, including a cesarean section. If everything goes well, clean the mother with Betadine while she cleans up the nest — eating the afterbirths is a normal part of the process.

An important after-birth problem to look out for: If your nursing mom becomes restless, agitated, and trembling, call the veterinarian and say you're on the way. She may need calcium treatments for a condition called eclampsia.

Birth to 3 weeks

Puppies are pretty helpless at birth. They can't see or hear and need their mother for everything. She is their source for food, warmth, and protection; they cannot even eliminate waste without her gentle licking to stimulate the process.

Newborn pups can crawl and right themselves when turned over, and they can seek out food by smell. They can also seek out the warmth of their littermates — they are unable at this stage to regulate their own body temperature. On the outside, this time seems quiet — puppies at this age sleep almost constantly — but a lot of development is going on inside their brains and central nervous systems.

Leave them alone, except for one thing: Handle them briefly and gently on a daily basis and subject them to the tiniest amount of stress in the process. Puppy-raising experts believe this little bit of stress — such as placing them on a scale — is as important as handling in the development of a confident dog.

Even this early in a puppy's life, some temperament patterns are set. If you watch, you can already see which puppies will later become dominant with their siblings. These pups are the ones who push others out of the way at nursing time —frequent weighings will prove that the pushier pups will grow faster. Other pups are more wiggly, act nervous, or cry during handling. Be sure to note all these things.

Toward the end of the second week, the puppies start to open their eyes, although they see little more than light at this point. In the third week, the first teeth appear, and puppies start to hear. By the end of the third week, the sausages look like puppies, and they're ready to start exploring the world.

What if you have a litter of black Labrador puppies? How can you possibly tell one from another enough to follow and record changes in the early weeks when personalities are not so obvious? Use this trick: Make little collars of rickrack, a decorative zigzag trim material available in fabric stores, using a different color for each puppy. You won't have to resort to this tactic, of course, if you can note the puppies' markings to keep things straight.

3 to 5 weeks

During this stage, puppies start relying less on their mother and begin to learn from each other. They learn to play and to eat solid food.

Even as all this activity is happening — a wealth of new experiences, overwhelming their new senses of vision and hearing — the puppies are learning the rudiments of canine communication and social structure. Puppies start to learn when to use their sharp little teeth and, more important, when they cannot use them. Their mother teaches them some of this behavior, using her teeth to correct but not hurt them. In play with each other, an observer hears plenty of cries and squeals as bites are delivered just a little too hard, and puppies learn to inhibit their bites, delivering them with a force that matches the situation. (When puppies don't learn to inhibit biting from their mother and littermates, problems are bound to occur when they're in their new homes.)

Although puppies are most interested in each other at this stage, you should be busy reminding them that there are people in the world, too. Make sure that their environment is always changing and continue to handle the puppies, making sure that each gets individual attention. Expose the puppies to both genders and to children as well as adults. If a cat lives in the house, even better — although do your cat a favor and let him choose his interactions. His mere presence is enough to expose the puppies to the existence of felines.

Start weaning the puppies after three weeks. Discuss with your veterinarian or mentor the type of soft food to offer the puppies, and help the pups get the idea by putting the food on your finger and helping it into their mouths.

Puppy pans — doughnut-shaped dishes with a low outer rim — are ideal for giving every pup a place at the "table."

When puppies are eating semisolid food, the mother will quit cleaning up the nest by eating their waste — so the task of keeping puppies clean falls entirely to you now. About this time, the mother will start helping the weaning process by spending more time away from her babies. Understandably, she's getting a little sick of them.

5 to 7 weeks

The biggest mistake you can make in this period is to remove a puppy from the litter and send him to a new home. This practice is probably based on the idea that weaning is the logical time for puppies to be sold — puppies can start on hard kibble around six weeks — but the research emphatically insists that this "logic" is wrong.

Puppies have a lot more learning to do during these two weeks, and they need to be with their littermates to do it. Think of this period as the time of *more*. Puppies can see more, hear more, and play more at this stage. They are starting to become more interested in the world beyond their enclosure. They are especially attracted to those funny two-legged dogs who have spent the last few weeks picking them up, talking to them, and petting them. Suddenly, they think humans are pretty cool.

This stage is when humans think puppies are pretty cool, too. Puppies are absolutely adorable now, with the softest fur and the cutest faces. They run with a rolling, bouncing puppy gait, tripping over their big paws at times. They roughhouse with each other and stalk their toys. They drive their mother crazy — she is interested in spending as little time with them as possible now.

They are still learning, but what a fun time they're having.

Spend a lot of time with them at this stage, because their socializing is in full swing. Keep exposing them to the sights and sounds of life all the way up to the time they go to their new homes — ideally, after their seventh week.

Finding Proper Homes for Puppies

If you've done your job right, you have something truly remarkable to offer puppy buyers: fat, friendly, well-socialized puppies who promise a lifetime of good health and companionship. You want to be sure that the people who take them are worthy of such wonderful pups.

To find good potential owners, you need to be extra careful in screening homes. You mustn't just accept money from the first half-dozen people who walk through your door. If you've been working with a reputable breeder, ask for her help in placing the puppies. Ask prospective buyers these questions:

- ✔ **What is your living arrangement?** You don't need a house with a yard — some dogs, even large ones, do just fine in apartments. But you do need a person who's aware of what a dog needs and is prepared to deliver it. Definitely say no to anyone who plans to stick one of your pups on a chain in the yard.

- ✔ **Have you had dogs before? What kinds, and what happened to them?** Wrong answers include "lots" and "they ran away," "we moved," or "he got hit." Accidents happen to even the most conscientious of dog lovers, but a pattern of mishaps says a great deal about the way the prospective buyer treats dogs.

- ✔ **Do you have any experience with this breed? What do you expect of it?** You want to educate — and possibly eliminate from contention — anyone who isn't prepared to deal with the reality of living with a dog like yours. Don't sell to a person who isn't prepared for the shedding of a long-haired dog or the activity level of a terrier, for example. Be honest with buyers about the drawbacks of the breed, and you're much more likely to put your puppies in homes that will keep them, because they know what to expect.

- ✔ **Do you have children? What ages?** Some dogs, as with delicate toys, just don't work out well with children. Still, be flexible. A thoughtful, gentle child could work out fine. Discuss your concerns and see what answers you get.

- ✔ **Do you intend to breed your dog? Show your dog? Train your dog?** Your pet-quality puppies — ones with obvious show faults, such as wrong markings — should be sold on contracts that require them to be spayed or neutered. (Some breeders have the surgery taken care of before their puppies go to their new homes.) People who are interested in training and competing with their dogs are people who plan to be involved in their pup's life, and that's the kind of thing you like to see. Look, too, for people who travel with their pets or obviously treat them like family.

Be cordial and informative, but be persistent. Check references, including calling their veterinarian. A person who has had numerous pets and doesn't have a veterinary reference is another to cross off your list. Don't be afraid to turn people down. Sure, it may not be pleasant, but you must do what's best for your puppies. You've put a lot of effort into them, and you want them to live with someone who will continue to love and care for them as you have. You want your puppies to go to good homes, and the only one who has a chance at making that happen is you. So do your best.

If you are considering breeding your dog again, you need to skip at least a season to give her time to recover. In any case, one or two litters are about all you should ask of her if she's to enjoy just being a member of your family. As soon as her motherhood days are behind her, arrange for her to be spayed, to give her the best chance at a healthy life.

Another reason to spay her quickly: If you keep a puppy, you may be positively shocked to find your girl pregnant again — thanks to her own son. Many folks have been surprised to find that their dog becomes pregnant, because the only male she'd been around was a pup from her last litter. "But that's incest!" these people say, shocked. "Don't they know better?"

Unfortunately, they don't.

Book II

Dog Nutrition and Health

Book III

Cleanliness Is Next to Dogliness: Grooming

The 5th Wave   By Rich Tennant

"We try to pay personal attention to the dog's grooming, but it's time consuming and lately Agnes has been hacking up hair balls."

In this book . . .

Keeping your dog clean and presentable becomes more important as your dog integrates into your life. It can also be a constant battle. These chapters cover the basics of bathing, grooming, nail trimming, and hair clipping — and taking care of lesser-known dog hygiene issues.

Chapter 1

What Good Grooming Is All About

In This Chapter

▶ Understanding why grooming is important to your dog's health

▶ Tallying the costs of grooming

▶ Determining which dogs (and coat types) need the most and least grooming

▶ Figuring out when to do it yourself and when to hire a pro

Grooming . . . the froufrou doggie beauty parlor, complete with bows, silly hairstyles, and nail polish. It doesn't have to be that way, but grooming is important any way you brush it. Your dog feels as uncomfortable as you do when his hair is all ratty and snarled. But grooming is also vital for his health. And it means more than just a bath — it includes brushing, combing, keeping his teeth and ears clean, clipping his nails, and keeping him in top shape. In this chapter, you get an overview of dog grooming and why it's so important for your dog's well-being. You also find out how much time and money it takes to keep your dog well groomed and when to call in a pro.

Big Hairy Deal: Why Grooming Is Important

Your dog isn't healthy if she doesn't look good outside. A lackluster coat or one that's plagued with external parasites and sores is just the tip of the iceberg. If she looks icky outside, she probably feels icky inside, too. A dog's coat mirrors her health. And her outward appearance can be a signal of internal problems that no amount of brushing can fix.

Keeping clean company

When your dog is clean, you want him around more so you can bond and enjoy each other's company. Sure, he likes to play in the dirt and roll in distasteful stuff, but he also likes how it feels to be clean, just like you do. In the end, you and everyone around you are less likely to enjoy having a dirty, smelly dog around. A clean, refreshing one is definitely a more enjoyable companion.

Presenting a positive public image

Keeping your dog clean says something about you; it says that you're a responsible dog owner and that you care for your dog. You may be able to take your dog places where dogs aren't usually allowed. If it takes only a glance to see that you take care of your dogs and that they're well mannered, rules can often be bent.

Your dog no doubt will join you on walks outside your home, but you may occasionally do other things together, such as go to special events or even compete in various dog sports and activities. Maybe you want to do some social work, such as visiting the sick or elderly. Your dog could become a therapy dog, but being clean and friendly is crucial under those circumstances. No one wants to pet a dirty dog, no matter how lovable.

Dogs aren't always allowed everywhere you want to take them, no matter how well behaved and well groomed they are. Sometimes health department regulations come into play, so make sure that you always get permission before you take a dog to a place that doesn't normally accept them.

Eliminating the spread of dirt and disease

Dirty dogs track dirt into your home and get dirt on your clothing, furniture, and carpet. Ungroomed dogs are also more likely to be infected by internal and external parasites — fleas and ticks — and can harbor dangerous diseases, such as bubonic plague (yes, really), typhus, Lyme disease, and Rocky Mountain spotted fever, which can make you and your family sick. If your dog is ungroomed, she may be carrying fungi such as ringworm that young kids and the elderly can catch. Keeping your dog clean through good grooming eliminates many potential health problems.

Coaching your canine to be groomed

Grooming your dog requires partnership. Although you don't necessarily need your dog's full compliance when grooming, it sure makes things easier. Good grooming starts when your dog is a puppy. Getting her used to routine tasks, like being brushed and combed and having her feet handled so you can clip her toenails, is all part of grooming. If you wait until the dog is grown, your dog may fight you, and you may end up with results neither of you like.

Teaching your dog simple cues, such as Sit, Down, and Stay, is important in wise grooming. If you can't keep your dog in one place, it's very hard to do anything. Chapter 3 in Book IV provides advice for training your dog to enjoy grooming (or at least tolerate it and cooperate).

Determining whether something's really wrong with your dog internally

Plenty of good reasons exist for grooming your dog. One of them is finding out the difference between a coat that looks bad because it's dirty and one that looks bad because something is wrong with your dog. Grooming also eliminates various problems associated with an ill-kept dog, such as external parasites or open sores caused by a matted and dirty coat that traps bacteria.

A lackluster coat can be a sign of one or more serious problems, including the following:

- Poor nutrition
- Allergies
- Internal parasites
- Hormonal imbalances or diseases
- External parasites
- Cancer
- Other diseases

Any one of these problems can severely shorten your dog's life or, in extreme conditions, kill your dog outright. Grooming your dog helps separate potential health problems from problems caused by not properly caring for your dog.

Considering the Necessary Investment

You may be wondering just how much it costs to have a good-looking dog. You may have even visited the local groomer to find out how much bathing and/or clipping your dog costs. If so, you know it can be a bit pricey. The truth is, when you start grooming your dog, you can take certain basic steps just to get by, all the while keeping an eye out for bargains on good equipment and supplies. It's not all about money, though. Your time is worth something, and grooming requires some of that, too.

You may find grooming expensive in time *and* money, or you may find it relatively inexpensive. Much of the cost of grooming depends on the breed, what type of hair your dog has, and whether you're grooming your dog as a pet or for show. The following sections can help you figure out how much time and money you need to keep your pup well groomed.

The cost in money

The bad news is that good grooming supplies are fairly expensive. The good news is that after you dole out the initial investment for your equipment, you probably won't encounter that expense again unless something breaks or wears out.

How much does at-home grooming cost compared to a year's worth of grooming sessions from a pro? Well, if you're paying from $20 to $50 a month in grooming, you're paying $240 to $600 a year. You can buy some pretty nice grooming equipment for that amount of money, meaning that doing it yourself pays off during the first year or two, and you're saving that much every year from then on.

Some dogs need more grooming equipment and supplies than others. For example, a dog who needs daily brushing and regular clipping will need more equipment than a dog with a wash-and-wear coat. (See "Getting Familiar with Your Dog's Coat" later in this chapter, for more on fur types.)

The cost in time

Think about both the work and the fun factors when you bathe or brush your dog. Grooming your dog is as much a necessity as housetraining your dog or taking him to the vet for an annual exam, but whether it's a joy or a chore is up to you. When considering doing the grooming yourself, be aware of the following:

External Anatomy of a Dog

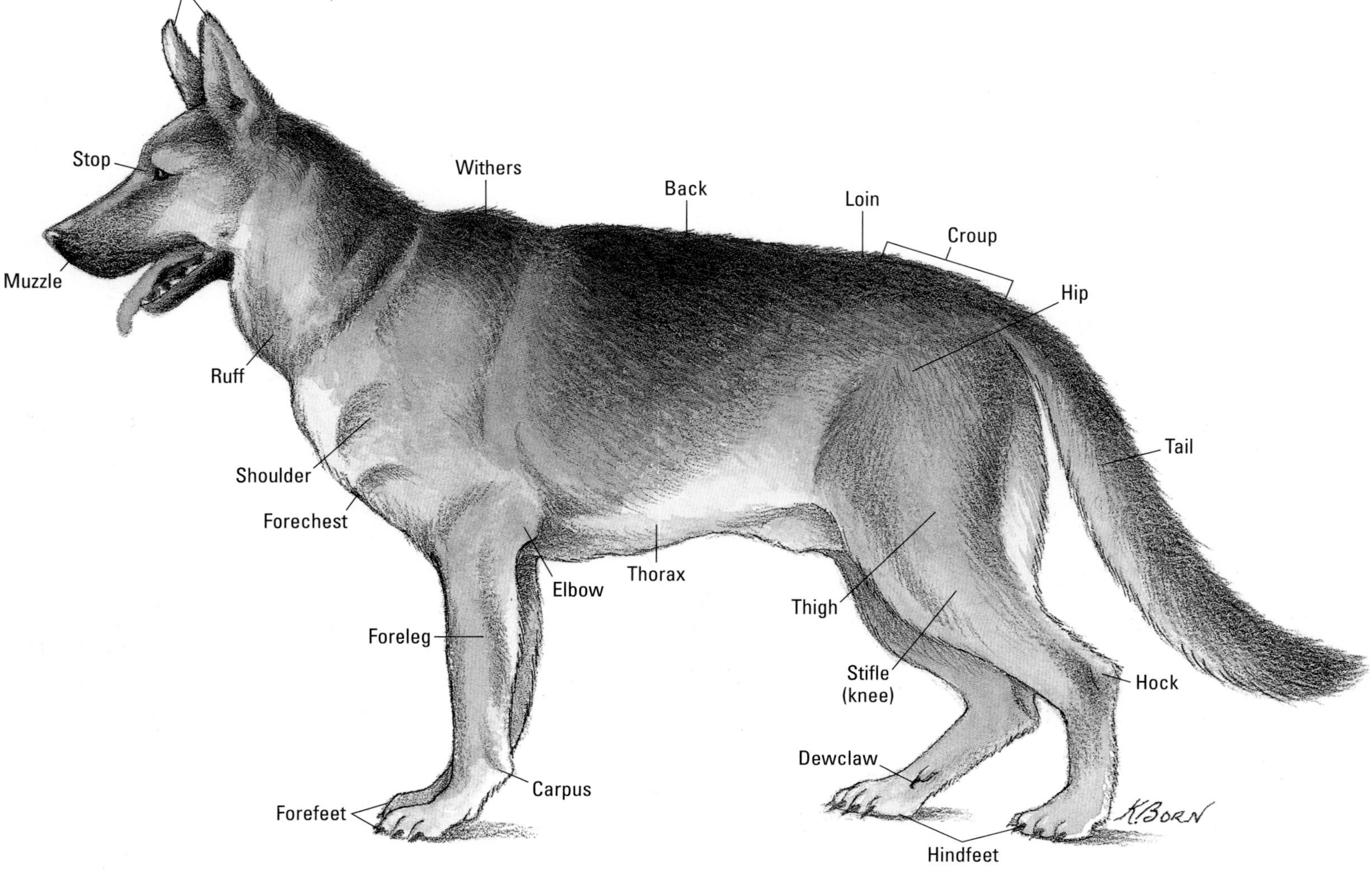

Ears

Stop

Muzzle

Ruff

Shoulder

Forechest

Withers

Back

Thorax

Elbow

Foreleg

Carpus

Forefeet

Loin

Croup

Hip

Tail

Thigh

Stifle
(knee)

Dewclaw

Hock

Hindfeet

K.BORN

Some of a dog's body parts have familiar, human-sounding names, but some are particular to the species.

Training classes are a terrific way for your dog to socialize, exercise, and have loads of fun — and they're usually just as fun for people.

Using treats to enhance dog training is a great strategy, especially for dogs who love food. Gradually stop giving treats when the dog performs as desired and replace with enthusiastic praise.

Dogs respond to praise for a job well done — go ahead and kiss, hug, pat, ruffle the ears, and scratch under the chin whenever your dog does what you want.

Agility training takes play instincts to a much higher level, into the realm of sports technique. Dogs appreciate the chance to up their game as much as human athletes do.

You're never too young to begin agility classes, as this happy puppy illustrates — in fact, the younger a dog starts, the more refined and ingrained agility skills become.

Most dogs retain the instincts that assist in the jobs they were bred for, even if those jobs are now obsolete. These dogs have been genetically developed to hunt foxes, and they are still very good at their jobs.

A sheep herding dog knows just how to handle stubborn livestock with a stern hand without actually doing them harm

These sled dogs are obviously in ecstasy pulling their sled through winter landscapes.

The primal hunting instinct to chase and capture easily translates to games that are a blast for canine and human alike.

Dog show judges check and examine every aspect of show competitors.

All show dogs must conform to breed standards, including color, size, and body form.

Breeding dogs involves getting out of the way so the mother can provide for her young.

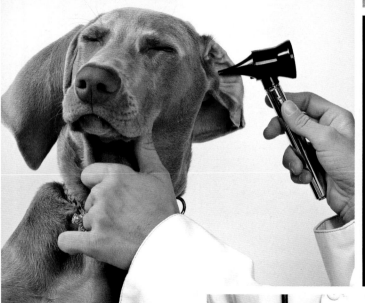

Most dogs don't like vet visits any more than people like going to the hospital.

Regular check-ups and staying up to date on vaccinations are key to taking care of a dog.

When it comes to dogs and leisure time, the more the merrier. Be sure to socialize your dog as much as possible.

Dogs and kids have always been best buddies. Kids teach dogs tolerance and patience toward people, and dogs teach kids respect and responsibility for other beings.

Many dogs are happiest in the company of other dogs and often develop lifelong friendships.

- The shorter your dog's coat, the less grooming he'll need.

- The smaller the dog, the less grooming he'll need.

- A dog with long hair or a double coat takes more time to groom than one with a medium- or short-haired coat.

- Different procedures take different amounts of time. A quick brushing with a well-maintained coat takes less time than a bath (see Chapter 2 in Book III for more).

- The condition of your dog's coat dictates the amount of time grooming takes. Brushing out a clean dog with a well-maintained coat takes very little time when compared to one with a dirty, matted coat.

- Dogs with wash-and-wear (short-haired) coats can usually get away with once-a-week grooming.

- Dogs with average coats can usually get away with twice-a-week grooming.

- Dogs with high-maintenance coats need to be groomed three times or more per week.

- When some dogs are adolescents or when they're shedding, they require coat care *every day*.

When planning your initial grooming session, set aside at least two hours, because you'll be going more slowly and your dog's coat may not be in the best condition. Later you can whittle down your grooming sessions to an hour or even a half hour as you get better at grooming and your dog's coat is better maintained.

If you don't have the time to groom your dog's coat into good shape, consider first taking him to a professional groomer and then maintaining the coat after the groomer works it into manageable shape. Your dog's coat can achieve the proper condition without using too much of your valuable time.

The added investment: Grooming for show

Grooming your dog for show costs plenty more in terms of time and money over what you'd spend on grooming a pet dog. Special show clips and stripped breeds (such as Terriers, whose grooming requires hair removal) usually take a while to develop and maintain. Many coats benefit from special leave-in coat conditioners, bodifiers, and coat dressings. (See Chapter 6 in Book IV for more information on showing your dog.)

Getting Familiar with Your Dog's Coat

Dogs have some amazing coats, ranging from curly to straight, puffy to wiry, short to long, and every variation in between. Some dogs even come equipped with dreadlocks!

It's hard to believe that the wolf produced descendants with such wide varieties of coats, but it did. You have to evaluate the type of coat your dog has, and that determines the grooming equipment and supplies you need. The following sections cover differences in the basic types of coats.

Coat types: Single versus double

Dogs basically have two types of coats:

- ✔ **Double coat:** Most dogs have a *double coat* (also called a *two-ply coat*) that consists of a top coat and an undercoat. The *top coat* is composed of stiffer *guard hairs,* which tend to be naturally water repellant. Top coats protect the dog's skin and undercoat, acting as a natural guard against the elements. The *undercoat* is a fleecy or downy type of fur that's shorter than the top coat. The undercoat serves as insulation to keep the dog warm during cold or inhospitable weather. Dogs shed (or *blow out*) the undercoat twice a year — it's a seasonal action.

- ✔ **Single coat:** Some dogs have a *single coat,* in which only a top coat is present without an undercoat. Dogs with this kind of coat shed less than their double-coated counterparts.

You can tell what kind of coat your dog has in two ways. The first is easy: Read the American Kennel Club (AKC) breed standard for your breed and look under the Coat listing (www.akc.org). The second way is to part the hairs on your dog's coat to find out whether it's a longer, harsh coat combined with soft, downy fur. If so, your dog has a double coat. If the hair is mostly even without an undercoat, your dog has a single coat.

However, both types of coats have different issues when it comes to grooming, so be aware that one type isn't necessarily better than another. Knowing coat type helps you determine how to groom your dog properly. Knowing whether she will go through a seasonal shed or blow her coat, can avoid surprises when she leaves enough hair on the rug to knit three more dogs her size.

Two types of double coats exist. One is called a *natural coat* — that is, a coat with two layers. The second is found on longer-haired breeds that have two-ply coats that obviously need more attention.

Defining coat terms

Many funny-sounding words are associated with dog coats. They're worth mentioning because you may come across them when working on a particular breed or reading a particular breed standard (see Book V). Peruse these various coat textures and what they mean:

- **Blow coat:** The yearly or biannual shedding that some dog breeds go through. The coat comes out in handfuls during a short period of time.

- **Bristle coat:** A wiry or broken coat, or a *bristly coat,* such as the one worn by the Chinese Shar-Pei.

- **Broken coat:** See *wire coat.*

- **Corded coat:** A coat that has dreadlocks.

- **Crinkly coat:** A wire coat found on the Wire (Haired) Fox Terrier.

- **Curly coat:** A coat with curls, like that of the Poodle or the Curly-Coated Retriever.

- **Double coat:** A coat with an undercoat and a top coat.

- **Guard hairs:** See *top coat.*

- **Linty coat:** A coat that has an unusual soft, downy texture. (Also what your light-colored dog gets when you carry her around while you're wearing black cashmere.)

- **Open coat:** A sparsely haired coat; usually a single coat.

- **Out of coat:** A dog who has shed his undercoat and is waiting for his new coat to grow in. Out-of-coat dogs usually are not as pretty as when they're in full coat.

- **Pily coat:** A coat with a dense, harsh top coat with a soft, fur-like undercoat. Usually found in Dandie Dinmont Terriers.

- **Single coat:** A coat that lacks an undercoat.

- **Smooth coat:** A short coat that lays back against the dog's skin.

- **Stand-off coat:** A long coat that does not lay flat against the body, but stands straight up. (Also the kind of coat your dog will have if you two can't come to terms with grooming.)

- **Top coat:** The outer coat that protects the dog's skin and undercoat. Usually harsh and weather resistant.

- **Two-ply coat:** See *double coat.*

- **Undercoat:** The downy second coat found beneath the top coat, usually shed once or twice a year.

- **Wire coat:** A type of harsh coat that may be single or double with stiff, wiry hairs.

Coat textures

Different coats have different textures. Understanding the texture of your dog's coat is crucial for proper grooming. Consider these different textures:

- **Smooth coats:** The smooth-coated or short-coated dog has very short hair that lays back against the dog's skin. A smooth coat can be either double-coated or single-coated, depending on the breed. These coats tend not to be much of a hassle when it comes to grooming — even though they do shed. Dalmatians and Bulldogs have this kind of hair.

✔ **Wire coats:** The wire coat (broken coat) is wiry on the outside and often has a soft undercoat on the inside, but it can be a single coat. Wire coats are wavy looking, but the hair feels a bit coarse. Think Terrier. Wire coats usually need to be stripped or clipped (removed or cut), adding an extra step to the average grooming routine.

✔ **Curly coats:** Curly coats are few in number, but you'll recognize them. They're the Poodles, the Portuguese Water Dogs, and the Irish Water Spaniels. These curly dogs require extreme maintenance, including clipping and brushing (see Chapter 4 in Book III).

✔ **Corded coats:** Dogs with "dreadlocks" need a fair amount of work upfront to prevent the hair from tangling into mats. After the cords are twisted, keeping them well maintained takes time. Dogs with corded coats include the Puli and the Komondor. Poodles can also be corded.

Coat length

Shorter coats generally are easier to groom than longer coats. Check out the other differences in the list that follows:

✔ **Hairless dogs:** On one end of the spectrum are the hairless or near-hairless dogs. They are lacking when it comes to hair, although some breeds, like the Chinese Crested, actually have some hair on the head or legs (and the Powderpuff variety is a hairy dog). But just because they're hairless doesn't mean that you don't groom them. Although you may not be brushing their hair, their skin requires plenty of attention.

✔ **Short coats:** Dogs with short coats are pretty much the wash-and-wear dogs. Their coats don't offer much protection against the elements, so they're more likely to have problems with cold climates than their furrier counterparts. They may be single- or double-coated. Examples include the Basenji and the Beagle.

✔ **Medium coats:** A medium coat is not so short that the hair doesn't give the dog protection, and not so long that the hair tangles or mats terribly. Medium-coated dogs usually are double-coated with a top coat and an undercoat, but unlike long-haired dogs, they're usually fairly easy to groom. Border Collies and Cardigan Welsh Corgis have medium coats.

✔ **Long coats:** Dogs with long coats often are the showstoppers of the dog world, attracting oohs and ahhs wherever they go. But all that beauty has a price. Long-coated dogs often are single-coated and prone to mats and tangles if the hair isn't kept up. If your dog has a long coat, you can expect long grooming sessions or trips to the grooming parlor. Afghan Hounds and Irish Setters have long coats.

Coat color

Dogs come in a variety of colors — everything from black to white and all shades in between, or so it seems. And their colors come in many different patterns, including bi-color, tri-color, and *brindle* (mottled with brown and black — often looking like stripes). Colors and color combinations depend a great deal on the breed and whether they are acceptable in the breed standard.

Some shampoos and conditioners help bring out the best in your dog's coat. When buying supplies, look for ones that make your white dog sparkling white, your black dog glossy black, or your brown dog look his very best.

Having the Proper Tools on Hand

Different coats require different grooming methods, and different grooming methods require different equipment and supplies. Analyzing your dog's coat should give you some idea of what tools and supplies you need to properly groom her. For example, depending on your dog's coat, you may be simply brushing and bathing, or you may be clipping or stripping it, too.

Good grooming requires more than brushing, bathing, and possibly clipping your dog. It also involves routinely trimming her toenails, brushing her teeth, cleaning her eyes and ears, and possibly expressing her anal sacs. Chapter 3 in Book III covers these jobs.

Book III

Cleanliness Is Next to Dogliness: Grooming

Choosing a low- or high-maintenance pup

Grooming can be a piece of cake or a nightmare, depending on your patience and the breed of dog you've chosen. Although other factors are probably more important, grooming also should go into the decision-making process when choosing a dog.

- ✔ Basenji
- ✔ Beagle
- ✔ Boston Terrier
- ✔ Dalmatian
- ✔ Doberman Pincher

Which dogs are low maintenance when it comes to coats? Think short and medium coats that don't need clipping and don't need a lot of brushing and detangling (but these dogs do shed). Consider this partial list of some dogs with low-maintenance coats:

- ✔ German Shorthaired Pointer
- ✔ Great Dane
- ✔ Labrador Retriever
- ✔ Pointer
- ✔ Rottweiler

(continued)

(continued)

Why would anyone want a dog with a high-maintenance coat? Well, as you've seen, they can be very beautiful. Owners and breeders like that certain look you don't see with a short-coated dog. The dog's temperament figures in, too — many people like certain temperaments that come in a particular package. This list includes some dogs with high-maintenance coats:

- Afghan Hound
- American Cocker Spaniel
- Dandie Dinmont Terrier
- Keeshond
- Kerry Blue Terrier

- Poodle
- Portuguese Water Dog
- Puli
- Samoyed
- Soft Coated Wheaten Terrier

Knowing When to Call a Pro

You may be ready to invest your time and money in grooming your pooch, but in some situations you need to rely on the skills and advice of an expert. Your Bearded Collie may tangle with a sticker bush, and you may not have the time or patience to pick every last sticker out of his coat. Maybe your Great Dane is easy to bathe and brush but a gigantic pain when you're trimming his nails and brushing his teeth. Perhaps you adopted a dog who's never been groomed, and you need help getting his coat into shape so you can then maintain it.

If you're an honest soul who has admitted to yourself that you have neither the time nor the inclination to do it right, there's no shame in that. And why should there be? You call a plumber when your sink faucet is spraying water. You have a teacher teach your kids. You buy an airline ticket to fly across the country instead of going to flight school. You pay someone else to do plenty of tasks that you can't or won't do, so there's nothing wrong with hiring a professional groomer for your dog.

Assigning children to groom the dog usually isn't a reliable alternative to routinely grooming the dog yourself. No matter how much your kids promise to take care of the dog (including grooming), don't believe them. This task ultimately falls on an adult in the household. Younger children are neither responsible enough to take care of a dog without adult supervision nor capable of tackling the grooming process.

Considering the cost

Most pet owners hesitate to look for a professional groomer because, quite frankly, it's costly. Yet that's all a matter of perspective. What's your time worth? If you take three or four hours to groom your Standard Poodle, paying someone $45 to $65 to bathe, brush, and clip your dog may actually be a deal.

The cost of having a professional groom your dog varies widely depending on where you live and what you want done. Time- and skill-intensive procedures like stripping or clipping coats cost more than a simple bath and brushing. Problem coats (matting and tangles) also add to the cost.

Keep these points in mind when considering the cost of grooming:

✔ Most groomers charge between $35 and $70 for complete grooming.

✔ Some groomers charge more or less, depending on the breed, the location (New York City is more expensive than Great Falls, Montana), the size of the dog, and the type of work done.

✔ Dogs with matted or dirty fur cost more, and so do dogs who need a show trim.

✔ Groomers add from $8 to $12 for mats and add at least $40 for show cuts, over the average cost of grooming.

TIP

Most, but not all, groomers offer baths, brushing, clipping, stripping, ear cleaning, and nail cutting as part of their services. Ask what the full grooming price includes. Some groomers don't quote a price until they see your dog and can gauge how much work grooming your dog will be.

Looking for a professional groomer

Now that you've decided to use a professional groomer, you can easily Google **dog grooming** with your city name included, or kick it old school in the Yellow Pages under the "Dog Groomers" section. But you may have a better method.

Finding a professional groomer

Finding a groomer is pretty easy. You're likely to see a shop on the corner in your neighborhood, but you may not be sure whether that groomer is any good. Take these steps to find a good one:

Book III

Cleanliness Is Next to Dogliness: Grooming

1. **Ask your dog-owning friends whether they use a groomer for their dogs or know of one they can recommend.**

   A good recommendation is worth its weight in gold. If your dog-owning friends praise a particular groomer, go with that one.

2. **Ask your veterinarian what groomer he recommends.**

   Sometimes vets employ a groomer onsite.

3. **Look for groomers near you online:**

   - **Find a Groomer directory (`www.findagroomer.com`):** This groomer directory is the pet owner's side of PetGroomer.com (`www.petgroomer.com`). Groomers list themselves here. You can search by city and state or even by zip code.

   - **BreederWeb.com (`breederweb.com/services/dogGroomers.asp`):** This resource is another good one to use in your search for a groomer.

   - **DexOnline.com (`dexonline.com`):** Use this Internet Yellow Pages site to do a search on **dog grooming** in your city and state.

Checking into Certifications

Certifications are a mixed bag. Plenty of good groomers who have well-established businesses and do an exceptional job are not certified. A groomer who is neither certified nor professionally trained may have a good reputation and references that check out. If so, that groomer probably is a good bet.

A certified groomer is someone who is professionally trained and certified to a certain standard. You don't know what level of expertise a groomer who hasn't been certified has achieved. An uncertified groomer may be better or worse than someone who is certified. With certification, at least you know the standard to which the groomer should be able to perform.

Certifications are offered through certain grooming schools and through the National Dog Groomer's Association of America (NDGAA). You can find out more about NDGAA certification at `www.nationaldoggroomers.com`.

Screening a professional groomer

After you find a professional groomer you're interested in using, you need to determine whether that groomer is the right one for your dog. Not all groomers are comfortable with all dogs; some groomers prefer to work only with certain breeds.

Some groomers may use tranquilizers, especially with difficult-to-handle or aggressive dogs. If you don't know whether a groomer uses tranquilizers, ask. Some dogs can experience seizures when administered certain common tranquilizers. Tranquilizers also make dogs more susceptible to problems caused by changes in temperature, such as hypothermia and heatstroke.

Knowing the right questions to ask

Let your fingers do the walking here. You can prescreen most professional groomers over the phone to find out whether they're right for you and your dog. Ask these questions:

- What hours are you open for business?
- Are you available for emergencies or after hours?
- How long have you been in business?
- What are your certifications? With what organization?
- How many clients do you see?
- What breeds do you see most of?
- How many of my breed do you see?
- Are you comfortable working on my breed?
- How much do you charge for a full grooming? What procedures does a full grooming include?
- How do you handle difficult dogs? Do you muzzle or tranquilize them?
- Do you use cage dryers? If so, how often do you check on dogs with cage dryers?
- What do you charge for just a bath and brushing? Nail clipping?
- How many staff members do you employ?
- What other services do you offer?
- Do you have an emergency on-call vet? Who is it?
- Do you have references?

Visiting a professional groomer

After you prescreen the professional groomer on the phone, it's time for a visit. Ask whether you can drop by and check out the groomer's facility some time. The grooming shop should be neat, clean, and organized. If the shop is especially busy, you may find hair and water on the floor, but overall the shop needs to leave you with a good impression.

Watch how the groomer and staff members handle dogs. Are they gentle and caring, or do they move the dogs around like commodities? Watch body language; you generally can tell whether the groomer is just going through the motions or sincerely likes what she is doing. Although everyone is entitled to a bad day, the groomer shouldn't take out any frustrations on the dogs.

When you're convinced that a particular groomer is the one for your dog, make an appointment. You may need one or two sessions to really decide whether the groomer is a good fit.

A dirty or terribly chaotic and disorganized grooming shop may be a sign that the groomer doesn't have enough staff and may not have time to care for and watch all the dogs, especially the ones in cage dryers (combination kennels/dryers). When that's the case, you may want to look for another groomer. For the lowdown on the basics of doing your own grooming, continue on to the other chapters in this Book. For the whole story on grooming, check out *Dog Grooming For Dummies* by Margaret H. Bonham (Wiley).

Chapter 2

The Basics of Brushing and Bathing

Good grooming is a part of caring for your dog, but most of what you do is maintenance work — that is, just keeping your dog clean and healthy. If you start with a clean dog and maintain a clean and healthy coat, you prevent headaches and disasters later.

This chapter covers the proper techniques for brushing, combing, bathing, and drying your dog. You can find out about other grooming basics, like clipping your dog's toenails and cleaning his ears and teeth, in Chapter 3 of Book III.

Do-It-Yourself Canine Hair Styling

Brushing and combing form the foundation of good grooming. Most dogs don't actually need baths all that frequently. They usually need them only when they get noticeably dirty or have to go to a show. However, they must be brushed and combed often — usually twice weekly or more often, depending on the breed and coat. Brushing and combing are great for your dog's skin and coat because they distribute oils from the skin throughout the coat and get rid of bits of dirt, tangles, and loose hair. This aspect of grooming is the one thing you really need to do, even if you hire a groomer.

Always brush and comb a dog *before* you bathe her. Doing so helps prevent tangles and keeps your dog cleaner (bathing is covered later in this chapter).

Beyond pulling hairs: Making the experience pleasant

Brushing and combing can be enjoyable or a total nightmare. Usually, dogs who hate to be brushed and combed are the ones with long hair or thick coats that tend to mat easily. Owners often don't tackle the thick coat early or often enough, and these sessions wind up being much more painful than they have to be. Brushing and combing don't have to become a hair-pulling event.

A few tricks can make brushing and combing easier for you and your dog:

- **Start young.** When your dog is a puppy, get her used to brushing. In many cases, dogs love the attention. However, even if you do start early, some dogs never quite take to grooming. In many instances, you may have to work through some bad behaviors, and in other rare cases, you may even need to muzzle or sedate the dog.

- **Stick to a routine.** Where on your dog you first start brushing, combing, and grooming doesn't matter, but being consistent does. By following the same routine every time you groom your dog, you won't forget to do anything, and your dog won't have any surprises.

- **Relax with your dog.** Taking time to relax — both dog and owner — goes a long way toward calming your dog's fears. Your dog may get nervous when she senses it's grooming time, regardless of whether you're breaking out a grooming table (highly recommended — find them online or at pet stores) or simply reaching for a brush and comb. Giving her treats, administering a good massage (see the "Massaging your dog" sidebar for advice), or just talking to her in a soothing tone helps relieve your dog's tension before and during a brushing session.

  If you use a grooming table to groom your dog, never leave her on it unattended. She can hurt herself jumping off or even strangle herself if she's hooked into a noose.

- **Brush your dog after she's exercised — when she's a little bit tired.** She'll be calmer.

- **Never hurry and always be gentle whenever possible.** One bad experience can be traumatic and turn your dog off grooming entirely.

- **Use the right tools.** The right tools make the job not only easier, but less stressful and less painful. If you use the wrong tools, you're more likely to pull on your dog's hairs (tools are covered in the next section).

Massaging your dog

Massaging your dog may sound a little odd, but it's a great way to bond with him. If your dog has never been massaged, he may find it a little strange at first. The first goal when massaging your dog is to get him to relax. Start with gentle stroking movements in areas where he's normally accustomed to being petted. Don't touch areas that your dog isn't quite comfortable with you touching, and don't use a lot of pressure until your dog gets used to it. Pick up a copy of *How to Massage Your Dog,* by Jane Buckle (Wiley), or *Dog Massage,* by Maryjean Ballner (St. Martin's Press), for the basics of massaging your dog.

Gathering the tools you need

Before you get started brushing or combing your dog, gather all the tools you need for the session. Having everything you need in one place and within reach makes the brushing and combing session go much more smoothly; it can make all the difference between an experience that's pleasant and one that's not.

If you live in a flea-prone area, make sure that you have a flea comb handy, especially during flea season (which begins in spring). Flea combs, along with all kinds of rakes, brushes, combs, and clippers, are available at all good pet stores.

Tools for long coats

If your dog has a long coat, you need the following tools:

- **An undercoat rake or long comb:** To remove the loose undercoat hairs.

  Some groomers prefer using wide-toothed combs first and then changing to progressively narrower or finer-toothed ones. This strategy is good whenever your dog has really snarly hair. However, if you're simply maintaining your dog's coat, you can choose to go over him with a fine-or medium-toothed comb and then a slicker brush.

- **Detangler solution and a mat splitter or mat rake:** For tangles and mats (use electric clippers in extreme cases).

- **Shedding tool:** For removing the soft undercoat when the dog is *blowing coat* (shedding profusely).

- **Slicker brush:** For removing hair and stimulating the skin and coat.

Book III

Cleanliness Is Next to Dogliness: Grooming

Tools for short coats

If your dog has a shorter coat, you need these grooming tools:

- **A Zoom Groom or short curry brush:** For removing hair and polishing the coat
- **A short-toothed comb:** For removing hair and getting through any tangles
- **Slicker brush:** For removing hair and stimulating the skin and coat

Brushing up on basic techniques

You can work from tail to head or vice versa. Just start at one end and work your way to the other — and don't miss anything in between.

Various methods of brushing include *line brushing and combing* — that is, parting the fur and combing and brushing out each section (which works well on long coats) — and *spiral brushing,* in which the dog's hair is brushed and combed in a circular pattern. Spiral brushing works well on any coat.

Regardless of the method of brushing and combing you use, you need to brush all the hair, not just the top coat. That means getting down to the skin and brushing upward.

You can brush out your dog's coat in a variety of ways. One common way is to brush backward against the lay of the fur and then brush it back into place (see Figure 2-1). Brushing that way usually loosens and removes hair and stimulates your dog's skin. Some breeds have hair types that don't go well with this method. Breeds with corded hair, in particular, just can't be brushed backward, so make sure that you remove all the tangles as you go.

Dealing with the dreaded mat

Because brushing or combing out mats and tangles can cause any dog a great deal of discomfort, don't keep pulling on them after you find them. Instead, follow these instructions to gently remove tangles and mats:

1. **Spray the mat with detangler solution and use an appropriate comb to slowly work the hairs in the mat free.**

   Work from the outside of the mat (where the hair isn't tangled) and slowly untangle the hair. Hold the base of the mat (closest to your dog's skin) as you work, to avoid pulling your dog's skin.

2. **If the mat doesn't come out with the comb, try using a mat rake next.**

   Mat rakes are equipped with sharp teeth that work at cutting through the mat. You use the mat rake the same way you do a comb, but you simply rake along the lay of the hair. The teeth will cut through the mat.

Figure 2-1:
Brushing
against the
grain to
remove
hair and
stimulate
the dog's
skin.

3. **If the mat rake doesn't cut it (so to speak), try using a mat splitter — but don't put away the rake just yet.**

   Start by splitting the mat of hair in horizontal or vertical strips and then using either a mat rake or a comb to tackle those smaller pieces individually. Watch to make sure that no skin is pulled up into the mat.

   Be careful when using mat rakes or mat splitters. They're quite sharp and can cause cuts if used improperly.

4. **In the worst conditions (that means the rake and the splitter have failed), use electric clippers (any blade should work) to slowly shave away the mat.**

   Be aware that this step should be considered as a last resort and that it can leave a bare patch that will ruin a show coat until it can grow out again. You can also ask a professional groomer or veterinarian to help you get rid of the mat.

Whatever you do, don't use scissors to cut out a mat! No matter how careful you think you are, accidentally cutting your dog's skin is all too easy, and that means a trip to the emergency vet for a suture.

Heading down the right grooming path

If your dog's coat or the hair on her face is short, use a soft slicker that's made specifically for the face — and even then, brush gently. The skin and hair around a dog's face are particularly sensitive. Also be especially careful when working around a dog's eyes with a dog comb or brush.

Book III

**Cleanliness
Is Next to
Dogliness:
Grooming**

On the other hand, if your dog has long hair on the face, such as the *fall* (hair over the eyes) or beard found in breeds such as the Old English Sheepdog or Soft-Coated Wheaten Terrier, lift the hair by putting your fingers behind the long hair and gently comb it out. You need to place your fingers behind these long facial hairs to protect your dog's sensitive skin and face from the comb.

If you find mats or tangles around your dog's face, don't spray them with detangler solution, because you risk getting some in your dog's eyes. Instead, dip a washcloth into the detangler solution, gently rub it into the hair, and then gently comb out the tangle, starting from the bottom of the hair. If the mat is really stubborn, use an electric clipper with a guarded blade to clip out the mat while also guarding your dog's face and skin (and keeping her reassured and still) with your other hand.

If your dog has long hair on her ears, you can use a comb to hold the hair so that your hand is between the comb and your dog's tender skin. If the ear fur is matted or in knots, use the washcloth dipped in detangler solution to slowly try to comb out the tangles. If the knots around the ear fur are too big (many dogs get them behind the ears), use electric clippers — sliding your hand between the skin and the clipper — to remove them. Or ask a professional to do it for you, to avoid cutting the skin.

If you don't have grooming clippers, ask a vet or a professional groomer to remove the mat for you. Most are happy to do so at little or no charge.

Smoothing the ruffles on the nape of your dog's neck

The *ruff* areas (the longer, thicker fur around the neck, shoulders, and chest) of your dog's coat may also be sensitive, so start brushing them with a soft slicker. Brush backward against the lay of the hair (if appropriate — otherwise, brush with the grain). If your dog is shedding, the slicker brush may fill up quickly. You can use the comb to dislodge the hair from the slicker and deposit the hair in the trash. If your dog has a ruff, pay particular attention to it; you need to use a comb or undercoat rake whenever your dog has a long or thick double coat in those areas. Comb through the hair you just brushed before brushing it back the way it should lay.

Brushing and trimming feathered forelegs

Short hair on a dog's forelegs usually doesn't need to be brushed, but if your dog has *feathering* — that is, long hair on the backs of the legs that runs from armpit to paw — you have to comb it out. Feathering, like the hair behind the ears, has a tendency to tangle more than the rest of your dog's coat, so use a detangler solution whenever the feathering on your dog's legs is tangled and comb it out carefully, or use a mat splitter or mat comb.

If your dog isn't a show dog but nevertheless has feathering that's either too matted or too much of a pain to brush out all the time, consider using a guarded clipper to remove the feathering on each side, for a cleaner look. Be sure to keep your fingers between the clippers and your dog to protect his skin, trimming the hair so that it looks neat.

Belly-rubbin' for laughs

The next step is to brush out your dog's chest and belly. Use a slicker to brush against the lay of the hair (if appropriate — otherwise, brush with the grain), remaining keenly aware that your dog's underside is sensitive, especially around the belly and private parts. If you can get your dog to lie down on one side, do so. Be gentle while brushing near your dog's privates.

Don't pull on any mats on your dog's sensitive underbelly, and don't use a mat rake, because one slip can cause problems in these sensitive regions. If you find any mats, take your dog to your vet or a professional groomer, who can use electric clippers to carefully remove them.

Sidewinding and backing up

Your dog's sides and top are probably the easiest areas to brush and comb. Take the slicker and brush backward against the lay of the fur (if appropriate — otherwise, brush with the grain), and follow up with a comb. Use detangler and mat splitters as required for removing any mats.

No butts about it

As with the belly and underside, your dog's rear end can be particularly sensitive, but it's also often the first area where a dog may shed. Use a slicker brush first to find out how tolerant of being touched your dog is, especially along the back legs, where the fur may be feathered or in *pantaloons,* tufts of hair that make your dog look like she's wearing bloomers. Brush the fur against the lay (if appropriate — otherwise, brush with the grain) and then follow up with a comb. Use detangler solution and a mat rake if you run into any mats, but be extremely careful around the base of the tail near the anus and around the dog's, um, equipment.

Handling those hind legs

Like the forelegs, your dog's hind legs shouldn't require much brushing, but if your dog has feathering, you have to comb it out. Feathering, like the hair behind the ears, tends to tangle a lot, so use a detangler solution if needed and comb out the feathering carefully or use a mat splitter or mat comb.

If your dog isn't a show dog and has feathering down his back legs, you can trim it just like you trim the front legs. Removing the feathering makes your grooming job easier. Don't forget to use an electric clipper with a guarded blade, and carefully trim the feathering back so that it's nice and neat.

Shedding time

Some double-coated breeds shed profusely once or twice a year. Others shed year-round. If your dog has little tufts of hair that look like pieces of cotton candy scattered throughout his coat, he's *blowing coat,* or shedding. You can pluck out these tufts of hair, but most dogs find that annoying. A better solution is to use a shedding blade or an undercoat rake.

The shedding blade looks like something you'd use on a horse. It's a flexible piece of steel with little sawlike teeth that catch the hairs. You can operate the blade in a one-handed U-shape configuration, or you can keep the blade straight and use two hands. The undercoat rake is a rake with either long sets of teeth to pull out the hair out or a dual set of teeth that work both the undercoat and top coat.

Shedding blades need to be used carefully on thin-coated dogs because the blades can scratch the skin. However, if you own a thick-coated dog, you're not likely to have this problem.

Tweaking that dratted tail

Depending on what your dog's tail is like — smooth and sleek, furry, or like a plume — you may need to carefully comb it out. If it's short, fuggetaboutit! Otherwise, if it's long and furry, you need to use a comb. If you find mats in your dog's tail, use detangler solution and a mat splitter or mat rake.

Getting pesky fleas to flee!

During flea season, which varies from one region to the next, you'll be using a flea comb in addition to the other grooming implements. After brushing, go over your dog again with a flea comb.

Talk with your veterinarian about putting your dog on a systemic flea-control product that's distributed throughout your dog's system either in topical (spot-on) form or pill form. The topical products are usually applied between your dog's shoulder blades and at the base of her tail; you feed products in pill form to your dog. These systemics have rendered other flea-control substances virtually obsolete, except when a dog exhibits undesirable side effects from using systemics. Ask your veterinarian what's right for your dog.

When using any systemic, read the directions thoroughly and follow them carefully. Otherwise, the product may be ineffective. For example, some topical systemics can be ineffective if your dog gets wet shortly after you apply them. Use common sense, and if you're not sure, ask your vet. Also, dosages and the amount of time the systemic is effective vary, so always have a clear understanding of the product you're using. These flea products often control ticks, too. Talk to your vet for other possible tick-control solutions as needed.

Rub-a-Dub-Dub: Washing Your Dog

One of the old wives' tales about grooming dogs is that you shouldn't bathe your dog unless she's really dirty or stinky. The story goes that if you do, you'll remove essential oils and dry out her coat. This story is so prevalent among dog people that it's repeated as a mantra by folks who should know better, namely breeders and dog experts.

At one time, dog shampoo really was harsh stuff that could strip a dog's coat, leaving it feeling pretty icky. However, today dogs enjoy some pretty decent shampoos, conditioners, cream rinses, mousses, gels, detanglers, and just about any other hair-care products that humans enjoy, only formulated for dogs. You're not hurting your dog's coat by bathing her.

Bathing, like brushing, doesn't have to be a pain, but it tends to be a pretty traumatic experience for many dogs. Most dogs try to avoid a bath when they've had bad experiences with it. Again, patience is the key.

Making bath time a pleasant experience

Because most dogs hate baths, getting your dog to a point where he actually likes them can be rough. A few tricks can help you smooth over those rough spots when bathing your dog:

- ✔ **Start young.** Get your dog used to bathing as a pup. Experience is key to preventing bad bath-time behavior. In many instances, you may have to work through the bad behavior. In fact, as with grooming, in some rare cases you may have to muzzle or sedate the dog.

- ✔ **Use the right tub, and give your dog easy access.** If you're using your bathtub, putting your dog in it may be as easy as walking him in. With a groomer's tub, you may have to use a ramp or stairs to walk a big dog into it, especially if you have a bad back (or a good back and you don't want to have a bad back). Use the sink only for small or toy-size dogs. Don't use the shower for any dog. And although you may be tempted to use an outdoor hose for bathing, don't. It isn't ideal because the water is usually too cold, and the dog will get dirty all over again from being outside.

- ✔ **Keep your dog in place in the tub.** Most dogs don't like to stay still in the tub, so you may want to use a special tub or bathing "noose" (available at pet stores — a poor name for a useful tool) that attaches to the tub to keep him in place. *Never* leave a dog alone restrained by a noose.

✔ **Don't hurry, and be gentle whenever possible.** One bad experience can be traumatic.

✔ **Make bathing as comfortable as possible.** To prevent a painful experience, gently put some cotton balls in your dog's ears — don't shove them into the aural canal at the base of the ear, mind you. The cotton balls help keep water out of your dog's inner ears.

Gathering the tools you need

Before you start to bathe your dog, gather all the tools you need. Having everything in one place makes the bathing process much smoother and means all the difference between a pleasant and an unpleasant experience.

When bathing your dog, you need the following supplies:

✔ pH-balanced shampoo for dogs (and possibly a pH-balanced conditioner)

✔ Cotton balls for ears

✔ Bathing noose (if required)

✔ Washcloth

✔ Blow-dryer

✔ Towels for drying

You may want to look into a tearless variety of shampoo if you're not used to bathing dogs. Read the labels to find a tearless shampoo.

Scrubbing bubbles: Bathing your dog

Thoroughly brush and comb your dog's coat before bathing her. If you don't brush out dogs before you bathe them, most dogs end up with nasty tangles and mats from those scrubbing bubbles. The same is true for a dog who's shedding heavily. Although warm water loosens the hair, clumps of shedded hair tend to mat and later make for a grooming nightmare.

Some dogs' coats require a pre-bath clipping. After thoroughly brushing out your dog and getting rid of all the tangles, you may need to use the clippers to lop off frizzy or flyaway split ends so they don't become a tangled nuisance during the wash. You can find out more about taking just a little off the top with the clippers in Chapter 4 in Book III.

The following steps explain the basics of bathing. Before you begin, you may want to place sterile cotton balls inside your dog's ears to keep water out while bathing. Just don't forget to take them out when you're done.

1. **To start, place your dog in a tub that's an appropriate size for your breed of dog.**

2. **Thoroughly wet down your dog's hair with lukewarm water; use a washcloth to gently wet your dog's face.**

   You may like a hot shower, but that temperature is too high for your pooch. Also, some bathtubs nowadays come equipped with sprayer attachments that enable you to focus the flow of water. They're great for soaking your dog's coat and for being gentle around the face.

   While your dog is wet but before you apply shampoo is a great time to express your dog's anal sacs, if you were planning to do it as part of your grooming routine (see Chapter 3 in Book III — if you dare).

3. **Lather up your dog's coat with a good pH-balanced dog shampoo, except around the face and sensitive eyes — which you must do separately with a wet cloth (see Chapter 3 in Book III).**

4. **Rinse thoroughly, sliding your fingers along your dog's skin so that you get out all that soap.**

   Soap attracts dirt, and a dog with dried soap in her hair is prone to those dreaded mats.

5. **Apply a good pH-balanced conditioner or cream rinse for dogs.**

   Using a conditioner that prevents tangles and also keeps the coat from drying out is a good idea for most coat types.

6. **Thoroughly rinse away the conditioner.**

   With regard to attracting dirt and causing mats, conditioner residues are as bad for your dog's hair as soap residue, so rinse even better than you did in Step 4.

7. **Get out those towels and start drying.**

   As you squeeze the towels into the coat, look for soapy water. If you find any, go back to rinsing. The next section provides additional advice about drying your dog.

Book III

Cleanliness Is Next to Dogliness: Grooming

Drying

After you've thoroughly rinsed your dog, dry his coat as thoroughly as possible, first using towels. Blot the coat. Meanwhile, your dog will shake off all that excess water and then shake some more. After toweling off and allowing for a few shakes, you can move him onto the grooming table, if you have one, for a blow-dry and style.

Some professional groomers like to use cage dryers, devices that attach to the outside of a cage or crate and force warm air inside to dry your dog. Cage dryers can be efficient, but watch your dog carefully when using them. A dog can quickly overheat in a warm area he can't escape.

Whenever you use a cage dryer, *never* leave a dog unattended in it. Dogs have overheated and died because the groomers forgot to watch them. Unless you're planning to open a grooming shop (or you care for several dogs), skip the cage dryer and work with the hand-held blow-dryers only.

When using a blow-dryer, make sure you use one that's made specifically for dogs (see Figure 2-2) or one that doesn't use any heat. Hot air from human blow-dryers is much too hot and can hurt your dog's skin and frazzle the fur. You can use a human hair dryer on the no-heat setting to dry small dogs, but blow-dryers intended for humans don't have enough power to handle drying a larger, long-haired dog.

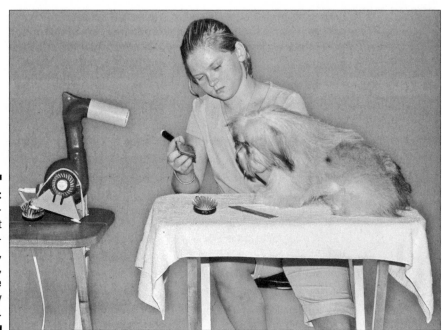

Figure 2-2:
Use a blow-dryer that has a no-heat setting, like this one, made specifically for dogs.

Always thoroughly dry your dog before you let him outside.

When your dog is dry, you need to brush him again. At this time, you can use mousse or other leave-in coat conditioners if you're getting him ready for a show.

Chapter 3

Caring for Nails, Teeth, Nose, Ears, Eyes, Face, and . . . Elsewhere

In This Chapter

▶ Keeping the toenails trimmed and ears clean

▶ Getting "expressive" with your doggie's derriere

▶ Brushing your dog's teeth and caring for her eyes

▶ Putting your dog's best face forward

After you discover the basics of dog grooming — brushing, combing, and bathing — you have to tackle some tougher jobs, like brushing your dog's teeth, cleaning his ears and face, trimming his toenails, and, yes, some less glamorous and even gross tasks. Don't panic! All dogs need these essential grooming tasks done regularly. This chapter tells you how you can do them without too much of a struggle.

The Art of the Paw-dicure

Many dogs' toenails have a habit of rapidly growing long. Unless your dog runs around on pavement or asphalt that help keep toenails short, you have to trim them. But clipping a canine's claws is delicate work and can be an agonizing chore, especially if your dog has had a bad experience with the nail clippers.

Making toenail trimming a pleasant experience

Despite your best intentions and skill level, your dog may never be comfortable having her nails trimmed. Dogs are usually sensitive about their nails. Knowing that you have a few options helps. If you can't do all your dog's nails at once, you can clip them in stages, one paw at a time. The trick is to be diligent so that you're trimming your dog's nails *before* they're overgrown. And be sure to read this *whole section* before you do anything.

If all else fails, there's no shame in having a professional groomer or veterinarian trim them.

Some tricks you can try when trimming your dog's toenails include the following:

- ✔ **Get your dog used to your handling her feet.** This tip is of utmost importance. Most dogs simply detest having their feet handled, so the sooner you get your dog used to enduring it, the better (and easier) giving your dog a weekly manicure can be.

- ✔ **Ask for help getting started.** If your dog's nails are too long the first time you think about trimming them yourself, ask your veterinarian or a groomer to show you how to trim them to the right length. After that, you can trim them every week or so.

- ✔ **Trim one paw at a time.** This technique is a good one for fussy dogs. You can trim one paw at a time, giving your dog a rest before moving on to another paw.

- ✔ **Provide a treat.** Giving your dog a yummy treat after trimming her toenails also helps, and so do big hugs, a boisterous "Good dog!" and a vigorous scratch behind the ears.

- ✔ **Try a nail grinder rather than clippers.** Sometimes dogs who can't tolerate nail trimmers can deal with a nail grinder. If you're experiencing major problems clipping toenails, a nail grinder (which looks like a rotary tool) may work.

- ✔ **Trim your dog's nails once a week:** Ideally, you need to trim your dog's nails once a week. Weekly nail trimming not only helps keep them in good shape and prevents problems like broken nails, but it also gets your dog used to having a routine manicure.

If you hear your dog's nails clicking as they touch a hard surface (floor or sidewalk), it's time for a nail trim.

Gathering the tools you need

Before wielding any sharp instruments like nail clippers, make sure that you gather all the tools you need for the toenail-trimming session. Having everything you need within reach can make the nail-trimming session go more smoothly, may ease the tension associated with it, and can make all the difference between a pleasant experience and one that isn't so pleasant.

You need these tools to trim your dog's toenails:

- **Nail cutters for dogs:** Use either the guillotine or scissors styles.

- **Styptic powder or a nail-cauterizing tool:** You need one of these products in case you cut the *quick* (blood supply in the nail) and cause bleeding. Find out more about this problem in the next section.

- **A slightly damp washcloth:** Use a washcloth to clean up any styptic powder or other messes you may make.

- **A nail file or nail grinder:** The file or grinder smoothes the rough edges of the nail.

- **Cotton swabs:** Use them to apply styptic powder.

- **A batch of yummy treats:** Rewarding your best bud for a toenail-trimming job well done helps ease your dog through the procedure.

Book III

Cleanliness Is Next to Dogliness: Grooming

Nailing trimming basics

A dog's toenail is made up of the nail and the quick. The *quick* is the pink (when it's visible) part of your dog's toenails; it's similar to the pink part of your own fingernails and toenails. The quick is pink because it provides blood supply to the nail. When trimming your dog's nails, you must avoid cutting into the quick, because it bleeds quite a bit and is sensitive (see Figure 3-1).

If your dog has white nails, you'll be able to see the quick. However, many dogs have black or dark-colored nails, and no matter what tricks you may have heard, seeing the quick in them is impossible. You have to snip *very* carefully and look closely at the nail. If the nail feels spongy while you're trying to cut it, stop immediately! Always err on the side of caution.

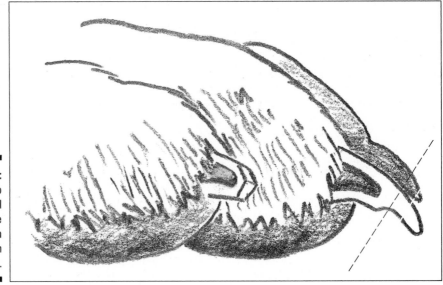

Figure 3-1:
Be sure to trim the nail below the quick. If in doubt, trim less.

If you cut the quick (often called *quicking*), you'll have an unhappy dog and a bloody mess. The quick bleeds a great deal, so if you cut it, you need either a nail cauterizer or styptic powder to stop the bleeding. Pack the nail with the styptic powder or use the cauterizer on the nail. Quicking hurts a lot, and most dogs remember the experience long afterward.

To trim your dog's nails, you must follow these steps:

1. **Hold the foot steady.**

   However, also hold your dog's foot gently.

2. **Snip off a small bit of the end of each toenail.**

   Place a tiny bit of the nail in the nail clipper and snip.

   Most people prefer to have their dog lying down or sitting when they cut the toenails. Use whatever method is most comfortable for you and your dog.

If you use a nail grinder rather than clippers, the same general method applies. Hold your dog's foot and grind a little off each nail.

The best time to trim nails is, of course, when they need it; however, some people like to do the trimming before a bath so that if they do quick the dog, they can wash off the blood.

Doing the dew

Some canine breed standards require dewclaws for animals that are intended for the show ring. For example, rear double dewclaws are the standard for Great Pyrenees. Other standards say that rear dewclaws need to be removed. Check the breed standard at www.akc.org.

Before removing dewclaws on a puppy you plan to show, check with the breed standard to find out whether removal is allowable. In working dogs, the breeder or vet needs to remove dewclaws when the puppy is 3 to 5 days old, to prevent injuries when dewclaws are torn. Removal of dewclaws any time after that requires surgery and anesthesia at the vet's office.

If you plan to remove the dewclaws from a litter, have your vet show you how. If it's not done right, you can end up with malformed dewclaws or worse — an injured or crippled puppy.

Don't forget the dewclaws — the dog's useless "thumbs." They're located on the inside of the leg above the foot. Most dogs have dewclaws in the front; some also have them in the rear. Some dogs have dewclaws; others don't. If your dog has them, pay special attention when trimming them. They tend to grow long because they don't normally touch the ground. If you don't cut them, they'll eventually grow back into your dog's foot, which is painful.

Book III

Cleanliness Is Next to Dogliness: Grooming

Do You Hear What I Hear?

All dogs have sensitive ears, and some can develop frequent ear problems. Others never seem to have any problems. Breeds that have a predilection for ear infections and injuries tend to be Sporting dogs and Hounds because of their *dropped* (hanging or drooping) ears. Dropped ears make an ideal place for bacteria to grow and mites to hide. Regardless of whether your dog has pricked-up or dropped ears, you have to keep them clean and sweet smelling. If an odor is present around your dog's ears, they may be infected.

Dog owners (usually Poodle owners) often pluck the hair inside their dog's ears. They use ear powder to dry the ear and yank out the hair. Ouch! Dogs don't like this procedure. But if your dog has hair growing in his ears and has a lot of infections, you may have to do some plucking. Ask your vet.

Making ear cleaning more pleasant

Dogs hate to have things stuck in their ears, so you're not likely to make it an enjoyable experience. Nevertheless, you can try to make it as comfortable as possible by following these tips:

- ✔ **Get your dog used to your gently handling his ears.** Get him used to your touching his ears (a gentle ear scratch), holding his ears, flipping them up (if he has hanging or dropped ears), and looking in his ears.

- ✔ **Clean your dog's ears when he's a bit tired.** The less your dog fights with you, the less he'll have his ears pulled.

- ✔ **Clean your dog's ears once a week.** The longer you wait to perform a grooming task like this one, the longer it takes and the worse the experience is likely to be for the dog and for you.

- ✔ **Give treats for behaving while you clean his ears.** Give him a goody even if he's good only long enough for you to touch his ears.

- ✔ **Never pull on your dog's ears or jab deep into them.** It's painful, and if you do it, your dog will never let you near his ears again.

Gathering the tools you need

Before you get started, gather all the tools you need for the ear-cleaning session. Doing so makes the ear-cleaning session go more smoothly. Having all your implements in one place makes all the difference between a pleasant experience and one that isn't so pleasant.

You need these tools to clean your dog's ears:

- ✔ **Mild otic (ear-cleaning) solution for dogs:** Don't use anything with insecticides. Otic solution is available at groomers' supply houses.

- ✔ **Sterile gauze, cotton swabs, or sponges:** Use these items to remove the otic solution or cleaner.

- ✔ **Surgical forceps or clamps:** No, you're not doing surgery. You wrap the clamp or forceps with the gauze and then wipe the gauze inside the ears to clean out any dirt and otic solution.

Cleaning your dog's ears

Cleaning your dog's ears is fairly uncomplicated. Proceed slowly and be sure not to enter the ear canal.

Follow these steps when cleaning your pup's ears:

1. **Gently hold your dog's head so that the open ear is exposed.**

   Sitting down beside your dog usually works.

2. **Squeeze some otic solution into the ear (follow the label directions).**

   Gently massage the outside of the ear canal to help the solution do its work.

3. **Using a sterile gauze pad or sponge, gently wipe out excess solution.**

   You can wrap the gauze or sponge completely around the forceps or the clamp to wipe around the ear.

   Don't use insecticides or mite treatments, because they can cause irritation. If you notice any red dirt, anything that looks like coffee grounds, or a waxy buildup and you suspect ear mites, see your vet.

4. **While your dog's ears are exposed, gently trim any excess hair from around the openings.**

Recognizing an ear problem

Ear infections are sometimes hard to clear up. Doing so takes commitment and determination. Watch your dog for the following signs of potential ear problems that a veterinarian may need to address:

- Blisters or abrasions on the ears
- Crusty or red ears
- Excessive or red or black waxy buildup
- Foul-smelling odor coming from the ears
- Your dog scratching or pawing her ears or shaking her head
- A yelping reaction when you touch her ears

No Butts About It: Getting Expressive

Has your dog suddenly taken to using your nice, new Berber carpet as a roll of toilet paper? If so, you may be in for a real treat. You may have the distinct pleasure of helping your dog remove the fluid from his anal sacs. And you thought dog grooming wouldn't be any fun!

Anal sacs, or a dog's anal *glands,* are located around or on either side of the dog's anus. These sacs carry some smelly fluid and occasionally need to be *expressed,* or emptied. Many dogs express them by themselves every time they poop, but occasionally these sacs fill with fluid, and your dog may need some help from you to release the fluid. Some dogs need their anal sacs expressed a lot; others don't. Failing to care for anal sacs may lead to infection. Whether you express the anal sacs depends on what your dog is feeling.

You can tell when your dog needs to have his anal sacs expressed. How? When you see him sliding his backside across the carpet, or when he chews or licks at his rear end or tail, you know it's time.

Ask your vet before attempting to express your dog's anal sacs for the first time. In bizarre instances, you can rupture the sacs.

You may try expressing your dog's anal sacs when you're bathing him. That way you can wash away the smelly liquid and you don't really care whether it misses the paper towel you're using.

Gathering the tools you need

If you have a thumb and a forefinger, you have all the tools you need. If you have a weak constitution, you may also want to have the following on hand:

- ✔ **Paper towels:** Having plenty of paper towels for any type of cleanup always helps. You may even want to try a diaper wipe or other moistened cleansing wipe.
- ✔ **A clothespin, heavy-duty rubber gloves, welder's apron, rubber boots, and tongs:** With these tools, you can glove up, cover up, and thus avoid the gag reflex the way Michael Keaton does while changing diapers in *Mr. Mom.*

Expressing yourself

Expressing anal sacs is relatively simple work (you may try and recruit someone to hold the dog's head still):

1. **Fold several paper towels together (about like the huge wad you normally need to take care of a spider or bug).**

   Doing so provides an absorbent pad to catch the liquid.

2. **Lift your dog's tail and place the paper towels over her backside.**

   Note the position of her anus in relation to the paper towels.

3. **Press gently on the 4 o'clock and 8 o'clock positions in relation to her anus (see Figure 3-2).**

   Keep your face out of the way! (You're welcome!)

4. **Wash and rinse your dog's rear end really well.**

   A clean doggie rump is a healthy doggie rump.

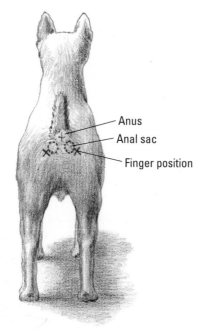

Anus
Anal sac
Finger position

Figure 3-2:
Apply
pressure
at the 4
o'clock and
8 o'clock
positions
to express
anal sacs.

If your dog shows discomfort back there and her sacs aren't producing fluid, she may have an impacted or infected anal sac, which requires veterinary intervention.

Care for Those Pearly Whites

Dogs don't get cavities the way humans do, but they do get plaque, tartar, and gingivitis — all of which can cause foul breath and tooth problems. Trips to the doggie dentist are costly, and your dog will have to be put under anesthesia, because no dog ever "opens wide" for any dentist or vet.

Brushing your dog's teeth obviously is important, but how often you do it depends on your dog and your motivation factor. Poor doggie dental care, however, can lead to dental infections that can travel to your pooch's heart, causing major problems and even death. How's that for motivation?

Making brushing doggie pleasant

Now that you're working with the end of your dog that has teeth, you need to keep not only your dog's dental health in mind, but also the safety of your fingers and hands. Working anywhere near your dog's mouth puts you at risk of an occasional frustrated nip or two. Use these hints and steps to make brushing your dog's teeth a little less tedious:

- **Brush frequently.** You *should* brush your dog's teeth every day, but realistically, you're better than most pet owners if you can brush them once or twice a week. Frequent brushing gets your dog used to the brushing routine and to the idea of having his mouth invaded.

- **Choose the best time.** A great time for brushing is right after your dog has exercised and is a little tired. At least, that time's preferable to when he's willing to fight with you over handling his mouth.

- **Train your dog to allow you to touch his mouth.** You can get him to tolerate having his mouth handled by doing so from an early age.

- **Get him ready to have his teeth brushed in this way:**

    1. Flip up his lips (see upcoming Figure 3-3).

    2. Wet the edge of a clean washcloth so you can rub your dog's gums and teeth; hold a corner of the wet portion of the washcloth with your index finger and use a gentle, circular motion.

    3. Talk to your dog in calm, soothing tones.

    4. If your dog grows impatient, do Steps 1 through 3 for only a few seconds, and then stop and give him a treat.

    5. Repeat Steps 1 through 4 again tomorrow, gradually lengthening the amount of time you spend doing them.

Eventually, you'll be able to build up the amount of time your dog allows you to touch his mouth to where you're giving your dog a nice tooth and gum massage without any fuss.

Gathering the tools you need

Before you get started, gather all the tools you need for the tooth-brushing session. Doing so makes the session go more smoothly. You need the following:

✔ **Toothpaste for dogs:** Don't ever use human toothpaste! Human toothpaste contains fluoride, which in large quantities is poisonous to dogs. Dogs can't rinse and spit, so they pretty much swallow everything you put on their teeth. Doggie toothpaste is flavored with malt, chicken, or some other yummy flavor that dogs can't resist. It makes the experience more enjoyable.

✔ **Toothbrush for dogs:** A finger toothbrush that's made for pets is best. You can use a human toothbrush, but it isn't as good as a finger brush.

Both items are available from your vet's office, pet supply stores, and mail-order catalogs.

Brushing your dog's teeth

When your dog is used to getting a gum massage with a wet washcloth, the next step is getting her used to the finger brush and pet toothpaste. You can start brushing your dog's teeth by using a technique similar to the way you use the washcloth in the preceding section.

At the risk of repeating this information, never use human toothpaste on a dog. Okay now, follow these steps to properly brush your dog's teeth:

1. **Squeeze some doggie toothpaste onto the brush and allow your dog to lick it off.**

   Most dogs like the flavor, but some don't. Don't worry about it one way or the other.

2. **Flip up your dog's lips and gently rub the toothbrush and toothpaste against your dog's teeth and gums for a few seconds (see Figure 3-3).**

3. **Give your dog a treat, even if she allows you to work on her teeth for only a few seconds.**

4. **Repeat Steps 1 through 3 again tomorrow, gradually lengthening the amount of time spent brushing.**

If you gradually increase the amount of time you spend working on this four-step process, you'll eventually build up enough time to give your dog's teeth a thorough brushing.

Some people like to purchase a *dental scalar,* a device they use to scrape away plaque from their dogs' teeth. Unfortunately, if you're not careful, you can injure your dog's gums, not to mention make one unhappy pooch. That form of teeth cleaning is better left to your vet, especially when your dog has a lot of tartar and buildup and big teeth. And if your dog has loads of tartar buildup, get your dog to a vet first to have her teeth cleaned.

Book III

Cleanliness Is Next to Dogliness: Grooming

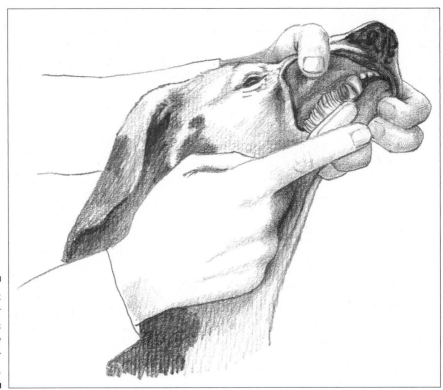

Figure 3-3:
Flip up your
dog's lips as
you gently
brush her
teeth.

Spotting a dental problem

Watch your dog for these signs of potential tooth or gum problems that a veterinarian needs to address:

- A lump above or below a particular tooth or under an eye
- Bad breath
- Broken teeth
- Loss of appetite
- Nasal discharge
- Red, swollen gums
- Sudden, unexpected chewing on inappropriate items
- A grayish or darkened tooth

Other ways of keeping your dog's teeth clean

If your dog doesn't handle brushing well, you can use one of several methods for keeping your dog's teeth clean. Most of these methods have something to do with feeding him the right kind of food and giving him appropriate kinds of chews. You can use these items to clean those pearly whites:

✔ **Dental toys intended to reduce plaque and tartar:** Some of these toys actually are made so that doggie toothpaste can be squeezed into them, so they sometimes take the place of brushing. Busy Buddy, Kong toys, and Nylabone all have products intended to clean teeth.

✔ **Certain premium dog foods:** Some premium dog foods have additives that make their products more dental friendly by making them more abrasive. Hill's and Iams each market a dental dog food, and so do many other brands.

✔ **Tartar-control biscuits:** Many pet food manufacturers sell tartar-control biscuits and snacks.

✔ **Appropriate kinds of dog chews:** Some chews, such as enzyme-treated rawhide chews and Greenies and Pedigree's Dentabone, are made to help reduce plaque and tartar.

✔ **Large bones:** Giving your dog a big marrow bone or knucklebone from a cow helps clean canine teeth. Some vets recommend boiling for safety or freezing them raw to make them harder. Bones are controversial because they harbor bacteria and can cause blockages when chewed or swallowed. Never give a dog small sharp bones that can splinter. Some vets don't recommend bones because they can break teeth.

Book III

Cleanliness Is Next to Dogliness: Grooming

Shiny, Bright Eyes

Dogs' eyes are pretty much self-maintaining, but occasionally they run into problems with their eyes and the areas surrounding them.

Dogs have various eye shapes and sizes. Some dogs, especially breeds with *brachycephalic* (short, pushed-in) heads — Pugs and Pekingese — tend to have large, protruding eyes that are more susceptible to accidental injury. Other dogs have almond-shaped eyes. Alaskan Malamutes, Siberian Huskies, and still others have rounded eyes.

Regardless of type, red eyes, lacerated eyes, and eyes that tear excessively are *not* normal, and dogs with these conditions need to visit the veterinarian as soon as possible. Excessive tearing, for example, may be caused by ear infection, tonsillitis, or infected teeth.

Making cleansing your dog's eyes pleasant

A dog's eyes are particularly sensitive, so you want to avoid bringing them into contact with soaps, chemicals, or anything that may cause irritation or abrasions. Unless directed by a vet, avoid using eye drops altogether. When you do use eye drops, make sure that they're made specifically for a dog's eyes.

When you clean around your dog's eyes, you need to do so in the gentlest way possible. Because you have to be able to touch your dog around and close to his eyes, help your dog get used to it in these ways:

- ✔ **Try cleaning the accumulated gunk from your dog's eyes.** Use a soft cloth or cotton ball moistened only with water. You'll be cleaning off gunk deposits, or "sleep," and other deposits that accumulate.

- ✔ **Avoid directly touching your dog's eyes.** This should be obvious.

- ✔ **Gently rub your pooch's jowls and forehead, and give him a scratch or two behind the ears as you talk to him in a calm, gentle, and reassuring voice.** Setting your dog at ease like this gives you better access for cleaning the areas around those sensitive orbs.

If you encounter excessive deposits of gunk, it's time for a trip to the vet to make sure that nothing's wrong. If your dog's eyes are watering all the time, it's another reason to visit the vet.

Don't cry for me Argentina: Addressing tear stains

Tear stains show up as brown gunky stuff that runs from the tear duct down the muzzle. Although they're unsightly, with some dogs, they're natural, and you don't have to do anything about them. Nonetheless, you *can* do plenty to get rid of them.

If your dog has tear stains, take her to a vet first to make sure she doesn't have some other problem. Tear stains are natural for a few breeds.

Dogs prone to tear stains typically are white or have light-colored coats and usually are single-coated with long hair. Many dogs with brachycephalic heads (with protruding eyes) pick up more gunk. In fact, the problem has a name. *Poodle eye,* as the name suggests, is common among Poodles, but that doesn't mean other dogs don't have tear stains. You probably don't notice it as much in other dogs because their fur is darker or seems to get rid of the gunk better.

In some breeds with serious congenital eye problems, the tear ducts can get clogged and require surgery. (See your vet if your dog shows any problems with her eyes or her tear ducts.)

Gathering the tools you need

A vet can help you get rid of tear stains — if that's indeed what the problem is — with a course of tetracycline, which usually helps get rid of the staining but not the tears.

At home, you need these grooming products to help you get rid of tear stains:

- **A soft cloth, makeup pad, or cotton ball:** Use these materials, or others like them that don't contain any soaps or chemicals, to apply grooming products to rid your dog of tear stains.

- **A 10 percent solution of hydrogen peroxide with water, or other grooming products for getting rid of stains:** These stain removers may or may not erase the total stain, depending on how bad it is. Always be extremely careful not to get any of these products in your dog's eyes.

- **Face cream, powder, cornstarch, or other coverup products:** Yes, you have a choice of either getting rid of the tear-stained hair or covering it up.

- **Electric clipper with an appropriate clipper guard or guarded blade:** Use with extreme care if you choose to get rid of stained fur altogether.

As you may have already guessed, you can get rid of tear stains by either wiping them clean, covering them up, or clipping or plucking them off. You've probably also surmised that tear stains are the nemesis of show dogs and their owners.

You get rid of tear stains in this way:

- **Wipe them off.** If you choose to wipe off the tear stains, use the 10 percent solution of hydrogen peroxide or another stain-removal product for dogs. Gently swab the solution over the tear stain, but don't get any of these products in your dog's eyes. Make sure that you rinse the residues from your dog's fur.

- **Clip them off.** If you decide to clip out the stain, do so very carefully with guarded clippers, or try plucking the stained fur. *Note:* Your dog must be extremely tolerant of clippers to remove tear-stained fur; otherwise, using the clippers can spell disaster.

Never use scissors around your dog's eyes or face for any reason.

- **Cover them up.** If you choose the face cream, powder, or cornstarch coverup route, you've chosen the safer but less permanent way:

  - **Cornstarch:** Use it in a pinch, because it can whiten or lighten the stained area.

  - **Face cream/powder:** Dampen the area and then use a small bit of cream or mousse to apply the powder. (Make sure that none gets in the eyes!) Then you can gently brush out the area. Some of the powder will stick, thus making your dog's face more appealing.

Technically, a show dog is never supposed to have chalk or powder left over. The truth is that some stays in, but the handler must get most of it out so that it doesn't *appear* that the chalk is still there.

Eyeing other eye issues

Some breeds are prone to eyelid conditions, such as *entropion* (eyelids that roll in) and *ectropion* (eyelids that roll out), in which the eyelids are malformed. These conditions aren't just cosmetic, and they can be quite painful. In most cases, surgery is needed to correct them. Other types of eye and eyelid problems include cherry eye, distichiasis, and conjunctivitis (pinkeye). Again, you can't correct these conditions by yourself, so be sure to seek out the advice of your vet.

As your dog grows older, he may develop eyelid tumors (such as papillomas) or clouding of the eye (or crystal eye) caused by cataracts. If your dog has any of these conditions, a trip to the vet is in order.

Knowing when your dog has an eye problem

Eyes are one area of your dog's grooming that you don't want to ignore, especially if your dog has an eye problem. Take your dog to the vet if your dog is squinting or pawing an eye or if your dog's eye looks like any of the following:

- Bulges or is out of its socket (a no-brainer!)
- Is red or tearing profusely or has a thick discharge
- Is lacerated or exhibits another apparent abnormality
- Appears opaque or cloudy
- Bleeds or shows other signs of injury
- Has foreign matter in it

Face Time

Your dog's face is the first thing you and other people see, so keeping her face clean and looking great makes sense, right? Some of the problems many dogs have in maintaining that glow usually have to do with wrinkles (if they have them) and beards (if they have them).

Making cleaning your dog's face pleasant

Get your dog used to your touching his face. Unless your dog is really comfortable with looking you right in the eyes, avoid making direct eye contact, because doing so exhibits a challenging behavior. Move slowly and carefully around his face, which is extremely sensitive.

Gathering the tools you need

Before you get started, gather all the tools you need for the face-washing session. Having all your implements in one place makes the difference between a pleasant face-washing experience and one that isn't so pleasant.

You need these items to wash your dog's face:

- A damp washcloth

- A mild soap, dog shampoo (the tearless variety works well), or groomer's *blue shampoo* (a great cleansing product that you don't have to rinse out)

- Cotton swab

Book III

Cleanliness Is Next to Dogliness: Grooming

Facing off

When cleaning your dog's face, use a damp washcloth (wet but not dripping) and some mild soap. If you use dog groomer's blue soap (waterless shampoo), you don't have to rinse it off. When using any kind of soap, your main objective is keeping it away from your dog's eyes, because it can sting. Gently go over your dog's face with the washcloth until it's clean. Be sure to wash the *flews,* or the hanging skin around the mouth.

If your dog has wrinkles, the crevices can harbor bacteria and can become infected. Clean wrinkles carefully. If your dog is small, like a Pug, you can use a cotton swab dipped in blue soap to go over the wrinkles.

Long hair and beards need to be brushed out first. If your dog naturally has long hair over her eyes (called not bangs, but a *fall*), brush out the hair first and then use a ponytail-type band to bunch it and get it out of your dog's face. Any stained hair that isn't going to fall back in the eyes can be washed with soap and water. Trim any discolored hair unless it's absolutely necessary for the show ring. If you can't trim the hair, try the hydrogen peroxide solution mentioned in the "Getting rid of your dog's tear stains" section earlier in this chapter, or try to cover it with chalk.

Chapter 4

To Clip or Not to Clip: Dog Haircuts

In This Chapter

▶ Knowing which dogs need to be clipped

▶ Choosing the right tools: Clippers, blades, and scissors

▶ Clipping your pooch

Clipping a dog is one of the more daunting tasks for pet owners. If you have a dog who needs to be clipped or one who needs a touch-up, this chapter is for you.

Several breeds need to be clipped. Most have single coats, the kind without an undercoat. The hair of these dogs grows like yours, and because these pooches don't shed, they're bound to look like a terrible mess of hair if you don't clip their coats. Other breeds are clipped for show or style reasons, or maybe just because the pet owner doesn't want to deal with all that hair.

Don't fear the electric clippers. You discover the basics of using them and what you can do with all those strange blades and plastic snap-on thingies in this chapter. You also discover how to safely handle scissors (also called *shears* in the grooming world), and even how to clip your dog yourself.

Deciding Whether to Clip Your Dog

Before going farther, you need to determine whether your dog actually needs to be clipped. Although many breeds need only a cursory neatening up, the following breeds generally need more serious clipping:

- ✔ American Cocker Spaniel
- ✔ American Water Spaniel
- ✔ Bedlington Terrier
- ✔ Bichon Frise
- ✔ Black Russian Terrier
- ✔ Bouvier de Flandres
- ✔ Brittany
- ✔ Cesky Terrier

- Cocker Spaniel (American and English)
- Curly-Coated Retriever
- English Setter
- English Springer Spaniel
- Field Spaniel
- Gordon Setter
- Irish Setter
- Irish Water Spaniel
- Kerry Blue Terrier
- Löwchen
- Poodle (all sizes)
- Portuguese Water Dog
- Soft Coated Wheaten Terrier
- Springer Spaniel

At first, you may be surprised that more breeds aren't on this list, but that's because some breeds aren't exactly clipped breeds — they're *stripped breeds,* or dogs who need excess hair stripped from their coats to attain the proper look. Most dog owners aren't into time-consuming stripping procedures, though, so they opt for clippers. Nothing is wrong with using clippers in that manner, but you won't get the right look for your breed if you intend to show your dog (see Chapter 6 in Book IV).

Getting Acquainted with Your Tools

You can find a dizzying array of electric clippers and blades sold on the grooming-tool market these days. Open up a grooming catalog, and you'll see a bunch of different clippers, ranging from the basic home-use, pet-grooming clippers to the fancy-schmancy ones the pros use.

Deciding which clippers to buy

The kind of clippers you need depends on how much clipping you need to do with your dog. These three hints can help you choose wisely:

- If you're using clippers just to neaten up Fido's feet or clean up a stray hair here or there, you likely need only a set of inexpensive home clippers that won't see a lot of use.

- If you want to maintain a nice show coat (or even a good pet coat) between trips to the groomer, you're probably looking at medium-priced clippers and a variety of blades.

- If you want to trim and style your own dog and perhaps other dogs, you're looking at professional-style clippers, maybe with more than one speed and certainly with several blades. Some of these clippers are cordless, so you don't always need an outlet handy.

Several different manufacturers make clippers, including Oster, Wahl, Andis, and Conair, among others. Oster is pretty much the leader when it comes to clippers, and its blades are universal enough that other manufacturers make their clippers so that Oster-style blades fit them. In fact, almost all clipper blades are made to fit Oster or similar products.

If you decide to purchase a brand of clippers other than an Oster, make sure that it's equipped to use Oster-style blades. Most clippers are, but you need to be sure; otherwise, you're stuck buying proprietary blades that may cost more. Besides, if your clippers breaks, you'll be forced to choose between buying new clippers of a brand that matches the blades you already have or tossing everything and starting from scratch. Also, the quieter the clippers, the better.

Becoming a blade-runner

Most clippers come with blades, but some don't. Blades are typically marked either by closeness of cut or by their Oster number (size 10, for example). The higher the number, the closer the cut. The lower the number, the more hair you'll have on your dog after each clipping. So a size 40 blade (surgical cut) produces a much finer cut than a size 5 blade (¼-inch cut).

Choosing your blades is a bit of an art form and depends on your dog's breed and coat type. Look at your breed standard and talk to other owners of your breed. Table 4-1 describes various blades.

Most blades are full-toothed, but you can also find some skip-tooth blades. *Skip-tooth blades* are for stand-up coats (Poodle-type coats). *Full-tooth blades* are for smooth or drop-coated dogs (Spaniel-type coats).

Table 4-1	Clipper Blade Types, Cuts, and Uses	
Blade Size	**Cut Length/Type**	**Uses**
40	$\frac{1}{100}$-inch/surgical	Hair trimming around wounds; can be used for ears and face as well
30	$\frac{1}{50}$-inch/very close	Show clips
15	$\frac{3}{64}$-inch/medium	General use; this blade is also referred to as a Poodle blade
10	$\frac{1}{16}$-inch/medium	General use, including hair trimming from around and between your dog's paw pads
9	$\frac{5}{64}$-inch/medium	Smooth finish, general use

(continued)

Table 4-1 *continued*

Blade Size	Cut Length/Type	Uses
8½	7⁄64-inch/medium	General use; this blade is also referred to as a Terrier blade
7F	⅛-inch	Full tooth, body clipping
7	⅛-inch	Skip tooth, body clipping
5F	¼-inch	Full tooth, body clipping
5	¼-inch	Skip tooth, body clipping
4F	⅜-inch	Full tooth, body clipping
4	⅜-inch	Skip tooth, body clipping
3F	½-inch	Full tooth, body clipping
3	½-inch	Skip tooth, body clipping
⅝	1⁄32–⅝-inch/wide	Hair trimming and finishing
⅞	1⁄32–⅞-inch/wide	Hair trimming and finishing

Snapping on guide combs

Snap-on guide combs (shown in Figure 4-1, along with electric clippers, blade-lubricating oil, and a cleaning brush) are plastic combs that you attach to your electric clippers to provide an even cut. So if you get a half-inch guide comb, you'll get a half-inch cut. Pretty simple, isn't it?

Some guide combs come with the clippers. Others you have to buy separately.

Using scissors

When you just can't get your dog's coat to even out with clippers no matter how hard you try, use scissors, but only with extreme caution. Scissors can injure you and your dog if you're not careful.

You can find plenty of reasons for using scissors on your dog's coat. One is that you just don't have the same control with clippers that you do with scissors. If you need to trim whiskers or stray hairs from your dog, for example, scissors probably work better than clippers. Scissors are best used on dogs who are already groomed properly and just need touch-ups. Consider these tips when using scissors:

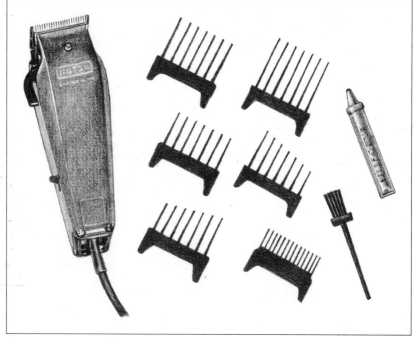

Figure 4-1:
Electric
clippers
(with oil and
a clean-
ing brush)
and guide
combs help
maintain
your
pooch's
coat.

✔ Choose scissors that are sharp and made for dogs.

✔ Never use dull scissors on a dog's coat.

✔ Go slowly when using the scissors.

✔ Always keep your fingers between the scissors and your dog's skin. Otherwise, you may easily suffer a mishap that requires you to take your dog to the emergency vet.

✔ Train your dog to stay still when you're using scissors, to avoid injury.

✔ Avoid distractions when using scissors. No TV, no chatty friends, no talk radio. Remember, you're working on your dog with a sharp instrument.

Thinning scissors (also called thinning shears) are used to thin the coat or blend one layer of hair with another. They have rows of skipped teeth that cut only every other hair. As with all scissors, thinning scissors can be dangerous if used incorrectly or without care.

Getting Down to Clipping Business

Before you cut your first dog hair, plan ahead. Your dog must be clean, with all mats and tangles brushed out, before you start clipping. Doing so makes clipping the coat evenly easier for you.

Preparing for success

You have your clippers and your dog. Now what? These handy tips can help you get your dog used to the clippers and keep your dog looking good:

- ✔ **Start clipping your dog as early as possible, even as a puppy.** Getting an older dog used to the clippers is much harder than training a puppy.

- ✔ **Read your dog's breed standard.** Often you can get clues about how your dog's coat should look and how to make it look that way.

- ✔ **Check out the breed club's Web site for tips on how club members clip their dogs.** Some clubs provide free guidelines.

- ✔ **Have a professional groomer or a breeder show you how your dog's coat needs to be clipped.** Most groomers and breeders are happy to spend a little time helping you — or have a pro do it the first time.

If you make a mistake, don't fret. Your dog may have a bad hair day, but it'll eventually grow out. Your main concern is using your clippers safely.

Using clippers safely

Follow these handy guidelines for safely using clippers on your dog's coat:

- ✔ Be sure your clipper blades are sharp. Dull clippers pull hair more.

- ✔ Choose the clipper blade that works best with your dog's specific type of coat so you achieve the result you want.

    If you're not sure about the cut of the blade you're using, you can try using one of the many available snap-on guide combs. These combs help you make a uniform cut.

- ✔ Always use clipper coolant or lubricant on your blades, to keep them from getting too warm and burning your dog. Coolant or lubricant is available through pet supply catalogs and on the Internet. Clipper blades can become extremely hot, especially when you use them for a long time. If you burn your dog, she won't soon forget and will decide that clippers are no fun. Make sure that you wipe off excess lubricant, or you'll end up getting oil all over that nice clean coat.

Frequently turn your clippers off and touch them to make sure that they're not too hot. If they become too warm, spray on coolant. It's made especially for cooling down hot clippers. (Follow the directions on the canister.) When the clippers become too warm, you can also

- Switch blades and let the hot ones cool down.
- Switch to another clippers (if you have one).
- Place the blade on a metal surface, which quickly cools it off (a cookie or baking sheet works).

Making your first clip

The best way to find out how to use your clippers is to start by neatening up areas where your dog has already been trimmed but where the fur has grown a little untidy.

Before jumping into the deep fur, however, make sure that you've chosen the clipper size that works best for your dog's coat and the right blade. Your dog also should be clean and free of tangles and mats.

Hold the clippers in a way that feels comfortable in your hand and gives you the most control over them. Check out Figure 4-2 to get a better idea.

Book III

Cleanliness Is Next to Dogliness: Grooming

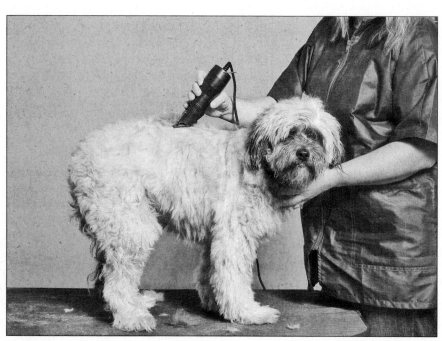

Figure 4-2: Clipping a dog can seem daunting, but when you and your dog get comfortable with the clippers, it can be fun.

By starting with an inconspicuous area that needs some neatening up, you can easily find out how much hair your clippers and blade take off. If the amount of hair you removed is too much or too little, you can adjust by switching to a different guide comb setting or blade.

The higher the number of the blade, the shorter and finer the cut. And always appraise your work as your clipping progresses — after you've trimmed a bit. That way, you know whether you're taking off too much or too little. Don't forget, however, that taking off too little is better than taking off too much. You can always trim off more, but you can't glue it back on.

And don't forget to trim the hair that sticks out around and between your dog's paw pads, if you like a neater look. Simply use an electric clippers with a size 10 blade and hold the foot in its normal shape (not splayed). Trim the hair that sticks out beyond the pads (don't clip down between the pads), and then use the clippers to trim any other hair around the foot that ruins a neat presentation.

Attempting a Pet cut

Unless you're set on giving your dog a *show cut* (usually because you're showing your dog), sometimes the best thing to do is to clip your dog in an easy-to-maintain cut. Often called a *Puppy cut,* a *Teddy Bear cut,* or a *Pet cut,* this cut doesn't require much work (see Figure 4-3). Follow these steps for giving your pooch a Pet cut:

1. **Equip your clippers with a size 30 or 40 blade and an appropriate snap-on guide comb set at the right length for your clip.**

2. **Go over your dog's body with the clippers, trimming her coat to an even length.**

3. **Remove the snap-on guide comb and gently trim the ears with either a size 10 blade or size 15 blade (if you want a closer shave).**

   Trim to the ear flaps, thus following the line of the ear.

4. **Using the size 10 or size 15 blade without the snap-on guide comb, gently trim your dog's underside — especially around the genitals and anus, to keep them clean.**

Oops! Righting a wrong

Everyone makes mistakes. It's a normal part of being human. Occasionally, you'll make goof-ups that don't hurt your dog but make her look pretty silly. No matter how hard you try, you'll make a mess, and now your dog looks like she's having a bad hair day. What do you do?

Figure 4-3:
Most like
the simple
Pet cut,
because
keeping it
looking good
doesn't take
much effort.

Take a deep breath before you panic, and try to relax. If your dog is injured, with cuts to the skin, see Chapter 3 in Book II on how to handle them. If your dog has suffered clipper burn, you can use a little aloe vera on the burn — and remember to keep your clippers cool next time.

If your dog has not been injured, remember that the mess you've made is only hair, and hair *does* grow back. You just need to figure out how to fix the problem so your dog won't be the laughingstock at the dog park.

Assess the problem first. What did you do that looks so awful? In most cases, you're probably looking at an uneven spot or two, so check to see whether you can blend the two layers of hair together. Thinning scissors or shears — see the "Using scissors" section earlier in this chapter — can sometimes fix a problem; sometimes they can't. Sometimes you can trim the area around the uneven spot to match, or vice versa. Your dog's coat may be a little short for a while, and if it's cold, she may have to wear a sweater.

If you're afraid you'll end up with a bald dog, put away all your grooming tools, take your dog off the table, and have a cup of coffee (or tea). When you've relaxed, evaluate your dog. Can you realistically fix the problem? Or do you need to call in the pros? And of course, try not to clip your dog's coat to the point where the only thing a pro *can* do is shave her.

Book IV
Training, Agility, and Shows

The 5th Wave   By Rich Tennant

"You know, you're never going to get that dog to do its business in your remote control dump truck."

In this book . . .

Training a dog not to pee in the house is your first step, but after that the sky's the limit. These chapters cover dog manners and basic commands, tricks, and agility. The last chapter takes you into the world of dog shows — the ultimate in showing off your training.

Chapter 1

Housetraining 101

Max, a 10-week-old Beagle, is delighting his new owner with his puppy antics but is dismaying her with his penchant for peeing all over her recently installed carpet. No matter how recently he tinkled outside, he always seems to have something left over with which to tinkle on the floor covering.

Allie, a 6-year-old Golden Retriever, would never pee on anyone's carpet. Her people can count on her to do her business three or four times a day: first thing in the morning, early in the afternoon, in the late afternoon (sometimes), and in the evening before she retires for the night. On the rare occasions that she needs an extra bathroom break, she lets her people know by heading to the back door and scratching it — or if her tummy is giving her trouble, by waking up one of her people to get her outside in time to avoid an accident.

Cody, a 3-year-old Chihuahua, can hold his water pretty well — sometimes. Other times, though, he seems to suffer from bathroom-manners amnesia or a sudden preference for taking a whiz any place except where he's supposed to.

Which of these dogs are housetrained? Which ones aren't? In this chapter, you not only find the answer to those two questions, but also discover why housetraining plays such an important role in whether you and your dog can live happily ever after.

What Housetraining Is and Why It Matters

To know whether your dog is really housetrained, you need to understand exactly what housetraining is. Simply put, *housetraining* is the process by which you teach your dog to eliminate when you want him to and where you want him to — and to refrain from eliminating at any other time or place.

That definition doesn't allow much room for errors or lapses. And clearly, when measured against those criteria, a dog who consistently does his duty outdoors or in a designated indoor area is fully housetrained. That's not the case, though, with a dog who usually tinkles outdoors, never tinkles outdoors, or only occasionally tinkles outdoors (or performs with similar levels of consistency in a predetermined indoor Bowser bathroom). Housetraining is one of those all-or-nothing cases. That being the case, Allie is the only dog in the chapter intro whom you can consider truly housetrained.

Why does such precision matter? Simple: An otherwise well-behaved, healthy dog who doesn't know proper pooch potty protocol is much more likely to lose his home than a similar dog who knows his bathroom basics. No human being likes to have his home turned into a multiroom canine toilet — and if such a human can't teach his dog to take his bathroom business elsewhere, that dog will likely find himself going elsewhere.

Why Your Dog Can't Be "a Little Bit Housetrained"

Housetraining is an either-or proposition: Either a dog is housetrained or not. To say that a dog is "a little bit housetrained" is like saying that a woman is "a little bit pregnant."

 If you consider your dog to be "a little bit housetrained," you're really saying that she hasn't completely learned proper bathroom manners yet. So you can't really rely on her to go to the bathroom only where and when you want her to.

Until your dog is totally housetrained, you always face the chance that Lassie will decide to use your brand-new area rug as her toilet or that Laddie will choose to anoint your mother-in-law's prized Chippendale chair. And of course, for some dogs, especially puppies, those chances are way better than even. That's certainly the case with Max, the young Beagle from the chapter intro who's been using that new carpet as his own personal potty.

But owners of adult dogs like Cody, the Chihuahua who's occasionally leaving unwelcome puddles throughout his owner's abode, also cope with unreliable canines. Cody appears to have forgotten the lessons in bathroom manners his owners taught him years ago — or perhaps he never quite understood those lessons in the first place. Or maybe Cody doesn't feel well.

But although housetraining is an either-or proposition, owners definitely can teach a dog proper potty behavior in more than one way.

Exploring Housetraining Methods

Most people who choose to live with dogs want to be able to regulate their canines' bathroom deportment. They want their dogs to poop and pee where and when *they* (the people) choose.

Fortunately, you can choose between two methods designed to help you achieve this goal. The right choice for you and your dog depends on many factors, some of which relate less to your dog's needs than to your way of living. This section discusses indoor and outdoor training and talks about some of the lifestyle issues that may help you choose one method over another.

Location, location, location: Outdoor versus indoor training

The two housetraining methods are all about location — as in, where you want your pooch to potty: indoors or outdoors.

Outdoor training

If the idea of turning part of your house into a canine bathroom doesn't thrill you, you're far from alone. That same lack of enthusiasm is probably the primary reason millions of dog owners train their four-legged friends to do their bathroom business outside. *Outdoor training* involves teaching a dog to eliminate in a potty area located outside your home. The potty area can be a designated spot in your backyard or wherever you allow your dog to do his business, such as on walks.

Outdoor training has plenty of advantages. First and foremost, as soon as your dog knows what he's supposed to do and where he's supposed to do it, you never again need to worry about canine waste marring your floors, staining your carpets, or otherwise stinking up your house. You also have more floor space to use and enjoy, because you don't have any newspapers, litter boxes, or other indoor canine bathroom paraphernalia to get in the way of household foot traffic. Finally, owners who choose to walk their dogs outdoors can get some healthful, enjoyable exercise and some special bonding time with their canine companions.

But outdoor training carries some disadvantages, too — just ask anyone who's had to go outside with his pooch on a cold or rainy night. Fortunately, a little extra training can go a long way toward alleviating the problem of the pooch who takes too long to do his business during bad weather.

Don't think that letting your pooch potty in your yard relieves you of the obligation to clean up those deposits. Unless you like having bright yellow patches in the middle of your green grass or stepping in the other stuff — because that stuff generally doesn't degrade fast enough for you to totally avoid such missteps — plan on cleaning up after your four-legged friend even if his potty is on your property.

Indoor training

Indoor training involves teaching a dog to eliminate in a potty area located inside your home. The potty area can be some newspapers spread on the floor in one room, a litter box tucked discreetly into a corner, or some other device located in a designated area of your abode.

A dog who's indoor trained makes a beeline for that indoor location whenever she feels the urge to eliminate. As soon as she's finished, cleanup is easy: You just flush the poop down the toilet and either throw away or clean the surface upon which the poop or pee landed.

Indoor training is a viable housetraining option if, for some reason, taking your dog outside to eliminate isn't practical. This method is also worth trying if your adult dog and her waste byproducts are very small.

But indoor training carries some disadvantages. It's impractical if your dog is much bigger than toy sized (consider how big that waste is likely to be). Moreover, if your canine companion is male, sooner or later he'll probably starting lifting his leg when he pees. When that happens, his ability to aim accurately may decline. Instead of hitting the litter box, newspaper, or other toilet, he may . . . well, you get the idea.

Looking at lifestyle factors to help you choose your method

How do you decide which housetraining method works best for you? The right answer depends as much on your way of living as it does on your dog's needs.

Maybe you're one of those lucky people who not only works from home during the day but also has some nice outdoor places within walking distance. For you, walking a dog can be a real pleasure — and at times even a sanity saver. A housetraining method that takes you and your dog outdoors is probably an attractive option.

Perhaps, though, you're an elderly person or a mobility-impaired individual who can't get out and around easily. The dog walk that's pure pleasure for your work-at-home neighbor may be torture for you. If this description fits you, the ideal housetraining method probably means never having to leave the house. Indoor training may be a better choice.

Maybe you live in a high-rise apartment building in the middle of the city. When your canine companion needs a potty break, you can't just snap on the leash, open the front door, and head out for a quick stroll or a trip to a designated doggie toilet area. Instead, your route to the great outdoors may require you and your dog to walk to the opposite end of a long hallway, wait for the elevator, ride down to your building lobby, and finally get yourselves to the proper spot outside. And all this time, your dog is expected to hold her water. If you and your dog face such obstacles *en route* to an outdoor bathroom, you may also want to consider keeping her potty indoors.

Although housetraining is generally a straightforward process, chances are, you'll encounter setbacks during the training period. And even when your four-legged friend becomes a housetraining graduate, she's bound to do some occasional backsliding. In any case, you'll likely see situations in which your consistently rock-solid housetrainee suddenly seems to lose her edge, and neither you nor she knows why.

Book IV

Training, Agility, and Shows

Understanding the Role You and Your Family Play

You and the other humans in your life play crucial roles in your dog's housetraining progress and ultimate success (or lack thereof). Not only do you teach your dog the ins and outs of proper potty protocol, but you also create the conditions that can make or break a housetraining program. For one thing, housetraining needs to be a family affair. Consider why:

- ✔ **To keep the diet consistent:** No matter how diligently you're trying to regulate Sparky's bathroom urges by regulating the kind and amount of food you feed him, such diligence is all for naught if your partner or child is sneaking the dog snacks all the while.

- ✔ **To help you avoid burnout:** Housetraining can be pretty simple, but it can also be pretty tedious when just one person is doing the day-in, day-out routine of feeding, walking, and confining the housetrainee.

But maybe getting your family on board isn't your problem. Maybe you're trying to deal with housetraining a dog while working away from home all day. Even well into the 21st century, corporate America isn't great about accommodating the needs of employees' family members, whether those members are human or canine.

Your dog or puppy has all the instincts and desire he needs to motivate him to acquire good bathroom manners — he just needs you to get him going. If you do the job right, not only will your dog become a housetraining ace, but the two of you will build a bond that goes the distance for years to come.

Scheduling Outdoor Training for Adult Dogs

Teaching an adult dog to do her bathroom business outside is similar to teaching a puppy. The difference between the two, and the good news, is that an adult dog doesn't need nearly as many bathroom breaks as a puppy does. But the principles and procedures are the same: showing your four-legged friend that her bathroom is outside and doing whatever it takes to keep her from eliminating inside.

Table 1-1 shows a sample schedule for outdoor-training an adult dog. As soon as your adult dog has mastered her housetraining basics — which can happen in just a few days — you can eliminate the noontime potty break and consider giving her a little more freedom in your home.

Table 1-1	Outdoor Training Schedule for an Adult Dog
Time	*Tasks*
7:00 a.m.	Get up. Take dog outside. Feed dog. Offer water. Take dog outside. Play with dog up to 15 minutes.
Noon	Take dog outside. Offer water. Play with dog 15 to 30 minutes.
5:30 p.m.	Take dog outside. Feed dog. Offer water. Play with dog for 1 hour and/or let her hang out with the family in the kitchen.
7:00 p.m.	Remove water.
Before bed	Take dog outside.

Training the Housetrainer: Taking the Right Approach

Before a person can teach any subject, he has to know not only the subject itself, but also how to convey that information to a student. The same is true for housetraining. For your puppy or dog to learn basic bathroom manners, you must teach him those manners in a way he can understand.

That said, your four-legged friend brings plenty of positive attributes to the housetraining process: a strong instinct to seek out a den, an equally strong instinct to keep that den clean, an ability to learn through repetition, and a desire to score rewards. But it's up to you to capitalize on those attributes and develop an approach to housetraining that enables him to get the hang of proper potty protocol with minimal stress on him — and on you.

Leaving behind housetraining methods of yesteryear

Housetraining a dog doesn't have to be hard. But a generation ago, not many people realized that fact. At best, housetraining was a difficult undertaking; at worst, it was a total failure. Unfortunately, failures occurred all too often.

Consider what may have been behind these failures. Mom (she was the one who usually got stuck with the housetraining task) would see a puddle or pile of poop on the floor. She'd freak — naturally, the little deposit would be gracing a just-mopped kitchen floor or freshly shampooed living room carpet — and go on the warpath to find the canine culprit. When she found him, she'd grab the culprit by the collar, drag him over to the puddle or pile, and yell, "Bad dog!" at him. Maybe she'd swat him with a rolled-up newspaper. She may even have rubbed his nose in the object of his offense. The terrified pooch would then creep away, and things would settle down, at least temporarily.

Maybe the dog would eventually figure out what Mom was trying to tell him. Often, though, he wouldn't. And so the dog would soon have another accident, and the whole miserable cycle would begin again. Still, the dog was learning something: He learned that he should avoid the rolled-up newspaper at all costs. He also learned that he should avoid screaming moms.

Most of the problems people had with housetraining their dogs weren't the dogs' faults; they were the people's faults. People knew very little about the canine instincts that make housetraining and other training easier. They knew only that they didn't want their dogs to do their business inside the house.

Since then, dog trainers and owners alike have discovered a lot about how dogs learn. And you can use that knowledge to make housetraining a much easier process than when your mother was trying to do the job.

The way you try to show your dog proper potty protocol lays the foundation for your efforts to teach him other maneuvers, such as coming when called, sitting when told, and walking nicely while leashed (see Chapter 3 in Book IV for details on these lessons). What you do now, in this most basic of lessons, can set the tone for your relationship with your dog in the years ahead. For that reason alone, it's worth taking the time to do the job well.

Using Your Pooch's Instincts to Lay a Foundation

When housetraining your pooch, you're not working with a blank slate. Your canine companion probably learned a lot about bathroom behavior before you ever met her — whether she came to you as a puppy or as an adult dog. And a lot of what she knows comes from her *instincts:* those feelings, drives, and desires that have been with your dog since the moment she was born. They're hard wired into her very being. No one taught her the behaviors that result from these impulses; they just came naturally.

The places where your dog chooses to sleep, her tendency to hoard things, her love of licking your face, her delight in fetching objects — these and countless other actions and reactions may all be inborn. And although some of these instincts don't affect her ability to be housetrained, others do. After you find out about some of these inborn impulses, you can begin to direct them in ways that help your dog learn to do what you want her to do. Your dog's instincts help her pick up not only potty deportment, but also just about anything else you want your dog to know.

The training your dog has already had, whether puppy or adult

You can housetrain almost any dog, but the challenges of teaching a puppy to go potty may differ from the challenges you encounter when you try to teach the same maneuvers to an adult dog. Some of these issues have to do with the kind of nurturing and training the dog has already received.

The wee ones: Preliminary training and physical limits

All a healthy puppy usually needs to become housetrained is some time to grow and to develop some self-control — and, of course, some guidance from you in the meantime.

If you got your puppy from a reputable breeder, he may already know the rudiments of proper potty behavior. After all, the well-bred pup has had lots of opportunities to learn about keeping clean and getting along with other dogs (and people) — both of which are important pre-housetraining skills. A puppy who has nailed those basics is easier to teach than one who lacks such knowledge.

Many breeders go even further. They take their puppies outside every morning and after meals, and they praise the little pups when they eliminate. If your puppy's breeder did that (ask when you're interviewing prospective breeders), she already did some of your dog's housetraining for you. The same may be true of a dog you adopt from a shelter, rescue group, or individual.

But even if your new puppy aced those preliminary lessons, one crucial lesson he's only starting to learn is the lesson of self-control. To put it simply, your little pup just can't hold it — at least, not for very long. A puppy younger than 4 months doesn't have a big enough bladder or sufficient muscle control to go more than a couple hours without eliminating. As he gets older, a pup's ability to control himself gradually increases. By the time he reaches adulthood, at about 1 year of age, a healthy dog usually has plenty of self-control. In fact, some adult dogs can hold it for a *very* long time.

Grown-up pooches: Unlearning bad habits

Even an adult dog who appears to have an iron bladder isn't necessarily housetrained. The fact that she *can* hold it doesn't necessarily mean that she *will* hold it. An adult dog may be burdened with mental baggage or just plain bad habits that can create additional obstacles to housetraining.

For example, if you adopted your young adult dog from an animal shelter, her previous owners may not have bothered to housetrain her — or if they did, they may have done a poor job. Either way, her failure to master proper potty deportment may well have been what landed her in the shelter in the first place.

Some shelter and rescue dogs have behavioral problems that manifest as inappropriate elimination — for example, a shy dog may roll over and pee whenever someone stands above her and looks directly at her. Even a dog who's been a model of proper bathroom behavior at one point in her life can later appear to forget what she's been taught.

Not surprisingly, then, housetraining an adult dog is often less straight-forward than housetraining a puppy. The grown-up pooch who has less-than-stellar bathroom manners often needs to unlearn some bad but well-entrenched habits before learning new ones. The person who lives with such a dog may need to develop his detective skills and figure out why his canine companion keeps making bathroom mistakes.

In any case, though, when you know something about your canine friend's instincts and impulses, you have a leg up on your efforts to housetrain her.

How long can a dog hold it?

Some dogs appear to have bladders made of iron. When the weather is bad, for example, they slap their floodgates shut. A storm-frightened dog can hold it for up to 24 hours, even if you give him ample opportunity to unload during that time period.

Still, just because your dog has an iron bladder doesn't mean you should put it to the test. Keep some guidelines in mind:

✔ Most experts say a dog needs a chance to pee at least every eight to ten hours.

✔ For puppies, the standard guideline is that they can hold it for the number of months they've lived plus one. In other words, your 3-month-old youngster can hold it for about four hours, max. But for many puppies of that age, even four hours is pushing their anatomical limits; they may need trips every three hours, or even every two hours for a while.

✔ Very small puppies, such as toy breeds, often need hourly potty breaks when they're under 4 months of age simply because their bladders are so small.

Learning from mom

Even while he's still with his litter, a puppy is learning a lot about life as a dog. From his littermates, he learns not to bite too hard (if he bites at all) and how to jockey for position at feeding time. He learns a lot about proper bathroom behavior, too.

Puppies can start learning elimination etiquette from the time they're about 3 or 4 weeks old — in some cases, even earlier. Generally, their bathroom manners start kicking in when they have sufficient motor skills to start wandering around the whelping box where they've been living with their mom, and perhaps outside the box, too.

The mama dog takes advantage of this ability. When the pups indicate that they're about to go potty, she may use her nose to push them outside the box if they haven't already gotten themselves out of there. Doing so keeps their poop and pee from stinking up the doggie domicile. If the mama dog and puppies are lucky enough to be residing in the home of a good breeder, several layers of newspaper will be at the other end of the box or other quarters for the puppies to eliminate on. After the puppies eliminate on the newspaper that the breeder placed on the floor for just that purpose, she whisks away the soiled papers and replaces them with fresh ones. A breeder reinforces the mama dog's efforts in this way.

By 7 or 8 weeks of age, most puppies have developed enough control to master this first bathroom lesson. They have to poop and pee every couple hours or so, but they've learned to listen to their bodies, and they can tell when they need to go. When they get those urges, they try to scurry away from their den before giving in to that compulsion to squat. This effort to eliminate away from the den signals that a puppy is ready to begin learning the rudiments of housetraining.

Den dynamics

The lessons a puppy learns about keeping clean go way beyond what her mom makes her do. The nest that a dog's mother teaches her to help keep clean is really her first den — and dens are a big deal in the lives of most dogs.

For a dog, the *den* is simply an area that she can call her own. Generally, it's a small place that's at least somewhat enclosed on two or three sides but is also open on at least one side. The area may be dark, but it doesn't have to be. What it *does* have to be is a place where the dog feels safe and secure.

Unlike her wolf ancestors, the domestic dog doesn't need a den to ensure her physical survival, but her urge to find a den is still very strong.

Cleanliness is next to dogliness

So-called dog people — humans who are enamored of anything and everything remotely canine — like to say that the word *God* is really *dog* spelled backward. They may espouse the motto of a magazine called *The Bark:* "Dog is my co-pilot." These dog people aren't being blasphemous. Dogs instinctively want to keep themselves clean.

Sometimes a dog's definition of cleanliness differs slightly from yours. You probably don't like the idea of Fido's splashing in a mud puddle, but Fido may not mind the mud at all. In terms of peeing and pooping, though, Fido and most of his canine compatriots draw the line between dirt and cleanliness — and they draw that line right smack in front of their dens.

Instinctively, a normal, healthy dog does just about anything to avoid having to use his den as a toilet area. The last thing he wants to do is deposit his bodily waste anywhere near his cherished domicile. You can make that impulse work in your favor as you housetrain your dog. The impulse to keep the den clean is the foundation of teaching dogs to poop and pee only where and when you want them to. The drive to use a den and the drive to avoid soiling that den form the basis of easy, effective housetraining — using a crate.

Life without guilt

Suppose your dog makes a mistake. Say that he anoints your freshly mopped kitchen floor or leaves a little pile of poop in the foyer. Do you think he feels bad about it? Do you think he's overcome with remorse? Do you think he even remembers he's done a dirty deed within five minutes of committing the act? The answers to those questions are no, no, and no. Guilt and remorse aren't in your dog's emotional repertoire.

"Now, wait a minute," you say. "When I come home at night from work and see that Fido's peed on the rug, he sure looks to me as though he's feeling guilty. And when I start yelling at him, his ears go back, his tail goes between his legs, and he kind of cringes. He *knows* he's done something wrong."

Fido knows something all right — but that something isn't any realization that he's messed up big time. What he does know is that you're angry. If you're yelling his name, he also figures out pretty quickly that you're angry at *him.* But he doesn't have a clue about why you're so upset; he's long since forgotten about his little rug-christening party. All he knows is that you're mad at him, and he's scared of you. Under such circumstances, he takes what looks to him like two prudent courses of action: literally making himself smaller (that's why he cringes) and beating a hasty retreat.

Does he understand that you don't want him to have any more accidents in the house? Nope. Does he realize that if he didn't have any accidents, you wouldn't become angry? No again. He's just doing everything he can to minimize your wrath and, when that fails, to get away from that wrath — and from you.

Your dog lives a life that's completely free of guilt. He doesn't connect one of his long-ago actions with the angry outburst you're having now, which is why yelling at your dog after the fact doesn't teach him anything except to be afraid of you. Time, patience, and consistency are much more likely to get you the results you seek.

Learning by repetition

Your dog's inability to remember past mistakes doesn't mean that she can't make connections. On the contrary, she's very good at linking cause and effect. You can use that linking ability to teach her proper bathroom behavior or just about anything else you want her to know. How? Behold the power of repetition.

In fact, many times your dog learns something that you didn't plan to teach her. Your dog may know when you're about to leave the house — and, in response to your near departure, may head down to her crate on her own. How does she know? You perform the same sequence of actions every time you leave the house: You may turn off some lights, close doors, grab your wallet and iPod, pick up your purse, get out your car keys . . . that sequence is an unmistakable signal.

Although repetition is the key to teaching your dog what you want her to know, you can do less repeating when you provide her with some sort of incentive for doing the right thing. Find out more about this positive approach in the later section, titled "Rewarding the good, ignoring the goofs."

The need for attachment

Puppies tumble over each other constantly and seem to be touching each other all the time. Rarely do you see one puppy consistently go off by himself. Puppies need each other for warmth and companionship; they thrive in each other's company.

But perhaps when you welcomed home your new puppy or dog, you made the mistake of having him sleep by himself in the kitchen or basement. If so, you undoubtedly experienced a night full of heart-rending wails, yips, and howls. Your canine companion didn't like being alone, away from his littermates or the companions of his previous home. Being away from *you* made those already bad feelings seem even worse.

Book IV

Training, Agility, and Shows

And of course, you may have a neighborhood dog whose owner leaves him alone in the backyard all day, every day, and who barks his head off — much to the annoyance of people who live nearby. Why does he do it? Boredom is one reason. Loneliness is another.

Dogs are social animals. When they have a chance to choose between being alone and being with another individual, they generally choose the latter.

What does this need for company have to do with housetraining? Plenty. Not only does your dog's desire to be with you help build a precious bond between the two of you, but it also helps you keep track of where he is and what he's doing during the housetraining process. No matter how you look at it, your dog's instinctive desire to be close to you is something you can use as part of his housetraining — and any other training, for that matter.

How instincts can be thwarted

Instincts play a big role in how quickly your dog masters the art of housetraining. Many puppies learn basic cleanliness and social skills — two important pre-housetraining accomplishments — from their mothers and littermates. But what if, for some reason, a puppy doesn't pick up those lessons in the first few weeks of her life? And how can that happen? One answer to how that happens is just two words: puppy mills.

Puppy mills: Inhibiting instincts

Puppy mills are substandard breeding operations in which female dogs are forced to mate as often as possible. Breeders raise mother and pups in deplorable conditions — tiny cages in which these poor animals barely have enough room to turn around. They also often have to live knee-deep in their own poop and pee.

Having to live in her own filth is a surefire way to short-circuit a dog's instinctive drive to do her bathroom business away from her den. She can't get away from her den. And especially if she's a puppy, she can't hold it long enough. Sooner or later, she has to go, and if the den is the only place where she can eliminate, that's where she does so. Eventually, she learns to deal with it.

What does this kind of situation mean for housetraining? Simple: A puppy-mill dog may take quite a while to recover her instinct to potty away from her den. And until she does, housetraining will be extremely difficult for everyone involved. This doesn't mean that a puppy-mill pooch can't be housetrained. Plenty of people have persevered until their canine companions finally understood where and when they were supposed to potty. But getting to that point takes lots of time and even more patience.

Unfortunately, many people lack such patience. Life with their puppy-mill potty delinquents may veer off in one of two directions. Either the owners put up with a dog they say is "partially housetrained" (which really means the dog isn't housetrained at all), or the owners decide that they can't tolerate the stains, smells, and aggravation of a dog who can't learn basic bathroom manners. In turn, they either relegate the dog to remote areas of the house or, worse, get rid of the dog. Any way you look at it, the outcome is unhappy for all concerned.

Clearly, avoiding such problems in the first place is a good idea. How? By not buying a puppy or dog who comes from a puppy mill. A large number of these pooches end up in retail pet stores, such as stores located in shopping malls. Others are sold by dealers who pose as breeders and advertise online or through print classifieds. Always visit the premises and ask to see the mama dog.

Many pet stores have stopped selling puppies themselves and instead hold adoption events to allow shelters and rescue groups to showcase the puppies and dogs who need new homes. Such stores clearly indicate that they're holding such events, and personnel from the shelter or rescue group are there to talk with you about the animals up for adoption. If that's the case with the pet store you're considering, assess the puppies and dogs up for adoption, and know that, in doing so, you may be saving a life. If you can't tell whether the store is selling puppies or is just giving a shelter or rescue group a place to display the animals in their care, think two, three, four, or more times before acquiring a puppy from that store.

Animal shelters and rescue groups: Lacking socialization?

Suppose you've opted for an older dog or a mixed breed from a shelter or rescue group. Will such a dog pose special housetraining challenges? That question has no single answer.

Lots of dogs from animal shelters and rescue groups do just fine with housetraining. In fact, quite a few of them have mastered basic bathroom behavior before they even arrive at their new home. Some, though, may not have done so. And some may be poorly socialized — in other words, they lack the exposure to everyday sights, sounds, and people that enables them to become emotionally well-adjusted animals. This poor socialization may make it tougher for such a dog to become bonded to you and may also make it tougher for you to help him unlearn some bad bathroom habits.

This certainly doesn't mean that the dog you adopt from a shelter or a rescue group can't be housetrained. The task simply may be a bit more challenging than you expected. You'll get a leg up on that challenge, however, if you find out as much as you can about your dog's background before you bring him home and start teaching him basic bathroom etiquette.

Book IV

Training, Agility, and Shows

Taking the 21st-Century Approach to Housetraining

Today more people understand that to get what they want from their dogs, they first have to tune in to what their dogs want. People have discovered a lot about how dogs think, feel, and learn. They now know that most dogs don't want to poop or pee anywhere near where they sleep and eat. They understand that every canine likes to have a den to call her own. They realize that dogs don't remember what they've done within a few minutes of having done it. Consistency, patience, and repetition are the tools you need to teach your dog what you want her to know.

Such knowledge enables you to develop a training approach that helps you help your dog express her instincts in ways that are acceptable to you. In other words, you can train your dog not only to do what you want, but to do what *she* wants, too. After you know what your dog can bring to the housetraining process, you have to realize what you need to bring to that same enterprise. This section covers some of the qualities that can help you be the best teacher your dog will ever have.

Seeing your dog's point of view

Any communications theorist, corporate trainer, or psychologist will tell you that to persuade someone to do what you want, you have to put yourself in his shoes. You need to imagine his thoughts and figure out what makes him tick.

Empathy is just as important when you're trying to reach a dog as when you're trying to persuade a person. You need to understand the way your dog views the world and relates to it. In terms of housetraining or any other teaching, you'll be miles ahead of the game if you can think like a dog.

When you think like a dog, you realize that

- ✔ Disciplining your dog after he's done something wrong doesn't do any good, because he has no idea what that "something wrong" is.

- ✔ For many dogs, peeing is much more than an act of elimination — it's a way to communicate with other canines.

- ✔ The shy little darling who rolls onto his back and dribbles a bit of urine when you come home hasn't mislaid his bathroom manners. Instead, he's paying homage to you, doggie style.

> ✔ When you're out walking with your four-legged friend at night and he stops suddenly in the middle of the sidewalk, he's not being stubborn; more likely, he sees something that scares him. To you, it's just another garbage can, but to him, it's big and bad and dark and menacing. When you realize what he's feeling and thinking, you can coax him past the object in question instead of yanking on his leash and dragging him to you.

You can't succeed with housetraining — or any type of dog training — by shoving your wishes down your dog's throat and expecting him to swallow them. Force isn't effective; it pits the two of you against each other. Instead, you and your canine companion should be on the same side. You should have a common goal: figuring out how to live happily together.

Being benevolent

A lot of dog-training literature, not to mention amateur trainers or people who think they know the scoop, tell you that dominance and leadership are the keys to training success. "Show your dog who's boss," they say. "Don't let her get away with anything."

Some "experts" even recommend that you punish a transgressing dog by grabbing her by the scruff of the neck and rolling her over onto her back (called an *alpha roll*). Still others advocate that the best way to deal with a fearful dog is to help her face her fear. You won't see any such advocacy here.

At times, a dog owner does need to be a leader. But even at such times, you can be a *benevolent* leader — the giver of all good things, the source of all things fun, the refuge in times of fear. Such a leader thinks not in terms of dominance and submission, but in terms of benevolence and cooperation. You can be your dog's best teacher, but you can also be her best friend — and dominance never needs to be a part of your vocabulary.

Working with your dog's instincts

You can housetrain your puppy or dog faster when you work with his tendencies. His need for a den, his desire to keep that den clean, and his ability to learn through consistency and repetition can all help him become a housetraining ace much faster than back in the day when all Mom had to work with was a rolled-up newspaper and a boatload of totally understandable frustration. You just have to use your dog's instincts to your advantage.

Book IV

Training, Agility, and Shows

Creating a schedule

Creating a schedule for the canine housetrainee is important because, quite simply, having a schedule is a great way to reduce the time it takes your dog to get the hang of housetraining. The training process becomes a whole lot easier when you feed your dog, play with him, and let him eliminate at the same times every single day.

A schedule plays right into your dog's need for repetition, consistency, and predictability. A schedule also makes it a whole lot easier for you to anticipate when your dog needs to pee and poop and then to get him to the right place before he has an accident. You won't find a one-schedule-fits-all timetable. You need to put together a regimen that fits your dog's age, his degree of housetraining prowess, and the housetraining method you're using.

Rewarding the good, ignoring the goofs

No, this section isn't an advertorial for the Reverend Norman Vincent Peale's treatise on *The Power of Positive Thinking*. But frankly, he had a point: A whole lot of power lies in positive thinking — and in positive training, too.

Think about the old approach to dog training. Basically, it revolved around finding your dog doing something wrong and then punishing her for doing so. But that approach doesn't work very well. All too often, dogs don't know what they're doing wrong, much less how to do something right.

The opposite, positive approach works much better than the negative one. Instead of pouncing on your dog for messing up, look for her to do the right thing — and when she does, reward her lavishly. That reward can come in the form of verbal praise, loving hugs and petting, tasty treats, or even all three. In any case, take a positive approach, not a negative one.

Of course, you don't just wait passively for your dog to do the right thing. As part of your approach, you need to actively guide her into performing the maneuvers you want her to perform, using her instincts to help her get the idea a little faster. And when she does get the idea, don't forget to praise her to the skies. You have to reward her for doing what you want her to do.

By consistently showing your dog what you want her to do and then rewarding her for doing so, you're conditioning your dog to do the right thing. You're upping the odds that she'll do what you want her to do every time you want her to do it.

Remember reading about Pavlov's dogs in science class? The Russian scientist actually got the dogs to salivate by giving each dog a food reward — a treat — every time a bell rang. The dogs learned that the ringing bell meant a treat, and they began to look forward to getting that treat. They were primed for that food reward, and as a result, their mouths mouth began to water when they heard the bell.

You don't have to wear a white coat and have a fancy laboratory to condition your dog the same way Pavlov conditioned his. Simply show your pooch what you want and immediately reward her for doing what you've shown her — whether it's the first time she pees in your backyard or the hundredth time she anoints a tree rather than the rug in your bedroom. By giving her that reward, you're letting her know that she's done something that pleases you, and you give her an incentive to do that something again.

What if she does something wrong? If she pees on your carpet, you clean it up without any comment. If she poops on your brand-new hardwood floor, you whisk the mess away. Period. You don't yell at her. You don't punish her. You certainly don't rub her nose in it. You just get rid of the mess and move on.

If you catch your dog in the act of peeing or pooping in the wrong place, view the situation as a teaching opportunity for you and a learning opportunity for her. Interrupt her in the act and take her to the right place — the place where you've decided she should do her bathroom business.

Being consistent

You've already got so much going on in your oh-so-busy life that you can't possibly remember what color your dog's pee was yesterday or when he last pooped. Everyone is on information overload. But take heart. Help for memory-impaired folks is here: consistency. In housetraining terms, *consistency* means having your dog eat, drink, pee, and poop at the same times and places every day. You create a routine that the two of you eventually can do in your sleep (or almost, anyway).

By adopting a consistent routine for your dog's dining and toileting activities, you help not only your own memory, but also your dog's ability to housetrain faster. Dogs learn through repetition, so when you and he do the same things at the same times in the same places each day, he'll come to expect that you'll be doing those things.

Book IV

Training, Agility, and Shows

This consistency affects your dog both physically and mentally. The repetition that you establish in feeding and housetraining your dog conditions his body as well as his mind. After all, you may be physically conditioned to expect that early morning jog or a second cup of coffee at the same time each day — and without the jog or joe, you don't feel quite right. You don't like that feeling, so you stick with your exercise and/or coffee routine; it becomes a habit. By establishing similar routines with your dog, you're helping to make housetraining a habit for him. When his body gets used to the routine you set up for him, he'll be primed to poop and pee when and where you want him to.

Don't worry, though. After your dog is truly housetrained, you don't have to be quite such a fanatic about repetition and consistency. Your dog will have the control he needs to hold it a little longer if your schedule hits an unexpected snag. Still, keeping to at least a semblance of routine is a good idea, even when your four-legged friend is a housetraining ace.

Attending to details

Have you ever toilet-trained a child? If so, you know the importance of paying attention to seemingly trivial details, such as when he last peed in the potty, when he last did a doo-doo in his diaper, or what he ate for dinner the night before he had a funny-colored bowel movement.

The same is true when you're housetraining your dog. During this process, you need to remember what you fed your four-legged friend and when you did so. Recalling how long it's been since he last peed or pooped is always a good idea. And knowing what his pee or poop normally looks like is important so that you can tell when he may be sick.

Paying attention to details also means taking the time to observe your dog and discover what makes him the unique individual he is. For example, do you know the answers to these questions?

- Does he lift his leg when he pees? Does he like to lift both legs (one at a time, of course)? Or does he not bother lifting his leg at all?

- Does he need to eliminate right after he eats, or does he like to wait awhile?

- Does he like to pee in the same spot all the time, or is he an I'll-do-it-anywhere piddler?

- Does he circle and sniff before doing his business? Or does he suddenly stop midstride and do the deed before you quite realize what's happening?

- Is he a little introvert who sometimes releases some urine when you greet him? Or is he an extrovert who offers a wagging tail and canine grin to everyone he meets?

Think of the stories you tell your friends about your dog. What are some funny things he's done? How about the sweet things, the poignant things? What are some of his quirks — potty related and otherwise?

What, you ask, do all these questions have to do with housetraining? A lot. The better you know your dog, the more you can empathize with him. The more you can empathize with him — to think the way he does — the better able you are to adjust his housetraining lessons to his unique character and perspective. And the better able you are to fine-tune your housetraining to his character, the more effective your housetraining efforts are overall.

This personalized — or, rather, dog-specific — approach is particularly true with respect to your dog's bathroom habits. By paying attention to what he does when he pees or poops, you can better anticipate when he's going to go — and intervene when he's going to go in the wrong place.

Chapter 2

Teaching Your Dog Manners

. . . .

In This Chapter

▶ Considering your attitude toward training

▶ Setting up for success and checking out teaching tools

▶ Crate-training your dog

▶ Teaching the basic stuff they don't always teach in obedience school

▶ Knowing how to travel with your dog

. . . .

An old dog-training adage still applies today: Every handler gets the dog he deserves.

In other words, the most important factor in training is not your dog, but you. You're the leader — or you should be — and you need to know enough about canine language so you can teach your dog your language. You need to show your dog what you want her to do and give her a reason for doing it — and an understanding that not doing the very reasonable things you ask of her is unacceptable.

Your dog gets trained whether you do anything or not. If you don't guide her toward good behaviors and praise her when she accomplishes them, she will fill her life with behaviors you don't like. If you don't lead, she will. And that's bad news for a dog. Shelters, rescue groups, and newspaper classifieds have plenty of dogs like that: dogs with problems. Their chances of finding happiness — or even staying alive — aren't very good at all.

That's not the way things have to be.

Resolve that you must train your dog, and that training is not a one-shot deal, but an intrinsic and ongoing part of the promise you make to your dog when you bring her into your life.

Then think of the rewards of dog training. The obvious reward is good manners, but the bigger payoff is that as you train your own dog, the bond between you and your dog grows stronger, the love deeper. In Chapter 1 of Book IV, you found out about housetraining. In the next chapter, Chapter 3, you get into basic training, including step-by-step commands. This chapter focuses on getting a handle on your dog's behavior and discovering how you can play your proper role in training your pup. The special relationship between an owner and a well-mannered dog is the Total Dog Experience — don't miss it.

A Few Words about Aggression

If you have ever, even for a moment, been afraid of your dog or what he may do, read the rest of this section carefully and then put the book down, for now. The rest of this chapter and the next are not for you. Not yet, anyway. You need serious one-on-one help, whether you realize it or not.

Aggression in dogs has both genetic factors and learned ones. Some dogs are born with the potential to be aggressive, and that potential can be fully realized in a home that either encourages aggressive behavior or is ill equipped to cope with it. Other perfectly nice dogs can become unreliable because of abusive treatment.

Is your dog potentially dangerous? Answer these questions, and be brutally honest:

- Has your dog ever stared you down? Not with a loving gaze, but with a hard, fixed, glassy-eyed stare that may be accompanied by erect body posture — stiff legs, ears forward, hackles raised.

- Do you avoid doing certain things with your dog because doing them elicits growling or a show of teeth? For example, are you unable to approach your dog while he's eating or ask him to get off the couch?

- Do you make excuses for his aggressive behavior or figure he'll grow out of it? Or do you think a growling puppy is cute?

- Do you consider your dog safe — except around a particular group of people, such as children? When he growls at the veterinarian, do you tell yourself that the behavior is reasonable and that a veterinarian should be able to cope with it, after all?

✔ Has your dog ever bitten anyone, even only once, because it was an accident, because he was scared (even though he's usually so good), or because of some other equally inexcusable rationalization? People often make excuses for the behavior of little dogs, but growling and snapping is no more acceptable from a Pomeranian than from a Pit Bull.

If, after answering these questions, you suspect that you have a problem, get help from a professional dog trainer or veterinary behaviorist. Now. You should no more attempt to cure aggression yourself than you should try to treat cancer. The reason is the same: You don't have the training and the expertise to do so. If you suddenly try to eliminate your dog's self-appointed role of leader of your pack, you'll find trouble. If you even attempt to make eye contact with such a dog, you may get bitten. So don't.

Ask your veterinarian for a referral to a trainer or behaviorist with experience handling aggressive dogs. And realize from the start that, just like cancer, aggression is a disease that is sometimes not curable. Have your dog neutered — most dogs involved in attacks are young, unneutered males — and follow the expert's advice. But if, in the end, you have a dog who still cannot be trusted, have him euthanized. It's upsetting, but this course is the only responsible one to take. If your dog is aggressive, he'll probably end up euthanized eventually. The difference is that if you wait, someone will get hurt first.

Finding an aggressive dog a new home — one with no children, perhaps — is not the answer. Children are everywhere, and you may be responsible for one of them being hurt if you pass a problem dog on to someone else — especially if you do so without admitting the real reason you're finding him a new home, knowing that no one wants to adopt a biter. You do the dog no kindness, and you put the new family at risk.

Maybe you prefer to live in a state of denial, hoping nothing awful involving your dog will ever happen. More than 4.5 million American dog owners are jolted into reality every year — 4.5 million being the number of bites estimated by the U.S. Centers for Disease Control and Prevention. Children are the most frequent victims.

Need more reasons to act? You could lose your homeowners insurance — or more. U.S. insurance companies shell out more than $1 billion a year to settle dog-bite liability claims. The companies say claims are rising in both number and value. Even one "minor" bite claim could cost you your homeowners insurance — and a vicious attack could cost you a lot more than that.

Aggressive behavior never improves on its own. It only gets worse. So get help — now.

Book IV

Training, Agility, and Shows

Developing the Right Attitude toward Training

If you don't have an aggressive dog, consider yourself lucky. Chances are, though, you probably have a dog who's a little out of control: one who drives you just a little bit crazy, and a canine adolescent, more often than not. You've given up waiting for her to outgrow her bad behavior — they never do! — and figure it's finally time to . . . (big sigh) . . . train her. You're thinking that you can't avoid training; it just has to be done, like cleaning leaves out of the rain gutters.

Stop!

Now consider the following: If you have a bad attitude toward training, so will your dog. If you think training is a joyless chore, she'll hate every minute of it. If you walk around jerking on her collar and swearing, she'll wonder what she's done to deserve your anger, and she'll be too busy worrying about that to learn anything.

Expect success from her and be willing to work for it. Praise her not only for succeeding, but also for trying. Learning is hard for her — and stressful. Think of your dog as a person who has just moved to your house from a country where the language and customs are different — a trans-species exchange student. After all, she was born a dog, and you're asking her to live as a member of a human family. You're asking her to learn the language and follow the rules. The fact that this feat is ever accomplished is nothing less than a miracle. So celebrate it *with* her.

Consider dog training not as a mechanical thing — if you do X, your dog does Y — but rather as something organic, alive, interconnected, and ever changing. A well-mannered dog becomes that way from the inside out. "Sit" and "Stay" are the least of it, really, and are only the visible manifestations of what that dog is on the inside: a confident, comfortable, and secure member of a loving human pack. That dog is, quite simply, a joy to live with.

We all get cranky sometimes. If you've had a horrid day at work, you've had a fight with your spouse, or the mechanic just told you the cost to fix your car is $2,700, you're probably better off skipping any efforts at teaching your dog something new. Instead, use your dog to ease out of your funk: Play fetch or just hang out with her. Pet her while you watch TV — it's good for your blood pressure.

Likewise, if you start a training session fine and feel yourself getting frustrated and angry, don't push things. End on a positive note. Ask your dog for something you know she knows well and, when she does it, praise her. Then call it a day. If you can't manage even that, just stop before you both get even more frustrated.

In either case, remember: Tomorrow is another day.

Dog fight!

Anyone who has ever walked a dog has experienced that terrifying moment when a vicious, unleashed dog is intent on doing harm to your dog. It's a dangerous situation, even for owners of big dogs; for small dogs, it could be a fatal encounter.

If you have a male dog, getting him neutered may help keep him out of fights. Even if your dog is a cupcake, one dominant unneutered male may take your dog's very presence as an insult to his dominance. If your dog is neutered, this particular fight trigger is usually not an issue.

Always try to avoid dogs who appear aggressive — dogs with erect body stances instead of the relaxed, ears-back attitude of a dog coming over to play — but sometimes you can't escape a dominant dog.

If the other dog's owner is nearby, demand that he put his canine terrorist on leash. If he's clueless enough to say "Mine's friendly," yell back "Mine's not," and make your demand again.

If a fight starts, stay out of it. You may be badly hurt. If you're willing to risk a bite and another person can help, pull the dogs apart by their tails — not their collars! If you're alone and there's a hose nearby, hitting them in the chops with a high-volume water spray usually stops the action.

If your own dogs are constantly fighting, call a trainer or behaviorist to help you develop strategies to make it clear that you require your dogs to get along. Realize, however, that peace may never be possible, and you may have to find a new home for one of the dogs.

Keys to Success

Ask a person who has never owned or trained a dog to teach one to sit, and he can probably come up with a successful plan without any prompting. Hold the front end up and push the back end down while saying, "Sit." The mechanics of training aren't that hard to understand. But to get your dog to mind you consistently and happily, you need to know a little more.

Dog training is not getting through eight Thursday-night group classes for the training to be over, forever. The training is never over. You teach, and then you practice, in ever-more-challenging circumstances. You correct or ignore the behavior you don't want. And you integrate your dog's lessons into everyday life so that he never loses the lessons. Remember the French or Spanish you learned in high school? How good are you at it now? If you don't use it, you lose it. The same is true of the skills you teach your dog.

After he knows the language, keep asking him to use it. Following are some tips that will help both of you.

Book IV

Training, Agility, and Shows

Be on the same team

Don't think of training your dog as a you-versus-your-dog endeavor. Instead, think about the two of you being on the same team, albeit in different positions. Consider yourself the quarterback, if you like: You call the plays. Maybe you've noticed that quarterbacks don't get very far without folks to follow those plays. Winning is a team effort.

Of course, your dog has to learn the plays first, and you're the one to teach her. But this relationship is still not an adversarial one. You show your dog what she needs to learn, and you do so with love and respect, which your dog will return in kind.

To bring your dog onto your team and show her the plays you'll be calling, you need to spend time with her. Bring her into your life. Let her sleep in your bedroom and practice her "Sits" in the kitchen. The more opportunities for interaction and practice you have, the faster and more reliably your dog will perform.

Be positive

This tip goes back to having the right attitude, of course, but it's more than that. Rewards — treats and praise — that are well timed and appropriate are essential to your dog's learning process. If all you ever do is tell your dog "no," your relationship isn't going to be a very good one. How would you like to work with a boss like that?

In particular, praise is cheap — free, in fact! — so use it a lot. Use praise when your dog tries to get it right. Use it more when your dog succeeds. Use it when your dog just pays attention to you, because as you'll find out in a moment, that's the first step in the training. You don't have to be some gushing goof, but you do need to let your dog know when you're proud of him.

Be fair with corrections

Make sure that your dog understands what you want before you correct her for not doing it. And let the punishment fit the crime.

A correction should not be a release of anger or a way to clear pent-up feelings by unloading them on your dog. Instead, a correction is another way to communicate with your dog, to foster in her a clear understanding of her place in your human pack. As such, a proper correction is another way to strengthen the bond between you and your pet.

A correction can be the absence of praise, the denial of attention, or a sharp rebuke. Always ask yourself if you're being fair before you give in to a desire to respond negatively toward your dog. A correction is one of many tools in the trainer's kit; it's not about anger or revenge. Use negative reinforcement selectively and always fairly — and never punish a dog for something she didn't know was wrong.

Be consistent

How would you do in your job if your boss kept changing the names of your tasks or asked you to do two things at once? Or had different rules for different places and times? It would drive you nuts, wouldn't it? Yet that's exactly what people do to their dogs. Consider these points:

- ✔ **Training consistency:** When your dog knows a command and demonstrates that knowledge consistently, use that command the same way each time; never change its meaning. The most common example of inconsistency is probably saying "Sit down" to a dog when you really mean "Sit." Now, you know that when someone says "Sit down" to you, it's the same as saying "Sit." But if you teach your dog "Sit" and "Down" as two separate commands, you can understand why it's confusing. Which do you want? The same applies for saying "Down" when you really mean "Off" (more on this in a bit).

- ✔ **Situational consistency:** Some dogs start to recognize situations in which ordinary rules don't apply. They learn, for example, that when you're in a hurry, you'll shrug off disobedience: You're in a rush to feed your dog, for example, and when you say "Sit," he doesn't. You throw the food down anyway.

  If "Sit" doesn't always mean "Sit," eventually it will never mean "Sit." Teach your dog that "Sit" means "Sit," no matter where or when you request the behavior.

  Another kind of inconsistency is when you never expect your dog to mind until you've repeated the command a few times. After a dog knows a command, follow through in having him perform the behavior. Then praise him.

Book IV

Training, Agility, and Shows

Build on your successes

Dog training succeeds by degrees and creativity. You continue to expand the length of time and the number of situations in which your dog will execute a command, and you look for new ways to use what she knows so you can continue to develop and strengthen the bond between you.

Build a little at a time, celebrating every step along the way. Living is learning, and learning is good.

Tools for Teaching

Dog training isn't expensive, or it needn't be. You need a leash, some treats, and a properly fitted collar, but your other tools are free for the asking. The trick is knowing what they are, how they work, and when to use them.

A 6-foot lead you can handle easily — leather or nylon, neither too wide nor too thin — is a must, as is a collar that is properly fitted and put on. Chapter 6 in Book I introduces leashes and collars, if you need a refresher.

Some trainers recommend a slip-chain collar for training; others prefer a flat collar, a head halter, or even a prong collar. All these pieces of equipment are right for some dogs and some people in some training situations. Start with what's easiest on you and the dog — a head halter or a flat collar — and focus on teaching, not forcing. Slip collars are often put on incorrectly — choking the dog,rather than correcting him — because the collars are difficult for most novice dog trainers to use properly. If you use a slip collar, you must attach the leash to the live ring and keep the chain loose except for the split second when it tightens and releases to correct your dog.

Getting your dog's attention

You're not going to be able to teach your dog anything if you can't get her attention. One of the best ways to do so is to teach her to give you eye contact at your request. Eye contact is one of the most important areas of communication for dogs, and mastering eye contact, dog style, immediately strengthens your relationship.

Catch your dog's eye by swooping your hand under her chin, bringing your fingers back up near your eyes while you make a clucking noise, and saying her name, followed by "Look" or "Watch." The motion upward and the sound orient your dog's eyes up so that she's looking right into your own. When they lock in, hold for a split second, smile, and praise. This command may take time to learn, because dogs avoid eye contact to show respect. Build up your time until your dog gives and holds eye contact until you release her. Practice this command several times a day, and always be loving and encouraging.

As your dog learns to respect and trust you more, you'll find that she looks at you more. She wants to see what you're doing, because you're where the action is.

Some dogs get a little bit carried away with this devotion thing, to the point that it becomes a way of controlling you. If your dog is becoming an attention addict, give her something to do to earn your praise — ideally, a half-hour "Down-Stay" on the other side of the room (see Chapter 3 in Book IV). Think of this activity as tough love, if you will, but it's better than spending the rest of your life unable to read your newspaper because your love-junkie dog is sticking her nose through it.

Your dog should know her name not as a command to go to you or as a swear word, but as a request for her attention. Praise her for looking at you when you use her name, and then build on that to help get her attention before giving a command. If you're doing your eye-contact exercises, she'll start looking at you at the sound of her name, before she even hears "Look." Praise her! Eventually, you won't even have to give the "Look" command. The sequence will be, "Luka (not yelled, but clear and encouraging) . . ." and then a slight pause, and then the command. Finish with praise, always.

On the cutting edge: Clicker training

One of the most exciting developments in dog training in recent years has been the widespread use of a little piece of plastic and metal known as a clicker (or sometimes a cricket). The clicker brings classic operant conditioning to dog training, and it first became known for training dolphins and whales for those popular shows at marine parks.

Consider the dolphin, if you will. You can't put a leash on him, and he's really too big — and too slippery — to force him into doing what you want to do. (Trying to wrestle in the water with an orca would be even harder — and dangerous, too!) So trainers had to come up with a way to communicate, to shape behavior in a nonphysical way. Enter the clicker.

Trainers — dog and dolphin alike — begin by associating the sound of the clicker with the reward: Fish, in the case of dolphins, and a dog treat for a canine pupil. Soon the animal understands that the clicker — which is easier to time properly than verbal praise — means

that he did right and that he's earned a reward. This technique is especially good for shaping complex behaviors — in the obedience ring, for example, where high-scoring dogs must not only sit, but sit square on their haunches and in proper position relative to their handlers to get a high score.

This level of precision is attained by shaping the behavior. The dog gets a click and treat for sitting, and when that's mastered, the trainer waits to click/treat until the dog offers a behavior that's just a tiny bit closer to the goal, and then a tiny bit more, and so on. Soon the dog is being clicked/treated for the perfect position only.

If you have a click trainer in your area, take a class — you'll enjoy it! If not, you can find the best selection of books on clicker training at the Dogwise Web site, www.dogwise.com.

You'll definitely be hearing more about clicker training for dogs in the future, and more trainers will be switching to this novel way to train.

Giving praise

All praise is good, but praise specially tailored to connect with the dog's way of reacting is ten times as effective. Consider these tips:

- ✔ **Use the right tone of voice:** Dogs communicate with one another through sounds easily duplicated by humans. If you're angry with your dog, for example, dropping your voice to a low rumble closely approximates the growling of a dog. For praise, use a sweet, high-pitched crooning voice: "Goooooooood, dooooogggg. Aaaren't youuuu a gooood doooog?"

- ✔ **Tailor your petting style to your dog:** Some dogs go crazy when petted; others hardly notice. Use a little chest pat or scratch for dogs who tend to be overly enthusiastic, and be a little more boisterous for the ones who really warm to being jollied. Don't let the dog use petting as an excuse to go crazy — lighten up on the pats, but don't correct him — and let your voice do most of the praising.

- ✔ **Smile:** Dogs understand many of our facial expressions because they use similar ones to communicate with each other. A smiling face is understood in both species, but if you really want to get through, make the smile as wide open as you can. You're trying to approximate that big, panting grin a happy dog has. Panting is optional (but kind of fun).

Training with treats

What about using treats to train your dog? They're a wonderful way to get through to your dog quickly, and probably the easiest way for beginning dog owners to train. Dog trainers have come a long way in developing training techniques by using food. Unfortunately, many people take away the wrong lesson: They come to believe in the treat not as a way to shape behavior, step by step — for which treats can work very well — but rather as the wages for obedience. Dog sits, dog gets a treat. Dog sits, dog gets a treat. And guess what happens? You end up with a dog who won't pay attention to you if you aren't in a position to pay the edible going rate.

And what about the relationship that's supposed to be developing from the inside out, that special bond? It doesn't. To your dog, you become a vending machine, not a leader. Food helps to form the bond with your dog — dogs quickly become attached to the person who feeds them, after all — but there's more to developing a solid relationship.

Treats are great for training — they're especially useful for trick training, or for teaching any behavior that requires your dog to be in precise positions, such as behaviors demanded of top-level competitors in obedience trials. But they're for training, not for life. You should not be carrying around a pocketful of treats to bribe your dog into doing what you want. Your dog needs to learn his proper place in your pack by using the commands without food after he learns them, or you're not really teaching him much of anything. Vary his rewards — always praise, but don't always treat after he's learned the lesson. When you teach a dog to figure out that a particular behavior gets him what he wants (food and praise), and then put a word on it (the command word), you are truly teaching, and he is truly learning.

Maintaining control and giving correction

During training, you maintain control and offer correction, using both a collar and leash and your body to help guide your pet into correct position and to keep her from getting into wrong ones — such as a full-out gallop, heading away from you.

You also correct your dog with your voice, and you need to be sure that you're using both your voice and your vocabulary properly. Maybe you don't use the word "no" much because it's so overused. Instead, you say "bad dog," often preceded by a very loud and dramatic intake of air, like the shocked gasp you make involuntarily when you find that your dog has chewed your favorite shoes. Use a sharp, guttural, and dramatic word or sound. Throw the sound at your dog, like a rock.

Put the emphasis on the correction word, not on your dog's name, to which there should never be any negative connotations.

Using a release word

You need a word to let your dog know he is done with the command you gave him. Probably the most common in use is "Okay." "Release" is another fine one, as is the one the sheepdog people use at trials: "That'll do." It sounds very gracious. Whatever you use, be sure that you're consistent in its use.

Your release word can mean more than the end of an exercise, such as allowing your dog to move about at the end of a "Stay" command. The release word is also a sort of an all-purpose "at ease" word. For example, if your dog is heeling along at your side, staying out of trouble on a crowded sidewalk, you can use your release word to let him know that doing a little sniffing is fine, and maybe a little leg-lifting, too.

Book IV

Training, Agility, and Shows

Using a Crate: A Playpen for Your Puppy

To speed the process of training, we strongly recommend that you use a crate or similar means of confinement from the time your dog is a puppy.

Initially, you may recoil from this concept as cruel and inhumane. Nothing could be farther from the truth. You'll discover that your puppy likes her crate and that you can enjoy your peace of mind. Think of a crate as a dog's playpen.

The proof is in the pudding: Dogs like crates. A crate reminds them of a den — a place of comfort, safety, security, and warmth (see Figure 2-1.) Puppies, and many adult dogs, sleep most of the day, and many prefer the comfort of their den. For your mental health, as well as that of your puppy, get a crate.

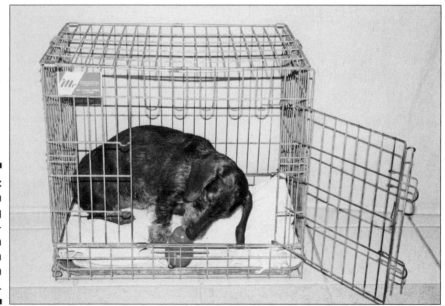

Figure 2-1:
In addition to helping with house-training, a crate is a comfy den for your dog.

Crate-training your dog offers many advantages. Consider just a few:

✔ A crate is a babysitter — when you're busy and can't keep an eye on your dog, but you want to make sure that she doesn't get into trouble, put her in her crate. You can relax, and so can she.

✔ Using a crate is ideal for getting her on a schedule for housetraining.

✔ Few dogs are fortunate enough to go through life without ever having to be hospitalized. Your dog's private room at the veterinary hospital will consist of a crate. Her first experience with a crate shouldn't come at a time when she's sick — the added stress from being crated for the first time can retard her recovery.

✔ A crate is especially helpful when you have to keep your dog quiet, such as after being altered or after an injury.

✔ Driving any distance, even around the block, with your dog loose in the car is tempting fate. Stop suddenly, and who knows what could happen? Having the dog in a crate protects you and your dog.

✔ When you go on vacation, you may take your dog. Her crate is her home away from home, and you can leave her in a hotel room knowing she won't be unhappy or stressed, and she won't tear up the room. (See the section "Traveling with Your Dog" later in this chapter for more on dogs and travel.)

✔ A crate is a place where she can get away from the hustle and bustle of family life and hide out when humans become too much for her.

A crate provides a dog with her own special place. It's cozy, secure, and her place to get away from it all. Make sure that your dog's crate is available to her when she wants to nap or take some time out. She'll use it on her own, so make sure that she always has access to it. Depending on where it is, your dog will spend much of her sleeping time in her crate.

Finding the right crate

Select a crate that's large enough for your dog to turn around, stand up, or lie down comfortably. If he's a puppy, get a crate for the adult-size dog so that he can grow into it.

Some crates are better than others in strength and ease of assembly. You can get crates in wire mesh–type material, cloth mesh, or plastic (called *airline crates*). Most are designed for portability and are easy to assemble. Wire-mesh crates are easy to collapse, although they're heavier than crates made of cloth mesh or plastic.

If you frequently take your dog with you in the car, consider getting two crates, one for the house and one for the car. Doing so saves you from having to lug one back and forth.

Book IV

Training, Agility, and Shows

Coaxing your dog into the crate

To coax your dog into the crate, use these helpful hints:

1. **Set up the crate and let your dog investigate it.**

   Put a crate pad, doggie bed, or blanket in the crate.

2. **Say a command, such as "Crate" or "Go to bed."**

   If your puppy isn't lured in, physically place her in the crate, using the command you've chosen.

3. **Close the door, tell her what a great puppy she is, give her a bite-sized treat, and then let her out.**

   There's no rule against gentle persuasion to get your pup enthused about her crate.

4. **Use a treat to coax her into the crate.**

   If she doesn't follow the treat, physically place her in the crate and then give her the treat.

5. **Again, close the door, tell her what a great puppy she is, and give her a bite-sized treat.**

6. **Let her out.**

   The treat doesn't have to be a dog biscuit, as long as it's an object the dog will actively work for.

7. **Continue using the command and giving your dog a treat when she's in the crate until she goes into the crate with almost no help from you.**

For the puppy who's afraid of the crate, use her meals to overcome her fear. First, let her eat her meal in front of the crate; then place the next meal just inside the crate. Put each successive meal a little farther into the crate until she's completely inside and no longer reluctant to enter.

Helping your dog get used to the crate

Tell your dog to go into the crate, give him a treat, close the door, tell him what a good puppy he is, and let him out again. Each time you do this, leave him in the crate a little longer with the door closed, still giving him a treat and telling him how great he is.

Finally, put him in his crate, give him a treat, and then leave the room — first for 1 minute; then 5 minutes; then 10 minutes; then 15 minutes, and so on. Each time you return to let him out, tell him how good he was before you open the door.

How long can you ultimately leave your dog in his crate unattended? That depends on your dog and your schedule, but for an adult dog, don't let it be more than eight hours.

Never use your dog's crate as a form of punishment. If you do, he'll begin to dislike the crate and it will lose its usefulness to you. You don't want him to develop negative feelings about his crate. You want him to like his private den.

Great Things They Don't Teach in Obedience Class

The lessons you can teach your dog have no end. This section gives you a taste of a few off-the-beaten-path lessons you can teach your dog.

Don't let your mind stop because a trainer's — or author's — suggestions do. After reading this chapter and the next, you'll know how to train a dog, so build on your own success. If you have something you want to teach your dog, give the behavior a name and do it!

Wait

This command is different from Stay because the dog is not required to hold a position — she just can't cross an imaginary line until the time of your choosing. To teach this command, position your dog in a doorway, call her name, say "Wait," and draw your hand, palm out, from frame to frame in front of her eyes. Walk back into the room and allow her to move around, and then step back out. If she follows across the imaginary line, give a voice correction and repeat the command and hand signal. Praise her and give her a treat for staying on the other side of the line; then release her to more praise and treats.

This command has many uses, such as when you open the car door and you don't want your dog to jump out into traffic, and before you and your dog enter people's homes or leave your own.

Go to Your Bed

The command Go to Your Bed means "Go there and plant it, pal" and is a great command for getting your dog out from underfoot. Call your dog's name, tell him "Go to your bed," lead him there, and tell him "Down." With practice — and consistency — the Down part becomes automatic.

Off

"Off" is what people often mean when they say "Down": "I want all four of your paws on the floor, now." Off is not a punishment: It's a command. If your dog's on the couch or the bed without an invitation, take her by the collar, say "Off," and then lead her down and praise. The same applies with the jumping dog, although then the command is best taught with a leash and slip collar. Say "Off," then use the leash in a downward motion until those feet hit the ground, say "Sit," and offer praise. (See Chapter 3 in Book IV for details.)

Don't Touch or Leave It

Teach this command with a physical correction from the get-go. With your dog in a Sit-Stay and your hand in a fist, flat surface up, offer your dog a biscuit with the other. As he reaches for the biscuit, say "Don't touch," and bop him gently under the chin, enough to close his jaw but not lift him off his feet. Offer the biscuit again, repeating "Don't touch," and if he hesitates or turns away, praise him. Few dogs need this command demonstrated more than twice.

This command is another one with many useful applications. A dog leads with his nose, after all, and a dog who knows Don't Touch isn't going to head in a direction you don't want him to go in. Use this command when you're walking and he dives for some dreadful leftovers in a fast-food bag. Use it to keep him from lifting his leg where you don't want him to on walks — because the sniff is the prelude to the leg-lift, this command works well. If you drop your sandwich in front of him, saying "Don't touch" ensures that you get to finish it — assuming you still want to, of course.

Fetch

For many dogs, retrieving is the easiest command to teach. They're retrievers: They were born with the desire to retrieve. You throw something, they bring it back. That's the way they're wired.

For other dogs, such as Rhodesian Ridgebacks, who were bred to hunt lions, which are hard to fetch, you throw something and they look at you as if to say, "Well, you obviously didn't want it, because you threw it away. Surely you don't expect me to do something about it. Fetch? You must be kidding!"

It's worth trying to teach your dog to retrieve, if only because it's the world's best way to get your dog the exercise she needs without you having to exert all that much time or energy. You don't have to jog — you can just throw.

If your dog isn't a natural-born retriever, realize that you must be very patient, and be content with small advances. The dog who first makes even the tiniest move forward to take an object on command has made a huge achievement. Recognize it, and build on your successes. Don't lose patience.

Before you start, go to pet supply store and get a *dumbbell* — a wooden or plastic retrieving tool that's a dowel with wide pieces on both ends to help keep it from slipping out of your dog's mouth. Dumbbells come in various sizes and weights; pick one wide enough for your dog to get her mouth on the dowel part comfortably, without being squeezed by the side pieces.

Several different methods exist for teaching fetch, including ones that involve force. For most people, a positive, patient approach works fine. Remember, think short, upbeat sessions in small increments, and offer lots of praise and treats. Work at your dog's own pace, and don't rush to the next level.

Start by teaching the dog to open her mouth. Say "Take it" and offer a treat. After your dog is opening her mouth in expectation when she hears you say "Take it," slip the dumbbell inside for a second. Praise her and offer her a treat. Try this sequence a few more times, and then end the lesson.

After your dog is accepting the dumbbell, put it in her mouth and say "Hold it" while you gently hold her mouth around the dumbbell for three or four seconds. Then tell her "Give" and let her spit out the dumbbell. Treat and praise.

The next step is to hold the dumbbell just in front of the dog's mouth and say "Take it." If you need to pull her head toward the dumbbell with the collar, that's fine. If she moves forward on her own, even better. Treat and praise.

From that point, it's a matter of building the distance slowly, lesson by lesson. One foot, 2 feet; then picking it up from the floor; then picking it up from the floor 3 feet away, and so on. You should be working separately on practicing the Hold It and Give commands, as well as the Come command described earlier in this chapter and detailed in the next chapter.

Fetching isn't just one skill: It's a combination of skills. Taking the object is one part of it. Holding the object is another, and so is bringing it to you. Releasing the object on your Give It command is the final part. Each piece must be taught, and then merged into a seamless behavior. Some dogs put it all together quickly and naturally; other dogs don't. But if you work slowly and patiently, your dog will learn.

Book IV

Training, Agility, and Shows

Traveling with Your Dog

It's one thing if your dog behaves at home under your supervision. It's quite another out in the wide world. Although dogs aren't as complicated to travel with as, say, babies, you do have to pick up and work out a few things in advance of any trip.

The well-equipped travel dog

You can really go crazy packing things to ensure your dog's safety and comfort. What should you bring? First, some basics.

✔ Your dog should be wearing a sturdy collar with a license and an up-to-date ID tag with at least one number, area code included, that's not yours — someone who'll be there to answer the phone if you lose your dog miles from home.

If your dog is more comfortable in a harness, put the tag on that, but remember, a harness isn't a good option for a dog who doesn't behave well on leash, because you have less control with a harness.

Ideally, your pet should also be "chipped" — see Chapter 3 in Book II for details.

✔ Bring along a 6-foot leash. A longer leash is handy, too, especially a reel-type leash such as the Flexi, which is great for giving your dog a little room to stretch his legs in areas such as rest stops. Think about bringing an extra leash, as well as a nylon, one-piece slip lead like the ones veterinary hospitals and kennel operators use. Keep it in your glove box.

✔ Pack two bowls: one for food, one for water.

Water bowls that either collapse for easy storage or don't spill are perfect for travel. Keep a collapsible bowl in your car trunk, along with a bottle of water.

✔ If your dog eats a widely available brand of food, pack enough to get you started and pick up the rest on the road, if you're going to an area with a market or pet supply store. If your dog eats prescription food or anything out of the ordinary, bring enough for the trip. If your pet eats canned food, you need a spoon or fork and a can opener, unless your pup's brand comes in pop-tops.

✔ Don't forget some treats!

✔ A comb, brush, and tweezers or ready-made device for pulling ticks come in handy, especially on back-country trips.

✔ Some basic first-aid supplies — scissors, gauze, tape, and Pepto-Bismol, for diarrhea — are handy to have around. Your veterinarian can prescribe some motion-sickness medication, if need be, and you certainly want to pack that.

✔ Don't forget to pack any regular medication your pet takes.

✔ Bring cloth towels, for drying off wet, dirty dogs, and paper towels for cleaning up more things than you can imagine. You may want to pack an old sheet and blanket, for covering bedspreads, furniture, and carpets in hotel rooms, and perhaps a multipurpose cleaner in a spray bottle.

✔ Plastic bags are a must-bring, too, for poop pick-ups.

✔ Bring dog shampoo. Trying to find shampoo at 10 p.m. in a resort town after your dog has rolled in something vile will convince you of this necessity.

✔ *For owners of little dogs only:* A shoulder bag for carrying your pet. With this tote — or any oversized bag — you can slip your dog into areas the big dogs can only dream of, and most of the people around you will never notice.

✔ Don't forget your pet's health records, including microchip number, and especially proof of rabies vaccination. The latter is absolutely imperative if the unthinkable happens and your dog bites someone or tangles with a rabid creature in the wild.

✔ Last, but certainly not least, from your dog's point of view: a couple of his favorite toys.

The standard travel advice has been to bring water from home, but that's just unfeasible for a trip of any decent length. Your dog will be fine drinking the same water you do in unfamiliar places. That said, bring a couple gallons of bottled water, from either the tap or the store, because you may stop to water and walk your dogs in areas where a source of safe drinking water isn't readily available.

The well-prepared dog lover

As with anything else, the key for traveling with a dog is to prepare for the worst, hope for the best. Carry some ready-made LOST DOG! flyers with your dog's picture on them and a place to write a phone number with a big marker (which you should also pack). (More on preparing these flyers is in Chapter 3 in Book II.)

Find a directory of pet-friendly lodgings. Some travel guides, such as AAA, mention whether pets are accepted, but calling ahead is always a good idea: Policies and ownership can change, after all.

Book IV

Training, Agility, and Shows

A good dog travel book is Maria Goodavage's *The California Dog Lover's Companion* (Avalon Travel Publishing). If you live in or are planning to visit California, this book is a must-buy. Others in the series are just as wonderful.

As with so many other things, the Internet has changed travel, and that's just as true of travel with dogs. Search the Web for "pet-friendly travel" or "pet-friendly lodging" and be prepared for an onslaught of options.

Travel by car

Given the worries most pet lovers have about air travel, it's no wonder that most doggie vacations are conducted in the family car. When they understand that car rides end up in exciting places like the beach, most dogs greet the prospect of a car ride with unabashed enthusiasm — a little too much, for some drivers.

Making car rides safer

As with all other training, ending up with a good car rider starts with molding correct behavior when your dog is a puppy. No matter how cute or how small, do not allow your pup to ride in your lap, and don't make a fuss over her while you're driving. On short neighborhood trips, ask your pup to sit quietly, and praise her for proper behavior.

Traveling with your dog in a crate is often easier and definitely safer. Depending on the size of your dog and the size and shape of your car, a crate may not be feasible. Do consider using a crate, though, especially if your dog is active enough to distract the driver. Collapsible crates are available for easy storage in the trunk when not in use.

Another safety tool is a doggy seat belt, which fits into a standard seat-belt buckle and then attaches to a harness on the dog. If you have a station wagon or similar vehicle, widely available metal barriers fit between the passenger and cargo areas, to keep your pet in her place. You can find these devices in pet stores.

Uneasy riders

If your dog's only exposure to riding in a car is an occasional trip to the veterinarian, don't be surprised if he's not the happiest of riders. Try to build up his enthusiasm by increasing his time in the car and praising him for his good behavior. The first short trips should be to pleasant locations, such as parks.

Hot dog

Just about everyone understands that dogs shouldn't be left inside a car on a hot day, but fewer realize that the danger is just as great on a warm one. It's a horrible way to die. A car functions similarly to a greenhouse, and heat can build up to lethal levels in minutes, even on a pleasant day in the 70s or low 80s. Even with the windows rolled down, a dog can show signs of heat stress — heavy panting, glazed eyes, rapid pulse, dizziness or vomiting, or a deep red or purple tongue — in the time it takes you to get a six-pack through the Ten Items or Less line. Brain damage and death can follow within minutes.

An overheated dog needs prompt veterinary attention to have a chance of survival. Don't delay! Better yet, don't risk your dog's life by leaving him in the car. Another danger to the unattended dog is theft, which, when combined with heat dangers, means a few minutes looking through that cute little shop really isn't worth the risk posed to your pet.

Dramamine prevents car sickness in dogs as well as people, but other remedies are available — talk to your veterinarian. A dog-handler's trick: Your dog should travel on little or no food, and the dog should get a jelly bean — or any other piece of sugar candy, except chocolate — before hitting the road.

Because most of the problems stem from fear, not motion sickness, building up your pet's tolerance for riding in a car is a better long-term cure than anything you can give him. Although fresh air is wonderful, don't let your pet hang his head out of the window. Small debris kicked up by other cars can strike him in the eye or nose and injure him. Roll down the window enough for a sniff, if you like — but no more.

On the road, remember to stop at regular intervals — about as often as you need to for yourself — for your dog to relieve himself and get a drink of fresh water. Remember to always keep your dog on a leash, for his safety.

When you're on the road, if you want to spend a few hours kicking around an area where dogs are not welcome, a local veterinary clinic is a safe place to leave your dog. You can usually manage to find one amenable to a short-term boarder within a couple calls, and you'll know your dog is in safe and secure surroundings while you're not with him. The price for this service is negotiable — a half-day's boarding is a good starting point.

Although leaving a dog loose in a hotel room is not a good idea — most places forbid doing so, in fact — you can leave a crated dog alone, provided he's not a barker. Just another reason why a crate is one of the most versatile pieces of canine equipment your dog can have.

Book IV

Training, Agility, and Shows

Travel by air

If you don't take your dog by car in the United States, air is your only other option. The major bus lines and Amtrak don't allow any animals except dogs serving the disabled. Other countries are far more liberal on this point — dogs are welcome in restaurants, too, in some places — but it's still hit and miss.

Although horror stories make the news, the truth is that airline travel is relatively safe for most dogs, and it will be for yours if you play by the rules, plan carefully, and are prepared to be a little pushy on your pet's behalf.

Animals move through the airline system in two ways: as cargo or as accompanied baggage. Most animals travel in a pressurized cargo hold beneath the passenger compartment. Although the accommodations aren't any nicer, it's better for your pet if she is traveling as your "baggage" so you can ask about her in person.

Some airlines allow small dogs in the cabin, if their carriers can fit in the space beneath the seat. This is by far the best way your dog can fly, because she never leaves your care during the course of the trip. Not all airlines allow dogs to travel in the cabin, however, and others put a limit on the number of dogs in the cabin, so making your arrangements far in advance pays.

The only larger dogs allowed in the cabin are service dogs traveling with a disabled person.

The Air Transport Association estimates that more than a half a million dogs and cats are transported on commercial airlines in the United States each year, and the industry group insists 99 percent reach their destination without incident.

To make sure that your dog is one of them, talk to the airline. Some carriers — especially the no-frills companies — don't take animals at all. Even the carriers that do have limits to the number of animals on a flight because a set amount of air is available in the sealed cargo holds. You also need to know where and when your dog has to be presented, and what papers — health certificate and so on — you need to bring.

Also consider these tips when flying with your dog:

✔ Be sure that your dog is in good health and isn't one of the pug-nosed breeds. These dogs find breathing a little difficult under the best of circumstances, and the stress of airline travel may be more than they can handle.

✔ Make sure that your dog is traveling in a proper carrier (crate) that has contact phone numbers at both ends of the journey. (Your home number won't help if you're not home.) The crate should be just big enough for your dog to stand up and turn around in. Be sure that all the bolts securing the halves of the carriers are in place and tightened.

✔ Although your dog shouldn't wear a collar in her crate — it's not safe, because it can get caught on other objects — put an ID tag on a piece of elastic around her neck; in addition, you may want to consider having her microchipped before travel.

✔ Don't ship your pet when the weather is bad or when air traffic is heaviest. Avoid peak travel days such as around the Christmas holidays, and choose flights that are on the ground when the temperature is neither too hot nor too cold, not only at the departure airport, but also at the connecting and arriving airports. In summer, a night flight is likely better, whereas the reverse is true in the winter. Many airlines have their own temperature restrictions.

✔ Fly with your dog whenever possible. Keeping on top of things is easier when you're on the same flight.

✔ Choose a direct flight; if that's not possible, try for a route with a short layover. Most canine fatalities occur on the ground, when dogs are left in their crates on the hot tarmac or in stifling cargo holds. Direct flights eliminate layovers, and short layovers reduce the time on the ground.

✔ Remember, your dog's life relies on the attentiveness of airline personnel. Most of these employees are excellent and caring, but mistakes do happen. Be prepared to pester airline personnel to confirm that your dog has been loaded and has made the same connections you have. If your pet is flying unaccompanied, talk to freight-handling personnel at every airport your dog will visit. Be polite but persistent; don't take "I'm sure she's fine — have some delicious honey-roasted peanuts" as an answer from a flight attendant. Make the staff check and report back.

Book IV

Training, Agility, and Shows

A piece of doggie heaven

It used to be that dog lovers were happy just to find lodgings that accepted dogs. How things have changed — some vacation options today are designed with dogs first in mind. These doggie vacations take two forms: Dog resorts with planned activities, and dog resorts without.

Places with planned activities are known as *dog camps.* The organizers rent a campground, school campus, or similar location for part of the year and bring in trainers, lecturers, and other experts to teach campers and their human companions about various dog sports. Dog camps leave plenty of time for hiking, fetch, silly games, and just plain hanging out with other dogs.

Camp Gone To The Dogs is the prototype and still a place many dogs and dog lovers dream of visiting someday. Honey Loring puts the camp together every year, offering everything possible to keep human and canine guests

deliriously happy. For information, check out the Web site at www.camp-gone-tothe-dogs.com.

The other kind of dog resort is typified by the strangely named Sheep Dung Estates in Northern California. Sheep Dung's cabin's are dog friendly to the maximum extent possible, with tile floors and easy-to-clean furnishings. And each cabin is set in a private setting away from the others, so staying at Sheep Dung is like having your own ranch — your dog can be off leash the entire stay. For more information, visit www.sheepdung.com.

While Camp Gone to The Dogs and Sheep Dung Estates are definitely pioneers, their trailblazing efforts have not gone unnoticed by others in the travel industry. Similar businesses have followed the great example set by these dog-friendly operations — and the trend is sure to grow.

Contrary to popular belief, it's generally better not to tranquilize your dog before flying. The combination of high altitude and limited oxygen is a challenge that your pet's body is better prepared to meet if she's not sedated. Still, your pet may be an exception. In the end, you and your veterinarian should decide on this issue.

Dog-friendly vacations

Just as vacations with children are different from adults-only trips, traveling with your dog works out better if you plan the journey with an eye to finding places where dogs not only are welcome but are also able to enjoy the surroundings.

Ruffing it

Some people spend their vacation not in some fancy resort, but in the great outdoors — and they want to take their dogs with them. Fortunately, sturdy, well-designed packs are on the market, designed to let your dog carry his share of the load and even some of yours. An adult dog in top condition can carry up to a quarter of his weight, evenly distributed in a properly fitting pack. Get your dog used to the feel of the pack on short walks and trips, and gradually build up the weight and distance.

Dogs aren't welcome everywhere, and the biggest danger to the future of canine backpacking is other hikers more than wild beasts. Don't give the dog haters any ammunition: Keep your dog under control, and that means on-leash in areas with other people or animals. Take either tools to bury waste or supplies to pack it back out.

You don't need to take much into the back country — food and water are the basics — but you do need a few extra things. Grooming tools — a brush or comb, and tweezers or a tick remover — keep your pet healthy and comfortable. Also include basic first-aid supplies for human and canine packers, and bring a light rope for tethering your dog when necessary.

Charlene G. LaBelle's *A Guide to Backpacking With Your Dog* (Alpine) is an outstanding book that offers invaluable tips on how to train and equip your dog, and where to take him.

In general, you'll want to emphasize the outdoors. But as you'll soon find in traveling with your dog, not all parks and beaches are the same. In some cities and towns, dogs aren't even allowed in municipal facilities; in other open areas, too many humans may make things tough for dogs.

Even camping can be a disappointment. The U.S.'s national parks aren't much fun for dogs, but national forests are. The difference: The crowded national parks — such as Yosemite — have strict leash laws and require dogs to stay off most trails. National forests, on the other hand, have wide open spaces with few people and fewer leashing requirements — although that doesn't relieve you of the responsibility for your dog's poor behavior. Requirements in other parks vary, so check them out in advance.

You may prefer to stay in lodgings where dogs aren't just tolerated — they're welcomed. The owners of dog-friendly inns and hotels are often dog lovers, and they're happy to give you clues on the best activities in the area. A less-popular resort area is almost always more laid back and tolerant where dogs are concerned.

Book IV

Training, Agility, and Shows

Whatever you do, call ahead! Even the most dog-friendly places may have only a couple rooms available for dog lovers, and if these accommodations are in popular resorts areas, they can be booked months in advance for prime vacation weekends. Better still, plan for an off-season vacation (and still call ahead).

Getting past "no dogs allowed" — it's possible

If you travel with your dog a lot, a time will come when you'll be stranded somewhere you weren't counting on — because of a car problem, perhaps — and you'll be trying to find a place to stay. You may be able to convince some hotels to let the rules slide. Consider some tips:

- ✔ Offer a deposit. If you're confident that your dog won't cause any damage — and if you aren't, you shouldn't be traveling with him — put your money where your mouth is and offer to guarantee your pet's good behavior.

- ✔ Show off your dog's good manners and well-groomed appearance. Obviously, this plan is not a good one for someone with a muddy, out-of-control, 125-pound shedding machine. But if your dog is clean and well behaved, show him off.

- ✔ Show the manager your crate. A dog who will sleep in a crate and not be left to his own devices is a much better risk for the manager to take.

If you're going to sneak a dog into a hotel room — and who would ever suggest such a thing? — it probably works best if your room is far from the office and you're prepared to sleep in your car, just in case. If you're planning to have your dog sleep in your car, you'd better be with him: Leaving your pet unattended is never a good idea.

Keeping the world safe for canine travelers

Even though more people than ever are traveling with their dogs, plenty of people out there still don't like sharing their space with the four-legged tourist.

You can see how the decisions to ban dogs get made. Liability concerns arise over dog bites and sanitation worries emerge over dog mess. But our job as caring, responsible dog lovers is to make sure people realize that more good dogs are around than bad ones. Remember a few pointers while on the road:

✔ **Keep 'em clean.** Your dog needs to be well groomed and clean smelling. Always dry off wet dogs and wipe off muddy feet — using your towels, not the hotel's — before allowing your dog inside. Cover furniture, carpets, and bedspreads with your old sheets and towels, and if you need to bathe your dog, be sure, again, to use your towels and to clean up all the fur.

✔ **Keep 'em under control.** Your dog should be obedient, friendly but not annoying, and never aggressive — to people, pets, or wildlife. Do not allow your dog to bark uncontrolled in a car, camper, or hotel room. Use your best judgment on when to let a dog off-leash — even in areas where doing so is allowed — and be sure that your dog isn't annoying other people or dogs.

✔ **Pick up after 'em.** Isn't it astonishing that well-mannered people who would never consider tossing a soft-drink cup on the ground will look the other way when their dog deposits something 5,000 times more vile? That "it's biodegradable" excuse doesn't wash, either. Pick up after your dog. Dog mess is the single biggest complaint dog haters have against our being in public areas, so don't give them any ammunition. When you check into a hotel, stress that you intend to pick up after your dog, and inquire if they have a place where they prefer you take her to relieve herself. Don't let a male dog lift his leg on the shrubs while you're walking there, either.

Book IV

Training, Agility, and Shows

Chapter 3

Basic Training and Beyond

. . . .

. . . .

*O*ne question almost every dog owner asks is, "How do I keep my dog from jumping up on people?" Dogs jump on people as a form of greeting, like saying, "Hello, nice to meet you!"

Dogs perceive jumping on people as a friendly gesture, a dog's way of letting the object of his affection know how happy he is to see him. He's literally jumping for joy. You can train your dog to greet people in a less rambunctious fashion, but you don't want to punish your happy pet simply because he's glad to see you.

Perhaps even more annoying is the dog's habit of sniffing parts of our anatomy we prefer he didn't. Although this behavior may be normal for the dog — he uses his nose to identify the rank, gender, and age of other dogs he meets — you need to insist that he get this information from people in a less-intrusive way.

So how do you get him to stop these behaviors without dampening his enthusiasm? By teaching Sit and Stay on command. Your dog can't jump on you when he's sitting — the two behaviors are mutually exclusive.

You also need to teach a release word to let him know that he can move again after you've told him to stay. If you don't release him from the command after a reasonable period of time, he'll release himself, and the length of time he stays will become shorter and shorter. The recommended release word is Okay, meaning "You can move now." Another common release word is Free.

The First Step: Leash Training Your Dog

Most dogs readily accept the leash. Some dogs, especially puppies, need a little time to get used to it. If your dog hasn't already been leash trained, you need to do it now.

Slip a correctly sized gentle leader — a head collar that controls your dog by her head, not her neck — or a chain training collar over your dog's head, attach a standard 6-foot leash to the *dead ring* on it (the one that doesn't move), and let her drag it around (see Chapter 6 in Book I for information on leashes and collars).

You must supervise your dog at all times so that she doesn't get tangled up. Never leave a dog alone with a training collar on. In fact, if you're not comfortable using a "choke" or training collar, you can try this method by attaching the leash to the dog's regular collar. More vets seem to be recommending against training collars these days. Others maintain that they are useful.

Do this over a period of a few days. After she ignores the leash, pick up the other end and follow her around. She'll happily wander off wherever her fancy takes her.

You're now ready to show her where you want her to go. First use a treat to entice her to follow you, and then gently guide her with the leash, telling her what a good dog she is. If you're teaching her outside, use the treat to coax her away from the house, and use the leash to guide her back toward the house. Before you know it, she'll not only walk on the leash in your direction, but she'll actually pull you along. (See the section "Born to pull" later in this chapter, to teach your dog not to pull.)

Puppies are sometimes reluctant to go away from the house, even for a treat. In that case, pick up your puppy, carry her away from the house, and then put her down; she'll lead you back to the house.

Teaching the Basics

Of all the commands your dog will learn, he must know the following to be a good house pet and socially acceptable companion:

- Sit
- Stay

✔ Okay (the release word)

✔ Down

✔ Go lie down

Sitting

The Sit and Stay is one of the simplest and yet most useful combination commands you can teach your dog. It gives you a wonderfully easy way to control him when you need to most. It's also one of the most basic commands that you and your dog can quickly accomplish.

The importance of teaching your dog to sit and stay can't be overemphasized. Not only will he stop jumping up on Grandma when she walks into the house, but when the door opens, he won't run into the street.

Use the Sit and Stay command when you want your dog to remain quietly in one spot.

Getting your dog to sit — the easy part

Teaching your dog to sit on command is quite simple.

1. **Show your dog a small, bite-sized treat, holding it just a little in front of his eyes, slightly over his head.**

2. **Say "Sit" as you bring your hand above his eyes.**

   When your dog looks up at the treat, he should sit.

3. **When he sits, give him the treat and tell him what a good dog he is.**

   Tell him without petting him. If you pet him at the same time as you praise him, he'll probably get up, but what you really want him to do is sit. *Praising* is verbal, such as saying "good" or "good dog" in a pleasant tone of voice. *Rewarding* is giving the dog a treat for a correct response while he's still in position. For example, if your dog gets up after you told him to sit, and you then give him a treat, you're rewarding his getting up and not the sit.

   When using this method of teaching your dog to sit, position your hand properly in relation to the dog's head. If your hand is held too high, your dog will jump up; if it's too low, he won't sit. Hold your hand about 2 inches above his head.

4. **If your dog doesn't respond on his own, say "Sit" again and physically place your dog into a Sit position by placing your left hand under his tail and behind his knees and placing your right hand on his chest, and then tuck him into a sit.**

Book IV

Training, Agility, and Shows

5. **Keep your hands still and count to five before giving him the treat.**

6. **Practice making your dog sit five times in a row for five days.**

   Some dogs catch on to this idea so quickly that they sit in front of their owner whenever they want a treat.

Getting your dog to sit on command — the next part

When your dog understands what Sit means, you can start to teach her to obey your command.

1. **Put the treat in your right hand and keep it at your side.**

2. **Put one or two fingers, depending on the size of your dog, of your left hand through her training collar at the top of her neck, palm facing up, and tell her to sit.**

   If she sits, give her a treat and tell her how good she is while taking your hand out of the collar. If she doesn't sit, pull up on her collar and wait until she sits, and then praise her and reward her with a treat.

3. **Practice until she sits on command — that is, without having to pull up on or touch the collar.**

4. **Give her a treat and praise her for every correct response, keeping her in position to the count of five.**

As your dog demonstrates that she has mastered sitting on command, start to reward the desired response every other time. Finally, reward her on a *random* basis — every now and then, give her a treat after she sits on command. A random reward is the most powerful reinforcement of what your dog has learned. It's based on the premise that hope springs eternal. To make the random reward work, all you have to do is use it and keep using it!

Now when your dog wants to greet you by jumping up, tell her to sit. When she does, praise her, scratch her *under* the chin, and then release her. Following this simple method consistently, you can change your dog's greeting behavior from trying to jump on you to sitting to being petted.

Sit-Staying

As a part of your dog's education, he has to learn the Sit-Stay in a more formal manner — not just at home, but anywhere. Because he already knows the Sit command, teaching the Sit-Stay will probably go relatively quickly.

How much time you have to spend and how many repetitions it takes for each progression depend on your dog's personality. How much time do you need to spend at any given session? As long as you and the dog enjoy it. You can also practice several different exercises at the same session — the Sit-Stay, the Down, Walking On Leash without pulling, and the Come. Whatever you do, there's no point advancing to the next progression until the dog masters the previous one.

Follow these steps in mastering the Sit-Stay:

1. **With your dog sitting at your left side, both of you facing in the same direction (called the Heel position), put the rings of his training collar on top of his neck and attach the leash to the dead ring of the collar (or fit the gentle leader/head collar over his head).**

   In the Heel position, the area from the dog's head to his shoulder is in line with your left hip, with both of you facing in the same direction.

2. **Put the loop of the leash over the thumb of your left hand and fold the leash accordion style into your hand, with the part of the leash going toward the dog coming out at the bottom of your hand.**

   Hold your hand as close to the dog's collar as you comfortably can. The farther away from the dog's collar you are, the less control you have.

3. **Apply a little upward tension on the collar — just enough to let him know the tension is there, but not enough to make him uncomfortable.**

4. **Say "Stay" and give the Stay signal — a pendulum motion with the right hand, palm facing the dog, stopping in front of the dog's nose, and then returning to your right side (Figure 3-1).**

   Keep your body as straight as you can, and don't bend over your dog. Before you step away from your dog, make sure that your right hand is at your side again.

5. **Take a step to the right, keeping the tension on the collar, count to ten, return to your dog's side, release tension, praise him, and release him, taking several steps forward.**

6. **Repeat, but this time step directly in front of your dog, count to ten, step back to Heel position, release tension, praise, and release.**

7. **With your dog in Heel position, put the rings of the training collar under your dog's chin and attach the leash to the *live* ring of the collar (the one that moves).**

8. **Neatly fold your leash accordion style into your left hand, and place it against your belt buckle, allowing 1 foot of slack.**

Book IV

Training, Agility, and Shows

Figure 3-1:
Giving the
Stay signal.

9. Say and signal "Stay" and then place yourself 1 foot in front of your dog, keeping your left hand at your belt buckle and your right hand at your side, palm open, facing your dog.

When you see that your dog's attention is drifting, he's probably about to move. You can tell your dog is thinking about moving when he starts to look around and begins to focus on something other than you. Any time you see that lack of attention, reinforce the Stay command by slapping the leash straight up with your right hand. Don't say anything, but smile at your dog when he's in position. Return your right hand to your side.

If your dog is thinking about moving or actually tries to move, take a step toward your dog with your right foot and, with your right hand, slap the leash straight up to a point directly above his head. Bring back your right foot and right hand to their original positions without repeating the Stay command. Count to 30 and pivot back to your dog's right side. Count to five, praise, and release.

Until you discover how to recognize the signs that your dog is going to move, chances are, you'll be too late in reinforcing the Stay, and he'll have moved. When that happens, without saying anything, put him back at the spot where he was supposed to stay, stand in front of him, count to ten, return to Heel position, count to five, and release him. Repeat over the course of several training sessions until your dog is steady on this exercise.

Playing the Sit-Stay game

The following steps, using the leash on the *dead* ring of the collar (or on the gentle leader), involve testing your dog's understanding of Stay, while extending the time and distance of the Stay command:

1. **Starting in Heel position, with your left hand holding the leash and placed against your belt buckle, say and signal "Stay" and then step 3 feet in front of your dog, with no tension on the leash.**

2. **Slightly rotate your left hand downward, against your body, to apply tension on the leash.**

   This test is called the Sit-Stay test. If your dog moves to come to you, reinforce the Stay with your right hand. Test three times, increasing the tension until you get physical resistance from your dog.

   Your tension needs to be commensurate to your dog's size and weight. In other words, Terrier-strength tension applied to your Golden Retriever isn't going to produce the desired results.

   For the Sit-Stay test, use a downward rotation of the left wrist. Maintain tension for a few seconds and then slowly release tension. You're looking for physical resistance from your dog. From now on, practice this quick test before you do a Sit-Stay. Remember to release at the end of the exercise.

3. **Starting in Heel position, with the leash now on the live ring, go 3 feet in front of your dog.**

   The goal is to have her stay for one minute. If she moves, reinforce the Stay.

4. **Move 6 feet in front, to the end of the leash.**

You need to practice the Sit-Stay on a fairly regular basis, but you don't want to bore yourself or your dog. After your dog understands what you want, once or twice a week is perfectly adequate. Start with the Sit-Stay test to refresh her recollection of what you expect from her. When she's reliable on leash, try her off leash in a safe place. First practice 3 feet in front, and then gradually increase the distance and the time you expect her to stay.

Book IV

Training, Agility, and Shows

Releasing: The magic word is "Okay"

When you say the release word, "Okay," your dog will know that he can move now and is on his own time. Make it a strict rule to give him the release word, which allows him to move again, every time after you tell him to stay. If you get lax about releasing and forget, he'll get into the habit of releasing himself. That teaches him that he can decide when to move — not a good idea and the opposite of what you want him to learn.

Your dog also needs to learn the difference between being praised for responding correctly and being released. Praise isn't an invitation to move. You say "good boy" when he responds to a command. Praise is when you use your voice. Petting is when you use your hands. You release him when the exercise is finished.

As quickly as you can, get into the habit of using only one command. If you don't get the desired response on the first command, show your dog what you want without repeating it. Repeating commands teaches your dog to ignore you. If you're consistent from the start, your dog learns he has to respond to the first command.

Getting the dog down (and staying down)

Your dog already knows how to lie down, but she needs to be taught to lie down on command. Down is the command to use when you want your dog to lie down in place, right now, and stay there until you release her. The following steps can help you teach this command:

1. **With your dog sitting at your left side and a treat in your right hand, put one or two fingers of your left hand, palm facing you, through her collar at the side of her neck.**

   Show her the treat and lower it straight down and in front of your dog as you apply gentle downward pressure on the collar, at the same time saying, "Down."

2. **When she lies down, give her the treat and praise her by telling her what a good dog she is.**

   Keep your left hand in the collar and your right hand off your dog while telling her how clever she is so that she learns she's being praised for lying down. With a small dog, you may want to do the exercise on a table.

3. **Reverse the process by showing her a treat and bringing it up slightly above her head with upward pressure on the collar as you tell her to sit.**

   Practice having your dog lie down at your side five times in a row for five days, or until she does it on command with minimal pressure on the collar. Praise her and reward her with a treat every time.

4. **Sit your dog at your left side and put two fingers of your left hand, palm facing you, through her collar at the side of her neck.**

   Keep your right hand with the treat at your right side.

5. **Say "Down" and apply downward pressure on the collar.**

   When she lies down, praise her and give her a treat every other time. Practice over the course of several days until she lies down on command without any pressure on the collar.

Make a game out of teaching your dog to lie down on command. Get her eager about a treat and, in an excited tone of voice, say "Down." Then give her the treat. After that, when she lies down on command, you can randomly reward her.

Although the Sit-Stay is used for relatively short periods, the Down-Stay is used for longer periods. Traditionally, the Down-Stay is also taught as a safety exercise — to get the dog to stop wherever she is and stay there. For example, she finds herself across the road. She sees you and is just about to cross the road when a car comes. You need a way to get her to stay on the other side until the car has passed.

The object of the Down-Stay command is to have your dog respond to your command whether she's up close or at a distance. Pointing to the ground won't work from a distance, so you need to train your dog to respond to an oral command. This point is where the Down-Stay command comes in — the theory being that the dog is least likely to move in the Down position. Be that as it may, you'll find this command not that hard to teach, and you do want to be able to stop your dog in her tracks.

Go lie down, doggy!

Go Lie Down is a useful command when you want your dog to go to a specific spot and remain there for an extended period until you release him. Use the command whenever you don't want him underfoot, such as at mealtimes or when you have visitors and don't want him making a pest of himself.

Select the spot where you want him to hang out — his crate, bed, chair, whatever:

1. **Depending on your needs, you can also use a movable object — a dog bed, crate pad, or blanket, which allows you to change locations.**

   Assume that you're going to use a dog bed.

2. **Take your dog to the bed and tell him, "Go lie down."**

   You may have to coax him with a treat.

3. **When he lies down on the bed, praise him, give him the treat, count to five, and release him.**

4. **Repeat until he readily lies down on the bed.**

5. **Next, start 3 feet from the bed, give the command "Go lie down," and lure him onto the bed with a treat.**

6. **Praise him when he lies down, give him the treat, count to ten, and release him.**

7. **Repeat several times, gradually increasing the time between the praise and the giving of the treat, from a count of 10 to a count of 30.**

Stop for now — you're getting bored and so is he. Come back to it another time.

For your next session, review the last progression two or three times and then send him from 3 feet. Stand still, but motion him to go to his bed. He may surprise you and actually go to his bed and lie down. If he does, praise him enthusiastically and give him a treat. If he just stands there with a befuddled look on his face, put one finger through his collar, guide him to his bed, and, when he lies down, praise him and give him a treat. You may have to repeat this process several times until he responds to the command.

When your dog responds reliably from 3 feet, gradually and over the course of several sessions, increase the distance from the bed, as well as the length of time — up to 30 minutes — you want him to stay there. If he gets up without being released, just put him back (finger through the collar).

The Go Lie Down command, although practical, isn't the most exciting exercise. Use common sense, and don't make it drudgery.

You must release him from the spot when he can move again. If you forget, he'll get into the habit of releasing himself, thereby undermining the purpose of the exercise.

Dashing Your Dog's Dashing Habits

Almost as annoying as unrestrained greeting behavior, but far more dangerous, is the dog's habit of dashing through doors just because they're open, racing up and down stairs — ahead of or behind you — and jumping in and out of the car without permission. These behaviors are dangerous to your dog because she may find herself in the middle of the road and get run over. They're dangerous to you because you may get knocked over or down the stairs.

Prevent such potential accidents by teaching your dog to sit and stay while you open the door and to wait until you tell her it's okay to go out.

Door and stair manners

After your dog knows the Sit-Stay, you can easily teach her door manners:

1. **Put your dog on leash, using the dead ring of the training collar, and review the Sit-Stay test described in "Teaching the Basics" earlier in the chapter.**

2. **Neatly fold the leash, accordion style, into your left hand, and approach the closed door you normally use to let her out.**

   Follow the same procedure as you did for sequence 1 of the Sit-Stay. Place yourself in such a way that you can open the door without your dog having to get out of its way.

3. **With a little upward tension on the collar, tell her to stay and open the door.**

   Release the tension, and she should stay. If she doesn't, apply a little upward tension. Close the door and try again.

4. **When your dog stays without any tension on the leash facing the open door, slowly walk through the door.**

   If she tries to follow, apply upward tension on the leash to remind her to stay. Repeat until she stays without having to be reminded.

5. **Walk through the door and release her so she can follow you.**

6. **Repeat the entire sequence off leash, beginning with Step 1.**

You'll find that after several repetitions, she begins to get the message and will sit and stay on her own as you approach the door.

Motion means more to dogs than words, so make sure that you stand still when releasing your dog. For this exercise, you don't want her to associate your moving with the release. Dogs are also time conscious, so vary the length of time you make her wait before releasing her.

Some people prefer to go through the doorway first, while others want the dog to go through first. It makes no difference, as long as your dog stays until you release her. Practice through doors your dog uses regularly, including the car door, especially when exiting the car. Every time you make her sit and stay, you reinforce your position as pack leader and the one in charge.

If you have stairs, start teaching her to stay at the bottom while you go up. First Sit her and tell her to Stay. When she tries to follow, put her back and start again. Practice until you can go all the way up the stairs with her waiting at the bottom before you release her to follow. Repeat the same procedure for going down the stairs.

Book IV

Training, Agility, and Shows

After your dog has been trained to wait at one end of the stairs, you'll discover that she'll anticipate the release. She'll jump the gun and get up just as you're thinking about releasing her. Before long, she'll stay only briefly and release herself when she chooses. It may happen almost as soon as she grasps the idea, or it may take a few weeks or even months, but it will happen.

When it does, stop whatever you're doing and put her back, use the stairs, turn, count to ten, and release her. Don't let her get into the habit of releasing herself. Consistency is just as important here as it is in teaching any other exercise.

The doorbell and guests

Your dog now knows to sit and stay when you open the door. It's doubtful, however, that he'll obey these commands when the doorbell rings or someone knocks on the door. The doorbell usually causes an immediate charge amid barking. Even though most people want their dog to display his protective side, they then also want him to stop, sit, and stay so they can answer the door.

To accomplish this goal, you need to enlist the aid of a friend or neighbor to ring the doorbell.

1. **Agree on a time and then put your dog on leash.**

   When the bell rings and your dog goes through his antics, tell him to Sit and Stay.

   To help make your helper's arrival as traditional as possible, have her ring the doorbell only once. Ask her to wait for you to open the door.

2. **Start to open the door, and when your dog gets up, which he surely will, reinforce the Sit-Stay with a check (a quick pull of the leash).**

   If your dog is an excitable soul, you may have to put him on the live ring of his training collar before he takes you seriously. Less excitable dogs catch on after two or three attempts.

3. **When your dog stays, open the door and admit your accomplice.**

   At this point, your dog wants to say hello. Again, reinforce the Stay and have your helper approach him while holding out the palm of her hand.

4. **Let your dog sniff the palm and then have your helper ignore him.**

   You may have to be right next to your dog to reinforce the Sit-Stay.

5. **You need to repeat this procedure several times until the dog is reliable and holds the Sit-Stay while you open the door.**

   Remember to release him. Successful training depends on who is more determined and persistent — you or your dog.

Paying attention to inflection

Give commands in a normal tone of voice. For example, when giving the Sit command, remember that it's "Sit!" — the command — and not "Sit?" — the question.

When releasing, say "Okay!" in a more excited tone of voice, as in, "That's it, you're all done!"

Unless impaired, a dog's sense of hearing is extremely acute, and when giving a command, there's absolutely no need to shout. In fact, the opposite is true — the more quietly you give your commands, the quicker your dog learns to pay attention to you.

The procedure to teach your dog not to jump on people is the same. Follow the same progressions as you did for the doorbell, and when he wants to jump on your helper, reinforce the Stay command. After several repetitions, he should be steady enough to try him off leash. The key to your ability to control him is a reliable Sit-Stay.

Having said that, you also need to remind your guests not to get your dog all riled up with vigorous petting or active solicitations to play. The less excitement, the better. The proper way to greet a dog on a Sit-Stay is to let him sniff the palm of the hand and perhaps give a little scratch under the chin. A dog doesn't like to have the top of his head patted any more than kids do.

When teaching a new command, you may have to repeat it several times during the initial introduction before your dog catches on. After the first session, teach him to respond to the first command. Give the command, and if nothing happens, show your dog exactly what you want by physically helping him. Consistency is the key to success.

Setting the Tone for Proper Table Manners

Teaching your dog table manners is your responsibility, and you have to remember only one rule: Don't feed the dog from the table. This concept sounds a lot simpler than it is, especially in a multiperson household. Moreover, don't ever underestimate your dog's ability to train you.

Every time you reward your dog's efforts with a treat from the table, you're systematically teaching her not to take no for an answer.

When she was a puppy, nobody thought much about occasionally slipping her something from the table. But now she is 6 months old, almost fully grown, and has started to beg at the table. Because her begging is no longer cute and is embarrassing when you have guests, the family resolves to put a stop to it.

At first, your dog doesn't believe you're serious; after all, you were the one who started it in the first place. She digs a little deeper into her repertoire of begging routines. She may sit up, nudge you, paw you, or whine in the most pathetic tone as though she's near death's door from starvation. Sure enough, little Sally takes pity on her and slips her something.

As this scenario repeats itself, often with longer intervals before someone gives in, your dog is systematically being trained to persevere at all cost and never give up. Looking at it from her point of view, you're rewarding, even encouraging, the very behavior you want to stop.

When you stop rewarding the undesired behavior (begging), your dog will stop begging at the table. As soon as you stop giving in to your dog, her efforts will decrease, until over time, and provided you don't have a relapse, she'll stop begging altogether. You have extinguished the undesired behavior by refusing to reward it.

You can also save yourself all this aggravation by teaching your dog the Go Lie Down command so you can enjoy your meals in peace. (See "Go lie down, doggy!" earlier in this chapter.)

Walking Your Dog

Taking your dog for a nice, long walk is balm for the soul and good exercise for both of you, provided he doesn't drag you down the street. Teaching him to walk on a loose leash makes your strolls with your dog a pleasure rather than a chore.

You want to be able to take your dog for a walk on leash and have him remain within the length of his leash without pulling. A leisurely stroll is an important daily routine, and for many dogs, it's the only opportunity to get some fresh air.

Even better from the dog's perspective is a good run in the park or the woods. For this privilege, your dog has to learn to come when called. You can teach him to respond to the Come command by playing the Recall Game.

Another command you want your dog to learn is Leave It. The command tells the dog to ignore whatever interests him at the time. The object of his interest can be a cat, another dog, a person, or something on the ground. Leave It is especially useful when your dog discovers something disgusting he perceives as edible.

Even if you don't ordinarily take him for walks, the well-trained dog knows how to walk on a leash without pulling your arms out. For example, at least once a year, you have to take him to the vet. If he's been trained to walk on leash, the visit will go much more smoothly than if he bounces off the end of the leash like a kangaroo.

Dogs pull on a leash because they're more interested in the sights and scents in their environment than in you. Your job is to teach your dog to become aware of and respect your existence at the other end of the leash.

Born to pull

To teach your dog not to pull, you need her training collar, her leash, and a few treats. Attach the leash to the live ring of the training collar (or to the gentle leader). Take her to an area without too many distractions — you don't need other people and dogs (especially loose dogs) in the vicinity right now — and where you can walk in a straight line or in a circle (about 30 feet in diameter).

Perform these steps:

1. **Put the loop of the leash over the thumb of your right hand and make a fist.**

2. **Place your left hand directly under your right.**

   Hold the leash in both hands as though it were a baseball bat. Plant both hands firmly against your belt buckle.

3. **Say "Let's go" and start walking.**

4. **Just before she gets to the end of the leash, say "Buddy, easy," (using her name instead) make an about-turn to your right, and walk in the opposite direction.**

   Be sure that you keep your hands firmly planted. As a safety precaution, don't put your entire hand through the loop of the leash or wrap it around your hand. If your dog catches you unaware and makes a dash, she may cause you to fall. By having the loop over your thumb, you can just let go, and it'll slide off.

5. **Step 2 produces a tug on your dog's collar and turns her in the new direction.**

   As she scampers to catch up with you, tell her what a clever dog she is, and give her a treat. Before you know it, she'll be ahead of you again, and you'll have to repeat the procedure. When you make your turn, do it with determination. Be sure that you keep your hands firmly planted against your belt buckle. Make your turn, and keep walking in the new direction. Don't look back, and don't worry about her; she'll quickly catch up. Remember to praise and reward her when she does.

The first few times you try this exercise, you'll be a little late — she's already leaning into her collar. Try it again. Concentrate on your dog, and learn to anticipate when you have to make the turn. Always give her a chance to respond by saying, "Buddy, easy" before you make the turn. You need to repeat this sequence several times over the course of a few training sessions until she understands that you don't want her to pull. Your goal is to teach her to walk within the perimeter of her leash without pulling.

Most dogs quickly learn to respect the leash, and with an occasional reminder, they become a pleasure to take for a walk. Some, on the other hand, don't seem to get it. If your dog seems particularly dense about this simple concept, or if the training collar or gentle leader just don't cut it, you may need to use a *pinch* or *prong collar* (see Chapter 6 of Book I for more on pinch collars). Put your dog in a position where you can praise her.

How readily your dog responds to her collar depends on these factors:

- How distracted she is by what's going on around her, including scents on the ground
- Her size and weight in relation to your size and weight
- Her personality
- Her touch sensitivity

The pinch collar is an equalizer for these factors. It lets you enjoy training your dog without becoming frustrated or angry. Your dog, in turn, will thank you for maintaining a positive attitude and for praising her when she responds correctly.

Heeling on leash

Heeling and walking on a loose leash are two different exercises. When you take your dog for a walk to give him exercise or to do his business, he's on his own time. He can sniff, look around, or just aimlessly wander about, as long as he doesn't pull. For those times when you walk him on a busy sidewalk or in an area with traffic, he needs to learn the Heel command.

Heeling means your dog has to walk at your left side, the traditional position, while paying strict attention to you and staying with you as you change direction or pace. When your dog is heeling, he's on your time, not his own. His responsibility is to focus on you, and you have to teach him to accept that responsibility. He has to learn to heel whether you make a right turn or a left turn, do an about-face turn, run, or walk slowly. The key to teaching heeling is to get him to pay attention to you.

Heeling is used for walking your dog in traffic — when you need absolute control — and for competitive obedience events. The American Kennel Club (AKC) definition of heeling is walking "close to the left side of the handler without swinging wide, lagging, forging, or crowding," either on a loose leash or off leash.

Teaching your dog to sit at heel

Before teaching your dog to heel with both of you walking, you're going to teach him what to do when you stop, which is called the Automatic Sit at Heel:

1. **Attach your leash to the gentle leader/head collar or to the live ring of your dog's training collar and have him sit at your left side with both of you facing in the same direction while you put the leash over your right shoulder.**

2. **Say "Buddy, heel."**

3. **Take a step forward on your right foot, and then a step with the left past the right; drop down on your right knee, put your right hand against your dog's chest, and fold him into a Sit at Heel position.**

Use the same technique to sit your dog described in Chapter 2 of Book IV, and avoid the temptation to push down on his rear. Keep your hands in place as you tell him how clever he is.

Your dog already knows the Sit command (right?), but you're now showing him exactly where you want him to sit. Practice the Sit at Heel about five times or until both of you feel comfortable with this maneuver (see Figure 3-2).

Teaching heeling

To teach heeling, choose a location relatively free of distractions (preferably a confined area, such as your backyard), and follow these steps:

1. **Attach your leash to the live ring of your dog's training collar and have him sit at your left side with both of you facing in the same direction while you put the leash over your right shoulder.**

   You need to allow about 4 inches of slack so there's no tension on the leash when you start.

2. **Make a funnel with both hands around the leash.**

   Keep both hands about waist high and close to your body. The object is not to touch the leash until necessary.

Book IV

Training, Agility, and Shows

Figure 3-2:
Preparing
to teach
heeling on
leash.

3. **In a pleasant, upbeat tone of voice, say "Buddy, heel" and start to walk.**

   Move out briskly, as though you're late for an appointment. Walk in a large, clockwise circle or in a straight line.

4. **When your dog leaves your left side, close your hands around the leash and bring him back to Heel position.**

   You'll notice that as soon as both of you are in motion, your dog wants to get ahead of you. Close your hands on the leash, and firmly bring him back to your left side. Work on keeping his shoulder in line with your left hip. Anytime he gets out of position, bring him back and tell him how clever he is.

5. **After about ten steps, stop and place him in a Sit at Heel, and verbally praise him.**

   It'll take you a few tries to get the hang of it. At first, you'll be a little slow on the uptake. He's joyfully bounding ahead of you, the leash has fallen off your shoulder, and you're scrambling to get it back. Just start over and work on *anticipating* what your dog is going to do.

When heeling your dog, walk briskly and with determination, as though you're trying to catch the next train home. The more energy you put into your pace, the easier it is to keep your dog's attention focused on you. If you dawdle, so does your dog. By paying attention to your dog, you'll discover when you need to bring him back to Heel. If you can see his tail, you've waited too long.

Your initial goal is to be able to heel your dog for ten paces without having to touch the leash. How long it takes you depends on these factors:

- ✔ Your dog
- ✔ What your dog was bred to do
- ✔ His response to the training collar
- ✔ Your attitude

Generally, if you have a Shetland Sheepdog, you'll reach that goal in maybe five minutes; if you have a Fox Terrier, you'll work on it considerably longer.

When your dog heels without your having to touch the leash for ten paces, gradually increase the number of steps before a halt. Bring him back to Heel whenever necessary, and then praise him. After about five training sessions, he should be getting the idea, at least in an area relatively free from distractions.

Changing direction

When you and your dog have pretty much gotten the hang of heeling, your next step is to introduce her to changes of direction while heeling. In this section, you find out about the three essential turns — a right turn, an about-turn to the right, and a left turn.

Right turn

To stay with you when you're making a right turn, your dog needs to speed up. At this stage in your training, she isn't yet giving you 100 percent of her attention, and you're going to anticipate that she needs help with the right turn.

If you want your dog to pay attention to you, you have to pay attention to your dog. Discovering how to anticipate what she's going to do is the first step to successful heeling. Just before you make the turn, enthusiastically say her name, make the turn, and keep moving. Using her name causes her to look up at you, and she then notices that you're changing direction, which causes her to stay with you. Without giving her that cue, as you make the turn and go one way, she'll probably keep going the other direction.

About-turn

An about-turn is a right turn times two. When you make your turn, keep your feet together so she can keep up. As you did for the right turn, use her name just before you make the turn, to encourage her to stay with you.

If your dog has a particularly difficult time remaining at your side for the right turn or about-turn, you can use a treat or other object of interest to help guide her around. Hold the treat in your right hand as you're heeling. Before you make the turn, show it to your dog by bringing the treat directly in front of her nose and using it to guide her around the turn, and then give her the treat.

This approach has a potential drawback. Some dogs become overly stimulated when they know you have a treat in your hand. Make no mistake about it, she knows. If you see that your dog becomes difficult to control under such circumstances, you may want to eliminate use of the treat. The hassle isn't worth the potential benefit.

Left turn

To make the left turn without bumping into her, she needs to slow down as you make the turn and then resume normal speed after you make the turn. Just before you make the turn, slow down. With your left hand, draw back on the leash, make the turn, bring your hand back to position, and resume your normal brisk pace. Practice heeling and doing the turns for a few times as a regular part of your daily outings.

Changing pace

You need to teach your dog to change pace with you while heeling. He has to learn that whether you walk slowly or quickly, he must stay in Heel position.

For the slow pace, cut the speed of your pace in half, but maintain the same length of stride. As you go into the slow pace, draw back on the leash to keep your dog in Heel position. For the fast pace, double the speed of your normal pace, again keeping the length of your stride the same. Just before you go into a fast pace, use your dog's name in an excited tone of voice to encourage him to stay with you.

You're still working with the leash over your shoulder. By now, you'll also be able to tell whether he is actually heeling. If heeling properly, he doesn't swing wide on right turns and about-turns, bump into you on the left turn, fall behind you as you go into a fast pace, or get ahead of you as you go into a slow pace.

Winning the Game of Coming When Called

One of the greatest joys of owning a dog is going for a walk in a park or the woods and letting her run, knowing she'll come when called. A dog who doesn't come when called is a prisoner of her leash and, if she gets loose, a danger to herself and others. This section offers some proven rules for helping you and your dog realize the benefits of coming when called.

Follow these basic rules to encourage your dog to come to you when you call her:

- **Exercise, exercise, exercise.** Many dogs don't come when called because they don't get enough exercise. At every chance, they run off and make the most of this unexpected freedom by staying out as long as possible.

  Consider what your dog was bred to do, and that tells you how much exercise she needs. Just putting her out in the backyard isn't good enough. You have to participate. Think of it this way: Exercise is as good for you as it is for your dog. A good source for exercise requirements is *The Roger Caras Dog Book: The Complete Guide to Every AKC Breed,* 3rd Edition (M. Evans & Co.).

- **Whenever your dog comes to you, be nice to her.** One of the quickest ways to teach your dog not to come to you is to call her to punish her or to do something the dog perceives as unpleasant. Most dogs consider it unpleasant to be called just before they're left alone in the house or given a pill. In these circumstances, go and get your dog instead of calling her to you.

  Another example of teaching your dog not to come is taking her for a run in the park and calling her to you only when it's time to go home. Repeating this sequence several times teaches the dog that the party is over. Soon she may become reluctant to return to you when called because she isn't ready to end the fun. You can prevent this kind of unintentional training by calling her to you several times during her outing, sometimes giving her a treat, sometimes just a word of praise. Then let her romp again.

- **Teach her to Come as soon as you get her.** Ideally, you acquired your dog as a puppy, which is the best time to teach her to come when called. Start right away. But remember, sometime between 4 and 8 months of age, your puppy begins to realize there's a big, wide world out there. While she's going through this stage, keep her on leash so she doesn't learn that she can ignore you when you call her.

Book IV

Training, Agility, and Shows

✔ **When in doubt, keep her on leash.** Work to anticipate when your dog is likely not to come. You may be tempting fate by trying to call her after she has spotted a cat, another dog, or a jogger. Of course, sometimes you goof and let her go just as another dog appears out of nowhere.

Resist the urge to make a complete fool of yourself by bellowing "Come" a million times. The more often you holler "Come," the quicker she learns she can ignore you when she's off leash. Instead, patiently go to her and put her on leash. Don't get angry with her after you've caught her, or you'll make her afraid of you, and she'll run away when you try to catch her the next time.

✔ **Make sure that your dog always comes to you and lets you touch her collar before you reward.** Touching her collar prevents the dog from developing the annoying habit of playing "catch" — coming toward you and then dancing around you, just out of reach. So teach her to let you touch her collar before you offer a treat or praise.

Training your dog to come when called

You need two people, one hungry dog, one 6-foot leash, plenty of small treats, and two whistles (optional). Some people prefer to train their dog to come to a whistle instead of using the verbal command "Come." Some people train their dog to do both.

What works best depends on the dog, and you may want to experiment. Consider trying the verbal command first, because you may need to call your dog sometime but don't have your whistle. You can then repeat the steps, using a whistle, which goes very quickly because your dog already has some understanding of what he's supposed to do.

For this exercise, you need to be inside the house, with your dog on a 6-foot leash. You and your partner sit on the floor, 6 feet apart, facing each other, and your partner gently restrains the dog while you hold the end of the leash.

1. **Call your dog by saying, "Buddy, come" and use the leash to guide him to you.**

   Avoid the temptation to reach for your dog.

2. **When he comes to you, put your hand through his collar, give him a treat, pet him, and praise him enthusiastically.**

   Now you can — and should — pet him so he understands how happy you are that he came to you. This situation is different from the Sit or the Down earlier in this chapter, when you want him to remain in place, and petting him will cause him to get up.

3. **Hold him and pass the leash to your partner, who says, "Buddy, come," guides the dog in, puts his hand through the collar, gives him a treat, and praises the dog.**

   Keep working on this exercise until your dog responds on his own to being called and no longer needs to be guided in with the leash.

4. **Repeat the exercise with your dog off leash, gradually increasing the distance between you and your partner to 12 feet.**

5. **Have your partner hold him by the collar while you go into another room and then call your dog.**

6. **When he finds you, put your hand through the collar, give him a treat, and praise him.**

   If he can't find you, *slowly* go to him, take him by the collar, and bring him to the spot where you called. Reward and praise.

7. **Have your partner go into another room and then call the dog.**

8. **Repeat the exercise until the dog doesn't hesitate in finding you or your partner in any room of the house.**

9. **Take your dog outside to a confined area, such as a fenced yard, tennis court, park, or school yard, and repeat Steps 1, 2, and 3.**

Now you're ready to practice by yourself. With your dog on leash, take him for a walk. Let him sniff around, and when he isn't paying any attention to you, call him. When he gets to you, give him a treat and make a big fuss over him. If he doesn't come, firmly check him toward you (you may have to use the live ring of his training collar), and then reward and praise him. Repeat until he comes to you every time you call him. After he's trained, you don't have to reward him with a treat every time, but do so randomly.

Adding distractions

Most dogs need to be trained to come in the face of distractions, such as other dogs, children, joggers, food, or friendly strangers. Think about the most irresistible situations for your dog, and then practice under those circumstances.

Put a 12-foot leash on your dog (you can tie two 6-foot leashes together) and take her to an area where she's likely to encounter her favorite distraction. When she spots it (jogger, bicycle, other dog, whatever), let her become thoroughly engrossed, by either watching or straining at her leash, and then call her. More than likely, she'll ignore you. Give a sharp tug on the leash and guide her back to you. Praise and pet her enthusiastically. Repeat three times per session until the dog turns and comes to you immediately when you call. If she doesn't, you may have to change your training equipment.

Some dogs quickly learn to avoid the distraction by staying close to you, which is fine. Tell her what a clever dog she is, and then try with a different distraction at another time.

Repeat in different locations with as many different distractions as you can find. Try it with someone offering your dog a tidbit as a distraction (*don't* let the dog get the treat), someone petting the dog, and anything else that may distract her. Use your imagination. Your goal is to have her respond reliably every time you call. Until she's steady on leash, she most certainly won't come off leash.

Advancing to off-leash distractions

How you approach adding off-leash distractions depends on your individual circumstances. For example, take your dog to an area where you aren't likely to encounter distractions in the form of other dogs or people. Let him off leash, and allow him to become involved in a smell in the grass or a tree. Keep the distance between you and him about 10 feet. Call him, and if he responds, praise enthusiastically and reward. If he doesn't, avoid the temptation to call him again. Don't worry; he heard you but chose to ignore you. Instead, slowly walk up to him; firmly take him by his collar, under his chin, palm up; and trot backward to the spot where you called him. Then praise and reward.

After he's reliable with this exercise, try him in an area with other distractions. If he doesn't respond, practice for the correct response with the 12-foot leash before you try him off leash again.

Can you now trust him to come to you in an unconfined area? That depends on how well you've done your homework and what your dog may encounter in the real world. Understanding your dog and what interests him helps you know when he's likely not to respond to the Come command.

Let common sense be your guide. For example, when you're traveling and have to let him out to relieve himself at a busy interstate rest stop, you'd be foolhardy to let him run loose. When in doubt, keep him on leash.

Mastering the "Leave It" Command

You'd prefer it if your dog didn't pick up anything from the ground that she perceives as potentially edible. What dogs find fascinating and, apparently, delicious, people often find disgusting. And if your dog gets hold of something rotten, she may get sick. The Leave It command is a good start for such situations.

Teaching this command is a wonderful opportunity to find out more about how your dog's thought processes work. You can truly see the wheels turning. Depending on how quickly she catches on, you may want to practice this exercise over the course of several sessions. Keep the sessions short — no more than five minutes at a time, and follow these steps:

1. **Hold a treat between your thumb and index finger.**

2. **With your palm facing up, show the treat to your dog.**

   She'll try to pry it loose. Say "Leave it," close your hand into a fist, and turn it so that your palm now faces down. (See Figure 3-3.)

3. **Observe your dog's reaction.**

   She may stare fixedly at the back of your hand, she may try to get to the treat by nuzzling or nibbling your hand, or she may start barking. Ignore all these behaviors. You're looking for the first break in her attention away from your hand. She may make eye contact with you or look away.

4. **The instant she breaks her attention away from your hand, say "Good" and give her the treat.**

5. **Repeat until your dog looks at you or away from your hand when you give the command and turn your hand over.**

   You're teaching her that looking at you and not at your hand is rewarded with a treat.

6. **To find out whether she is responding to the command or to the turning of your hand, repeat Step 1 without turning your hand.**

   If she responds, praise and reward. If she doesn't, close your hand into a fist and wait for the break in attention. Repeat until she responds to the command.

7. **Make yourself comfortable on the floor and show your dog a treat; put it on the floor and cover it with your hand.**

   When her attention is on your hand or she tries to get to the treat, say "Leave it."

Figure 3-3:
Working on
the Leave It
command.

8. **Wait for the break in attention, and then praise and reward.**

9. **Repeat Steps 6 and 7, but cover the treat with just your index finger. Then try it when placing the treat between your index and middle finger.**

10. **When successful, place the treat 1 inch in front of your hand, and repeat Steps 6 and 7.**

    Here you need to be watchful: She may be faster at getting to the treat than you can cover it.

11. **Put the dog on leash and stand next to her (Heel position), neatly fold the leash into your left hand, and hold your hand as close to her collar as is comfortable without any tension on the leash.**

    Make sure that the amount of slack in the leash isn't so much that her mouth can reach the floor.

12. **Hold the treat in your right hand and show it to her, and then casually drop the treat.**

    When she tries to get to the treat, say "Leave it." If she responds, praise her, pick up the treat, and give it to her. If she doesn't, check straight up. Repeat until she obeys the command.

    Test her response by taking off the leash and dropping a treat. If she makes a dive for it, don't attempt to beat her to it or yell "No." She's telling you she needs more work on leash.

Now go outside — but first you need to do some preparation. Select a food item that's readily visible to you in the grass or the ground, such as some crackers or popcorn. Drop four or five pieces of food in the area where you're taking her for the big test. Put some of your regular treats in your pocket, and take her for a walk on leash in the area where you left the food. As soon as her nose goes to the food, say "Leave it." If she responds, praise enthusiastically and give her a treat. If she doesn't, check straight up.

If she manages to snag a cracker or kernel of popcorn, you're too slow on the uptake. Practice walking around the food-contaminated area until she ignores the food on command.

Your dog should now know and obey the Leave It command. Test her off leash, and her response will tell you whether she needs more work. Still, as with any other command, you need to review it with her periodically on leash.

Book IV

Training, Agility, and Shows

Chapter 4

Teaching Your Dog Tricks

*L*ike people, every dog has different likes and dislikes, games they enjoy, and routines that they count on. When your training comes from a consistent, patient, and understanding place that takes these canine preferences into consideration, your dog will master tricks and activities quickly and enthusiastically.

Teaching interactive skills is your first trick. And as you'll see, it isn't complicated at all. In this chapter, you find out some tricks you can teach so your dog uses those barking, chewing, and jumping instincts in a socially acceptable way, and some simple tricks and games you can play together.

Before you dive into the dog tricks in this chapter, keep the following tips in mind:

- ✔ **Know when to practice.** Some games are designed to burn energy. Play these when your dog is full of beans. Other tricks are just for fun; when your dog catches on, she'll want to practice as much as you.

- ✔ **Keep the sessions short and sweet — no more than five to ten minutes.** Several short lessons are better than one long one. With a positive attitude and the building-block approach, your dog can master these techniques in no time.

- ✔ **Try a clicker.** In Chapter 2, I discuss the use of a clicker. Although this little hand-held device isn't mandatory for trick training, it can be useful when teaching complex tricks like the ones in this chapter. The sharp sound paired with a tasty food reward helps your dog know exactly which behavior you're after.

> ✔ **Avoid forcing your dog to do certain tricks.** Tricks like rolling over and begging are very entertaining, but please don't force your dog if she's not into it. Some dogs love to act silly; others don't or can't do it without discomfort. How do you know? If your dog naturally rolls around or easily sits back on her haunches, you have the green light! If rolling on the floor is beneath her standards or physical capabilities, don't force it.

Some Simple Moves: Tricks for a Happy, Loving Dog

One of the fastest ways to get addicted to trick training is to teach your dog some easy tricks that showcase that puppy love. And dogs, like people, love to succeed, so the surest way to get your dog addicted to trick training is to start with a few surefire winners. Here are a few tricks that everyone can master — people and dogs of all ages.

Wag Your Tail

If you're happy and you know it, wag your tail. Teaching your dog how to wag his tail on command is so easy. If a tennis ball brings the tail into action, hold up a ball; if food gets the tail to wag, use that. Catch your dog wagging, praise him for it, and think of a clever cue word to command each time (like "Wag"). Use your cue word in a positive, inviting tone and watch your dog come alive.

Now add a hand signal like waving your right hand back and forth. Start out with a pronounced sweep, and then phase off until you can make small motions with your index finger.

If you're in front of a crowd, you can ask really difficult questions and tell your dog that if he agrees, all he has to do is wag his tail. It goes like this: "I'm going to ask you a hard question and if you agree, all you have to do is wag your tail. Ready? Would you like everyone to give you a hug?" Signal your dog, and voilà — a surefire crowd pleaser.

Give Me a Hug

Give Me a Hug is a breed-selective exercise. If your dog is injured, has dysplasia, or is skeletally challenged (like a Basset, a Bulldog, or a giant breed), avoid this trick. And don't forget — if your dog refuses, move on.

You can teach this command in several ways. If your dog loves to wrapher paws around you, you can reinforce this behavior when it's happening by using a clicker or you can cue your dog by luring her and pairing her cooperation with a word like "Hug." Reward your dog when she's in the hug position — this method works best for calm dogs who are not prone to excessive jumping.

For jumpy dogs, try a more sedate method. Ignore the behavior when she jumps all over you and then sit with her and organize it this way:

1. **Kneel down on the floor or sit in a chair and give your dog the "Sit" command.**

   Check to make sure that your dog is sitting square on the floor, not leaning to either side.

2. **Lift your dog's front paws gently and place them on your shoulders as you say "Hug."**

   Give your dog a thorough pet and/or a reward.

3. **Say "Okay" and help her down.**

Do Steps 1 through 3 only three times per session — stop if your dog becomes too energetic or starts to nip. Leave the leash on and give a tug on the leash as you say "Shhh!" if your dog gets too excited while on two paws. Also, try practicing "Hug" when your dog has less energy.

The silent signal for Give Me a Hug is to cross your arms over your chest and tap your shoulders with your fingers. You can demonstrate the signal each time you say "Hug." Be patient while teaching this sign language — it may take a while for your dog to make the connection.

Kisses!

Getting your dog to give you kisses is a real delight — unless you hate dog kisses. You can teach this trick quickly by association, simply saying "Kisses" whenever you're getting a licking.

If your dog is licking out of control, make it more of a two-step process:

1. **First teach your dog "Enough" to signal him to stop licking.**

   Keep a short (8- to 12-inch) leash on your dog and say "Enough" in a pleasant but serious tone. If your dog doesn't listen, tug the leash as you withdraw your attention.

   When discouraging licking, look away and not at your dog. If you look at your dog, you're essentially saying, "Do it again!"

2. **Teach your dog to lick on cue.**

   To teach your dog to lick you, take a frozen stick of butter and rub it on the back of your hand. During a period when your dog is calm, go to him, extend your hand, and command "Kisses" as he licks your hand. When you've had enough, just say so — "Enough!"

   To teach your dog to give someone else a kiss, such as the next-door neighbor or a member of your audience, use a stick of butter during the teaching phase. Ask a few people to help you out, and rub the backs of their hands with butter before you instruct your dog to give them a kiss. Have them extend their hands to your dog and say "Kisses" as you point to the buttered hand. Soon your dog will be seeking out hands to kiss, butter coated or not. This trick is handy if you have kids over; putting butter on their hands encourages licks, not jumping.

When your dog knows the trick, you can add a hand signal: Rub your right index finger on the back of your left hand, as though your finger is your dog's tongue.

Introducing Interactive Play

Dogs love to play. The more you can let go and roll with their enthusiasm, the more fun you'll have. Some games, like tug of war and wrestling, inspire confrontation, so use the games in this section instead to increase your fun. Interactive activities like Hide and Seek and Catch Me can build your bond and inspire respect.

Hide and Seek

Hide and Seek is a great game and also reinforces that indispensable "Come" command. You need one to four players and a treat cup, and your dog needs to know his name and the "Come" command. "Stay" also comes in handy.

Start with this game inside, one-on-one:

1. **While your dog is occupied, go into an adjoining room with a treat cup; call out his name and shake the cup.**

   Use a disposable plastic cup filled halfway with small treats, such as Cheerios.

2. **When you hear him running, say "Come" clearly.**

   Praise him, offer a treat, and let him return to whatever he was doing, putting the treat cup away — or he may never leave your side.

3. **Increase the level of difficulty by calling him from two rooms away.**

   You should still be in sight, not hard to find.

4. **After a couple of days of hiding in plain sight around the house and calling from room to room, go into the adjoining room and hide behind a chair.**

After your dog catches on to this game, you can increase the difficulty of your hiding places and add another teammate. Eventually, your two-legged geniuses can play a game to see who gets found first and who gets found last. Gradually phase off using your treat cups.

Where's Sally? The name game

Teaching your dog everyone's name couldn't be easier. Pick one person at a time and have the person sit across the room with a treat cup. Instruct your dog to find that person by name. For example, say "Where's Sally?" and have Sally shake the cup the moment she hears her name. Progressively ask Sally to distance herself from you, having her in various rooms of the house so your dog will always be curious to find her location.

After your dog is eager to track Sally (and her treat cup), reintroduce her nearby — but phase off using treats. Sally can call and encourage your dog with praise instead. Soon just her name will inspire enthusiasm.

The Shell Game

Dogs love to be included in the Shell Game. Whether you're sitting at home or on an adventure, you can use shells, cups, or even sand piles to hide your dog's treat or toy under one of three stacks. After you shift the stacks about, ask your dog, "Where's your bone?" or "Where's your toy?" If your dog's confused, pretend to sniff each pile — he'll copy your example and find the bone or toy soon enough.

Book IV

Training, Agility, and Shows

Catch Me

Games that encourage your dog to focus on and follow you are a real prize when it comes to training and having fun. These games also reinforce the extinction of bad habits, such as nipping and jumping.

To play Catch Me, a variation of the children's game Red Light, Green Light, you need one or two players and a dog toy. Your dog needs to know "Sit," "Wait," "Down," "Stay," "Okay," and "No."

1. **Turn and face your dog from about 3 to 6 feet away; say "Catch me" and then turn and run.**

2. **After a few feet, pop back to face your dog and command "Wait!"**

3. **Treat your dog when she stops; then say "Okay, catch me," and run again.**

4. **Now that she'll stop, try another quick command like "Sit" or "Down," luring your dog into position if she's confused by the excitement.**

5. **Follow each stationary command with "Okay, catch me" to continue the game.**

6. **When you're through, tell your dog "Okay" and give her a favorite toy.**

   Keep the game short, just one or two minutes.

Some dogs get too excited or overwhelmed by this game. If yours isn't cooperating, try a different game. If she goes wild, racing in a big circle playing hard to get, guess what — this isn't the game for you.

Don't high-energy games encourage mouthing and jumping? If it escalates the dog's bad behavior uncontrollably, leave it out. If your dog enjoys the game and you can curb naughtiness with a sharp "No," then go for it. Catch Me is a fun activity and sharpens your dog's impulses, teaching her to follow — but not jump or nip at you.

Digging for China

Have you considered hiring your dog out to the local excavating company? The prerequisite, of course, is to teach him to dig on command. Equip yourself with a clicker, garden gloves, and treats, and then follow these directions to play Digging for China:

1. **Find a private area in your yard to teach your dog to dig; bury some treats 1 inch under the ground to pique his interest.**

2. **Start blissfully digging yourself, unearthing the treats as you go and handing them to your dog.**

3. **Reward your dog for joining in, saying "Go dig!"**

4. **Now try hiding a few treats or a toy before bringing your dog to his digging spot; then give the command "Go dig."**

   Like an archeologist discovering treasures, he'll unearth them with obvious delight.

You may be worried that without your approval, your dog will unearth your shrubbery and carpets. However, although there's no guarantee, most dogs who are reinforced for digging in one area usually stick to it. By teaching your dog to dig in specific locations, you may be able to discourage him from digging in other places.

Playing with the Plain Ol' Paw

Nothing like starting with a classic: Giving a paw. Some dogs are naturally predisposed to giving a paw, so much so that you're probably wondering how to teach "No paw" (see the sidebar "Getting dogs to keep their paws to themselves").

After your dog masters "Paw," you can really start being creative, teaching her to wave, give high fives, and turn out the lights. But everyone's got to get started somewhere — after you master the basic "Paw," the sky's the limit.

Doing the basic Paw

To teach the basic "Paw," first get your dog (on a leash if he's antsy) and some favorite treats, and go into a quiet room. Then do the following:

1. **Kneel or sit in front of your dog.**

2. **Command "Sit," positioning your dog's hindquarters if necessary, and offer praise.**

3. **You can try two methods at this point:**

   - **Physical:** Using a thumb, press your dog's shoulder muscle gently until his front leg lifts. Then lay your hand under his foot pad as you say "Paw."

   - **Treat-based:** Hold a treat in a closed hand a couple of inches in front of your dog's foot. When he paws it, open your hand to reward him. With each repetition of this step, gradually raise your hand to your dog's elbow. Now add the Paw step. Keep the treat in your other hand, as you extend your closed hand. As he hits your hand, say "Paw" and gently grasp his paw with an opened palm. Treat him the moment your palm connects to his paw.

4. **Now signal and command "Paw."**

   Is he catching on? If not, help him complete the Paw by pressing his shoulder blade gently. Praise him warmly, whether he caught on or needed your help.

The hand signal for Paw is to stretch out your hand, as if to shake hands.

Paw variations: Shaking things up

Shaking paws is great, but you can easily teach a few variations that will delight you, your pup, and any onlookers. In this section, you find some new cue words and variations on the basic Paw.

Say Thank You

Hold out your hand as if to shake hands. At first, say, "Paw — Thank you." Fairly soon she'll respond to both your signal and your new directional cue. Praise your dog for placing her paw in your hand and give her a treat.

Now get a human pal to help you out. As your human pal extends a hand, command "Paw — Say thank you" and encourage your dog to offer her paw to your friend. Now you're ready to spread your dog's good manners everywhere.

The hand signal for Say Thank You is the same as for the Paw trick — extend your hand to the dog with your palm up.

Wave

A dog who knows how to wave hello and goodbye — miraculous, you say? Actually, it's not hard to teach at all. Here's how:

1. **Place your dog in a sit-stay and show her that you have a treat in your left hand.**

2. **Standing in front of her, say, "Paw" and signal with your right hand (as if you were going to shake hands).**

3. **As she lifts her paw, wave your signal hand and say "Paw — Wave" as you reward her with the treat.**

4. **Repeat this, slowly weaning off the initial Paw signal in place of a wave signal, simply waving to your dog while saying, "Wave hello" or "Wave bye-bye!"**

Other One

As your dog gets into the Paw trick, you may notice that he favors eitherhis left or right paw. To prevent having a one-dimensional dog, teach the cue Other One. Here's how:

1. **Say "Paw" and lovingly praise your dog when he raises his paw.**

2. **Extend your hand to the other paw and say, "Other one," using the treat-on-on-the-floor trick or shoulder press to inspire hiscooperation.**

   Hold the treat in a closed hand a couple of inches in front of your dog's foot until he paws it, or press the shoulder muscle gently with your thumb until he lifts his paw, as described earlier in the section "Doing the basic Paw."

3. **If your dog lifts his favored paw, use a sound such as "Nope" and repeat your original request while you put pressure on the shoulder muscle of the other leg.**

   When your dog lifts the other paw, praise, treat, and give him a big hug (if your dog likes that sort of thing).

The hand signal for Other One is to stretch out your hand to the specified paw.

Right Paw, Left Paw

By using Other One to get your dog to pay attention to which hand you extend, you can pull off a trick that makes it seem as if your dog can tell her right paw from her left, the little genius!

While in a quiet room, decide which paw your dog gives most frequently. For this example, say it's the right paw. Exaggerate the Paw hand signal as you hold your right hand to her right side and say, "Right paw." Praise and offer a treat. Have your dog do this right three times in a row so she gets plenty of positive reinforcement. If by chance your dog swaps and offers a left paw, say "Nope" and wait to reward until she offers the right paw.

Now for the other paw. Exaggerate your hand signal toward the left side and say "Left paw." Your dog will probably try the right paw. If she does, say "Nope — Other One." Show her physically if you have to. Practice three lefts, and then stop.

The next time you go to practice, start with "Right paw," accentuating your signal. Help your dog out if you must. Do three rights; then three lefts, accentuating the left signal. Soon your dog will catch on, and you can mix it up: two rights, two lefts, two rights, one left, one right, and so on. Vary the pattern each time and keep these mind-puzzler sessions short. As your dog becomes clued in to your body language, you can exaggerate the hand signal less and less.

Book IV

Training, Agility, and Shows

Celebrating success: High Five and Go for Ten

Getting your dog to give you five — or ten — is easy to teach, and dogs love it. Afterward, you'll both have something to celebrate. Here's how these tricks work:

- **High Five:** To teach High Five, simply hold your hand palm out at the same height you normally do when you say, "Paw." If the command High Five gets a puzzled look, then say, "Paw" to request the action and say, "High Five" as the dog's paw makes contact with your hand. Drop the Paw command when your dog makes the connection. Slowly lift your hand higher to accentuate the High Five.

  When asking for the High Five, stay within your dog's height capabilities. If you hold your hand too high, your dog will leap up to try to please you, but you don't want to encourage jumping. High Five is a three-paws-on-the-floor trick.

- **Go for Ten:** This trick involves two hands and two paws. When saying "Go for ten," keep your hands at about the level of your dog's head. Any higher will encourage jumping. At first your dog may only reach up to hit you with one paw . . . after all, that's what he's used to. Reaching up will encourage him to stretch up and bring his other paw off the floor — at this point, tuck your free hand under his paw and praise him the moment both paws connect with your hands.

  Some dogs simply can't sit up on their hind legs. You know if your dog can't do Go for Ten. So what? You love him anyway.

Hit It! Targeting paw tricks with lights, doors, and music

After your dog knows how to Paw, you can teach her to target an object and then use the object's placement to help her learn to play music, close doors, and work the light fixtures . . . before you know it, your dog will be saving you a bundle in electric bills.

Hit It

After your dog knows Paw (see the earlier section, "Doing the basic Paw"), establish a target object, such as a container lid or business card. Then do the following to teach your dog to strike it with his paw:

1. **Present the target object in the palm of your hand and command "Paw."**

2. **The moment your dog hits the object, say, "Hit It"; give your dog a treat (or click and treat) and offer praise.**

3. **Phase off holding the object flat in your hand, holding it at the same level but pinched between your thumb and forefinger.**

   Repeat this until you're able to hold the object out and your dog will paw it when directed with the Hit It command.

Your next goal is to place the object in various locations to encourage your dog to do things like turn out the lights and close doors. This section includes three tricks that do just that.

Close It

After your dog learns how to Hit It, you can parlay that one behavior into a whole host of cool, helpful, and unique tricks, such as closing the cabinet, turning out the lights, and playing the piano! Though these tricks might sound like magic, it all boils down to the placement of the target object.

When teaching your dog to close cabinets and doors, she may be initially startled by the sound the door makes as it shuts. Before asking her to tidy up for you, place her in a Sit-Stay next to the hinge and give her a treat as you open and shut the door gently. She will soon get used to the sound of its opening and shutting.

At first, hold the target object near a cabinet door at what would be a normal Paw level for your dog — about her elbow. Do a couple Paws (see the earlier section, "Doing the basic Paw"), holding your hand near the door. Next, encourage her to paw the object by saying "Hit it." If she has a light touch, encourage her to really whack the object by egging her on and withholding the reward until she does.

Next, tape the object to the outside of the opened cabinet door. Kneel close to your dog and point to the object. Reward each attempt to strike the door with her paw. After two days, withhold the reward until a successful closing.

Over the course of four days, gradually start combining the new command with the familiar cue: Hit It — Close It. Phase out the Hit It command so Close It will mean just that.

Lights

Teaching your dog to turn out the lights requires blending the Hit It command with a jumping sequence. If your dog is tall and agile enough to reach the switch, he'll be more than happy to oblige you.

Book IV

Training, Agility, and Shows

To begin, get a light switch like the ones on your wall. Use your target object to teach your dog to Paw It and to get comfortable with its feel. Tape the target object above the fixture and hold the fixture in your hand initially.

At first, hold the switch at a normal Paw level — about your dog's elbow — and pair the command Hit It with "Lights" as you encourage his cooperation with praise and rewards. This will seem awkward at first for your dog, who isn't used to things moving when he paws them. Use your praise to encourage him and rewards to emphasize the moment his paw connects with the switch.

Separately teach your dog to jump up on the wall by the switch. Pat the wall and teach Up, guiding your dog there with a treat if necessary. At first, all your dog needs to do to earn a reward is jump up and stand against the wall.

Gradually lift your practice switch higher and higher until it's at the height of the real switch. Each time, prompt your dog with the command Hit It — Lights. At first, reward and praise your dog if he touches the switch. After four days of practice, reward him only if he activates the switch. When he's got it down pat, phase off the Hit It command and emphasize Lights.

Now that you've connected the dots, try this trick in the real world. Move to other switches in your home, using the pretend switch step if your dog acts confused.

Piano

All you need to teach your dog to play the piano is a keyboard, a target object, and the Paw command. Here's how it works:

1. **Teach your dog to paw a target object.**

   See the earlier section, "Hit it: Targeting paw tricks with lights, doors, and music."

2. **Place the keyboard on the ground and place your target object on it.**

3. **Pair the command Hit It with "Piano."**

4. **Move the object to various spots on the piano.**

The hand signal for this trick is to pretend your fingers are tapping an imaginary keyboard.

Getting dogs to keep their paws to themselves

Is your dog too paw-expressive? It happens to the best of them. If your dog constantly paws, you have two options: Ignore her, or use a mild correction. Ignoring is self-explanatory; you may simply walk away. If that doesn't work, try one of the following corrections:

✔ Keep a short *tab* (a very short loop of leash) on your dog and snap it downward while saying, "Not now." (You can buy a short lead — 8 to 12 inches — at a pet supply store.)

✔ Say "No" and command "Sit."

Remember that dogs usually paw because they want something: a treat, a toy, or attention. Avoid giving in to your dog's pestering. You're just teaching her that it works. Wait for more mannerly behavior, such as sitting quietly or lying down, before you give your dog what she wants.

Roll Over

Dogs who are as comfortable on their backs as they are on their paws really groove with Roll Over. How will you know whether your dog qualifies? He'll roll anywhere, anytime, and often of his own volition.He'll sleep on his back. He'll scratch his back by rolling on the carpet. He'll come in with a grass-stained coat from rolling in the yard.

Although teaching Roll Over requires some patience, it demonstrates the importance of *sequencing* — breaking the sum of a trick into parts and then linking the parts to perform the trick.

Before you begin, bring your dog into a quiet room and place treats on a nearby table. Find your clicker if you're using one. Here are the three training sequences:

1. **First sequence:** Call your dog to you and put him in a Down-Stay. Kneel next to your dog and scratch his belly until he lies on one side. As he does so, say, "Roll"; then reward and praise him. Repeat this sequence 10 to 20 times until your dog responds comfortably to this direction.

2. **Second sequence:** Repeat the preceding steps. Then take a treat and circle it from under your dog's chin to just behind his ear. As his head twists to follow the treat, his body will rock to the side. Say, "Roll," offer a treat, and praise him. Repeat this sequence 10 to 20 times until your dog responds quickly.

Book IV

Training, Agility, and Shows

3. **Final sequence:** Repeat the preceding steps. Now circle the treat slowly backward over the back of your dog's head as you say, "Roll Over."

When your dog is first learning to roll over, he may need some help. Guide him over by gently pushing his top front leg to the other side as you say the command.

Click (or say "Yes!") and give your dog a treat whenever he does a full roll, whether you helped your dog or not.

As soon as your dog gets the full roll sequence, practice a few times and then quit on a high note.

Roll Over with a hand signal

When your dog is comfortable rolling over, you can teach a simple hand signal to prompt this trick:

1. **Continue to kneel next to her when commanding "Roll Over," but lean backward in the direction you want her to roll.**

2. **Hold your index finger parallel to the floor, and draw small circles in the air as you give your verbal command.**

3. **Help your dog initially if she seems confused, praising her as you assist and jumping up with her to end the trick.**

4. **As soon as she responds to the cue without your help, stand up and give the command and the hand signal, always accentuating your hand signal.**

Your end goal is to direct your dog from a standing position. Gradually move up from a kneeling position to a one-knee bend to eventually standing up, as you overaccentuate your hand signal.

After your dog seems able to follow the command, you can teach her to keep on rolling or to jump up after the first roll. Using enthusiastic body language, you can easily communicate when you want your dog to jump up. Toss your arms in the air and jump like a bunny when you're encouraging your dog to leap up.

If you want your dog to continue rolling, lean in the direction she's rolling and exaggerate your signal initially.

Pump your clenched fist in an enthusiastic hooray to signal your finishing roll!

Roll Over from a distance

When your dog knows the hand signal — drawing circles in the air with your index finger — you're ready for control at a distance. Here's how to cue your dog to roll from farther away:

1. **Place your dog in a Down-Stay and stand back 3 feet.**

2. **Use your hand signal, leaning your body in the direction you're sending your dog, as you command "Roll Over."**

   If your dog looks confused, go to him calmly and help out, getting back into your starting position as he finishes the trick.

   When he performs on his own, give him a jackpot — a whole fistful — of treats and end with a fun game.

3. **Back up 2 feet at a time during your subsequent practice sessions, until your dog will roll over at a reasonable distance from you.**

Visualization helps you teach a trick, so create a picture in your mind of your dog performing the trick flawlessly. Can dogs read minds? Who can prove they can't?

Ain't Too Proud to Beg

"Beg," "Ask nicely," "Put up your paws" — take your pick of a verbal command — they all mean the same thing! Getting your dog to sit up on her back legs (or *haunches*) is a real charmer. Some dogs come by this trick fairly easily. Others aren't as coordinated and need help up. Either way, this section explains how to teach your dog to beg.

The naturals: Teaching the art of begging

Some dogs are born beggars. Your dog may have even discovered the begging trick by himself during one of his more-successful ploys to get attention. If your dog is a natural beggar, praise him each time he offers you the begging behavior. Soon you'll have a smart aleck on your hands who sits up at every opportunity, and you'll have no trouble getting him to beg on cue.

Here's how to teach the begging trick:

1. **Command "Sit" and make sure that the dog is sitting squarely (not leaning to either side).**

   If your dog is relatively coordinated but often gets a little too excited about food rewards —he's jumping, turning inside out, and basically unable to sit still — make him part of the "Corner Crew": Start the dog out in a corner of the room to help him feel more secure. Tuck his back end toward the wall. The walls on either side help limit and guide his movements. If he's super-excited, practice when his energy is lower, such as late in the evening or after a good romp.

2. **Take a treat and hold it an inch above his nose.**

3. **As he stretches to sniff the treat, bring it back slowly between his ears as you command, "Ask Nicely."**

    The dog should rise up to follow the path of the treat.

4. **Click (or say "Yes!") and reward the dog's split-second attempt to sit up.**

    After he catches on, hold out on rewarding treats for performances that are more balanced.

The hand signal for this trick is to move your palm upward, facing the sky. Start your hand at your hip and move it to your chest level.

Bowser bracers: Begging for a little help

If your dog is not that, uh, coordinated, you need to be a more active participant in the learning phase of begging. Try this approach:

1. **Sit your dog squarely (not leaning to either side) and instruct "Stay."**

    Stand directly behind her tail with your heels together and your toes out to either side of her spine.

2. **Hold a treat above her nose and bring it upward and back toward her ear.**

3. **Give the command "Ask nicely," and as your dog begins to rise, brace her back with your legs for support.**

4. **Click (or say "Yes!") and reward the slightest lift.**

    Gradually hold out for routines that are more balanced (though still supported).

5. **When you see that she can balance well with your help, try supporting the dog with just your knees.**

    Eventually, she'll perfect a steady balance while supported by your knees.

6. **Withdraw your support in increments until you're just standing there cheering your pal on.**

    Fairly soon, you can begin to step away. See how she shines!

Expanding Your Repertoire with Stretching Tricks

Stretching is a simple trick to teach because you can reinforce it simply by catching your dog in the act. Of course, you can build on the simple stretch technique in this section and get your dog to even take a bow after he's done performing.

Super stretching

Certain tricks don't involve more than catching your dog acting normally and attaching a cue word to the behavior. The Stretch trick is one of these. To teach your dog the "Stretch" command, just follow these easy steps:

1. **Watch your dog as she wakes up, is excited in play, or is preparing to rest.**

2. **Use the command word "Stretch" as she stretches forward.**

3. **Praise and reward her enthusiastically.**

Taking a Bow

Of course, no performance is complete without a bow. To teach your dog to bow, utilize all three of the following approaches. Soon all of them will meld together and your dog will be dazzling his audience to the very end of the act.

✓ **Caught in the act:** Whenever you catch your dog stretching his front paws with his bum in the air, command "Bow" as you flip twirl your arm out for a signal. Praise enthusiastically.

Or if your dog's feeling spunky and playful and crouches on his front legs with his bottom in the air, take a bow as you command "Bow." Praise enthusiastically and reward him with his favorite game.

✓ **Jury-rigged:** Take your dog aside into a quiet room with some favorite treats and a clicker if you have one. Hold his belly up as you hold the treat to the ground, just in front of his paws, and command "Bow." Slowly fade off the belly hold, simply using the cue word Bow.

Book IV

Training, Agility, and Shows

✔ **Smush face:** In a quiet room, take a treat and hold it against your dog's nose. Press the treat gently back and downward, thus encouraging your dog to bend forward on his elbows to get the reward. As he does, say "Bow" and reward him!

Other cues words besides Bow fit the stretching behavior just as well. Your dog can learn multiple words for the same behavior. Just make sure that you start with one command cue before adding others, and always use the same hand signal.

Chapter 5

The Ins and Outs of Agility Training

In This Chapter

▶ Showing your dog where to jump and how to race through tunnels

▶ Exploring chutes and mastering the table

▶ Getting your dog to nail the contacts every time

▶ Navigating the A-frame and dog walk

*I*n an introductory agility class, you find out how to direct your dog through a simple agility course, navigating obstacles with commands and body cues. This chapter gives you an overview of some of the obstacles in an agility course and prepares you for the adventures that lie ahead. If you want to pursue teaching more tricks, check out *Dog Tricks and Agility For Dummies* by Sarah Hodgson (Wiley).

Planning for a Good Training Session

After you've decided to take the plunge into agility, you'll be sharing the journey with other participants in various stages of learning. Some will be way ahead of you, making you feel like an eternal freshman. But in time, you'll find yourself lending a hand to a new team, and you'll realize — "Hey! We're getting somewhere!"

In the meantime, keep the following advice in mind as you get started:

✔ **Make it simple.** Many of the obstacles have adjustable heights, so start at the lowest position. This ensures your dog's safety and success.

✔ **Find a helper.** Many introductory steps require an extra set of hands. Partner up with another newbie, and you'll be doing each other a favor.

✔ **Use leash control to start.** Keep your dog on leash in the beginning, and listen to your instructor. Think of holding the leash as holding a child's hand: In the early days of agility, it will make you both feel more secure. Your dog will need to be off leash eventually to execute the course, but the leash is helpful when directing your dog in the early stages. Wait until your dog really understands the program and your instructor tells you it's okay to go off leash.

✔ **Keep your lessons short and sweet.** If you're taking a group class, chunks of time will be spent listening to your instructor and taking turns with the various participants. Your dog won't be "on" for long stretches of time. If you're practicing on your own, a good rule of thumb is to do three to five repetitions on no more than three obstacles. Use lots of treats and end each practice session with a game. Though every dog is different, and some breeds or personality types might enjoy hours of practice, these dogs are the exception — most dogs burn out (physically and mentally) when pressed to perform.

✔ **Stay positive.** Throughout the learning phase, you'll have days where you feel confused and awkward. Confusion is a little contagious, and your dog may catch it like a cold. She'll show her confusion by acting up or racing around. If you compound the problem by showing frustration, your dog will misunderstand your displeasure and begin to associate it with the equipment or the activity. She'll want to go home, where everything is predictable and safe.

✔ **Listen to your dog.** Some days, everything will be going right. Your dog will be eager, your signals will be crystal clear, and the sun will be shining. Other days, your dog will bolt, your knees will hurt, and everything will be just . . . muddy. On those days, lighten your practice load: Simplify the routine, end on a high note, and toss in the towel until another day.

✔ **As you practice, be mindful of your dog's stress signals.** Repetitive motions such as scratching, lip-licking, and barking can be a sign that your dog is losing focus or has overexerted herself. If you've just started your practice session, see whether a walk, ball toss, or some soothing pats will get her on track. If you've been out on the course a while or the weather is extreme, go home and chill. No one — dog or person — likes to be pushed beyond their limits.

✔ **Have fun.** Agility is about having fun and being together. Repeat it like a mantra — "Having fun and being together. Having fun and being together!"

✔ **Keep it slow and simple, and smile!** Remember the three-part cardinal rule when introducing any new obstacle: Keep it *slow* and *simple,* and don't forget to *smile!*

The Jumps: Taking a First Leap into Agility Training

Most dogs love to jump. Teaching them to do it on command can be the easiest step in agility, but there's more to a good jumper than meets the eye. Dogs must not only clear the object but also be able to take a jump at any angle and land squarely.

This section gives you advice on setting up the jumps for training. It also explains how to get your dog used to clearing obstacles — at your direction — in different combinations and from various angles. Finally, you get some quick tips for tackling the specific kinds of jumps you'll see in an agility trial.

Setting up the jumps for training

Regardless of competition jumping heights, set your jumps very low for training purposes. Make each one easy to clear and fun to do. A jump for a novice jumper should be below the dog's elbow. Got a toy breed? Set the bar on the ground to start. When arranging a set of jumps, leave enough space between them for a proper five-stride approach and a clear landing.

Repetitive stress on your dog's body increases the risk of injury.

As you and your dog get more comfortable with the jumps, you should vary the height to keep your dog ever mindful of the jump set in front of him. Lower the jump during routine practice or on days when the workout is demanding.

Going over: Making the jumps

To teach your dog the agility jumps, you follow a step-by-step process that ends with your ability to direct your dog to any jump from various locations on the field.

Step 1: Calling your dog over the jump

Your dog's first introduction to jumping should be easy and fun. Set up a low jump, say "Over," and trot over the jump with your dog. As you move with her, try to get a feel for her movement — ideally give her five full strides to clear the jump and three more when she lands before interrupting her movement. Praise and reward her enthusiasm.

Now you're ready to have her jump on her own:

1. **Have your helper stand and hold your dog in front of the jump as you walk to the far side of the jump.**

   Stand, but don't turn around and face her.

2. **Twist back and make eye contact with your dog; wave a toy or treat cup from the hand on the same side.**

3. **Call, "Over — Come," as your helper releases your dog.**

4. **Click or call out a praise word like "Yes!" as your dog clears the jump.**

   Reward and praise your dog from the side you've twisted from when she reaches you.

Practice twisting, calling, and rewarding your dog from either side. This conditions her to move toward either the right or the left side as you indicate, which will become important as you sequence to other prepositioned obstacles.

Step 2: Running alongside

Next, your dog will learn to take jumps as you run alongside him next to the jump. Here's how to accomplish this step in jump-training:

1. **Hold your dog in front of the jump and let him watch your helper execute the next step.**

2. **Ask your partner to walk ahead of you, indiscreetly placing a toy or treat on the far side of the jump.**

   Place the reward several strides past the jump to allow your dog to land squarely. Have your helper ready to remove it in case your dog races around the jump.

3. **Release your dog as you say "Over!" and run with him toward the jump. Let him run just ahead of you and take the jump as you navigate to either side of the jump.**

   As you shout "Over," signal, too, with an exaggerated bowling motion directed at the jump. Your signal arm should be closest to the jump.

4. **Click or shout your praise as your dog clears the jump.**

   As he lands, let him enjoy his reward and/or break for a favorite game!

   If your dog runs around the jump, have your helper remove the reward quickly. Calmly return your dog to his starting position, and show him the baited target before you release him. If he still dodges the jump, try trotting over the jump with him to let him see the reward, but don't let him have it until he's cleared the jump on his own.

Practice running and signaling from both directions. You dog should be comfortable jumping with you strategically positioned anywhere on the field.

Step 3: Encouraging your dog to run ahead

The term *Velcro dog* refers to a dog who clings to her owner and can't think well or enthusiastically on her own. Although your dog's affections may reassure you, discourage overdependence by teaching her to go forward and tackle life . . . one obstacle at a time.

Set the jump very low or lay it on the ground. Then follow these steps:

1. **Have your helper set the lure just beyond the jump or set the target on the other side of the jump yourself.**

2. **Send your dog out with "Go on over" as you let her go.**

   Click or mark the moment she clears the jump. If your dog races around the jump, have your helper remove the reward before she reaches it.

3. **Follow your dog past the obstacle and then turn to play with, praise, and reward her for her efforts.**

Phase out placing the target on the far side of the jump. But don't forget to praise and reward your dog enthusiastically when she clears the jump.

Step 4: Setting up multiple jumps

Now you're ready for multiple jumps. Lay them out in a direct line, allowing your dog five paces between each one.

Go back to Step 1, working with your assistant to help your dog understand your new focus. Place the treat at the end of the jump sequence and keep the hurdles low to ensure success and safety.

Step 5: Adding angles

Enter "dog agility" in the search box on YouTube (www.youtube.com), and watch a competitive run. Notice how each jump's placement sets up the overall performance.

Before you think sequencing, however, practice your jumps one at a time. Teach your dog how to approach and clear each one from any angle, as you encourage him to watch you for direction. Send or run your dog over jumps at different angles, varying your position to the left or the right to simulate a competitive agility experience.

Book IV

Training, Agility, and Shows

Working on specific types of jumps

A professional course includes many different types of jumps. Here are some tips on approaching specific kinds of jumps:

- ✔ **Single jump and panel jump:** These jumps are straightforward: A single bar or flat, wall-like board is positioned for your dog to jump over. Your main goal is to build your dog's success rate and enthusiasm so she doesn't become a "bar knocker." Dogs who clip the jump or dislodge a bar lose points or, worse, are disqualified in competition.

  Keep the jumps low, giving your dog room to clear each one. Positively reward each step of this learning phase. Your enthusiasm and patience will ensure that your dog learns to jump high and clear.

- ✔ **Spread jump:** Spread jumps are a spread-out arrangement of several ascending bar jumps that your dog must clear. When practicing, keep the bars low to ensure your dog's success every step of the way.

- ✔ **Broad jump:** These low, angled boards are spread out on the ground to simulate a wide environmental obstacle that your dog must jump over. If you're experienced in trial obedience, you'll notice the similarity.

  Tip the boards on edge so they're progressively more pronounced and harder to walk over. After your dog is jumping up and across them, you can lay them down one at a time, back to front, till the series is laid flat.

  If your dog hits the boards, try laying an uncomfortable surface over them, such as chicken wire.

- ✔ **Tire:** A "tire" obstacle is usually an elaborate hoop suspended in a wooden frame. This jump may jar your dog's concentration. When first introducing the tire, make sure that it's braced tightly to prevent both motion and sound as your dog acclimates to it. Stay positive, and use plenty of tantalizing food lures and toys. Lower the tire to floor level and kneel down as you bait your dog to come through the circle.

  If your dog's still resistant, use a leash to steady her and lead her through. Toss a toy or treat ahead of her, or let her watch a favorite friend manage the obstacle. Leash her and cheerfully guide her through several times. After she's coming through when you call her, raise the tire slightly. Good with that? Go back and practice Steps 1 through 4 in "Going over: Making the jumps."

  Never force your dog through this obstacle. Frustration will ensure one thing: She'll never get near a hoop again. Watch your temper.

Going Through Tunnels

The difficulty here isn't so much teaching a dog to run through a tunnel as it is teaching him to avoid it to work on other obstacles.

There are two different types of tunnels:

- ✔ **Open-ended:** A 15- to 20-foot-long open-ended tunnel that can be positioned straight or curved

- ✔ **Closed:** A 12- to 15-foot-long closed tunnel or chute with a barrel opening and a collapsible fabric tail that a dog must push through to get out

Make sure that each tunnel is secured: Flexible tie-downs are best. You can make one with an overlying strap or tether that's affixed to sand-filled water jugs on either side. Dogs who love the tunnels are called *tunnel suckers*.

Introducing open-ended tunnels

Begin training on the straight, open-ended tunnel. Let your dog explore the tunnel as you walk along the outside of it together. Look down the hollow as though you were exploring a cave. If your dog grows wary, avoid looking at or reassuring her — your attention will reinforce her concern. Instead, crawl into the opening in sheer amazement, rewarding any sign of confidence.

Two unusual-looking tunnels are used to compete for UKC titles. The hoop tunnel and crawl tunnel are open frames that your dog must navigate in the same way she moves through the tunnels discussed in the following sections.

When practicing your tunnel runs, direct your dog from both the right and left side. Later, your position will help orient her toward the next obstacle.

Step 1: Calling your dog through

Ask a helper to assist you. If possible, scrunch up the tunnel to shorten its length. Then proceed as follows:

1. **Ask your helper to hold your dog at the mouth of the tunnel.**

2. **Walk around to the opposite end, kneel down, and wave toys or treats as you call out to your dog.**

Book IV

Training, Agility, and Shows

3. **Have your helper release your dog when you shout, "Tunnel!"**

   If your dog shoots through, reward and praise him enthusiastically. If he balks, stay calm and do whatever it takes to fan his enthusiasm . . . find more tasty treats, use a host of favorite toys, or position his favorite dog friend at the far end of the tunnel.

Super-sized tall breeds will need to scrunch to get into the large tunnel. To encourage your large breed into the tunnel, make it as short as possible. Lure him in with a tantalizing treat or favorite toy.

Step 2: Running alongside

The next step is to teach your dog to run through the tunnel as you run alongside it.

1. **Set up and secure the tunnel in a straight line.**

2. **Hold your dog at the mouth of the tunnel while your helper maneuvers to the far end with a baited target.**

   When your helper has your dog's attention, ask him to set the target on the ground.

3. **Release your dog, saying "Tunnel!" with enthusiasm. Thrust the arm closest to your dog forward in a bowling motion.**

   If your dog ducks in, run alongside her, cheering her on as you do so she can better orient herself to your position as she exits. Reward her enthusiastically. If your dog runs around the tunnel or is confused, ask your helper to remove the reward, ignore her, and start over again.

Practice running along both sides of the tunnel. As you learn sequencing, the side you'll stand on will depend on the location of the other obstacles.

This obstacle is very, very exciting. Some dogs get wound up and forget their manners. To help ground your dog, let her drag a light leash. Should she start to zoom off, you'll have an easy way to stop her. Laugh it off; then up the quality of your food rewards or practice just before mealtime.

Step 3: Sending your dog out

Next, you teach your dog to race ahead of you to take the tunnel:

1. **Keep the tunnel straight and shortened.**

2. **Stand way back, and run toward the tunnel saying "Go on–Tunnel!"**

3. **Slow your pace so that your dog gets ahead of you.**

4. **Ask a friend to toss a treat pouch or a toy to your dog as he emerges from the tunnel (or, if you're fast enough, greet him yourself!).**

The chute: Introducing closed tunnels

The closed tunnel is slightly more complicated than the open version. Here your dog must run into an open barrel without being able to see her way out. What's blocking her view? A collapsed fabric tail, known as the chute.

Make sure that your dog doesn't get tangled in the chute. Fluff it before and after each use.

Getting your dog to navigate a closed tunnel is similar to the preceding section on open-ended tunnels, but with the following variations.

Step 1: Variations on the call-through

If possible, get your dog used to going through the tunnel without the cloth section attached. Remove the cloth section and call your dog through the barrel. Repeat Steps 1 through 3 as outlined in the previous section on open tunnels. When your dog's familiar with the equipment, place the collapsible section on the barrel and proceed:

1. **Fold the fabric section back like a pant cuff, making it as short as possible.**

2. **Hold the fabric open so that your dog is able to see through the tunnel.**

3. **Have your helper hold your dog back; then call your dog through as described in the earlier section, "Step 1: Calling your dog through."**

   Praise and reward him enthusiastically as soon as he enters the chute.

4. **After your dog is confidently racing through the tunnel, drop the fabric on his back gently as he exits the chute.**

5. **Gradually drop it earlier and earlier — using your cheerful enthusiasm to reassure him that everything is okay.**

Some dogs freak out when the chute covers their head. Delay this as long as possible — when you're first dropping the fabric, make sure that it doesn't cover his eyes.

You can practice a game of peek-a-boo with a lightweight towel and some favorite treats. Toss the towel over your dog's head and say, "Peek-a-boo," as you whisk it off and reward her.

Step 2: Variations on running alongside

Here you repeat Step 1, but you enlist the help of a friend, freeing you to run alongside your dog.

Book IV

Training, Agility, and Shows

1. **Ask your friend to fold back and hold the chute open.**

2. **Have her wave the baited target so your dog sees it, and then drop it on the ground at the end of the opening.**

3. **Shout "Chute" and signal with your full-arm swing (the bowling motion) as you release your dog and let her race through.**

4. **Run out to meet and congratulate your dog with praise and play.**

5. **Have your friend lengthen and drop the fabric as you did in the preceding section.**

Run on either side of the chute to condition your dog to locate you as he moves through.

Step 3: Variations on sending your dog out

When your dog is comfortable moving through the chute, you're ready for the last step. Ask your friend to hold the tunnel open for the first send-outs.

1. **Stand back and run toward the tunnel, shouting "Go on — Chute" as you signal and release your dog from your grasp.**

2. **Slow your pace to let her race on ahead of you.**

3. **Ask your helper to toss a toy or treat bag down so that your dog is rewarded the moment she emerges.**

    Alternatively, run alongside the chute and do this yourself. When you reach your dog, play with and reward her some more.

Modifying tunnel positions

In competition, your dog will have to navigate the tunnel on-course. At higher levels, the open tunnel may be curved so that your dog will have to run to an opening that's out of sight. Here are a couple exercises to challenge your dog's tunnel comprehension:

✔ **Curved open tunnel:** Curve the tunnel, both to the left and right. Send your dog from either side, conditioning him to take your direction from anywhere on the field.

✔ **Hidden opening:** From the same curved layout, gradually angle back away from the curve so you're sending your dog around the tunnel to enter it. Use dramatic bowling signals to urge your dog to navigate around to the opening. Toss a toy/treat out as he races through. Bend the tunnel the other way and work the same exercise from the opposite side.

Waiting on Tables

The table obstacle tests your dog's ability to put on the brakes. While the rest of the agility course is pure form, function, and speed, the table is the one obstacle where your dog must come to a complete stop and hold a specific position for a full five seconds.

If you're planning on getting some equipment to practice at home, put "table" near the top of your list. Why? The skills you teach here have side benefits in everyday life: For instance, when the doorbell rings or your dog sees a squirrel, the table can help ground your overstimulated dog. A dog who has mastered the table has been taught the obstacle with a fine balance of patience and enthusiasm. You can spot this dog a mile away. She'll

- ✔ Run directly to the table without hesitation.
- ✔ Quickly respond to "Sit" or "Down" as directed.
- ✔ Stay steady as a rock, yet be poised to spring on her release cue.
- ✔ Fly off tilt and onto the next obstacle, when given the cue.

But aren't you supposed to be teaching your dog to stay *off* the table? Well, yes, when it comes to your furniture, but the agility table is a different type of table. It's low and square with a roughened surface area to prevent slipping (you can even jury-rig a table out of a low, sturdy, resurfaced coffee table — sanded and coated with sand-textured paint or nonslip vinyl strips). The height of the table is adjustable to your dog's height.

Step 1: Encouraging quick positioning

The first step is done off the table: You need to speed up your dog's reaction time to the "Sit" and "Down" commands. Use your dog's favorite lures and a clicker or word cue to highlight his speediest renditions. Begin with the speedy "Sit." When your dog gets the knack of that, move on to the speedy "Down." Follow these steps:

1. **Give the "Sit" or "Down" command as you lure your dog into position.**
2. **Reward your dog's initial cooperation — no matter what his speed.**
3. **Then withhold the treat for faster positioning, urging him with faster luring motions and more urgent tones.**
4. **When he nails his first speedy posture, give him a jackpot reward — a fistful of treats.**

Book IV

Training, Agility, and Shows

Step 2: Going to the table

After your dog has mastered the speedy "Sit" and "Down," teach her to run to the table and get on it with eager enthusiasm.

Make table time special by pulling the table out when practicing, but storing it away when not in use.

When you first approach the table, let your dog explore it . . . allow her to sniff it, put her paws on it, jump on it, and so on. If your dog gives you a double-take, do your best to erase her skepticism by staying enthusiastic and encouraging your dog to climb up. You're ready for the send-off.

1. **Ask a friend to stand behind the table with a loaded target disc — an object laced with a treat.**

   Have your friend wave the object to get your dog's attention.

2. **Stand back 5 to 10 feet. Shout "Table" as you let your dog go.**

3. **Mark the moment she lands on the table with a clicker or a praise cue such as "Yes," or "Good!"**

   Let her have the reward by approaching behind her and praising galore.

Always use your release word, for example, "Okay," to end the praise fest. You're conditioning your dog to get off when she hears the word cue. Increase your dog's understanding by practicing from different angles and increasing the send-off distance.

After you've accomplished all this, try practicing solo:

1. **Show your dog the target and place it back and slightly off the table's center.**

2. **Bring your dog back, and then release her with the command, "Table!"**

3. **Run with her to the table. If she leaps on, mark it with your word cue and/or clicker, and stop in front of the table and praise her.**

   If she's hesitant or runs by, move to the opposite side and encourage her to get on from the front.

   If she ducks behind and tries getting up on the far side, put her on a short tab leash and calmly maneuver her back to the front side.

4. **When she has mastered jumping on the table, send her from different angles and distances.**

   Always release your dog from the table with "Okay."

Some dogs approach the table with such force and excitement that they slip off. If this happens to your dog, shout her name as she nears the table.

Now phase out your use of the target object:

1. **Put the object up on the table without lures.**

   Mark the moment she hits the target, and then run up and reward her by hand.

2. **Remove the target altogether.**

   Reward your dog instead with a marker cue (click or word) and treats.

Step 3: Practicing table positions

When your dog is super-happy about the table, you're ready to introduce your stationary commands, combining quick positioning (Step 1) with going to the table (Step 2):

1. **Bring out the table. Practice a few familiar runs (see the preceding section) to stoke your dog's enthusiasm.**

2. **Send your dog to the table by commanding "Table!" When all four paws hit the table, direct "Sit."**

   Verbalize clearly and with urgency. Command from an upright posture — your dog may misconstrue any bending forward as threatening.

3. **Cue or click and reward your dog the instant he nails the posture.**

   At this stage, get close enough to your dog to treat him while he's in position. Otherwise, you'll be conditioning a position-pop-up — a big no-no in this sport.

4. **Work on the quick "Down" the same way you approached the "Sit" cue in Steps 1 through 3.**

Your only focus at this point is to teach quick positioning.

Step 4: Holding — 1-2-3-4-5 go

When your dog will assume whatever posture you direct on the table, you're ready for the final move: holding still. In trial, the judge will stand near you and count to five: Initially, vary the holding time from five toten seconds.

Book IV

Training, Agility, and Shows

You can practice this move at home with or without a table. Do your quick "Sit" or "Down," count out loud, and then release with "Okay!" Use a more urgent tone than that of your everyday command voice so your dog will know these short counts to five are different than your other, lengthier, expectations. Follow these steps:

1. **On every third "Table" run, add the command "Stay" after your "Sit" or "Down" positioning cue.**

   Vary the stay time from 5 to 10 seconds.

2. **Hold the treat in your hand while your dog holds the position, giving her the food just before you release with "Okay!"**

3. **Is your dog holding her stay? Ask someone to volunteer as the judge — standing next to the table and counting "1-2-3-4-5 GO!"**

The bottom line? You don't want this obstacle to dampen your dog's enthusiasm for agility. Make it a fun and exciting challenge, and your dog will look forward to it as much as the other obstacles on the field!

Acing the A-frame

The A-frame is a truly beautiful thing. To condition your dog's movement, practice the dismount first (known as *back-chaining*) to help your dog learn to run through the contact zones (colored areas your dog must touch). After this is accomplished you can work on your approach to and motions over the frame as you chain together the rest of the steps, as follows:

1. **Find a helper for the initial learning stages.**

2. **Lower the frame to its lowest point.**

3. **Put your dog on leash, and surprise him with food or toys.**

   When practicing on leash, do your best to keep the leash loose. A tightened collar can throw your dog off balance and slows your dog on the very obstacles for which he needs momentum the most.

4. **Lure him up the frame saying a chosen command, such as "Frame!" or "Climb!"**

   If your dog balks, ease off. Let him watch other dogs manage the frame. Climb it yourself. Do whatever it takes to help him overcome that initial trepidation.

5. **Don't allow your dog to stop on the obstacle, even as you're rounding the top of it.**

   Encourage him to move quickly as you lure him forward.

6. **After your dog is cooperating on leash, raise the frame to its normal position (5 to 6 feet).**

Perfected that? Is your dog excited to scale the A-frame? You're in good shape. Now you're ready to practice off leash. Your helper should continue to spot your dog. Move toward the frame, using your familiar command and a bowling signal with the arm closest to the obstacle.

If at any point your dog reverts back or tests the crazy jump-off maneuver, back-chain it, and start over. Stay happy — you need your dog's pumped enthusiasm to complete all the obstacles on an agility course.

Staying Balanced on the Dog Walk

The dog walk is a bit precarious. A raised, 12-foot-long, 4-foot-high, 12-inch-wide bridge extends between two planks — a balance beam for dogs. Mindful of their footing, few dogs will fall off if they walk it, but you will eventually be asking for speed. A slow and steady training regime ensures that your dog will be more mindful of her footing when you speed things up. Here's how to get your dog ready for the dog walk, both on and off the agility course.

Off-course

Introduce this fun game in a nondistracting setting. Here's what to do:

1. **Lay a wooden plank along the floor.**

   Ideally, set the plank against a wall to discourage darting.

2. **Use treats to lure your dog (or puppy) onto the plank on leash.**

3. **Guide him down the entire length of the board, praising and treating your dog as you go.**

4. **Lead him straight off the end — straight off, every time.**

5. **When he's comfortable with this exercise, begin to use your agility command word: "Plank!" or "Walk it!"**

6. **Direct your dog to run the plank in both directions, pairing the command with a bowling arm signal whenever possible.**

7. **Remove the leash, but keep enforcing the entire run — straight off, every time.**

8. **Elevate one end of the dog walk a few inches (use a big book or a brick). It will seem awkward. Go back to Step 2. Lure your dog on leash as you command and reward him. Proceed through Step 7, using this configuration.**

Book IV

Training, Agility, and Shows

9. **Now elevate both ends and repeat Steps 2 through 7.**

Got that? You're ready for the real deal!

On-course

When possible, introduce your dog to using the *Baby Dog Walk* — it's lower and safer than the raised version, and it seems less scary to your dog. Here's how it works:

1. **Find a helper to spot your dog on the opposite side of the plank.**

2. **Lure your dog on leash, as you did for the A-frame (see the earlier section, "Acing the A-frame").**

If your dog is hesitant, create a Hansel-and-Gretel pathway with favorite treats. Use this grazing method a few times (and only if necessary) to encourage your dog's enthusiasm on this obstacle. Hold the leash loosely to prevent unconsciously slowing your dog's progression.

When your dog can manage this obstacle with comfort, you're ready to try the official dog walk. For the raised dog walk, repeat the preceding steps, asking your helper to channel your dog's movements to prevent early slipping. If your dog does fall, stay as calm and cheerful as possible. As they say in horseback and bike riding: If you fall off, get up, get back on.

Chapter 6

Best in Show: Showing Your Dog

So you think that you have the best dog in the world? Your Bichon, Border Collie, Pug, or Portuguese Water Dog is perfect, and you want everyone to know it. Fortunately for you, a whole sport is dedicated to doing just that — the fascinating world of dog shows.

Conformation trials, or dog shows, are sporting events in which dogs compete against other canines to see who is top dog. Although dogs today can compete in a whole host of events — agility, flyball, herding, and earthdog among them — a dog's overall appearance and structure is judged in conformation.

Shows of all sizes and shapes take place in the United States each year; leading the pack is the Westminster Kennel Club Dog Show, one of the most famous dog shows in the world. Held each year in New York City, this show has been running since 1877 and draws an interesting mix of fierce competitors (including the humans), unified fanciers, and devoted spectators.

Dog shows like Westminster are popular and very competitive, and the whole scene can seem quite overwhelming for beginners — even people who simply buy a ticket so they can sit back and watch. This chapter helps answer questions about the different types of shows, the breed standards, and how to get started, plus it aims to give you enough information to help you decide whether dog showing is right for you and your dog.

Discovering the World of Dog Shows

Some basic information about dog shows is helpful in understanding this fascinating and sometimes strange world. Hype and glitz aside, keep in mind the original goals of the sport set down by canine devotees more than a hundred years ago.

Achieving high standards

According to the American Kennel Club (AKC), breeders must work to "produce a dog who most closely conforms to the breed standard." In competitions of conformation, judges examine dogs and rank them according to how closely each compares to the dog described in the breed's official *standard*, a description of the characteristics that allow a breed to perform the function for which it was bred. Standards often include a description of general appearance, as well as detailed specifications on the following:

- ✔ **Structure:** Size, proportion, color, coat, and so on
- ✔ **Temperament:** The personality, described in such terms as "alert," "even-tempered," "cheerful," "confident," and "reliable"
- ✔ **Movement:** How a breed should move ("at a gallop," "powerful," "purposeful")

Despite the razzle-dazzle, dog shows are not beauty contests. When it comes to conformation, the standard rules. How else can judges objectively choose one magnificent, gorgeous dog over another?

Breeds were developed to perform specific duties, and a written standard describes the ideal structure for the breed. Terriers, for example, needed a rough, protective coat to allow them to chase vermin under brush and underground. A long-legged, smooth-coated breed just wouldn't hold up to the work of chasing down rats and badgers.

Standards for breeds are developed and maintained by the breed's national club, and those breeds registered by the AKC are included in the AKC's *Complete Dog Book*. The AKC's Web site, www.akc.org, lists each breed's standard and includes a link to the breed's parent club.

Who can compete?

Not just any good-looking pooch can compete in a conformation event. To be eligible to compete, a dog must be

- ✔ A purebred.

✔ **Registered with a kennel club.** For an AKC-sponsored event, a dog must be individually registered with the American Kennel Club. In other words, the dog must have papers proving its registration as a purebred. (See the nearby sidebar, "The kennel clubs: Playing for papers.")

✔ **The correct age,** often 6 months or older.

✔ **Intact** (not spayed or neutered).

Because conformation has always been about judging a dog's potential as breeding stock, show dogs are required to be intact — whether or not you plan to breed your own. Serious health risks are associated with intact dogs, and individual owners need to decide whether showing a dog is worth the potential health problems.

Don't despair if one of these requirements excludes your dog from competition. Not to compare apples to oranges, so to speak, but altered cats have been able to compete in a special class at pet shows for years, and some shows offer a special altered class for competition. Three kennel clubs offer signs of hope for pups that don't fit the standard show mold:

✔ **The United Kennel Club** offers, in addition to its purebred registry, a program to all dogs who are spayed or neutered — including mixed breeds, purebred dogs of unknown pedigree, and purebred dogs with "faults" that disqualify them from UKC breed standards. Included in the program are trials for agility and obedience, dog sports, weight pulls, and the group's junior program.

✔ **The Canadian Kennel Club** allows unregisterable dogs of CKC breeds to participate in competitive events, as long as the owner has obtained a Performance Event Number from the organization. Such dogs must be spayed or neutered.

✔ **The American Kennel Club** has a program for spayed and neutered mixed breeds (see Chapter 8 in Book V), as well as a program for unregistered dogs of AKC breeds. For more information, go to www. akc.org/reg/ilpex.cfm.

Book IV

Training, Agility, and Shows

The Mixed Breed Dog Clubs of America (MBDCA), a national registry for mixed breeds, provides many opportunities for mixes, which *must* be altered to participate. In addition to obedience, lure coursing, tracking, and other performance events, mixed breeds can compete in conformation. Before dogs can earn an MBDCA championship title, they must earn the organization's obedience titles, ensuring a mix of both brains and beauty.

Individual breed clubs may also be making changes to accommodate owners who are not interested in breeding or, for some other reason, want to show an altered dog. For example, the Australian Shepherd Club of America allows spayed and neutered Aussies to compete in all club programs, including an Altered Conformation Program, in which dogs can earn points toward breed championships.

The kennel clubs: Playing for papers

Dogs who compete in conformation must be registered with a kennel club. But what does that really mean? A dog can be registered with a kennel club if it is the offspring of two purebreds of the same breed. Such a dog gets *papers* — paperwork that certifies the dog as a purebred. Does this mean that a dog with papers is better or healthier than a dog without papers? Nope, not necessarily. Kennel clubs register dogs as a way to track them. You can register your dog with one club or with many, depending on the breed and where you live (owners near the border of Canada and the United States may choose to register with both the AKC and the CKC). Although there are countless kennel clubs in the world, these clubs are a few of the big players:

American Kennel Club (AKC), oldest and largest in the United States, with more than 160 breeds

United Kennel Club (UKC), second-oldest in the United States, with more than 300 breeds

States Kennel Club (SKC), formed in the 1980s, with limited geographic reach

American Rare Breed Association (ARBA), a newer registry, with limited geographic range

Canadian Kennel Club (CKC), somewhat aligned with the AKC, with 175 breeds

Kennel Club (in Great Britain), the oldest kennel club in the world and organizer of the Crufts show

Federation Cynologique Internationale (FCI), with member clubs from European, Asian, and Latin American countries

Types of conformation dog shows

You're faced with a host of new terminology as soon as you start looking into dog shows. *All-breed*, *specialty*, *group* — what do they all mean? Here's a head start on the three types of conformation dog shows:

✔ **All-breed shows:** An all-breed show offers competitions for more than 150 breeds and varieties of dogs recognized by the AKC or one of the other major dog registries. These shows are the ones you're most likely to see on TV. The first-place dog from each of the seven breed groups competes in a final round to be Best in Show. The Westminster Kennel Club Dog Show is one of the best-known all-breed shows.

- **Specialty shows:** Often hosted by breed clubs, specialty shows are open only to dogs of a specific breed or to varieties of one breed. For example, the Border Collie Society of America specialty show is for, not surprisingly, Border Collies only.

- **Group shows:** These shows are for dogs who belong to one of the AKC's seven groups: Hound, Herding, Sporting, Non-Sporting, Terrier, Working, Toy, and Miscellaneous. Beagles, for example, are in the Hound Group, so they compete with other hounds such as Bassets, Bloodhounds, and Dachshunds.

Dog shows can be indoors or outdoors, benched or unbenched. In a *benched* show, dogs are kept on assigned benches when not in the show ring. This arrangement gives visitors attending the show a better chance at seeing the breeds and talking to breeders and handlers. Few shows these days are benched; Westminster is one of them.

But wait — there are shows and there are *matches*. In the three types of shows, dogs compete for points toward a championship. Matches are more informal, and dogs do not earn points toward a championship. Don't discount this level of competition, though; matches can be very useful for practicing and getting your feet wet in the ring. Dogs can enter three types of matches:

- **Workshop:** The most informal type of match, in which dogs are not judged by breed or group. Judges typically give advice, not ribbons.

- **Fun match:** The next level up from a workshop. Dogs are judged by breed, usually with ribbons awarded.

- **Sanctioned match:** The most formal type of match, the closest thing to a sanctioned show. Clubs use sanctioned matches as part of the approval process for being able to hold shows.

You can check the events calendar of different breed clubs to find out when matches and shows are being held in your area. Many dog magazines also list dates for upcoming shows.

A group by any other name

This book primarily refers to the AKC breed groups, and other clubs break down the breeds differently. The UKC has eight groups that are based on purpose: Companion, Guardian, Gun Dog, Herding Dog, Northern Breed, Scenthound, Sighthound and Pariah, and Terrier. The FCI relies on ten groups. The Canadian Kennel Club uses the same seven groups as the AKC.

Getting to know the cast of characters

Putting on a dog show is no small feat. Consider the time and energy involved in scheduling and coordinating what are often multiday events. Although many people work hard behind the scenes to make a show a success, you can familiarize yourself with a few of the key characters you'll come across in the world of dog shows.

✔ **Breeders:** More than a matchmaker, the *breeder* is responsible for the health of the father (sire) and mother (dam), as well as any puppies in the litter. Breeders must have a thorough knowledge of AKC regulations and breed standards; they are also responsible for seeing to it that the proper AKC documentation is submitted for new puppies. Although a breeder is there at the start of a show dog's life, a breeder may or may not be an owner or handler.

✔ **Owners:** An *owner* is typically the person who decides whether to show a dog. Does a dog conform to the breed standard? Is the dog trainable? Will the dog have a winning personality in the ring? An owner considers a number of factors — time and expense among them — before launching a dog on a show career. An owner may or may not be a breeder or handler. It's becoming more common for people to be more interested in showing than breeding, and that's fine.

✔ **Handlers:** The person in the ring with a show dog is the *handler*. Some handlers are professionals (sometimes referred to as *agents*). A good handler is well versed in the breeds and understands all the rules of competition. Handlers are not limited to showing — most devote a lot of time to training and grooming. A handler can show one dog or many.

✔ **Judges:** A *judge* is the person who examines the dogs in a show and awards them based on how closely they match the breed standard. Judges need to be breed experts, able to examine everything from a dog's teeth and muscles to the way the dog moves and behaves. Judges have to meet various requirements to be approved by a registry; although they vary, most judges have to be active in the dog fancy for at least ten years, with dogs whom they've bred having gone on to championship level.

Though some people take on multiple roles — breeder, owner, and handler — a dog usually has more than one person involved in its show career.

Understanding the basics of competition

Sure, there's camaraderie with other fanciers and bonding between dogs and owners, but the goal for most dogs who compete in conformation shows is to win points toward a championship. Depending on the show and sponsoring kennel club, points are accumulated based on some fairly complicated formulas, some of which change each year (see your club's Web site for details). For example, to become an AKC champion, with a Champion of Record title, dogs must earn 15 points, with two stipulations:

- ✔ Points must be awarded by at least three different judges.

- ✔ Points must include two *majors* — shows in which at least three points are awarded.

The number of championship points awarded at a show depends on the number of males and females of the breed actually in competition. The more entries, the greater the number of points that can be won, with five points being the maximum number awarded to any dog at any show. A dog who earns a Champion of Record title can compete for Best of Breed and Best of Show awards. So just as in any other sport, points are important.

The following simplified description explains a complicated process (entire books are devoted to it), but you can use this information as an introduction to the way competition works. In a show, dogs are divided by breed first and then by gender. For example, a Greyhound is separated from other breeds and then divided into groups of males and females. At that point, the males and females are divided into seven regular classes:

- ✔ **Puppy:** Dogs between 6 and 12 months of age are usually divided into 6 to 9 months and 9 to 12 months. Dogs in this class have not yet achieved champion status.

- ✔ **12 to 18 Months:** For dogs 12 to 18 months old. These dogs have not yet achieved champion status.

- ✔ **Novice:** For dogs 6 months and over who have not won three first prizes in the Novice class or a first prize in the Bred By Exhibitor, American-bred, or Open classes. The dog may also not have been awarded any championship points as a puppy.

- ✔ **Amateur-Owner-Handler:** A new AKC class (started in 2009) for dogs at least 6 months of age who are not champions. Dogs must be handled by the owner of the dog, and that person cannot have been, at any point, a professional dog handler, an AKC-approved conformation judge, or an assistant to a professional handler.

- ✔ **Bred By Exhibitor:** For dogs who are exhibited by their owner and breeder. These dogs have not yet achieved champion status.

- ✔ **American-Bred:** For dogs born in the United States from a mating that occurred in the United States. These dogs have not yet achieved champion status.

- ✔ **Open:** A catchall class, and typically the biggest of a show, for any dog registered with the AKC who is at least 6 months old and not yet a champion.

Book IV

Training, Agility, and Shows

Looking back: A short history of dog shows

Undoubtedly, people have been comparing their dogs to others since ancient canines first became companions. What began as friendly get-togethers of breeders eventually morphed into informal dog shows, but it wasn't until June 1859 that the first *official* dog show took place. The location was the English town of Newcastle-on-Tyne, and the competitors were Pointers and Setters, with 60 dogs shown. Other shows soon followed in Birmingham, England, with Spaniels and then Hounds included.

Not to be outdone, fanciers in the United States began organizing their own dog shows, and the first was held in Chicago in 1874. Three years later, the Westminster Kennel Club held its first show, with more than 35 breeds competing. The club has held the annual Westminster Kennel Club show for more than 133 years, making it the second-longest continuously held sporting event in the country.

Another big player entered the scene in 1884 when the American Kennel Club (AKC) was established; the group's primary goal was as a *dog registry,* to maintain the breeding records of purebred dogs in the United States; today the organization maintains the records of more than 15,000 events a year. The United Kennel Club (UKC) followed on the heels of the AKC in 1898. The group's founders believed it was important to focus more on the original function of the dog breeds. Although the UKC held dog shows, the shows were geared more toward performance events such as gun dog and obedience competitions.

After brief stints with AKC rules, Canadian dog shows were held under the rules of the Canadian Kennel Club and have remained that way since 1896. The Fédération Cynologique Internationale, the World Canine Organisation, recognizes 83 member countries and licenses international shows in those countries. One of these shows, the World Dog Show, held annually since 1971, is hosted by a different country each year. Billed as the world's largest dog show, Crufts, run by England's Kennel Club, hosts an estimated average 28,000 canine competitors each year, with about 160,000 spectators and visitors.

Dogs shows are big business, and some of the larger organizations televise competitions and build interactive Web sites for fanciers. With thousands of dogs and their entourages, New York City is taken by storm each February when the Westminster Dog Show hits Madison Square Garden. The canine version of the Super Bowl brings with it great fanfare, extensive television coverage, and media events. Dog show culture probably peaked in the limelight when the hilarious film spoof *Best in Show* was released in 2000.

After the male (dog) and female (bitch) winners are chosen in each class, they are brought back and judged against each other to determine which dog is the best of those winning dogs, known as the *Winners Dog* and the *Winners Bitch.* Judges award championship points to these dogs, from 1 to 5, depending on the number of dogs competing.

The Winners Dog and the Winners Bitch then compete with each other and with any dogs who have already earned their champion title, called the Best of Breed Competition. Three awards are usually given during this part:

✔ **Best of Breed:** The dog judged best in its breed category

✔ **Best of Winners:** The dog deemed better between the Winners Dog and the Winners Bitch

✔ **Best of Opposite Sex:** The best dog who is the opposite sex of the Best of Breed

Only the Best of Breed advances to the next step: competing in the Group competitions. And only the dogs who win in the Group competitions go on to compete for the coveted top prize: Best in Show.

Deciding If Showing Is Right for You

Maybe you've been to a dog show or two and loved the camaraderie, or your friend shows her dog and has raved about the experience. Maybe you've dreamed about showing a dog since you were a teen and saw the Westminster show on television. Whatever it was, it got you thinking about getting a show dog or showing the dog you already have.

Take some time to think about whether you have what it takes to be a show dog's human. Are you outgoing enough to mix with other show people? Do you like to travel with your dog? Keep in mind that most newcomers to showing will lose and lose badly. It will most likely take some time before a win comes your way. Are you prepared for the mental beating your confidence will take? Are you the type who can smile as the awards are handed out to others? Will you be able to make sure that your dog doesn't feel as though she let you down? Be honest and give these questions some thought.

What about your pooch? If you're thinking about showing a dog you already have, consider the dog's temperament and tolerance for excitement. If your dog has never even been to a dog park, let alone a loud, crowded arena full of other dogs, she may be in for a shock. Puppies destined for showing are socialized and trained from an early age, both of which help with temperament and tolerance of noise and crowds.

A good way to test both you and your dog is to try a local workshop or fun match (see the earlier section, "Types of conformation dog shows"). Some dogs may enjoy a smaller outdoor setting but will tremble or yawn their way through a large indoor match. And if you don't have a dog to show, maybe someone you know has an experienced dog you can take for a test run.

Book IV

Training, Agility, and Shows

Taking it all in: Being an informed spectator

As with any sport, it's a good idea with dog showing to spend some quality time watching from the sidelines. Attend as many different types of shows as possible and really soak it all in.

- ✔ **Grab a show catalog:** The show catalog is the official listing of the dogs entered in a show, categorized by breed. Dogs are assigned a number in the catalog; the dog's name, registration number, date of birth, parentage, and owner are typically listed.

- ✔ **Check out the grooming area:** Talk to professional groomers, whether about your current dog or a breed you may be interested in owning.

- ✔ **Look at the dogs:** Compare different dogs of the same breed at a specialty show, or many different breeds at an all-breed show. What looks good to you? As tempting as it may be, don't pet any dog unless given permission (some of those doggie do's take hours to perfect!).

- ✔ **Try to follow the action:** Use your show catalog to track the progress of the show — the breeds, groups, judges, and winners.

- ✔ **Chat with anyone and everyone:** Here's your chance to schmooze with people who have experience. Ask questions, listen, and take it all in.

Pros of showing

People have strong opinions about nearly everything having to do with dogs, and dog showing is no exception. The advantages of being involved with dog showing vary with the people you talk to. Some pros include the following:

- ✔ **Better bonds:** Owners who show their dogs spend a good deal of time with each other, helping to ensure a strong bond.

- ✔ **New friends:** People who enter the show world are likely to meet a host of new people, some of whom may turn out to be lifelong friends, supporters, and even mentors.

- ✔ **Education:** Understanding the complex world of dog showing can take years. Look at it as a learning experience, with regard not only to dogs, but also to life (winning, losing, playing nice, and so on).

- ✔ **Breed insight:** Being surrounded by dogs of the same breed may give you valuable insight about the breed and ways to improve the health of your dog or, if you're a breeder, future dogs.

Considering Junior Showmanship

Think you're too young to show your dog? Perhaps not. Junior Showmanship competitions typically are open to boys and girls who are at least 9 years old and under 18. These competitions give young fanciers the chance to develop handling skills, practice good sportsmanship, and learn about dogs and dog showing. In fact, many professional handlers started off in Junior Showmanship, so it's a good way to get experience early on, and maybe even decide whether a career as a pro handler is in the cards. Conceived as Children's Handling in the 1920s, Junior Showmanship competitions vary according to kennel club; the UKC's youngest class is for 2- and 3-year-olds! Though the junior competitions share some similarities with the adult competitions, judges evaluate the children's handling methods, but not the animals.

Cons of showing

Dog showing is not without its downsides, as even the most ardent fanciers will attest. Others see more controversy in the sport. Some cons include the following:

- ✔ **Ego:** Yours, not the dog's. Though dog showing should be about promoting good health and temperament in dogs, that focus can be eclipsed by breeders, owners, and handlers who think it's all about them.

- ✔ **The money:** Though most breeders don't make much, if any, money on breeding, dog showing is big business. Some people are discouraged by others in shows who are motivated more by financial gains than interest in dogs.

- ✔ **Your money:** Or lack thereof. It costs money to pay entry fees for shows, buy equipment, and foot the bills for travel.

- ✔ **Breeding issues:** Some believe that dog showing encourages unhealthy breeding practices. In 2009, the BBC refused to broadcast the annual Crufts Dog Show, citing concerns that intensive breeding of pedigree dogs in the United Kingdom is leading to health problems in breeds such as Boxer dogs with epilepsy and Pugs with breathing problems. The Kennel Club, which runs Crufts, has since introduced regulations to encourage responsible breeding.

- ✔ **The scene:** Sabatoge, snarkiness, rumors, and fakery are alleged issues of dog shows, although these problems are certainly not typical of the general dog-showing community.

Book IV

Training, Agility, and Shows

Of course, these points are just some food for thought, and individuals are responsible for making their own decisions.

Getting in Gear to Show

After you've decided to enter the wonderful world of dog showing, you need to prepare yourself and your dog before bounding into the ring. The homework items to check off your list include the following:

- **Register your dog:** Dogs must be registered with a kennel club before they can compete. You can register your dog with one club or many (see this chapter's sidebar "The kennel clubs: Playing for papers"), but if you're like many people, you'll show your dog at AKC events, so your dog must be registered with the AKC. Club rules vary, but for a new puppy to register, both the puppy's sire and dam must have papers. Typically, a breeder is responsible for registering the new litter, and you work with the breeder to register your individual puppy.

- **Join your local breed club:** Local clubs are a great resource for information on classes for conformation, handling, obedience, agility, and other activities. Depending on where you live, clubs can be all-breed or breed specific. Search for a state-by-state listing of clubs affiliated with the AKC at www.akc.org/clubs/search/index.cfm.

- **See a vet:** A vet checkup is a critical piece of the preparation puzzle. Your vet may be able to offer helpful advice about your dog's show potential and spot issues that may get in the way of a successful show career. Your vet can also guide you in the area of vaccinations, ensuring that your dog is healthy and able to join the pack. However, a vet may not be an expert on any specific breed standard.

- **Get some identification:** You're not likely to lose your dog, but it's best to be prepared. Collars with identification tags are one option, tattoos another, but many people prefer a recent technology, microchipping. No technique is foolproof, so your best bet for bringing Fido home safe may be to use more than one method.

- **Make nutrition a priority:** All dogs should be fed quality nutritional food, but a dog getting ready for competition needs to be in top form, both inside and out. The right foods will help keep your show dog trim and his coat shiny (see Chapter 1 in Book II for more on food).

- **Begin a grooming regimen:** Although the level and intensity of grooming varies from breed to breed, bathing, brushing, scissoring, and plucking are important parts of a dog's show life. If you're showing a Poodle or Bichon, you may need to take a grooming course or hire a groomer. It's never too early to get started, though. Go to shows, get advice from groomers, and try out a bath or two.

✔ **Get an anatomy lesson:** Personality, charm, and temperament are factors that help sway a judge in the ring, but conformation is really about how closely the dog conforms to the breed's official standard. The standard refers to how the breed's form follows its original function, and it has everything to do with hocks, rib cages, tails, ears, and shoulders — and, critically, how a dog moves in the ring. Familiarize yourself with the breed standard and the basic terms of dog anatomy (see the illustration in this book's color insert).

✔ **Make friends:** Plenty of Web sites and books offer advice on showing, but one of the best ways to get advice is to meet and talk to actual show people. These folks are doing exactly what you want to do, and many are happy to share their personal stories and tips for getting ahead. Mentoring is a big thing in the show world, and you may find someone willing to take you on as an apprentice, so to speak.

✔ **Submit your entry forms:** Dog showing comes with a daunting amount of paperwork. Be sure to carefully complete all entry forms. Then be certain to send them in on time so they are received before the entry period closes.

✔ **Set some goals:** Thinking about your goals will better prepare you for the amount and level of work you're in for when it comes to dog showing. Will showing be a hobby? A career? Something in between? Be realistic when it comes to your dog — not every pup is destined to be a champion. Preparing for fun matches will be very different from preparing for your dog's debut at Westminster.

Packing: Checking your list twice

Packing for a show is no small matter. You need plenty of gear, and it's a big nuisance if you forget something. Although your list may be different, here's one to get you started:

✔ Grooming equipment (tack box or bag, grooming table, supplies)

✔ Regular collar and lead

✔ Show collar and lead

✔ Bait (treats)

✔ Water bowl and gallon jugs of water

✔ Crate and/or exercise pen

✔ Dog bed or blanket

✔ Cart to carry equipment

✔ Tarp, canopy, or umbrella for shade

✔ Chair

✔ Towels

✔ Bags or other method of scooping poop

✔ Confirmation of entry paperwork and show/parking pass

✔ Show clothes/apron

✔ Extra shoes/socks/hosiery

✔ Sunscreen

✔ Cooler with lunch and drinks

Book IV

Training, Agility, and Shows

Throwing yourself into training

As with any sport, dog showing requires a fair amount of training. Neither you nor your dog will be very happy — or successful — if you show up and compete without first training. To get yourself and your pooch in top form, consider the following:

- **Obedience training:** A prerequisite. Impeccable behavior is a must for any dog, but especially those at a dog show. No nipping or jumping allowed. Given the excitement, crowds, doggie hormones, and noise — not to mention the somewhat invasive poking of the judges — a show dog needs to have passed obedience training with flying colors. Start early; many breed clubs offer training classes.

- **Conformation and handling classes:** Another prerequisite, especially if you plan to handle your dog yourself. Although you'll do some training at home, classes taught by experienced handlers give novices a chance to do the following:

  - Practice their dogs in a controlled showlike setting

  - Use show-style collars and leads

  - Get used to being surrounded by other dogs

  - Learn to *stack,* or pose your dog to best show off his conformation and features

  - Learn the secrets of *gaiting,* or moving your dog around the ring in a trot

  Your dog will need to use his manners in class (no impolite sniffing, please) and you'll need to make sure that your dog's shots are up-to-date.

- **Conditioning:** You guessed it, a prerequisite. A swimmer needs to do laps, a soccer player needs to run on the track, and a show dog needs to do whatever it takes to stay fit. The type of conditioning a dog needs will vary. For some, conditioning means regular walks; for others, it means herding trials or a treadmill. Check with your veterinarian for guidance.

Mastering the stack

A good conformation class teaches you a lot about stacking, but practice really makes the difference when you're presenting to a judge. Although most dogs are stacked with all four feet square and even, some breeds are stacked differently, so be sure to find out if your breed's pose is unusual in any way. Small breeds are stacked on a table. Some tips for great stacking practice include the following:

✔ Practice often — once a day, if possible — but keep sessions short, about three minutes. A weekly class is helpful until you're both at ease.

✔ Use a mirror so you can see what the judge will be seeing, and set your dog facing to your right.

✔ Always handle your dog gently.

✔ Don't mess around with your dog's feet — dogs don't like it. Instead, when placing the front or back legs into position, hold the leg above the elbow (for the front) and above the hock (for the rear), and move the entire leg into place.

✔ Use lots of praise. Then add some more.

✔ Practice the *free stack,* letting your dog pose herself. Bait (a treat) is useful for this move; some say that tossing a piece of bait for a dog to catch can help put a dog in a nice free stack.

This practice is important for both you and your dog. Neither one of you will be able to look relaxed or natural if you're nervous — and a judge is likely to notice.

Getting ahead with gaiting

Gaiting doesn't come naturally to most people or their dogs, so classes are critical in getting this part of the competition down. Not surprisingly, practice makes perfect. During competition, you're asked to *go around;* all the dogs then trot around the ring at once, as well as gait individually. Gaiting gives the judge the greatest chance of seeing your dog's best qualities and structural features. Keep the following tips in mind as you practice gaiting:

✔ Control the lead, holding it taut but not tight. Keep excess lead tucked into your hand, to prevent it from distracting your dog or the judge.

✔ Use a command that lets your dog know what's going on: "Let's go," "Let's show," or some other phrase.

✔ Watch the *dailies* — that is, view some video of your gaiting techniques. Too bouncy? Collar too low? Watching both of you from a different perspective gives you a chance to make corrections before you get into the ring.

✔ Figure out the best speed for your breed. Faster is not always better. When you find that speed, practice until you can match it with some consistency.

✔ Learn the patterns — "take them around," "up and back," "triangle," "L," and "T." Then practice them.

✔ Praise and encourage your pup. Stay positive!

Book IV

Training, Agility, and Shows

The question of bait: To use or not to use?

The show ring is a place of great commotion and excitement, and it's not unusual for a dog to get distracted by another dog or sounds from the crowds. Handlers rely on *bait,* an edible treat of some sort, to entice a dog or get a dog's attention when necessary, often when stacking. Bait can be bits of cooked liver or steak, cheese, sausage, or even popcorn — whatever makes your dog pay attention. Handlers carry bait in a pouch or in a pocket and dole out a piece to achieve an alert look or have a dog stay focused (some handlers hold the bait in their mouth, but that's an individual choice). Bait is not allowed at all shows, however. If you're showing at a UKC event, you can't have food in the ring. Alternatives to edible bait include balls and any toys with squeakers. Edible or not, you may have to test a few different methods before you find the one that works best.

Good gaiting comes from practice and experience, but remember one other point: Listen. If you miss what a judge is saying, you miss out on the chance to show him what your gait is made of.

Choosing a handler

Yes, it's possible to do it alone — be the breeder, groomer, handler, secretary, travel agent, chauffeur, and pooper scooper. But it's not easy. Many in the dog show world rely on a team of people to help ensure a successful dog-showing experience. Because some handlers take care of everything from transportation, to grooming, to piloting around the show ring, a professional handler can be a key component in any team.

A professional handler has the skill and knowledge to present your dog in the ring as a winner. In general, the dog show handler's job includes the following tasks:

✔ Grooming your dog according to the breed standard

✔ Presenting your dog in the ring when called

✔ Moving the dog around the ring to show him off to his best advantage

✔ Making sure that your dog looks good at all times

The best handlers have a way of disappearing in the ring so the spotlight stays only on the dog. Good handlers have a knack for making it fun, which can make all the difference for some dogs, giving them that extra gleam in their eyes or extra something in their trot. Handlers may also take care of other aspects of showing:

> ✔ Boarding, conditioning, grooming, and training
>
> ✔ Getting your dog to and from the show (if you choose not to attend)

The fees handlers charge vary; some charge per class entry, per day, with additional charges per each point won, and more for dogs who go on to win Best of Breed or Best in Show. Expect to pay more for handling a dog who requires extensive or finicky coat care.

Breeders and local breed clubs can suggest where to find handlers. The Professional Handlers' Association (www.phadoghandlers.com) has membership requirements and a code of ethics; the AKC also has a program for handlers who commit to following the organization's criteria and standards for professional handlers.

Competing: Let the Games Begin!

You've done your homework, your pooch is primped and poofed, and you're prepared in every way possible. It's show time!

Arriving at the show

Your first show will be a whirlwind of emotion, nerves, and excitement. You need to keep your head about you to take care of a few important steps:

✔ **Get settled:** Because most shows today are unbenched, you want to find the area for exhibitors so you can set up for the day; benched shows assign each exhibitor a section of bench. Take your dog for a quick walk to see the layout, and then secure her in her crate or pen and take care of unpacking.

✔ **Check in:** Visit the check-in table or ring and pick up your armband from the *ring steward* (judge's assistant); have your entry confirmation handy. Stash your armband somewhere safe or put it on, securing it in an armband holder or with a rubber band.

✔ **Study the catalog:** Although you'll probably buy at least the first few catalogs for the shows you attend, you can also look through the catalog available at the superintendent's table. Check your dog's listing to make sure that it's correct; your pooch's wins will be tracked in this way.

Book IV

Training, Agility, and Shows

Dressing the part

The dress code for dog showing is a serious matter. Although proper, smart attire is a must, a dog show isn't a fashion show for you. What you wear needs to help your dog look her best, not detract attention from your dog. Simple and conservative works best, with solid colors; the color of your suit needs to complement your dog's coat but not be the same color. For example, don't wear a black suit if you're showing a black Labrador — the judge may not be able to see the outline of your dog. Men wear dress trousers, a shirt, and sometimes a jacket. Women choose skirts, dresses, or slacks, and some top it all off with a jacket. Typically, the formality of dress matches the formality of the show. Of course, whatever you wear has to be practical and comfortable — skirts with sufficient length and shoes with rubber soles.

Entering the ring

This moment can be nerve racking, so try to relax and follow the lead of the ring steward. The steward, sometimes a volunteer, is responsible for getting each class into and then out of the ring. You're called in by your number (the one on your trusty armband) or by group. If you go in by group, you can pick your spot in the line; if you're called by number, you have no choice. Give your dog one last look, but too much fussing may make him nervous.

When you're in the ring you're in the hands of the judge. Hopefully, you've watched the judge with other classes and have a good idea of her routine. You take your place, stack your dog, and wait for what comes next.

Judging: The process

Most judges share a fairly simple routine when it comes to show time. Some room exists for variation, so it's always a good idea to get a preview before it's your turn. This section presents a typical scenario.

When a class of dogs first enters the show ring, the judge stands back and looks at a dog from a distance to get a general impression. Then he begins an individual examination, usually in the direction of head to toe, starting with the eyes, ears, and mouth. While in the mouth region, a judge often looks at the number of teeth (missing teeth can mean a disqualification in some breeds), as well as the dog's *bite,* or how the teeth come together.

When the judge is done with the head area, he "goes over" the rest of the dog, judging coat texture and feeling the parts of the dog's body: hips, shoulders, ribs, and so on. By using his hands, especially with heavy-coated breeds, he can tell a great deal about a dog's bone structure and musculature. If a judge thinks a dog may be too big or small for the standard, he may ask for a measuring wicket to check the shoulder height.

When judging male dogs, a judge has to make sure that there are two fully descended testicles. At this moment, many handlers try to distract their dog, often with some bait. Distraction isn't a bad idea, because most dogs — male or female — don't like to have their nether regions examined.

When that business is over, it's time to move. The judge asks the handler to trot the dog in a pattern that allows him to see the animal from every direction — from the front, rear, and side. Throughout this part of the judging, the judge is watching the smoothness of the dog's gait and structure and deciding how well the dog can perform in its original function.

A dog may be disqualified for a number of reasons: missing teeth, a missing testicle, or some other physical trait defined in the standard. Aggression toward a judge or another dog is not a good sign and may also spell disqualification.

You've spent weeks or months preparing, and the whole experience may take only about two minutes per dog. Then the judge may simply point to the winners or, if the class is large, ask for additional gaiting for some dogs so he can compare them a final time before making his decision and handing out the ribbons. Game over.

Playing nice: Good sportsmanship

Whether your dog wins or loses, practicing good sportsmanship is essential. Think back to the lessons of childhood: "Play nice," "Don't brag," "Don't pout," and "If you can't say something nice, then don't say anything at all."

Book IV

Training, Agility, and Shows

Book V
Meet the Breeds

The 5th Wave   By Rich Tennant

OVER 54 BREEDS

RUFFIES DOG PARLOU

| TERRIERS | HOUNDS | TOY | HERDING |

"Sorry, I'm all out of chocolate Labs. I got
strawberry, caramel, and vanilla."

In this book . . .

1t's crazy and wonderful how many different breeds of dog there are, and these chapters introduce you to all the ones the American Kennel Club recognizes — plus some surprising mixes that are gaining in popularity.

Chapter 1

Profiling the Toy Group

*L*ooking for a canine companion that packs a lot of personality into a small package? A pooch that fits in a pocketbook? A dog who's happy walking around the block rather than over the river and through the woods? A Toy may be just what you need. From the tiny Chihuahua to the perky Papillon, 21 little Toy breeds have a great deal to offer.

Although a few started out as rodent hunters, Toys were primarily bred to be companions for the wealthy and as elegant accessories of royalty. In many cases, though not all, the Toy breeds are smaller versions of larger counterparts (the Toy Poodle from the Standard Poodle, say, or the Pug from the Mastiffs). However, the Miniature Pinscher, which does look like a "Mini Me" Doberman Pinscher, was not bred down in size from the Doberman.

Because the Toy breeds were developed from so many other groups, it's impossible to characterize them together. Although Toys are typically mild mannered and sweet, their personalities are quite different. Compare the sensitive nature of the Italian Greyhound, for example, to the fearless Min Pin or the spunky Brussels Griffon.

The Toy breeds' small sizes make them perfect for any lap, but also for any home — even the smallest studio apartment. Toys are very popular with city dwellers, especially people who live in condos or retirement communities that impose size limits on pets. A Toy's small size also makes it transportable, which means you can pick up and carry your petite pooch with you wherever you go, even on many airlines. Try that with a Labrador Retriever!

Don't be fooled by the small stature of a Toy, though; many are tougher than you think. Nearly all Toy dogs make decent little watchdogs: They will certainly let you know (by barking, most likely) that a stranger has entered their territory. Top alert breeds include the Affenpinscher, Brussels Griffon, Chihuahua, Toy Manchester Terrier, Min Pin, Pomeranian, and Yorkshire Terrier. Keep in mind, of course, that their greatest strength is probably their bark (as opposed to the implied bite of a German Shepherd, for example).

Toys are an ideal choice for many because of their minimal exercise needs. That's not to say that they should lie around eating canine bon-bons all day. Even the tiniest Toy needs a short daily walk, romp, or play session to stay fit. On the other hand, elderly owners or others who can't walk their dog every time it needs to go out manage to train their pooch to use puppy pads or a litter box. Toys also require less grooming and vacuuming time in general (smaller dogs, smaller shedding surface).

Older people find great comfort in the affectionate and devoted nature of the Toy breeds. A source of companionship and comfort for the lonely, Toys also do well with the physically challenged. Toys are excellent therapy dogs, and many nursing homes have live-in Toys that provide great joy to residents, who benefit from the endless snuggles.

A Toy breed is likely to cost less to maintain than a large breed (they eat less food). On the other hand, Toy breeds tend to live longer (mid-to-late teens for many), so the cost differences may not be significant in the long run. Although not a major consideration, insurance liability is a factor for some people. Certain homeowner insurance policies restrict coverage, or charge more, for specific large dogs. A Toy breed saves you the hassle of dealing with a change or increase in your insurance coverage.

Clearly, the Toy breeds have a lot to offer many types of people — not everyone, though. People who probably shouldn't get a Toy breed include the following:

- ✔ **Families with young children (six and under):** Toys can be fragile, and most may not be able to stand up to the horseplay and extra-big hugs of little tykes. Even a Toy dog will have to defend itself with a nip if a small child is pulling its tail or poking. Better safe than sorry.

- ✔ **Busy people who aren't home much:** Toys breeds exist to be canine companions. They love their people and do best with plenty of attention, whether on your lap, at your feet, or sitting nearby.

- ✔ **Active people looking for running partners:** Although an Italian Greyhound enjoys a jog, most toys do better with a walk or play session. Some Toys are sensitive to overheating; others have trouble breathing.

Unless you're interested in getting into the show ring, pet owners should look for a larger-sized individual within a breed. Though too big for competition, they may be sturdier.

Affenpinscher

History/Evolution: One of the oldest of the Toy breeds, the Affenpinscher is believed to have originated in Germany in the 1600s; the name means "monkeylike terrier" in German. In their early years, Affenpinschers excelled at hunting rodents on farms and in homes. The breed's hunting skills come from its Terrier roots, but its wiry hair stems from the German Pinscher. Less common today, this monkey-faced breed is still a beloved companion, amusing owners with playful antics.

Size: Tiny, 8 to 11 inches, average 7 to 9 pounds.

Color: Black, gray, silver, black and tan, beige, red.

Temperament: Inquisitive, bold, alert, mischievous. Loyal and affectionate with family and friends, but will bark when threatened or attacked. Fearless for its size.

Photograph © Isabelle Francaise

Energy level: Medium to medium high. Can be busy.

Best owner: Active owner with a sense of humor.

Needs: Exercise and play (indoors or out), socialization, regular brushing, and periodic clipping and stripping.

Life expectancy: 12 to 14 years.

Brussels Griffon

History/Evolution: The Brussels Griffon originated in Belgium in the early 1800s, the result of crossing the Affenpinscher and the Belgian street dog. The breed's cocky demeanor served it well as a guard of cabs in Brussels, attracting customers and deterring robbers. It was crossed with the Pug in the late 1800s, accounting for the head type and the breed's smooth-coated individuals, known as *Petit Brabancon.* Recognized by the AKC in 1910, the Brussels Griffon is known for its sensitive nature and comical ways.

Size: Small, 9 to 11 inches, 8 to 10 pounds.

Color: Red, beige, black and tan, black.

Temperament: Intelligent and confident, sometimes to the point of self-importance. Usually enjoys other pets; protects with a fierce bark. May experience separation anxiety.

Photograph © Isabelle Francaise

Energy level: Low to medium.

Best owner: Upbeat, patient trainer; a family, preferably with older children.

Needs: Exercise and mental stimulation, fenced yard, some brushing, patience with housetraining.

Life expectancy: 12 to 15 years.

Cavalier King Charles Spaniel

Photograph © Jean Fogle

History/Evolution: The Cavalier King Charles Spaniel, a descendant of European toy Spaniels, was a pet of aristocratic families during Tudor times. In the 1700s, King Charles II favored it so much it was given its royal name. The breed changed over the years until the 1920s, when an American fancier generated enough breeder interest to revive the original spaniel. The first Cavaliers were sent to America in 1952, but the AKC didn't recognize the breed until 1996.

Size: Small, 12 to 13 inches, 13 and 18 pounds.

Color: Red and white, tricolor, black and tan, mahogany red.

Temperament: Gentle, sweet, and easy to please. An affectionate, nonaggressive breed that is friendly with other dogs, pets, and strangers.

Energy level: Medium.

Best owner: Active seniors, families with considerate children.

Needs: Exercise, regular grooming, and cuddling.

Life expectancy: 12 to 15 years.

Chihuahua

Photograph © Jean Fogle

History/Evolution: Although much of the Chihuahua's history is based on speculation, most believe that the tiniest of the toys descended from the Techichi, a dog ancient Aztecs used as companions and in religious ceremonies. The Chihuahua of today, both smooth- and long-coated varieties, differs from the native dog, perhaps due to breeding with dogs introduced by New World explorers. Thanks to its size and saucy personality, the Chihuahua is one of the most popular breeds in the U.S.

Size: Tiny, 6 to 9 inches, less than 6 pounds.

Color: Any color.

Temperament: Lively, alert, and swift, with a Terrier-like sense of confidence and self-importance. Intense devotion is common. Some bark.

Energy level: Medium to high.

Best owner: A gentle person with time for daily companionship.

Needs: Little exercise or grooming needed, but warmth is appreciated; urban living suits its minimal space requirements.

Life expectancy: 16 to 18 years.

Chinese Crested

History/Evolution: It's no easy task to trace the origins of the Chinese Crested, but the breed appears to have evolved from African hairless dogs, which the Chinese bred down in size as early as the 13th century. Chinese Cresteds are thought to have sailed with Chinese mariners, serving as ratters during times of plague. By the late 1800s, a handful of American breeders had begun to popularize the Chinese Crested with dog show enthusiasts; the AKC recognized the breed in 1991.

Size: Small, 11 to 13 inches, about 10 pounds.

Color: Any color or combination of colors.

Temperament: A devoted companion; alert, gentle, playful, and sensitive. Agreeable with dogs, other pets, and strangers.

Photograph © Jean Fogle

Energy level: Medium to high.

Best owner: Someone with dander allergies.

Needs: Hairless varieties require regular skin care (including sun block) and protection from cold; dogs with a powder-puff coat require normal brushing.

Life expectancy: 15 to 16 years.

English Toy Spaniel

History/Evolution: Like its relative, the Cavalier King Charles Spaniel, the English Toy Spaniel was a beloved companion of royalty and families of privilege in Europe. Mary, Queen of Scots, is believed to have favored this spaniel; the story goes that one of the dogs even refused to leave her side at the scaffold. Though English Toy Spaniels are perfectly content as lapdogs, they retain their natural hunting instinct. The breed achieved AKC recognition in 1886.

Size: Small, 10 to 11 inches, 8 to 14 pounds.

Color: Red and white, tricolor, black and tan, mahogany red.

Temperament: Not overly active, but bright and interested, willing to please. May be shy with strangers or in new situations.

Photograph © Isabelle Francaise

Energy level: Low.

Best owner: Loving, calm owner who is open to plenty of lap time.

Needs: Long coat needs brushing twice weekly.

Life expectancy: 10 to 12 years.

Havanese

History/Evolution: A descendant of breeds brought to Cuba from Spain, the Havanese is Cuba's national dog. By the mid-18th century, the breed's popularity included such notable companions as Queen Victoria and Charles Dickens. Some Cubans who left the country during the Cuban revolution brought their Havanese with them, and a handful ended up in the U.S. By the end of the 1970s, the breed was gaining popularity, and the AKC recognized it in 1996.

Size: Small, 8½ to 11½ inches, 7 to 13 pounds.

Color: All colors.

Temperament: Busy, curious, trainable and intelligent; affectionate with all — animals and humans alike.

Photograph © Isabelle Francaise

Energy level: Medium.

Best owner: Someone who wants a small dog who isn't too yappy or too fragile for kids. Nonshedding coat is okay for people with allergies.

Needs: Brushing every other day, exercise in the form of walks or play sessions.

Life expectancy: 12 to 15 years.

Italian Greyhound

History/Evolution: The smallest of the sighthounds, the Italian Greyhound is believed to have originated more than 2,000 years ago in the Mediterranean basin. During the 16th century, the breed was in high demand in Italy and came to be known as the Italian Greyhound. Its appeal spread through Europe, and the breed was often depicted in Renaissance paintings. A true greyhound, the Italian Greyhound is as skilled at hunting as it is comfortable as a lapdog and companion.

Size: Small to medium, 13 to 15 inches, 8 to 12 pounds.

Color: Any color, but no brindle markings or the tan markings normally found on black-and-tan dogs of other breeds.

Temperament: Gentle, sensitive, and timid with strangers but devoted to its family; like its sighthound relatives, likes to run and chase.

Photograph © Jean Fogle

Energy level: High, but mellows with age.

Best owner: Family with gentle children, owners who can give daily exercise and plenty of attention.

Needs: Daily exercise, sprints in a fenced area, regular brushing of teeth.

Life expectancy: 13 to 15 years.

Japanese Chin

History/Evolution: The Japanese Chin originated in China, where it was prized by the aristocracy. The Chin eventually moved to Japan via a royal gift. In 1853, Commodore Perry brought the first of the breed to Europe in 1853 as a gift to Queen Victoria. The Chin made its way to the U.S., although the supply was temporarily cut off during World War I. Playful and entertaining, the Chin has enjoyed some popularity in the United States, but most of its devotees are in Japan.

Size: Tiny, 8 to 11 inches, 4 to 7 pounds.

Color: Black and white, red and white, black and white with tan points.

Temperament: Sensitive, intelligent, and willing to please. Devoted dogs who will follow their owners anywhere.

Photograph © Jean Fogle

Energy level: Adaptable.

Best owner: Seniors or invalids interested in close companionship.

Needs: Sensitive to heat and humidity — air conditioning a must. Prolific shedders requiring twice-weekly combing. Suited to apartment living.

Life expectancy: 12 to 14 years.

Maltese

History/Evolution: The most ancient of the toys, the Maltese has been popular for centuries with people of wealth. As with other ancient breeds, the origin of the Maltese remains a mystery; the dogs appear in Greek art dating back to the fifth century. Most associate the breed with the Isle of Malta. Maltese likely were distributed as exotic items of trade from Malta, eventually making their way throughout the civilized world. The breed was recognized by the AKC in 1888.

Size: Tiny, 9 to 10 inches, 4 to 6 pounds.

Color: Pure white.

Temperament: Gentle, playful, and energetic; fearless for its small size. Showers affection on family and friends.

Photograph © Jean Fogle

Energy level: High.

Best owner: Someone with a lot of time for a dog.

Needs: Lots of attention; extensive daily care of long, silky coat; frequent dental care. Apartment living is fine with walks and playtime.

Life expectancy: 12 to 15 years.

Miniature Pinscher

History/Evolution: Despite its name, the Miniature Pinscher is not a miniature version of the Doberman Pinscher. Native to Germany, the Min Pin is most likely the result of breeding the German Standard Pinscher with the Italian Greyhound and the Dachshund. Though it originated several centuries ago and has been bred extensively in Germany and Scandinavia, the Miniature Pinscher did not become popular in the United States until the 1920s.

Size: Tiny, 10 to 12½ inches, 8 to 10 pounds.

Color: Black or chocolate with rust-red markings, or solid red.

Temperament: Energetic, busy, and inquisitive, sometimes aggressive if not well trained; fearless watchdog. Usually affectionate with family, reserved with strangers.

Photograph © Jean Fogle

Energy level: High.

Best owner: Active owner with fenced yard and ability to supervise; families with older children.

Needs: Lots of exercise and activity in areas where the curious dog can be left alone when necessary (think toddler).

Life expectancy: 14 to 15 years.

Papillon

History/Evolution: The dog who became the Papillon started off as the dwarf spaniel of the 16th century. Though its name — French for "butterfly," for the butterfly effect of dog's fringed ears — and much of its development can be traced to France, the breed gained a good deal of its popularity in Spain and Italy. Both erect-eared and drop-eared Paps can be born in the same litter and are judged together by the AKC, which first represented the breed in 1935.

Size: Tiny, 8 to 11 inches.

Color: Parti-color or white with patches of any color(s).

Temperament: Happy, obedient, and playful. Friendly toward other pets, and strangers, but a capable watchdog.

Photograph © Jean Fogle

Energy level: High.

Best owner: Fun-loving, active owner who can take charge.

Needs: Playtime, positive training methods, twice-weekly brushing of coat, regular teeth brushing.

Life expectancy: 14 to 18 years.

Pekingese

History/Evolution: With legends that can be traced back to ancient Chinese dynasties, the Pekingese is truly a regal creature. The small, maned dogs resembled the symbol of Buddha, the lion, and were developed to accentuate this resemblance. Later, Queen Victoria was given one, causing great demand for the dogs in Britain. First registered by the AKC in 1906, the Pekingese continues its role as charming, loyal companion.

Size: Small, less than 14 pounds (dogs 6 pounds and under are called *sleeves,* because they could be carried in the sleeves of their Chinese masters).

Color: All colors, but the exposed skin of the muzzle, nose, lips, and eye rims is black.

Temperament: Regal, intelligent, independent, and self-important. Affectionate to family; often aloof with strangers. May not be sturdy enough for a child's handling.

Photograph © Jean Fogle

Energy level: Low.

Best owner: Low-key owner who is a gentle and patient trainer, and tolerant of snoring.

Needs: Leisurely walks or indoor romps, regular combing, air conditioning, daily cleaning around nose wrinkle and hind end.

Life expectancy: 13 to 15 years.

Pomeranian

History/Evolution: A descendant of the Spitz family of dogs, the Pomeranian gets its name from the historical region of Pomerania (split today between Germany and Poland), where the Poms served as able sheepherders. The breed gained popularity after Queen Victoria brought one back from a trip to Italy, and a smaller-size Pomeranian then became more fashionable. Today the animated, fox-faced Pom remains a popular show dog and companion.

Size: Tiny, 8 to 11 inches, 3 to 7 pounds.

Color: Red, orange, cream and sable, black, brown and blue, brindle, beaver, white, and parti-color.

Temperament: Extroverted, busy, and curious. Attentive and playful; reserved with strangers. Can bark a lot.

Photograph © Jean Fogle

Energy level: High.

Best owner: Loving, gentle family/owner.

Needs: Minimal daily exercise, but lots of attention; twice weekly brushing, training, supervision with young children, secure fenced yard.

Life expectancy: 12 to 15 years.

Pug

History/Evolution: Much of the Pug's origins are a mystery, but the miniature mastiff-type dog appears to have been developed in ancient Asia. A favorite pet of Tibetan Buddhist monasteries, the Pug was brought by traders to Holland. By the late 1700s, the breed had arrived in France, where Napoleon's imprisoned wife, Josephine, used her Pug to deliver messages to Napoleon. The Pug's official motto, *multum in parvo,* meaning "a lot in a little," suits it well. In 1885, the AKC accepted the Pug for registration.

Size: Small, 10 to 11 inches, 14 to 18 pounds.

Color: Fawn or black.

Temperament: Adaptable, even-tempered, pleasant, playful; exudes charm and dignity.

Photograph © Jean Fogle

Energy level: Low to medium.

Best owner: One with plenty of time for interaction and who can tolerate wheezing and snoring.

Needs: Low heat and humidity; minimal coat care; daily cleaning of facial wrinkles.

Life expectancy: 12 to 14 years.

Shih Tzu

History/Evolution: Although the Shih Tzu is typically associated with China, many believe the breed was brought to the Chinese court from Tibet. The Shih Tzu as we know it was most likely developed in China around the late 1800s during the reign of Dowager Empress Cixi. The breed faced extinction during the Communist Revolution, but 14 dogs imported to England formed the foundation of every Shih Tzu today. The Shih Tzu remains a gentle and devoted companion.

Size: Small, 8 to 11 inches, 9 to 16 pounds.

Color: All colors.

Temperament: Positive, playful, and affectionate; sweet, occasionally stubborn.

Photograph © Jean Fogle

Energy level: Low to medium.

Best owner: Everyone from families to seniors, but a patient trainer with time for daily grooming or funds for professional appointments.

Needs: Socializing, daily exercise, positive training methods, diligent grooming.

Life expectancy: 10 to 14 years.

Silky Terrier

History/Evolution: Developed in Australia in the late 1800s, the Silky Terrier is the result of crosses between Yorkshire Terriers from England and Australian Terriers. Known as the Syndey Silky Terrier, the Australian Silky Terrier and, finally, in the United States in 1955, the Silky Terrier. This toy breed's pleasant and inquisitive nature has made it a moderately popular companion.

Size: Small, 9 to 10 inches, 8 to 11 pounds.

Color: Blue and tan.

Temperament: Alert, feisty, inquisitive, and playful. Terrier instincts make it an adept hunter. Intelligent, stubborn, mischievous. Tends to bark a lot.

Photograph © Isabelle Francaise

Energy level: Medium to high.

Best owner: Relatively active owner with a fenced yard for exploring.

Needs: Daily exercise (games of fetch or walks with family), training and socialization, regular bathing and brushing, routine dental care, and attention.

Life expectancy: 12 to 15 years.

Toy Fox Terrier

History/Evolution: The Toy Fox Terrier was developed in the early 1900s by American fanciers who crossed small Smooth Fox Terriers with Toy breeds such as Miniature Pinschers and Manchester Terriers. The breed retains the working abilities of the Terrier but has a mild and amusing character that makes these dogs wonderful home companions. Accepted by the AKC in 2001, the Toy Fox Terrier does well on the farm, in the show ring, and in conformation, agility, and obedience trials.

Size: Small, 8½ to 11½ inches, 3 to 7 pounds.

Color: Tricolor; white, chocolate, and tan; white and tan; white and black, all with predominately colored head.

Temperament: Alert, spirited, determined. Animated, playful, loyal; may not warm to strangers right away.

Photograph © Isabelle Francaise

Energy level: Medium to high

Best owner: Active individual or family with post-toddler children.

Needs: Exercise, training and attention to divert it from digging and barking; fenced yard for hunting and exploring.

Life expectancy: 13 to 14 years.

Yorkshire Terrier

History/Evolution: Despite its long coat and lovely looks, the Yorkshire Terrier began as a hunter of rats and other vermin in Yorkshire, England. The breed is the result of crosses that likely include the Waterside Terrier, Clydesdale Terrier, Paisley Terrier, and Black-and-Tan English Terrier. The Yorkshire Terrier soon became a popular show dog and companion of the wealthy. Don't be fooled, though — the breed is still a Terrier, with Terrier instincts.

Size: Tiny, 8 to 9 inches, 5 to 7 pounds.

Color: Blue and tan.

Temperament: Busy, inquisitive, and bold; can be stubborn and surprisingly aggressive for its size. May bark a lot, but can be trained not to.

Photograph © Isabelle Francaise

Energy level: High.

Best owner: Active owner or family with gentle, considerate children.

Needs: Daily short, leashed walks or play sessions; firm and fair discipline, brushing every other day, routine dental care, attention.

Life expectancy: 12 to 15 years.

Chapter 2

Profiling the Working Group

. . . .

. . . .

*T*he Working Group is a formidable assemblage, made up of dogs of great strength, courage, and devotion. The AKC category of Working Dog describes breeds that were originally bred for jobs other than herding or hunting: carting, sledding, guarding, and rescuing. Though many machines now do these jobs (snowmobiles rather than sledding dogs, for example), plenty of Working breeds are still doing their jobs throughout much of the world.

The breeds in the Working Group are built to perform tough tasks. They are sturdy and strong and capable of carrying heavy loads. They are brave enough to guard against predators and intruders, as well as accompany soldiers into war. They have specialized skills that allow them to dive underwater, perform rescues, and detect drugs and explosives. These breeds are intelligent and able to think for themselves, a true asset when a dog must act alone to get a job done.

Though they excel at these tasks, the Working breeds are typically large to giant — Great Dane, Akita, Mastiff, and Doberman Pinscher, to name a few — which may make them a challenge for the average person interested in a pet. Fortunately, they are also quick to learn, and early and proper training can help a dog stay on track as a home companion. Without training, however, the typical owner will be challenged to control such large and powerful dogs. Socialization should be done early and throughout a dog's life, to prevent the dog from becoming overprotective, especially if you ever plan to bring new people into your life.

Working dogs may be similar in size, but they vary greatly in other aspects of appearance. From the corded white coat of the Komondor to the baggy, smooth coat of the Neapolitan Mastiff, the dogs of the Working Group have quite a range of hair types. Being workers, of course, coat type has everything to do with job performance: The Komondor's cords protect it from the elements and allow it to blend in with its flock; the Neapolitan Mastiff's unusual appearance is enough to stop any intruder in his tracks.

In general, Working dogs are territorial and make excellent guard dogs because of their physical size and the volume of their bark. What burglar would hear the booming alarm bark of a Rottweiler and decide to come on in?

Despite their size, some of the Working breeds are perfectly content with a minimal amount of exercise and can even live happily in a small home or apartment. The Mastiff types, for example, don't require strenuous exercise and can do well with a daily leisurely stroll. The sled dogs are a different story, however, and are quite active. Be prepared for more exercise and play if you have an Alaskan Malamute, Samoyed, or Siberian Husky. Dogs like the Portuguese Water Dog, the Boxer, and the Standard Schnauzer also benefit from more activity than others in the Working Group.

Whether guardian or powerhouse, Working dogs love nothing better than having a job to do. For some that means being a drug-sniffing police dog, a therapy dog at a nursing home, or a sled dog in the Iditarod. For others, it means keeping a careful eye on a backyard full of children. And nothing is better than celebrating a job well done with a well-deserved snooze at your master's feet.

Akita

History/Evolution: The largest of Japan's seven native breeds, the Akita specialized in hunting and guarding. Beloved in Japan as loyal pets and companions, the breed was named one of the country's national monuments in 1931. Helen Keller brought the first Akita to the U.S. when she returned from a trip to Japan; American servicemen also brought back the dogs from World War II. Recognized by the AKC in 1972, the Akita continues to gain admirers.

Size: Large; females 24 to 26 inches, 75 to 95 pounds; males 26 to 28 inches, 85 to 115 pounds.

Color: Any color, including white, brindle, or pinto.

Temperament: Bold, alert, dignified, and courageous; devoted and protective of family members; can be aggressive toward other dogs.

Photograph © Isabelle Francaise

Energy level: Medium.

Best owner: Experienced in obedience training and time for daily physical exercise.

Needs: Daily outdoor runs (leashed or in a yard with a 6-foot fence), weekly brushing (more often during seasonal shedding) and cool climate.

Life expectancy: 10 to 12 years.

Alaskan Malamute

History/Evolution: One of the oldest sled dogs, the Alaskan Malamute evolved in Alaska. There they hunted with native peoples for seals and polar bears, and then hauled the catch back to the village. The arrival of white settlers brought mixed breeding until the 1920s, when people interested in sled dog racing began to breed the traditional malamutes. A noted contributor to Admiral Byrd's trek to the South Pole in 1933, the AKC recognized the breed in 1935.

Size: Large; females 23 inches, 75 pounds; males 25 inches, 85 pounds.

Color: Light gray to black, red, or sable with white markings, also all white; brown eyes (unlike the blue eyes of its Siberian cousin).

Temperament: Affectionate, friendly, playful, and loyal. Behaves well if given enough exercise; can be territorial with other pets.

Photograph © Jean Fogle

Energy level: Low to medium.

Best owner: Active owner with time for adequate exercise (long walks, runs) maintaining firm, consistent methods of training.

Needs: Daily doses of vigorous exercise, daily brushing, cool climate.

Life expectancy: 10 to 12 years.

Anatolian Shepherd Dog

History/Evolution: More guard dog than herder, the Anatolian Shepherd Dog has origins in ancient Turkey, with probable ties to the Tibetan Mastiff and Roman Mallosian war dogs. The dogs served as staunch defenders of livestock and are still valued for their hardiness, loyalty, and independence. The breed became more widely known and appreciated by the 1980s; the AKC accepted it in 1996.

Size: Giant; females from 27 inches, 80 to 120 pounds; males from 29 inches, 110 to 150 pounds.

Color: Fawn, brindle, tricolor, white, black mask.

Temperament: Serious about its job as protector, yet calm and easygoing. Intelligent, adaptable, and territorial; may perceive children as part of flock to be guarded.

Photograph © Isabelle Francaise

Energy level: Low (except when a threat is perceived).

Best owner: Strong owner in a rural or suburban home.

Needs: A job (guard, patrol, slipper fetcher) and socialization from an early age; daily exercise and securely fenced yard.

Life expectancy: 10 to 13 years.

Bernese Mountain Dog

History/Evolution: The Bernese Mountain Dog is perhaps the most well known of the four varieties of Swiss Mountain Dogs, distinct from the other three by its long, silky coat. A hardy dog who can thrive in cold weather, the Bernese Mountain Dog retains its original skills as a draft dog, herder, and watchdog. Prized in Switzerland for centuries, the breed is now popular throughout Europe and the United States, and acquired AKC recognition in 1937.

Size: Large; females 23 to 26 inches, 70 to 100 pounds; males 25 to 27½ inches, 70 to 120 pounds.

Color: Tricolor (black with white and rust markings).

Temperament: Alert, good natured, and calm. Extremely devoted, does well with children; gets along with other pets but is aloof with strangers.

Photograph © Jean Fogle

Energy level: Low to medium.

Best owner: Families who include a dog in the family's schedule and activities.

Needs: Daily moderate exercise and twice-weekly coat brushing; quality time with human family (isolation leads to bad habits and unhappiness).

Life expectancy: 8 to 10 years.

Black Russian Terrier

Photograph © Isabelle Francaise

History/Evolution: Developed in the mid-1900s in the Soviet Union, Black Russian Terriers were bred to be large, highly trainable dogs who could work with security forces as guard dogs. The breed is the result of crossings with many breeds, primarily Airedale Terrier, Giant Schnauzer, and Rottweiler. Spreading through Europe and then to the U.S., the Black Russian Terrier was accepted into the AKC's Miscellaneous Class in 2001 and the Working Group in 2004.

Size: Large, 80 to 145 pounds; female 26 to 29 inches; male 27 to 30 inches.

Color: Black (sometimes with a few gray hairs).

Temperament: Calm, confident, and courageous; protective and attached to their family. Bred to guard; reserved toward strangers.

Energy level: Low.

Best owner: An active owner who has the time and energy for obedience training and daily exercise.

Needs: Job or activity such as obedience or agility training; exercise, socialization, and human contact.

Life expectancy: 10 to 11 years.

Boxer

Photograph © Jean Fogle

History/Evolution: Boxer origins trace back to the 16th century, with ancestors that include Tibetan fighting dogs, central European hunting dogs, and bulldogs. Today's Boxer owes much of its development to German breeders in the 1800s. One of the first breeds to serve as police and military dogs in Germany, by 1900 the Boxer had become a beloved pet. Recognized by the AKC in 1904, the Boxer soared in popularity in the 1940s to its current high ranking.

Size: Medium to large; female 21 to 23½ inches, 50 to 65 pounds; male 22½ to 25 inches, 65 to 80 pounds.

Color: Fawn or brindle, usually with white markings.

Temperament: Intelligent, alert, courageous, and self-assured. Playful and exuberant, but patient with children.

Energy level: High (not hyperactive), mellows with age.

Best owner: Active family with a fenced yard.

Needs: Human contact (obedience, therapy, and companionship) and exercise (agility, play, leashed walks).

Life expectancy: 8 to 12 years.

Bullmastiff

History/Evolution: The Bullmastiff was developed in England in the 1800s to help gamekeepers keep poachers out of estates and game preserves. The dog needed to track quietly and pin and hold poachers without mauling them. The winning combination of size, speed, and ferociousness turned out to be 60 percent Mastiff and 40 percent Bulldog. Today, as a companion, the Bullmastiff still can be counted on for its watchdog abilities. The AKC recognized the breed in 1933.

Size: Large; females 24 to 26 inches, 100 to 120 pounds; males 25 to 27 inches, 110 to 130 pounds.

Color: Red, fawn, and brindle.

Temperament: Gentle, quiet, devoted guardian and companion. Intelligent, stubborn when it comes to obedience training.

Photograph © Isabelle Francaise

Energy level: Low.

Best owner: Firm but loving owner who has time and patience for training.

Needs: Moderate daily exercise (leashed), socialization, roomy indoor accommodations (soft, comfy bed), slobber maintenance.

Life expectancy: 8 to 10 years.

Doberman Pinscher

History/Evolution: The Doberman Pinscher, which originated in Germany around 1900, gets its name from Louis Dobermann, a tax collector who wanted a dog to accompany and protect him as he worked. The German Pinscher, Rottweiler, Black and Tan Terrier, and Weimaraner were probably used to develop the Doberman. Intelligence and ability makes it among the finest police dogs, guard dogs, and war dogs. A noted show dog, the Doberman has also become a beloved and loyal family pet.

Size: Medium to large, 60 to 85 pounds; females 24 to 26 inches; males 26 to 28 inches.

Color: Black, red, blue, or fawn, all with rust markings.

Temperament: Energetic, watchful, and fearless. Loyal and intelligent. Reserved with strangers and may be aggressive with strange dogs.

Photograph © Jean Fogle

Energy level: High.

Best owner: Active owner; a firm person who has time and energy for training.

Needs: Daily mental and physical exercise (vigorous runs, long walks, agility), indoor companionship.

Life expectancy: 10 to 12 years.

Dogue de Bordeaux

History/Evolution: Although the history of the Dogue de Bordeaux is steeped in mystery, it is generally agreed that the ancient breed shares its ancestry with Molossers such as Mastiffs and Bulldogs. The Dogue de Bordeaux was a prized hunter, fighter, and guardian, found in homes of wealthy French. The breed suffered setbacks during the French Revolution and World War II, but rebounded and realized its fame in the U.S. after one of its kind co-starred in the 1989 film *Turner and Hooch*.

Size: Giant; females 23 to 26 inches, from 99 pounds; males 23½ to 27 inches, from 110 pounds.

Color: Shades of fawn to mahogany.

Temperament: Gifted and courageous guardian, but not aggressive; loyal and affectionate. Can coexist with older children with supervision.

Photograph © Jean Fogle

Book V

Meet the Breeds

Energy level: Low.

Best owner: Confident, active owner able to handle the breed's size and strength.

Needs: Extensive socialization, daily exercise, patient and positive obedience training.

Life expectancy: 10 to 12 years.

German Pinscher

History/Evolution: Although the German Pinscher resembles other Pinschers and the Doberman, it is more closely associated with the Standard Schnauzer. Traced to Germany in the 1600s, the German Pinscher was known as a hard-working ratter around stables. It faced extinction after World War II but was rescued by dedicated breeders. It was accepted into the Working Group of the AKC in 2003. These dogs are loyal, high-energy companions that retain natural hunting abilities and protective instincts.

Size: Medium, 17 to 20 inches, 25 to 35 pounds.

Color: Fawn to red to stag red; black and tan, blue and tan.

Temperament: Alert, vivacious, and courageous; a guard dog with highly developed senses. Intelligent, independent, and playful.

Photograph © Isabelle Francaise

Energy level: High.

Best owner: Active owner able to dole out consistent discipline; families with older children.

Needs: Daily exercise (fenced yard or twice-daily walks), socialization, companionship, and obedience training.

Life expectancy: 12 to 15 years.

Giant Schnauzer

Photograph © Jean Fogle

History/Evolution: Developed in Germany, the Giant Schnauzer is joined in the Schnauzer breed by the Miniature and Standard Schnauzers. Through crossings with smooth-coated cattle dogs, sheepdogs, Great Danes, and probably others, the breed developed into a capable cattle and driving dog who could withstand varying weather conditions; butchers and breweries also used them as guard dogs. The intelligent dogs later excelled as trained police dogs during World War I.

Size: Large; females 23½ to 25½ inches, 65 to 80 pounds; males 25½ to 27½ inches, 80 to 95 pounds.

Color: Solid black or pepper and salt.

Temperament: Bold and protective, reserved with strangers; playful and boisterous. Happy when working. May herd children or tend toward overprotective.

Energy level: Medium to high.

Best owner: Confident and firm with time to dedicate to training and companionship.

Needs: Daily exercise and play, obedience training, fenced yard; daily beard cleaning, weekly combing and professional shaping twice a year.

Life expectancy: 10 to 12 years.

Great Dane

Photograph © Jean Fogle

History/Evolution: The distinguished Great Dane's origins can be traced to ancient crossings that included English Mastiff, Irish Wolfhound, and Greyhound. By the 14th century, Great Danes were prized in Germany as swift and powerful wild boar hunters. As time went on, the breed gained in popularity with wealthy landowners because of its imposing and noble appearance. Though their size can be limiting, Great Danes continue to impress show people and pet owners alike.

Size: Giant; females 30 inches or more, 100 to 135 pounds; males 32 inches or more, 145 to 185 pounds.

Color: Brindle, fawn, blue, black, mantle, and harlequin (white with black patches).

Temperament: Spirited, courageous, friendly, and dependable. With proper training and supervision, makes a fine family companion.

Energy level: Medium.

Best owner: Confident owner in a suburban or rural home with time for training and exercise.

Needs: Fenced yard, early socialization, companionship; soft bedding and elevated food bowls (to help prevent bloat).

Life expectancy: 7 to 10 years.

Great Pyrenees

Photograph © Jean Fogle

History/Evolution: The Great Pyrenees gets its name from the European mountain range where it has long guarded flocks of sheep, but its origins can be traced to Asia Minor around 10,000 BC. In medieval France, the imposing white dogs were prized by royalty and nobility. Although the Great Pyrenees has suffered setbacks, conscientious and focused breeding has allowed the breed to continue, achieving moderate popularity in the U.S. The Great Pyrenees achieved AKC recognition in 1933.

Size: Giant; females 25 to 29 inches, 85 pounds; males 27 to 32 inches, 115 pounds.

Color: White or white with markings of gray, badger, reddish brown, or tan, especially on the head.

Temperament: Confident, territorial, and protective; affectionate, loyal, but reserved and serious. May try to dominate and wander off-leash, and tends to bark.

Energy level: Low to medium.

Best owner: Active owner with a large, fenced yard; someone strong enough to manage a giant, strong-minded dog.

Needs: Early training and socialization, kind firmness, daily exercise, leashed outings, weekly brushing (more when shedding).

Life expectancy: 10 to 12 years.

Greater Swiss Mountain Dog

Photograph © Isabelle Francaise

History/Evolution: The Greater Swiss Mountain Dog is the largest and oldest of the Swiss Mountain Dogs native to Switzerland. With a heritage traced to Mastiff-type dogs that ancient Romans introduced to the area, the breed is a skilled herder, drafter, and guardian of home and livestock. Although machines have taken over many of its duties, the breed has enjoyed a slow but steady growth in interest as companions. In 1995 the breed achieved recognition by the AKC.

Size: Giant; females 23½ to 27 inches, 85 to 90 pounds; males 25½ to 28½ inches; 90 to 130 pounds.

Color: Black and rust and white.

Temperament: Faithful, sensitive, devoted family companion. Calm and easygoing, but territorial, alert, and vigilant.

Energy level: Medium.

Best owner: Family with roomy, fenced yard.

Needs: Moderate exercise, early socialization and training, an owner who is a leader; participant in family goings-on.

Life expectancy: 10 to 12 years.

Komondor

History/Evolution: The Komondor is a breed that has worked for centuries guarding livestock in Hungary. The breed's unusual coat allows it to blend in with sheep and also serves as armor against the jaws of predators. Although uncommon everywhere but in Hungary, Komondors were brought to the U.S. in 1933 and have been effectively used in the to guard livestock and fend off coyotes and bobcats. As pets, Komondors require extra consideration for their corded coat and independent nature.

Size: Large to giant; females 25½-plus inches, 80-plus pounds; males 27½-plus inches, 100-plus pounds.

Color: White.

Temperament: A natural protector; vigilant, courageous, and faithful. Calm; reserved with strangers, may be overprotective of children.

Photograph © Isabelle Francaise

Energy level: Low to medium.

Best owner: Active owner with time for exercise and consistent training.

Needs: Fenced yard, daily exercise, obedience training, fair but firm handling, socialization. Coat care requires separation of unusual cords and time-consuming bathing.

Life expectancy: 10 to 12 years.

Kuvasz

History/Evolution: An ancient breed, the Kuvasz can trace its origins to Hungary in the Middle Ages and Tibet and Turkey before that; the name probably is derived from the Turkish *kawasz,* meaning "armed guard of the nobility." Although the Kuvasz declined during the two World Wars, breeders continued the breed. Kuvaskok (plural) were brought to the U.S. in the 1930s; the AKC recognized the breed in 1935. Today the Kuvasz remains a noble addition to family and farm.

Size: Giant; females 26 to 28 inches, 70 to 90 pounds; males 28 to 30 inches, 100 to 115 pounds.

Color: White.

Temperament: Spirited, fearless, and protective. Devoted companion but not demonstrative; sensitive to praise and blame. Independent thinker.

Photograph © Isabelle Francaise

Energy level: Medium.

Best owner: Confident, active owner in a rural or suburban home; may be overprotective when children are playing.

Needs: Daily exercise, fenced yard, twice-weekly brushing (more during shedding), socialization and obedience training. Enjoys colder climates.

Life expectancy: 10 to 12 years.

Mastiff

History/Evolution: Evidence of ancient Mastiffs is peppered with uncertainty, but traces of the giant breed are found in Egyptian monuments and in images of Roman gladiators. Later, the English prized them watchdogs against wolves and thieves. Today's Mastiffs are descendants of a noble line of dogs from the Lyme Hall Mastiffs of England. Although some believe the Mastiff arrived in the U.S. on the Mayflower, more concrete evidence suggests the late 1800s. Sometimes called "Old English Mastiff."

Size: Giant; females 27½ inches, 120 to 165 pounds; males 30 inches, 165 to 225 pounds (pets often 10 to 40 pounds smaller).

Color: Fawn, apricot, or brindle.

Temperament: Devoted and courageous guardian, but good natured, docile, and surprisingly gentle; well mannered as a house pet and not overly excitable.

Photograph © Jean Fogle

Energy level: Low.

Best owner: Owner in a roomy suburban or rural home; resources for vet care, food, and a large automobile.

Needs: Daily moderate exercise (walks or games), socialization and companionship; drool maintenance, room to stretch and lounge.

Life expectancy: 8 to 10 years.

Neapolitan Mastiff

History/Evolution: An ancient breed with roots going back to war dogs used by the Romans, the Neapolitan Mastiff retreated into obscurity until the breed was rediscovered in Italy in the 1940s. With its massive size and imposing look created by its loose folds of skin, the Neapolitan is a daunting and commanding guard of livestock, estate, master, and family. The AKC recognized the Neapolitan Mastiff as a member of the Working Group in 2004.

Size: Giant; females 24 to 29 inches, 110 pounds; males 26 to 31 inches, 150 pounds.

Color: Gray, black, mahogany and tawny; with or without brindling.

Temperament: Watchful, steady, and loyal to owner; calm yet wary. Good with children, but can be overprotective, and massive size can cause accidents. Does not get along with other dogs.

Photograph © Isabelle Francaise

Energy level: Low.

Best owner: Owner with a large home and no other pets; sufficient financial resources for food and vet bills.

Needs: Roomy living quarters, minimal exercise, drool and food cleanup.

Life expectancy: 8 to 10 years.

Newfoundland

History/Evolution: The exact origin of the Newfoundland is unclear, but the breed is widely believed to have developed on the coast of Newfoundland. Thanks to webbed feet, powerful muscles, and a thick coat, the dogs excelled in the island's cold waters and were used to drag heavy fishing nets. On land the dogs are superb draft and pack dogs. Beloved for its easygoing, sweet temperament and working ability, it has fans in the U.S. and Canada as well as throughout Europe.

Size: Giant; females 26 inches, 100 to 120 pounds; males 28 inches, 130 to 150 pounds.

Color: Black, brown, gray, and white and black.

Temperament: Sweet, calm, gentle, intelligent, and patient. Ideal for training. Friendly to all, but will protect family if threatened.

Photograph © Jean Fogle

Energy level: Medium to low at maturity.

Best owner: Active family with fenced yard in suburbs or countryside.

Needs: Brushing (lots of it), daily exercise (walking, swimming, pulling, playing), room to stretch out, indoor companionship, drool duty, obedience training.

Life expectancy: 8 to 10 years.

Portuguese Water Dog

History/Evolution: Bred to help fishermen, the Portuguese Water Dog is native to Portugal, where its name *Cao de Agua* means "dog of water." Exceptional swimmers and divers, the dogs would guard boats, dive for fish, and retrieve broken nets. Although technology has taken over its duties, the Portuguese Water Dog is proving itself as a family companion. This nonallergenic breed is enjoyed by those with allergies; President Obama and the First Family adopted a Portuguese Water Dog in 2009.

Size: Medium; females 17 to 21 inches, 34 to 50 pounds; males 19 to 23 inches, 42 to 60 pounds.

Color: Black, white, various tones of brown, parti-color.

Temperament: Spirited, gregarious, brave, and water loving. Intelligent and loyal, obedient.

Photograph © Jean Fogle

Energy level: High.

Best owner: Active owner who wants an affectionate, playful, adventurous canine companion.

Needs: Daily mental and physical exercise (with obedience, swimming, and retrieving), regular combing and grooming (clipping or scissoring), inclusion in family activities.

Life expectancy: 10 to 14 years.

Rottweiler

History/Evolution: The Rottweiler probably originated from Roman dogs who drove and guarded the cattle that accompanied Roman soldiers on marches. Some of the dogs settled in Germany, where the herding and guarding instincts were further developed. Dog fanciers reestablished the breed after a brush with extinction; in the 1990s the Rottweiler was the second-most-popular breed in the U.S. A current concern is that the powerful, highly territorial dogs are not always placed in suitable homes.

Size: Large; females 22 to 25 inches, 80 to 100 pounds; males 24 to 27 inches, 95 to 135 pounds.

Color: Black, with rust to mahogany markings.

Temperament: Alert, confident, and imposing. Self-assured, aloof, and protective of home and family; not likely to form immediate friendships.

Photograph © Jean Fogle

Energy level: Medium.

Best owner: Strong, confident owner with a fenced yard; someone able to administer fair and consistent discipline.

Needs: Daily exercise, obedience training, and socialization. Happiest as protector, herder, service dog, obedience competitor, therapy dog.

Life expectancy: 8 to 10 years.

Saint Bernard

History/Evolution: The Saint Bernard is believed to have origins in the Molossian dogs brought to Switzerland by the Romans, but the dog's most relevant history began in the mid-1600s. At that time, the original Saint Bernard was introduced to the Hospice, a refuge for travelers crossing the Swiss Alps. The dogs proved invaluable; guarding, carting, and locating and rescuing lost travelers and people trapped in avalanches. Saint Bernards saved more than 2,000 lives during their service in the Alps.

Size: Giant, 130 to 180 pounds; females 25½ inches and up; males 27½ inches and up.

Color: Red and white, with the red in varying shades.

Temperament: Devoted, gentle, dignified, and patient. Willing to please, but can be stubborn. Protective nature should be controlled, not encouraged.

Photograph © Jean Fogle

Energy level: Medium to low.

Best owner: Confident, strong owner who can provide a cool living environment.

Needs: Daily exercise (to prevent obesity), outside time in a fenced yard (except when it's hot), obedience training, weekly brushing, drool patrol.

Life expectancy: 8 to 10 years.

Samoyed

History/Evolution: The Samoyed has remained relatively unchanged for centuries. Reindeer herder, work dog, guardian, and companion of the nomadic Samoyed peoples of northwestern Siberia, the Samoyed possesses great intelligence and strength. Samoyeds were included in sled teams that explored Antarctica and the South Pole. Although the breed's primary purpose has changed from reindeer herder to sled puller and companion, the Samoyed has retained its gentle, protective temperament.

Size: Medium; females 19 to 21 inches, 38 to 50 pounds; males 21 to 24 inches, 50 to 65 pounds.

Color: White (can have cream or biscuit-colored spots, especially on the head).

Temperament: Gentle, amiable, and playful; loves everyone. Intelligent, but bores quickly and may bark and dig. May tend to herd children.

Photograph © Isabelle Francaise

Energy level: Medium.

Best owner: Active family with fenced yard and year-round pile of snow.

Needs: Daily vigorous exercise (long walk, jogs, sled pulling, play sessions), coat brushing twice a week (more during shedding), cool climate or air conditioning.

Life expectancy: 12 to 15 years.

Siberian Husky

History/Evolution: The Siberian Husky was bred as a sled dog and has retained the endurance and willingness to work. Sled dogs were the primary means of transportation in northeastern Asian subarctic communities, and Huskies were utilized during the Alaskan Gold Rush and early long-distance sled races. Air travel and snowmobiles have largely replaced them, but the dog's agreeable temperament and a growing interest in recreational races such as the Iditarod have kept its popularity high.

Size: Medium; females 20 to 21 inches, 35 to 50 pounds; males 21 to 23½ inches, 45 to 60 pounds.

Color: All colors, from black to white, usually with markings; brown, blue, parti-colored eyes.

Temperament: Friendly, gentle, outgoing, adventurous, and fun loving.Not overly suspicious, possessive, or aggressive. Not to be trusted with small domestic pets.

Photograph © Isabelle Francaise

Energy level: Medium to high.

Best owner: Athlete or active lover of the outdoors with a firm handle on obedience.

Needs: Frequent brushing, fenced yard, outlet for vigorous daily exercise.

Life expectancy: 12 to 14 years.

Standard Schnauzer

History/Evolution: Of the three Schnauzers — Miniature, Standard, and Giant — the Standard is the prototype. It may be the result of crossings between Wire-Haired Pinschers, black German Poodles, and Gray Wolf Spitz. With early jobs that included guard, rat catcher, and yard dog, the Standard Schnauzer went on to work with German police and as dispatch carriers and Red Cross aides. Although still at work in some sheep ranches, the Standard Schnauzer is a beloved and loyal companion.

Size: Medium; females 17½ to 18½ inches, around 35 pounds; males 18½ to 19½ inches, around 45 pounds.

Color: Pepper and salt, or black.

Temperament: Bold, lively, and fun loving; headstrong (training exercises channel such traits toward positive behaviors). Good at obedience, agility, and tracking.

Photograph © Jean Fogle

Energy level: High.

Best owner: Active, confident owner with a fenced yard.

Needs: Daily exercise (runs, games, agility courses), training, socialization, twice-weekly combing and quarterly professional shaping.

Life expectancy: 12 to 14 years.

Tibetan Mastiff

History/Evolution: Although much of the history of the Tibetan Mastiff is lost, the breed is believed to be the basic stock from which most modern working breeds developed. The Tibetan Mastiff was prized by Tibetans living in the Himalayas; the massive dogs were traditionally tied to gates or stakes and let loose at night to protect livestock and masters. A few Tibetan Mastiffs trickled out of the region, eventually gaining the attention of fanciers in England and beyond.

Size: Giant; females 24 inches and up, 80 to 110 pounds; males 26 inches and up, 90 to 150 pounds or more.

Color: Black, brown, and gray, with or without tan markings, and shades of gold.

Temperament: Independent, strong willed, and reserved. Territorial and protective of family; aloof with strangers. Gentle with children, but may be overprotective.

Photograph © Isabelle Francaise

Energy level: Low, but more active outside.

Best owner: Strong, confident owner with fenced yard.

Needs: Daily exercise, regular brushing, integration into family activities and home life.

Life expectancy: 11 to 14 years.

Chapter 3

Profiling the Herding Group

*T*o see a Herding dog in action is to see something quite amazing.

Whether by staring, nipping, stalking, circling, or barking, Herding breeds have an incredible ability to control the movement of other animals. The work requires great endurance, with constant running and patrolling to keep herds or flocks together. These breeds are highly intelligent and able to work with a shepherd or rancher to follow commands, but they are also perfectly capable of thinking on their own when necessary.

Created in 1983, the Herding Group is the newest AKC classification, made up of breeds that were formerly members of the Working Group. Although the group is diverse, the breeds are known for their stamina and obedience, and are able to follow the signals of their master and execute them with great skill.

The job of herder should not be taken lightly; some farmers use one dog to herd more than a thousand animals at a time!

Consider the diminutive Cardigan Welsh Corgi: At about a foot tall, this remarkable dog can drive an entire herd of cows to their destination. Never losing sight of the job at hand, a Corgi runs circles around a herd, moving cows together and collecting strays that may escape from the group.

The Shetland Sheepdog, only slightly larger than the Corgi, was bred down to its current small size to better control the smaller livestock common to the rugged Shetland Islands of the British Isles. The dogs were hardy enough to endure the harsh climate and smart enough to even be left in charge of the animals when the farmers weren't around.

Today most Herding dogs live as household pets, with little or no contact with farm animals. With or without livestock, these dogs are still instinctual herders and will herd whoever and whatever they can, including other dogs and children.

Herding breeds need socialization and close contact with humans, and they should have access to both home and yard.

Members of the Herding Group are described as follows:

- ✔ Loyal
- ✔ Energetic
- ✔ Smart
- ✔ Territorial
- ✔ Inclined to chase

Herding dogs are happiest when they have a job to do. People who live with herders find that exercise, training, and activities such as agility, and obedience activities and training provide an outlet for all the energy they possess.

Because they are alert and protective, Herding breeds are capable watchdogs in the home. Some, such as the German Shepherd and Malinois, are excellent police and military dogs and are used in search-and-rescue efforts.

Australian Cattle Dog

History/Evolution: The Australian Cattle Dog was developed in Australia in the 1800s when it became clear that European herding dogs could not withstand the country's rough terrain and climate. Australian cattlemen needed a dog who could herd a wilder type of cattle; crosses may have included Dingos, Highland Collies, Black and Tan Kelpie, and the Dalmatian. Though the breed was slow to catch on in the U.S., it has proved an untiring and effective herder. The AKC recognized the breed in 1993.

Size: Medium, 35 to 45 pounds; females 17 to 19 inches; males 18 to 20 inches.

Color: Blue or red (mottled or speckled), with or without black, blue, or tan markings.

Temperament: Intelligent, independent, tenacious, energetic, hardy, and untiring. Loyal and protective; suspicious of strangers. Needs a job. Herds children, sometime with nips.

Photograph © Jean Fogle

Energy level: High.

Best Owner: Active owners with time and energy for hard, daily exercise; a family with older children and a fenced yard.

Needs: A lot of physical and mental activities (more than a walk — think agility course and obedience lessons), opportunities to herd, regular brushing.

Life expectancy: 10 to 13 years.

Australian Shepherd

History/Evolution: Despite its name, the Australian Shepherd probably originated in the Pyrenees Mountains between Spain and France; the name comes from association with shepherds who came from Australia to the western U.S. in the 1800s. Ranchers continued to develop the breed to its current high level of versatility, intelligence, and trainability. Appearances in movies, television shows, and rodeos helped boost popularity. The breed excels as guide, hearing, therapy, and search-and-rescue dogs.

Size: Medium; females 18 to 21 inches, 40 to 55 pounds; males 20 to 23 inches, 50 to 65 pounds.

Color: Blue merle, red (liver) merle, and black or red, all with or without copper and/or tan markings.

Temperament: Bold, alert, confident, independent, and smart; difficult if lacking a challenge. May try to herd children and small animals by nips.

Photograph © Jean Fogle

Energy level: Medium to high.

Best Owner: Active owner in a rural or suburban home.

Needs: Daily workouts with mental and physical challenges (agility, flyball, obedience, tracking, freestyle), fenced yard, weekly brushing, companionship.

Life expectancy: 12 to 14 years.

Bearded Collie

History/Evolution: Developed in Scotland, the Bearded Collie may trace its ancestors to the Komondor, British Isles herding dogs, and the Poland Lowland Sheepdog. In Scotland, the energetic Beardies were tireless sheepherders and later gained popularity as show dogs. The AKC recognized the breed in 1977. The Bearded Collie has loads of fans who enjoy the breed as a companion who likes plenty of activity, whether in the form of agility, Frisbee, or herding a backyard full of children.

Size: Medium; females 20 to 21 inches, 40 to 45 pounds; males 21 to 22 inches, 50 to 60 pounds.

Color: Black, brown, blue, or fawn, usually with white markings.

Temperament: Lively, playful, and enthusiastic; devoted, intelligent, and self-confident. Exuberant with kids; may try to herd young children while playing.

Photograph © Jean Fogle

Energy level: Medium to high.

Best Owner: Active owner or family with post-toddler children.

Needs: Family bonding, vigorous daily exercise, fenced yard, weekly brushing and combing sessions.

Life expectancy: 12 to 14 years.

Beauceron

History/Evolution: The Beauceron is a French herding dog dating back to the 1500s, highly valued as a farm dog, drover, and guardian of sheep and family. In 1863, the breed was differentiated into long-coated (Briard) and short-coated (Beauceron). During World War I and II, the military used them as messenger dogs and mine detectors. Although the breed has been relatively unknown outside of France, the Beauceron has recently begun to gain the attention of fanciers in the U.S. and elsewhere.

Size: Medium to large, 65 to 85 pounds; females 24 to 26½ inches; males 25½ to 27½ inches.

Color: Black and tan, or black, gray, and tan.

Temperament: Self-assured, courageous, calm, and intelligent. Loyal and devoted to family, but without training, can take over. Very protective; may herd children.

Photograph © Jean Fogle

Energy level: Medium to high.

Best Owner: Active owner or family with fenced yard.

Needs: Daily mental and physical exercise, firm obedience training, some time outdoors, human contact.

Life expectancy: 10 to 12 years.

Belgian Malinois

History/Evolution: The Belgian Malinois shares a foundation with other Belgian sheepherding breeds, including the Belgian Sheepdog and the Belgian Tervuren — Belgian dogs share a breed standard in all countries except the U.S. Developed in the city of Malines, Malinois is prized as a confident herder and guard. Although it has experienced uneven growth in popularity outside Belgium, the Malinois is considered a preeminent security and police dog, ranking even above the German Shepherd.

Size: Medium to large; females 22 to 24 inches, 50 to 60 pounds; males 24 to 26 inches, 55 to 75 pounds.

Color: Fawn to mahogany, with black mask and ears.

Temperament: Confident, intense, alert; protective without being overly aggressive. Happiest with plenty of activity and a job; quick and responsive to commands.

Photograph © Isabelle Francaise

Energy level: High.

Best Owner: Active, confident owner with experience handling dogs and time for training and socialization.

Needs: A lot of exercise (not leashed strolls) and mental stimulation (obedience training and tracking), fenced yard, weekly brushing.

Life expectancy: 10 to 12 years.

Belgian Sheepdog

History/Evolution: Known as the *Groenendael,* or *Chien de Berger Beige* in most parts of the world, the Belgian Sheepdog traces its origins to the late 1800s. Like all Belgian shepherds, the breed was an accomplished herder and guard. In the early 1900s Belgian Sheepdogs were gaining a reputation as police dogs. During World War I and II, they served as sentry dogs, message carriers, and ambulance dogs. Today they continue to serve society well, as guide and therapy dogs and as devoted companions.

Size: Medium to large; females 22 to 24 inches, 40 to 60 pounds; males 25 to 26 inches, 50 to 75 pounds.

Color: Black.

Temperament: Watchful, attentive, courageous, and intense; possessive and aggressive toward dogs and animals. Intelligent but independent. Aloof with strangers.

Photograph © Isabelle Francaise

Energy level: High.

Best Owner: Patient but firm owner with time for training and socialization.

Needs: Tolerance with shedding and weekly brushing, fenced yard, cool climate, plenty of mental and physical stimulation (herding trials).

Life expectancy: 10 to 12 years.

Belgian Tervuren

History/Evolution: One of the four Belgian shepherd breeds, the Belgian Tervuren's protective instincts and herding abilities made it an ideal dog for rural farmers in Belgium. The dogs continued as beloved companions even after machines gradually took over the breed's farm duties. A drop in numbers nearly caused the Belgian Tervuren to disappear by 1930, but fanciers have rescued the breed to its current moderate popularity.

Photograph © Jean Fogle

Size: Medium to large; females 22 to 24 inches, 45 to 60 pounds; males 24 to 26 inches, 65 to 80 pounds.

Color: Fawn to mahogany, with black overlay.

Temperament: Alert and energetic; affectionate and possessive with family, but observant and aloof with strangers. Given exercise and challenges, can be well-mannered companion. May nip at children's heels.

Energy level: High.

Best Owner: Active, confident owner who has time for training.

Needs: Strenuous daily activity (jogging, serious play or working session) and mental challenges of obedience, agility, tracking; regular brushing and interaction; fenced yard.

Life expectancy: 10 to 14 years.

Border Collie

History/Evolution: The Border Collie is the consummate sheepdog. The energetic breed's origins can be traced back to the 1800s, in the border country between Scotland and England. One accomplished individual, named Hemp, is considered the father of the breed; his herding skills were considerable, especially his intimidating stare. Although many of the breed's devotees wanted to keep the Border Collie out of the show ring, the AKC recognized it in 1995. Studies suggest that the Border Collie may be the most intelligent dog.

Photograph © Jean Fogle

Size: Medium; 18 to 20 inches, 30 to 45 pounds.

Color: Black, blue, chocolate, and red, with or without white markings or merling.

Temperament: Energetic, intelligent, and an intense worker who can be destructive if not sufficiently challenged. Loves to chase (not the best choice for families with children).

Energy level: High.

Best Owner: Active owners with time for exercise or someone who lives on a farm.

Needs: Daily exercise, a job, obedience training, fenced yard, regular brushing.

Life expectancy: 12 to 14 years.

Bouvier des Flandres

History/Evolution: *Bouvier* means "cowherd" in French, and that's exactly what the Bouvier des Flandres did best. Because early individuals of the breed were strictly working dogs, the dogs came in a variety of sizes and colors. Interest in the breed developed in the early 1900s, and an accepted standard soon followed. Although the Bouvier des Flandres is not extremely popular, it is recognized for its excellence in dog shows and herding trials.

Photograph © Jean Fogle

Size: Large; females 23½ to 26½ inches, males 24½ to 27½ inches, 60 to 90 pounds.

Color: Fawn to black, salt and pepper, gray, and brindle.

Temperament: Steady, resolute, and fearless. Loyal, devoted, and protective; reserved with strangers and can be aggressive with strange dogs. Independent and confident, but willing to please.

Energy level: Medium to high.

Best Owner: Strong, confident owner with time for training, exercise, and grooming.

Needs: Daily interaction and exercise (herding is ideal, but running and playing work), fenced yard, cool climate, early training, and regular brushing and grooming.

Life expectancy: 10 to 12 years.

Briard

History/Evolution: Records of the Briard, the oldest of the four French sheepdog breeds, date back to the 1300s. Though the Briard originally defended estates and flocks against wolves and human intruders, its role developed into more of a peaceful herder. The tale goes that the breed surfaced in the U.S. with either the Marquis de Lafayette or Thomas Jefferson. In 1922 the AKC registered the first litter of Briards. The breed is still a popular sheepherder in France.

Photograph © Isabelle Francaise

Size: Large; females 22 to 25½ inches, 50 to 65 pounds; males 23 to 27 inches, 75 to 100 pounds.

Color: Black, gray, and tawny.

Temperament: Naturally protective, fearless, reserved with strangers; loyal, loving, gentle with friends and family. Intelligent and independent, easily trained. May try to herd children.

Energy level: Medium.

Best Owner: Firm, confident owner.

Needs: Daily exercise (long walk or jog, play session) and interaction (training), early training and socialization, frequent brushing to prevent matting.

Life expectancy: 10 to 12 years.

Canaan Dog

History/Evolution: The Canaan Dog has a long and eventful history, beginning in ancient times in the biblical Land of Canaan as an adept guard and herd dog of the ancient Israelites; when the Israelites were dispersed by the Romans 2,000 years ago, many dogs survived on their own or lived with Bedouins, who raised them as guard and livestock dogs. Later, Canaan Dogs were trained as sentry dogs, messengers, and land mine locators. The first Canaan Dogs arrived in the U.S. in 1965.

Size: Medium; females 19 to 23 inches, 35 to 45 pounds; males 20 to 24 inches, 45 to 55 pounds.

Color: White with black, brown, or red markings; brown or black, with or without white markings.

Temperament: Devoted, docile, and willing to please family; reserved and aloof with strangers. Alert, vigilant, and territorial; vocal and persistent.

Photograph © Sarah O'Neill

Energy level: Medium.

Best Owner: Active owner in a suburban or rural home.

Needs: Plenty of exercise and mental and physical challenges; secure fencing, training, human contact, weekly brushing, and early socialization.

Life expectancy: 12 to 15 years.

Collie (rough and smooth)

History/Evolution: Long used as herding dogs in Scotland and England, the Collie became fashionable after Queen Victoria was smitten with the breed in 1860. Two varieties of Collie exist: rough coated and smooth, the smooth and rough varieties are identical in standard except for their coats. Settlers brought Collies to the U.S. to work sheep farms, and the breed continued its rise in popularity. Lassie, the most famous rough-coated Collie of all time, further solidified the breed's place in popular history.

Size: Medium to large; females 22 to 24 inches, 50 to 65 pounds; males 24 to 26 inches, 60 to 75 pounds.

Color: Sable and white, tricolor, blue merle, and white.

Temperament: Sensitive, intelligent, gentle, and mild mannered. A devoted family dog; especially good with children, but may nip at heels. Some bark when left alone.

Photograph © Jean Fogle

Energy level: Medium.

Best Owner: Active family.

Needs: Daily exercise (herding is an excellent choice), close bonding with family, gentle handling, weekly brushing.

Life expectancy: 10 to 13 years.

German Shepherd Dog

History/Evolution: The product of much development, the German Shepherd Dog is the result of breeder efforts to produce the ideal herder and guarder of flocks. The German Shepherd possesses it all: strength, dependability, intelligence, and courage. Off the farm, the breed was quick to prove itself a capable police and war dog, and later as a guide, search-and-rescue dog, and show dog. Thanks to movie stars such as Strongheart and Rin Tin Tin, the breed's popularity soared in the 1920s and 1930s.

Size: Large; females 22 to 24 inches, 60 to 70 pounds; males 24 to 26 inches, 75 to 95 pounds.

Color: All colors except white; typically black and tan, sable, and black.

Temperament: Direct, fearless, and protective but not hostile; suspicious of strangers. A poised, intelligent guardian. Devoted to family; dogs from well-bred lines are great with children.

Photograph © Jean Fogle

Energy level: Medium.

Best Owner: Active, confident owner or family.

Needs: Daily mental and physical challenges (exercise, play sessions, and learning), fenced yard, obedience, close human contact, lots of brushing (heavy shedder).

Life expectancy: 10 to 12 years.

Old English Sheepdog

History/Evolution: A relatively new breed, the Old English Sheepdog originated in the 1800s in the west of England, probably a descendant of the Scotch Bearded Collie and the Russian Owtchar. The dogs drove sheep and cattle to market, and were known as "Bobtail" because of their docked tails (a sign that they were working dogs and exempt from taxes). The dog's coat insulates it from cold, heat, and dampness. Though the profuse coat can be a deterrent, the Old English Sheepdog is an ideal house dog.

Size: Large; females 21 inches and up, 60 to 80 pounds; males 22 inches and up, 70 to 90 pounds.

Color: Gray, grizzle, blue, or blue merle, with or without white.

Temperament: Energetic, adaptable, intelligent, gentle, and clownish. Devoted, thrives on companionship; protective of family members and will herd children. Can be headstrong or bossy.

Photograph © Jean Fogle

Energy level: Medium.

Best Owner: Active, confident owner; families, if someone has time for grooming.

Needs: Daily exercise (consider herding), fenced yard, human contact, serious brushing every other day to prevent matting.

Life expectancy: 10 to 13 years.

Norwegian Buhund

History/Evolution: The Norwegian Buhund traces its history to the Vikings, with whom they traveled by sea and land; remains of the earliest Buhunds were found in a Viking grave from about the year 900. The modern Norwegian Buhund resembles the refined Buhunds of Norway, which guarded farms and herded sheep. Today's Buhund still works with livestock and guards home and family — and is happy lying at an owner's feet at the end of the day. The AKC recognized the breed in January 2009.

Size: Medium; females 16 to 17½ inches, 26 to 35 pounds; males 17 to 18½ inches, 31 to 40 pounds.

Color: Wheaten, with or without black mask; black.

Temperament: Energetic, lively, with great stamina; quick learners. Alert, self-confident, and independent, but affectionate with people.

Photograph © Isabelle Francaise

Energy level: High.

Best Owner: Active, firm owner or family in a suburban or rural home.

Needs: Daily exercise and lots of playtime (running/walking, herding, Frisbee, agility), firm obedience training, fenced yard, and family contact.

Life expectancy: 13 to 15 years.

Polish Lowland Sheepdog

History/Evolution: Known to much of the world as the Polish Owczarek Nizinny, the Polish Lowland Sheepdog goes by the nickname PON. The breed's origins go back to the early history of Poland, with crossings that may include Tibetan Terrier and Puli. Because the PONs were smaller than some of the larger flock-guarding dogs, they didn't scare the sheep as much and had better endurance. The PON survived World War I and remains a valued sheepherder and companion; its size makes it suitable to apartment life.

Size: Medium, 30 to 50 pounds; females 17 to 19 inches; males 18 to 20 inches.

Color: Any color.

Temperament: Self-confident, independent, willful; more serious than its appearance. Affectionate, but territorial and wary with strangers. Barks often. Good with children, especially when raised with them.

Photograph © Isabelle Francaise

Energy level: Medium to high.

Best Owner: Active, firm, and consistent owners.

Needs: Daily exercise for mind and body (herding and agility are ideal), fenced yard, firm training, socialization, considerable brushing and combing of coat.

Life expectancy: 12 to 14 years.

Puli

History/Evolution: Some believe that Tibetan Terriers and sheepdogs of France and Germany played a role in this breed's development in Hungary in the Middle Ages. The Puli's small size, speed, and agility made it an excellent sheepherder; the unusual corded coat is the breed's natural protector. Crossbreeding nearly led to the Puli's extinction, but Puli devotees worked to reconstitute the breed in the early 1900s. Today the Puli is more a trusted watchdog and companion than sheepherder.

Size: Medium, 30 to 35 pounds; females 16 inches; males 17 inches.

Color: Rusty black, black, gray, and white.

Temperament: Energetic, curious, and smart. Protective of family, suspicious, and watchful; barks and can be aggressive toward other dogs. Home loving and affectionate.

Photograph © Isabelle Francaise

Energy level: High.

Best Owner: Active owner who can handle firm and fair training.

Needs: Daily exercise, a job to do (herding children or sheep), serious coat care (cording and cleaning), training.

Life expectancy: 12 to 16 years.

Pyrenean Shepherd

History/Evolution: Remains of ancient sheepherding dogs have been found in the Pyrenees Mountains of Southern France, and many Pyrenean Shepherds still herd in those mountains, but exact origins remain unclear. The dogs are relatively small, and so are quicker and require less food than larger sheepherder dogs. Two varieties exist: Rough-Faced and Smooth-Faced. First brought to the U.S. in the 19th century, the breed earned AKC recognition in the Herding Group in January 2009.

Size: Medium; between 15 and 21 inches, 15 to 30 pounds.

Color: Fawn or fawn with a black overlay, brindle, and gray; solid black and blue merle.

Temperament: Energetic and active, dominated by a love of work. Devoted and affectionate with immediate family, but distrustful of strangers. Strong barking instinct.

Photograph © Isabelle Francaise

Energy level: High.

Best Owner: Active owner able to devote time to training.

Needs: Daily exercise, fenced yard, inclusion in owner's/family's activities, training, early socialization, regular brushing.

Life expectancy: 12 to 15 years.

Shetland Sheepdog

History/Evolution: The Shetland Sheepdog's history goes back to the Border Collie, which was brought to the Scotland's Shetland Islands and crossed with other breeds to develop the Sheltie. The miniature Shetland proved itself to be a hard worker, protecting home, flock, and herd — and found its way into the hearts (and homes) of farm families. The breed earned it AKC recognition in 1911 and has continued to excel as a dedicated worker, loyal companion, and able competitor in obedience, herding, and agility trials.

Size: Small to medium; 13 to 16 inches.

Color: Black, blue merle, and sable, with white and sometimes tan marking.

Temperament: Loyal, affectionate, and obedient; devoted to family and excellent with children. Intelligent and highly trainable. Reserved toward strangers and barks a lot.

Photograph © Jean Fogle

Energy level: Medium to high.

Best Owner: Family or active owner who has time for keeping company with a dog.

Needs: Daily exercise and activity (agility, herding, conformation), lots of family contact, early socialization, brushing every other day.

Life expectancy: 12 to 14-plus years.

Swedish Vallhund

History/Evolution: The Swedish Vallhund is an ancient breed with origins that go back to the Vikings, when it was known as the *Vikingarnas Hund,* or "Viking Dog." A small, powerful, sturdy breed, the Swedish Vallhund excels as cattle drover, watchdog, ratter, and general farmhand. Although the Corgi and the SV share some similarities, the SV is longer legged and not as stocky. The dog faced extinction in Sweden in 1942 but was rescued by a devoted fan. The AKC recognized the breed in 2005.

Size: Small to medium; 12 to 16 inches, 25 to 35 pounds.

Color: Gray through red and combinations of these colors in various shades.

Temperament: Alert, fearless, intelligent. Responsive, devoted, and affectionate; loves attention and craves leadership. Can be overprotective if not trained and socialized; may bark a lot.

Photograph © Jean Fogle

Energy level: Medium.

Best Owner: Active owner with yard or time for daily walks.

Needs: Daily exercise, early socialization and training, regular brushing.

Life expectancy: 12 to 14 years.

Cardigan Welsh Corgi

History/Evolution: The older of the two Corgi breeds, the Cardigan Welsh Corgi was brought to Cardiganshire (South Wales) from Central Europe by the Celts around 1200 BC. Later the Corgis served their masters well by driving cattle from the farmers' meager acreage out to the common land owned by the Crown. Although the breed became less useful when the land was sold off and fenced in, it has survived, with the Cardigan and the Pembroke officially divided into two types in 1934.

Size: Small to medium, 10½ to 12½ inches; females 25 to 35 pounds; males 30 to 45 pounds.

Color: All shades of red, sable, and brindle; also blue merle or black, both with or without tan or brindle points; white markings common.

Temperament: Loyal, affectionate, and even tempered; devoted to family, but reserved with strangers. Fun and high spirited, with a love of antics and tricks. Barks.

Photograph © Jean Fogle

Energy level: Medium.

Best Owner: Active owner with time for exercise.

Needs: Daily exercise (walk, herding, or play session), fenced yard, regular brushing.

Life expectancy: 12 to 14 years.

Pembroke Welsh Corgi

History/Evolution: The Pembroke Welsh Corgi's history goes back to Pembrokeshire in South Wales, where it was brought over by Flemish weavers around 1100. Though it shares some obvious similarities with the Cardigan Corgi, the Pembroke has a shorter body than the Cardigan; pointed, erect ears, compared to the Cardigan's rounded ears; and a shorter tail than the Cardigan's. Like the Cardigan, the Pembroke is a high-spirited, amiable herder that makes a fine farmhand, competitor, and home companion.

Size: Small; 10 to 12 inches, 25 to 30 pounds.

Color: Red, sable, fawn, black and tan; with or without white markings.

Temperament: Bold, active (more easily excited than the Cardigan Corgi), and quick witted. Devoted, amiable, and willing to please. Alert; reserved with strangers. Barks. May nip at heels.

Photograph © Jean Fogle

Energy level: Medium.

Best Owner: Active owner or family.

Needs: Daily physical and mental exercise (herding sessions are ideal, but walks or off-leash training sessions work), weekly brushing, human companionship.

Life expectancy: 12 to 14 years.

Chapter 4

Profiling the Hound Group

Dogs are known for their keen eyesight and acute sense of smell. After all, who hasn't seen a pup take off after a leaf skittering down a path? And what about those wet noses poked out of car windows? Dogs love to set their sniffers on a scent. But Hounds, by far, boast the best of these senses.

Most Hounds are bred to be hunters — to spot quarry or follow a trail and then have the stamina to keep going for as long as it takes. Part of the Hound group's appeal is that the breed is independent, with instincts so strong that commands often aren't necessary. These dogs understand their job and are happy and focused on doing it.

For owners, the problem lies in the fact that a Hound may not be inclined to obey a command when one is given, especially if there's an enticing scent on the breeze or a squirrel making a mad dash across the yard. Worse yet is the unleashed Hound who sets its sights on the squirrel and takes off without regard to safety.

Though all Hounds live to pursue prey, the group is a diverse lot. From the showy Afghan to the stocky Basset, the Hounds come in all shapes, sizes, colors, and coat types. Consider the Pharaoh Hound: Its stately form, going back to ancient times, is built like a Greyhound for speed, but with large, upright ears that can home in on animals underground. The Otterhound is a sturdier dog built for hunting in and around cold water, equipped with large, webbed feet for slippery terrain and a rough coat with an oily undercoat that protects it from brambles and chilly English streams.

Hound temperaments vary as widely as looks. Although all are wired to hunt, most are happy to hit the couch or curl up at your feet at the end of the day. The desert Hounds such as the Saluki and Pharaoh tend to be aloof and less demonstrative. Feisty dogs in small packages, the Dachshund and Basenjis, are confident, bold, and often described as Terrier-like. Friendly are the Beagles, and Coonhounds are known for their sweet and mellow natures.

Hunters are an obvious choice for Hound ownership, but plenty of athletic people — runners, hikers, and other sporty types — can give a Hound the outlet he needs for sniffing and chasing. This chase instinct is strong, so all Hounds need leashed outings and secure fencing.

Some Hounds, Foxhounds and Beagles among them, produce a unique sound called *baying* — that chattering howl you may have heard in movies when Hounds are hunting. Be sure you can live with this sound before bringing one of these Hounds into your life.

The Hound Group is divided into two subgroups:

- ✔ **Sighthounds:** Also called Gazehounds, these Hounds are some of the fastest breeds around, bred to spot and chase prey. The Sighthounds, which tend to be sleeker than their Scenthound cousins, include the Afghan, Basenji, Borzoi, Greyhound, Ibizan, Irish Wolfhound, Pharaoh, Saluki, Scottish Deerhound, and Whippet. Today's Sighthounds are rarely used for hunting; most, however, excel at lure coursing, running with their human partners, or competing on racetracks. The typical Sighthound is quiet, aloof, and calm.

- ✔ **Scenthounds:** Whether they're tracking scent in the air or on the ground, Scenthounds are driven by the need to sniff down prey. These dogs typically are solidly built and include the Basset, Beagle, Black and Tan Coonhound, Bloodhound, Dachshund, American and English Foxhounds, Harrier, Norwegian Elkhounds (though of the Spitz family), Otterhound, Petit Basset Griffon Vendéen, Plott, and Redbone Coonhound. This group tends to be social; dogs often work in packs and live and play together. The group's sociable nature has helped earn the Scenthounds a reputation for being amiable and adaptable companions.

With both talented nose and eyes, the Rhodesian Ridgeback fits into the Sighthound and Scenthound groups.

Afghan Hound

History/Evolution: Although some link its origins to ancient Egypt, the Afghan Hound was developed in Afghanistan; in the early 1900s, it was brought to England. Primarily a coursing Hound, the Afghan was a fast, agile, and accomplished hunter that at times was paired with specially trained falcons. The breed's dignified appearance and silky coat helped bring it into the spotlight in the show ring. Although the glamorous Afghan was fashionable in the 1970s, the breed's popularity has since dwindled.

Size: Large; females 25 inches, 50 pounds; males 27 inches, 60 pounds.

Color: Any.

Temperament: Aloof and dignified, but with a clownish side. Independent hunter. Not overly demonstrative with family, reserved with strangers.

Photograph © istockphoto.com/ Jerzy Czarkowski

Energy level: Medium, higher when young.

Best owner: Active owner in a suburban or rural home.

Needs: Daily exercise (long walks, sprints, and runs), fenced yard, leash, regular and consistent coat care.

Life expectancy: 12 years.

American Foxhound

History/Evolution: A native U.S. breed, the American Foxhound traces its origins to the late 1600s and early 1700s, when it was developed from various Hound breeds imported from France, England, and Ireland. George Washington, who ran a breeding program for the breed, is sometimes called the father of the American Foxhound. Although the breed's great speed and agility have made it a popular choice for hunters, the American Foxhound has experienced limited popularity as a pet for nonhunters.

Size: Large, 40 to 65 pounds; females 21 to 24 inches; males 22 to 25 inches.

Color: Any.

Temperament: Tolerant, gentle, amiable; reserved with strangers, but can be a well-mannered household companion. A hunter at heart; may be stubborn or independent.

Photograph © Isabelle Francaise

Energy level: High.

Best owner: Active owner in suburban or rural area.

Needs: Daily exercise (long walks or runs), fenced yard, minimal brushing to remove dead hair, tolerance of baying, companionship, a patient trainer.

Life expectancy: 11 to 13 years.

Basenji

History/Evolution: The lightly built Basenji was used for hunting game in its native Central Africa and was prized for its speed and intelligence and for its very specialized trait: Known as the "Barkless Dog," the Basenji is a silent hunter. However, the Basenji emit joyful yodels during play and when greeting family. Despite some unsuccessful attempts to bring the breed to England in the late 1800s, the Basenji eventually was established outside of Africa in England and, in 1941, the U.S.

Size: Small; females 16 inches, 22 pounds; males 17 inches, 24 pounds.

Color: Chestnut red, black, black and tan, or brindle with white markings.

Temperament: Feisty, intelligent, curious, and independent; affectionate with friends and family, but reserved with strangers. Fastidious about grooming.

Photograph © Jean Fogle

Energy level: Medium to high.

Best owner: Active owner with fenced yard and time for canine exercise.

Needs: Daily mental and physical exercise (walks, games, free runs), fenced yard, minimal coat care.

Life expectancy: 12 to 14 years.

Basset Hound

History/Evolution: Developed in France as a low-legged trailer of small game, the Bassett Hound was highly popular during the reign of Napoleon. The Marquis de Lafayette brought them to the U.S. as a gift to President George Washington to use in his hunting expeditions. In 1884, the first Basset Hound was exhibited at the Westminster Kennel Club show. Beloved companion of many, the Basset Hound continues to prove itself in conformation, obedience, tracking, hunting, and field trials.

Size: Medium, but heavy boned; 14 inches, 40 to 60 pounds.

Color: Hound colors: black, tan, and white markings; red with white; piebald.

Temperament: Sweet, gentle, good natured; easygoing with children, other dogs, and pets. Can be stubborn and slow moving when on the trail of a scent.

Photograph © istockphoto.com/ Phil Berry

Energy level: Low, but can have great stamina when hunting.

Best owner: Patient trainer who lives in a home with a backyard.

Needs: Daily leashed walk; great tolerance of drool and dirt distributed by big feet and trailing ears; minimal grooming, but regular ear cleaning to avoid infections and odor.

Life expectancy: 10 years.

Beagle

History/Evolution: Though details of the Beagle's origins are somewhat uncertain, Beagle-type dogs were used to hunt rabbits in England as early as the 14th century. The sturdy breed has undergone changes, but today's Beagle comes in two height varieties. Beagles are still used for hunting in packs, but they are equally valued for their merry personality and loyal companionship. Their intelligence, compact size, and care-free coat have made them one of the most popular breeds in the U.S.

Size: Small; 13 to 15 inches, 16 to 30 pounds.

Color: Hound colors: usually black and tan, red, or lemon, with or without white markings.

Temperament: Amiable, tolerant, good with children, curious, and mischievous if not provided with enough exercise. Independent thinker when he detects a scent.

Photograph © Jean Fogle

Energy level: Medium.

Best owner: Active owner with securely fenced backyard.

Needs: Daily exercise and playtime, leash, adequate fencing to prevent digging, companionship, minimal grooming, tolerance of barking, howling, and begging.

Life expectancy: 12 to 15 years.

Black and Tan Coonhound

History/Evolution: An all-American breed, the Black and Tan Coonhound was developed from other Scenthounds used to hunt raccoons and bears in rugged terrain. Following in the footsteps of their Bloodhound ancestors, the Black and Tan trails with nose to the ground and is a determined hunter even in the worst conditions. The dog's deep voice enables a hunter to find him after he's treed his quarry. Registered with the AKC in 1945, the breed is favored more for hunting than as a show dog or pet.

Size: Large, 65 to 100 pounds; females 23 to 25 inches; males 25 to 27 inches.

Color: Coal black with tan markings.

Temperament: Mellow, even tempered, calm; friendly and playful, but reserved with strangers. Strong trailing instincts make training difficult.

Photograph © Isabelle Francaise

Energy level: Moderate.

Best owner: Hunter or family with large, secured backyard.

Needs: Daily exercise, leash, consistent training, tolerance of loud baying and drooling, weekly ear cleaning to prevent odor and infection.

Life expectancy: 10 to 12 years.

Bloodhound

History/Evolution: One of the oldest Scenthounds (some have traced the Bloodhound to Mediterranean countries in the third century), most believe that the breed was developed in Europe during the Middle Ages. The name refers to *blooded hounds,* meaning they were of pure blood and noble breeding. The Bloodhound's trailing skills in the field of law enforcement have earned the breed high honors. This highly recognizable dog excels in shows and trailing but has enjoyed moderate popularity as a pet.

Size: Large, 80 to 110 pounds; females 23 to 25 inches; males 25 to 27 inches.

Color: Black and tan, liver and tan, and red.

Temperament: Trustworthy, extremely affectionate, calm; tolerant of children and playful. Reserved with strangers. Ruled by its nose.

Photograph © Jean Fogle

Energy level: Lots of energy until 3 or 4 years of age; then low.

Best owner: Active owner with a firm approach to training.

Needs: Daily exercise, securely fenced yard, leash, drool tolerance, facial cleaning (ears and wrinkles pick up food and water), soft bedding, weekly brushing.

Life expectancy: 7 to 10 years.

Borzoi

History/Evolution: A graceful, elegant Sighthound, the Borzoi was developed by the Russian aristocracy. Known as the Russian Wolfhound before 1936, the Borzoi was originally bred to hunt wolves, often in packs of more than a hundred dogs. The first Borzoi was brought to the U.S. from England in 1889; today the breed is prized for its beauty and talent in the show ring, as well as its skill in lure coursing. Farmers in Western states still rely on the Borzoi to control coyote populations.

Size: Large; females 26 to 30 inches, 65 to 85 pounds; males 28 to 33 inches, 85 to 105 pounds.

Color: Any color, with or without markings.

Temperament: Intelligent, sensitive, and well mannered; described as catlike in their independent nature. Affectionate with family, but reserved with strangers. Strong chase instinct.

Photograph © Jean Fogle

Energy level: Low.

Best owner: Runner or active owner with fenced yard.

Needs: Daily exercise (leashed walk plus a sprint in a well-secured area), patient and consistent obedience training, socialization, regular brushing and bathing, cool quarters.

Life expectancy: 10 to 12 years.

Dachshund

History/Evolution: Developed hundreds of years ago in Germany, the Dachshund was bred to be a fearless, long-bodied dog who could dig a badger out of its burrow and kill it (the breed's name means "badger dog" in German). The Dachshund has a sharp sense of smell and is an eager hunter, both above and below ground. One of the most popular AKC breeds, the friendly Dachshund comes in three different coat varieties (smooth, wirehaired, and longhaired) and can be miniature or standard size.

Size: Small; miniature less than 11 pounds; standard usually between 16 and 32 pounds.

Color: Sable, chocolate, black and tan, or chocolate and tan, all with or without brindling or merling.

Temperament: Bold, curious, and courageous; toddlerlike and comical. Independent, but playful and family oriented; longhairs a good choice for families with children.

Photograph © Jean Fogle

Energy level: Medium to high.

Best owner: Confident owner with time for training.

Needs: Daily exercise, regular grooming (varies with coat type), obedience training, precautions against back injuries, mindfulness about overeating.

Life expectancy: 12 to 14 years.

English Foxhound

History/Evolution: Breeding records for the English Foxhound date back to the late 1700s in Great Britain, where the breed was developed to have great stamina and trailing skills. By the late 1800s, foxhunting had become extremely popular with the wealthy, who built up great fanfare around the hunts. The English Foxhound was brought to the U.S. and bred with other dogs to create the American Foxhound. Many people still regard the English Foxhound as the first choice when pursuing a traditional hunt.

Size: Large, 24 to 26 inches; females 60 to 80 pounds; males 75 to 90 pounds.

Color: Hound colors: black, tan, and white.

Temperament: A pack Hound at heart; can be strong, stubborn, and independent. Amiable, gentle, tolerant. Reserved with strangers.

Photograph © Jean Fogle

Energy level: High.

Best owner: Active, patient owner in a rural or suburban house.

Needs: Daily exercise (long leashed hikes) and activity to prevent boredom and destructive behaviors, fenced yard, consistent obedience training, companionship, occasional brushing.

Life expectancy: 10 to 13 years.

Greyhound

History/Evolution: With origins going back to ancient Egypt, the Greyhound is one of the oldest breeds known. Important breed developments were made in Great Britain when the Greyhound was kept and bred by royalty. The Greyhound pursued game by using both vision and speed, and was used to hunt deer, fox, and hare. Spanish explorers brought the breed to the U.S. in the 1500s; the AKC recognized the Greyhound in 1885. Today the Greyhound is regarded as a sweet and lively companion.

Size: Large; females 60 to 65 pounds; males 65 to 70 pounds.

Color: Immaterial.

Temperament: Quiet, well mannered, and calm. Possesses independent Hound spirit, loves to chase. Can be timid and sensitive; reserved with strangers.

Photograph © Jean Fogle

Energy level: Medium to high, lower in dogs older than age 3.

Best owner: Active owner in rural or suburban home.

Needs: Daily exercise (long leashed walks with sprints), fenced yard, patient training, soft bedding and warm surroundings, occasional brushing.

Life expectancy: 10 to 13 years.

Harrier

History/Evolution: Developed in England during the Middle Ages, the Harrier was bred to hunt hare in packs. The sturdy, large-boned breed was tireless and tough but not particularly fast, making it a good companion for hunters on foot. Harriers have been used in the United States for hunting since Colonial times. Though not ranked particularly high by the AKC, the Harrier serves as a family companion and fine competitor in tracking and agility.

Size: Medium; 19 to 21 inches, 45 to 60 pounds; females slightly smaller than males.

Color: Any.

Temperament: Outgoing, intelligent, friendly; amiable, tolerant, good with children. Most reserved with strangers. Strong hunting instinct; easily bored.

Photograph © Isabelle Francaise

Energy level: High.

Best owner: Hunter or active owner in a rural or suburban home.

Needs: Daily exercise and activity, leash, tall and secure fencing, canine companionship, occasional grooming.

Life expectancy: 10 to 12 years.

Ibizan Hound

History/Evolution: The Ibizan Hound's roots can be traced back to the days of ancient Egypt, when sea traders are believed to have brought Hounds to the island of Ibiza off the coast of Spain. A skilled runner and jumper, the Ibizan was used in packs to hunt rabbits in the rough terrain of its native land. The elegant Hound with amber eyes was brought to the U.S. in the mid-1950s. Though a rare breed, the Ibizan is a highly regarded competitor and makes an excellent family pet.

Size: Large; females 22½ to 26 inches, 45 pounds; males 23½ inches to 27½ inches, 50 pounds.

Color: White or red, solid or in combination.

Temperament: Even tempered, affectionate, loyal; intelligent and trainable. Aloof with strangers; some can be timid. Good with children and other pets.

Photograph © Jean Fogle

Energy level: Moderate to high.

Best owner: Active owner in a rural or suburban home.

Needs: Daily exercise (long walks with chances for sprints), tall fences, warm surroundings and soft bedding, occasional brushing (weekly for wire coat).

Life expectancy: 12 to 14 years.

Irish Wolfhound

History/Evolution: An ancient breed, the Irish Wolfhound can be found in records dating back to AD 391, when royal gifts of the giant hunters were made to Rome. Irish Wolfhounds fought with their masters, guarded castles, and hunted wolves and elk, nearly to the point that the dogs' own existence was at risk. Breeders restored the Irish Wolfhound in the 1800s. Potential owners must consider the amount of space and attention required to keep the Irish Wolfhound happy and healthy.

Size: Large; females 30-plus inches, 105 pounds; males 32-plus inches, 120 pounds.

Color: Gray, brindle, red, black, white, and fawn.

Temperament: Gentle, easygoing, patient, sweet. Good with children and pets; friendly with strangers. Can be stubborn and may be sensitive to harsh training methods.

Photograph © Jean Fogle

Energy level: Low, unless in pursuit of game.

Best owner: Owner with a spacious home.

Needs: Daily exercise, fenced yard, ample room indoors, soft bedding, attention and companionship, weekly brushing and occasional scissoring.

Life expectancy: 5 to 7 years.

Norwegian Elkhound

History/Evolution: Though the Norwegian Elkhound has its roots in the Spitz family, the breed's tracking abilities have earned it a place of honor in the Hound Group. An ancient breed that hunted with the Vikings, the Norwegian Elkhound is hardy and has the stamina to outlast moose, bear, and hunter alike. The breed is devoted to the chase but also thrives on human companionship, making it a good candidate for an active family's pet.

Size: Medium; females 19 ½ inches, 48 pounds; males 20½ inches, 55 pounds.

Color: Gray.

Temperament: Playful, bold, independent. Alert and ready for adventure, preferably in cold weather. May be destructive if not given enough exercise. Good with children and strangers, but not other dogs.

Photograph © Isabelle Francaise

Energy level: High.

Best owner: Active owner with plenty of time for exercise.

Needs: Daily strenuous exercise, fenced yard, training, a social life, tolerance for shedding, patience with barking, cool weather, attention to overeating.

Life expectancy: 10 to 12 years.

Otterhound

History/Evolution: Although the Otterhound was used to prevent otters from preying on fish in the rivers and streams of England, the breed's origins are believed to be in France. Otter hunting has since been banned, but the Otterhound has found a place with some as an amiable companion. The breed's webbed feet help facilitate its love of being in the water, whether it's a river, pool, or puddle. The AKC recognized Otterhounds in 1909.

Size: Large; females 23 to 26 inches, 65 to 100 pounds; males 24 to 27 inches, 75 to 115 pounds.

Color: Any — usually black and tan, grizzle, red, liver and tan, tricolor, or wheaten.

Temperament: Boisterous, amiable, easygoing; good with children. May be stubborn and less than responsive to training, especially when outdoors and a scent is detected.

Photograph © Isabelle Francaise

Energy level: Medium to high as a youngster.

Best owner: Hunter or some other outdoorsy type.

Needs: Daily exercise, leash, fenced yard, training, companionship (human and canine), tolerance of baying, acceptance of wet beard, weekly brushing and occasional bathing.

Life expectancy: 12 to 14 years.

Petit Basset Griffon Vendéen

History/Evolution: The Petit Basset Griffon Vendéen, or PBGV, originated in the Vendéen area of France around the 16th century. Closely related to both the Basset Hound and the Grand Basset Griffon Vendéen, the low, rough- or wire-coated breed was developed to hunt small game such as hare over difficult terrain. The AKC recognized the PBGV in 1990; since then, the breed's fuzzy appearance and merry manner have drawn many fans.

Size: Small to medium; females 12 to 14 inches, 25 to 35 pounds; males 13 to 15 inches, 30 to 45 pounds.

Color: White, with lemon, orange, black, tricolor, or grizzle markings.

Temperament: Bold, active, extroverted; independent but willing to please. Good with older children, dogs, and strangers. Hunter at heart; loves to sniff, explore, dig, and bark.

Photograph © Isabelle Francaise

Energy level: High (males may be less so), but more moderate as adults.

Best owner: Active, experienced dog owner in a rural or suburban home.

Needs: Daily exercise to prevent barking, digging, and other canine amusements; well-fenced yard, leash, socialization and training, weekly combing/brushing.

Life expectancy: 11 to 14 years.

Pharaoh Hound

History/Evolution: With origins that can be traced back to Egypt circa 3000 BC, the Pharaoh Hound is truly an ancient breed. The Pharaoh of today bears a close resemblance to its Egyptian ancestors: noble, graceful, powerful, and fast. The breed has also retained its unique tendency to "blush," with nose and ears turning a rose color when the dog is excited. The Pharaoh Hound is prized for companionship, hunting, lure coursing, and obedience.

Size: Medium to large; females 21 to 24 inches; males 23 to 25 inches.

Color: Tan to chestnut, with white markings.

Temperament: Affectionate, playful, sensitive, willing to please. Intelligent, alert, active; will chase with no regard to safety. Good with children, reserved with strangers; some timid.

Photograph © Jean Fogle

Energy level: High.

Best owner: Active owner in a rural or suburban home.

Needs: Daily exercise (some recommend two hours a day), fenced yard, leash, soft bedding and warmth, socialization, occasional brushing.

Life expectancy: 11 to 15 years.

Plott

History/Evolution: When 16-year-old Johannes Georg Plott immigrated to America with five Hanoverian Hounds in 1750, he probably had no idea that a noted hunting dog breed would bear his name less than 200 years later. Plott, who settled in the mountains of North Carolina, developed the powerful breed to hunt boar and bear. His dogs earned a reputation for their skills, and subsequent crossings only improved the breed. Today the Plott is the state dog of North Carolina and is used for coonhunting.

Size: Medium to large; 23 to 25 inches, 50 to 60 pounds.

Color: Brindle, blue, may have black saddle.

Temperament: Loyal, eager to please, alert. Courageous, aggressive, headstrong; can be a challenge with obedience. Good with children and wary with strangers. Likely to bay.

Photograph © Isabelle Francaise

Energy level: High.

Best owner: Hunter or active owner in suburbs or rural area.

Needs: Daily exercise (hunts or woodland hikes are best; swims are enjoyed), leash, fenced yard, human companionship, minimal coat care.

Life expectancy: 11 to 13 years.

Rhodesian Ridgeback

History/Evolution: Developed in South Africa, the Rhodesian Ridgeback is the result of crossings between European hunting dogs and a native dog who had a ridge of hair growing down its back. European settlers developed the breed to hunt in the African wild and guard the farm and family. Originally bred to hunt lions — earning its earlier name of African Lion Hound — the Rhodesian Ridgeback is still a formidable hunter and competitor. Its good looks and protective nature have made it a popular pet.

Size: Large; females 24 to 26 inches, 70 pounds; males 25 to 27 inches, 85 pounds.

Color: Light wheaten to red wheaten.

Temperament: Dignified, even tempered, loyal. Good with children, reserved with strangers. Strong willed; some domineering. Bored if not properly exercised.

Photograph © Jean Fogle

Energy level: High as youngsters.

Best owner: Active owner with previous dog experience.

Needs: Daily mental and physical exercise (jogging, hiking, agility), leash, fenced yard, consistent obedience training, weekly brushing and occasional baths.

Life expectancy: 10 to 12 years.

Saluki

Photograph © Jean Fogle

History/Evolution: The swift and noble Saluki is perhaps the most ancient domesticated breed of dog, its image visible on pottery from Iran circa 3500 BC. Arab nomads used the Saluki to run down gazelles, Egyptians depicted the breed on tombs and mummified Saluki remains to be buried with pharaohs, and English hunters relied on Salukis to course hare. Today the Saluki's talents are a bit less dangerous, serving as exotic companions and graceful competitors in the show ring.

Size: Large, 40 to 70 pounds; females usually 23 to 28 inches; males 23 to 29 inches.

Color: White, cream, fawn, golden, red, grizzle and tan, tricolor, black and tan, and more.

Temperament: Independent and devoted. Fine with older children, but not with rough play. Aloof with strangers. Chases anything that moves.

Energy level: High outside, low indoors if properly exercised.

Best owner: Active owner in a rural or suburban home.

Needs: Daily exercise (running free in an enclosed area is best), leash, fenced yard, patient training, soft bedding, weekly brushing.

Life expectancy: 12 to 14 years.

Scottish Deerhound

Photograph © Jean Fogle

History/Evolution: An accomplished deer hunter since at least the 16th century, the Scottish Deerhound was valued for its hunting prowess by Scottish nobility; for a time it could not be owned by anyone ranking lower than earl. The breed faced extinction, but breeders revived it in the early 1800s. Though relatively rare, the Scottish Deerhound can still be found in lure-coursing events, in the show ring, and in homes of people who have room for such a noble giant.

Size: Giant; females 28-plus inches, 75 to 95 pounds; males 30 to 32-plus inches, 85 to 110 pounds.

Color: Dark blue gray, gray, brindle, yellow and sandy red, and red fawn.

Temperament: Quiet, dignified, and mellow in the home; inclined to run and chase outdoors. Willing to please, but independent. Good with children; reserved with strangers.

Energy level: Low to moderate.

Best owner: Athletic owner in a home with a good-size backyard.

Needs: Daily exercise, leash, fenced yard, care to prevent bloat, human companionship, soft bedding, combing with occasional scissoring and stripping.

Life expectancy: 8 to 10 years.

Whippet

History/Evolution: The Whippet is a medium-sized Sighthound developed in England in the 1700s, most likely from small Greyhounds and other smaller dogs. At times peasants used the Whippet for poaching rabbits, as well as in "snap dog" contests, in which dogs competed to see which could "snap up" as many rabbits as possible before they escaped from a circle. Today some people race Whippets; others believe the dog belongs in the show ring, in lure-coursing events, or in the home.

Size: Medium; females 18 to 21 inches, 20 to 30 pounds; males 19 to 22 inches, 25 to 40 pounds.

Color: Immaterial.

Temperament: Amiable, gentle, friendly, devoted, and demonstrative. Good with children. Not good with harsh correction or rough treatment. Intense chaser.

Photograph © Jean Fogle

Energy level: Moderate.

Best owner: Active, athletic owner.

Needs: Daily exercise (long walk or run), fenced yards, leash, soft bedding, warmth (coats or sweaters a requirement for the cold), minimal grooming.

Life expectancy: 12 to 15 years.

Chapter 5

Profiling the Terrier Group

*I*n name and in spirit, the dogs of the Terrier Group are down to earth. The name *terrier* is derived from *terra*, Latin for "earth." Farmers relied on Terriers to control pests — mice, rats, foxes — in fields and stables. These dogs were developed to pursue and kill vermin, and many did so by digging, or "going to ground," after their prey. These Terriers had to be energetic, brave, and tenacious. For many Terriers, survival depended on their ability to fend for themselves.

During the group's history, some were bred for sport, to kill rats in pit contests, and later to fight against each other. Fortunately, such activities are no longer legal, but the breeds as a group have retained their original feisty nature.

Today's Terriers appeal to people who are looking for a lot of dog in a small package. In general, dogs in this group have a good disposition and can become attached to their families.

However, Terriers are not for everyone. True, they are engaging, but they require an owner with enough spunk to cope with the Terrier's distinctive personality. On top of that, a Terrier's level of high-energy play can be overwhelming to some people.

Although they don't demand a lot of attention, a Terrier is likely to become bored and destructive without activities to challenge the body and mind. One way to fulfill the challenge is to test your dog in Terrier trials. Earthdog tests allow Terriers to test their skills in man-made tunnels and courses. Border, Wire Fox, Lakeland, and Scottish Terriers are just some of the breeds who live for the moment when they're set loose to pursue some sort of critter scent or caged prey.

With their strong prey instinct intact, typical Terriers have little tolerance for other mammals, including other dogs, gerbils, and cats. They are also confident and cocky when challenged, displaying a "You talking to me?" attitude. This is good news for someone looking for a protective breed; even the smallest of the Terriers will bark to alert you to visitors, whether it's a messenger at the door or a squirrel at the gate.

In general, Terriers are

- ✔ Feisty
- ✔ Self-assured
- ✔ Busy
- ✔ Inquisitive
- ✔ Bold
- ✔ Tenacious
- ✔ Dominant

Terriers range greatly in size and shape — the fluffy Westie and the muscular Bull Terriers bear little resemblance, although all have strong jaws to take on prey.

The Australian, Border, and Cairn Terriers are on the small side; the Airedale and American Staffordshire are bigger. The vermin-catching Terriers are roughly divided into long-legged and short-legged breeds.

Although coats can be smooth or coarse (wiry), medium or long, most Terriers are known for their wiry coats that need to be maintained with a special grooming technique known as stripping (see the chapters in Book III for information on different aspects of grooming).

Airedale Terrier

History/Evolution: Known as the "King of Terriers," the Airedale is the largest of the group. Like other Terriers, it is believed to be a descendant of the extinct Old English Terrier. English hunters fancied its versatile hunting skills (badger, otter, and fox are just a few of the breed's quarry). The Airedale's intelligence, protective nature, and looks earned it many admirers when it was imported to the U.S. Whether companion, police dog, show dog, or hunter, the Airedale is truly a champion.

Size: Medium to large; males 23 inches, females slightly smaller; 45 to 70 pounds.

Color: Tan with black.

Temperament: Bold, adventurous, intelligent; can be headstrong. Good ability to learn, if things are kept fun and interesting. Protective; some can be domineering.

Photograph © Jean Fogle

Energy level: High.

Best owner: Outdoorsy owner in a suburban or rural home.

Needs: Daily vigorous exercise (long walks, hunting excursion), leash, obedience training, plenty of interaction, twice weekly combing plus scissoring and shaping.

Life expectancy: 10 to 13 years.

American Staffordshire Terrier

History/Evolution: Both the American Staffordshire Terrier (AmStaff) and the Staffordshire Bull Terrier descended from the Bulldog and a game Terrier breed. The powerful AmStaff was used in the illegal sport of dog fighting in England in the 1800s. Although sweet and docile, improper handling and training by people for fighting has left the AmStaff with a less than favorable reputation. Because of its intelligence and build, the AmStaff excels at obedience, agility, tracking, and conformation.

Size: Medium; females 17 to 18 inches, males 18 to 19 inches; 40 to 75 pounds.

Color: Almost any solid, particolored, or brindled.

Temperament: Playful, affectionate, and friendly, but protective of family; can be aggressive with other dogs. Stubborn and prone to destructive behaviors if not properly exercised.

Photograph © Jean Fogle

Energy level: Medium to high.

Best owner: Active owner with previous training experience.

Needs: Daily exercise, leash, secure fences, bonding and socialization, a job, early training, minimal grooming

Life expectancy: 10 to 12 years.

Australian Terrier

History/Evolution: Developed in Tasmania, the Australian Terrier was the first native breed to be recognized and shown in that country. A versatile dog, the Australian Terrier was bred to be an all-purpose companion and worker, able to control livestock, manage pests such as snakes and rats, and guard against intruders. Suited to life on the farm, in the city, or somewhere in between, the Australian Terrier thrives on equal doses of activity and companionship.

Size: Small; 10 to 11 inches, 14 to 18 pounds.

Color: Sandy, red, or blue and tan.

Temperament: Self-confident, spirited, and courageous. Keen and alert, although easier to quiet than some other Terriers. Friendly and affectionate; adaptable.

Photograph © Isabelle Francaise

Energy level: Medium to high as puppies, mellows later.

Best owner: Family or active owner who enjoys training.

Needs: Daily exercise (walk or romp in park), leash, fenced yard, companionship, weekly combing plus twice yearly stripping.

Life expectancy: 12 to 15 years.

Bedlington Terrier

History/Evolution: Named for England's Bedlington Mining Shire, where it was developed in the 1800s, the Bedlington Terrier is one of the more unusual members of the Terrier Group. The lamblike appearance of the breed is deceiving; the Bedlington was bred to be a fast and skilled hunter of rat, badger, and other vermin. The Bedlington's curly, woolly coat requires work and skill to maintain, but owners of the breed often rely on professional groomers to keep their dog's coat in top condition.

Size: Medium; females 15 to 16½ inches, males 16 to 17½ inches; around 20 pounds.

Color: Blue, sandy, liver — each with or without tan points.

Temperament: Gentle, mild, and tractable; a loyal family pet. Good with children and other pets (except squeaky rodents); reserved with strangers.

Photograph © Jean Fogle

Energy level: Medium.

Best owner: Active family or individual.

Needs: Daily exercise, leash, fenced yard, plenty of companionship, regular ear cleaning, combing once or twice a week, grooming to maintain shape.

Life expectancy: 15 to 16 years.

Border Terrier

History/Evolution: The Border Terrier may be the oldest of Britain's Terriers, originating in the 1700s in the border country between England and Scotland. The breed was used to hunt fox, which were considered a nuisance to farmers. The agile Terrier was fast enough to keep up with horses on a hunt, but small enough to go underground after a fox. Today the Border Terrier excels in agility and earthdog trials; the people-oriented breed makes a fine home companion.

Size: Small; females 11½ to 14 inches, 12 to 16 pounds; males 12 to 15½ inches, 12 to 20 pounds.

Color: Red, grizzle and tan, blue and tan, wheaten.

Temperament: Good tempered in the home; independent, curious chaser in the field. Good with children and pets other than rodents. Enjoys digging and barking.

Photograph © Jean Fogle

Energy level: Moderately high.

Best owner: Active family or owner.

Needs: Daily exercise, leash, securely fenced yard, weekly brushing plus stripping about four times a year.

Life expectancy: 12 to 15 years.

Bull Terrier

History/Evolution: Bull baiting and dog fighting were in vogue in England in the early 1800s, and patrons worked to breed dogs into fighting champions. Crosses between Bulldogs, various Terriers, and Dalmatians yielded the Bull Terrier, which captured the attention of the public. Despite the breed's somewhat unapproachable appearance, the Bull Terrier is a friendly and fun-loving dog who has become popular as a devoted family pet and exceptional competitor in agility and conformation.

Size: Medium; 21 to 22 inches, 50 to 70 pounds.

Color: White, colored variety may be brindle or any color.

Temperament: Playful, mischievous, natural clowns; may be too exuberant for young children. Prone to bursts of energy; can be destructive chewers. May be aggressive with other dogs and small animals.

Photograph © Isabelle Francaise

Energy level: High.

Best owner: Active owner in a suburban or rural home.

Needs: Daily mental and physical exercise, leash, fenced yard, human companionship, obedience training, minimal grooming.

Life expectancy: 11 to 14 years.

Cairn Terrier

History/Evolution: With roots that lie in the Isle of Skye and the Highlands of Scotland, the Cairn Terrier was originally grouped with Scottish and West Highland White Terriers; the breeds began to be separated in the early 1900s. The Cairn was skilled at hunting prey such as fox that lived in the ledges and rock piles (cairns) that dotted the farming countryside. A working Terrier, the Cairn likes to be busy; today's dogs excel in agility and tracking trials. Made famous by Toto in the *Wizard of Oz.*

Size: Small; females 9½ inches, 13 pounds; males 10 to 12 inches, 14 pounds.

Color: Any color except white.

Temperament: Intelligent, spirited, curious, quick to learn. Can be stubborn and independent. Good with children, but may be aggressive with other dogs. Enjoys chasing and digging; some bark.

Photograph © Jean Fogle

Energy level: High, but not high strung.

Best owner: Active family or owner.

Needs: Daily exercise, leash, secure fencing (to prevent digging), obedience training, weekly brushing.

Life expectancy: 12 to 15 years.

Dandie Dinmont Terrier

History/Evolution: Named after Dandie Dinmont, a character in Sir Walter Scott's 1814 book *Guy Mannering,* the Dandie Dinmont Terrier is an interesting combination of unusual but dignified appearance and hunting prowess. Overflowing with confidence for such a small dog, the Dandie would take on otters, badgers, and foxes without hesitation. Although the Dandie has retained its strong hunting instincts, the breed has somewhat "retired," instead serving as a loyal family pet and companion.

Size: Medium to small; 8 to 11 inches, 18 to 24 pounds.

Color: Pepper or mustard.

Temperament: Intelligent, dignified, independent. Affectionate with family but reserved with strangers; aggressive toward strange dogs. Good with kids if raised with them. Bold, determined, a hunter in the field.

Photograph © Isabelle Francaise

Energy level: Moderately high.

Best owner: Active, confident owner in a suburban or rural home.

Needs: Daily exercise (walk or exploring in a safe area), leash, secure fencing (some will dig), obedience training, twice weekly brushing plus regular scissoring and shaping.

Life expectancy: 12 to 15 years.

Glen of Imaal Terrier

History/Evolution: One of the four Terrier breeds native to Ireland, the Glen of Imaal Terrier was a working Terrier, able to survive in a difficult terrain and conditions. These tough canines not only hunted rats, foxes, and badgers, but they worked the turnspit at the hearth (a dog-powered rotisserie) and fought in the pits at night. Even though the breed's numbers dwindled for a time, the Terrier's charm and spirit ensured its survival into modern times.

Size: Small to medium; 14 inches, 35 pounds.

Color: Wheaten, blue, or brindle.

Temperament: Spirited, inquisitive, and game for fun; ready for a chase. Docile and content with plenty of exercise. Good with older children; can be aggressive with other dogs.

Photograph © Isabelle Francaise

Energy level: High.

Best owner: Active owner able to train a strong-willed dog.

Needs: Daily exercise (brisk walk or off-lead romp in a secure area), leash, fenced yard, involvement in family activities, regular combing as well as stripping twice a year.

Life expectancy: 10 to 15 years.

Irish Terrier

History/Evolution: Though the Irish Terrier's origins are uncertain, clues have led some to believe that the old Black and Tan Terrier and the Irish Wolfhound may have contributed to this long-legged Irish breed. Black and tan, gray, and brindle were once common colors, but the solid red became standard in the late 1800s. A bold, courageous, and intelligent breed, the Irish Terrier was used as a messenger and sentinel during World War I. The breed is uncommon today.

Size: Medium; 18 to 20 inches, 25 to 27 pounds.

Color: Shades of red or wheaten.

Temperament: Assertive, brash, playful, independent; Affectionate, loyal, protective of family; usually good with children but reserved with strangers. Aggressive toward other animals.

Photograph © Isabelle Francaise

Energy level: High outdoors but calm indoors.

Best owner: Active owner in a suburban or rural home.

Needs: Daily mental and physical exercise (hiking, hunting, agility); leash; fenced yard; early, firm, and obedience training; twice weekly combing plus shaping twice a year.

Life expectancy: 12 to 15 years.

Kerry Blue Terrier

Photograph © Jean Fogle

History/Evolution: Developed in Ireland, the Kerry Blue Terrier was an all-purpose farm dog — herding livestock, hunting vermin, and retrieving over land and water. It wasn't until the 1920s that the breed became known outside of Ireland. Kerry Blues are born black, but the breed's striking coat changes color with maturity. Though the breed has experience limited popularity as a pet, it has excelled as a police dog, as well as in herding and trailing.

Size: Medium; females 17½ to 19 inches, 30 to 35 pounds; males 18 to 19½ inches, 33 to 40 pounds.

Color: Blue gray when mature.

Temperament: Fun-loving, energetic, and enthusiastic. Independent; a hunter. Can be protective with strangers and aggressive toward other dogs and small animals.

Energy level: Medium.

Best owner: Active owner with training experience.

Needs: Daily mental and physical exercise, leash, fenced yard; early, firm, and consistent training; companionship, weekly brushing and combing plus monthly scissoring and shaping.

Life expectancy: 12 to 16 years.

Lakeland Terrier

Photograph © Isabelle Francaise

History/Evolution: One of the oldest working Terrier breeds, the Lakeland Terrier was used by farmers in the lake districts of England to kill troublesome fox and vermin. With its narrow frame, the breed was able squeeze into rocky dens to chase after quarry; later, when fox hunting became fashionable, the Lakeland Terrier joined the hunt scene. Although this former working breed is best known today as a show dog or companion, Lakelands also do well in earthdog trials.

Size: Medium to small; 13 to 15 inches, 14 to 20 pounds.

Color: Blue, black, liver, red, and wheaten; the wheaten may have a saddle of blue, black, liver, or grizzle.

Temperament: Bold, friendly, confident, and spunky. Quiet and well mannered with enough exercise. Reserved with strangers and usually aggressive toward animals.

Energy level: High.

Best owner: Active owner with training experience.

Needs: Daily exercise (walks, games), leash, fenced yard, patient and consistent training, combing once or twice a week plus some scissoring and shaping.

Life expectancy: 12 to 16 years.

Manchester Terrier (Standard)

History/Evolution: Developed in England, the Manchester Terrier is a descendant of the oldest Terrier breed, the Black and Tan. The breed's development centered on Manchester, and it was officially dubbed "Manchester Terrier" in 1860. In 1959, the Toy and the Standard Manchester were classified as one breed with two varieties. The Manchester is well suited to home life; however, its hunting instincts come to life when it detects a rodent or some other small creature that needs to be chased.

Size: Small to medium; 15 to 16 inches, 12 to 22 pounds.

Color: Black with mahogany tan.

Temperament: Observant, busy, independent, sensitive. Devoted to family, usually one person in particular; reserved with strangers. Described as catlike. Some dig.

Photograph © Isabelle Francaise

Energy level: High, but not hyper.

Best owner: Active owner with time for companionship.

Needs: Daily exercise (moderate walk on leash, off-lead romp in a secure area), leash, fenced yard, consistent obedience training, soft bedding, minimal coat care.

Life expectancy: 15 to 17 years.

Miniature Bull Terrier

History/Evolution: Truly a smaller version of the Bull Terrier, the Miniature Bull Terrier shares the Bull Terrier's early history. When the Bull Terrier breed was developed in the 1800s, many were as small as today's Miniatures; eventually, differences in size led breeders to divide the Bull Terriers into the Miniature and Standard groups. The AKC accepted the Miniature Bull Terrier in 1991.

Size: Small; females 12 to 14 inches, males 13 to 15 inches; 15 to 35 pounds.

Color: White or colored — any color, including brindle.

Temperament: Lively, playful, mischievous, fearless. Even tempered, sweet, but not overly devoted. Independent and stubborn. May be too boisterous for small children.

Photograph © Jean Fogle

Energy level: Moderate.

Best owner: Confident owner with time for daily walks and play.

Needs: Daily exercise, leash, fenced yard, patient obedience training, a rodent-free home (for example, hamsters and guinea pigs), occasional brushing.

Life expectancy: 10 to 14 years.

Miniature Schnauzer

History/Evolution: Developed in Germany in the 1800s, the Miniature Schnauzer may have been the result of crossing Affenpinschers and Poodles with small Standard Schnauzers. The Miniature, the smallest and the most popular of the Schnauzers, was exhibited in Germany as a distinct breed in 1899; the AKC separated the Standard and Miniature in 1933. Today the breed is prized for its protective nature, charm, and dapper good looks.

Size: Small; 12 to 14 inches, 13 to 20 pounds.

Color: Salt and pepper, black and silver, and solid black.

Temperament: Alert, spirited, playful, and friendly. Intelligent, but can be stubborn. Good with children. Some bark. Thrives when included in a family's activities.

Photograph © istockphoto.com/ Simon Ivarsson

Energy level: Moderately high.

Best owner: Active, attentive owner.

Needs: Daily exercise (moderate walk will do), leash, fenced yard, human companionship, fun training methods, combing once or twice a week plus scissoring and shaping every two months, regular dental care.

Life expectancy: 12 to 14 years.

Norfolk Terrier

History/Evolution: For much of their early history in England, the Norfolk Terrier and the Norwich Terrier were believed to be different varieties of the same breed — the Norfolk with drop ears and the Norwich with prick ears. Not until the 1930s did breeders begin to separate the varieties. Though today's Norfolk is not the ratter of its heyday, the breed still loves a good chase when out and about with its owner.

Size: Small; 9 to 10 inches, 11 to 12 pounds.

Color: Red, wheaten, black and tan, and grizzle.

Temperament: Energetic, bold, and feisty. A Terrier at heart; curious, independent, stubborn, loves to hunt and dig. Affectionate and loyal. Good with children when raised with them.

Photograph © Jean Fogle

Energy level: High.

Best owner: Active owner in a suburban or rural home.

Needs: Daily exercise (short to moderate walk, hike), leash, fenced yard, positive training methods, human companionship, combing once or twice a week plus hand stripping three or four times a week.

Life expectancy: 12 to 15 years.

Norwich Terrier

History/Evolution: Developed in England, the Norwich Terrier and Norfolk Terrier were once believed to be separate varieties of the same breed; eventually, the two were separated into distinct breeds (see Norfolk Terrier), with the prick-eared dog as the Norwich. Though small, the Norwich was an eager worker and a formidable force in ratting and fox hunting. Today the breed excels in the show ring but has experienced limited popularity as a pet.

Size: Small; 10 inches, 10 to 15 pounds.

Color: Red, wheaten, black and tan, and grizzle.

Temperament: Fearless, amusing, affectionate, adaptable. Independent; can be a training challenge. Loyal, sensitive companion; good with children, especially when raised with them.

Photograph © Jean Fogle

Book V

Meet the Breeds

Energy level: High, but can vary with owner.

Best owner: Active, patient owner.

Needs: Daily exercise (short walk or run; avoid heat and humidity), leash, fenced yard, patient housebreaking, obedience training, combing once or twice a week plus stripping twice a year.

Life expectancy: 12 to 15 years.

Parson Russell Terrier

History/Evolution: Named for the Reverend John Russell, an English huntsman of the 1800s, the Parson Russell Terrier was first bred to hunt fox. Subsequent crossings led breeders to change the name to the more commonly recognized Jack Russell Terrier, but the AKC reinstated the original name in 2003. The breed's weatherproof coat can be wire-haired or smooth. Although the breed has experienced a jump in popularity (as "Eddie" on the sitcom Frazier), it is not a breed for everyone.

Size: Small; 12 to 14 inches, 13 to 17 pounds.

Color: White; white with black or tan markings, or a combination of these; tricolor.

Temperament: Outgoing, friendly, energetic, adventurous. A true hunter. Good with strangers and older children; may have issues with other dogs. Thrives on exercise and activity. An escape artist.

Photograph © Jean Fogle

Energy level: High.

Best owner: Active owner with training experience.

Needs: Daily mental and physical exercise, leash, fenced yard, training. Weekly brushing for the smooth type; the broken coat also needs occasional hand stripping.

Life expectancy: 13 to 15 years.

Scottish Terrier

History/Evolution: The Scottish Terrier's early history is confusing, at best, but it's clear that the feisty, bearded "Scottie" was one of a rugged group of Terriers used to hunt vermin in the Highlands of Scotland. Like other Terriers, the Scottie is a fast, strong breed that excelled at pursuing prey. The Scottish Terrier has enjoyed great popularity over the years, with admirers such as King James VI and President Theodore Roosevelt, and President George W. Bush.

Size: Small; 10 inches; females 18 to 21 pounds, males 19 to 22 pounds.

Color: Steel or iron gray, brindled or grizzled, black, wheaten or sandy.

Temperament: Spirited, alert, determined, ready for adventure. Loving and gentle with family (best with children over 5); friendly but reserved with strangers. Can be aggressive with other dogs. May dig or bark.

Photograph © Jean Fogle

Energy level: High.

Best owner: Active owner with training experience.

Needs: Daily exercise (moderate walk, vigorous game), leash, fenced yard, obedience training, regular brushing and shaping.

Life expectancy: 12 to 14 years.

Sealyham Terrier

History/Evolution: Developed in the 1800s in Wales, the Sealyham Terrier was named after the estate of a noted breeder of the time. A small package of power and determination, the Sealyham was an exceptional hunting dog, facing badgers, foxes, and otters without fear. Although the breed was once a fashionable accessory, associated with Alfred Hitchcock, Cary Grant, and Elizabeth Taylor, its popularity has waned.

Size: Small; 10½ inches; females 21 to 22 pounds, males 23 to 24 pounds.

Color: White with lemon, tan, or badger markings.

Temperament: Friendly, charming, playful, and outgoing. Inquisitive and always ready to explore; may dig if bored. Devoted to family — best with older children — but reserved with strangers.

Photograph © Isabelle Francaise

Energy level: Moderate to low.

Best owner: Patient owner with time for grooming.

Needs: Daily exercise (short walk or play session), leash, fenced yard, firm and consistent obedience training, early socialization, brushing two or three times a week plus shaping every three months.

Life expectancy: 12 to 14 years.

Skye Terrier

History/Evolution: One of the oldest Terrier breeds, going back to the 1500s, the Skye originated off the coast of Scotland on the Isle of Skye. Farmers relied on the plucky, long-haired Skye to hunt vermin such as fox, badger, and otter. The Skye's popularity surged in the mid-1800s when Queen Victoria declared her affection for the breed. The Skye brings its natural enthusiasm to whatever task it takes on — agility competitor, tracking champion, or loyal home companion.

Size: Short but substantial; females 10 to 12 inches, males 11 to 14 inches; 25 to 40 pounds.

Color: Black, blue, gray, silver, fawn, or cream.

Temperament: Mild mannered, loyal, and friendly; fearless hunter with surprising strength and stamina. Affectionate with family and friends; cautious with strangers, a good watchdog.

Photograph © Isabelle Francaise

Energy level: Moderate.

Best owner: Active owner with Terrier experience.

Needs: Daily exercise, leash, fenced yard, obedience training, regular combing and an occasional bath.

Life expectancy: 12 to 14 years.

Smooth Fox Terrier

History/Evolution: Though its ancestry is somewhat uncertain, the Smooth Fox Terrier originated in England in the 1700s. With its keen nose, excellent eyesight, and stamina, the Smooth Fox Terrier helped farmers eradicate vermin such as foxes. Until 1984, the Smooth and the Wire Fox Terriers were considered one breed with two varieties. Though the breed isn't used much for hunting today, the Smooth Fox Terrier is highly trainable and does well in agility and earthdog trials.

Size: Medium; females 14 to 15½ inches, 15 to 18 pounds; males 15 to 15½ inches, 18 to 20 pounds.

Color: Mostly white with black and/or tan markings.

Temperament: Energetic, feisty, lively, playful; good playmate for children over 6. Reserved with strangers, excellent watchdog. Strong digging instincts; some may bark. Independent, adventurous, loves to chase.

Photograph © Jean Fogle

Energy level: High, mellows with age.

Best owner: Active owner or hunter with training experience.

Needs: Daily exercise (vigorous game or walk), leash, fenced yard, firm and patient training, weekly brushing.

Life expectancy: 12 to 14 years.

Soft Coated Wheaten Terrier

Photograph © Isabelle Francaise

History/Evolution: One of the three large Terriers of Ireland, the Soft Coated Wheaten Terrier is prized for its abundant silky coat. Earlier in its history, the breed was developed as an all-purpose farm dog who could herd, guard, and hunt. The Soft Coated Wheaten Terrier came to the United States in 1946, and the AKC recognized it in 1973. The breed is versatile — a fine competitor in obedience and agility trials, as well as an affectionate companion in the home.

Size: Medium; females 17 to 18 inches, 30 to 35 pounds; males 18 to 19 inches, 35 to 40 pounds.

Color: Wheaten.

Temperament: Affectionate, happy, gentle, adaptable. Good with considerate children; can be too boisterous for some. Active and alert. Less aggressive than some Terriers. Adaptable. May jump and dig.

Energy level: Medium to high, mellows with age.

Best owner: Active owner with training experience.

Needs: Daily exercise, leash, fenced yard, firm and consistent training, brushing or combing every two days, and bathing and trimming every other month.

Life expectancy: 12 to 14 years.

Staffordshire Bull Terrier

Photograph © Isabelle Francaise

History/Evolution: The Staffordshire Bull Terrier's history begins in England in the 1800s, at a time when popular sports included rat killing and dog fighting. The breed, developed from crossings between the Bulldog and the Black and Tan Terrier, was fearless, quick, and strong for its size. Today less a fighter than lover, the Staffie's temperament has earned him a spot in many families as a devoted and affectionate companion. The breed earned AKC recognition in 1974.

Size: Medium; 14 to 16 inches; females 24 to 34 pounds, males 28 to 38 inches.

Color: Red, fawn, white, black, blue, or brindle; may have white markings.

Temperament: Amiable, fun loving, docile; good with children, but may be too strong and lively for little ones. Intelligent and determined; owners may need to earn respect with training. Perceived association with pit bulls will keep intruders away.

Energy level: Medium to high.

Best owner: Active owner with training experience.

Needs: Daily exercise, leash, fenced yard, sturdy chew toys, human companionship; early, fair, and consistent training; low heat and humidity, weekly brushing.

Life expectancy: 12 to 14 years.

Welsh Terrier

Photograph © Jean Fogle

Book V

Meet the
Breeds

History/Evolution: The Welsh Terrier originated
in Wales in the 1700s, one of only two Terriers
native to that country. The compact breed was
renowned for its gameness and hunted otter,
fox, and badger. Little has changed about the
Welsh Terrier in appearance and spirit, and
owners of today's Welsh Terriers need to be
mindful of the breed's tendency to take off
and chase. The breed was first brought to the
United States in 1888.

Size: Medium; 15 to 15½ inches, 20 to 25 pounds.

Color: Black and tan.

Temperament: Spirited, alert, friendly, and
mischievous; will create own fun if not provided
with outlets. Good with considerate children,
but not as much with strangers and other pets
(cats beware!). Tends to dig and bark.

Energy level: Medium to high.

Best owner: Active family, including a "master"
with training experience.

Needs: Daily walk or play session, leash, fenced
yard, obedience training and socialization,
patient housetraining, combing two to three
times a week plus shaping every three months.

Life expectancy: 12 to 14 years.

West Highland White Terrier

Photograph © Jean Fogle

History/Evolution: The West Highland White
Terrier originated in Scotland in the 1800s,
one of the Scottish Terriers used to hunt fox,
badger, and other pests. The compact but hardy
"Westie" was originally known as the Poltalloch
Terrier, after the home of a Westie breeder;
the breed was also known for a time as the
Roseneath Terrier, named for the estate of the
Duke of Argyle. The confident Westie excels in
competitions and has become one of the most
popular pet Terriers.

Size: Small; females 10 inches, 13 to 18 pounds;
males 11 inches, 15 to 20 pounds.

Color: White.

Temperament: Affectionate, happy, friendly,
devoted. Alert, curious, determined, loves to
bark and dig. Good with considerate children
but not with small animals.

Energy level: High.

Best owner: Active owner or family.

Needs: Daily exercise (short to moderate walk,
backyard game), leash, fenced yard, consistent
training, combing two to three times a week
plus shaping every three months.

Life expectancy: 12 to 14 years.

Wire Fox Terrier

History/Evolution: A descendant of the rough-coated Black and Tan Terrier, the Wire Fox Terrier was developed in England in the 1800s to go to ground for fox and other small game. Until 1984, the Smooth and the Wire Fox Terriers were considered one breed with two varieties. Today the Wire Fox Terrier excels in the show ring as well as earthdog trials. Owners with patience, some training experience, and a sense of humor find the breed to be a delightful home companion.

Size: Medium; females 14 to 16 inches, 15 to 20 pounds; males 15 to 17 inches, 20 to 25 pounds.

Color: Mostly white, with black and tan markings.

Temperament: Playful, energetic, adventurous, mischievous. Vocal and loves to dig. Thought to be scrappier with other dogs than the Smooth variety. Good with children, but best for those under 6.

Photograph © Jean Fogle

Energy level: High, mellows with time.

Best owner: Active owner in a rural or suburban home.

Needs: Daily hike, long walk, vigorous play session, leash, fenced yard, early and obedience training and socialization, combing two to three times weekly plus shaping every three months.

Life expectancy: 12 to 14 years.

Chapter 6

Profiling the Sporting Group

. . . .

In This Chapter

▶ Getting to know the modern hunters

▶ Understanding the finer points of the breeds

▶ Choosing a breed that suits your lifestyle

▶ Learning to live with an energetic dog

. . . .

The "sporting" in Sporting Dogs is less about soccer and baseball than it is about hunting. The dogs of the Sporting Group — the Pointers, Setters, Retrievers, and Spaniels — were bred to be active, alert, and athletic hunting companions. Their primary purpose: to search for and retrieve game. For some, this meant flushing small game out of brush; for others, it meant diving into icy waters to retrieve fallen waterfowl. The Sporting breeds are known as the modern hunters of the canine world because they accompanied hunters with guns rather than nets.

Thanks to supermarkets and convenience stores, today's Sporting dogs are not a critical part of stocking the icebox. If you don't hunt, you'll need to divert your Sporting dog's boundless energy in other directions. Consider jogging, field trials, brisk walks, play sessions, and obedience training as potential hunting alternatives. Because Sporting breeds typically are gentle, enthusiastic, and eager to please, they're well suited to family life — as long as they get a good dose of strenuous exercise each day. Without it, you risk damage to your backyard and home.

If you're happy to spend a weekend at home reading a good book or devoting an entire day to your model airplanes, a Sporting dog probably is not the breed for you. If, however, you and your dog can start the day with a good jog and then head out in the afternoon for a short hike, your companion will happily settle down at your feet for an evening of popcorn and the latest movie release. Sporting dogs are real social animals who were bred to enjoy working closely with people. Without their people, these breeds are not happy campers. Ever seen the look in a black Lab's eyes as he waits for his owner to come out of a store? Dogs such as Spaniels and Retrievers crave interaction with humans and truly appear to suffer if ignored or left alone too long.

The Sporting breeds have long been admired for their instincts and skills in water and woods. This group is divided into four types: Pointers, Retrievers, Setters, and Spaniels. The breeds presented in this chapter are grouped according to these types, each with its own talents and physical characteristics. Pointers, Retrievers, and Setters are large; Spaniels run smaller. Retriever coats range from short to medium, and most Pointers have short hair (some are wiry). The Setters have long hair, and the Spaniels' coats range from medium to long, some with gorgeous curls.

When you're not out hiking or hunting with your Sporting breed, you may find a fenced yard to be a useful part of satisfying your dog's need for fresh air and room to explore. Even better, head out there for a game of catch or fetch. You'll be amazed at how long your dog is capable of playing; Retrievers, in particular, are perfectly happy to fetch sticks, balls, Frisbees, and so forth for you until your arm is numb.

Brittany

History/Evolution: Named for the French province where it originated around 1900, the Brittany may have been the result of crosses between native Brittany Spaniels and English pointing dogs. A fine hunter with a strong nose, the Brittany became popular in France, arriving in the U.S. in 1925. Equally suited for sport and companionship, the Brittany's popularity has surged. Originally called the Brittany Spaniel, the "Spaniel" was dropped in 1982 because the breed's hunting style is more like a Setter than a Spaniel.

Size: Medium; 17½ inches to 20½ inches, 30 to 40 pounds.

Color: Orange and white, liver and white (white can be clear or roan).

Temperament: Alert, quick, and curious; loves to run and play. Independent but responsive, eager to please, affectionate. A good house pet if given mental and physical exercise.

Photograph © Jean Fogle

Energy level: High.

Best owner: Hunter, an active family in a suburban or rural home.

Needs: Abundant and daily exercise (runs, obedience), fenced yard, regular brushing once or twice a week.

Life expectancy: 12 to 13 years.

Pointer

History/Evolution: Though unclear, the Pointer's lineage likely can be linked to Greyhounds, Foxhounds, Bloodhounds, and a type of setting Spaniel. Pointers were first used in the mid-1600s in England to point hares for Greyhound coursing. Pointers later became popular for recreational bird hunting and, in the 19th century, as show dogs. Today's Pointers still have the stamina, determination, and skill of capable hunters, but are also treasured as family dogs and companions.

Size: Large; females 23 to 26 inches, 35 to 65 pounds; males 25 to 28 inches, 55 to 90 pounds. (Field-trial lines tend to be smaller than show lines.)

Color: Liver, lemon, black, orange; all with or without white.

Temperament: Alert, independent, and dignified. Happiest with a job (obedience, agility, field trials); can be destructive if not exercised enough. Exuberant but tolerant of children.

Photograph © Jean Fogle

Energy level: Medium to high.

Best owner: Hunter or active, outdoorsy owner.

Needs: Vigorous physical and mental exercise every day, fenced yard, plenty of outside time, companionship, regular brushing.

Life expectancy: Field lines 10 to 12 years; show lines 12 to 14 years.

German Shorthaired Pointer

History/Evolution: Various scent and track breeds were crossed to produce what became the German Shorthaired Pointer in the late 1800s. Proficient with trailing, retrieving, and pointing game of many varieties, the German Shorthaired Pointer eventually became known as an ideal all-purpose hunting dog. First recognized by the AKC in 1930, the breed remains a gifted hunter as well as a loyal, obedient companion.

Size: Medium; females 21 to 23 inches, 45 to 60 pounds; males 23 to 25 inches, 55 to 70 pounds.

Color: Liver, liver and white ticked, spotted or roan.

Temperament: Intelligent, active, enthusiastic about hunting. Devoted, friendly, and willing to please. Playful and loving, but can be too boisterous for small children.

Photograph © Jean Fogle

Energy level: High.

Best owner: Hunter or active family in a suburban or rural home.

Needs: Consistent exercise and mental stimulation to prevent boredom and destructive behaviors, gentle training, fenced yard, minimal brushing.

Life expectancy: 14 to 16 years.

German Wirehaired Pointer

History/Evolution: With traces of Griffon, Pointer, German Shorthair, and Poodle, the German Wirehaired Pointer is an accomplished and versatile hunter. Able to withstand weather and water, the German Wirehaired can point and track game, retrieve waterfowl from water or land, and serve as a reliable guard dog. Recognized by the AKC in 1959, the breed enjoys moderate popularity in the United States, but not nearly as much as it has in its native Germany.

Size: Medium to large; females smaller, but not less than 22 inches; males 24 to 26 inches.

Color: Solid liver, liver and white; may have spots, roaning, and ticking.

Temperament: Energetic, rugged, independent, and driven. Prone to boredom and destructiveness if not physically and mentally challenged. Loyal and affectionate; aloof and protective, but not unfriendly to strangers.

Photograph © Jean Fogle

Energy level: Medium to high.

Best owner: Active, outdoor-oriented person.

Needs: Regular exercise or a job to do, training, fenced yard, human companionship, minimal grooming.

Life expectancy: 12 to 14 years.

Chesapeake Bay Retriever

Photograph © Jean Fogle

History/Evolution: The Chesapeake Bay Retriever's history begins in 1807 in Maryland with the arrival of two Newfoundlands who were rescued from an English brig shipwrecked off the coast. Crossings with various retrievers and others eventually produced the Chessie, a breed that excels at retrieving waterfowl both on land and in water. The Chesapeake Bay Retriever's reputation later spread beyond the Bay, and the AKC recognized the breed in 1885. The Chessie is a true working dog who requires a master who is a skilled trainer.

Size: Large; females 21 to 24 inches, 55 to 70 pounds; males 23 to 26 inches, 65 to 80 pounds.

Color: Brown, from straw to reddish sedge.

Temperament: Hardy, intelligent, and active, with a love of water. Independent but eager to learn. Strong willed and protective; reserved with strangers.

Energy level: Medium to high.

Best owner: Active owner, outdoorsy family with considerate children.

Needs: Daily exercise (swims are preferred), early socialization, obedience training, fenced yard, weekly brushing of oily coat.

Life expectancy: 10 to 12 years.

Curly-Coated Retriever

Photograph © Isabelle Francaise

History/Evolution: One of the oldest of the Retrievers, the Curly-Coated Retriever is believed to have roots in such breeds as the English Water Spaniel, a smaller Newfoundland, and the Poodle, from which it gets its tightly curled coat. Developed in England to be a multipurpose hunting Retriever, the Curly is favored for its excellent field ability, endurance, and courage. Unsurpassed in the water, the Curly-Coated makes a fine family companion when challenged with exercise and activity.

Size: Medium to large; 22 to 27 inches, 55 to 75 pounds.

Color: Black or liver.

Temperament: Eager, self-confident, and steadfast; determined in the field, sensitive at home. Independent; sometimes appears aloof or self-willed.

Energy level: High.

Best owner: Hunter or active, outdoorsy owner in suburban or rural home.

Needs: Daily exercise (swimming and retrieving are best) and training to prevent boredom (and undesirable behaviors), fenced yard, companionship, and occasional combing.

Life expectancy: 8 to 12 years.

Flat-Coated Retriever

Photograph © Jean Fogle

History/Evolution: The Flat-Coated Retriever's history can be traced to the 1800s, to dogs who served fisherman by retrieving fish and objects from the cold waters of Newfoundland. Crosses with these Retrievers and British Setters and Pointers eventually led to the Flat-Coated, which had the skills of both water dogs and bird dogs. Originally suited for hard work in the field, the Flat-Coated is an enthusiastic competitor and family member.

Size: Medium to large, 60 to 70 pounds; females 22 to 23½ inches; males 23 to 24½ inches.

Color: Black, liver.

Temperament: Lively, sweet, eager to please, outgoing, and playful; one of the most devoted breeds. Known for its ever-wagging tail. Determined in the field, with a great desire to hunt.

Energy level: High.

Best owner: Hunter, athlete, or active family.

Needs: Vigorous exercise and mental challenges (agility and obedience), fenced yard, early and consistent training, family bonding, occasional brushing and bathing.

Life expectancy: 10 years.

Golden Retriever

Photograph © Jean Fogle

History/Evolution: The Golden Retriever was developed in Scotland in the late 1800s as a hunting dog. Lord Tweedmouth, who wanted a Retriever suited to the Scottish terrain and climate, is credited with the breed's beginnings. The Golden's popularity grew, and the breed was brought to the United States in the 1920s. Although the breed is still valued for its hunting abilities, its intelligence, beauty, and eager-to-please attitude has made it one of the top breeds in the U.S.

Size: Medium; females 21½ to 22½ inches, 55 to 65 pounds; males 23 to 24 inches, 65 to 75 pounds.

Color: All shades of gold, from pale to rich reddish gold.

Temperament: Friendly, devoted, and obedient; eager to please as a family companion, with excellent rapport with children. Active and boisterous; needs exercise and activity.

Energy level: Medium to high; field lines higher than show lines.

Best owner: Active, social family in suburban or rural home.

Needs: Daily physical and mental exercise (games, retrieving, obedience), human interaction, fenced yard, twice-weekly brushing.

Life expectancy: 10 to 14 years.

Labrador Retriever

History/Evolution: Originally from
Newfoundland in the 1800s, Labs were bred to
work with fisherman to pull nets and retrieve
fish. Later the dogs were honed to be game
retrievers. Although black Labs were initially
preferred, chocolate and yellow were accepted
by the early 1900s. The breed's intelligence and
adaptability has propelled it into such canine
careers as guide dog, search and rescue, and
police work. Extremely gentle and eager to
please, the Lab is incredibly appealing as a pet
and remains *the* most popular breed in the U.S.

Size: Large; females 21½ to 23½ inches, 55 to 70
pounds; males 22½ to 24½ inches, 65 to 80 pounds.

Color: Black, yellow, and chocolate.

Temperament: Outgoing, amiable, gentle, and
obedient; nonaggressive toward all. Intense in
the field, but calm and playful as a home
companion; patient with kids.

Photograph © Jean Fogle

Energy level: High, especially in puppyhood.

Best owner: Active owner or family in suburban
or rural home.

Needs: Daily physical and mental challenges
to stay occupied (and avoid pudginess),
obedience training, secure fencing (around
yards *and* pools), weekly brushing.

Life expectancy: 10 to 12 years.

Nova Scotia Duck Tolling Retriever

History/Evolution: The smallest of the retrievers,
the Nova Scotia Duck Tolling Retriever was
developed in the 1800s to toll and retrieve
waterfowl. *Tolling* — having dogs play and
retrieve sticks or balls along the shoreline —
aroused the curiosity of ducks offshore and lured
them within gunshot range. The first Tollers
arrived in the U.S. in 1984, and the AKC recognized
the breed in 2001. Since their arrival, the dogs
have proven themselves as able retrievers,
skilled competitors, and loyal companions.

Size: Medium; females 17 to 20 inches, 35 to 42
pounds; males 18 to 21 inches, 45 to 52 pounds.

Color: Any shade of red, usually with white
markings.

Temperament: Energetic, playful, alert, outgoing,
ready for action; fast learners but bored easily.
Affectionate and gentle; boisterous when young.
Good with other animals and children.

Photograph © Isabelle Francaise

Energy level: High.

Best owner: Active owner or family in a
suburban or rural home.

Needs: Lots of exercise, play, and activity; a job
to do, fenced yard, weekly brushing.

Life expectancy: 11 to 13 years.

English Setter

History/Evolution: With a history going back 400 years, the English Setter is one of the oldest gundog breeds. Likely developed from Spaniels, the breed would find birds and crouch down or "set," allowing the hunter to (before guns) throw a net over the catch. Breeders developed the English Setter into two types: the Laverack (show setters) and the Llewellin (field setters). An elegant and accomplished Sporting dog, the English Setter is also a fine show dog, agility competitor, therapy dog, and companion.

Size: Medium to large; females 24 inches, 50 to 55 pounds; males 25 inches, 60 to 65 pounds.

Color: Orange, blue, lemon, or liver belton (white background with colored flecks or roan shading), tricolor.

Temperament: Athletic and energetic; a calm housedog with enough exercise. Gentle, affectionate, and laid back; exuberant, but good with children. Thrives on human contact, though not a good obedience student.

Photograph © Jean Fogle

Energy level: High.

Best owner: Active owner or family with a suburban or rural home.

Needs: Vigorous daily exercise (hard runs), fenced yard, companionship, brushing every two to three days (with occasional clipping and trimming).

Life expectancy: 10 to 12 years.

Gordon Setter

History/Evolution: The Gordon Setter's origins can be traced to the 17th century in Scotland; its name comes from the fourth Duke of Gordon, who kept many of the dogs at his castle. Known at times as the Gordon Castle Setter and the Black and Tan Setter, the breed is the heaviest of the three setters. Hunters favored the sturdy and muscular Gordon for its bird-setting and retrieving skills. Though not as popular a pet as the other setters, the Gordon is a lively and devoted companion that thrives on exercise and love.

Size: Large; females 23 to 26 inches, 45 to 70 pounds; males 24 to 27 inches, 55 to 80 pounds.

Color: Black with tan (mahogany or chestnut) markings.

Temperament: Intelligent, fearless, and capable bird dog. Alert, energetic, and enthusiastic; devoted to family. Can get bored or frustrated without enough exercise and activity.

Photograph © Jean Fogle

Energy level: High, calmer when mature.

Best owner: Athletic, confident owner.

Needs: Daily exercise (a 3-mile walk *plus* a short run), fenced yard, firm and consistent obedience training, human interaction, daily brushing to prevent mats.

Life expectancy: 10 to 12 years.

Irish Red and White Setter

History/Evolution: Although the Irish Red and White Setter is rare in the U.S., recognized by the AKC only in 2007, the breed has a long history that began in 17th-century Ireland. A valuable hunting dog and companion, the breed was known for its power and skill in the field. Thought to be the older of the two Irish Setters, the Red and White's popularity was eclipsed by that of the solid-red Irish Setter. It faced extinction by the end of the 1800s, but devotees revived the breed in the early part of the 1900s.

Size: Large, 50 to 75 pounds; females 22½ to 24 inches; males 24½ to 26 inches.

Color: White with solid red patches.

Temperament: Friendly, spirited, determined; can be high strung without proper exercise. Good with children.

Photograph © Isabelle Francaise

Energy level: High.

Best owner: Hunter, active owner in a suburban or rural home.

Needs: Daily exercise (long walks or off-leash runs); fenced yard; early, firm, and consistent training; brushing two to three times a week.

Life expectancy: 11 to 15 years.

Irish Setter

History/Evolution: A probable blend of spaniels, pointers, and other setters, the Irish Setter was developed by Irish hunters who needed a skilled bird-setting and retrieving dog large enough to be seen from a distance. Originally bred as red and white, the solid red of the Irish Setter gained favor in the 1800s. The breed's elegant, striking looks have made it a champion in the show ring; its good-natured attitude and clownish personality have made it a beloved companion.

Size: Large; females 25 inches, 60 pounds; males 27 inches, 70 pounds.

Color: Mahogany or chestnut red.

Temperament: Tireless hunter and an amiable companion if exercised enough. Rollicking personality, full of gusto, eager to please. Good with children, but may be a bit rambunctious for toddlers.

Photograph © Jean Fogle

Energy level: High.

Best owner: Active owner or family in a suburban or rural home.

Needs: Lots of exercise (minimum one hour of exertion a day), a social life, brushing every two to three days, consistent and gentle training methods, fenced yard.

Life expectancy: 12 to 14 years.

American Water Spaniel

Photograph © Isabelle Francaise

History/Evolution: The history of the American Water Spaniel is something of a mystery, but the breed is likely a product of ancestors that include the Irish Water Spaniel and the Curly-Coated Retriever. Developed in the mid-1800s in the Great Lakes region of the U.S., the American Water Spaniel was, and is, a remarkable hunting companion, the first American breed that could retrieve from boats. Although the AKC recognized the breed in 1940, it is still uncommon in the show ring or the home. It's the state dog of Wisconsin.

Size: Medium, 15 to 18 inches; females 25 to 40 pounds; males 30 to 45 pounds.

Color: Solid liver, brown, or dark chocolate.

Temperament: Intelligent, friendly, and fun loving; a good family dog if given enough exercise (if not, prepare for barking and digging). Whining and drooling can be a problem.

Energy level: High, calmer when mature.

Best owner: Hunter of upland birds or waterfowl, active family in suburbs or country.

Needs: Daily exercise (swims are appreciated), fenced yard, human attention, short obedience sessions, weekly brushing, attention to ears (clean regularly).

Life expectancy: 10 to 15 years.

Clumber Spaniel

Photograph © Isabelle Francaise

History/Evolution: One of the oldest of the Spaniels, the Clumber dates back to 18th-century France and counts the Basset Hound and the Alpine Spaniel among its ancestors. The breed was valued for its low build, quiet nature, and slow gait, which helped it approach game very closely. English nobility favored the breed and discouraged its popularity with commoners. Although the Clumber is one of the original nine breeds recognized by the AKC, it remains generally unknown to the public.

Size: Medium; females 17 to 19 inches, 55 to 70 pounds; males 18 to 20 inches, 70 to 85 pounds.

Color: White with lemon or orange markings.

Temperament: Gentle, affectionate, and devoted; the most low key of the spaniels. Intelligent and independent; may be aloof with strangers.

Energy level: Medium.

Best owner: Hunter, social family in suburban or rural home.

Needs: Daily exercise (long walk or leisurely hike), fenced yard, positive training, tolerance for shedding and drool, brushing two to three times a week.

Life expectancy: 10 to 12 years.

Cocker Spaniel

History/Evolution: The American Cocker Spaniel is derived from the English Cocker Spaniel, which was brought to the United States in the late 1800s. Wanting a smaller dog for small game birds such as quail, breeders likely crossed the English Cocker and smaller dogs to produce the American version; the two varieties were separated into two breeds in 1946. Although few hunt with the Cocker today, the breed — one of the most popular of all time — is a favorite at shows and treasured as a pet.

Size: Small, 24 to 28 pounds; females 14 inches; males 15 inches.

Color: Solids — black, black and tan, silver, buff, red, chocolate, chocolate and tan; parti-color — black and white, red and white, chocolate and white, tricolor.

Temperament: Merry, jovial, playful; a social dog who loves family. A true Sporting dog, but hunting instincts can be satisfied with a walk in the country. Some bark a lot.

Photograph © Isabelle Francaise

Energy level: Medium to high.

Best owner: Loving owner with a penchant for hair care.

Needs: Daily exercise, a social life, almost daily brushing, clipping every month or so, special attention to eye and ear care.

Life expectancy: 10 to 14 years.

English Cocker Spaniel

History/Evolution: The English Cocker Spaniel is one of the oldest land Spaniels, a descendant of the original spaniels of Spain. In the 1800s, the Spaniels were divided based on size and hunting ability. The English Cocker, a small land Spaniel, was used to hunt woodcock. Fanciers worked to differentiate the English Cocker from the American type that was gaining recognition; the two breeds were accepted as separate breeds in 1946. Today the English Cocker is an active Sporting dog and loyal companion.

Size: Medium; females 15 to 16 inches, 26 to 32 pounds; males 16 to 17 inches, 28 to 34 pounds.

Color: White with black, blue, liver, or red markings with roaning or ticking; solid black, liver, or red with or without tan markings.

Temperament: Affectionate, cheerful, and devoted; sociable and likes its humans. More of a hunter than the American Cocker Spaniel and needs a bit more exercise.

Photograph © Jean Fogle

Energy level: High as a puppy, medium as matures.

Best owner: Active, social person or family.

Needs: Daily exercise, socialization, consistent brushing and combing, monthly clipping, special attention to eye and ear care, companionship.

Life expectancy: 12 to 15 years.

English Springer Spaniel

Photograph © Jean Fogle

History/Evolution: English Springer Spaniels and Cocker Spaniels were originally born in the same litters, and not until 1902 did the English Kennel Club separate the breeds. English Springers, the larger of the two, were used in the field for flushing or "springing" animals in hiding. The Springer Spaniel continues to thrive, gaining popularity with hunters as a versatile, vigorous gundog who can both flush and retrieve game. Many consider the breed to be the ideal family canine companion.

Size: Medium; females 19 inches, 40 pounds; males 20 inches, 50 pounds.

Color: Black and white, liver and white, or tricolor; may have ticking.

Temperament: Cheerful, playful, and energetic; affectionate and devoted to family. Good as a house pet if outlets for energy are provided.

Energy level: Medium-high.

Best owner: Active owner in a suburban or rural home.

Needs: Daily mental and physical exercise (hunting preferred, but obedience sessions and field outings will do), fenced yard, twice-weekly brushing plus clipping every couple months.

Life expectancy: 12 to 14 years.

Field Spaniel

Photograph © Isabelle Francaise

History/Evolution: Originating in England in the mid-1800s, the Field Spaniel shares its beginnings with the Cocker Spaniel but was deemed a separate breed in 1892. The long-eared Spaniel survived misdirected breeding efforts that nearly brought it to the point of extinction. Dedicated breeders revived the breed in the mid-1950s, honing not only its looks, but its hunting abilities. Though admired for its level headedness, the Field Spaniel remains one of the rarest breeds in the U.S.

Size: Medium, 35 to 50 pounds; females 17 inches; males 18 inches.

Color: Black, liver, golden liver, roan.

Temperament: Cheerful, affectionate, fun loving, and willing to please. Independent, but happy to have human companionship and a job. May be reserved with strangers.

Energy level: High.

Best owner: Hunter, active owner with training experience.

Needs: Daily exercise, fenced yard, human companionship, inclusion in family activities, weekly brushing, tolerance of sloppiness (eating and drinking) and shedding.

Life expectancy: 10 to 12 years.

Irish Water Spaniel

Photograph © Isabelle Francaise

History/Evolution: The largest Spaniel, the Irish Water is an interesting blend of several dogs: a Poodle-like coat, a Retriever's fetching instincts, a Spaniel's affectionate nature, and a Sporting dog's love of water. The Irish Water Spaniel has a smooth face framed with curls and its body covered in dense, water-repellent ringlets, ending with a signature "rat tail." An adept water retriever, the breed entered the American and British show rings in the late 1800s. Though popular for a time, the Irish Water Spaniel is relatively rare these days.

Size: Medium; females 21 to 23 inches, 45 to 58 pounds; males 22 to 24 inches, 55 to 65 pounds.

Color: Liver.

Temperament: Energetic, enthusiastic, even clownish. Can be independent and stubborn; needs patient, firm training. Alert and inquisitive; reserved with strangers.

Energy level: High as puppy.

Best owner: Hunter, outdoorsy type.

Needs: Daily mental and physical exercise (runs, strenuous play, obedience sessions), brushing and combing two times a week, scissoring every few months.

Life expectancy: 10 to 12 years.

Sussex Spaniel

Photograph © Isabelle Francaise

History/Evolution: The Sussex Spaniel owes it name to the kennel in Sussex, England, that was an important part of the breed's development in the early 1800s. This small land Spaniel, though not as fast as others of its type, had a good nose and was skilled at working through dense underbrush. Unfortunately, the breed's popularity with hunters was short lived, and the Sussex came close to extinction during the 1900s. Still rare, the Sussex is treasured by people who appreciate its lovely coat and deceptively somber expression.

Size: Small to medium; 13 to 15 inches, 35 to 45 pounds.

Color: Rich golden liver.

Temperament: Cheerful, and mellower than other spaniels. Calm in the home, but may bark or howl if left out of activities. Fine with animals and children.

Energy level: Medium.

Best owner: Family or owner in a suburban or rural home.

Needs: Daily exercise (a walk or backyard romp), fenced yard, human attention, obedience training, early socialization, brushing two to three times a week.

Life expectancy: 11 to 12 years.

Welsh Springer Spaniel

History/Evolution: The exact origins of the Welsh Springer Spaniel are unclear, but the breed likely was developed around the 1600s in Wales. The breed enjoyed a rise in popularity as a hunting dog of the nobility but lost footing as the English Springer and other Spaniels came into favor. Brought to the U.S. in the late 1800s, the Welsh Springer gained AKC recognition in 1906. The breed is an accomplished all-purpose, all-terrain hunter that excels beyond the field into the show ring and home.

Size: Medium, 35 to 45 pounds; females 17 to 18 inches; males 18 to 19 inches.

Color: Red and white.

Temperament: Active, steady, easygoing. Loyal, affectionate, and totally devoted to family, but independent; reserved with strangers. Usually gentle with children.

Photograph © Jean Fogle

Energy level: High as puppy, mellows with age.

Best owner: Active, loving owner in a suburban or rural home.

Needs: Daily exercise (long walks and strenuous games), socialization, fenced yard, weekly brushing, and occasional trims with scissors.

Life expectancy: 12 to 14 years.

Spinone Italiano

History/Evolution: The Spinone Italiano's origins are somewhat mysterious, although most experts credit the Piedmonte district of northwest Italy with its development. Theories abound; some link the dog to coarse-haired Italian Setters, dogs left behind by Greek traders, and even French Griffons. Italy's all-purpose hunting dog, the Spinone Italiano is an excellent retriever that can hunt on any terrain. Although popular in Italy and some other European countries, it has not taken off in the U.S.

Size: Large; females 22 to 25 inches, 70 to 80 pounds; males 23 to 27 inches, 80 to 90 pounds.

Color: White, orange and white, orange roan, chestnut and white, chestnut roan.

Temperament: Gentle, devoted, eager to please, and affectionate; cautious about new people and situations, but good with children. Calmer than most pointing breeds.

Photograph © Isabelle Francaise

Energy level: Medium.

Best owner: Hunter, athletic owner in suburban or rural home.

Needs: Daily exercise (long walk or off-leash run), fenced yard, socialization, training, weekly brushing and occasional hand stripping, tolerance of messy beard.

Life expectancy: 12 to 14 years.

Vizsla

History/Evolution: The Vizsla's history can be traced to Hungary in the Middle Ages. The country was rich in game, and the Vizsla's superior nose, speed, and hunting ability met the needs of the hunters. The breed excelled at both pointing and retrieving and was a favorite of barons and warlords by the 1700s. Although the Vizsla's numbers declined by the end of the World Wars, devotees worked to reestablish the breed; the AKC recognized the Vizsla in 1960.

Size: Medium, 45 to 65 pounds; females 21 to 23 inches; males 22 to 24 inches.

Color: Golden rust.

Temperament: Lively, active, highly trainable; a natural hunter. Gentle, affectionate. Well-developed protective instinct. Can be frustrated and destructive without enough exercise.

Photograph © Jean Fogle

Energy level: High.

Best owner: Hunter, athlete, or active family in suburbs or country.

Needs: Strenuous daily exercise (long runs), fenced yard, lots of outdoor activity with its family, regular brushing to control shedding.

Life expectancy: 12 to 15 years.

Weimaraner

History/Evolution: Developed in Germany in the 19th century, the Weimaraner is believed to be a descendant of the Bloodhound and early pointing breeds. Originally bred to be an all-around gundog who could hunt wolves, deer, and bear, the Weimaraner later transitioned to more of a bird dog and hunting companion. The distinctly gray dogs were highly valued, and breeding was strictly managed to keep lines pure. Not until 1929 did the first Weimaraners leave Germany, when an American was allowed to bring two to the U.S.

Size: Large; females 23 to 25 inches, 50 to 70 pounds; males 25 to 27 inches, 70 to 85 pounds.

Color: Mouse gray to silver gray.

Temperament: Friendly, fearless, and obedient; can be stubborn or headstrong, but learns easily. Needs to run and hunt. Good with children, but may overwhelm little ones.

Photograph © Jean Fogle

Energy level: Very high.

Best owner: Hunter or outdoorsy, confident owner.

Needs: Serious daily exercise, fenced yard, human companionship, obedience training, brushing.

Life expectancy: 10 to 12 years.

Wirehaired Pointing Griffon

History/Evolution: The history of the Wirehaired Pointing Griffon begins in the mid-1880s. Eduard Korthals of Amsterdam is credited with developing the breed, which he hoped would be a dog who could hunt in marshes and other terrain. He took the dog to France, where it was well received and quickly gained a following. Known for a time as the Russian Setter, the Griffon gained AKC recognition in 1887. Today the breed still has loyal followers who value it for its pointing and retrieving as well as for its companionship.

Size: Medium to large, 50 to 60 pounds; females 20 to 22 inches; males 22 to 24 inches.

Color: Chestnut, solid or with roaning.

Temperament: Skilled, independent field dog, easily trained. Outgoing, eager to please, comical, and amiable in the home with enough exercise. Generally friendly toward others.

Photograph © Jean Fogle

Energy level: Medium to high.

Best owner: Hunter, athletes in suburban or rural home.

Needs: Daily exercise (jogging, field runs, games), fenced yard, consistent training, weekly brushing and some hand stripping, attention to ear care.

Life expectancy: 12 to 14 years.

Chapter 7

Profiling the Non-Sporting Group

*O*kay, so what's the deal with the Non-Sporting Group? Is it truly a group made up of non-sporting types, or is it a catchall category of groupless pooches?

In truth, the answer may be a bit of both. The Non-Sporting Group was created back in the early days of dog shows, when all the other breeds were neatly classified in the Sporting Group. Now that we have several other groups to choose from, each of these Non-Sporting breeds could probably fit — or almost fit — into another group. But what's done is done, and there they remain.

Members of this group are wonderfully diverse, with great variety in appearance, size, temperament, and conformation. The group's 17 breeds have backgrounds that can be traced to retrievers, mastiffs, spaniels, Nordic dogs, and more. As far as origins go, the breeds came from all over the globe — the Shiba Inu from Japan, the Tibetan Spaniel from the Himalayas of Tibet, the Keeshond from the Netherlands, and the Boston Terrier from, well, Boston.

These days most of the Non-Sporting breeds dedicate themselves to careers as devoted companions, but going back to their roots, these dogs were workers of all types: ratters, guard dogs, retrievers, performers, fighters, hunters, carriage dogs, herders. Two were lapdogs extraordinaire (a cushy job, for sure), and one was even a "good luck" companion.

Because they come from such different stock and were developed for such different purposes, the breeds in the Non-Sporting Group are quite distinct in appearance and character. Talk about a smorgasbord of personalities, not to mention a cornucopia of ears, tails, and coat types!

American Eskimo Dog

History/Evolution: A member of the Spitz family, the American Eskimo Dog, or "Eskie," descended from a variety of German spitz, with influences from other spitzes such as the Keeshond and Pomeranian. Known for its beauty, intelligence, and agility, the Eskie was an extremely popular performer in traveling circuses throughout the U.S. Today's Eskies are primarily companion dogs, although some compete in conformation, obedience, and agility.

Size: Tiny to medium. Toy 9 to 12 inches, Miniature 12 to 15 inches, Standard 15 to 19 inches.

Color: White, white with biscuit cream.

Temperament: Intelligent, alert, and friendly; trainable and willing to please. Protective and wary of strangers. Not the best choice if there are children or other pets.

Photograph © Jean Fogle

Energy level: High, especially with smaller sizes; mellows with age.

Best owner: Active owner in a home with a fenced yard.

Needs: Daily exercise, fenced yard, patient housetraining, cool climate; brushing and combing twice weekly, more often when shedding.

Life expectancy: 12 to 15 years.

Bichon Frise

History/Evolution: Originating in the Mediterranean area in the 13th century, the Bichon Frise is believed to be the descendant of large water spaniels and small, often white, dogs. Spanish sailors traded the cheerful breed and transported dogs from continent to continent, and Bichons found their way into French royal courts and Spanish paintings. In the late 1800s, the breed fell out of favor, but it survived by performing with street artists and in circuses and fairs. Bichons make excellent pets.

Size: Small; 9½ to 11½ inches, 14 to 16 pounds.

Color: White.

Temperament: Playful, cheerful, friendly, and affectionate. Good with children, other dogs and pets, and strangers. Doesn't like to be alone. Some bark a lot.

Photograph © Jean Fogle

Best owner: Aspiring pet groomer.

Needs: Daily exercise, attention, patient housetraining, intense grooming (daily brushing to prevent mats, occasional trims).

Life expectancy: 12 to 15 years.

Boston Terrier

History/Evolution: An all-American dog, the Boston Terrier was developed in the 1800s in Boston, the result of a cross between an English Bulldog and an English Terrier; the Bulldog (named Hooper's Judge) became the ancestor of nearly all true Bostons. The breed is nicknamed "the American gentleman" because of its characteristically gentle disposition. Highly intelligent, the Boston Terrier is an unrivaled companion, ranking as one of the most popular breeds since the early 1900s.

Size: Small; 15 to 25 pounds.

Color: Brindle, seal, or black, all with white markings.

Temperament: Friendly, lively, gentle. Intelligent, well mannered, and playful. Reserved with strangers and other dogs. Some bark.

Photograph © Jean Fogle

Energy level: Moderate to high, mellows with age.

Best owner: Active owner with plenty of time for companionship.

Needs: Daily exercise, fenced yard, positive reinforcement, low heat and humidity, human interaction, occasional brushing, patience with snoring.

Life expectancy: 10 to 14 years.

Bulldog

History/Evolution: Bulldogs are so gentle it's hard to imagine the life these dogs led in their early history, when bull baiting was popular. The dogs' role was to attack the bull, grabbing it by the nose. Fortunately, dog fighting became illegal, and breeders bred out ferocity while retaining the Bulldog's distinctive physical characteristics. The efforts paid off within a few generations; today the Bulldog's lovable dispositions and adorable mugs make it one of the most popular breeds.

Size: Medium to large; 40 to 60 pounds.

Color: Red brindle, brindle, white, red, fawn, and piebald.

Temperament: Kind, amiable, mellow, comical. Willing to please but can be stubborn. Forms bonds and is good with children.

Photograph © Jean Fogle

Energy level: Low.

Best owner: Mellow family or individual.

Needs: Daily exercise (a short walk will do), air conditioning, motivational training, tolerance of drooling and snoring, daily cleaning of facial wrinkles.

Life expectancy: 8 to 10 years.

Chinese Shar-Pei

Photograph © Jean Fogle

History/Evolution: The Chinese Shar-Pei goes back to ancient China, when the dogs were general farm dogs, used for hunting, herding, and guarding. The Chinese believed the breed's characteristic scowl and black pigmented mouth would scare off evil spirits. Although most dogs were eliminated after China became communist, some Shar-Peis survived in other countries. American fanciers rescued the breed from extinction, and the breed is one of the most recognizable in the U.S.

Size: Medium; 18 to 20 inches, 45 to 60 pounds.

Color: Any solid color.

Temperament: Dignified, sober, self-assured, self-possessed. Independent and stubborn. Devoted and protective; suspicious of strangers and aggressive with other dogs.

Energy level: Low to moderate.

Best owner: Confident owners with previous training experience.

Needs: Daily mental and physical exercise, training and socialization, weekly brushing, attention to ears and wrinkles, regular nail clipping.

Life expectancy: 8 to 12 years.

Chow Chow

Photograph © Jean Fogle

History/Evolution: Though its origins are unclear, the Chow Chow can be traced back to ancient China. An all-purpose working dog, the powerful and lionlike dog was used for guarding, hunting, and herding. The name Chow Chow was adopted after the breed was brought to England, and its popularity rose after Queen Victoria took an interest. Like the Shar-Pei, the Chow Chow is known for its blue/black tongue and makes an extremely protective and loyal companion.

Size: Medium, 17 to 20 inches; females 50 to 65 pounds; males 60 to 75 pounds.

Color: Red, black, blue, cinnamon, and cream.

Temperament: Serious, independent, dignified; devoted to family, not demonstrative. Suspicious of strangers and aggressive with other dogs.

Energy level: Low.

Best owner: Confident owner who doesn't need a cuddly canine.

Needs: Daily exercise (casual walks), low heat and humidity, socialization, firm training, daily brushing for rough coats and weekly for smooth coats (more when shedding).

Life expectancy: 8 to 12 years.

Dalmatian

History/Evolution: The Dalmatian's origin is a mystery, but we do know that the breed served as war dogs, sentinels, shepherds, ratters, retrievers, and even circus dogs. The Dalmatian found its true calling as a coach dog in Victorian England, protecting horses and adding a touch of style. When the auto arrived, the Dalmatian continued as a coach dog for horse-drawn fire engines. Movies with Dalmatians have spurred their popularity, but most people are unprepared for the training involved.

Size: Medium to large; 19 to 23 inches, 45 to 60 pounds.

Color: White with black or liver spots.

Temperament: Outgoing, energetic; daily exercise ensures better manners. Good with children when raised with them. Reserved with strangers; can be aggressive with dogs.

Photograph © Jean Fogle

Energy level: High.

Best owner: Active owner in a suburban or rural home.

Needs: Daily strenuous exercise, leash, fenced yard, consistent training, lots of attention and companionship, soft bedding, regular brushing.

Life expectancy: 12 to 14 years.

Finnish Spitz

History/Evolution: Originally known as the Finnish Cock-Eared Dog and the Finnish Barking Bird Dog, the Finnish Spitz excelled at hunting birds and small game; hunters relied on the vocal breed to alert them to prey. Although interbreeding threatened the breed's survival, two Finnish sportsmen were able to salvage the "Finkie." More of a companion in the U.S., the breed is still used for hunting in Finland. With its erect years and plumed tail, the Finnish Spitz resembles a lively red fox.

Size: Medium; females 15½ to 18 inches, 23 pounds; males 17½ to 20 inches, 29 pounds.

Color: Shades of golden red.

Temperament: Active, lively, friendly, eager; good with children but often devoted to one person. Aloof with strangers, aggressive with strange dogs. Barks.

Photograph © Taru Korrensuo

Energy level: Moderate.

Best owner: Active owner or hunter.

Needs: Daily exercise, leash, fenced yard, human interaction, reward training, tolerance of barking, brushing twice a week (more when shedding).

Life expectancy: 12 to 14 years.

French Bulldog

History/Evolution: The French Bulldog probably owes much of its good looks to the English Bulldog. English lacemakers fancied toy versions of the bulldogs, taking their dogs with them when they were displaced to France. With their small size and "bat ears," the little bulldogs became popular; in the late 1800s, they became known as French Bulldogs. The clownish breed continues to be prized for its affectionate nature and even disposition.

Size: Small; 11 to 14 inches, 20 to 28 pounds.

Color: A variety — often brindle, cream, black-masked fawn, and pied.

Temperament: Amiable, sweet, adaptable, well behaved. Affectionate and cuddly. Alert and active, but not boisterous or barky.

Photograph © Jean Fogle

Energy level: Moderate.

Best owner: Senior citizen or family.

Needs: Minimal daily exercise, leash, tolerance of drooling and snoring, cleaning of facial wrinkles, weekly brushing, low heat and humidity.

Life expectancy: 9 to 11 years.

Keeshond

History/Evolution: One of the spitz breeds, the Keeshond has a history that can be traced to Holland in the 1700s, where it served as a watchdog on the barges and riverboats of the Rhine River. The breed, named for Kees de Gyselaer, the leader of the Dutch Patriot party, became a symbol of that party. Although many of the dogs were disposed of when the party lost, the breed survived, aided by farmers and boatmen. The Keeshond is now the national dog of Holland.

Size: Medium; females 17 inches, 35 pounds; males 18 inches, 40 to 45 pounds.

Color: Gray, black, and cream.

Temperament: Outgoing, friendly, intelligent, affectionate; thrives in a family. Alert but a friend to all; good with children and other dogs.

Photograph © Jean Fogle

Energy level: Medium.

Best owner: Family in a home with a backyard.

Needs: Daily moderate exercise, companionship, brushing once or twice a week and more when shedding.

Life expectancy: 12 to 15 years.

Lhasa Apso

History/Evolution: The Lhasa Apso originated in Tibet's Himalayan Mountains near the city of Lhasa. The bold, hardy dogs served as watchdogs in Buddhist monasteries; Buddhists believed that the souls of lamas entered the dog's bodies when they died. The breed was first brought to the U.S. around 1930, as gifts of the 13th Dalai Lama. With a cloak of hair that parts down the back from head to tail, the Lhasa is not a breed for those who don't care for grooming.

Size: Small; 10 to 11 inches, 11 to 18 pounds.

Color: All.

Temperament: Independent, alert, bold; stubborn but trainable. Content after exercise. Good with older children; reserved with strangers.

Photograph © Isabelle Francaise

Book V

Meet the Breeds

Energy level: Low to medium.

Best owner: Dog groomer in training.

Needs: Daily exercise, leash, early socialization and training, dedicated grooming (brushing every or every other day).

Life expectancy: 12 to 14 years.

Lowchen

History/Evolution: The Lowchen's history began about 400 years ago, most likely in Germany, where the breed served as a foot warmer and companion to ladies of the court. The name means "little lion dog" in German; the breed's trademark is its traditional lion trim, with the coat left untrimmed on the forequarters (the mane) and clipped close on the hindquarters. Although the breed nearly disappeared in the 19th century, dedicated breeders ensured its continued existence.

Size: Small; 12 to 14 inches, 12 to 18 pounds.

Color: Any.

Temperament: Affectionate, lively, devoted, outgoing, inquisitive. Intelligent, highly trainable. Alert; may bark or dig a lot.

Photograph © Isabelle Francaise

Energy level: Medium.

Best owner: Retiree or quite family.

Needs: Daily exercise, mental challenges (obedience, agility), plenty of attention; brushing or combing every other day, clipping.

Life expectancy: 14 to 16 years.

Poodle (Standard and Miniature)

History/Evolution: Today's Poodles were developed in Germany as water retrievers; the trademark poodle clip was designed by hunters to help the dogs move through the water, the remaining hair left on to keep vital organs warm. The breed, which became popular in France, comes in three varieties: Standard (the oldest), Miniature, and Toy. The Poodle's low-shed coat may reduce allergic reactions but requires extensive grooming. Poodles are one of the top ten most popular breeds.

Size: Small and large; Miniature 10 to 15 inches, 12 to 20 pounds; Standard 22 to 27 inches, 40 to 80 pounds.

Color: Blue, gray, silver, brown, café-au-lait, apricot, cream

Temperament: Miniature is playful, responsive, obedient, devoted; good with children, may bark a lot. Standard is intelligent, obedient, active, playful; good with older children.

Photograph © Jean Fogle

Energy level: High.

Best owner: Active owners with dedication to grooming.

Needs: Daily exercise (more for Standards), mental challenges (obedience), leash, fenced yards, companionship, daily grooming plus clipping and scissoring every five weeks.

Life expectancy: Miniature, 14 to 16 years; Standard 10 to 13 years.

Schipperke

History/Evolution: It's possible that this bold dog originated in Belgium, a smaller version of a black Belgian Sheepdog. Schipperke dogs worked as watchdogs and ratters on river barges, where the breed likely got the name *Schipperke,* after the Flemish word *schip,* meaning "boat." Known for its mischievous expression, bold nature, and watchdog qualities, the Schipperke does well with supervision and training. Enjoys conformation, agility, and obedience competitions.

Size: Small; females 10 to 12 inches, males 11 to 13 inches; less than 18 pounds.

Color: Black.

Temperament: Active, confident, curious. Interested in everything, faithful watchdog; protective, reserved with strangers. May bark.

Photograph © Jean Fogle

Energy level: High.

Best owner: Active owner with time for training.

Needs: Daily exercise, mental challenges, leash, fenced yard, patient housetraining, air conditioning, weekly brushing (more during sheds).

Life expectancy: 12 to 15 years.

Shiba Inu

History/Evolution: The Shiba Inu is the smallest and perhaps oldest of the six dog breeds native to Japan. Of Spitz heritage, the Shiba was originally developed for hunting small game and boar. Although the bombing raids of World War II and distemper nearly caused the breed to die out, bloodlines were interbred to produce the breed as it is known today. Alert watchdogs and adaptable companions, the Shiba Inu has established itself as the number-one companion dog in Japan.

Size: Small to medium; females 13½ inches to 15½ inches, males 14½ inches to 16½ inches; 18 to 25 pounds.

Color: Red, red sesame, black/tan, black sesame, and brindle; may have white markings.

Temperament: Bold, spirited, headstrong. Adaptable and well mannered if properly exercised. Reserved with strangers; an excellent watchdog.

Photograph © Jean Fogle

Energy level: Moderate.

Best owner: Active owner in a rural or suburban home.

Needs: Daily vigorous exercise, leash, fenced yard, early and continuing obedience training, socialization, brushing once a week.

Life expectancy: 12 to 15 years.

Tibetan Spaniel

History/Evolution: Originating in Tibet in ancient times, Tibetan Spaniels were prized as pets and companions in Tibetan monasteries. Like the other two Tibetan breeds — the Lhasa Apso and Tibetan Terrier — the Tibbies were highly valued. The lionlike dogs were excellent watchdogs and would sit on monastery walls and bark when strangers or wolves approached. Tibbies are popular primarily in Tibet but are found in conformation, obedience, and agility rings in the U.S.

Size: Small; 10 inches, 9 to 15 pounds.

Color: All.

Temperament: Outgoing, friendly, intelligent. Aloof with strangers, alert; excellent alarm system. Good; considerate with children and other dogs.

Photograph © Isabelle Francaise

Energy level: Medium to high.

Best owner: Retiree with time for socializing.

Needs: Daily exercise (minimal), leash, twice-weekly combing and brushing (more during seasonal shed).

Life expectancy: 15 to 18 years

Tibetan Terrier

History/Evolution: The Tibetan Terrier was bred and raised in Tibetan monasteries almost 2,000 years ago. The dogs, developed to withstand the harsh terrain and climate of the remote "Lost Valley" of Tibet, were often given as a "luck bringer" to safeguard visitors on the return trip. One such visitor returned to England with a dog, obtained another, and then began a breeding program. The Tibetan Terrier is not a terrier at all, having only been given the name because of its terrier size.

Size: Medium to small; 14 to 17 inches, 18 to 30 pounds.

Color: Any.

Temperament: Devoted, sensitive, and affectionate; Intelligent, independent, even mischievous. Cautious and reserved with strangers. Best with gentle children.

Photograph © Isabelle Francaise

Energy level: Moderate, low to moderate with age.

Best owner: Family with older children.

Needs: Daily exercise, fenced yard, leash, brushing or combing twice a week, patient training.

Life expectancy: 12 to 15 years.

Chapter 8

Profiling the Mixed Breeds

. . . .

. . . .

*W*hat is a mixed breed? A mutt? A devoted companion? A Cockapoo? How about a Chiweenie? The answer to all these questions is yes. Although mixed breeds sometimes get an undeserved bad rap from the more snooty purists, these types of pooches have legions of devoted fans and are becoming increasingly popular, no doubt because of the relatively recent trend of so-called "designer dogs," such as Goldendoodles, Puggles, and Schnoodles.

Mixed breeds are nothing new. From the dawn of canine history, intact male and female dogs have met and, during the heat of the moment, started something new. The results of these couplings come in a rainbow of colors, weigh from 5 to 95 pounds, and have coats that are wiry or silky, long or short, straight or curly. But what they do have in common is their uniqueness — no two are alike.

Mixed breeds taken to the next level are called designer dogs, combinations of two purebred dogs. These pups are purposely crossed (no random unions, thank you) to create a specific appearance and temperament. The idea of designer mixes took off in the 1990s, thanks to a crossbred pioneer called the Labradoodle, a mix of Labrador Retriever and Poodle. Once an accessory of celebrities, today's crossbreeds are often sought after by people with deep pockets who are looking for small, agreeable, or low-allergy versions of purebreds.

This chapter tells the story of mixed breeds, from Heinz 57 to designer, including the famed Labradoodle. Though trendy today, designers are not without controversy, so their pros and cons are both considered. Because all mixes — intentional and unintentional — combine the characteristics of the parent breeds, this chapter covers the general characteristics of the various dog groups and gives profiles of 17 mixed breeds and designer dogs.

Introducing the Mixed Breeds

The mixed breeds are a diverse lot — mutts and designers, companions and competitors. By definition, a *mixed breed* is a dog conceived by two different purebreds or mixed breeds (or a purebred and a mixed breed). Because the terminology is important and can seem confusing, some additional definitions may be in order:

- **Purebred:** Dog with ancestors who are members of a recognized breed; the ancestry of a dog remains consistent over many generations.

- **Crossbred:** Dog who is the offspring of two different purebred dogs of different breeds. The Cockapoo, a cross between a Poodle and a Cocker Spaniel, is a well-known crossbreed.

- **Hybrid:** Although the word *hybrid* technically refers to the result of crossing animals of two different species (horse and zebra, for example), it is generally accepted to use the term interchangeably with *crossbred*.

- **Designer dog:** The name associated with crossbred dogs deliberately developed, most during the last few decades (see this chapter's "Delving into Designer Dogs" for more information).

Some mixed breeds may be more mixed than others. In fact, a mix may have some purebred ancestors in its lineage; other mixes come from a long line of mixed breeds. In many cases, a mix's ancestors are vague, at best, and some are simply identified by the most recognizable breed of the mix — "Shepherd mix," "Beagle mix," or "Lab mix," to name a few.

Making sense of mixed breed history

Take a look at the history of nearly any purebred dog, and you'll read about breeders who played the mating game, introducing other breeds to early purebreds to improve coat, temperament, height, weight, strength, and so on. Along the way, some accidental intermingling occurred as well.

So if mixed breeds have been around for so long, then what's all the fuss about crossbreeds, hybrids, and designer dogs? Consider the Silky Terrier, developed in Australia in the late 1800s by crossing native Australian Terriers with Yorkshire Terriers imported from England. The breeders were successful in improving the Australian's coat color, and a standard was developed and accepted in 1926. Although the breed hasn't topped the Yorkshire in terms of popularity, the Silky earned its place with the AKC as a breed and continues to attract followers.

The mix heard 'round the world

When Wally Conron, a breeding manager for an Australian guide dog association, set out to help a visually impaired woman find a guide dog that her allergic husband could live with, he had no idea he was embarking on an adventure in genetics that would change the way people think of mixed breeds. It seemed simple enough: Breed a Labrador Retriever (the center's choice for guide dogs) with a Poodle, a breed known for a low-shed, curly coat.

After a good deal of trial and error, in the late 1980s, Wally found himself with the Labradoodle, a crossbreed with a Poodle-type coat and Labrador-type temperament. The Labradoodle has led to a great deal of change in the dog breeding world. This dog was the first mixed breed that people were willing to pay thousands of dollars to have. It's the breed that launched the careers of many other Poodle hybrids. It's also the breed that replaced the classic Scottish Terrier game token in a special edition of the Monopoly board game. Go figure.

The mating game continues today. In the 1950s, it was the Cockapoo and the Pekapoo. Then came the Labradoodle in the late 1980s (see "The mix heard 'round the world" sidebar). Breeders discovered that certain crossbreeds had traits that made them popular companions, so they worked to produce dogs who had these characteristics:

- Low-shedding, low-dander coats, a benefit for people with allergies

- Fewer physical problems found in some purebreds, such as the breathing issues of short-nosed breeds like the Pekingese, Shih Tzu, and Pug

- Improved temperament and trainability

At play here is the concept of *hybrid vigor,* which means that careful breeding of mates from two different breeds can result in a stronger or improved mix. Although some breeders use the term indiscriminately when discussing mixed breeds, offspring likely will have a combination of good and bad traits from both parent breeds.

Hitting the big-time

With all the attention focused on mixed breeds these days, it's no surprise that organizations are getting involved. Since 1978, the not-for-profit Mixed Breed Dog Clubs of America (MBDCA) has supported owners of mixed breeds. Unlike the American Hybrid Club of America, the MBDCA is an actual club, not just a registry, and has members and elected officers as well as a code of ethics. Under the code, all members must agree to spay and neuter their mixes. Through the club, which has a limited number of local chapters throughout the United States, owners of mixed breeds can enter their dogs in competitions of obedience, conformation, tracking, and more.

After years of consideration, the American Kennel Club announced in 2009 that it was creating a program for mixed breeds. Owners of mixes can now enroll their pets and receive an AKC competition card. Since April 2009, enrolled dogs have been able to compete in mixed breed classes at stand-alone AKC agility and obedience events, as well as in rally events, the organization's newest performance competition. Although the mixed breeds will not be registered as breeds with the AKC, this move signals a big step for all mixes.

Delving into Designer Dogs

With catchy names and celebrity owners, designer dogs have certainly captured attention. Some people are taken by the dogs' unique looks; people with allergies are interested in particular designers strictly for the promise of a low-sneeze companion. Why else, some would ask, would anyone pay thousands of dollars for a dog they could just as easily find at an animal shelter?

Now, most mixed breeds — as wonderful as they are — are products of unplanned coupling. When handled responsibly, designer dog mixes are bred for specific characteristics, whether appearance, temperament, or both.

Although they have quickly risen in popularity, designer dogs are not without controversy. This section covers the pros and cons of designer dogs.

The Pros

Because such a wide variety of designer dogs are available, prospective owners may be able to find a dog who suits their individual needs — size, coat, temperament, protective nature, and so on.

Many of the designer dogs are bred to have specific characteristics, and in doing so, breeders may reduce or eliminate certain problems associated with the purebred parents.

Some people believe that the offspring of two different breeds will have hybrid vigor and, because of greater genetic diversity, may be less likely to inherit generic diseases carried from one purebred generation to the next — problems including epilepsy, hip dysplasia, and dental issues. Of course, this theory applies to all mixed breeds, not just hybrids and designer dogs.

The Cons

Although each designer dog is bred to have specific traits, there are no guarantees. The mating game is a game of chance, and breeders can't determine which traits the hybrid offspring will inherit from the parents. This truth applies to both appearance and personality. In fact, in some cases, offspring may inherit negative traits from both parents.

Designer dogs are pricey, which is a major drawback for many people. Many designer dogs cost as much as or more than purebred dogs, with price tags that can reach into the thousands of dollars, particularly for trendy breeds.

Although the idea of hybrid vigor — that mixing two breeds can improve the offspring's health — has some truth, it is not an absolute. A designer dog's health cannot be guaranteed to be better than the health of the purebred parents.

Many people believe that the practice of breeding designer dogs is contributing to the already overwhelming problem of unwanted dogs in this country. Dogs who are less than desirable or unsellable may end up in shelters, taking up much-needed space and resources.

Some people worry that the trendy nature of designer dogs will lead to unscrupulous breeding practices by breeders who see this fad as a quick way to make a buck. This type of breeder is not concerned about health, of either the parents or the offspring.

Getting Some Breed Insight

A certain degree of the unknown arises when it comes to predicting the outcome of a pairing between mixed breeds. The same is true, perhaps to a lesser extent, with crossbreeding. Will your Shepadoodle be more German Shepherd or Poodle? Your Beagalier more Beagle or Cavalier King Charles Spaniel?

Compounding the unpredictable nature of crossbreeding is the sheer number of combinations that are possible (just because a hybrid is possible doesn't mean it's a good idea). The American Canine Hybrid Club, a registry service for hybrid dogs, currently lists nearly 600 different crossbreeds (www.achclub. com/modules.php?name=Breeders). This chapter can cover a mere fraction of these crosses, but understanding the personality and appearance of some of the breed groups can help you understand a mix, whether it's a cross of two breeds or a mixed breed of unknown descent. Other chapters in this book profile the seven groups the American Kennel Club uses to categorize dogs. Although all dogs are individuals, look to these chapters for insight about the general characteristics of each group:

✔ **Sporting:** Includes the Retrievers, Setters, and Spaniels; 27 breeds.

✔ **Hound:** Includes Sighthounds like the Greyhound and Afghan, and Scenthounds such as the Basset and the Beagle; 23 breeds.

✔ **Working:** Includes breeds such as the Bullmastiff and Newfoundland that were developed for guarding and pulling sleds; 26 breeds.

✔ **Terrier:** Includes energetic dogs such as the Bedlington and Scottish Terriers that were bred to hunt and kill vermin; 27 breeds.

✔ **Toy:** Includes small breeds such as the Maltese and Pekingese that were developed as lapdogs and companions; 21 breeds.

✔ **Non-Sporting:** Includes an eclectic variety, such as Dalmatian and Poodle crosses; 17 breeds.

✔ **Herding:** Includes a variety of dogs, like the Chow Chow and the Shiba Inu; 17 breeds.

In addition to the 20 crossbreeds profiled in this chapter, looking at some general characteristics of some of the popular types of mixes may be helpful when it comes time to choose your special mix.

Poodle pairings

Beginning with the Cockapoo and the Labradoodle, some of the most popular crossbreeds have been dogs with a Poodle parent. Poodles have a lot to offer when it comes to crossbreeding — four sizes, high intelligence and trainability, and a low- to no-shed coat that makes the breed very appealing to people with allergies. Other poodle crosses include the following:

✔ Goldendoodle (Golden Retriever and Poodle)

✔ Yorkiepoo (Yorkshire Terrier and Poodle)

✔ Shepadoodle (German Shepherd and Poodle)

✔ Pekapoo (Pekingese and Poodle)

✔ Schnoodle (Schnauzer and Poodle)

✔ Terripoos (various terriers and Poodle)

Pug pairings

Currently the most popular cross is the Puggle, an appealing mix of Pug and Beagle that first rose to stardom in cities, often attached to such celebrities as Uma Thurman and James Gandolfino. Pugs typically are sweet, loyal, and intelligent, with easy-to-care-for coats. Unfortunately, their short noses make them prone to respiratory problems. The Puggle often inherits the longer snout of the beagle, which reduces or eliminates the breathing problems associated with the Pug. Other Pug mixes include these:

- Pugland (West Highland Terrier and Pug)
- Pugshire (Yorkshire Terrier and Pug)
- Bassug (Basset and Pug)
- Buggs (Boston Terrier and Pug)

Toy pairings

The Puggle appeals to many because of its compact size. Other diminutive and Toy breeds have become popular crossbreed candidates because of their small stature. Known as pocket dogs, they are usually a cross between two Toy breeds, such as Maltese, Pekingese, and Shih Tzu; many tend to have good personalities and longevity. Though they may look like fluffy accessories, these Toy crosses require the same care as any dog. Some of the smallest hybrids include these:

- Silkese (Maltese and Silky Terrier)
- Yorkinese (Yorkshire Terrier and Pekingese)
- Poshies (Pomeranian and Shetland Sheepdog)
- Snorkie (Miniature Schnauzer and Yorkshire Terrier)

Bichon Frise pairings

With a low-shed, low-dander coat, the Bichon Frise is a likely candidate for crossings. A small, white dog with a perky personality, the Bichon has been matched with Toy breeds to produce dogs who may inherit some of the breed's qualities. Bichon hybrids include these:

- ChiChon (Bichon Frise and Chihuahua)
- Havachon (Bichon Frise and Havanese)
- Maltichon (Bichon Frise and Maltese)
- Pekachon (Bichon Frise and Pekingese)
- Poochon (Bichon Frise and Poodle)
- Shihchon (Bichon Frise and Shih Tzu)

Playing detective

Not sure of your mixed breed's ancestry? Join the club. It's not uncommon for mixes to be a puzzling blend of a little of this and a little of that. But you may just figure out the breeds that make up your dog by doing a bit of research. Look at photos of purebreds to see if you can find similarities in appearance. You say that your dog's tongue is spotted? Chances are, a Chow Chow or Chinese Shar-Pei is part of your pooch's family tree. Your canine companion has a short nose and snores like your grandfather? Hmm . . . check out the Pug, Pekingese, or other brachycephalic types. The same goes for personality. Traits associated with Herders, Hounds, Terriers, and the other groups can tip you off to your dog's origins. If you're willing to put down some cash, you can check out companies that test dog DNA for you, such as www.canineheritage.com.

Border Collie pairings

Border Collies are hardy, intelligent, and highly trainable dogs, and hybrids of this breed are often developed to take advantage of these qualities. Bred more for intelligence than coat type, Border Collie crosses are typically focused and hardworking. The Borador, a cross with the Labrador Retriever, is one of the most popular of the Border mixes.

The Border Jack is a cross between the Border Collie and Jack Russell (now Parsons Russell) Terrier. With the speed of the terriers and the trainability of the Border Collies, the Border Jack has the best of both breeds — and loves to prove it in the competition arenas of flyball and agility.

For more information on many of these crossbreeds, read this chapter's individual breed profiles, which include details on size, temperament, history, and needs.

Aussiedoodle

History/Evolution: Also known as the Aussiepoo, the Aussiedoodle is a cross of the Miniature or Standard Australian Shepherd and the Toy, Miniature, or Standard Poodle. Although the Australian Shepherd is a heavy shedder, the Aussiedoodle may inherit the Poodle's low-shedding, low-dander coat — a plus for people with allergies. Aussiedoodles may also retain the Australian Shepherd's herding skills and merle coat colors.

Size: Varies: A miniature Aussiedoodle is about 13 to 18 inches, 15 to 30 pounds; a medium or large Aussiedoodle is about 20 to 30 inches, 25 to 50 pounds.

Color: A variety, including black, blue merle, red merle, and red.

Temperament: Intelligent, even tempered, energetic, loyal. Reserved with strangers; patient with children when raised with them.

Photograph © Pecan Place Kennels/ Joyce M. Wallace

Energy level: Active without being hyper.

Best owner: Active family in a rural or suburban home.

Needs: Daily exercise (brisk walk, agility), leash, fenced yard, socialization, regular grooming (shaggy or poodle clip), training, ear cleaning (removing hair).

Life expectancy: 12 to 15 years.

Bagel

History/Evolution: The Bagel is a cross between the Beagle and the Basset Hound. Though not as popular as some of the more well-established mixes, the short-coated Bagel has the loving personality one would expect from two Hounds, plus the potential for some stubbornness. The crossing may prove beneficial to some problems associated with the long-backed Basset. Potential owners should ask about back problems as well as epilepsy, inherited in Beagles.

Size: Small to medium; 10 to 15 inches, 20 to 50 pounds.

Color: Tricolor hound colors.

Temperament: Loving, devoted, even tempered. Also independent and willful. Usually good with children and other dogs and pets.

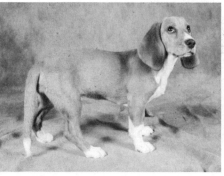

Photograph © Chelle Rohde / www.DesignerDoggies.com

Energy level: Medium.

Best owner: Active family.

Needs: Daily exercise, leash, fenced yard, early socialization, training, regular brushing.

Life expectancy: 10 to 15 years.

Beagalier

History/Evolution: A cross between a Cavalier King Charles Spaniel and a Beagle, the Beagalier was first bred in Australia in the 1990s, focused on reducing the Beagle's scent-hunting drive and wandering tendencies. The crossbreed may have a positive effect on health problems associated with the Cavalier, including heart conditions and other issues related to the shortened face. The typical Beagalier has a good temperament and resembles both parent breeds.

Size: Small to medium; 12 to 16 inches, 10 to 25 pounds.

Color: Black, white, or tricolor.

Temperament: Sweet, intelligent, playful, good natured, calm; good with considerate children. May get distracted by scents. Does not like to be alone.

Photograph © Louise Moon

Energy level: Medium.

Best owner: Active individual or family in suburban or rural home.

Needs: Daily exercise, leash, fenced yard, regular brushing (both parent breeds are shedders), obedience training.

Life expectancy: 12 to 14 years.

Borador

History/Evolution: The Borador's combination of Border Collie and Labrador Retriever seems to make sense. The two breeds excel at agility and trainability, raising breeders' hopes that they'll come up with a flyball or agility champion. Plus, the Lab influence may help to mellow out the Border Collie's need to chase and work all the time. The Borador pairing typically yields a friendly, easy-to-train breed with an attractive short or medium-length coat.

Size: Medium to large; 17 inches, 35 to 45 pounds.

Color: Varies; typically black with white Border Collie markings on nose, paws, and neck.

Temperament: Sweet, affectionate, friendly. Some herd children; may be overexuberant at times. Loyal to family, not usually aggressive to strangers.

Photograph © Corbin Collins

Energy level: Medium.

Best owner: Active owner in suburban or rural home.

Needs: Daily mental and physical exercise (long walks, fetch, agility), leash, fenced yard, chew toys, weekly brushing.

Life expectancy: 12 years.

Border Shepherd

Photograph © tbkmedia.de / Alamy

History/Evolution: Like the Borador, the Border Shepherd's combination of Australian Shepherd and Border Collie was made in the hopes of creating a canine performance champion. Also known as the Border-Aussie, the Border Shepherd is high energy and intense and may not be particularly friendly; look for parents with good temperaments who enjoy human companionship. The breed has a short-to-medium coat that sheds.

Size: Medium; 15 to 22 inches, 35 to 55 pounds.

Color: Varies; includes black and white, blue merle, red merle, and tricolor.

Temperament: Energetic, intelligent, intense, trainable. Reserved with strangers; some can be snappy and less tolerant of children.

Energy level: High.

Best owner: Athlete or someone who enjoys performance training.

Needs: Daily strenuous exercise, job or activity (flyball, agility), socialization, obedience, weekly brushing (more when shedding).

Life expectancy: 10 to 15 years.

Cavachon

Photograph © Silver Paw Kennels

History/Evolution: The Cavachon (or Cavashon) is a cross between the Cavalier King Charles Spaniel and the Bichon Frise. The Bichon, like the Poodle, has a high-maintenance but low-shedding and low-dander coat. The Cavalier is small and sweet tempered, so Cavachons may suit allergy sufferers looking for a small, good-natured companion. Research and careful screenings help identify potential health issues, such as eye problems found in both breeds.

Size: Small; 11 to 17 inches, 12 to 25 pounds.

Color: Black and white, red and white, sable and white; solid or tricolor.

Temperament: Affectionate, intelligent, lively, good natured. Family oriented, nonaggressive. Good with considerate children. Loves family activities.

Energy level: Medium.

Best owner: Family or owner who enjoys grooming.

Needs: Daily exercise (walk, fetching games); leash, socialization, housetraining; regular bathing, brushing, clipping, and grooming.

Life expectancy: 10 to 12 years.

Cockapoo

History/Evolution: Bred since the 1950s, the Cockapoo is one of the older crossbreeds. Two types exist: the American Cockerpoo (Poodle crossed with American Cocker Spaniel) and English Cockapoo (Poodle crossed with English Cocker Spaniel). The cross varies in size, depending on the size of Poodle. Cockapoos may inherit the Poodle's low-shedding, low-dander coat and the sweet disposition of the Cocker. The Cockapoo Club of America was founded to assist breeders.

Size: Small, but ranges: Teacup, less than 6 pounds; Toy, less than 12 pounds; Miniature, 13 to 18 pounds; Maxi, more than 19 pounds.

Color: All combinations of colors.

Temperament: Affectionate, vigorous, loyal, friendly. Intelligent and trainable. Usually fine with children and other animals. People oriented; may bark if left alone.

Photograph © Chuck Franklin / Alamy

Energy level: Low to medium, but playful.

Best owner: Active family.

Needs: Daily exercise, leash, early socialization and training, daily brushing and combing plus professional grooming several times a year, regular ear care.

Life expectancy: 12 to 15 years.

Goldador

History/Evolution: Two extremely popular breeds — the Labrador Retriever and the Golden Retriever — are crossed to get the Goldador, a large dog known for its good temperament and intelligence. Bred for its ability to serve as guide, search-and-rescue, and drug-detection dogs, the Goldador is increasingly popular as a social and trainable family dog. Generally healthy, the Goldador may be prone to eye disorders, as well as hip and elbow dysplasia.

Size: Large; 22 to 24 inches, 60 to 80 pounds.

Color: Usually yellow, but can be any shade of gold, red to yellow, and black.

Temperament: Loving, devoted; family oriented, would rather not be alone. Intelligent and trainable. Good with children and other pets. Good watchdogs.

Photograph © Seth Casteel / LittleFriendsPhoto.com

Energy level: Moderately high.

Best owner: Active family, someone interested in training a working dog.

Needs: Physical and mental exercise (retrieving, swimming, work as therapy dog), leash, fenced yard, early socialization and obedience, regular brushing, care to prevent obesity.

Life expectancy: 10 to 14 years.

Goldendoodle

History/Evolution: The Goldendoodle is a relatively new mix, a cross between the Poodle and the Golden Retriever. Like the Labradoodle, the Goldendoodle may inherit the Poodle's low-shedding, low-dander coat. Bred in different sizes, depending on the size of Poodle, the Goldendoodle is a larger alternative to the Cockapoo. The cross is the product of two intelligent breeds and is an able working dog, serving as a guide dog, sniffer, and therapy dog.

Size: Varies: Miniature, up to 20 inches, 15 to 35 pounds; Medium Standard, 17 to 20 inches, 40 to 50 pounds; Large Standard, 20 to 24 inches, 50 to 80 pounds.

Color: Usually golden, but with red and cream variations.

Temperament: Gentle, eager to please, even tempered, friendly. Intelligent and highly trainable. People oriented, good with children. Disapproves of being alone.

Photograph © istockphoto.com/ Jennifer Sheets

Book V

Meet the Breeds

Energy level: Medium to high.

Best owner: Active family in a suburban or rural home.

Needs: Daily exercise (retrieving and swimming), leash, fenced yard, consistent training, combing every week or so, regular ear care.

Life expectancy: 10 to 15 years.

Labradoodle

History/Evolution: The Labradoodle is the product of the Labrador Retriever and the Poodle, developed as a dog who could assist visually impaired people with allergies. The cross was a success, yielding some dogs with low-shed and low-dander coats; the Labradoodle has become popular, and breeders have continued with multigenerational crossings. Labradoodle associations try to establish the multigenerational Labradoodle as a recognized breed.

Size: Varies: 15 to 65 pounds; Miniature, 14 to 16 inches; Medium, 17 to 20 inches; Standard, 21 to 24 inches.

Color: Varies: chalk, cream, gold, apricot, red, black, blue, silver, chocolate, and cafe.

Temperament: Energetic, sociable, friendly, joyful; affectionate, gentle, and sensitive. Clever and highly trainable. Excellent with children.

Photograph © Jerry Zimmermann

Energy level: Medium to high.

Best owner: Active family in suburban or rural home.

Needs: Daily exercise, leash, fenced yard; early, fair and consistent training; regular grooming (varies according to coat type), regular ear care.

Life expectancy: 12 to 14 years.

Maltese Shih Tzu

History/Evolution: A cross of two low-shedding, low-dander dogs — the Maltese and the Shih Tzu — the Maltese Shih Tzu was developed in Australia in the 1990s. Also known as the Mal-Shi or Malt-Tzu, this small crossbreed may be a good choice for people with allergies; the cross may also avoid the eye and breathing problems associated with the Shih Tzu's flattened face. With enough exercise, the Maltese Shih Tzu is content in an apartment situation.

Photograph © istockphoto.com/ Jani Bryson

Size: Small; 10 to 20 inches, 15 and 30 pounds.

Color: Varies; usually white or a mix of brown, white, and black.

Temperament: Good natured, affectionate, playful, clever. Devoted to family, but best with older children. Alert, cautious with strangers. Needs chew toys).

Energy level: Medium.

Best owner: Attentive owner with time for grooming.

Needs: Daily exercise, early and consistent socialization and training, regular ear and dental care, daily brushing and clipping every three or so months, patient housetraining.

Life expectancy: 12 to 14 years.

Maltepoo

History/Evolution: The Maltepoo (or Maltipoo or Moodle), a cross between the Maltese and the Poodle, adorns the arm of more than a few celebrities. The Maltepoo may inherit the low-shedding, low-dander coat of the Poodle, making the cross attractive for people with allergies. The diminutive dog can be a successful therapy dog, especially with the elderly. Responsible breeders are alert to health issues such as endocrine disorders, skin diseases, and eye disorders.

Photograph © Lauren Garson

Size: Small; 7 to 14 inches, 5 to 17 pounds.

Color: Varies; black, but light colors such as white and cream more common.

Temperament: Affectionate, loving, loyal, and sweet. Some prone to barking and aggression. Alert, active, and trainable.

Energy level: Medium.

Best owner: Attentive individual or family with considerate children.

Needs: Daily exercise (walk, play session), leash, early socialization and patient training, regular ear care, daily brushing and combing plus clipping.

Life expectancy: 10 to 15 years.

Puggle

History/Evolution: A recent star in the world of crossbreeds, the Puggle is a cross between two popular breeds, the Pug and the Beagle. This sturdy dog with a distinctive face may inherit the Pug's good nature and the Beagle's longer snout, which may help to reduce the breathing problems often associated with the Pug's brachycephalic head. Urban dwellers attracted to the compact size of the Puggle need to provide it with plenty of exercise and attention.

Size: Small; 13 to 15 inches, 18 to 30 pounds.

Color: Fawn, tan, red, black, lemon; may have white markings and a black mask.

Temperament: Active, affectionate, good natured, playful, sociable. Will bark/bay if bored or lonely. Good with children and pets.

Photograph © Chelle Rohde / www.DesignerDoggies.com

Energy level: Medium.

Best owner: Active owner or family.

Needs: Daily exercise (brisk walk), mental stimulation (play and toys), leash, secure yard, patient housetraining, socialization and training, occasional brushing, daily facial (wrinkles) washing, ear care.

Life expectancy: 10 to 15 years.

Schnoodle

History/Evolution: A cross between the Schnauzer and the Poodle, the Schnoodle was developed in response to demand in the 1980s for Poodle mixes. Schnoodles vary in size and temperament, depending on the parents involved. Schnoodles may inherit the Poodle's coat and intelligence; health issues such as skin conditions, eye problems, and epilepsy may occur. Some breeders work with multigenerational lines, with the goal of developing the Schnoodle as a recognized breed.

Size: Varies greatly — parents may be Toy, Miniature, or Standard Poodles crossed with Miniature, Standard, or Giant Schnauzers.

Color: Gray, silver, black, apricot, brown, white; often a mix.

Temperament: Loving, affectionate, devoted. May bark or become destructive if bored. Wary of strangers. Better with older children; may not be good with other pets.

Photograph © Michael Beach

Energy level: Medium.

Best owner: Family or active owner in a suburban or rural home.

Needs: Daily exercise, leash, fenced yard, daily brushing and regular clipping, early training and socialization, ear care, patient housetraining.

Life expectancy: 10 to 15 years.

Shepadoodle

History/Evolution: With less than a decade of breeding, the Shepadoodle is a relatively new mix — a cross between the German Shepherd and the Poodle. The Poodle parentage may help reduce the shedding associated with German Shepherds. Both breeds are intelligent and do well with a dominant owner. Some believe the cross has potential as a working dog, perhaps in herding or as a therapy dog. Be aware of genetic problems such as eye disease and hip dysplasia.

Size: Varies: Standard size 20 to 28 inches, 50 to 90 pounds; Miniature 17 to 20 inches, 20 to 50 pounds.

Color: Black, chocolate, chalk, cream, apricot, silver, blue; may have markings.

Temperament: Energetic and sociable. Family oriented; may herd family members. Intelligent and highly trainable. Wary of strangers; better with older children.

Photograph © Kimberly Babins

Energy level: Medium to high.

Best owner: Active family or individual in a suburban or rural home.

Needs: Daily vigorous exercise, mental stimulation (herding trials), early socialization, firm training.

Life expectancy: 12 to 15 years.

Shihchon

History/Evolution: The Shihchon (also Bi-Tzu and Zuchon) is a cross between the Shih Tzu and the Bichon Frise. The Shihchon coat may have the low-shedding, low-dander qualities of the Bichon; it may also benefit from having fewer problems associated with the brachycephalic head of the Shih Tzu. The mix doesn't like to be alone and enjoys the company of humans, whether on a lap or on a neighborhood walk, making it an ideal companion for retirees.

Size: Small; 8 to 11 inches, 9 to 16 pounds.

Color: Any.

Temperament: Energetic, social, outgoing, and affectionate. Good with older children. Usually nonaggressive but alert; will bark to announce visitors.

Photograph © Donna Roach

Energy level: Medium to low.

Best owner: Attentive owner with time for grooming.

Needs: Daily exercise, leash, training, brushing and combing two to three times a week, regular trimming, patient housetraining.

Life expectancy: 10 to 15 years.

Yorkiepoo

History/Evolution: The Yorkiepoo (also Yorkipoo) has been bred for a decade or so, the result of a cross between the Yorkshire Terrier and the Toy or Miniature Poodle. Like other Poodle crosses, the Yorkiepoo may be low-shedding and is often soft and silky. The typical small size of the dog is appealing to older owners and people who live in apartments; keep in mind, however, that the Yorkiepoo is a lively dog who still needs exercise.

Size: Small; 7 to 15 inches, 4 to 14 pounds.

Color: Many, including white, sable, cream, silver, tan, chocolate, and black.

Temperament: Energetic, playful, curious, self-confident; Intelligent and trainable; some may be stubborn. Alert and watchful; tends to bark.

Photograph © istockphoto.com/ Stan Conti

Energy level: Medium.

Best owner: Attentive owner or family with older children.

Needs: Daily exercise, leash, training, daily brushing and combing plus regular clipping (keep eyes clear of hair), ear care.

Life expectancy: 10 to 15 years.

Book VI
Resources

The 5th Wave   By Rich Tennant

@RICHTENNANT

"Okay, this is getting ridiculous! Either teach your dog not to run away, or name him something other than 'Fire.'"

In this book . . .

When you've absorbed all this book has to offer, you can find plenty more detailed dog stuff to discover. These chapters include a glossary to help you comprehend some of the more esoteric terms you might hear bandied about, as well as a list of the best books, magazines, Web sites, and organizations, to take your dog obsession to the next level.

Appendix A
Glossary Plus

• •

*M*ost ordinary books have what is simply called a Glossary. But the world of dogs is wide-ranging, with specialized terms for anatomy, veterinary medicine, and breeding. The following is called a "Glossary Plus" because it includes scientific definitions (simplified), commonly used terms, and some of that extra-special lingo you probably hear only when you're at the vet's office or when you're hanging out with doggie-expert friends.

achondroplasia: A form of dwarfism that affects growth in certain breeds of dogs. Usually affected are the leg bones, so that the breed has a normal-sized head and torso, but the legs are severely foreshortened. Examples are the Basset Hound and the Dachshund. Chondrodysplasia is another term commonly used for this condition.

Addison's Disease: A low adrenal function.

American Kennel Club (AKC): Organization that registers purebred dogs and sanctions dog shows and other competitions.

angulation: The angles formed by the meeting of the dog's bones. Usually in respect to the bones of the forequarters and rear quarters.

ataxia: Wobbly, affecting a dog's ability to walk or stand properly

axonal dystrophy: A rare brain disorder.

BAER: (Brain stem auditory-evoked response) A hearing test.

balance and proportion: Used to signify that a dog is symmetrically and proportionally correct for its breed.

Best in Show (BIS): Designation for best dog at an all-breed show.

Best in Specialty Show (BISS): Designation for best dog at a specific-breed-only show.

Best of Breed (BOB): Designation for best dog/bitch of each breed at an all-breed show.

Best of Winners (BOW): Winners Dog (WD) and Winners Bitch (WB) compete to see which is the better of the two.

Best Opposite Sex (BOS): After Best of Breed (BOB) is awarded, the best individual of the opposite sex is chosen to receive this award.

bitch: A female dog (even the well-behaved ones!). This term can also be used to describe what some exhibitors do about not having won with their dog.

Bitter Apple: A liquid used to discourage dogs from licking or chewing on themselves or household objects.

bloat/torsion/GDV: Swelling and twisting of the stomach.

body language: A dog's method of communicating his reactions.

breed character: The sum total of the mental and physical traits that define what a breed should look like and how it should act.

Canine Good Citizen: Basic test of a dog's good manners and stability. Passing the test earns an official CGC designation, which can be added to the successful dog's name on the pedigree.

castration: Surgical removal of the testicles of the male dog. Also known as neutering.

CERF: (Canine Eye Registry Foundation) Certifies normal eyes; must be renewed annually.

Champion (CH): Winner of 15 American Kennel Club (AKC) championship points under three different judges. Two of the wins must be "majors" (three or more points).

character: The general appearance or expression that is considered typical of the breed.

cherry eye: A red, swollen gland at the inner corner of the eye.

Chondrodysplasia (Chd): Dwarfism.

chromosomes: Threadlike structures that consist of deoxyribonucleic acid (DNA) and protein, and which carry the factors for heritable characters, the genes. All living creatures are made up of microscopic cells, each of which has a membrane-bound nucleus containing chromosomes.

CMO: (Craniomandibular osteopathy) A painful, thickened lower jaw.

coat: In dog parlance, the coat includes amount, color, texture, and often trim.

collapsing trachea: A condition of small dogs in which the supporting cartilage of the trachea (windpipe) is not formed correctly, resulting in coughing spells.

Collie eye anomaly: Malformation of the retina.

colostrum: The milk secreted by the mother immediately after birth and during the next several days.

Companion Dog (CD): Official initial Obedience degree that can be earned by competing in the Obedience Novice class. Comparable to a person's high school diploma.

Companion Dog Excellent (CDX): Next up from the initial Companion Dog Obedience degree. Comparable to a person's college degree.

condition: A dog's overall appearance of health or lack thereof.

conformation: Form and structure of a dog as required by the respective breed standard of perfection.

corneal dystrophy: White patches on the eye surface.

cryptorchid: Male dog whose testicles are not descended into the scrotum.

Demodectic mange: A skin disease caused by mites.

dentition: Arrangement of the teeth.

dermoid sinus: A tubelike cyst in the back or spine.

dewclaw: A thumblike extra claw on the front foreleg.

distichiasis: An extra row of eyelashes, causing tearing.

dog: This is a tricky one because it can mean any member of the species *Canis familiaris,* or it can mean only the male of the species. Examples: "All dogs enjoy a romp in park," or "The litter contained three dogs and four bitches." To further complicate matters, dog fanciers are inclined to use the term interchangeably.

Book VI

Resources

dominant gene: A gene that masks the presence or appearance of an unlike gene.

dysplasia: Abnormal tissue development often used in reference to the skeletal system in dogs.

ectropion: A hanging lower eyelid (one that "rolls out").

EKG: (electrocardiogram) A heart examination.

elbow dysplasia: A crippling disease of the elbow.

elongated palate: Extra mucous membrane tissue of the soft palate (back of the throat) that can cause a partial airway obstruction.

entropion: Eyelids turned inward, causing irritation.

estrus: See *oestrus.*

expression: The resultant facial expression created by the formation of a breed's head characteristics. Examples: the "Oriental" and "faraway" expression of the Afghan Hound, the "lordly" expression of the Chow Chow, the "keen" expression of the Wire Fox Terrier, the "inquisitive" expression of the Bichon Frise, and the "keen, piercing, varminty" expression of the Scottish Terrier.

"eye" for a dog: A natural ability to assess quality in dogs.

Fanconi's Syndrome: Degeneration of the kidney tubes.

FCI (Federacion Cynologique Internationale): Controlling body of pedigreed dogs in most of the European and Latin American countries.

free whelper: A female dog (bitch) who has her puppies naturally. Because of their conformation, the females of some breeds frequently require Caesarean section.

gangliosidosis: Lack of brain enzymes, causing retardation and blindness.

gene: The basic unit of heredity, carrying individual characteristics.

genetics: The science and study of heredity.

genotype: The genetic makeup of an individual.

geriatric spinal demyelinization: Old-age destruction of the spinal nerves.

Glomerulonephritis: A kidney problem.

GM-1/ GM-1 N: (glycogen storage disease) A liver enzyme deficiency.

Group First–Fourth: Designation indicating that a dog has earned a placement in Variety Group competition at an all-breed show.

head: In a general sense, *head* refers to skull–muzzle configuration. In dogs, there are three basic types but many variations within the three: **1.** *Dolichocephalic* (narrow skull and muzzle, usually of great length, as in a Collie or Borzoi). **2.** *Mesaticephalic* (typified by medium skull and muzzle proportions as one might see in the Springer Spaniel or German Shepherd). **3.** *Brachycephalic* (broad skull and short muzzle length, as in a Pekingese or Bulldog).

hemolytic anemia: An autoimmune disease that destroys red blood cells.

hepatopathy: Liver damage.

herding trials: Trials designed to test a dog's ability to control livestock.

hip dysplasia (HD): Abnormal development of the hip, causing degenerative joint disease in the dog in varying degrees of intensity.

histiocytosis: A rare malignant tumor in various organs.

hybrid: The offspring of parents who have dissimilar genetic makeup.

hypertrophic osteodystrophy: (HOD) Painful, swollen joints and bones.

International Championship (Int.Ch.): An award given only by the FCI.

laryngeal paralysis: Paralysis of the larynx.

Legg-Perthes: Disintegration of the hip joint, usually occurring in small breeds.

lens luxation: Lens slips, leading to glaucoma.

liver shunts: Congenital liver malformation.

lure coursing: Working trials for sight hounds.

Lymphangiactasia: Abnormal lymph vessels.

malabsorption: An inability to absorb digested food.

Book VI

Resources

microphthalmia: Abnormally small eyes.

mitral valve defect: (MVD) A heart anomaly.

monorchid: A male dog that has only one testicle descended into the scrotum.

movement: The action taken by a dog's legs as he goes from one place to another. The respective breed standard dictates correct movement for a breed.

National Research Council (NRC): The company that researches ingredients before they are permitted to be used in dog foods.

neutering: Surgical removal of the testicles of the male dog. Also known as castration.

oestrus (estrus): Stage of the reproductive cycle in which the female will stand willing for mating.

OFA (Orthopedic Foundation for Animals): Certifies X-rays of hips and elbows.

optic nerve hypoplasia: Underdeveloped optic nerve.

osteochondritis dessicans: (OCD) A growth disorder of the cartilage within joints. Usually affects shoulders and the stifle joint (the "knee").

pannus: An eye condition leading to blindness.

patellar luxation/knee palpation: A kneecap that moves out of place/ determining whether the kneecap slips. Common in small breeds.

PDA: (patent ductus arteriosus) A heart anomaly.

pemphigus: An autoimmune disease of the skin.

perianal fistulas: Open, draining tracts around the anus.

phenotype: The physical appearance of a living thing; the physical expression of genotype.

PKD: (Pyruvate kinase deficiency) A hemolytic anemia.

PRA: (Progressive retinal atrophy) Causes blindness.

recessive gene: A genetic trait that is not expressed unless matched with a matching gene; is completely covered in the presence of a dominant gene.

renal cortical hypoplasia: Degeneration of the kidneys.

Schutzhund: German dog sport that tests a dog's excellence in obedience, protection, and tracking.

sebaceous adenitis: (SA) Inflammation of hair follicles and oil glands.

Sieger: Best male in a German Rottweiler show.

silhouette: An outline portrait in profile of a dog. The proportions called for in a breed standard, or in its origin and purpose, establish the correct silhouette for each breed.

skin punch for SA: Test for sebacious adenitis.

sound: Overall good construction and health of a dog.

spay: Surgically removing the ovaries and uterus of the female dog.

specialty show: A show restricted to only one breed of dog.

splenic torsion: Twisting of the spleen.

spondylosis: Spinal arthritis.

stacking: The act of posing the dog for examination or for having its picture taken.

stenotic nares: Pinched nostrils.

stop: The juncture at which there is a step-up from muzzle to skull.

subaortic stenosis: (SAS) A heart anomaly.

SV: (Verein fur deutsche Schaferhunde) Largest and most influential breed organization in the world, of which Schutzhund training is an integral part.

therapy dogs: Dogs trained to bring comfort and companionship to hospitalized and elderly people.

tracking: Trials that test a dog's ability to track humans or lost articles.

type: The distinguishing characteristics of a breed, as called for in the standard of the respective breed.

undershot: When the front or incisor teeth of the lower jaw extend beyond the front or incisor teeth of the upper jaw.

utility dog: Advanced Obedience trial degree, comparable to a person's Master's degree.

VWD: (Von Willebrand's disease) A hemorrhagic (clotting) disorder. Most common in Doberman Pinschers.

withers: The highest part of the body just behind the neck. Often referred to as the top of the shoulders.

wobblers: A disease caused by an instability in the cervical vertebrae, affecting a dog's ability to walk. Mostly seen in large/giant breeds.

Appendix B

Dog Resources

This appendix lists a variety of information sources that you can explore as you develop your dog-related pursuits. You'll find plenty of resources, from books and magazines, to videos, Web sites, and trade organizations.

Books

The Art of Raising a Puppy, The Monks of New Skete. Little, Brown & Company.

A–Z of Dog Diseases & Health Problems, Dick Lane and Neil Ewart. Book House.

Born to Win, Patricia Craig. Doral Publishing.

Breeding and Genetics of the Dog, Anne Fitzgerald Paramoure. Denlinger's.

The Breeding and Rearing of Dogs, R. H. Smythe. Arco Publishing Company, Inc.

Bring Me Home: Dogs Make Great Pets, Margaret H. Bonham. Howell Book House.

Canine Terminology, Harold R. Spira, DVM. Harper & Row Publishers, Sydney.

Canine Terminology, Harold R. Spira. Dogwise Publishing.

Cesar's Way: The Natural, Everyday Guide to Understanding and Correcting Common Dog Problems, Cesar Millan. Three Rivers Press.

Choosing a Dog For Life, Andrew De Prisco and James B. Johnson. TFH Publications, Inc.

The Complete Dog Book, American Kennel Club. Howell Book House.

The Dog Owner's Home Veterinary Handbook, James M. Giffin, MD, and Lisa D. Carlson, DVM. Howell Book House.

The Dog Repair Book, Ruth B. James, DVM. Alpine Press.

The Domestic Dog, James Serpell. Cambridge University Press.

Don't Shoot the Dog! The New Art of Teaching and Training, Karen Pryor. Bantam Doubleday Dell.

The Dry Dog Food Reference, Howard D. Coffman. Pig Dog Press.

The Encyclopedia of Dogs, Fiorenzo Fiorone. Thomas Y. Crowell Company.

For the Love of a Dog: Understanding Emotion in You and Your Best Friend, Patricia McConnell. Ballantine Books.

Genetics of the Dog: The Basis of Successful Breeding, Marca Burns and Margaret N. Fraser. J.B. Lippincott Company.

Good Owners, Great Dogs, Brian Kilcommons and Sarah Wilson. Grand Central Publishing.

The Heritage of the Dog, Colonel David Hancock. Nimrod Press Limited.

How to Be Your Dog's Best Friend, Monks of New Skete. Little, Brown & Company.

K-9 Structure & Terminology, Edward M. Gilbert, Jr., and Thelma Brown. Howell Book House.

The Life, History and Magic of the Dog, Fernand Mery. Grosset & Dunlap.

Marley & Me: Life and Love with the World's Worst Dog, John Grogan. Harper.

The Merck Veterinary Manual, Merck and Co., Inc.

The Natural History of Dogs, Richard and Alice Fiennes. The Natural History Press.

Poodle Clipping and Grooming: The International Reference, Shirlee Kalstone. Howell Book House.

Practical Genetics for Dog Breeders, Malcolm B Willis, BSc, PhD. Howell Book House.

Tricks of the Trade, Pat Hastings and Erin Ann Rouse. Dogfolk Enterprises.

Ultimate Dog Grooming, Eileen Geeson. Firefly Books.

Magazines

American Kennel Club Gazette: www.akc.org/pubs/gazette/

Bark: www.thebark.com

Dog and Kennel: www.petpublishing.com/dogken/

Dog Fancy: www.dogfancy.com

Dog World: www.animalnetwork.com/DogWorldMag/

Dog's Life: http://dogslifemagazine.com

Dogs In Canada: www.dogsincanada.com

Dogs in Review: www.dogchannel.com/dog-magazines/dogsinreview/

Fido Friendly: www.fidofriendly.com

Good Dog!: www.gooddogmagazine.com

Groomer to Groomer: www.groomertogroomer.com

Journal of Veterinary Medical Education: www.jvmeonline.org

Modern Dog: www.moderndogmagazine.com

The Whole Dog Journal: www.whole-dog-journal.com

Your Dog: www.yourdog.co.uk

Videos

AKC and the Sport of Dogs, American Kennel Club

Breed Standard Videos, American Kennel Club

Canine Legislation: Taking Command, American Kennel Club

Dog Steps, Rachel Page Elliot, American Kennel Club

Puppy Puzzle, Pat Hastings, Dogfolk Enterprises

Right Dog for You, American Kennel Club

Web Sites

American Kennel Club: www.akc.org

American Rare Breed Association: www.arba.org

American Veterinary Medical Association: www.avma.org

Australian National Kennel Council: www.ankc.aust.com/

Canadian Kennel Club: www.ckc.ca/info

The Kennel Club (England): www.the-kennel-club.org.uk

Pet Sitters International: www.petsit.com

Tattoo-a-Pet: www.tattoo-a-pet.com

United Kennel Club: www.ukcdogs.com

National Registry Sources

American Kennel Club
260 Madison Ave., Fourth Floor
New York, NY 10016
Web site www.akc.org

American Rare Breed Association
9921 Frank Tippett Rd.
Cheltenham, MD 20623
Phone 301-868-5718

Australian National Kennel Council
P.O. Box 285
Red Hill South

Victoria 3937
Australia
Phone 011-61-2-9-834-4040

Canadian Kennel Club
89 Skyway Ave., #200
Etobicoke, Ontario
Canada M9W 6R4
Phone 416-674-3672

Field Dog Stud Book
American Field Publishing Co.
542 S. Dearborn Street
Chicago, IL 60605

North American Dog Agility Council
HCR 2, Box 277
St. Maries, ID 83861
Web site www.nadac.com

States Kennel Club
1007 W. Pine St.
Hattiesburg, MS 39402
Phone 601-583-8345

The Kennel Club
1 Clarges St.
London W1J8AB
England
Phone 011-44-870-606-6750

United Kennel Club
100 East Kilgore Rd.
Kalamazoo, MI 49002-5584
Phone 616-343-9020
Web site www.ukcdogs.com

United States Dog Agility Association
P.O. Box 850955
Richardson, TX 75085-0955
Phone 972-231-9700
Web site www.usdaa.com

Grooming and Grooming Supplies

American Pet Pro: www.americanpetpro.com

Find A Groomer Directory: www.findagroomer.com

Groomer's Choice Pet Products: www.groomerschoice.com

Groomtech: www.groomtech.com

Intergroom: www.intergroom.com

International Pet Groomers: www.ipgcmg.org

International Society of Canine Cosmetologists: www.petstylist.com

National Dog Groomers Association of America: www.national doggroomers.com

Pet Supplies 4 Less: www.petsupplies4less.com

Petgroomer.com: www.petgroomer.com

The Shampoo Lady: www.theshampoolady.com

Veterinary Groups

American Animal Hospital Association: www.aahanet.org

American College of Veterinary Internal Medicine: www.acvim.org

American Veterinary Medical Association: www.avma.org

Canadian Veterinary Medical Association: www.crma-acmv.org

Canine Eye Registration Foundation: www.vet.purdue.edu/~yshen/cerf.html

Orthopedic Foundation for Animals: www.offa.org

PennHip: www.synbiotics.com/html/pennhip.html

Pet Supplies

Cherrybrook Pet Supplies: www.cherrybrook.com

Dogwise: www.dogwise.com

Drs. Foster & Smith Pet Supply: www.drfostersmith.com

J-B Wholesale Pet Supplies: www.jbpet.com

Jeffers Pet and Equine Supplies: www.jefferspet.com

KV Vet Supply: www.kvvet.com

Petco.com: www.petco.com

Petedge: www.petedge.com

PetSmart: www.petsmart.com

UPCO Discount Pet Supply: www.upco.com

Dog Training

Association of Pet Dog Trainers: www.apdt.com

Complete Guide to Dog Training: www.dog-obedience-training-review.com

North American Dog Obedience Instructors: www.nadoi.org

Animal Charities

American Kennel Club Animal Health Foundation: www.akcchf.org

American Society for the Prevention of Cruelty to Animals: www.aspca.org

American Veterinary Medical Foundation: www.avmf.org

Canine Companions for Independence: www.caninecompanions.org

The Delta Society: www.deltasociety.org

Dogs for the Deaf: www.dogsforthedeaf.org

Guide Dogs for the Blind: www.guidedogs.com

Guiding Eyes for the Blind: www.guiding-eyes.org

Morris Animal Foundation: www.morrisanimalfoundation.org

Index

Business/Accounting & Bookkeeping

Bookkeeping For Dummies
978-0-7645-9848-7

eBay Business
All-in-One For Dummies,
2nd Edition
978-0-470-38536-4

Job Interviews
For Dummies,
3rd Edition
978-0-470-17748-8

Resumes For Dummies,
5th Edition
978-0-470-08037-5

Stock Investing
For Dummies,
3rd Edition
978-0-470-40114-9

Successful Time
Management
For Dummies
978-0-470-29034-7

Computer Hardware

BlackBerry For Dummies,
3rd Edition
978-0-470-45762-7

Computers For Seniors
For Dummies
978-0-470-24055-7

iPhone For Dummies,
2nd Edition
978-0-470-42342-4

Laptops For Dummies,
3rd Edition
978-0-470-27759-1

Macs For Dummies,
10th Edition
978-0-470-27817-8

Cooking & Entertaining

Cooking Basics
For Dummies,
3rd Edition
978-0-7645-7206-7

Wine For Dummies,
4th Edition
978-0-470-04579-4

Diet & Nutrition

Dieting For Dummies,
2nd Edition
978-0-7645-4149-0

Nutrition For Dummies,
4th Edition
978-0-471-79868-2

Weight Training
For Dummies,
3rd Edition
978-0-471-76845-6

Digital Photography

Digital Photography
For Dummies,
6th Edition
978-0-470-25074-7

Photoshop Elements 7
For Dummies
978-0-470-39700-8

Gardening

Gardening Basics
For Dummies
978-0-470-03749-2

Organic Gardening
For Dummies,
2nd Edition
978-0-470-43067-5

Green/Sustainable

Green Building
& Remodeling
For Dummies
978-0-470-17559-0

Green Cleaning
For Dummies
978-0-470-39106-8

Green IT For Dummies
978-0-470-38688-0

Health

Diabetes For Dummies,
3rd Edition
978-0-470-27086-8

Food Allergies
For Dummies
978-0-470-09584-3

Living Gluten-Free
For Dummies
978-0-471-77383-2

Hobbies/General

Chess For Dummies,
2nd Edition
978-0-7645-8404-6

Drawing For Dummies
978-0-7645-5476-6

Knitting For Dummies,
2nd Edition
978-0-470-28747-7

Organizing For Dummies
978-0-7645-5300-4

SuDoku For Dummies
978-0-470-01892-7

Home Improvement

Energy Efficient Homes
For Dummies
978-0-470-37602-7

Home Theater
For Dummies,
3rd Edition
978-0-470-41189-6

Living the Country Lifestyle
All-in-One For Dummies
978-0-470-43061-3

Solar Power Your Home
For Dummies
978-0-470-17569-9

Available wherever books are sold. For more information or to order direct: U.S. customers visit www.dummies.com or call 1-877-762-2974.
U.K. customers visit www.wileyeurope.com or call (0) 1243 843291. Canadian customers visit www.wiley.ca or call 1-800-567-4797.

Internet

Blogging For Dummies,
2nd Edition
978-0-470-23017-6

eBay For Dummies,
6th Edition
978-0-470-49741-8

Facebook For Dummies
978-0-470-26273-3

Google Blogger
For Dummies
978-0-470-40742-4

Web Marketing
For Dummies,
2nd Edition
978-0-470-37181-7

WordPress For Dummies,
2nd Edition
978-0-470-40296-2

Language & Foreign Language

French For Dummies
978-0-7645-5193-2

Italian Phrases
For Dummies
978-0-7645-7203-6

Spanish For Dummies
978-0-7645-5194-9

Spanish For Dummies,
Audio Set
978-0-470-09585-0

Macintosh

Mac OS X Snow Leopard
For Dummies
978-0-470-43543-4

Math & Science

Algebra I For Dummies,
2nd Edition
978-0-470-55964-2

Biology For Dummies
978-0-7645-5326-4

Calculus For Dummies
978-0-7645-2498-1

Chemistry For Dummies
978-0-7645-5430-8

Microsoft Office

Excel 2007 For Dummies
978-0-470-03737-9

Office 2007 All-in-One
Desk Reference
For Dummies
978-0-471-78279-7

Music

Guitar For Dummies,
2nd Edition
978-0-7645-9904-0

iPod & iTunes
For Dummies,
6th Edition
978-0-470-39062-7

Piano Exercises
For Dummies
978-0-470-38765-8

Parenting & Education

Parenting For Dummies,
2nd Edition
978-0-7645-5418-6

Type 1 Diabetes
For Dummies
978-0-470-17811-9

Pets

Cats For Dummies,
2nd Edition
978-0-7645-5275-5

Dog Training For Dummies,
2nd Edition
978-0-7645-8418-3

Puppies For Dummies,
2nd Edition
978-0-470-03717-1

Religion & Inspiration

The Bible For Dummies
978-0-7645-5296-0

Catholicism For Dummies
978-0-7645-5391-2

Women in the Bible
For Dummies
978-0-7645-8475-6

Self-Help & Relationship

Anger Management
For Dummies
978-0-470-03715-7

Overcoming Anxiety
For Dummies
978-0-7645-5447-6

Sports

Baseball For Dummies,
3rd Edition
978-0-7645-7537-2

Basketball For Dummies,
2nd Edition
978-0-7645-5248-9

Golf For Dummies,
3rd Edition
978-0-471-76871-5

Web Development

Web Design All-in-One
For Dummies
978-0-470-41796-6

Windows Vista

Windows Vista
For Dummies
978-0-471-75421-3

Available wherever books are sold. For more information or to order direct: U.S. customers visit www.dummies.com or call 1-877-762-2974.
U.K. customers visit www.wileyeurope.com or call (0) 1243 843291. Canadian customers visit www.wiley.ca or call 1-800-567-4797.

How-to?
How Easy.

From hooking up a modem to cooking up a casserole, knitting a scarf to navigating an iPod, you can trust Dummies.com to show you how to get things done the easy way.

Visit us at Dummies.com

Dummies products make life easier!

DVDs • Music • Games • DIY • Consumer Electronics • Software • Crafts • Hobbies • Cookware • and more!

For more information, go to **Dummies.com®** and search the store by category.

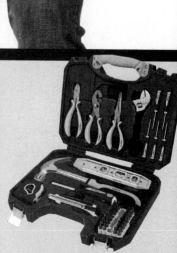

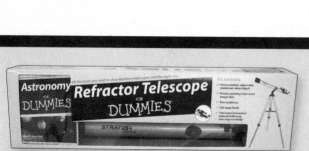

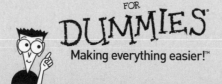